GLOBAL  STUDIES

COMMONWEALTH OF INDEPENDENT STATES
AND CENTRAL/EASTERN EUROPE

Fourth Edition

STAFF

Ian A. Nielsen	Publisher
Brenda S. Filley	Production Manager
Lisa M. Clyde	Developmental Editor
Charles Vitelli	Designer
Cheryl Greenleaf	Permissions Coordinator
Shawn Callahan	Graphics
Libra Ann Cusack	Typesetting Supervisor
Juliana Arbo	Typesetting
Diane Barker	Editorial Assistant

GLOBAL STUDIES

COMMONWEALTH OF INDEPENDENT STATES AND CENTRAL/EASTERN EUROPE

Fourth Edition

Minton F. Goldman
Northeastern University

The Dushkin Publishing Group, Inc., Sluice Dock, Guilford, Connecticut 06437

The Commonwealth of Independent States and Central/Eastern Europe

OTHER BOOKS IN THE GLOBAL STUDIES SERIES

Africa
China
India and South Asia
Japan and the Pacific Rim
Latin America
The Middle East
Western Europe

Library of Congress Catalog Number 90–081836

ISBN: 1–56134–076–6   ISSN: 1061–2823

Global Studies® is a Registered Trademark of The Dushkin Publishing Group, Inc.

Fourth Edition

Printed in the United States of America

The Commonwealth of Independent States and Central/Eastern Europe

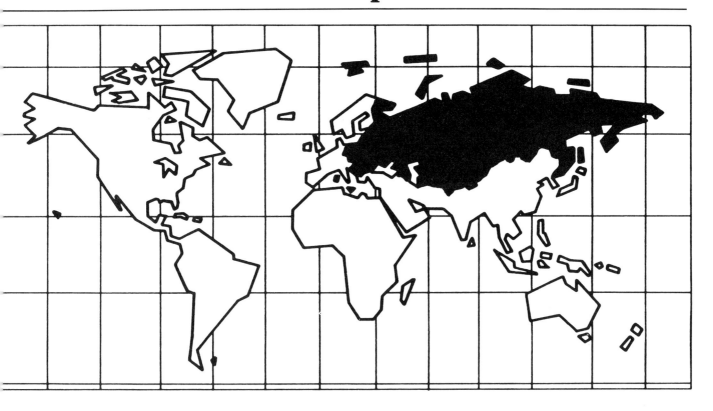

AUTHOR AND EDITOR

Dr. Minton F. Goldman

The author and editor of *Global Studies: The Commonwealth of Independent States and Central/Eastern Europe* is Associate Professor of Political Science at Northeastern University in Boston, Massachusetts. He has published book reviews and articles on European diplomacy and Soviet foreign policy in the *Journal of Southeast Asian Studies, Revue d'Histoire Maghrebine, Polity, East European Quarterly*, and *Il Politico*, and has contributed chapters to *Dynamics of the Third World* and *The Presidency and National Security Policy*. Dr. Goldman has traveled extensively in Central/Eastern Europe and the former Soviet Union and has presented numerous papers on panels of professional conferences.

SERIES CONSULTANT

H. Thomas Collins
Washington, D.C.

Contents

Global Studies: The Commonwealth of Independent States and Central/Eastern Europe

Page 8

Page 71

Page 82

Page 116

Page 146

Introduction

THE GLOBAL AGE

As we approach the end of the twentieth century, it is clear that the future we face will be considerably more international in nature than ever believed possible in the past. Each day of our lives, print and broadcast journalists make us aware that our world is becoming increasingly smaller and substantially more interdependent.

The energy crisis, world food shortages, nuclear proliferation, and the regional conflicts in Central America, the Middle East, the dissolution of communism in what was the Soviet Union and Eastern Europe, and other areas that threaten to involve us all make it clear that the distinctions between domestic and foreign problems are all too often artificial—that many seemingly domestic problems no longer stop at national boundaries. As Rene Dubos, the 1969 Pulitzer Prize recipient stated: "[I]t becomes obvious that each (of us) has two countries, (our) own and planet Earth." As global interdependence has become a reality, it has become vital for the citizens of this world to develop literacy in global matters.

THE GLOBAL STUDIES SERIES

It is the aim of this Global Studies series to help readers acquire a basic knowledge and understanding of the regions and countries in the world. Each volume provides a foundation of information—geographic, cultural, economic, political, historical, artistic, and religous—that will allow readers to better understand the current and future problems within these countries and regions and to comprehend how events there might affect their own well-being. In short, these volumes attempt to provide the background information necessary to respond to the realities of our Global Age.

Author and Editor
Each of the volumes in the Global Studies series has been crafted under the careful direction of an author/editor—an expert in the area under study. The author/editors teach and conduct research and have travelled extensively through the countries about which they are writing.

In this Commonwealth of Independent States and Central/Eastern Europe volume, the author/editor has written the regional essays and the country reports. In addition, he has been instrumental in the selection of the world press articles that relate to each of the regional sections.

Contents and Features
The Global Studies volumes are organized to provide concise information and current world press articles on the regions and countries within those areas under study.

(United Nations photo/Yutaka Nagata)

The Global Age is making all countries and all people more interdependent.

Regional Essays
Global Studies: The Commonwealth of Independent States and Central/Eastern Europe, Fourth Edition, covers the Commonwealth of Independent States and the eight countries of Eastern Europe—Albania, Bulgaria, Czechoslovakia, Eastern Germany, Hungary, Poland, Romania, and Yugoslavia. For the Commonwealth of Independent States and the Central/Eastern European regions, the author/editor has written narrative essays focusing on the cultural, sociopolitical, and economic differences and similarities of the countries and people in the regions. The purpose of the regional essays is to provide readers with an effective sense of the diversity of the areas as well as an understanding of their common cultural and historical backgrounds. Accompanying the regional essays are full-page maps showing the political boundaries of each of the countries within the regions.

Country Reports
Concise reports are written for each of the countries within the region under study. These reports are the heart of each Global Studies volume. *Global Studies: The Commonwealth of Independent States and Central/Eastern Europe, Fourth Edition*, contains eight country reports, covering the Central/Eastern European countries.

The country reports are comprised of five standard elements. Each report contains a small map visually positioning the country amongst its neighboring states; a summary of statistical information; a current essay providing important historical, geographical, political, cultural, and economic information; a historical timeline offering a convenient visual survey of a few key historical events; and four graphic indicators, with summary statements about the country in terms of development, freedom, health/welfare, and achievements, at the end of each report.

A Note on the Statistical Summaries

The statistical information provided for each country has been drawn from a wide range of sources. The nine most frequently referenced are listed on page 272. Every effort has been made to provide the most current and accurate information available. However, occasionally the information cited by these sources differs to some extent, and, all too often, the most current information available for some countries is dated. Aside from these discrepancies, the statistical summary of each country is generally quite complete and reasonably current. Care should be taken, however, in using these statistics (or, for that matter, any published statistics) in making hard comparisons among countries. We have also included comparable statistics on the United States, which follow on the next two pages.

World-Press Articles

Within each Global Studies volume are reprinted a large number of articles carefully selected by our editorial staff and the author/editor from a broad range of international periodicals and newspapers. The articles have been chosen for currency, interest, and their differing perspectives on the subject countries and regions. There are a total of twenty-six articles in *Global Studies: The Commonwealth of Independent States and Central/Eastern Europe, Fourth Edition.*

The articles section is preceded by a *Topic Guide* as well as an *Annotated Table of Contents.* The Annotated Table of Contents offers a brief summary of each article, while the Topic Guide indicates the main theme(s) of each article. Thus, readers desiring to focus on articles dealing with a particular theme, say, human rights, may refer to the Topic Guide to find those articles.

Glossary, Bibliography, Index, and Appendices

At the back of each Global Studies volume, readers will find a *Glossary of Terms and Abbreviations*, which provides a quick reference to the specialized vocabulary of the area under study and to the standard abbreviations (KGB, CMEA, etc.) used throughout the volume.

Following the Glossary is a *Bibliography*, which is organized into general-reference volumes, national and regional histories, current-events publications, and journals that provide regular coverage on the Soviet Union and Eastern Europe.

The *Index* at the end of the volume is an accurate reference to the contents of the volume. Readers seeking specific information and citations should consult this standard index.

Currency and Usefulness

This fourth edition of *Global Studies: The Commonwealth of Independent States and Central/Eastern Europe*, like other Global Studies volumes, is intended to provide the most current and useful information available necessary to understand the events that are shaping the cultures of the region today.

We plan to issue this volume on a regular basis. The statistics will be updated, regional essays rewritten, country reports revised, and articles completely replaced as new and current information becomes available. In order to accomplish this task we will turn to our author/editor, our advisory boards and—hopefully—to you, the users of this volume. Your comments are more than welcome. If you have an idea that you think will make the volume more useful, an article or bit of information that will make it more current, or a general comment on its organization, content, or features that you would like to share with us, please send it in for serious consideration for the next edition.

(United Nations photo/P. Teuscher)

Understanding the problems and lifestyles of other countries will help make us literate in global matters.

United States of America

Comparing statistics on the various countries in this volume should not be done without recognizing that the figures are within the timeframe of our publishing date and may not accurately reflect today's conditions. Nevertheless, comparisons can and will be made, so to enable you to put the statistics of different countries into perspective, we include here comparable statistics on the United States. These statistics are drawn from the same sources that were consulted for developing the statistical information for each country report.

The United States is unique. It has some of the most fertile land in the world, which, coupled with a high level of technology, allows the production of an abundance of food products—an abundance that makes possible the export of enormous quantities of basic foodstuffs to many other parts of the world. The use of this technology also permits the production of goods and services that exceeds what is possible in a majority of the rest of the world. In the United States are some of the most important urban centers in the world focusing on trade, investment, and commerce as well as art, music, and theater.

GEOGRAPHY

Area in Square Kilometers (Miles):
9,578,626 (3,618,770)
Capital (Population): Washington, D.C.
(639,000)
Climate: temperate

PEOPLE

Population

Total: 253,978,000 (adjusted 1990
census)
Annual Growth Rate: 0.8%
Rural/Urban Population Ratio: 21/79
Ethnic Makeup of Population: 80%
white; 11.5% black; 6.2% Spanish
origin; 1.6% Asian and Pacific
Islander; 0.7% American Indian,
Eskimo, and Aleut

Health

Life Expectancy at Birth: 72 years
(male); 79 years (female)
Infant Mortality Rate (Ratio):
9.1/1,000
Average Caloric Intake: 138% of FAO
minimum
Physicians Available (Ratio): 1/410

Religion(s)

55% Protestant; 36% Roman
Catholic; 4% Jewish; 5% Muslim and
others

Education

Adult Literacy Rate: 99.5% (official)
(estimates vary significantly)

COMMUNICATION

Telephones: 182,558,000 (79.1/100
Newspapers: 1,679 dailies;
approximately 63,000,000 circulation

TRANSPORTATION

Highways—Kilometers (Miles):
6,229,633 (3,871,143)
Railroads—Kilometers (Miles):
270,312 (167,974)
Usable Airfields: 16,685

GOVERNMENT

Type: federal republic
Independence Date: July 4, 1776
Head of State: President George Bush
Political Parties: Democratic Party;
Republican Party; others of minor
political significance
Suffrage: universal at 18

MILITARY

Number of Armed Forces: 2,127,940
*Military Expenditures (% of Central
Government Expenditures):* 27.1%
Current Hostilities: none

ECONOMY

Per Capita Income/GNP:
$18,400/$5,200 billion
Inflation Rate: 4%
Natural Resources: metallic and
nonmetallic minerals; petroleum;
arable land
Agriculture: food grains; feed crops;
oilbearing crops; cattle; dairy
products
Industry: diversified in both capital-
and consumer-goods industries

FOREIGN TRADE

Exports: $363 billion
Imports: $492 billion

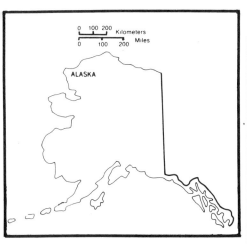

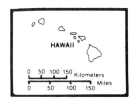

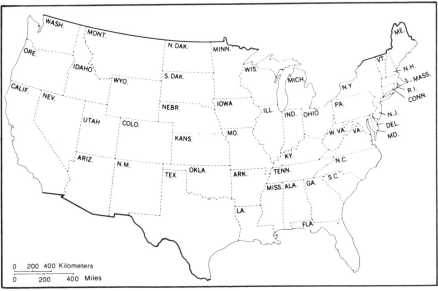

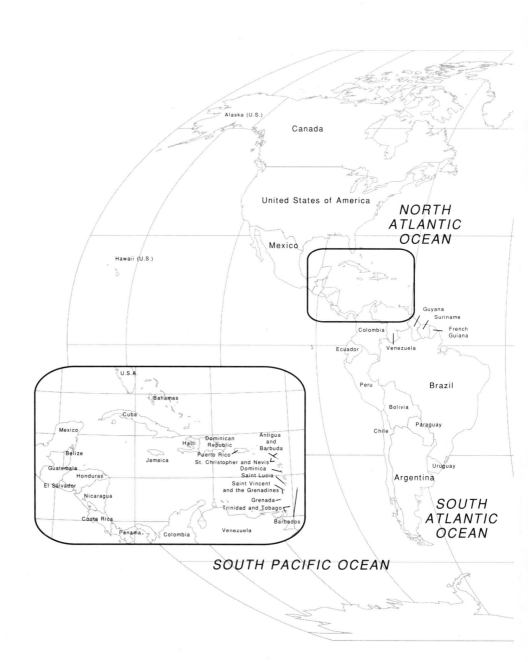

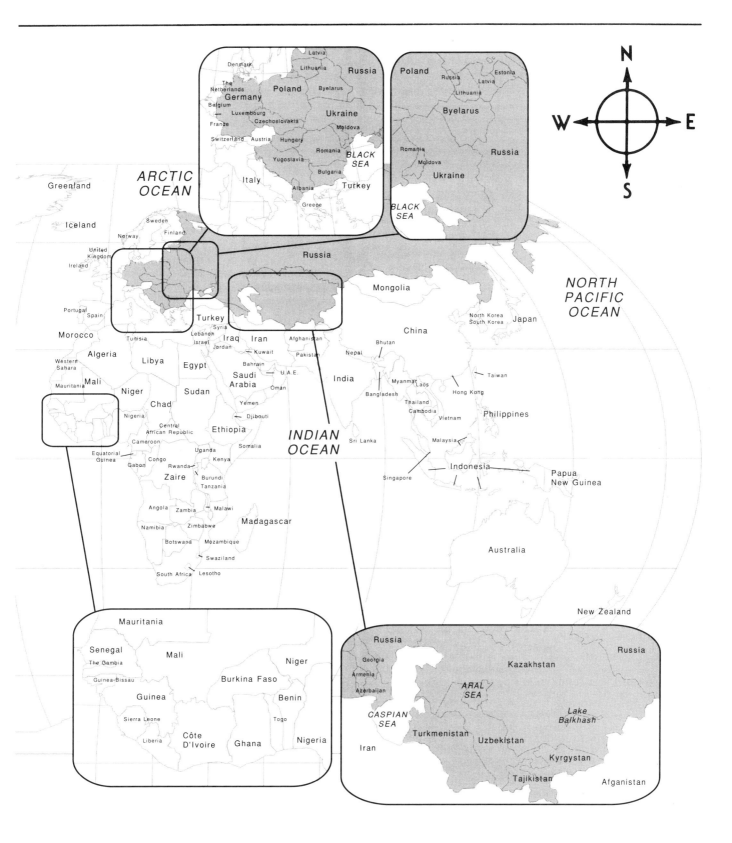

This map of the world highlights the Soviet Union and the Eastern European countries that are discussed in this volume. All of the following essays are written from a cultural perspective in order to give the readers a sense of what life is like in these countries. The essays are designed to present the most current and useful information available today. Other books in the Global Studies series cover different global areas and examine the current state of affairs of the countries within those regions.

The Commonwealth of Independent States

THE 11 REPUBLICS OF THE COMMONWEALTH OF INDEPENDENT STATES		
Republic	Capital	Population (in millions, according to 1990 census)
1. Russia	Moscow	(148.0)
2. Ukraine	Kiev	(51.8)
3. Uzbekistan	Tashkent	(20.3)
4. Kazakhstan	Alma-Ata	(16.7)
5. Byelarus	Minsk	(10.3)
6. Azerbaijan	Baku	(7.1)
7. Tajikistan	Dushanbe	(5.3)
8. Moldova	Kishinev	(4.4)
9. Kyrghyzstan	Bishkik	(4.4)
10. Turkmenistan	Ashkhabad	(3.6)
11. Armenia	Jerevan	(3.3)

THE 4 REPUBLICS THAT DID NOT JOIN THE COMMONWEALTH OF INDEPENDENT STATES		
Republic	Capital	Population (in millions, according to 1990 census)
1. Georgia	Tbilisi	(5.5)
2. Lithuania	Vilnius	(3.7)
3. Latvia	Riga	(2.7)
4. Estonia	Tallin	(1.6)

The area that makes up what was the Union of Soviet Socialist Republics (U.S.S.R.) is a mosaic of ethnic groupings and nationalities, with approximately 130 different languages. After the dissolution of communism in the Soviet Union in 1991, this very diverse population reacted with nationalistic fervor, and the 15 republics of the Soviet Union contended with the question of whether or not it was in their best interest to unite into a new union. Eleven did, into what is now called the Commonwealth of Independent States (C.I.S.), with 4 choosing independence of the Commonwealth.

The Commonwealth of Independent States

GEOGRAPHY
Area in Square Kilometers (Miles):
22,032,000 (8,506,563) (this is the area
for the 11 republics that make up the
C.I.S. and is approximately 2½ times
the size of the United States)
Capital (Population): Moscow
(8,800,000)
Climate: varied; generally, long, cold
winters and short summers

PEOPLE
Population
Total: 270,800,000 (11 republics of
C.I.S.)
Annual Growth Rate: 0.8%
Rural/Urban Population Ratio: 34/66
Ethnic Makeup of Population: 52%
Russian; 16% Ukrainian; 5% Uzbek;
4% Byelorussian; 23% others

Health
Life Expectancy at Birth: 60 years
(male); 74 years (female)
Infant Mortality Rate (Ratio):
25.2/1,000
Average Caloric Intake: 130% of FAO
minimum
Physicians Available (Ratio): 1/232

Religion(s)
18% Russian Orthodox; 9% Muslim;
3% Jewish, Protestant, Georgian
Orthodox, or Roman Catholic; 70%
atheist

Education
Adult Literacy Rate: 99% (official)

COMMUNICATION
Telephones: 41,800,000 (14.5/100)
Newspapers: 8,285; 176,000,000 daily
circulation

A DYNAMIC PLACE IN HISTORY
A man of Mikhail Gorbachev's achievements is not ready for retirement, although
his job as Soviet president no longer exists. For more than 8 years Gorbachev was
the world's boldest, most original political thinker and tactician. He made the arms
race an anachronism, he ended the Cold War, and he led his people as well as the
people of Central/Eastern Europe to abandon faith in communism. The ripple
effect of that move will be seen in not only those nations still committed to
communism, in particular China, Cuba, North Korea, and North Vietnam, but
also in the West, which no longer has to mobilize enormous resources to contain
Soviet political and military aggrandizement.

Gorbachev's experience gives him much to offer the C.I.S. as well as the
international community. But even if he does nothing more in his life, Gorbachev
has already carved out a deep niche in history. If the former Soviet lands that make
up today's Commonwealth are successful in moving away from totalitarian
dictatorships, future historians will credit Gorbachev for this achievement. They
will call him a visionary, and they will see him as a Churchillian giant of his time.

TRANSPORTATION
Highways—Kilometers (Miles):
1,584,400 (988,665)
Railroads—Kilometers (Miles): 145,600
(90,854)
Usable Airfields: 4,530

GOVERNMENT
Type: confederation of 11 former Soviet
republics (Russia, Byelorus, Ukraine,
Moldova, Armenia, Azerbaijan,
Kyrghyzstan, Turkmenistan, Uzbekistan,
Tajikistan, Kazakhstan)
Independence Date: 1991
Head of State: varies from republic to
republic
Political Parties: vary from republic to
republic
Suffrage: universal over 18

MILITARY
Number of Armed Forces: n/a
*Military Expenditures (% of Central
Government Expenditures):* 12%–14%
Current Hostilities: none

ECONOMY
Currency ($ U.S. Equivalent): 170
ruble = $1 (official); actual value is a
fraction of this figure
Per Capita Income/GNP: $3,000/$2,300
billion
Inflation Rate: 13%
Natural Resources: fossil fuels;
waterpower; timber; manganese; lead;
zinc; nickel; mercury; potash;
phosphate
Agriculture: wheat; rye; oats; potatoes;
sugar beets; cotton; sunflowers; flax
Industry: diversified: highly developed
capital-goods industries; consumer-
goods industries comparatively less
developed

FOREIGN TRADE
Exports: $97 billion (in Soviet Union
before 12/91)
Imports: $89 billion (in Soviet Union
before 12/91)

*Since the dissolution of the Soviet Union,
statistics should be viewed as approximate.

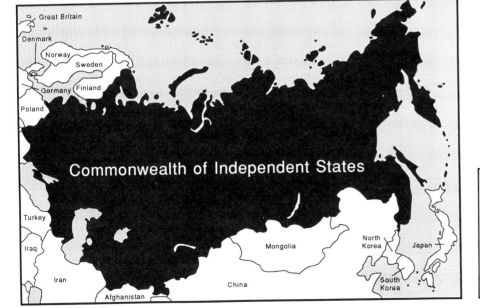

Commonwealth of Independent States

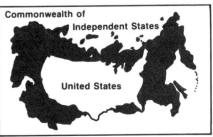

Commonwealth of Independent States

United States

The Commonwealth of Independent States:
Building New Political Orders

WHY STUDY THE C.I.S.?

A study of the Commonwealth of Independent States (C.I.S.), established on December 8, 1991, casts the Soviet Communist experience in a new light. Soviet communism for generations had been like the proverbial cat with 9 lives, able to maintain itself, despite its many flaws, by whatever means. People abroad, as well as in the Soviet Union, thought that Soviet communism would endure indefinitely. But the collapse of the Soviet state and the establishment of the Commonwealth suggests that Soviet communism was a transitional political order which had the seeds of its own self-destruction and which led to the emergence of a new political order called, for lack of a more precise term, post-Communist.

Within the framework of the C.I.S., the former Soviet republics are experimenting to find an ideal or, at least, a workable and improved political order. So far they are retaining some of the egalitarianism and paternalism of the old Soviet system while trying to adopt some of the political and economic liberalism of the parliamentary democracies in the West. Their attempts are complicated by the fact that the peoples of the Commonwealth inhabit an enormous landmass which stretches across 2 continents and contains more than 286 million people with well over 100 ethnic groupings, 100 nationalities, and about 130 different languages.

A WORD ON TERMS

Many foreigners failed to differentiate between the terms *Russia* and *Soviet Union*. Russia referred to the largest, most populous, and most politically influential of the 15 constituent union-republics that comprised the Union of Soviet Socialist Republics, commonly known as the Soviet Union. Thus, Russia was part of the Soviet Union, not synonymous with it.

The Soviet Union was a federation that was formally established by the Soviet Communist Party in 1922. The word *Soviet* referred to the conciliar or parliamentary type of government of the federation and its constituent union-republics. The Soviet type of government prevailed in all levels of administration in the Soviet Union, down to small villages and towns. *Soviet* derived from a Russian word meaning "council." It came into popular usage in the Russian Revolutions of 1905 and 1917, when insurgent workers, peasants, and soldiers formed soviets or councils in St. Petersburg, Moscow, and other Russian cities to oppose Czarist authority and create an alternative to it.

Sometimes people intentially used the word *Russia* when they really meant the *Soviet Union*. They did this because Russians in fact created the Soviet state and retained control of it from 1917, despite the multinational character of its society.

The former Soviet Union, which the C.I.S. replaces, was the second—or possibly the first, depending on one's viewpoint—most militarily powerful political entity in the world, the leading rival and antagonist of the United States. With its enormous military power, including the most technologically advanced conventional and nuclear weapons, the former Soviet state controlled most of Central/Eastern Europe and exerted influence throughout the developing Third World. And, as the first country to develop Marxist ideas and practices, it was a role model for other societies that suffered from the same hardships that had inspired the Communist ascendancy in Russia in 1917 and the subsequent establishment of the Soviet state. How the C.I.S. will manage and allocate this vast military resource is now a source of considerable discussion and disagreement.

What is happening in the Commonwealth is important to the outside world, especially the United States, where there had been much prejudice toward the now-defunct Soviet Union, born of a historic lack of American interest in foreign affairs as well as the absence of reliable information about the Soviets. The C.I.S. is important to the outside world, especially the West, also because international peace and stability depend on the success of its movement away from socialist authoritarianism toward political and economic democracy; the West does not want a return to Soviet imperialism. At the same time the newly emancipated peoples of the former Soviet republics are not only a huge potential market for the goods and services of foreign countries, especially those that are highly industrialized, but also a reservoir of opportunities for the development of new and extensive cultural and scientific interactions that can benefit the entire international community.

HOW TO STUDY THE C.I.S.

Before one can understand and evaluate the C.I.S., one must understand the past, especially the recent past, of the traditional Soviet system. This essay analyzes that system, in particular its roots, how it worked, its performance problems, its effort at profound restructuring to resolve those problems, called *perestroika,* and its collapse. Following this analysis is a discussion of major problems confronting the Commonwealth and of the chances of its survival.

The roots of Soviet communism include the pre-Communist past, notably the historic, economic, and sociocultural characteristics of the Czarist political system; the principles of communist ideology; and the birth and evolution of the Soviet Communist system following the 1917 Bolshevik Revolution. A look at how the Soviet system worked, which shows how Russian Marxists used power to achieve socialism (the prerequisite for communism), describes methods of popular political participation, such as voting, interest groups, and the role of the Soviet Communist Party; and the formal structures of the Soviet government, such as the executive, legislative, and judicial branches, the bureaucracy, the economy, and the social-welfare system. The performance section analyzes the Soviet system in terms of its promises to transform the Czarist Russian empire into a new, egalitarian, democratic, and prosperous society and examines problems in the economic, political, and sociocultural spheres of Soviet life. The section on restructuring, or perestroika, shows how former Soviet President and party leader Mikhail Gorbachev tried to address these problems by making sweeping changes in all aspects of the traditional Soviet system. It also examines the circumstances that led to the August 1991 coup attempt, the reasons for its failure to oust President Gorbachev, and the subsequent establishment of the Commonwealth in December 1991.

The discussion of problems and prospects of C.I.S. development focuses on the efforts of the former Soviet republics to move away from a Communist-dominated authoritarianism toward parliamentary democracy; policies to replace socialism with a market-driven economy; the reorganization of the former Soviet military; the persistence of interrepublic rivalries and conflict; and the consolidation of new international relationships with the late Soviet state's rivals in the West as well as with its former satellites in Central/Eastern Europe and countries in the developing world. This discussion ends with an assessment of the Commonwealth's chances of survival and, in the event it does endure, the possible kinds of interrepublic cooperation and coexistence likely to occur.

THE TRADITIONAL SOVIET SYSTEM

ROOTS

The traditional Soviet political system refers to the Marxist-Leninist polity established by the Bolsheviks (Russian followers of Karl Marx led by Vladimir Lenin in the early years of the twentieth century) after their successful revolution against the Czarist empire in November 1917. This new polity, called *socialist* and committed to the development of a communist society, transformed rural and agrarian Russia into an industrialized, semiurbanized modern society under the rule of the Communist party until the collapse of party rule 74 years later, at the end of 1991. Much of the traditional Soviet system prevails today in Russia and the other former Soviet republics that make up the Commonwealth of Independent States. One can speak of at least three major roots or sources of influence on the Soviet system: Czarist history, communist ideology, and the Bolshevik Revolution of 1917 to the ascendancy of Gorbachev, the last leader of the Soviet state, in 1985.

CZARISM

To understand the traditional Soviet political system as well as the new Commonwealth of Independent States, one has to understand Czarism. It is necessary to define Czarism; to determine why, as an almost medieval political phenomenon, it endured until 1917, centuries after many other nations in

(Eugene Gordon)

The Winter Palace in Leningrad is famous as the home of Romanov czars from the mid-eighteenth century to the end of their reign in 1917. Today it is a museum with nearly 3 million objects of art.

the West had outgrown their medievalism and adopted modern liberal political institutions; and to know how its opponents, especially the Russian Marxists, overthrew it and set up the Soviet system.

The Meaning of Czarism

In the 3 centuries preceding the 1917 Bolshevik Revolution and the Marxist seizure of power, the Czarist government was relentlessly authoritarian. The first czar of the Romanov family, Michael, ascended the Russian throne in 1614. Nicholas II, the last Romanov czar, abdicated in 1917. Throughout these 3 centuries of Romanov rule the power of the Czarist regime remained as autocratic, centralized, and extensive as the technology of the times permitted. The political theory of the Czarist regime—that the czar could do no wrong and accounted only to God—remained unchanged for 300 years.

The Romanov czars devised a variety of administrative measures to enforce political obedience, including a gargantuan bureaucracy and a ruthless secret police. Their power was nearly absolute, and the vast majority of their subjects had almost no way to influence them. Late-nineteenth-century czars, notably Alexander III (1881–1894) and Nicholas II (1894–1917), also had an obsessive drive to unify their multinational empire and reinforce their autocratic rule. They tried to impose the Russian language and the Russian Orthodox faith on non-Russian minorities under their rule. This "Russification" also involved harassment of Russian Jews to induce their abandonment of Judaism and to oblige them to accept Russian culture.

Czarism and Industrialization

Czarism was especially oppressive during the nineteenth and early twentieth centuries, as a result of the Industrial Revolution, which brought to Russia the same social miseries it had caused in the West. The last Romanov czars were indifferent to the plight of the growing Russian proletariat, who endured terrible living and working conditions as a result of the factory system in the cities of European Russia. These czars shared the assumption of other laissez-faire societies that the misery of the workers was inevitable, that the industrialization process was good for the entire society, and that government should not interfere to remedy its problems.

Why Czarism Endured

Why did the Czarist system endure past the time when other European political systems, notably those of England, France, and Germany, had begun to transform themselves into liberal democracies? One reason was a pervasive sense of insecurity, a result of the vulnerability of the enormous Russian landmass to the intrusions of hostile neighbors such as Swedes, Poles, Lithuanians, Mongols, Turks, and Germans. The Russian people tolerated the Czarist autocracy because it was the only certain means of assuring their defense and survival.

Serfdom reinforced Czarism. Most of the landless Russian peasantry had been serfs since the thirteenth century. Serfdom, which was really a form of slavery, kept Russians impoverished, ignorant, and servile. As long as serfdom flourished, the Russian people were politically, economically, and psychologically incapable of challenging Czarism.

Serfdom reinforced the czar's power and authority in another way. By providing the Russian landed aristocracy with a cheap source of labor, it rendered that class loyal to and supportive of the czar.

The czars encouraged and protected serfdom until the mid-nineteenth century. But even after the formal abolition of serfdom by Czar Alexander II in 1861, the dreadful conditions caused by serfdom—the poverty and ignorance of the Russian peasantry—continued.

The peculiar development of the Russian entrepreneurial middle class also helps to explain the endurance of Czarism. Since the money for industrial development in Russia at the end of the nineteenth century came from the czars, the Russian middle class, which was the beneficiary of industrialization, was beholden to the Czarist system and, like the aristocracy, supportive of it. Moreover, political reforms sought by the middle class were limited and of little practical value to the poverty-stricken Russian peasantry and workers who craved radical social and economic change.

Finally, the Russian Orthodox church buttressed Czarism. The church taught lessons that encouraged the deeply religious Russian people to accept and obey the Czarist order. Orthodox clergy preached the subordination of the individual to the congregation or group, the inevitability of suffering, the promise of a life after death in return for endurance and passivity, the evil of dissent and disobedience, and the sanctity of secular as well as spiritual authority.

Opposition to Czarism

While there was much to explain the endurance of Czarism, it is also true that there was a continuing opposition to it during the rule of the Romanovs. Opposition was at first sporadic, ineffectual, and ruthlessly suppressed by a regime fearful of change. In the seventeenth and eighteenth centuries this opposition consisted of periodic outbursts of rebellion by a depressed peasantry seeking relief from the burdens and cruelties of serfdom.

In the early nineteenth century the intelligentsia, including some military officers, offered some resistance. Influenced by liberal ideas developing in Western Europe during and after the French Revolution, they sought political and social change in Russia. But these critics had little impact on the regime's behavior until the reign of Alexander II (1855–1881).

Sympathetic to complaints that serfdom had destroyed peasant incentive and thus undermined Russian agricultural output, Czar Alexander II decreed the emancipation of the serfs in 1861. The newly emancipated serfs also received allotments of land purchased by the Russian government. They were to pay for this land on the "installment plan," over a 49-year period, and therefore did not really own it. Nor were they assured of enough land to support their families.

Czar Alexander II also carried out major political reforms in the countryside to permit some self-government in the form of local legislatures, called *zemstvos*, and a more rational court system modeled after judicial systems in Western Europe. But there was no liberalization of the Czarist government.

Consequently, opposition to the Czarist order continued in the 1870s and involved young political activists called *narodniki* ("nationalists"), who worked with the peasantry to pressure the czar to introduce further agricultural reform to relieve their poverty. The narodniki, however, found the peasantry more angry about their staggering indebtedness to landlords than about the conservatism of the czars.

During the 1870s more-violent political groups appeared. They were fervently hostile to the regime because of its stubborn resistance to reform. Some were called terrorists. They openly attacked Czar Alexander II and finally succeeded in assassinating him in March 1881.

The Russian Social Democratic Party (RSDP) was another kind of opposition to Czarism. Founded in 1898 and inspired by Marxist ideas, it sought to improve the living and working conditions of the depressed wage-earning proletariat who appeared in the cities of European Russia during the second half of the nineteenth century. Because of Czarist repression, the RSDP remained underground until legitimized in 1906 by Czar Nicholas II. A wing of the party made up of revolutionary Marxists believed in violence as the only way to improve the condition of the workers.

The Bolshevik Challenge

By 1912 the revolutionary Marxists had become a majority within the RSDP; hence, they were called *Bolsheviks*, from the Russian word meaning "greater." Their cohesiveness and sheer persistence under the leadership of Vladimir Lenin had enabled the Bolsheviks to expand their influence within the RSDP.

Czar Nicholas II's refusal to consider major social and economic reforms for workers helped to vindicate the Bolshevik commitment to violence. Indeed, he responded to the demands of the workers with excessive brutality. A workers' peaceful protest led by a Russian Orthodox priest, Father Gapon, ended in a massacre on Sunday, January 22, 1905.

Bolshevik radicalism also gained support within the RSDP as a result of the Revolution of October 1905, when workers in St. Petersburg and other cities waged a general strike to improve working conditions. The Revolution, in which the Bolsheviks actively participated, brought few concessions for the poor. Instead, Czar Nicholas II promised political reforms sought by the middle class, namely, a constitution, a new national Parliament called the *Duma*, and the introduction of ministerial accountability.

The Bolsheviks bided their time in the aftermath of the Bloody Sunday Massacre and the 1905 Revolution. Another opportunity to challenge the Czarist order came during World War I, which increased the hardships of workers and peasants. In March of 1917 workers again expressed their discontent by a general strike in St. Petersburg and other Russian cities. This massive popular action, along with the dissatisfaction of middle-class political groups in the Duma over the failure of Czar Nicholas to liberalize his rule despite the promises of reform in 1905, led to his abdication.

A provisional government of liberals and moderate socialists succeeded the czar. But this new government, of which Alexander Kerensky became prime minister in May, could not make real changes in Russian society. It refused to accommodate popular demands for an end to the war, for

(New York Public Library)

Nicholas II (1894–1917), the last of the Romanov czars, with his family. The czar, who abdicated in March 1917, his wife, and his children were murdered by the Bolsheviks on July 16, 1918.

further redistribution of land to poor peasants, and for immediate alleviation of widespread food shortages. This provisional government lasted only from March to November 1917.

During this 7-month period the Bolsheviks waited for the right moment to seize power. They were ready not only to destroy the provisional government, but also to oppose any groups, no matter how reformist, that did not support their revolutionary strategy. Their ultimate goal was the creation of a communist society.

The Bolshevik moment of action came on November 7, 1917, a point at which the provisional government was at its weakest because of the tremendous strain on all sectors of Russian life caused by the country's continuing involvement in the world war. The Bolsheviks seized control of key centers of administration and communication in St. Petersburg and other Russian cities. The provisional government, lacking popular support, collapsed.

To this day, the success of the Bolsheviks seems miraculous. After all, the Bolsheviks were only a very small minority of the Russian opposition to Czarism; the Russian state was the largest landmass of any European country; and previous revolutionary groups that had tried desperately to obtain change, let alone the destruction of the Czarist system, had failed.

Several reasons explain the success of the Bolsheviks. The most important, perhaps, was the leadership of Lenin, who was not only a masterful strategist but also an inspiring unifier and energizer of those who accepted his revolutionary beliefs. In his commitment to destroy Czarism and achieve communism in Russia, Lenin at all times believed that the end justified the means. This meant a willingness to take whatever steps necessary to win and hold power.

The Bolsheviks were successful also because of their highly disciplined, cohesive internal organization, which always had given them a strength out of proportion to their numbers. They loyally accepted Lenin's strictures about the need for unity, laid down in his famous 1902 treatise on the nature of the revolutionary party, called *What Is to Be Done?*

Events of 1917 played into the hands of the Bolsheviks. The most important for Bolshevik success were the intensification of material hardship as a result of World War I and the failure of the provisional government to alleviate it and to address major political and socioeconomic problems, including popular demands that Russia leave the war. Another important factor was the absence of any viable reformist alternative to the Bolsheviks. Other political opponents of Czarism had been in disarray. They had lacked the leadership and organization of the Bolsheviks.

COMMUNIST IDEOLOGY

Following their seizure of power from the provisional government, the Bolsheviks quickly established a new political and socioeconomic order based upon their Marxist ideology. This ideology, Soviet communism, explained the purposes and methods of the Soviet state from its inception in 1917.

The Role of Ideology

Soviet communist ideology was the inspiration for much Soviet political organization and behavior. It was the political language of all Soviet citizens and their government. It encouraged unity within the ethnically and culturally diverse Soviet society. It also legitimized the structure and behavior of the Soviet political system in the eyes of Soviet citizens and provided them with a basis for judging societies committed to other ideologies.

The Marxian Critique of Capitalism

The core of Soviet communist ideology was the Marxian critique of capitalism and advocacy of violent revolution by workers to replace capitalism with a stateless and classless society. In the mid-nineteenth century Karl Marx, a German, addressed the problems of Western industrial societies. But his ideas appealed to Russian revolutionaries, since the Czarist regime stubbornly refused to reform Russian society. By 1917 it was clear that Russia was a fertile place for Marxist ideas, even though it was predominantly agrarian and rural and had a very small urban proletariat.

According to Marx, those who own the means of production (capitalists) exploit those who are without property

(New York Public Library)

Karl Marx, the theorist whose ideas inspired revolutions against the European capitalist order in the nineteenth and early twentieth centuries, had more influence on underdeveloped, agrarian Russia, of which he knew little, than on his native Germany and its developed industrial neighbors, whose social and economic ills were the focus of his many writings.

(workers). Capitalists, motivated by greed and selfishness, will not do anything for workers that might diminish profits. Since those who own the means of production dominate the governments of capitalist societies, Marx believed that workers have no chance of relief. Thus, he said, to end their misery, workers must destroy not only the capitalistic economy but also the political system that protects it.

Marx also believed that workers in different national societies could unify against capitalists because they share a class consciousness. This consciousness of common economic complaint could override differences of religion, country, and ethnic background. A workers' movement, therefore, could be international and become a truly broad, unified opposition to capitalism. Marx also assumed that the workers have the physical and intellectual wherewithal to make a successful revolution against capitalism.

Marx described the ideal communist society, which would follow the workers' revolution against capitalism. It would have no social classes because there would be common ownership of the means of production. And since there would be no exploitation, there also would be no need for a state. Communist society would be egalitarian and democratic.

Socialism vs. Communism

The political and socioeconomic conditions in Russia caused Vladimir Lenin to modify Marxism. According to Lenin, Russia would need a transition period of undetermined length before the achievement of communism. During this transition period there would be a socialist system, in which the workers would create preconditions for the communist society, such as unity, social equality, economic prosperity, and political stability.

In the Russia of 1917, unity meant bringing Russian and non-Russian peoples together under a centralized administration that would permit cultural diversity but simultaneously assure the administrative unity essential to developing socialism and ultimately communism. Social equality involved the elimination of distinctions based on wealth, religion, race, and other causes of societal conflict.

Prosperity meant a redistribution of economic wealth through the elimination of private ownership of farms and the nationalization of industry and trade. It also meant creation of a comprehensive social-security and welfare system for all citizens that would end the misery of workers once and for all. This would be done by guaranteeing to all citizens a minimum material well-being in the areas of health, education, employment, and housing.

To achieve these conditions, Lenin believed that the workers would have to establish a dictatorship similar in some respects to the recently overthrown Czarist government. The socialist dictatorship would be coercive. It would suppress all protest and dissent. But politics in this new workers' state would be different from that in the old Czarist order. The new government would be of, by, and for workers and peasants and, hence, "democratic."

Lenin's socialism also called for a single political party of dedicated Marxists to lead the workers to their promised land of communism. This party always would be a small, highly disciplined organization of motivated revolutionaries who had successfully fought capitalism and were committed to the construction of a new socialist order essential to the achievement of communism. Since this party represented the workers, it would tolerate no rivals.

The Soviet Union was a socialist state striving to achieve communism. Therefore, it was not, strictly speaking, communist—it was socialist. Communism was not what the Soviet Union had but what it hoped to have.

Developed Socialism

In 1971 the Soviet Communist Party General Secretary Leonid Brezhnev introduced the concept of "developed socialism" to signify the Soviet Union's achievement of a new, higher level of overall socioeconomic and political development. But Soviet ideologists downplayed this new representation of socialism because of the wide gap between Soviet and Western standards of living. In 1977 a revised Constitution used less coercive language to define the Soviet state, which was no longer a "dictatorship" of the proletariat but a "state of the whole people" in which organs of local self-government, called soviets, had newly expanded administrative responsibilities.

Official Ideology and Popular Beliefs

While the principles of socialism were the basis on which Soviet administrative organization and behavior rested, other, popular political beliefs, derived from the official ideology, helped to explain the values and attitudes of ordinary Soviet citizens. The most widely held beliefs were the superiority of the community over the individual; the responsibility of the state to assure Soviet citizens a minimum level of material well-being in the areas of education, employment, health care, and housing; the notion that politics was not the job of ordinary private citizens but of the Soviet Communist Party; and the importance of societal order and stability.

These beliefs explained many well-known characteristics of the Soviet population, in particular the difficulty Soviet citizens had in understanding the self-reliance of ordinary people in the West and the Soviet citizenry's apparent willingness to accept with little question the Communist party's monopoly of power. It is also apparent why Soviet citizens had a strong sense of pride in the achievements of their socialist society, as Western visitors to the Soviet Union quickly found when they tried to make comparisons between Western and Soviet living conditions; and why Soviet society had very strong conservative instincts, seen clearly in the popular suspicion of political dissent and deviance and the lack of sympathy for Soviet dissidents.

POLITICAL EVOLUTION FROM 1917

The Soviet political system experienced six phases from 1917. Four of these phases coincided with the leaderships of

Vladimir Lenin, Joseph Stalin, Nikita Khrushchev, and Leonid Brezhnev. The fifth phase, the post-Brezhnevian phase, coincided with the leaderships of Yuri Andropov and Konstantin Chernenko. The sixth phase coincided with the leadership of Mikhail Gorbachev.

There was enormous continuity in Soviet political development. Yet a close look at what happened to Soviet institutions established in the early years of the Soviet system suggests that there also was much change. Indeed, the Soviet political system of the 1980s was far from what it was in the 1920s and 1930s.

The Lenin Phase (1917–1927)

Under Lenin, the Bolsheviks sought legitimacy by destroying enemies, creating a new political system, and inaugurating socioeconomic change in accordance with ideology. It was a harsh and brutal phase in terms of the condition of the individual, who was ruthlessly subordinated to the system's commitment to radical change and reform.

The achievements of the Soviet regime during the Lenin phase were monumental. The Bolsheviks concluded a long civil war against military remnants of the Czarist system. They established institutions of government, in particular the Soviet Federal Union. They affirmed the Communist party's supremacy in Soviet politics and abolished all other political parties.

The Bolsheviks suppressed criticism and dissent outside the Communist party by means of censorship and the subordination of interest groups, including the trade unions. Inside the party, criticism and dissent were discouraged by curtailment of discussion and debate and the imposition of a militarylike discipline of its membership.

Under Lenin, the Soviet leadership took the first steps toward socialism. First it tried, but quickly abandoned, a plan called "War Communism," to eliminate private enterprise. The Soviet leaders did too much too fast, and there was great popular resistance.

Lenin decided to move more slowly and cautiously in the development of socialism. The new Soviet regime established a mixed economy in which some private ownership of the means of production continued, especially in agriculture. But other sectors of the economy, notably industry, were nationalized. The creation of this mixed economy was called the "New Economic Policy," or NEP.

When Lenin died, in 1924, the change of leadership took place with virtually no popular involvement. There was competition between prominent political figures like Leon Trotsky, Lev Kamenev, Nikolai Bukharin, Gregori Zinoviev, and Joseph Stalin for the position of party general secretary. Stalin was successful because he isolated, discredited, and ultimately destroyed those who opposed him. He shrewdly advocated policies (notably a continuation of Leninist initiatives like the NEP) that he knew the party rank-and-file supported, even if he himself preferred alternatives. Finally, Stalin had the advantage of a political machine of supporters whom he had been able to appoint in preceding years to positions of influence within the party.

The Stalin Phase (1927–1953)

In the Stalin phase, which began with the Soviet Communist Party's endorsement of Stalin's victory over Trotsky and his supporters at its 15th Congress, in December 1927, many administrative characteristics of the later political system developed. The process of autocratization begun by Lenin continued, and ultimately the system became totalitarian.

Under Stalin, the Soviet system came under the rule of a single, omnipotent leader. Through his personal control of the major instruments of political power, especially the Communist party and the secret police, Stalin became the object of intense fear and respect. He also became something of a religious symbol.

Real and suspected critics and opponents of Stalin's policies were liquidated during Stalin's "Great Purge" of the 1930s. The Great Purge depended upon police use of unprecedented powers of investigation and interrogation. A politically subservient court system also played a significant role in the purges. Defendants had little protection against a state

(New York Public Library)

Vladimir Lenin strikes a familiar pose, haranguing workers and other Soviet citizens in 1919. Leon Trotsky stands listening at the right of the platform.

bent on destroying all challenges to its power. Arrests during the Great Purge ran into the millions. The targets were people as diverse as top political figures with whom Stalin had worked in earlier years, like Trotsky, Kamenev, Zinoviev, and Bukharin, high-ranking military officers, lower-level Communist party members, government workers, and ordinary citizens. Indeed, anyone even suspected of criticism of the regime was caught up in this terrifying nightmare.

Stalinist totalitarianism had other dimensions. One was a highly centralized bureaucracy. Another was the virtual extinction of representative institutions. Legislatures on the national and local levels of government lost political influence. They did not meet regularly and were subordinated to executive bodies. The judiciary became a pliant tool of the executive and of the Communist party, dutifully obeying the will of the leadership.

The justification for this totalitarianism was social discipline to accelerate the process of socialist development, which required enormous material sacrifice by an already impoverished society. Some people believe also that Stalin accumulated enormous power for personal reasons, to make himself a "Marxist czar."

Stalin presided over a profound socioeconomic transformation of the Soviet Union. He was responsible for the destruction of whatever capitalism remained in Soviet agriculture. Under Stalin's first 5 Year Plan, beginning in 1928, privately owned farms were seized and converted into self-governing collective farms or state-controlled farms on which farmers worked for regular wages like workers in factories. Those who resisted collectivization, notably well-off peasant farmers called *kulaks* who had benefited from the reforms of Lenin's New Economic Policy, were arrested and imprisoned.

Stalin also undertook a crash program to industrialize the Soviet Union, which was predominantly agrarian at the time of the 1917 Revolution. He pursued industrialization not only because it was a necessary component of socialist development (industrialization would lessen the Soviet Union's dependence on foreign manufacturers) but also because it would strengthen Soviet military power and the nation's defense capability.

Stalin's economic policies were carried out by a highly centralized administrative machine in which bureaucrats in Moscow made most of the key decisions on allocation of resources, production, and distribution. The high degree of centralization resulted from a strongly held assumption that the most efficient way to achieve rapid and sweeping socioeconomic change was by a concentration of decision-making power at the center of the country to assure a disciplined social response to changes that involved, in the short run, huge sacrifices by the individual.

Soviet society experienced great hardships in the Stalinist phase. Agricultural output declined, causing severe food shortages. The regime intensified the shortages by exporting food in order to pay for industrial imports. In addition, in pursuing industrialization, Stalin gave priority to the production of so-called producer goods, such as machine tools, rather than to consumer goods, like clothing and other necessities.

Stalin led the Soviet state in World War II, during which it is believed that 20 million Soviet citizens perished. Although the war was a terrible drain on an already impoverished and exhausted society, it resulted, paradoxically, in strengthening the Soviet dictatorship. The war distracted the Soviet people from the hardship of Stalin's excesses of the 1930s. It generated patriotism and national unity. It also greatly strengthened the Soviet military machine. The Soviet Union emerged from the war as second in power only to the United States.

The Khrushchev Phase (1953–1964)

When Stalin died, in March 1953, no one in the leadership had the equivalent of his power. Consequently, several influential senior party officials, including Nikita Khrushchev, shared power. Khrushchev was the most influential because of his power base in the popular and resource-rich Ukraine; his administrative expertise in agriculture, a critical area of the Soviet economy; and his apparent closeness in earlier years to Stalin. Moreover, there was support for his becoming Stalin's successor as party general secretary (Khrushchev subsequently changed the name of this office to first secretary) on the understanding that he would continue to share power with others; that decision-making in the party

(New York Public Library)

The famous and forbidding Soviet leader Joseph Stalin at a meeting with other Soviet leaders in 1937, the time of the purges. The man directly to Stalin's left is V. M. Molotov, who would become Soviet foreign minister in March 1939, at the time of the German dismemberment of Czechoslovakia.

would be by consensus; and that there would be an end to some of Stalin's abusive policies, particularly mass purges, indiscriminate use of terror, and fostering of the personality cult.

In the mid-1950s Khrushchev consolidated his power base shrewdly and carefully, making appointments of his supporters to key positions in the upper echelons of the party bureaucracy. He adopted a platform calculated to appeal to the party rank-and-file, promising a new concern with the quality of life, and he tried to cultivate a grass-roots popularity to strengthen his power within the party.

Khrushchev's accumulation of power climaxed in June 1957, when he crushed the opposition of the so-called anti-party group. This group consisted of several of Khrushchev's earlier colleagues whom he had pushed out of power because of their criticisms of him. They tried, but failed, to oust Khrushchev. With the help of supporters like the influential Minister of Defense Marshal G. D. Zhukov, Khrushchev defeated the anti-party group and had its members expelled from the party. He then forced the resignation of Premier Nikolai Bulganin. Khrushchev's power now reached its apex.

Under Khrushchev, Soviet society moved away from—and Khrushchev even denounced—the most rigid aspects of Stalinism. The new Soviet leadership recognized that many of Stalin's actions had been unnecessary, even counterproductive.

The most conspicuous change occurred in politics. Khrushchev openly discredited Stalin's policies in order to change or abandon them. For example, to mitigate Stalinist repressiveness, he condemned the personality cult, removed known supporters of Stalin from positions of responsibility in the Communist party apparatus, and placed the secret police under party control, affording a relief from terror. There was limited opportunity for mild criticism of government policy in the press.

There was an increase in popular involvement in government, although the essence of the dictatorship remained. For example, Khrushchev called for the reinvigoration of legislative bodies on all levels of administration. They were to increase their role in monitoring the economy, especially the performance of farms and factories. They were to report production problems to higher authorities.

There were also modest changes in the judicial system to provide individuals with more opportunity to defend themselves in trials. For example, defense attorneys were allowed to be more aggressive in their protection of clients. Judges were occasionally allowed to find for the defendant in political trials.

Khrushchev initiated economic change as well. The regime expressed concern for the material well-being of the individual. Khrushchev tried to increase food supplies, to make available more manufactured goods like home appliances and automobiles, and to provide more housing.

The Khrushchevian leadership showed a new interest in efficiency and quality in economic production. To improve performance, Khrushchev divided the Communist party

(United Nations photo)

The late Soviet leader Nikita Khrushchev addressing the 21st Congress of the Soviet Communist Party in 1959.

bureaucracy into separate industrial and agricultural hierarchies. He fostered a measure of administrative decentralization, giving line officials, such as factory managers and collective-farm directors, more autonomy in the running of their production units.

The Khrushchev phase ended in 1964, with the first secretary's sudden ouster by the Central Committee, which had become dissatisfied with not only his domestic and foreign policies but also his political style. Despite his condemnation of the personality cult, Khrushchev had begun to re-create it around himself. Following the anti-party crisis he took both the offices of premier and first secretary in 1958. He thereby ended the collegialism (shared authority) in top-level decision-making he had agreed to accept when he first took power.

Other factors contributed to Khrushchev's ouster. Acute shortages of grain and dairy products in the early 1960s were an embarrassment. His efforts to streamline party organization produced chaos and conflict among party administrators. And he was blamed for alienating China, letting the United States get the better of the Soviet Union in the Cuban Missile Crisis, and accomplishing nothing toward the reunification of Berlin under East German rule.

The Brezhnev Phase (1964–1982)

Leonid Brezhnev succeeded Khrushchev as Soviet party general secretary (the term first secretary was dropped) in

October 1964. His personal and political closeness to Khrushchev had not stopped him from mobilizing the support of Khrushchev's critics. Brezhnev was the choice of his Politburo/Presidium colleagues because he seemed to be the kind of quiet, professional, and conservative leadership they wanted.

Under Brezhnev, there was a reappraisal and alteration of Khrushchevian policies. Brezhnev considered many of Khrushchev's policies to be impractical and ineffective, such as his administrative decentralization and the division of the Communist party into industrial and agricultural hierarchies. The Brezhnev regime sought to discredit Khrushchev—in a way that calls to mind Khrushchev's criticisms of Stalin years earlier—as a means of ridding the party and state bureaucracies of some of Khrushchev's close supporters.

Brezhnev also cautiously rehabilitated Stalin. His purpose was a discreet restoration of some Stalin-like discipline in Soviet society. Stalin was now praised as a war hero, and his hometown of Gori, in Georgia, was made a museum. Some Stalinists imprisoned by Khrushchev were released. High-ranking party figures who had been associated with Stalinism, like Central Committee Secretary Mikhail Suslov, were kept on in positions of power.

Along with this renewal of interest in Stalin were more direct measures to reemphasize political discipline and ideological orthodoxy inside the Communist party. Brezhnev extended the activities of party control commissions on the union and regional levels.

There was an equivalent tightening up outside the party. The Brezhnev regime began an all-out attack on dissident members of the literary and scientific intelligentsia. There were sudden invasions of the privacy of suspected dissidents by KGB agents; prolonged imprisonment of convicted dissidents in labor camps, penitentiaries, and insane asylums; pressures on some of the dissidents to emigrate from the Soviet Union into permanent exile; and all kinds of harassment of individuals, such as loss of jobs, restrictions on travel, and loss of special privileges. The regime also acted punitively and retributively toward Jews who wanted to emigrate.

Brezhnev did not completely de-Khrushchevize Soviet society; nor did he thoroughly re-Stalinize it. For example, the top party leadership remained collegial. Brezhnev never really became more than "first among equals" in the party Politburo. Despite his accumulation of enormous political influence, Brezhnev never duplicated Stalin's mastery of the system. The Brezhnev leadership seemed determined to eschew the personality cult and the excessive accumulation of political authority in the hands of one person. Brezhnev also tolerated development of what has been termed *institutional pluralism,* namely, wider discussion and debate in newspapers, periodicals, and books; regime sensitivity to bureaucratic interests on different levels of the party organization; and an increasing articulation of special interests, such as party bureaucrats, the KGB, the army, industrial managers, economists, jurists, and writers, seeking to influence leadership policy-making. Finally, Brezhnev called for

a larger measure of independence for local legislative bodies in dealing with economic, financial, and other matters that came within their jurisdiction. They were told to become more active in the working of local agricultural and industrial enterprises.

Now called "the period of stagnation," the last years of Brezhnev's rule witnessed a slowdown of economic growth. The regime stubbornly refused to abandon Stalinist policy. With its traditional emphasis on expansion of *quantity* rather than on *quality* of output, Brezhnev's adherence to this outmoded growth model of the 1930s made for inefficient use of the country's land, labor, and capital resources and resulted in inadequate or shoddy output in industry and agriculture and the persistence of a low standard of living.

Another cause of the economic slowdown was political. An indulgent Brezhnev regime paid for the loyalty of bureaucrats by allowing them to place personal interests ahead of the public good in the performance of their official duties and by ignoring their inefficiency, negligence, indifference, and corruption.

By the early 1980s there was a marked deterioration of living conditions for most Soviet citizens. A new generation of Soviet citizens—well educated, articulate, and knowledgeable about better conditions in the West—was disgusted by the regime's perceived failure to deliver the material well-being promised in the ideology of communism. Moreover, a growing number of strikes and demonstrations against the authorities threatened the stability of the country and a collapse of what in the West has been called a "social contract" between the rulers and ruled. According to this contract, which seems to prevail in most socialist societies, the Soviet people gave up many political rights to the party and state leadership in return for a guarantee of security, free health care, and a minimum material well-being, including guaranteed employment. By the time of Brezhnev's death and during the brief tenure of his successors, Andropov and Chernenko, from 1982 until 1985, there was, indeed, the possibility of a major social upheaval in the Soviet Union.

The Post-Brezhnev Phase (1982–1985)

A series of successions quickly followed Brezhnev's death in November 1982: Yuri Andropov (1982–1984), Konstantin Chernenko (1984–1985), and Mikhail Gorbachev (1985–1991). Andropov and Chernenko were in power for too brief a time to leave their imprint on Soviet society; there were no significant changes in the structure and functioning of the Soviet system under their leadership.

The Gorbachev Phase (1985–1991)

Following his promotion within the Communist party Politburo in March 1985 to the position of general secretary, Gorbachev spoke often of a "pre-crisis" in Soviet society. By this he meant the flaws and errors of his predecessors, notably Brezhnev, whose era of rule Gorbachev condemned as one of stagnation. He predicted social upheaval unless the country addressed this pre-crisis by a program of broad and profound systemic reform. This perestroika, or restructuring, at first focused on the economy with a view to raising the depressed Soviet standard of living. But Gorbachev discovered that economic improvement depended on the introduction of other changes—notably, a more tolerant and open political environment; greater popular influence over the civil and military institutions of government and over the organization and behavior of the Communist party; and a foreign policy responsive to domestic needs and priorities.

Perestroika was meant to be a long-term program intended to transform the Soviet Union into a completely different kind of polity, comparable in scope to the transformation of Czarist Russia by Lenin and Stalin into the Soviet Union. Although Soviet citizens as well as people abroad were pessimistic about the chances of Gorbachev's success and even of his political survival, nobody expected that life in the Soviet Union would ever go back to what it was before Gorbachev. However, few imagined the scope of the changes that exploded in the early 1990s.

HOW THE SOVIET SYSTEM WORKED

Major components of any political system are instruments of popular political participation and institutions of government. Citizens of a state participate in politics through voting, interest groups, and political parties. Institutions of government are concerned with policy-making and include executives, legislatures, judiciaries, and bureaucracies. In socialist countries, other important aspects of government are the planned, regimented, centralized economy and the comprehensive social-security and welfare system.

POPULAR PARTICIPATION

Soviet citizens were educated to perform a political role essential to the achievement of socialism and communism. "Ideal" Soviet citizens were supposed to place the well-being of the community ahead of individual self-interest and personal gain. Most willingly accepted the view of government that opposition to its policies was immoral and illegal and that those who opposed them were criminals. They also accepted the Communist party's monopoly of political power. They were expected to be self-disciplined, devoted to work, and to contribute to civic activities.

Political Education

The Soviet system used a variety of methods to foster these characteristics, not least of which was the pervasive use of political symbols and messages. These glorified the progress of the Soviet state toward socialism and exhorted the Soviet people to work harder for further socialist development. Slogans and ubiquitous pictures of Marx and Lenin and the current leadership everywhere evoked the pride of Soviet citizens and reminded them of what was expected.

The mass media were an important way in which Soviet citizens received lessons on behavior. Television and radio programs, newspapers, magazines, and books told Soviets the political values and attitudes they were expected to have as members of a society that was building socialism. This relentless education by the media was reinforced by restrictions on foreign travel, which discouraged Soviet citizens from contact with non-Soviet ideas; and by heavy-handed censorship, which prevented widespread dissemination of domestic criticism and dissent.

Soviet citizens were taught proper political behavior also by a comprehensive system of punishment and rewards. Rewards were given to those citizens whose behavior in the workplace, neighborhood, and elsewhere in society was above reproach; who were never "troublemakers," in the sense of shirking their work or being nonconformist or socially deviant in personal lifestyle; and who thereby had some or all of the ideal characteristics of the "new Soviet person." Exemplary Soviet citizens could obtain more easily than would otherwise be the case improved living conditions in preferred areas; promotion to higher rank, greater responsibility, and more pay on the job; and the award of medals and honors that called public attention to them and improved their status.

The process of political education started early in life and continued to the end. It took place everywhere and was truly impossible to escape. For example, ideological and political education occurred on the preschool, elementary-school, and high-school levels, and in universities. The classroom and the teacher fostered the collective mentality by group learning. Children were taught not only the importance of submerging the individual personality to that of the group but also responsiveness to peer pressure for conformity. Indeed, by belaboring the individual's obligation to conform, schools and teachers discouraged children from questioning commonly accepted norms and saying what they really thought. There was hardly a kindergarten room without a picture of Lenin, and no child went through the system without achieving some familiarity with Lenin's life, work, and stature in Soviet society.

Political education also occurred in such official youth organizations as the Young Pioneers and the Komsomol as well as in other social groups. It went on in the workplace—in factories, farms, mines, and business offices—where time was regularly set aside for "study sessions" on political and ideological issues conducted by members of the Communist party. Political education occurred also in apartment houses, recreation facilities, and in all military units at home and abroad. One even got a political education while walking down a street or riding a subway train, where one's eyes could not avoid contact with advertisements that contained a political message.

As a consequence of this education process, most Soviet people tolerated the values of their political system. Most citizens did not question the restricted voting and interest-group activity or the dominance of the Communist party.

(UN photo/Philip Teuscher)

Moscow's Red Square was the main square of the capital of the Soviet Union, not only for the military parades regularly held there but also because it was the symbolic political center of the Soviet state. On the left are the Kremlin Wall and the Lenin Mausoleum.

Although some complained, they did not oppose, and they certainly did not challenge, the system.

Voting

The most frequent opportunity for popular political participation was voting in legislative elections on the national and local levels of government. The important phase of these elections seemed to be the nomination process, which until the Gorbachev era was carefully supervised by the Communist party to assure that candidates for office were politically reliable and not critical of the regime and its policies. Several kinds of organizations were legally authorized to nominate candidates: local agencies of the Communist party, the Komsomol, trade unions, cooperatives, work collectives, and meetings of servicemen in their military units.

Although voting for most of the Soviet Union's history did not provide citizens with the opportunity to change leadership and policies, as it does for citizens in Western democracies, it was not inconsequential. Voting provided at least the illusion of popular involvement in the political system. It helped to legitimize the system, its leaders, and its policies by giving to citizens the appearance of having some say in how the country developed socialism.

Interest-Group Activity

Pre-perestroika interest-group activity, another opportunity for popular political participation, was limited, primarily because the Communist party jealously guarded its political monopoly and was sensitive to challenges of its policies. Well-defined organizations committed to the special interests of particular groups, such as industrial workers, educators, jurists, economists, physicians, and writers, certainly did exist in the Soviet Union. But while their leaders may have been listened to, the organizations had little independence and could not aggressively pressure the Soviet regime to pursue policies favorable to their supporters.

On the other hand, some special-interest groups did have substantial influence over policy-making by the top Soviet leadership. The most important of them were the army and the KGB. Their leaders were in the top echelons of the party, where they could lobby for preferred policy alternatives.

Some interest groups were illegal. Among these were the Helsinki Watch Group, which was concerned with human rights in the Soviet Union; Jewish émigrés who sought freedom to leave the Soviet Union; and antinuclear peace demonstrators. When members of these groups tried to influence government policy by public demonstrations or even by peaceful written petitions, they frequently were arrested or harassed.

Finally, there were amorphous interest groups within the rank-and-file of the Soviet military, civilian bureaucracies, and legislatures. Soldiers, civil servants, and elected political officials constituted a potential source of interest articulation. But these people had no organization, no leadership, and no independent funding to enable them to express grievances and influence policy-making.

The Communist Party

The Communist Party of the Soviet Union (CPSU) was the most important vehicle of popular participation. According to Soviet ideology, the Communist party was the agent of the working masses, charged with leading them to communism. It took responsibility for all successes and failures of Soviet political development. Few Soviet Marxists believed that the achievement of socialism and communism was possible without the leadership of the party.

The party enjoyed a central, dominant, and omnipotent role in Soviet life. It was the real source of power and leadership in Soviet society. It had something to say about almost every aspect of Soviet life and was the ultimate source of all policies. The party was the object of reverence and admiration of most ordinary Soviet citizens, who trusted its judgment in the management of Soviet national affairs.

Party Membership

Communist party membership was elitist, in accordance with Marxist-Leninist ideology. Its membership rarely exceeded 6 to 12 percent of the total Soviet population. While the party claimed that more than half of its membership was drawn from workers and farmers, after several years members become bureaucrats within the party organization and no longer had the outlook of the large social groups in which they grew up. As this happened, the party became less a reflection of the people it served. Furthermore, party membership did not represent all of Soviet society, because its membership tended to be overwhelmingly Russian and male. For a long time its top leaders were mostly over age 60.

It was also true that some people joined the Communist party less out of ideological fervor than out of the desire for career advancement, which the party could assure. Nonideological incentives for joining the Communist party were the vast array of perquisites available to many party members. Attractive perks were access to scarce items of food, clothing, and appliances imported from abroad and beyond the reach of most Soviet citizens and a top spot on a long waiting list for good apartments in preferred locations or for scarce new automobiles, for which many ordinary Soviet citizens had to wait up to 10 years.

Party Organization: Leadership Organs in Moscow

Essential to its leadership of Soviet society was the Communist party's traditionally disciplined and cohesive internal organization. It was based upon the principles of democratic centralism, which stipulated that leading party bodies on all levels of organization were elected and must account for their behavior in periodic reports to their constituents and to higher bodies within the party. Democratic centralism called for strict party discipline and subordination of minority to majority. It also required the obedience of lower party agencies to higher agencies.

Democratic centralism was much more restrictive in fact than the theory implied. Before the late 1980s, the top leadership was not elected; it self-selected its membership, and there were no limits on the time of service in office. The top leadership's reports to the party were not open to criticism and debate, and factionalism within the rank-and-file was strictly forbidden. In effect, the practice of democratic centralism made the internal organization of the Soviet Communist Party highly autocratic, with the selection and behavior of the leadership not subject to any real influence from or control by the rank-and-file membership.

The All-Union Party Congress. According to party rules, the All-Union Party Congress was the supreme organ of the party, the locus of sovereignty, and the agency that selected the party leadership and determined party policy. The Congress was supposed to meet at least once every 4 to 5 years. It consisted of delegates chosen by party agencies on all levels of organization.

In practice, the Congress did little of substance before the perestroika era. It rarely discussed but always approved the general secretary's report. It had little choice in the election of the Central Committee. It had virtually no role in the selection of either the membership of the Politburo or the general secretary, the titular head of the party.

The proceedings of the Congress, however, were important symbolically, in the sense of helping to legitimize the leadership and its policies by giving the appearance of all-party support. The Congress also provided the party leadership with an opportunity to communicate with rank-and-file members to obtain their support of its policies. And because representatives of foreign Communist parties attended—but did not participate in—the Soviet party Congress, the leadership had an opportunity to engage in shoulder-rubbing diplomacy to help achieve foreign-policy objectives.

The Central Committee. Another and somewhat more important leading organ of the Communist party was the Central Committee, which was elected by and accountable to the Congress. The rules of the party charged the Central Committee with appointing the leading functionaries of the party, with directing their work, and in particular with originating and executing the party budget. The Central Committee was also supposed to direct the work of administrative agencies and nonparty organizations throughout the country in which party members participated.

The authority of the Central Committee was broad and significant—at least on paper. In practice, however, the role of the Central Committee was much more restricted than the rules of the party prescribed. This was partly because it had become a very large and unwieldy body since Lenin's time. In the 1930s Stalin had packed it with his supporters. As its membership expanded and its capacity to deliberate declined, it was obliged to delegate day-to-day decision-making authority to a small group made up of its most influential members: the Politburo.

In the Khrushchev and Brezhnev years the Central Committee regained some influence over policy-making. It debated policies of the top party leadership in the Politburo, which sought its approval and support, especially when difficult and controversial decisions had to be made, like the intervention in Czechoslovakia in August 1968. Because Central Committee membership, which consisted mainly of secretaries from intermediate-level party agencies responsible for implementing party policies, could provide the Politburo with the administrative support it needed to lead, the Central Committee's influence on the Politburo increased somewhat.

The Politburo. The Politburo consisted of 12 to 17 of the most senior party leaders, who served as a collective leadership of the Communist party. The presiding officer of the Politburo was the general secretary, who was usually the choice of the Politburo. The Politburo conveyed its wishes to the Central Committee, which nominated the general secretary and presented him to the Congress for its approval.

The Politburo's members were influential primarily because they held other important posts in either the party or the state. The Politburo included key members of the Secretariat. The Politburo membership also included high-ranking

government officials, such as the chair of the Presidium of the Supreme Soviet (who was also the Soviet president, the chair of the Council of Ministers, or premier), the minister of Foreign Affairs, the minister of Defense, and the chair of the KGB. The chief of the Leningrad party organization, which was responsible for supervising a substantial portion of Soviet heavy and defense industries, sometimes was in the Politburo. Other members usually were the premier of the Russian Soviet Federative Socialist Republic (R.S.F.S.R.), the largest and most populous of the 15 constituent republics, and the first secretary of the Ukrainian party organization in Kiev, who was in charge of the most fertile and productive agricultural region of the Soviet Union.

Given the influence of its individual members, Politburo decision-making was based upon consensus. It was no longer possible for a single person, say, the general secretary, to dictate policy. The Politburo and the Central Committee no longer tolerated a Stalin-like leader. The best a general secretary could do was to mediate and persuade.

The Secretariat. Another important leadership organ of the Communist party was the Central Committee's Secretariat. It had the critical responsibility of directing the party bureaucracy. In theory, the Secretariat's membership was selected

(Gamma-Liaison/Bernard Charlou)

The top Soviet leadership appears in a familiar pose in front of the Lenin Mausoleum in Red Square, observing the traditional May Day parade. Foreigners could gauge the political influence of particular leaders by their locations relative to that of the Soviet Communist Party general secretary, who in this picture is the late Leonid Brehznev (standing fourth from the right).

by and accountable to the Central Committee but, in practice, the Politburo made the appointments. According to party rules, the Secretariat selected the personnel of the party bureaucracy, supervised its behavior to ensure execution of Politburo decisions, and in general supervised the ebb and flow of party life throughout the Soviet Union.

The General Secretary. The head of the Secretariat, who was also the leader of the Soviet Communist Party, was the general secretary (called first secretary in the time of Khrushchev). His leadership authority came from the support of colleagues in the Secretariat, the Central Committee, and the Politburo. While the general secretary was supposed to be elected by the All-Union Party Congress, in fact he was the choice of his colleagues in the other leading organs of the party. The Congress simply ratified their choice.

Party Organization on the Local Level

Party organization on the intermediate and local levels of Soviet administration followed the model of organization at the top. There was a congress on the republic level; its equivalent on the city and district levels was the conference. On the very local level, in villages, towns, factories, and farms, the equivalent was the general meeting. Accompanying these legislative bodies were executive organs comparable to the Central Committee and Secretariat in Moscow. Below the republic level, executive organs were called executive committees and bureaus. As was true of the top level, legislative bodies did not meet for long periods of time; they generally allowed executive bodies to transact business in their name.

Local party organization proliferated everywhere. There was hardly a village, town, urban center, factory, farm, neighborhood, large apartment house, military unit, organization meeting, or other gathering place where the party did not have some kind of official presence. The larger the number of people in a particular place, the more complex the party organization there was likely to be.

A given local agency of the party was always subordinate to the next higher level of administration, to party organization on the union-republic level, and to the leading bodies of the party in Moscow.

Through this ubiquitous local organization, the Communist party was able to monitor the development of Soviet life to ensure progress in the development of socialism. Its local organization enabled the party to interact with institutions of all kinds—administrative, social, and military—to assure that their behavior conformed to predetermined norms and in particular that party-originated policies were successfully carried out.

The Party and the Government Bureaucracy

The Soviet Communist Party monitored and controlled the government bureaucracy on all levels of Soviet administration, from the top of the bureaucratic pyramid in Moscow to the local, grass-roots level. The party thus maintained its supremacy over government and made sure that state administrators carried out its policies.

On all administrative levels of the Soviet government there was an interlocking relationship between party and state agencies, which one might refer to as parallelism. There were two important features of parallelism. First, for most agencies of local administration, there was an equivalent party agency that continually surveilled, supervised, and scrutinized its government counterpart to assure conformity and obedience to decisions of higher party authorities. Second, in many instances, local party officials held positions in the government agencies they were supervising in the same manner that party leaders in the Politburo simultaneously held top positions in the national governments.

Finally, the Communist party assured a continuing subordination of the government bureaucracy on all administrative levels by its control of appointments to both civilian and military positions of responsibility, through a system called *nomenklatura*. This was the list of government positions over which the party legally had control of appointments. The party used its appointment power to make sure that people in responsibility in the government bureaucracy were politically loyal, or properly "red," as well as professionally qualified, or adequately expert.

In sum, the Soviet Communist Party had enormous influence over the workings of the government bureaucracy. It is not an exaggeration to say that there was very little that bureaucrats could do that was outside of party purview or beyond its control.

The Party and Trade Unions

Soviet trade unions confined their activities to helping workers increase fringe benefits and to interceding with management on behalf of workers who had gotten into trouble as a result of absenteeism, poor performance on the job, or some other unsatisfactory conduct that could have led to punishment. Soviet unions also were expected to mobilize workers to expand output to meet goals set by the party. Unions were expected to ensure that workers make their contribution to socialist development and to resolve problems that interfere with stable labor/management relations.

The Soviet Communist Party closely controlled Soviet trade-union organizations. The general secretary of the All-Union Council of Trade Unions was usually a high-ranking member of the Communist party. Party members were found in trade-union organizations throughout the country. And local party agencies maintained regular contacts with union officials in factories and other units of industrial production.

The Party and the Army

Party ties to the army and other military services were equally important. But they were somewhat more complex and uncertain than ties to the trade unions, if only because the Soviet Army was a powerful and influential institution in its own right.

The party/army relationship went through several phases of evolution, although the party leadership was nearly always suspicious of the military. In the 1920s and early 1930s the army was still officered by personnel trained under the czars. Its leadership was suspected of the same self-interest characteristic of military organizations everywhere else and aroused party doubts about its loyalty to communist ideology. Officers suspected of political unreliability were eliminated during Stalin's purges of the 1930s.

Party distrust of the military decreased considerably in the era of World War II. The army proved its loyalty by expelling the Nazi invaders and extending Soviet control into Central/Eastern Europe.

After World War II the Soviet Army acquired new political influence. Apart from the fact that it had aroused much patriotic admiration as a result of its heroic achievements in the war, the army was given responsibility for directing Soviet space exploration and developing nuclear weapons. In the 1950s, 1960s, and 1970s the army's influence increased as a result of the Sino-Soviet dispute and a perceived Chinese threat to Soviet territory in East Asia, as well as because of growing Soviet political and military difficulties in Central/Eastern Europe, such as in Hungary in 1956 and Czechoslovakia in 1968.

Beginning in the late 1950s, moreover, the army leadership saw opportunities to make allies within the party and thereby gain a role in policy-making. In the July 1957 antiparty crisis, which threatened the political dominance of Khrushchev, Army Chief Marshal Zhukov supported Khrushchev against his rivals and critics, enabling Khrushchev to retain power.

Army leaders in Brezhnev's time, in particular the late marshals Gretchko and Ustinov, supported the general secretary's policies in return for his commitment to an expansion of the country's conventional and nuclear capabilities. The army wanted to avoid the kind of humiliation suffered in the Cuban Missile Crisis in 1962, when military weakness required Soviet accommodation of U.S. demands for a withdrawal of offensive missiles from Cuba.

But the party still monitored the army and the other military services carefully. For example, party agents in military uniform proliferated the various units at home and abroad to assure the participation of enlisted and nonenlisted personnel in political study meetings. To the dismay of commanding officers, such meetings could at times interfere with performance efficiency. The party also made sure that only politically reliable officers were promoted to positions of responsibility through its control of the nomenklatura.

FORMAL STRUCTURES OF GOVERNMENT

The formal structures of government in the Soviet Union were in appearance not unlike those of many other modern political systems, in particular those in the West. But the Soviet government was, from the Western vantage point, a highly centralized dictatorship. The starting point of an analysis of this discrepancy between appearance and reality is the Soviet Constitution.

The Soviet Constitution

There were four Soviet constitutions, although the substance of them did not change much. The Soviet Constitution described, legitimized, and reinforced the administrative order that the Bolsheviks established following their seizure of power in November 1917. The Constitution signified where the Soviet regime perceived itself to be in the process of socialist development. It also was intended to serve as a guide to where Soviet society would go in the future.

The last Constitution, promulgated in 1977, was distinctive in several ways. It identified the Soviet Union as a developed socialist state, signifying the achievement of a new, higher level of socialist development. It confirmed the Communist party as the leading and guiding force in Soviet society in much more explicit terms than were used in the earlier documents. The 1977 Constitution indicated the continuing need for social discipline. It stressed the citizen's responsibility for meeting obligations as a prerequisite for the enjoyment of political rights and privileges.

Soviet Federalism

The Soviet Union had a federal type of administrative system in which there was at least the appearance of a dispersal of power between central (federal) administration in Moscow and local administrative agencies. The country was divided into 15 constituent republics, which in turn were subdivided into smaller units of government called autonomous republics; and into national areas, which were further subdivided into districts, cities, towns, and villages. The constituent republics were each inhabited by the largest of the many—more than 100—culturally and linguistically diverse national groups that comprised Soviet society. Autonomous republics and national areas were inhabited by somewhat smaller ethnic groups.

Established in 1922, this Soviet federal structure recognized the separate cultural identities of the large national groups that the Soviet state inherited from the Czarist empire. To this end, Soviet federalism provided for *cultural autonomy,* which meant the right of local inhabitants to use their own language in local administration (although local party and government officials were supposed to be fluent in Russian as well) and the right of newspapers and schools to use the local language. To reinforce cultural autonomy, the Soviet federal system guaranteed the inviolability of union-republic boundaries and the representation of the constituent union-republics and other ethnically based administrative units in the national government at the center, notably in the Council of Nationalities of the Supreme Soviet, which was the second chamber of the national Legislature in Moscow.

Soviet federalism was intended to encourage the loyalty to the new Soviet system of the different national groups that had made up the old Russian empire. It was also intended to provide for a substantial administrative unity to assure socialist development throughout the Soviet landmass. Thus Soviet federalism did not allow for the kind of political autonomy enjoyed by constituent units in the federal systems of Western countries like West Germany and the United States. Despite the appearance of a dispersal of authority, the Soviet federal system was characterized by a high degree of administrative centralization. Decision-making authority was concentrated at the center of the country—in Moscow—where the federal organs of government were located. Agencies of the central government, in particular the Presidium of the Supreme Soviet, had the right to interfere with and reverse local actions. Other reasons for the reality of centralization in the Soviet federal system were the weakness of representative institutions, notably the Council of Nationalities in the Supreme Soviet; the supremacy of the Communist party and its insistence on nationwide conformity to norms determined by its central and essentially Russian leadership; and the commitment to a planned and regimented command economy, which required a concentration of economic decision-making authority in Moscow.

The Federal Government

As is true of most modern governments, the Soviet federal government in Moscow was divided into three branches: the executive, legislative, and judicial. The bureaucracy, a fourth aspect of the national government, was sufficiently important to merit separate discussion here, even though in a technical sense it belonged with the executive.

The Executive Branch

Before changes enacted into law in December 1988, the Soviet executive branch consisted of a president (who was simultaneously the chair of the Presidium of the Supreme Soviet, the national Legislature, and whose position we discuss within the context of the Legislature) and a Council of Ministers, which was the real source of day-to-day administrative control of the country. The Council of Ministers was a large body of approximately 180 members who were responsible for running the bureaucratic departments that were in charge of almost every aspect of Soviet life.

Inside the Council of Ministers was a Presidium, or inner group, of the most senior, most experienced, and most politically influential members of the state apparatus. Members of this inner group were the premier, the minister of Foreign Affairs, the Defense minister, the Agriculture minister, the chief of the KGB, and heads of other key departments of government.

The Presidium of the Council of Ministers was the day-to-day leadership of the state. Its members were powerful administrators not only because of their authority as heads of critical government departments but also because some of them simultaneously were top-ranking members of the Communist party leadership, in either the Politburo or the Central Committee.

The Soviet Council of Ministers' responsibilities for management of the state bureaucracy were broad and complex because of the country's commitment to socialist development. The Council of Ministers performed all the functions of executives in Western democracies. In addition, it con-

trolled those aspects of economic, social, and cultural life that are normally left to the private sector in Western societies. The Soviet Council of Ministers, therefore, was one of the most powerful executive bodies in the world.

Although theoretically chosen by and accountable to the Supreme Soviet, in practice the membership of the Council of Ministers was determined partly by its own inner leadership and partly by the Communist party's Politburo, of which some ministers were members. The Council of Ministers functioned quite autonomously of the Supreme Soviet, and there was little accountability. In this respect, Soviet ministers were different from ministers in Western European democracies, who are responsible to their parliaments. There were no popular checks on the behavior of the Soviet executive beyond those imposed by the party. Ministers accounted for their behavior only to the premier, who in turn answered for the working of the state to his Politburo colleagues. If the party leadership was satisfied, the Council of Ministers in effect could wield virtually unlimited administrative authority.

The Legislative Branch

Until changes were enacted into law in December 1988, the national, or federal, Legislature in Moscow had always been the Supreme Soviet, which was bicameral. Its two houses were the Council of the Union and the Council of the Nationalities. The primary purpose of bicameralism seemed to be to give the different national groups in Soviet society representation at the center. But this representation was never very meaningful because the Legislature never played a significant role in the working of government; it was virtually a rubber stamp, approving and ratifying policies presented to it with little discussion or debate. Votes taken were almost always unanimous. Rarely were there no-votes or abstentions. Proceedings were routinized and uninspiring as compared to the legislatures of Western democracies. There was little interaction between deputies, no deals were struck, no spontaneous questions were asked, no amendments to policies were proposed. Speeches by Supreme Soviet members tended to be bland, boring, and confined to encomiums for the leadership. When party and state leaders spoke, there were no interruptions. Applause was mechanical.

Several factors explain the weakness of the Supreme Soviet as a legislative body. To begin with, the Supreme Soviet was always too big to accomplish anything of consequence. The two houses of the Supreme Soviet had a combined membership of about 1,500. The Supreme Soviet met for only a few days at a time, usually twice a year. There was little opportunity for legislative deputies to become deeply involved in and knowledgeable about anything brought to their attention.

Another weakness of the Supreme Soviet was the exclusion of mavericks, critics, and would-be opponents of the regime, who found it impossible to be elected to seats. And once candidates who had been elected took their seats, they

(Intourist, Moscow)

Built between 1838 and 1849, inside the Kremlin Wall overlooking the Moscow River, the Grand Palace became the meeting place of the Supreme Soviet and the soviet of the Russian republic. The flag of the Soviet Union or of the Russian republic was flown when either of these bodies was in session.

were subject to rigorous in-house discipline, which discouraged spontaneous outbursts or expressions of assertiveness.

Having said all this, it is also true that the Supreme Soviet did play a positive role. Its convening on a regular basis helped to legitimize the Soviet system by giving at least the appearance of popular involvement. Moreover, it could and sometimes did provide a forum, albeit a very restricted one, for the expression of concerns that citizens had on the grass-roots levels of administration. Mild criticism of government policies and questions about shortages and other problems were important sources of information about the impact of policy for party and state leaders.

The Presidium of the Supreme Soviet was more important in the administrative process than its parent body. The Presidium's membership reflected the diversity of Soviet society. It had 36 members in addition to a chair (who was also the president of the Soviet Union), a first vice chair, and 15 other vice chairs representing the 15 constituent republics. These vice chairs usually were themselves chairs of the supreme soviets of their own republics. The membership of the Presidium also included a variety of party and state notables and famous personalities.

While the Presidium theoretically was elected by the Supreme Soviet, in practice it determined its own replacements, who, of course, had the approval of the Communist party leadership. Also, the Presidium acted independently of the parent body to which, in theory, it was accountable.

The Presidium of the Supreme Soviet had a lot of power and its activities were extensive. It issued enforceable decrees and ordinances, thereby acting as an interim legislature. It could amend the Constitution. It supervised the work of the Council of Ministers and could dismiss its members, although in practice dismissal was done on signal of the Politburo. It ratified treaties and received ambassadors. The Presidium could deprive individuals (for example, political dissidents) of their Soviet citizenship. It supervised the military, which involved removal of the high command and the ordering of a partial mobilization—again, however, on signal from the top party leadership. The Presidium also received complaints and criticism from citizens throughout the country, enabling it to collect much information about administration on the local levels. Finally, the activities of all local governing bodies, called soviets, were subject to its supervision and control.

The chair of the Presidium was very powerful. He not only presided over and directed its proceedings but also could simultaneously hold the position of general secretary of the Communist party.

Brezhnev used the chair of the Supreme Soviet Presidium or Soviet presidency (to which he was elected in 1977, following the Supreme Soviet's approval of a constitutional amendment allowing the general secretary of the Communist party to run for that office) to strengthen his influence within the government apparatus. Because Brezhnev's successors as president, Andropov and Chernenko, held office for very short periods, it was difficult to know if they were able to increase their power as a result of holding simultaneously the office of Soviet president and party general secretary.

(Gamma-Liaison/APN)

The Supreme Soviet, the Soviet Union's national parliament housed in the great Kremlin Palace visible from Red Square, in session. The seating arrangement of parliamentary deputies in the audience with the top party and government leaders on raised platforms in the front (directly under the statue of Lenin) suggested that deputies were supposed to be the listeners and leaders were supposed to be the performers.

Unlike Brezhnev, Gorbachev initially refrained from seeking the presidency, which was held by former Foreign Minister Andrei Gromyko from 1985 to 1988. But in October 1988, after Gromyko's resignation, Gorbachev finessed his own election to the presidency, presumably for the same reason as Brezhnev in 1977: to strengthen his personal political power and leadership authority, in this instance to facilitate implementation of his sweeping reform program.

Law and the Judicial Branch

Soviet law had a very broad application and dealt with aspects of personal behavior that in Western societies are usually the concern of the private individual. Soviet law was intended to promote a respect for the process of socialist development on the part of both private citizens and public agencies. Soviet law was supposed to inculcate a sense of the moral rightness of behavioral norms established by the regime and of the impropriety—indeed, the absolute wrongness—of violating those norms.

Law seemed to play a much more important role in the daily life of the Soviet citizen than is true in Western democracies. Very young children were taught the importance of law-abiding behavior and obedience to rules. With the help of the mass media, which propagandized the impor-

tance of respect for rules, this process of law socialization continued through adolescence and adult life.

Finally, law in the Soviet Union traditionally had been closely connected to and supportive of economic planning and development and thus had a much wider area of concern than public law in Western democracies. Soviet law included a variety of economic subjects having to do with the running of collective farms, employee/employer relations in factories, and worker behavior. For example, Soviet law forbade what was called a "parasitic way of life," which meant avoidance of what the regime termed "socially useful work." Thus, the law could make criminals of citizens who did not fulfill the state's expectations of their roles in the national work force.

Legal procedure worked differently in the Soviet Union from how it does in the West. For example, the role of Soviet judges was unique. There was much more give-and-take between judges and witnesses. Judges might criticize witnesses and defendants in a court trial. While judges were elected for 5-year terms, they were subject to the same kinds of political scrutiny as other state officials and could not act with an independent mind to the extent that judges do in Western courts.

People's assessors, who were lay individuals, assisted judges and in theory provided them with the opinion of the

(UN photo/Saw Lwin)

Former Soviet Foreign Minister Andrei Gromyko addressing the UN General Assembly in New York in 1984. To Americans, Gromyko was one of the most familiar Soviet officials.

ordinary person. People's assessors were elected for 2 years and might not have any judicial training. Because they were frequently overshadowed by judges, who were better trained and more aggressive, their real role seemed to be political and symbolic. They gave the impression of popular involvement in a judicial process that had the reputation of being compulsive and severe. At the same time, their involvement helped to increase popular sensitivity and obedience to the law.

The behavior of Soviet attorneys also was quite different from that of their counterparts in the West, especially in handling a defense. Lest they become targets of the court's wrath, Soviet defense attorneys had to be very careful not to appear overzealous in the protection of clients who were fighting the state. The most that defense attorneys could hope to do for their clients was to present a balanced case. It was difficult for attorneys to combat the state aggressively, to outwit it, and to oblige it to admit error, especially in political cases.

Another contrast between Soviet and Western courtroom practice concerned the role of the Soviet bench (judges and

people's assessors), who frequently lectured, scolded, or intensively cross-examined witnesses. This behavior was further evidence of the educative function of Soviet law as well as the inherently paternalistic character of much of the Soviet administrative system.

From a Western vantage point, perhaps the most striking feature of Soviet law and legal procedure was the inequity that apparently occurred whenever the exercise of individual rights challenged the purported interests of the state. Soviet courts, in the Western view, had been political instruments of the Soviet leadership. Furthermore, public trials rarely involved members of the Soviet procuracy, or state attorney's office, Soviet police officers, prison-camp commanders, informers, or other state officials who might have abused their authority. The Soviet regime often ignored the constitutional rights of Soviet citizens, as seen in Alexander Solzhenitsyn's arrest, expulsion, and loss of citizenship in 1974 without any judicial hearing or procedure.

The KGB. The Committee for State Security, or KGB, one of the most publicized instruments of Soviet law enforcement, was responsible for protecting Soviet society against its real or imagined enemies everywhere. The KGB's powerful and pervasive influence in Soviet society was a result not only of its extensive intelligence-gathering apparatus and its exaggeration of the dangers and threats to Soviet domestic and external security but also of the climate of intense distrust or watchfulness that governed the Soviet state's relations with its citizens and citizens' relations among themselves.

The KGB could be very abusive because of operatives who were not always accountable for their behavior and who were not always easily controlled by their superiors. Examples of the KGB's abuses of power were the pervasiveness of its surveillance activity, its threats and annoying searches, and its use of entrapment devices, blackmail, and intimidation. It could arrange an individual's loss of employment, eviction from housing, and other forms of harassment. It was especially aggressive in dealing with dissidents in the late 1970s, virtually crushing the entire dissident movement in 1977 and 1978.

A practice developed in the Brezhnev era was KGB incarceration of political dissidents in mental hospitals. With the help of unscrupulous doctors, KGB operatives badgered political inmates to the point where they confessed error or truly went insane. All this was done, of course, without a costly and potentially embarrassing trial.

The Soviet regime traditionally defended this KGB behavior, saying that the interests of the party were synonymous with those of society and that there was no reason to tolerate the behavior of a few people seeking to obstruct socialist development and prevent Soviet workers from achieving their ultimate goal of communism. Indeed, from the Soviet vantage point, the workers, through their state and in particular its security and police apparatus, had to take whatever steps necessary to resist their enemies.

The Bureaucracy

The Soviet bureaucracy was unique and interesting for many reasons, not the least being the sheer enormity of its responsibilities and personnel, the result of the nation's commitment to the socialist transformation of its socioeconomic environment. Indeed, the regime became self-conscious about this gargantuan administrative machine, which contradicted the Marxist promise of a withering away of the state.

Perhaps the most publicized evil of the Soviet bureaucracy was bribery. It had been with the Soviet system since its inception; Lenin called it the worst enemy of the revolution. Bribery may have even worsened over the years because the Soviet bureaucracy expanded substantially to cope with accelerated socioeconomic change.

The persistence and pervasiveness of bribery in the Soviet bureaucracy were the result of many factors endemic to the Soviet system. Shortages of food, apartments, automobiles, and many other luxuries and necessities encouraged bureaucrats to accept bribes for favors rendered. The temptation to accept bribes was increased by the poor salary and poor living conditions of many state employees, especially in the service industries. But even highly paid bureaucrats wanted more and found it difficult to resist the temptation to accept "tips."

Furthermore, bribery was a way of Soviet life that generally was not been considered bad, if only because it always had been done. And because it was so ingrained and so pervasive, it was difficult to stamp out completely, no matter how determined the regime was. The most that any Soviet leadership could accomplish against bribery was an isolated attack for symbolic and educative purposes.

A serious flaw in the bureaucracy under Brezhnev was the manipulation of information or, simply, the telling of lies about conditions in the society. To satisfy their superiors, bureaucratic managers on all levels of administration transformed the dissemination of misleading and deceptive information, called *paradnost*, into a fine art. Each year lies were piled on top of lies about the true state of affairs, in a veil of impenetrable secrecy—to the point where, when Gorbachev became general secretary, the government and party leadership had no precise idea of the true state of the economy.

This "government by officials" had other problems. Employees often relied on family-type relationships that involved mutual accommodations at the expense of the state. There were widespread efforts to hoodwink superiors in order to conceal fraud and ineptitude, pervasive pilfering, cronyism, and nepotism.

To cope with some of these problems, the state made superiors responsible for the levels of achievement of their subordinates, and all state employees were responsible for damage done to state property by their negligence or carelessness. They were obliged to pay back to the state up to 3 months of their wages as compensation. But, ironically, these remedies worsened the problems that they were supposed to resolve. For example, to protect their own positions, managers concealed the failures of their subordinates and of entire units for which they were responsible.

To control its bureaucracy, the Soviet regime developed a multiplicity of party and nonparty controls. There were five different types of control: by party agencies, by government agencies other than the Ministry of Finance, by the Ministry of Finance, by the procuracy, and by the local soviets. Soviet administrators could be called upon at any time by one or more of these control agencies to account for their behavior or that of the people working for them.

These extensive controls, however, did not correct the problems from which the Soviet bureaucracy suffered. The sheer size and complexity of the bureaucracy made it difficult and many times impossible for control personnel to track down the source of a problem and remedy it. Bureaucrats became adept at hiding their misdeeds from inquisitive controllers, who were at best outsiders in dealing with the bureaucratic maze. On other occasions, controls became counterproductive, not only in the sense of encouraging what they were supposed to correct but also because they were intrusive and disruptive of routine and to that extent contributed to bureaucratic inefficiency.

It is not surprising that the last Soviet leaders gave much attention to the problem of corruption and incompetence in the bureaucracy. Gorbachev went after abuses like bribetaking, concealment, and falsification, and the display of indifference to citizens as part of his campaign to improve the Soviet administrative efficiency. There were other reasons why so much publicity was given to corruption and other ills of the Soviet bureaucracy. Accusing managers and ministers of incompetence or malfeasance and forcing their removal from office—and even their arrest, conviction, and imprisonment—provided the leadership with an opportunity to dispose of critics or enemies who might otherwise use their authority to sabotage policies they secretly opposed.

THE ECONOMY

The scope of Soviet economic control was staggering by Western standards. The Soviet state ran most of the economy and had much to say about the few economic areas not under its direct control. The state controlled allocation of land, labor, and capital, production, distribution, and a very large aspect of consumption.

The basis of state control of the Soviet economy was the state plan, which determined all phases of Soviet economic life. The state plan, which was drawn up by the Gosplan (State Planning Agency), set the goals of most areas of Soviet production. These goals were based on decisions made by the Communist party leadership. However, the Gosplan also took into account input from production units like factories and farms, which were obliged to estimate their future production output and their resource input. But in the drafting of the state plan, advice from lower echelons about future production was far less important than decisions of the party leadership.

To carry out the provisions of the state plan, the Soviet economy was divided into the following units of economic organization:

(United Nations photo)

The power station in Frunze, the capital of the Kirghiz republic in Soviet Central Asia, symbolized the achievement of industrial modernity in an agrarian and underdeveloped part of the Soviet Union.

- *Institutions*—all government administrative financial and commercial agencies.
- *Industrial enterprises,* which resembled the manufacturing companies and corporations of capitalist economies, consisted of factories, mines, and other basic units of production.
- *Agricultural cooperatives*, which were divided into 1) *collective farms,* which were large, self-governing farm communities with some decision-making autonomy and with remuneration to farmers based on earnings of the farm as a whole; and 2) *state farms,* which were run directly by the state and which paid farmers a regular wage. Both types of farms could be very large, consisting of thousands of acres and incorporating several villages.
- *Societal organizations*, including trade unions, professional associations, and social clubs and groups.

The Soviet economy also had a very limited private sector. It consisted of small garden plots owned by farmers employed by collective and state farms, who worked on their plots part time and marketed what they produced for extra income. The private garden plots were embarrassingly efficient as compared to collective and state farms. By the end of the 1970s more than half of the Soviet potato crop and almost a third of Soviet vegetables, meat, and milk came from the cultivation of private plots.

Like most other aspects of Soviet society, the economy was kept under close surveillance by the Communist party. Virtually all economic administrators, from ministers to factory managers to collective-farm directors, were party members. Many economic posts were on the so-called nomenklatura, or civil-service list, indicating further party influence over them.

The Soviet economic system had impressive accomplishments. Within a little over 60 years it achieved a radical redistribution of wealth and transformed an agricultural country to a highly industrialized and urbanized one. It raised the standard of living of the overwhelming majority of Soviet citizens as compared to the lifestyles of their parents in the 1920s and 1930s and their grandparents before the Revolution of 1917.

SOCIAL SECURITY AND WELFARE

The scope of the Soviet social-security and welfare system went beyond anything in Western societies. It guaranteed the usual benefits of modern state welfare systems, like insurance for illness, unemployment, and retirement. Soviet citizens also enjoyed guaranteed housing and cradle-to-grave health care.

Housing

The state was able to guarantee housing to all citizens because it owned most of the housing facilities in the country. Rents were very low for most apartments in state housing. There was also cooperative housing built by financially self-sustaining cooperatives of renters who were willing to pay higher rents in return for better-quality accommodation.

Soviet housing policy, however, was flawed. The regime was not always able to provide living quarters when people needed them. There was always a housing shortage, mainly because of the unwillingness of the Soviet leadership to invest sufficiently in housing construction. People frequently had to wait a long time for the assignment of an apartment, especially one located in a preferred urban area. Because of a steady influx of people from the countryside, housing shortages were so acute in cities like Moscow and Leningrad that authorities had to restrict private movement to those cities.

Guaranteed housing, moreover, did not always mean high-quality and comfortable housing. Much of Soviet housing was shabby by Western standards. New construction often showed careless workmanship, the use of cheap materials, and faulty planning. Older units were not in good repair. When something went wrong, it was very difficult for Soviet workers to repair and restore it. Hence, the state found it necessary to allow more construction of housing by private cooperatives and, in a very few instances, by private individuals.

Health Care

Like Soviet housing policy, the health-care system was comprehensive. It provided an extensive network of hospitals and clinics. There was unlimited hospitalization, and the ratio of physicians to population was among the highest in the world.

The achievements of the Soviet health-care system were impressive. In recent years life expectancy increased; infant mortality declined; and epidemic and endemic diseases like malaria, cholera, and typhus, to which the country was prone years ago, were brought under control.

On the other hand, the system also had many weaknesses. Participating physicians were overworked; they had to see a requisite number of patients per hour to meet quantitative targets set by authorities in Moscow. When there were mistakes or problems, physicians were always held responsible to superiors in the usual bureaucratic manner. The health-care system was highly centralized and thus a bureaucratic nightmare.

As was true of other areas of Soviet life having to do with the material well-being of the individual, the depth of stated official concern was never matched by an equivalent willingness to spend and improve. The expansion of health-care facilities, especially the construction and maintenance of clinics and the acquisition of technical equipment, did not receive the same priority as, say, defense industries. There was a scarcity not only of costly medical equipment standard in most large American hospitals, such as kidney-dialysis machines, but also of low-cost and simple equipment, like needles and tubing.

The health-care system seemed geared more to curing illness than to preventing it. Some diseases that are easily controlled in other countries ran rampant in the Soviet Union. Influenza, for example, killed tens of thousands of Soviet babies. Rickets continued to be a childhood scourge. Whereas 70 percent of cervical cancers were detected in their early and potentially treatable stages in the United States, 60 percent of the Soviet Union's cases were not recognized until they were terminal.

Despite these criticisms, one must commend the Soviet health-care system for revolutionizing medical treatment and for doing so in a relatively brief period, considering the size and diversity of the Soviet population as well as the country's broad territorial expanse. As far as is known in the West, there were no major breakdowns in the medical system and no major cutbacks in medical-care expenditures.

The cost of this welfare program was substantial and borne by the beneficiaries themselves, primarily in the form of low wages and a pervasive tax, called the turnover tax, which was levied on almost everything the consumer needed and used. By forgoing the discretionary income that workers can earn in capitalist societies, the Soviet citizens paid a high price for their extensive social benefits. Thus, there was the anomaly that Soviet citizens had more protection but lower living standards than the citizens of capitalist societies.

SOVIET FOREIGN POLICY

Communist ideology influenced Soviet international behavior. The Soviets always believed that capitalist countries were inherently expansionist and thus threatened Soviet security and that capitalism inevitably would collapse in consequence of its own inherent weaknesses and flaws,

(United Nations photo)

Collective farm villages were compact and self-contained, with cooperative banks and post offices. Farm families had their own homes, with backyards where they could raise ducks, pigs, chickens, and vegetables for their own consumption or for sale in local markets.

(Intourist, Moscow)

Kalanin Prospect, one of the major and more modern of downtown Moscow thoroughfares. The architecture of the high-rise office buildings built in Khrushchev's era contrasts with the Stalinist architectural style of the Hotel Ukraine in the foreground.

especially if Marxists aggressively fought against it. This belief explained the traditional undercurrent of suspicion and hostility in Soviet relations with the West. It also helped to explain the special relationship of the Soviet state with the socialist countries of Central/Eastern Europe and with Communist parties elsewhere. Finally, it provided some understanding of the intense Soviet interest in the developing societies of the Third World which were searching for ways to achieve modernization.

But nonideological considerations also played a role in explaining Soviet policy toward the West; toward ruling and nonruling Communist parties; and toward the developing countries of Asia, Africa, and Latin America. These considerations included protection of Soviet security abroad, the need for extensive foreign trade to promote economic development and modernization, and the craving for prestige and recognition as a global superpower.

The West

The Soviet Union pursued détente with the West from the 1950s. Détente involved occasional summit meetings between Soviet and Western leaders and treaty-making diplomacy, which led to the conclusion of agreements on trade, arms control, cultural and scientific exchanges, and other political matters. Détente diminished the likelihood of confrontation and conflict with the West, thus allowing the

Soviet regime to focus attention on other places in the world where its interests were threatened, such as the Middle East, Central Asia, and along the Soviet frontier with China. In making possible the conclusion of arms-control agreements like SALT II, détente allowed the Soviets to protect advantages they had acquired vis-à-vis the West in the development of weapons arsenals and to minimize unnecessary and costly weapons production so that scarce investment capital could be invested elsewhere in the Soviet economy.

Détente was essential to an expansion of Soviet trade with the West. The Soviets wanted to purchase high-technology products that they could not produce themselves but which they needed to increase the quality and quantity of their industrial and agricultural output. Improvement of Soviet economic performance was essential to the success of overall Soviet socialist development and in particular to the achievement of societal material well-being to assure political stability.

Only through détente could the Soviets induce the West, in particular the United States, to recognize them as a global superpower. The Soviet leadership always sought international respect, because it contributed to the legitimization of the Soviet system not only in the international community but also with the Soviet people.

The Soviets may have had an ulterior and, arguably, a sinister motive for their pursuit of détente in the Khrushchev and Brezhnev years: namely, to lull the West into a false sense of security and diminish its sensitivity to a Soviet arms buildup. The Soviets may also have wanted an opportunity to exploit differences between the United States, which believed that détente had a worldwide application, and the North Atlantic Treaty Organization (NATO) allies in Western Europe, which argued at times that détente applied mainly to Europe.

The Soviets showed, however, that when détente was an obstacle to the protection of their interests, they were willing to ignore it. Hence, they virtually destroyed political dissent in the Soviet Union in the late 1970s, despite U.S. President Jimmy Carter's aggressive campaign in support of human rights. They simultaneously tightened restrictions on the emigration of Soviet Jews, despite strong American opposition. And they assisted Marxists and other left-wing political groups in Third World countries, in the name of socialist internationalism. In their pursuit of détente, therefore, the Soviets seemed willing to risk a heightening of tensions in their relations with the West and to forfeit benefits of détente in order to obtain other advantages.

Socialist Countries in Central/Eastern Europe

The Soviets insisted upon substantial loyalty among the socialist countries established in Central/Eastern Europe after World War II. They wanted this loyalty for reasons of security. Central/Eastern Europe was a historic invasion route to the Soviet Union; this route was used most recently by Nazi Germany in World War II. The socialist countries of

Central/Eastern Europe were a strategic buffer between the Soviet state and the capitalist West.

Throughout the post–World War II era the Soviet Union also insisted that the socialist political systems of Central/Eastern Europe conform to the Soviet model, in particular the single-party dictatorship. The Soviets believed that a liberal political order in Central/Eastern Europe could lead to an erosion of their commitment to socialist development and a westward shift of foreign-policy orientation, to the detriment of Soviet security. The Soviets also saw Central/Eastern European conformity to the Soviet model of socialism and acknowledgment of Soviet leadership as essential to the legitimization of the Soviet system inside the Soviet Union itself.

To assure the loyalty of the Central/Eastern European states to Soviet foreign and domestic policies between the 1940s and 1980s, Moscow maintained close ties with their leaderships. The Soviets conferred with them in periodic bilateral summit meetings and at either local party congresses or international party gatherings; they maintained strong links with them through the Soviet-led regional military and economic organizations like the Warsaw Pact and the Council for Mutual Economic Assistance (CMEA).

The Kremlin had other means of influencing the behavior of its allies to assure conformity with Soviet policy. There always was the option of military intervention, which was used in August 1968 to prevent the Czechoslovak government from experimenting with liberal reforms. The so-called Brezhnev Doctrine asserted the right of socialist countries to intervene in one anothers' internal affairs to protect socialism against internal as well as external challenges. Gorbachev repudiated the doctrine by saying that the Soviet Union would never use force in Central/Eastern Europe, but what a conservative successor might do if confronted with a threat to Soviet security in Central/Eastern Europe was another matter.

The Soviets also had powerful sources of leverage other than outright military force. For example, the Kremlin dominated the Warsaw Pact command structure, paying 80 percent of the operating costs and cycling allied commanders through mid-career training in Soviet military academies. Moscow also controlled promotion to high ranks within the Soviet Bloc military establishments and monitored their political loyalty and morale through the Main Political Administration of the Soviet Army and Navy. Furthermore, although the Central/Eastern European armies were equipped with all the latest conventional weaponry to enable them to fulfill their role vis-à-vis NATO, they were kept short of ammunition and operated with a command and communications structure that would have been ineffective without Soviet control. Finally, various status-of-forces agreements with Soviet Bloc nations governing the movement of Soviet troops allowed for their mobilization and deployment without prior approval of the host governments.

The Soviet Union also had substantial economic leverage over the Central/Eastern European countries, to discourage domestic or international policies the Kremlin considered prejudicial to Soviet interests. The Soviets provided the countries with cheap raw materials, especially oil and gas, without demanding precious hard currency. The Soviets also bought their less-than-world-class products.

At times the Soviets tolerated a limited amount of Central/Eastern European deviance from their wishes. Sometimes enforcement of conformity was physically impossible, as in the case of Yugoslavia and Albania. In other instances, deviance did not threaten the domestic commitment to the single-party dictatorship and to continuing membership and support of the Warsaw Pact military alliance, as in the case of Romania. The Soviets said in 1956 that they were willing to acknowledge the legitimacy of "different paths to socialism" which individual Central/Eastern European countries wanted to follow for reasons of national self-interest, as long as they did nothing to jeopardize their commitment to socialism and/or their loyalty to the socialist community and to the Soviet Union.

China

China had been a relentless competitor of the Soviet Union in the world communist movement since the late 1950s. China not only refused to acknowledge Soviet leadership of the world's Communist parties but also challenged and rejected

(United Nations photo)

Eduard Shevardnadze, the former Soviet foreign minister under Gorbachev.

important principles of Soviet ideology. China, the most populous country in the world and the dominant power in Asia, rivaled the Soviet Union for influence not only in Asia and elsewhere in the Third World but also in the European movement of Communist parties. At times this rivalry was quite dangerous, because of China's geographic proximity to the Soviet Union, its expanding military capability, especially in the nuclear arena, and its ties with the United States.

The Third World

The Soviets always understood that Third World countries were reluctant to embrace Marxist-Leninism, despite their commitment to sweeping socioeconomic reform and their opposition to laissez-faire capitalism. Thus, in their relations with Third World countries, the Soviets did not make a fetish of ideology—they were never out to "communize the world."

Communist ideology nevertheless did influence Soviet behavior toward the Third World. In the 1960s and 1970s the Soviets wanted Third World countries to expand their public sectors and limit capitalism. They also supported political parties and groups that were on the ideological left, especially Marxist and other groups waging wars of national liberation against local and/or foreign capitalist forces. Indeed, the Soviets said they had an obligation to support Marxists whenever they were fighting capitalists.

The Soviet Union also had important nonideological ambitions in the Third World. The Kremlin wanted the friendship and cooperation of Third World governments at the United Nations, where it needed votes to block measures sponsored by rivals and opponents. In the economic realm, the Soviets wanted sources of raw materials and markets for manufactured exports.

Strategic considerations helped to explain Soviet policy in the Third World. Countries near Soviet territory, such as Iran, Afghanistan, and Pakistan, along with neighboring countries in the Middle East and around the Persian Gulf, were important to Soviet security. The Soviets never wanted dangerous antagonists like the Americans or the Chinese to obtain a foothold in these places. At the same time the Soviets saw opportunities to shift the balance of strategic forces vis-à-vis the United States to their advantage by cultivating certain Third World countries.

The Soviets tried to achieve their ambitions in Third World countries by giving them economic and technical assistance on very easy terms. They granted loans with low interest rates and with few strings attached and provided easy means of repayment by accepting local currency or export commodities. Sometimes Soviet economic aid led directly to an expansion of Soviet political influence, as when, for example, the recipient country appointed Soviet advisers to key administrative positions to help it make the best use of sophisticated equipment the Soviets had given it. And the sale of arms to Third World countries not only resulted in a weapons dependency that gave Moscow some political leverage but also facilitated trade to provide the Soviet Union with needed resources.

Political diplomacy was still another instrument of Soviet policy in the Third World. The Soviets signed treaties of friendship, cooperation, consultation, and mutual defense. The exchange of visits by Soviet officials with leaders of Third World governments also was useful in flattering them and enhancing Soviet influence with them. Sometimes Soviet diplomacy also supported Third World causes, such as black nationalism in Southern Africa, Palestinian self-determination in the Middle East, and opposition to U.S. initiatives in the United Nations.

As a measure of last resort to protect their vital interests in the Third World, the Soviets intervened militarily in Third World countries. They did so directly, as in Afghanistan in 1979; and indirectly, by means of proxies like Cuba, in Angola and Ethiopia in the mid- and late 1970s.

These methods did not always assure success. Indeed, the Soviets confronted many obstacles to the achievement of their ambitions in the Third World. Some obstacles had to do with the attitudes and policies of the Third World countries themselves, while other obstacles were thrown up by the United States, China, and other countries with opposing interests. Additional obstacles to Soviet success in the Third World were the Soviet Union's limited capabilities.

Third World governments sometimes found the Soviets to be pushy, overbearing, rude, and even prejudiced. This was true not only because the Soviets occasionally may have behaved in these ways but also because leaders of the Third World countries may have been hypersensitive to their countries' newly won independence and resented pressure on them. Moreover, some Third World governments that were recipients of Soviet weapons lost patience when these weapons did not work properly. They also became flustered when Soviet diplomacy did not seem adequately supportive of their interests abroad, especially in relations with the United States. Finally, many Third World leaders governed deeply religious societies that were offended by the atheism of Soviet communism. This was especially true of Islamic countries, whose leaders sometimes suspected that local Communist groups were linked closely to Moscow and were secretly working to overthrow their governments.

The Soviets always were constrained in what they could do in the Third World by their own finite political, economic, military, and strategic capabilities. It is an oversimplification to say that, because there were constraints on the formation of a critical public opinion within the Soviet Union, Moscow could pursue any policy it wished. The regime could never ignore the possibility that costly, belligerent, and dangerous excursions into the Third World could arouse popular dissatisfaction, provide encouragement to dissidents, and excessively burden a problem-ridden economy.

Indeed, Soviet resources for ambitious foreign-aid programs were limited. The regime nearly always had to give priority to domestic needs, especially in moments of economic scarcity. The Soviets, therefore, could not afford to export precious fuel or grain to Third World countries in unlimited amounts. Nor could the Soviets wage Afghanistan-like exercises to support policies in Third World countries far from their border. Their military capability was limited not only by investment priorities but also by the uncertain quality of military weapons needed in special situations, like desert warfare, and logistical equipment needed to sustain action in far-off areas.

Large-scale strategic considerations also limited Soviet policy in the Third World. Soviet leaders had to be wary of the way in which a distraction in the Third World encouraged Chinese political and territorial ambitions in Asia at the Soviet Union's expense. The Soviets had to be careful not to allow their policies in the Third World to compromise their freedom of action in Soviet Bloc countries, where they had substantial security interests. Soviet leaders had to be sensitive to the way in which Central/Eastern European countries could exploit Soviet distractions in the Third World to seek more autonomy and to increase their orientation toward the West. Nor could they ever dismiss the possibility of a clash with the West, in particular the United States, which considered Soviet expansionism in the Third World to be incompatible with détente and dangerous to Western strategic, economic, and military interests.

Foreign Policy-making

The Politburo and Secretariat were intimately involved in foreign policy-making. The Politburo deliberated on important foreign-policy initiatives. Its role seemed to be to set the large principles of policy. It relied on the Secretariat and other agencies for information and for implementation of its decisions.

The Central Committee itself had only an occasional involvement in foreign policy-making. It did not have a policy-originating role. Its major responsibility appeared to be concerned with ratification and communication. On the other hand, the Politburo would seek Central Committee approval of a major foreign-policy initiative carrying substantial risk, such as the decision to intervene in Czechoslovakia in 1968. It would appear, then, that the Central Committee was not without some influence, even though the likelihood of its veto over Politburo policy was minimal.

The Ministry of Foreign Affairs was the chief state agency concerned with foreign policy. It was organized for that purpose in much the same way as foreign-affairs ministries in other modern political systems. It had a large bureaucracy of experts in Moscow and it controlled the embassies and consulates of the Soviet Union abroad. The Ministry of Defense was involved when the implementation of foreign-policy decisions required military support.

Other state agencies that cooperated with the Ministry of Foreign Affairs in the implementation of foreign policy were the Ministry of Foreign Trade and the KGB. The Ministry of Foreign Trade was concerned with most economic measures needed to carry out foreign policy. The KGB did what most strategic intelligence-gathering agencies do: it acquired information about foreign countries, especially secret data, and engaged in espionage and counterespionage activities. The KGB also monitored the Soviet frontier.

Another important state agency that exerted influence on foreign policy-making was the Institute for the Study of the United States and Canada, located within the Soviet Academy of Sciences. This so-called USA Institute provided party and state leaders with up-to-date, accurate, and jargon-free explanations of American domestic and international behavior. It had access to American materials unavailable to the Soviet public. Some of its members—and many were distinguished scholars—advocated détente in Soviet-American relations.

PERFORMANCE PROBLEMS

Serious problems threatened the Soviet Union's domestic tranquillity and external security. The most intractable of these were interethnic tensions, social problems, political dissent, economic underperformance, and deterioration of the environment.

PERFORMANCE PROBLEMS

Relations between the different ethnic groups that comprised Soviet society were characterized by suspicion, resentment, and sometimes open hostility. There are many reasons for this disharmony among the nationalities of the former Soviet Union, especially the largest ones. Not least of the reasons were the weakness of their sense of belonging to the large Soviet national community in which they resided since the Bolshevik Revolution in 1917; the strength of their separate cultural identities, which, paradoxically, the Soviet regime sought to preserve in order to conciliate the nationalities and encourage their loyalty to the Soviet system; and different levels of material well-being, which were the result of different levels of economic development and wealth endowment. But the most serious cause of interethnic tensions was the dominant influence of Russians over key institutions of the Soviet national government and its insistence on the use of the Russian language almost everywhere in society.

Russian Dominance

Russians predominated in leading Soviet party and state agencies. Sixty percent of all Soviet Communist Party members were Russian. The All-Union Party Congress, which convened periodically in Moscow, was dominated by Russians and transacted its business in Russian, even though many party members were ethnically non-Russian. A substantial majority of the party Politburo consisted of Russians. Russians also held key party and government posts in the non-Russian republics.

The Soviet leadership tried to strengthen this Russian influence. The regime encouraged Russians to colonize, or settle areas inhabited predominantly by non-Russian peoples, and aggressively promoted the Russian tongue as the first language of all Soviet peoples. Despite the official policy of cultural autonomy, Soviet authorities in Moscow went to excessive and sometimes controversial lengths to foster the use of Russian in non-Russian areas. Large

(Intourist, Moscow)

The Mother Armenia Monument, or Soviet Power Monument as it was known officially, located in Akhtanak Park in Yerevan. It was built in 1970 to commemorate the 50th anniversary of Soviet power in Armenia.

(Intourist, Moscow)

This monument to the victims of the massacre of more than 1 million Armenians by the Turks in 1915 contains an open-air mausoleum in which an eternal flame burns. A column to its right symbolizes eternal life and brotherhood. The monument is sacred to Armenians.

amounts of money were spent on teacher training and modern equipment for the instruction of Russian in the schools and universities of the non-Russian republics. The Russian language became the official language of administration throughout the country and had to be used in all official communications between local areas and Moscow. Career advancement for non-Russians depended on their fluency in Russian and their acceptance of Russian culture, say, in the areas of dress and other aspects of personal lifestyle.

Russian dominance resulted also from the absence of any meaningful opportunities for the non-Russian peoples to influence the policy-making process at the center. This was true because the institutions in which the non-Russian national groups were represented by law—namely, the Council of Nationalities in the old Supreme Soviet and the All-Union Party Congress—actually had very little power.

Apart from the selfish, ethnocentric desire of Russian Marxists to perpetuate Russian control of the Soviet system, Soviet leaderships promoted Russian dominance to develop a new Soviet nationality based on Russian culture. This Soviet-nationality policy took advantage of communist ideology, which held that national differences were a relic of the discredited bourgeois-capitalist society to be replaced by

socialism. But it was also intended to strengthen administrative unity essential to successful economic development and the establishment of an effective defense of the country against foreign subversion.

The Soviet leadership was determined to maintain Russian dominance also because of a declining birth rate among the Russian people. In the 1980s the Russian population slipped somewhat, from about 54 percent to about 52 percent of the total population, while the birth rates of non-Russian groups, especially those of the Muslim peoples of the Central Asian republics, rose.

Russian dominance of the Soviet system aroused the anger of many non-Russian peoples, who resented Russification of their cultures, especially in the area of language. The non-Russian peoples also resented political control by Russians as well as an absence of ways to resist it except by protest and dissent. They were frustrated by the contradiction between Russian dominance, for whatever reasons, and the historic constitutional commitment of the Soviet system to respect their separate cultural identities.

The Baltic peoples in Estonia, Latvia, and Lithuania, who were very nationalistic, and the Muslim peoples of the Soviet Central Asian republics, who were very sensitive about their

Islamic cultural traditions, reacted strongly to Russian dominance. In response, the Soviet regime tried in a variety of ways to counter and control these perceived anti-Russian feelings. The result was conflict and tension between non-Russian and Russian peoples.

Baltic Nationalism

The Baltic peoples of Estonia, Latvia, and Lithuania who remembered the days of independence before annexation by the Soviet Union in April 1940 were very nationalistic and resentful of the highly centralized rule imposed upon them by Moscow. They knew that they were distrusted by the Soviet central leadership because of their nationalism and suspected anti-Russian feelings.

The Baltic peoples tried in a variety of ways to exploit the limited amount of autonomy they did enjoy. They stubbornly preserved their languages and local customs. Indeed, local Communist party newspapers in the Baltic republics perennially complained about popular indifference to the Russian language and a lack of fluency in it. In a gesture of protest—albeit a mild one—many Estonians in the 1979 Supreme Soviet elections either did not participate in voting or, when they did, they actually marked their ballots against the official candidate. In that election, Estonia had the highest "no-vote" of any socialist republic.

Muslim Grievances

Another source of interethnic tensions was the resentment of Muslim citizens of the former Soviet Union's Central Asian republics over the presence in their local government of Russians. The Russians sometimes seemed to Soviet Muslims to be abrasive, especially when they put on airs of superiority and acted as if they were civilizers of a primitive people.

Some Soviet Muslims were concerned by the possibility of large-scale population transfers to inhospitable places elsewhere in the country where there were labor shortages. On one occasion the regime moved a number of Central Asian Muslims to the north. The Muslims had such difficulty becoming acclimated to the new environment because of climatic contrasts and Russification pressures that other plans to move large numbers of people from the south to the north were abandoned.

Soviet Muslims demonstrated their strong anti-Russian feelings in 1986, when students in Alma Ata, the capital of Kazakhstan, protested the Kazakh party leadership's decision to replace as first secretary Dinmukhamed Kunaev, a Brezhnev appointee and a Kazakh, with Gennadi Kolbin, a supporter of Gorbachev and an ethnic Russian. Although the Kremlin accused Kunaev of corrupt and incompetent leadership and viewed him as an obstacle to the success of its reform policies in Kazakhstan, Kazakhs saw his removal as an effort by Gorbachev to strengthen his personal power and to reinforce Russian influence over the Kazakh party organization.

Moscow's worst fear was that Pan-Islamic sympathies encouraged by broadcasts from Iran, Pakistan, and Saudi Arabia would encourage a spirit of independence in Central Asia. At the least, the Islamic revival abroad, spearheaded by Iran, was likely to stimulate a demand of Soviet Muslims for more national and religious freedom and for greater political and cultural autonomy.

But Soviet Muslims showed no serious signs of alienation, and there seemed to be no major movements for secession in the Muslim republics. The Soviet government tried to encourage Muslim acceptance of Marxist rule by an intensive socialization of the youth. Soviet propaganda constantly compared the relative modernization and affluence of Soviet Central Asia with the underdevelopment and poverty of neighboring Muslim societies in Iran, Afghanistan, and Pakistan.

Still, the Gorbachev regime did have cause for anxiety and was not complaisant about sources of Muslim dissatisfaction with the central government. Because the birth rate of the Muslims was increasing at a much faster rate than that of other national groups, including the Russians, and because of the innumerable contacts Soviet Muslims began to have with coreligionists in Afghanistan and other neighboring Islamic societies in the 1980s, the Soviet regime expected Muslim pressures for a larger role in the Soviet political system to become more intense.

SOCIAL PROBLEMS

The persistence of deep-rooted social problems not only belied what the Soviets said about the achievements of their socialist society but also threatened its political stability. One problem involved religion. Other problems were alcoholism, juvenile delinquency and adult crime, discrimination against women, and weaknesses in the education system.

Religious Harassment

Before Gorbachev, the Soviet regime was consistently hostile to religion, which was considered a relic of the society's bourgeois past. The official attitude toward religion was also the result of history. The complaisance of Russian orthodox clerics toward, and their profit from, Czarism discredited the Orthodox church in Soviet eyes.

The Soviets saw religion also as a potential threat to political stability. Soviet officials considered the church, synagogue, and mosque to be rivals of the Communist party and a threat to its monopoly of power. They also believed that religion could undermine loyalty and obedience of citizens to the party and state.

But from the beginning of the Stalinist era the Soviet leadership gave up trying to annihilate religion. The Soviet government allowed the major religions—Russian Orthodoxy, Islam, and Judaism—to exist. However, party and state agencies relentlessly disseminated the message of atheism to remind those who were religious of the official attitude and to discourage people, especially the youth, from being religious. School textbooks were laced with antireligious propaganda, describing faith in God as antiquated and antiscientific. The hope of officials was that in the long term organized religion would disappear.

Russian Orthodoxy

The Soviet state permitted the Russian Orthodox church's religious practice, paid its maintenance costs, and provided seminaries to train clergy. The government had to give permission for any religious activity such as fund-raising, publications, and the organization of a congregation.

At the same time, however, the regime discriminated against and harassed the Orthodox church. It converted many churches into museums instead of keeping them as places of worship. Those open for religious services were in disrepair and frequently were located in out-of-the-way places. The regime also made it awkward or uncomfortable for people who openly professed religious commitment. Religion was something you didn't talk about in public if you wanted to get ahead in your career.

These efforts to discredit and discourage religious practice among those who professed the Orthodox faith were not successful. People packed existing churches at holiday times, especially at Christmas. And many young couples sought a religious marriage ceremony along with the required secular administrative one performed by a state official. Historic fascination with the divine and supernatural seemed to be an indestructible trait of the Russian people.

Islam

While Islam had the second-largest religious following in the Soviet Union, it was potentially the most troublesome for the Soviet state. The Soviets faced a dilemma with Islam that they had with no other religion. They had to be careful in their domestic antireligion policies to avoid antagonizing foreign Islamic countries, especially influential ones like Saudi Arabia, concerned with the condition of Muslims living under Communist rule.

Nevertheless, the Soviets continued unabashedly to try to weaken the Islamic faith by extensive and unrelenting pressures. Local party agencies actively promoted atheism, not only in schools, newspapers, and exhibits in former mosques converted to museums, but also by usurping old customs, creating new rituals extolling Soviet life, and enlisting elder *asksals,* or venerable storytellers, to talk about "the falsehood of religious concepts, the futility and harm in the worship of dark forces invented by clergymen for their own enrichment." Schoolteachers also helped the party in attacking Islamic religious practice.

The Soviet state tried to make attendance in mosques difficult. The number of mosques remained small. Those used for worship were left in disrepair and were located in hard-to-reach places. Official figures showed only 200 mosques for all of Soviet Central Asia's more than 20 million people of Muslim faith.

Another means of discouraging Islamic religious practices was a contrived scarcity of Korans. In a 1976 printing, only 10,000 copies were made and were available only in Arabic, not in Russian or any other languages and alphabets that young Soviet citizens in the Muslim constituent republics could read and write. A religious official obviously sympathetic—at least outwardly so—to regime policy on the printing of Korans explained that confining the book to an Arabic edition was a way of preserving its purity.

The Soviet regime also restricted pilgrimages and the pursuit of formal religious study. Muslim pilgrims were apparently hand-picked by Soviet authorities, and some of them were actually KGB agents.

Despite these gestures, the Soviet regime did not succeed in smothering the Islamic religion. Older people with influence over the youth continued to practice some Islamic religious traditions in the privacy of the home. And Muslims in the Soviet Army in Afghanistan apparently were repelled by commands to kill Afghan coreligionists. These soldiers had to be replaced by military personnel from non-Muslim parts of the Soviet Union.

Judaism

Many Soviet Jews, as well as Jews in the United States and other parts of the world, spoke of an official Soviet discrimination that went beyond anything endured by other religious groups. They accused the Soviets of discriminating against Jews in much the same way as their Czarist predecessors did. Many Soviet Jews likened their situation to that under Czars Alexander III and Nicholas II, who persecuted and harassed Russian Jews in the 1880s and 1890s, causing many to emigrate to the United States.

Alleged Soviet discrimination against Jews involved the same kind of policies the regime pursued toward other religions. Jewish synagogues fell into disrepair because little public money was made available for maintenance. There were restrictions on the training of rabbis, the publication of books in Hebrew, and the production and distribution of special foods like matzos. Synagogues, like mosques and many Orthodox churches, were located in hard-to-find places. It was easy for a foreign visitor seeking a synagogue to pass it by because of the absence of distinctive markings.

There was, allegedly, official discrimination of a more sinister kind. It was said to occur when Jews sought entry into and advancement in the professions, especially education and the bureaucracy. They met roadblocks at every turn, starting with their efforts to gain admission to universities and graduate schools. Some Soviet Jews said that it was impossible to climb the professional ladder while they practiced their religion.

The problem of discrimination was complicated by the impossibility of discussing it openly. People of influence refused to acknowledge its existence. There was an implicit threat that forceful efforts to bring it out into the open would invite retribution, such as dismissal from a job and harassment of family and even of friends who showed sympathy. Ultimately, the only escape was emigration.

Discrimination against Jews provoked an aggressive interest group of Soviet Jews who wanted to emigrate from their homeland. In an angry, perhaps vengeful, response to this embarrassing phenomenon, an image-conscious Soviet leadership from time to time tightened restrictions on emigration by all kinds of impediments, including repeated denial of exit visas and the payment of an exorbitant departure tax. The regime considered emigration to be an act of disloyalty and punished not only those who applied for exit visas but also others, like employers for whom would-be emigrants worked.

Soviet discrimination led to international complications, especially with the United States, which showed great sensitivity to the condition of Soviet Jewry. Influential American Jews lobbied aggressively and persuasively with their government to put pressure on Moscow to liberalize its policy on Jewish emigration.

Alcoholism

Alcoholism predominated among Soviet peoples. It was chronic and caused serious political, economic, and social problems. Alcoholism contributed to disorderliness and crime, resulted in missed hours at work, and made people weak, docile, and subservient. Many Soviet citizens seemed to drink for the express purpose of getting drunk and would drink until they were in a stupor.

A major reason for excessive drinking seemed to be escape from the monotony and deprivation of everyday life in the Soviet Union. The shabby and crowded living quarters, the limited means of recreation affordable for the average citizen, the perennial shortages of necessities and the few luxury items—in short, the harshness and drabness of everyday life—led people to seek distraction through drinking. The problem of excessive drinking, therefore, was linked closely to living and working conditions that could not easily be changed by the Soviet government. Without distracting people with alcohol, the state would have had to spend heavily on the development of alternative means of public relaxation, such as expensive sports facilities. Consequently, while Moscow spent a lot of money to discourage alcoholism, it carefully refrained from going all out to make alcohol unavailable.

The Soviet government was ambivalent on the issue of controlling alcohol consumption for another reasons. The state imposed high taxes on hard liquor. It did not want to lose this lucrative source of revenue.

Still, the Gorbachev leadership seemed bent on continuing the efforts of its predecessors to reduce at least heavy consumption of alcohol. In 1985 there were sharp increases in the prices of liquor, beer, and wine. The long lines of Soviet citizens outside the wine shops on the eve of the announced price increases confirmed the widely held view that people would find a way to continue past drinking habits, because the "nip" remained the only easy and certain means of achieving relief from the stress of everyday Soviet life. Indeed, as a result of strong popular antipathy to the regime's antidrinking campaign, Gorbachev relented and made alcoholic beverages a bit more accessible.

Juvenile Delinquency and Adult Crime

Juvenile delinquency and adult crime were embarrassments to the Soviet leadership because they confirmed the existence of problems and imperfections found in other, nonsocialist, "inferior" bourgeois polities. With some reluctance, the Soviet regime began to acknowledge that the causes of juvenile delinquency and adult crime in the Soviet Union were not so different from the causes in nonsocialist societies. The Soviets themselves said that juvenile delinquency was caused by parental neglect and indifference, narcotic and alcohol addiction, boredom, and a profound amorality and lack of belief in Marxist-Leninism.

To some extent, primary schools were implicated by encouraging difficult, misbehaving youngsters to leave school after the eighth grade. Thus, some teenagers were thrown onto the street. Since those under 16 could not hold full-time jobs, some young people were beyond the supervision of parents and society. They became prone to drug addiction and drinking.

The Soviets railed against three kinds of misbehavior that had serious impact on society: hooliganism, parasitism, and economic crime.

Hooliganism was a mindless violation of public order by young people as well as others. It was said by the Soviets to be inspired by a contempt for society.

Parasitism was a reluctance to work or study or in some other way to avoid the performance of one's responsibilities to the family and the state. Parasitism was a willingness to live at the expense of others. People who did not want to do a job assigned to them because they did not like it or were not trained for it ran the risk of being charged with parasitism. At the same time, people who intentionally evaded employment also were liable to charges of parasitism. Soviet authorities took a dim view of parasitism because of the lengths to which the state went to prepare people for gainful employment and because of the loss to the economy due to unemployment.

Economic crimes were considered to be the most serious and consisted of stealing state property, falsification, and embezzlement of state funds for private use. The state mandated the death penalty for some economic crimes. Crimes were a source of embarrassment to the Soviets because they suggested that Soviet citizens possessed the same acquisitiveness characteristic of citizens of capitalistic societies.

Discrimination Against Women

Marxist ideology preached equality, but in Soviet society women were not equal. They were the object of a systematic and pervasive discrimination outside the home. They were expected to work at a job while simultaneously discharging their traditional responsibility for home management and childrearing. Women in the Soviet Union confronted inequities everywhere. Most educated women could find jobs only in prestigious but low-paying jobs, like family practice in medicine. They were grossly underrepresented in the party and state bureaucracies, and there were no women in the party Politburo.

Several factors accounted for discrimination against women. While Soviet husbands needed and expected their wives to work in order to survive, never mind obtain a longed-for but very expensive luxury like an automobile, they did not want to do housework to help their working mates. They looked forward to the day when they could afford to have their wives stay at home and confine their work to family. There was a strong tradition of male chauvinism in the Soviet Union that was only barely affected by the egalitarianism of communist ideology. Assumptions of male superiority and female subservience endured.

In the predominantly Muslim republics of Soviet Central Asia, the Islamic religion discouraged female assertiveness and female employment in jobs outside the home. There were examples of families everywhere in the Soviet Union—not only in the Islamic republics—that, for reasons of tradition, did not want their daughters to receive a higher education and enter as equals the world of men. And some educated women who held responsible and well-paying jobs voiced privately a preference for part-time work and more time for family life.

The Soviet state tried to diminish discrimination. Women were given maternity and child-care leave to lessen the disadvantage of caring for family while developing a career. The state also provided stipends to encourage women to have more children without detriment, at least in theory, to their economic status. Indeed, the state recognized and rewarded fecundity. Mothers of 10 or more children were designated "heroines of socialist labor."

Soviet women made important gains. Women accounted for one-quarter of the Soviet equivalent of Ph.D.'s. Nearly one-third of ordinary judges were women, and almost one-third of the 1,500 members of the Supreme Soviet were women. Seventy percent of all physicians were women.

But discrimination persisted. For example, in the late 1980s there was still a striking absence of women from positions of leadership. Only a very small percentage of collective farm directors, factory managers, and construction supervisors were women. And while women had a much higher representation in the teaching profession, they held only about one-fourth of school principalships. Even more striking evidence of discrimination was the fact that women continued on average to earn lower salaries than their male counterparts.

Despite the bitterness and cynicism of many Soviet women, there appeared to be little feminist activism. On the surface, most women remained satisfied with their roles and were unwilling to lobby aggressively for equal treatment by the system. Women who did enter positions of responsibility and leadership seemed to want to avoid the controversy that would result from championing women's equality. Moreover, government censors would not allow blunt charges of sex discrimination by the regime.

Education

The Soviet school system was another area of Soviet society where there were problems, although they were less subversive of domestic tranquillity than religious harassment, abuse of alcohol, and juvenile delinquency. One weakness of Soviet schools was the way in which they fostered a tension-producing inequality, despite the regime's commitment to the ideological goal of egalitarianism. The best schools, those with better-trained teachers and up-to-date equipment for classroom instruction, were located in the large cities, especially in the European regions of the Soviet Union. Because of their locations, the best schools were not always open to citizens from all parts of the country and from all walks of life. Children of farmers and workers had to attend the schools close to where their parents worked.

One aspect of the school system that caused considerable tension was the ritual of assigning students employment following their graduation. Graduates had to accept the jobs assigned them and had to hold those jobs for at least 3 years. One rejected an assignment at great peril to one's future career development. Consequently, there was much personal anxiety as graduation neared. Students were not above trying to influence the assignments by bribery or "pulling strings" with officials responsible for making assignments. Sometimes disappointment with one's assignment was so great that it led to depression, demoralization, and even suicide. The price of a secure job after graduation thus came very high.

Another problem in Soviet education—and one that was admitted by Soviet authorities—was the way in which emphasis on education led many young people to disparage the kind of manual work that required only a minimum of schooling. A large portion of Soviet young people did not express much interest in becoming workers on the assembly line. They preferred jobs that required more education and had greater prestige than those held by manual workers. As a result, the authorities had to propagandize the importance of assembly-line work in this proletarian society.

Health Care

The Soviets acknowledged massive shortcomings in their health-care system, symbolized by a decrease in life expectancy and a steady worsening of the infant mortality rate. In the 1980s there was a slow erosion in hospital services and general health care. Other weaknesses of the health-care system included the very poor state of Soviet hospitals and polyclinics. They were underequipped, lacked modern facilities, and did not have sufficient pharmaceutical supplies. Doctors' and nurses' salaries were too low.

Poor standards of sanitation and public hygiene and high levels of alcoholism caused a striking increase in death rates in the Soviet Union, especially among working males. By the late 1980s the average Soviet male could expect to live for only about 60 years—some 6 years less than he could in the mid-1960s. Conditions of maternity care were unsatisfactory, especially in Soviet Central Asia. Only 30 percent of maternity hospitals in the Soviet Union met acceptable hygiene standards, and only a few maternity wards in all of Central Asia were properly equipped.

Nearly as shocking was infant mortality. The infant mortality rate for the entire Soviet Union was 25.2 deaths per 1,000 births. In some underdeveloped regions in the Central Asian republics, the rate was 60 and sometimes even more than 100 deaths for every 1,000 births.

These shortcomings were mainly the result of inadequate funding in consequence of the Kremlin's application of the "leftover" principle in Soviet investment policy. According to this principle, heath care received whatever was left of investment after other priorities, such as defense and domestic heavy industry, had been met. As a result, there was a continuous reduction in the share of national income allocated to medical services. In 1989 it was below 4 percent, as compared to the 8 to 12 percent allocated to medical services in other countries.

POLITICAL DISSENT

Dissent was a logical consequence of the Soviet regimes's intolerance of most forms of criticism and protest. It was inevitable in a society that promised in its ideology a paradise on earth and in its propaganda insisted upon the need of citizens to make great personal sacrifices to achieve that paradise, while delivering far less than what people needed and wanted simply to survive, never mind thrive. The complexity, intensity, and relentlessness of the Soviet dissident movement, despite the regime's best efforts to obliterate it—and sometimes the Soviet authorities came close to that—were in proportion to the regime's flaws and its failure to mitigate them.

Major Groups of Dissidents

In the Brezhnev era there were at least five well-known groups of Soviet dissidents. One large and somewhat diverse group included people like the late Andrei Sakharov and human-rights activists Yuri Orlov and Anatolyi Shcharansky. This group was critical of the Soviet dictatorship, in particular its refusal to allow serious criticism or opposition to its policies, and sought liberalization along Western democratic lines. They asked for civil liberties, truly representative government, relaxation of censorship, and establishment of a system of checks and balances to limit governmental power and prevent abuses. Human-rights activists also demanded Soviet compliance with the human-rights provisions of the 1975 Helsinki agreements.

A second group of dissidents included Jews seeking to emigrate because of official discrimination. They were concerned primarily with pressuring the Soviet government to give them exit visas.

A third group of dissidents advocated the causes of the non-Russian nationalities against the Russifying and homogenizing policies of the central government. In this group were Georgian, Ukrainian, and Baltic national dissidents.

A fourth group consisted of people who protested the regime's harassment of them for religious reasons. Catholic, Lutheran, Baptist, and Pentecostal dissidents demanded a lessening of regime discrimination and the right to emigrate.

Finally, other dissidents, notably Alexander Solzhenitsyn, advocated a return to historic Russian values and traditions. These people sought a separation of Russia from the non-Russian peoples, whom they distrusted. (They have been called "chauvinistic reactionaries.") They also displayed a somewhat un-Marxist admiration of the Russian Orthodox church.

External Stimulants of Political Dissent

International circumstances encouraged Soviet dissident groups. For example, the Helsinki agreements of 1975, signed by the Soviet Union and other socialist countries in Central/Eastern Europe as well as by Western democracies, focused international attention on alleged violations of human rights of Soviet citizens by their government. Another example was the aggressive human-rights campaign of American governments. Washington frequently accused the Soviet Union of violating the human rights of its citizens. The French also criticized the Soviet government for human-rights violations. This international concern inspired Soviet dissidents to publicize their complaints.

Dissident groups in other socialist countries inspired dissent in the Soviet Union. The Charter 77 movement in Czechoslovakia, which protested human-rights violations by the Communist government in Prague, and the emergence of the Committee for Social Self Defense in Poland, which tried to help workers arrested by the Warsaw authorities for their role in the 1976 food strikes, attracted the attention of Soviet dissidents. The Eurocommunist phenomenon of the 1970s, in which Western Marxists, notably the leaders of the French, Italian, and Spanish Communist parties, advocated a liberal parliamentary path to socialist development and criticized the Soviet system for its violations of human rights, also influenced and encouraged dissent in the Soviet Union. The independent Polish trade union, Solidarity, in the 1980s had an impact on Soviet dissidents, especially in the Baltic republics, although it was not clear how much influence Solidarity had on Soviet workers.

Soviet workers—who had much to complain about—traditionally were a source of only very mild and restrained dissidence in the Soviet Union, for several reasons. Spontaneous and illegal union activities were ruthlessly suppressed by the state. Soviet industrial centers were widely dispersed, discouraging communication and cooperation among workers in different factory locations. Soviet workers themselves were divided along nationality lines. Moreover, Soviet workers had no allies in other social groups, such as farmers, the intelligentsia, and the Russian Orthodox clergy. The intelligentsia, from which most Soviet dissidents came, seemed to have little interest in helping the workers obtain redress of their grievances against the system.

Dissident groups in the Soviet Union were always weak. Dissidents lacked strong and cohesive organization and effective leadership. They showed little of the discipline and unity that the Marxists of Lenin's time had in their opposition to Czarism. Many dissidents tended to be individualistic, absolutist in their thinking, and antagonistic toward one another as well as to other social groups. Their very Russian-like dogmatism, in particular the intolerance some had of alternative ideas and positions, contradicted their self-professed affection for Western-style liberalism and political pluralism.

Forms of Political Dissent

Political dissent had many forms from its apparent beginning during the Khrushchevian "cultural thaw." It first appeared in literary expression, perhaps because literature provided an opportunity to express criticism obliquely and with minimum risk. The *Samizdat,* or materials reproduced privately and clandestinely (the opposite of *Gosizdat,* which meant government-published and thus officially sanctioned), included literature not likely to pass Soviet censors.

An important watershed in the early development of political dissent through literature was the Andrei Sinyavsky-Yuli Daniel trial in 1966. These two Soviet writers were arrested for having their works, which were critical of the regime, published abroad under pseudonyms. They were accused of anti-Soviet agitation and were convicted in a trial that provoked much opposition in Western Europe as well as among Soviet dissidents at home. Indeed, many Soviet dissidents, notably Alexander Ginzburg, who published an unofficial record of the trial, dated their participation in the movement from this time.

Shortly after the trial the most important Samizdat publication, *The Chronicle of Current Events,* was launched. The *Chronicle* was an underground journal that covered a variety of political criticism. Other Samizdat publications focused on specific nationality and religious grievances. There was also a spate of terrorism, such as a 1977 bomb explosion in a Moscow subway train by disgruntled Armenians, airplane hijackings, and even self-immolations. But the most persistent, and possibly the most embarrassing, forms of dissidence were the less violent ones. The frequent public criticisms of Soviet policy by Andrei Sakharov and the activities of human-rights activists known as the Helsinki Watch Committee received publicity in the Western press.

Regime Responses to Political Dissent

The Soviets always reacted vehemently to the behavior of dissidents because of deep-seated hostility to and fear of opposition of any kind. This attitude toward opposition was historic, dating back to the governments of Czarist Russia. There was always a characteristically Russian fear of things different, of alien ideas, and of popular challenges to the established order.

A measure of anti-intellectualism contributed to regime hostility to dissent. Those in positions of administrative authority and responsibility for the day-to-day operation of the Soviet system, notably censors, police, and many members of the Communist party, were usually not intellectuals. Many had only the minimum of formal education and little sympathy for people with ideas they did not understand.

One never knew—and perhaps the regime itself did not know—what might happen to particular dissidents until they were actually taken in hand by the authorities. Official reactions depended upon circumstances of the moment, such as the particular kind of dissent being dealt with, the state of the economy, the international situation, and relations with the United States.

Specific regime reactions to dissent occasionally included warnings to dissidents by legal officials. Other, more draconian, responses consisted of arrest, conviction, and punishment by imprisonment, ranging from a few years in an ordinary penitentiary to many years at hard labor, under difficult and even life-threatening physical conditions, in maximum-security institutions. The regime also resorted to the ancient punishment of forced exile to either obscure places in the Soviet Union or abroad.

There were also unofficial and informal responses to dissent, such as harassment of individuals by KGB agents, who could intrude on any aspect of a citizen's life with near impunity. This intrusion might have involved an unexpected rifling of an apartment, constant surveillance, or "trailing" and entrapment. The KGB also could arrange for the confinement of dissidents in mental hospitals for indefinite periods, where they would be harassed until they recanted.

Another indirect means of dealing with dissidents was contrived discrimination against them and their families in the workplace, at school, and elsewhere. Known critics of regime policies were demoted or fired from their jobs, denied privileges to travel within the Soviet Union and abroad, prevented from sending their children to preferred schools, and prohibited from participating in professional activities.

In 1983 the Andropov regime went beyond its predecessor in trying to reduce dissent. It revived old laws that limited the contact Soviet citizens could have with foreigners. This move was intended to curtail the practice of Soviet dissidents meeting with Western visitors, especially journalists, and informing them of their complaints and grievances against the regime, which would then, in some instances, promptly appear on the front pages of major Western newspapers. A similar move was the revival of laws that extended the terms of troublesome prisoners in labor camps. This prolonged the incarceration of certain dissidents for whom the regime had a special dislike, without having to impose a publicity-provoking trial.

The Impact of Dissent

Beyond provoking a defensive and stubborn regime's anger, dissent did not have any appreciable impact on the development of Soviet society in the pre-Gorbachev era. Certainly dissent did not achieve the objectives of the extravagant critics who called for a Western-type liberalization of the Soviet political system. On the other hand, dissent did lead to some policy change when it received, as it frequently did, extensive international publicity. For example, the Soviet government relaxed restrictions on the emigration of Soviet Jews from time to time in response to American pressure.

ECONOMIC UNDERPERFORMANCE

Economic underperformance plagued the Soviet system from its inception. It was dangerous because it prevented the regime's fulfillment of its elaborate promises to improve the material well-being of the Soviet peoples and thereby contributed to societal discontent and the possibility of political instability.

Agriculture

The most intractable and perhaps most serious aspect of economic underperformance was in agriculture, especially in the failure of agricultural output to meet food needs. And while every Soviet leader did much to cope with this problem, none succeeded in correcting it.

Many different and complex factors explain the inadequacy of Soviet agricultural output. At the head of the list was a scarcity of arable land. Only about 10 percent of the enormous Soviet landmass was designated arable; and much of this was not ideal for farming because of climatic extremes, water erosion, and other problems that undermine soil fertility.

Another reason was incentive—or, rather, the lack of it. Most Soviet farmers were little more than wage earners with no stake in excelling. Moreover, many Soviet farmers did not earn as much as industrial workers, and the fact that they were better off than were earlier generations was little consolation.

Soviet agriculture also suffered from an inadequacy of machinery. That which Soviet farmers did have was either underutilized or abused. Because of the absence of spare parts, many machines in need of repair stood idle, and there was poor maintenance and storage. Finally, the Soviet leadership diminished the supply of agricultural machinery available for domestic use by exporting abroad.

The Soviets had poor storage facilities for grain harvests when they exceeded anticipated consumption requirements. About 20 percent of the grain harvests, even in bad periods, was lost to rot, partly because storage was inadequate. Invariably, grain reserves were low and never sufficient to make up for unexpected shortfalls of annual harvests.

Distribution was another problem. Perishable food products could not be moved swiftly to market and frequently rotted on freight platforms while awaiting shipment. Part of the distribution problem had to do with the inefficiency of the Soviet railway system as well as the lack of first-class roads needed by heavy trucks.

Soviet agriculture also lacked enough good mineral fertilizers. Soviet farmers were obliged to use smaller amounts of fertilizer than their American counterparts, and the quality of Soviet fertilizers was lower than in the West. Consequently, it was difficult to maximize yield.

Another and by no means insignificant factor that contributed to inadequate agricultural output was the conservatism of Soviet leaders who showed great reluctance to inaugurate changes that might improve productivity. When reforms were discussed and tried, as Khrushchev found, to his dismay, there was much resistance from the bureaucracy, which had a vested interest in preserving the centralized agricultural decision-making process. Indeed, the bureaucracy bitterly resisted any leadership efforts, however slight, to boost food production by encouraging private garden plots that were beyond its control. The bureaucracy also resisted any efforts to increase the autonomy of collective and state farms.

Finally, the Soviet leadership was reluctant to commit to agriculture the level of investment needed to achieve a significant improvement in output. There was an increase in agricultural investment between 1961 and 1975 over that of the preceding period, but the total investment only involved a decrease in the traditional investment advantage of industry over agriculture. It did not bring agriculture up to parity with industry.

Industry

Soviet industry suffered from underperformance in the form of poor quality, high costs, and economic waste, for some of the same reasons as agriculture. Chief among these reasons was an excessively centralized decision-making apparatus. Managerial personnel had little decision-making discretion. They also were obsessed with protecting themselves against criticism and punishment by superiors. They were evasive and defensive. They hesitated to use what little discretion allowed them by central planners and administrators to innovate or develop improved technology to increase the quality and quantity of output.

Furthermore, central planners, who had the bulk of decision-making authority, tended to ignore consumer demand. They set targets for output based upon somewhat arbitrary assessments of need. They also determined output goals in many industries in terms of number of tons or in ruble value and paid little attention to the quality and marketability of what was to be produced. This helps to explain why much of Soviet industrial output, when measured by Western standards, was shoddy and why there was much waste of scarce resources. At the same time, the Soviet industrial machine needed, but lacked, labor-saving automation based on modern computer technology. In general, it simply took too many people too long to make decisions at the center and to implement them in the production unit.

Disproportionate growth caused by overinvestment in some industries and underinvestment in others was another reason for underperformance. The Soviet leadership tended to overinvest in heavy industry, for reasons of ideology and defense. But profits in heavy industry were small when compared to the profits that could be made in the production of consumer goods. Furthermore, the regime continued to invest in inefficient units of production, for the sake of full employment. This unbalanced investment policy also encouraged problems of poor quality, to say nothing of high production costs.

Perhaps a critical reason for underperformance had to do with the behavior of workers. Soviet workers protested low wages and the absence of goods they needed and wanted by slackening their pace of work, because the unions to which they belonged were controlled by the Communist party and did not provide them with adequate means of obtaining satisfaction of grievances.

Strict obedience to the decisions of the Gosplan led to disastrous economic losses. For example, billions of rubles were spent building the Baikur-Amur extension of the Trans-Siberian railway before there was anything to haul on it; it is now falling into disrepair. The highly centralized method of determining prices also produced absurdities. Arbitrarily low prices for fuel and raw materials in the past stimulated excessive use, creating waste and inefficiency in industry and agriculture and raising real costs of production. Ultimately, a very costly program of price subsidies was required to avoid penalizing the consumer.

The Consumer

Not surprisingly, another economic problem potentially threatening to political stability involved the Soviet consumer, who suffered from inadequate quantity and quality of goods. There was never enough food, housing, clothing, and durable goods like automobiles and household appliances. Soviet citizens became inured to long lines in grocery stores and long waiting periods for cars, housing, and appliances.

Some of the reasons for consumer neglect in the Soviet Union already have been identified in our discussion of the problems of production in Soviet agriculture and industry. Other causes of this neglect were political. Consumers never had an effective interest group able to lobby for government policies to improve their lot. And while in its final years the Soviet government began to study poverty levels, noting that some segments of the society were "underprovisioned," very little was done to address the large problem of consumer neglect, beyond frequent promises of improvement and abundance.

Neglect of consumer goods compromised other sectors of the economy by discouraging workers from expanding output. Because consumer goods were not produced and made available for sale to the workers, the bonus and extra pay given for increased productivity were meaningless and provided no incentive for workers to excel.

Shortages of consumer goods also encouraged workers to patronize the black market, which thrived in Soviet society because most shortages were chronic. The black market experienced constantly rising prices for continuously scarce commodities, with the long-term effect of encouraging the development of barter. In barter, citizens traded their talents and possessions and paid no taxes on any of this activity.

Remedies

While Soviet leadership had made many promises to improve economic performance, for a long time they did little to fulfill them beyond a mere tinkering with existing institutions and policies. For example, agricultural shortfalls were dealt with by allowing expansion of the private garden plots and by massive importation of foreign grain. Underperformance in industry was addressed by modest amounts of administrative decentralization, which involved small increases in the discretionary authority of factory managers in such areas as plant renewal, wages, and working hours. Even these gestures were bitterly resisted by a bureaucracy determined to oppose any change that involved reducing its authority.

On the other hand, there was evidence in the mid-1980s of official interest in a major overhaul of the Soviet economy. A confidential memo, prepared by a group of economists associated with the Siberian division of the Soviet Academy of Science in Novisibirsk and circulated in the Soviet economic administration, supported market-driven planning, flexible prices, and incentives to workers. The memo said that economic bureaucrats (the personnel of the Gosplan, the industrial ministries, and other state economic agencies) had to be restricted and their opposition to innovation curtailed. It charged that the bureaucracy frequently blocked reform because change would have required a high level of competence many bureaucrats did not possess and would have resulted in their loss of privilege.

The recommendations apparently inspired a joint Central Committee-Council of Ministers decree in 1984 giving plant managers authority over their budgets and discretion in matters of investment, wages, bonuses, and profit retention. To spur technological innovation, management was to have authority to reward innovative engineers and workers. The criteria for measuring factory performance were simplified in order to emphasize production of goods that would sell, particularly abroad. This meant lower priority for the traditional performance indicators in Soviet industry, notably the overall value of output, which encouraged factories to turn out large volumes of goods regardless of quality or need.

THE ENVIRONMENT: A NEW CONCERN WITH POLLUTION

A major socioeconomic problem that only in the late 1980s began to arouse both official and public concern was industrial pollution of the environment. For example, Soviet writers and scientists complained about the pollution of Lake

Baikal, an inland sea of fresh water in Siberia. For years a large pulp plant on the southwest tip of the lake had spilled contaminants into its waters, disrupting the fragile ecological balance and endangering public health. In response to this and other expressions of concern about pollution, the Soviet government enacted new laws to protect forests, air quality, water resources, and animal life. In 1987 the Communist party ordered a halt to the pulp plant's polluting of Lake Baikal.

Another major environmental problem with very serious political implications involved the cotton economy in Uzbekistan, in Soviet Central Asia. Moscow's obsession with expanding cotton production caused an enormous amount of environmental deterioration, in particular pollution with pesticides, defoliants, and fertilizers, and the shriveling of the Aral Sea.

The ravaging of the Aral Sea by pollutants was especially striking. Soviet authorities diverted its waters to irrigate the cotton fields of Uzbekistan and Turkmenia. As a result of the diversion, the sea began shrinking and its pollutants condensed, turning the two rivers that feed it, the Amu Darya and the Syr Darya, into little more than sewers. The contaminated water, often the only potable water in places like Karakalpak, spread infection and disease, especially among the weakest infants. Moreover, the chemical pesticides and defoliants used in cotton-growing were absorbed by the people who worked in the fields and were washed into the river water, which they drank.

The Environment and Nuclear Energy: Chernobyl

Beginning in the Brezhnev era the Soviet leadership gave a high priority to the development of nuclear power, in order to diminish dependence on limited oil and natural-gas reserves. By the end of 1985 Soviet nuclear facilities had achieved a total generating capacity of 20,000 megawatts. Nuclear-fuel power-generating plants were responsible for 11 percent of the nation's total power output, placing the Soviet Union in third place among countries with nuclear-generated electricity, after the United States and France. But in the spring of 1986 the meltdown of a nuclear reactor in the Chernobyl nuclear plant in the Ukraine brought home to Soviet authorities the dangers of its hell-bent-for-leather commitment to double the Soviet Union's nuclear power-generating capacity by 1990.

The Chernobyl nuclear accident on April 26, 1986, was the world's worst civil nuclear disaster. A cloud of this fallout drifted hundreds of miles northward and westward beyond the Ukraine into other parts of the Soviet Union, Scandinavia, and Central/Eastern Europe, ultimately affecting areas as far away as Italy, West Germany, France, Britain, and even North America.

Soviet investigators accused workers and managers at the plant of negligence, incompetence, complacency, irresponsibility, and lack of discipline—in sum, a carelessness born of a conviction, untempered by careful and thoughtful supervision from above, that what did happen could not happen. In addition, Western scientists concluded that there had been serious flaws in the construction of the number-four reactor at the Chernobyl plant, which had outdated technology and inadequate safety devices.

The accident had a profound effect on the health and well-being of people within the immediate area of the plant. Radiation levels within that area were 2,500 times greater than normal. At least 235 people contracted radiation-induced diseases. Medical treatment was difficult because Soviet doctors lacked the technical skills needed to handle cases of extreme radiation. No one knew what the long-term health consequences for this population would be.

Evacuation of residents in highly contaminated areas was difficult because there had been little preparation for a disaster of Chernobyl proportions. In the month after the meltdown it was necessary to move 92,000 people and provide them with food, clothing, and shelter. Local authorities had to disperse hundreds of thousands of children in Kiev and nearby cities to contamination-free areas in summer camps located in the south. Finally, authorities also had to worry about other people who voluntarily left their homes out of fear of contamination to stay with friends or in temporary housing, where they waited to hear from officials when it was safe to return. Not since World War II had Soviet authorities had to deal with the movement of so many people.

Contamination of the rich food-producing topsoil of a large region surrounding the Chernobyl plant destroyed most of the Ukrainian grain crop for 1986. The Soviets were unprepared for this agricultural calamity, because of their limited grain-storage capacity. There also was a temporary loss of nuclear-generated energy output.

The task of decontamination was horrendous in cost and complexity. Major clean-up activities included protection of the Pripyat River and the ground water in the area against contamination; prevention of the spread of radioactive dust around the plant, in part by paving the ground with concrete; reduction of the spread of contamination through runoff of rain water, achieved by seeding clouds before they reached the power-plant area; the extinguishing of a large number of small fires around the reactor building; and the construction of a concrete containment structure, which would permanently encase the number-four reactor while ensuring ventilation so that residual heat would not build up. Some of these remedial activities continued well into 1987; problems and complications slowed down the processes of repair and reconstruction.

While the Chernobyl accident did not appear to dampen the enthusiasm of Soviet leaders for continued expansion of nuclear generating capability, it at least increased their sensitivity to safety in the construction and maintenance of nuclear facilities. They also knew better the problems likely to occur in a Chernobyl-type disaster, notably the care of large numbers of potential victims of a nuclear disaster. They may also have become more aware of the liabilities of secrecy in nuclear development and thus more willing to interact with other countries in this area of policy-making.

THE IMPACT OF PERESTROIKA

Beginning in 1986 the Gorbachev leadership embarked upon a radical program of reform, called *perestroika,* or restructuring, which eventually involved all aspects of the traditional Soviet political system: the economy, political environment, party, government, military, society, and foreign policy. The purpose of perestroika was to enable the system to improve the quality of life of average Soviet citizens and thereby assure their loyalty to and the survival of socialism. Perestroika profoundly transformed—and ultimately destroyed—the Soviet polity.

In countless and endlessly long public and party speeches in the mid-1980s Mikhail Gorbachev spoke of a pre-crisis in the Soviet state, brought on by a long period of economic stagnation for which his predecessor Brezhnev was responsible. Gorbachev spoke of the urgency of resolving this pre-crisis situation, first, so he said, by accelerating output. Subsequently, when he realized that underperformance was the result of profound flaws in the system's organization and behavior, he advocated restructuring to make it function more efficiently. Gorbachev warned that failure to restructure the system would eventually jeopardize it by provoking a violent social turmoil, an oblique reference to the popular uprising in Poland in the summer of 1990. That crisis theatened Polish socialism and in the long term was the cause of its demise.

Writers in the West identified this pre-crisis as a failure of the so-called social contract, an implicit understanding between Communist leaderships and their societies that, in return for popular loyalty and obedience to party rule, the peoples of socialist countries would obtain a radical improvement in the standard of living. By the time of Gorbachev's ascendancy in the Soviet Union, in 1985, it was plain to all Soviet citizens that the utopian ideal was far from having been achieved and that, while life was tolerable for most, the standard of living was still low as compared to not only the West but also other socialist countries—and even, embarrassingly, to some countries in the Third World.

In particular, it was obvious to most Soviet citizens that the system had not redeemed its promises of improvement in the areas of food, clothing, housing, medical care, and other amenities important in daily life. And it was an open secret that party and state managers, the lieutenants of the ruling elite, were abusive to the point of irrationality in their treatment of the citizenry they were supposed to serve. They were also personally corrupt, incompetent, apathetic, dishonest, and, worse, obsessed more with career-building than with socialist development—this despite the enormous perquisites available to them that in effect made them a privileged class in a society that was supposed to eschew class distinctions.

Gorbachev and his close advisers, such as Eduard Shevardnadze, Abel Aganbegyan, and Aleksandr Yacovlev, knew that the time had come for systemic reform. This, they believed, was necessary to assure the Soviet system's legitimacy at home, to enforce its claims to superpower status abroad, and to protect and further its global interests. They believed that, unless the Soviet system was thoroughly overhauled to make it serve its citizens better, it would never be able to achieve the place that its size and wealth justified in the international community.

The time for radical reform had come also because the people in power in the Kremlin in the mid-1980s were a new generation, sensitive to the flaws of the past and confident in their ability to improve the system once and for all. This was Gorbachev's generation, born well after the Revolution of 1917 and coming of age in the post-Stalin era, sensitive to the excesses of the earlier formative period of Soviet development. They were also proud of the new Soviet society because of the essentially humanitarian rationale on which it was based. They did not accept the long-held view of early Soviet leaders, notably Lenin and Stalin, that the end justified the means. They were in these as well as other respects very different in their political outlook and behavior from their tyrannical predecessors.

From the 27th party Congress in early 1986 to the collapse of the Soviet state in December 1991, perestroika affected all major areas of Soviet national life. Most of the changes that took place involved a loosening of state control and an increase in individual initiative and responsibility—a new respect for individuals in their relationship with the state.

The first area of Soviet life to experience change was the economy, perhaps the area most in need of profound alteration to improve performance. The next area of Soviet life affected by perestroika was the political environment; this involved changes called *glasnost,* or openness and candor. Gorbachev and his advisers believed that a relaxation of the political environment must accompany change in the economy. Changes in the political environment inevitably required changes in the party, in terms of not only personnel (Gorbachev removed from positions of power those who resisted perestroika) but also the style and substance of party behavior. Eventually there had to be changes in the structure and performance of government, called *democratization.* And finally, perestroika had a large impact on foreign policy, requiring changes in past thinking about and actions in the international arena, to the point where it was possible to speak of a revolution in Soviet foreign policy accompanying the revolutionary events at home.

Perestroika and the Economy

Gorbachev's restructuring of the Soviet economy had several dimensions: 1) substantial curtailment of the power of central administrators to control agriculture, industry, prices, and foreign trade; 2) the use of profitability as an economic indicator in the functioning of economic enterprises, with provision for their contraction or liquidation on the basis of their profit-and-loss record; 3) expansion of worker participation in the management of enterprises that employed them; 4) official acceptance and encouragement of a limited private entrepreneurialism in selected areas of the economy having to do with consumer services and food production; 5) the introduction of major agricultural reform, involving a gradual movement away from the traditional system of collectivization toward private control and ultimately private ownership of land as the most efficient way of expanding food output; 6) the closing of a massive gap between production and consumption to raise the standard of living of Soviet citizens in areas of health, education, and welfare, an effort sometimes referred to as the "human factor" in Soviet perestroika; and 7) the pursuit of joint ventures with foreign enterprises, to facilitate Soviet acquisition of investment capital and technology needed to improve both production and distribution of goods and services.

Decentralization

The most conspicuous targets of Gorbachev's program of decentralization were the historically sacrosanct administrative control agencies known as Gosplan (the Soviet government's central planning agency) and Gosnab (its sister agency, in charge of fixing prices for all goods produced by state-run enterprises). Gorbachev asked for and received in June 1987 Central Committee approval to transfer the Gosplan's responsibility for determining the quality and quantity of all Soviet economic output to lower administrative levels, in particular to enterprise managers themselves; and to overhaul the elaborately controlled and subsidized system of pricing that set the value of more than 200,000 goods and services.

Unfortunately, the decentralization of economic decision-making did not go far enough. Central authorities still had too much opportunity to interfere. Central ministries, which were supposed to be primarily reservoirs of research and technology with overall responsibility for quality control, still meddled in enterprise-level decision-making through so-called state orders, or government contracts, which got top priority. This back-door way of running the economy from Moscow required enterprises to manufacture a certain amount of goods regardless of need, for the sake of attaining "notorious gross output levels," as Gorbachev put it; and undermined factory managers who were supposed to be in charge of production, buying, selling, and the disposition of profits.

Nor was there a real decentralization of pricing. Extensive state subsidies still kept prices artificially low. Soviet leaders feared that freely fluctuating prices would generate inflation and provoke a violent popular reaction. Moreover, the government intended to cushion the negative impact of price reform on Soviet consumers by increasing availability of consumer goods in the short term by importing more of them from abroad.

Profitability

The use of profitability as a determinant of an enterprise's survival was a striking departure from the traditional practice of keeping production units going when they were demonstrably inefficient and unprofitable, simply to assure

the continuing employment of their workers and managers. In June 1987 the Central Committee approved new rules whereby unprofitable enterprises were to be closed down even at the risk of causing unemployment. Enterprises that had difficulty making ends meet were supposed to control costs not only by technological innovations to increase efficiency of production but also by cutting wages.

Enterprises were supposed to meet a standard of financial accountability. They were to work closely with banks to obtain credit and to use it efficiently. Financial accountability was to encourage enterprises to meet delivery dates and to promote quality control to meet standards assuring sales and profits.

Although in theory by 1990 all of Soviet industry was to function according to financial accountability, in practice this did not occur. Ministries did not allow crucial enterprises, like those belonging to the military industrial complex, to declare bankruptcy; they also ensured that important but unprofitable enterprises continued to receive subsidies.

Another problem in achieving financial accountability was unemployment caused by failed enterprises. Soviet workers had never experienced massive layoffs; the Kremlin, anticipating unrest, in 1988 provided for the establishment of job-placement centers, a system of retraining for workers who lost their jobs as a result of restructuring, and continuation of pay for at least 2 months. The Soviet regime had never acknowledged the existence of an unemployment problem and had no experience in dealing with one.

Worker Incentives

To encourage workers to improve their productivity, the Central Committee in 1987 authorized a significant expansion of existing opportunities for workers to participate in the management of the enterprises that employed them. A new rule required workers to elect all members of their enterprise's management team, from the director down. The rule also established a new workers' institution, the labor-collective council, a continuing executivelike body of the labor collective, to be elected by its members and to function on a day-to-day basis. These requirements were supposed to increase the opportunity of Soviet workers to influence management.

Another effort to provide workers' incentives involved a reversal of the traditional policy of wage-leveling. This policy, which maintained the fiction that everyone was economically equal, brought a measure of political stability, but it alienated the most industrious members of society.

Under Gorbachev, the Soviet regime sought to link pay to performance. In 1986 a decree on reforming the wage system in the production sector stipulated that workers' pay had to be linked to job performance and that raises and bonuses must be paid for out of enterprise profits.

The issue of wage differentials proved particularly controversial. The economic inequality resulting from increased wage differentials was anathema to Soviet ideologists. Furthermore, it threatened the stable and secure employment arrangement to which the Soviet labor force had become accustomed.

Private Entrepreneurialism

In still another effort to increase the quality and quantity of Soviet output in the consumer-goods sector, Gorbachev asked for and received the Communist party's approval for the legitimization and extension of existing private entrepreneurial activities. According to new laws, Soviet citizens could work for themselves instead of for the state as owners of cafes, tailoring establishments, repair shops, and other areas of business where there was pent-up demand for service.

In 1988 private entrepreneurial undertakings, referred to as cooperatives, assumed increased importance in economic restructuring. Soviet economic planners, frustrated by the prospects of reviving the industrial sector, began to turn to cooperatives as a way of delivering a jolt of competition to stimulate a sluggish economy. A new law allowed cooperatives to conduct business with foreign companies and to receive hard currency as payment; to own property; to hire consultants; and to receive guarantees against government interference in their day-to-day operation. This law also gave prospective cooperatives the opportunity to appeal government rejection of their applications to start a business and established the right of state-run enterprises to join cooperatives.

Problems hindered rapid development of cooperatives in the service sectors. With an almost total absence of wholesale trade, it was hard to obtain the necessary resources and materials. The credit system for cooperatives was not developed. There was also mounting popular hostility to the new entrepreneurialism because of alleged price gouging; because of the appearance of a new group of egregiously affluent promoters and hustlers in the new cooperatives; and because there was little sympathy for the entrepreneurial spirit, which, in emphasizing rugged individualism and initiative, contradicted the moral teachings of the socialist system of the previous 7 decades against personal aggressiveness in economic and social life.

In response to the growing and pervasive popular resentment against the new entrepreneurialism—especially the way in which it was leading to an accumulation of individual wealth—the Soviet government announced in April 1989 imposition for the first time of a progressive income tax. The government also curtailed development of medical cooperatives, ordering state hospitals to cease renting expensive medical equipment to private doctors. While not against medical cooperatives in theory, the government was critical of them in practice because they abused the system. For example, they leased valuable state equipment and used it to "extract personal gain."

Nevertheless, expansion of private entrepreneurialism occurred in March 1990, when the Supreme Soviet passed a law giving private citizens the right to own small-scale factories and other businesses for the first time since the 1920s. The controversial term *private property* was not used, and the law was framed in accordance with prevailing Marxist terms, including a prohibition against the exploitation of one person's labor by another. Still, the law represented a striking departure from more than a half-century of Soviet policy. Furthermore, one of Gorbachev's chief economic advisers, Leonid Abalkin, promised other advances toward private entrepreneurialism, like the creation of a new banking system to help underwrite new privately owned businesses.

Agricultural Reform

Gorbachev's agricultural-reform program involved a gradual transfer of farms from collective to individual control and ownership. By expanding private farming, he hoped to foster the personal initiative and diligence of rural workers essential to an expansion of their productivity.

Beginning in 1985 Gorbachev began to shift decision-making power from central and republic ministries to local agricultural enterprises. He encouraged different kinds of entrepreneurial activities, such as farm cooperatives and contractual leasing arrangements by individual farmers for the renting of land on long-term leases from state authorities. He also increased state support for personal auxiliary farming. In addition, most farms moved to so-called contract leasing, in which brigades of workers managed plots of land within a vast state farm.

In 1989 the leadership decided to carry agricultural reform a step further and approved the most far-reaching departure yet from the traditional collectivized and state farm system: individual farmers were now allowed to lease state land for life and to pass on the leasehold to their children. Thus, the farm population had a chance at independent land management for the first time since the 1920s. In 1990 Gorbachev finally obtained legislation that gave farmers who chose to lease land and engage in private farming equal legal and financial footing to compete with the big state farms. Other changes included a restructuring of the existing collectives and state farms, which were to continue to be the mainstay of Soviet agriculture. These farms, as well as farms on private leaseholds, were free to sell whatever was not purchased by the state in private markets (although the percentages of what could be sold privately were not defined). The state, however, continued to be the largest purchaser and had priority of purchase, leaving only a small amount of output for non-state-controlled distribution.

The Human Factor

Gorbachev said that the success of economic restructuring depended on the human factor. This referred to the need to provide Soviet citizens with adequate food, clothing, shelter, and other amenities of life. The efficiency of workers was linked to their satisfaction with living standards.

In developing policy to address the human factor, Gorbachev seemed to be listening to the advice of reform economists like Nikolai Shmelyev and Vasily Selyunin, who urged that he disavow the country's traditional obsession with industrial growth and shift emphasis to expanding the quality and quantity of consumer goods. Therefore, the regime spent precious gold and hard currency for imports of foreign-produced consumer goods and expanded investment in its own consumer industries, especially housing construction; increased investment in health care; and paid more attention to the plight of impoverished groups like elderly people, whose pensions in many cases placed them below even the regime's meager poverty level.

Still another effort to improve the human condition in Soviet society was the government's decision to reverse policy and allow private charity organizations to work among the elderly and poor. These organizations began to appear in 1988.

Joint Ventures

Joint ventures permitted foreigners to share in the equity and management of both private and state-owned Soviet industrial and service enterprises. They were intended to bring into the Soviet Union the kind of technology and management experience needed to expand local consumer-goods production.

The program of joint ventures was both radical and controversial. It represented a departure from the Soviet Union's historic protection of its domestic economy against competition from the highly efficient capitalist economies of the West. It also ended a long period of economic isolation, because joint ventures engaged in a kind of international division of labor that involved joint production with firms outside the Soviet Bloc.

Joint ventures were formed in a wide range of economic activities, with hotel and restaurant services for foreign tourists a natural area for cooperation. Typical industrial agreements between Soviet and Western firms involved the production of machinery and computer software for managing petroleum production in Soviet refineries, the equipping of Soviet fertilizer plants with high-technology machinery manufactured in the United States, and the development of plastic manufacturing in the Soviet Union for food packaging.

Problems in the operation of joint ventures were numerous. For example, Soviet domestic prices were artificial and the ruble was not convertible. Therefore, it was not clear how the Soviet share of a joint venture could be measured to make sure that the reliability and quality of what the Soviets contributed could equal that of the other side. Other questions had to do with ability of the foreign partner to select and retain the Soviet engineers and workers it wanted. Another problem involved the need of foreigners to deal with the Soviet bureaucratic maze. Finally, no one knew what would happen if a joint venture had to be liquidated.

In the absence of arrangements that provided otherwise—and such arrangements were difficult to make with the Soviet foreign-trade bureaucracy—foreign investors had to take their profits in rubles, for which U.S. and other Western companies had little use. Some American companies found ways around this currency problem. The Pepsi-Cola company, which built two Pizza Hut shops in Moscow, accepted rubles at one outlet and collected foreign currencies at another one in a tourist neighborhood. Occidental Petroleum, on the other hand, exported 25 percent of the plastics produced in Soviet factories for sale in Western Europe and other markets and was allowed to take out of the Soviet Union hard-currency earnings equivalent to returns from sales outside the Soviet market.

Insofar as Soviet joint ventures with American firms were concerned, there were specific difficulties, not least of which were American regulations governing the export of certain kinds of technology, the acquisition of licenses, and the extension of credit. U.S. firms did not always find Washington receptive to joint ventures, on grounds of national security.

Problems and Limits of Economic Restructuring in 1990

Soviet citizens apparently had difficulty being enthusiastic about economic restructuring, because they did not understand and therefore did not have much sympathy for the changes it was supposed to bring about in their traditional values and behavior patterns. Soviet society was inherently conservative, fearful of the new and unknown. This was especially true if change involved a deemphasis of the system's traditional paternalism, in particular subsidized prices, egalitarian wages, and protection from unemployment. Indeed, the benefits of economic restructuring were not at all apparent to many Soviet citizens.

Conservatives warned that efforts to liberalize the Soviet economic system would fail because the economy could not be half free and half controlled. They worried that Gorbachev's policies, by encouraging individualism and group interests at the expense of collectivism, would lessen social discipline, encourage anarchy, and compromise socialism and the struggle to achieve communism. There also was a silent but nonetheless effective opposition of middle-level party and state bureaucrats likely to lose power and influence, and in some instances their jobs, as a result of the reduction of central control over the country's economic life.

Making matters worse for economic restructuring were two major tragedies that befell the Soviet Union in this critical era of change: the 1986 Chernobyl nuclear accident and the 1988 Armenian earthquake. They caused an unexpected and severe drain on already scarce goods and services and increased the hardship of Soviet citizens as they grappled with the changes wrought by economic restructuring.

Perestroika and the Political Environment

Perestroika also led to a liberalization of the repressive Soviet political environment through a set of policies known as glasnost, which called for full, frank, and public discussion of what Soviet citizens thought was wrong with their society. This was a stunning departure from the rigid and repressive control over thought and speech practiced by all previous Soviet leaderships. Glasnost also called upon party and state officials to respond to public inquiries and public criticisms about policy-making in different sectors of the administration, from economic enterprises to the KGB. Glasnost thus called upon state officialdom to abandon the secrecy practiced by all Soviet political officials as a matter of course throughout the history of the Soviet state.

The purpose of glasnost was to foster a new dialogue between citizens and the state to identify problems, especially in the economic sphere, to build public support for radical reforms of the economy and other sectors of Soviet soviety, and to pressure the bureaucracy to accept and implement changes it might not like. Glasnost was supposed to have many advantages for perestroika: 1) more open mass media would better reflect the leadership's commitment to reform; 2) public discussion of social and economic problems by individuals in the party, bureaucracy, and state apparatus would pressure officials to keep pace with the times and to be accountable for mistakes and abuses; 3) more open media would act as a barometer, providing Soviet reformers with necessary feedback on the general acceptance or rejection of their policies; and 4) glasnost would facilitate popular political participation and therefore be linked closely with policies designed to promote democratization.

In the late 1980s glasnost led to a substantial expansion of the permissible limits of public debate on national problems. For example, the Soviet press published criticisms of economic slackness and some of its causes, such as alcoholism, drug abuse, bureaucratic corruption, and economic waste. There was more media coverage of major accidents and disasters, injustices of the court system, and homosexuality. Perhaps one of the most striking aspects of the new candor of the official press involved public discussion of national problems such as poverty and homelessness, which former Soviet officials always insisted were absent from Soviet socialism and found only in capitalist societies.

Glasnost also included historical revisionism, or the rewriting of history. Gorbachev condemned Stalinism anew; cast the Khrushchev era in a much more favorable light than Brezhnev did; and referred in noncondemnatory ways to early Soviet revolutionary figures reviled by Stalin, like Trotsky and Bukharin, anticipating the official rehabilitation of these antiheroes and their ideas and policies.

Glasnost and Religion

Glasnost involved a new Soviet tolerance of religion. Leading newspapers reported on religious conferences and congresses in the Soviet Union. They even published stories about the infringement of rights of people seeking to practice their religion openly. Many presented the Russian Orthodox church in a favorable light, describing its key role in Russian history; its emphasis on values of family, work, and environ-

mental protection; and its potential contributions to charity work and to world peace.

The Soviet government made significant concessions to the Orthodox church. It returned three monasteries to church jurisdiction. It granted permission to the All-Union Council of Evangelical Christian Baptists to receive 100,000 Bibles from England; and approved a visit of Mother Teresa in 1987 to Moscow, Kiev, and the area around Chernobyl. In 1988 the Gorbachev leadership also approved of and participated in the extensive publicity given to the celebrations of the millennial anniversary of the establishment of Christianity in Russia. Gorbachev used the occasion of the celebrations to tell church leaders of his opposition to past religious repression and of the government's intention to guarantee religious freedom.

Gorbachev wanted to enlist the support of the Russian Orthodox church in his perestroika policies, and he undoubtedly wanted the church's assistance to alleviate the suffering of ordinary people from the hardships of economic reforms. The regime, moreover, had no reason to fear that its new indulgence of the church would lead to unwanted consequences, at least insofar as the clerical hierarchy was concerned. The leadership of the church remained conservative—conditioned to obedience and accommodation under the long, repressive rule of Stalin, Khrushchev, and Brezhnev—and therefore reluctant to go further than expanding church influence in Soviet society.

Atheistic feeling continued to permeate the Soviet political establishment, suggesting that liberalization of policy toward the church was based more on expediency than on alteration of the historic aversion to religion inspired by Leninism. In 1987 there was still some official discrimination against minority religious groups, such as the Lithuanian Catholics, Pentecostals, and Baptists, that may well have been ignored by an Orthodox church leadership sensitive to the competition coming from other religious groups.

The Soviet regime's softer approach toward religion had a mixed impact on Soviet Jews. On the positive side was an effort to improve cultural conditions for Soviet Jewry. The regime legalized the instruction of Hebrew in 1988 and agreed in 1989 to the establishment of a Jewish Cultural Center in Moscow, the first in the Soviet Union in 50 years. On the negative side was a new outbreak of anti-Semitism among the public at large, as seen in the emergence of a new chauvinistic movement called *Pamyat* ("Memory" in Russian). Pamyat encouraged popular prejudice against Soviet Jews by blaming them as well as other non-Russian groups for the Soviet regime's repressive policies in the 1920s and 1930s.

Glasnost and Dissent

Under glasnost, the Gorbachev leadership seemed willing to tolerate new, unofficial, and critical organs of public political expression. A new magazine, *Glasnost,* addressed Soviet national problems, as did discussion groups in Moscow and Leningrad, like the Perestroika Club, which was composed primarily of intellectuals, especially scientists working for Soviet government research institutions.

The most prominent and pervasive of the new unofficial journals, independent of party and state control, was *Ogonyok*, which was started up by Vitaly Korotich, a Ukrainian physicist-turned-editor. With revelatory articles on the seamier side of Soviet life, such as fascist tendencies among Soviet youth, corruption in Soviet sports, and the torturing of a criminal suspect by police—subjects that had been taboo in the official press—*Ogonyok* circulation increased in 1987 to 1.5 million copies.

But glasnost, as it applied to political criticism and dissent, had limitations. Gorbachev always viewed glasnost as a means to an end rather than an end in itself. The freer political environment existed to serve a purpose: economic reform. Glasnost-inspired dissent was limited by the Communist party, which controlled the media. Official censorship severely reduced the ability of the press, radio, television, and journals to pursue a truly open information policy. Party Secretary Yegor Ligachev, a critic of the more tolerant political environment fostered by glasnost, deplored the new permissiveness of the Soviet media, calling upon them to show restraint and responsibility in publishing material that reflected negatively on the country's socialist system. He also criticized historical revisionism, saying that there was too much stress on negative aspects of past Soviet development. The KGB was another obstacle to real freedom of expression. KGB operatives throughout the country, in cooperation with conservatives in the party and state bureaucracies, watered down or circumvented directives from the top leadership aimed at increasing personal political freedom.

Gorbachev himself would have been the first to acknowledge the shortcomings of the permissiveness engendered by glasnost. And he shared, to a degree, Ligachev's view that at times glasnost encouraged an all-too-aggressive criticism of national problems and policies. Gorbachev believed that by emphasizing the negative aspects of his reform program, the press discouraged and demoralized the Soviet public.

Glasnost and the Nationalities

One of the most important consequences of glasnost was an increase of nationalism and ethnic self-consciousness among the major non-Russian peoples of the Soviet Union. With more freedom of the press, these peoples expressed their needs, desires, and values, exploding with pent-up feelings of resentment and hostility toward Russians. They openly demanded liberalization, autonomy, and eventually complete independence of Moscow in administrative, cultural, and economic affairs.

Not surprisingly, the non-Russian groups welcomed the introduction of glasnost and took advantage of it to lobby for greater recognition by Moscow of their special needs and interests. For example, in June 1988 representatives of six non-Russian national movements met in the former Polish city of Lvov in Ukraine and founded a coordinating commit-

tee of Patriotic Movements of the Peoples of the U.S.S.R. The committee was supported by national-rights campaigners from Ukraine, Lithuania, Estonia, Latvia, Georgia, and Armenia and called for political and economic decentralization of the Soviet Union as well as the eventual transformation of the Soviet Union into a confederation of separate sovereign states. The Kremlin reacted more tolerantly than ever before to demands of the national minorities, listening extensively, tolerantly, and sympathetically to their complaints and their demands for change. But Gorbachev resisted their demands for changes that would have significantly altered the highly centralized Soviet administrative system, still dominated by Russians.

The challenge for Gorbachev was to remain sensitive to the nationalistic susceptibilities of the ethnic minorities while at the same time to assure the administrative unity he needed for the success of perestroika. In looking for a moderate long-term solution to the problem of controlling the increasing assertiveness of the large and small minorities, Gorbachev was willing to allow the minorities an extremely large amount of control over their local affairs, in return for their acceptance of nominal Soviet authority and continued membership in the Soviet federal union.

Glasnost and Baltic Nationalism

When glasnost began there was a veritable explosion of nationalist-inspired protest and dissent in the Baltic republics. In 1987 thousands of people in Estonia, Latvia, and Lithuania publicly protested the anniversary of the 1939 Hitler-Stalin pact in which Germany gave the Soviets a green light to annex the Baltic states that had received their independence from Russian rule at the end of World War I. These demonstrations were significant in two respects. First, they affirmed the intensity of anti-Russian feelings among the Soviet Union's Baltic citizens, despite Moscow's efforts to integrate them into Soviet society. Second, they revealed Moscow's hypersensitivity to the way such public expressions of anti-Russian sentiment were reported—and, in the Kremlin's view, sensationalized—by the Western media, which were accused by Soviet authorities of gratuitous mischief-making, as if to suggest that the existence of hostility toward Russia in non-Russian areas like the Baltic republics was the result of outside interference rather than of popular discomfort over subordination to Russian rule.

A proliferation of nationalist organizations emerged from cultural groups and professional unions. These organizations fielded candidates in local and national parliamentary elections in 1988 and 1989. They also publicly commemorated important historical events that were anniversaries of national tragedies. They staged a dramatic cross-border handholding of several hundred thousand citizens of Estonia, Latvia, and Lithuania in August 1989 to mark the 50th anniversary of the Nazi-Soviet Non-aggression Pact and to protest continuing communism and Soviet control. Representatives from these republics lobbied directly with the

Soviet leadership for political, economic, and sociocultural change.

The Baltic nationalist organizations—the Estonian Popular Front, the Latvian Popular Front, and the Lithuanian Sajudis and Movement for the Support of Perestroika—publicized a long list of grievances against Moscow. Their most important grievance was that the Soviet Union unlawfully destroyed the independence of the Baltic countries with the complicity of Nazi Germany in April 1940. A commission of the Lithuanian Legislature in August 1989 publicly declared the Soviet annexation of Lithuania illegal, the first official effort of the Baltic republics to lay the legal groundwork for declarations of independence.

Baltic nationalists also complained that Moscow's excessive centralization of economic power stifled economic life and forced the Baltic peoples to endure a low standard of living. Lithuanian nationalists in particular advocated the equivalent of states' rights, and the republic's government approved a constitutional amendment establishing a right—opposed by Moscow—to reject national laws with which they did not agree, a measure that violated the Soviet Constitution, which established the supremacy of national over republic law.

Baltic nationalists called for the deployment of Baltic soldiers of the Soviet Army in their native republics rather than to posts elsewhere in the Soviet Union. They insisted that Baltic soldiers be under the command of Baltic officers. In effect, they sought a breakup of the Soviet Army into nationality-based divisions.

In the economic sphere, they demanded and obtained a near-total independence from Moscow's administrative and planning agencies. They also sought policies to address environmental issues long ignored by Moscow and advocated freedom to develop closer economic ties with Western Europe.

In addition, Baltic nationalists criticized the past influx of Russians into their republics. In Latvia, where ethnic Latvians numbered less than 50 percent of the republic's total population, they sought both to curtail this Russian immigration and to limit the political influence of Russians on local government. The Estonians enacted a law defining residency requirements for voting in local elections that discriminated against recent Russian immigrants. And nationalists in all three republics lobbied aggressively to establish the local language as the state language, in place of Russian. (The Russian minorities protested this action as a violation of their rights under the Soviet Constitution.)

These explicitly anti-Russian gestures provoked a backlash by Russians living and working in Estonia, in the form of strikes and demonstrations against local authorities. Estonian citizens of Russian origin and other non-Estonian groups formed their own popular-front organization, the Intermovement, to resist the discriminatory policies of the Estonian majority and the majority's efforts to achieve autonomy of Moscow. One of Intermovement's first acts was to protest an Estonian law requiring non-Estonians working in Estonia to learn the language within 4 years or face dismissal.

Gorbachev sympathized with legitimate Baltic demands for reform. He approved the promotion of reform-minded party members to positions of leadership in the Baltic branches of the Soviet Communist Party. And he made striking concessions in the economic sphere, granting most of the Baltic demands for near-total local control over their economic life. And, in another conciliatory gesture, in 1989 the Kremlin acknowledged the existence of the secret protocols of the 1939 pact with Germany assigning the Soviet Union paramouncy in the Baltic states, on which basis the Soviet forces invaded and occupied them in 1940.

Gorbachev's conciliatory approach stemmed from his commitment to glasnost and his belief that the political ferment in the Baltic republics was a logical and healthy consequence of glasnost and democratization—healthy, that is, as long as it did not get out of control and lead to secession (as it eventually did). Also important in understanding Gorbachev's policy was his view that the Baltic peoples, with their already high degree of overall socioeconomic development as compared to other parts of the Soviet Union, were the most likely to make a success of his economic-restructuring policies, which, incidentally, they strongly endorsed.

Gorbachev hoped that Soviet flexibility in regard to Baltic nationalism would help to keep the region inside the Soviet administrative system. Many Baltic nationalist figures were sensitive to Moscow's anxiety over the possible loss of the Baltic republics and for a time avoided demands for immediate independence. There was a strong economic logic for postponing discussion of secession; Baltic economists believed that most of the region's trade would continue to be with the Soviet Union.

But Gorbachev always opposed Baltic secession, which would have set a dangerous precedent for other national minorities in the Soviet Union. Indeed, the mere prospect of secession strengthened the hand of skeptics, especially conservatives in the top party leadership, the state security establishment, and the army high command, who were determined to preserve the integrity of the historic Soviet domain bequeathed by Lenin and Stalin.

On several occasions in 1988 and 1989 the Kremlin warned Baltic nationalist leaders against promoting secession and against policies that violated the Soviet Constitution, such as discriminatory behavior by local authorities toward Russians and other minorities. And in 1989 Soviet Politburo member Yacovlev publicly declared that there was no link between the Nazi-Soviet pact and the current status of the Baltic republics and therefore no legal basis for secession.

The Lithuanian Crisis in Early 1990

Despite Gorbachev's warnings, a crisis over secession did occur, on March 11, 1990, when the newly elected Lithuanian Supreme Soviet voted a declaration of independence from the Soviet Union. This momentous act was predictable after the independence movements in Central/Eastern Europe and after the overwhelming victory of candidates who supported independence in the February 1990 Lithuanian parliamentary elections.

In the weeks immediately following the Lithuanian Legislature enacted laws to reinforce the republic's independence. The Parliament called for the issuance of Lithuanian identity cards and for the rejection of the Soviet military draft. Moreover, Lithuanian authorities refused to cooperate in the apprehension and prosecution of young Lithuanian men who defected from the Soviet Army. Lithuanian President Landsbergis made a point of addressing Gorbachev as if he were the head of a foreign state.

The Soviet reaction to this challenge was swift but also, at least initially, restrained. After declaring the Lithuanian action a violation of the Soviet Constitution and therefore illegal, Gorbachev told the Lithuanian government that Moscow would not oppose eventual secession if it occurred within the framework of the Constitution, which was in the process of being amended to provide the means for secession, which always had been accepted in principle, if not in practice. He also appealed to the Lithuanians, as supporters of perestroika, to remain in the Soviet Union to help him implement his reform program from which they, as well as the rest of the country, stood to benefit. Finally, he promised all of the republics a new "union treaty" giving real autonomy to republic governments in return for their acceptance of central-government control over defense.

The Lithuanian Parliament refused to go back on its declaration of independence, and eventually Gorbachev threatened Lithuania. Gorbachev exerted tremendous psychological pressure. He criticized the Lithuanian Parliament for voting on independence precipitously—only hours after its election and without having provided all of the republic's citizens, including minorities like the Russians, who constituted about 9 percent of the republic's 3.7 million inhabitants, an opportunity to express their point of view, such as in the form of a republic-wide referendum.

Gorbachev warned of dire economic consequences if the Lithuanians implemented secession. He reminded Lithuania of its dependence on trade with the Soviet Union and the difficulties of developing economic links with the West. An independent Lithuania would have to pay $33 billion for economic property in the republic which technically belonged to the Soviet state. Lithuania would lose to the neighboring republic of Byelorussia territory previously controlled by Byelorussia and transferred to Lithuania following its admission to the Soviet Union in 1940. Furthermore, Gorbachev expressed deep concern for the well-being of the Russian minority in Lithuania, suggesting a moral as well as political justification for a possible military interference in Lithuania to preserve its legal membership in the Soviet Union.

By the end of March Gorbachev had moved toward more stringent actions to sway the Lithuanians from their independence course. He sealed off the republic to prevent outsiders,

including tourists and journalists, from entering the republic, thus isolating it from the West. He sent limited military contingents into the republic to protect federal buildings and installations as well as to intimidate the local populace and the government in Vilnius. Federal authorities moved to establish control over local law-enforcement and criminal-justice agencies in the republic. And in mid-April Gorbachev threatened an economic boycott of the republic if its government did not rescind various legislative enactments that violated the Soviet Constitution.

Gorbachev's responses to Lithuania were influenced by several considerations. One was fear that the Lithuanian move might set off the feared chain reaction of secessionist movements, not only in the other Baltic republics but in any republics where there was nationalist agitation. What was also at stake was the possible disintegration of the traditional Soviet state. In particular, the Soviet military worried about the strategic liabilities of the Soviet Union's loss of control over Lithuania and perhaps the Baltic republics. Indeed, the reduction of Soviet political influence and military power in Central/Eastern Europe in 1989, while possibly encouraging the Lithuanian independence movement, probably strengthened the Kremlin's determination to maintain control over the Baltic republics, which would have had to take the place of the former Soviet Bloc countries as the first line of Soviet defense against a threat from the West.

In its confrontation with the Kremlin over independence, the political leadership of Lithuania did not have much support from the West. Most of Western Europe remained silent on the issue. The Bush administration responded cautiously, despite the United States' past refusal to acknowledge the legality of the Soviet incorporation of the Baltic republics in 1940. Washington, however, did urge Gorbachev to resolve Moscow's differences with Vilnius peacefully. Both President Bush and Secretary of State James Baker warned the Kremlin of very negative consequences for Soviet-American relations if it tried a forceful Brezhnev-style Soviet crackdown in Lithuania. The U.S. Congress was more adamant than Bush and wanted the United States to recognize Lithuanian independence; its views undoubtedly strengthened the impact of the Bush administration's warnings to Moscow about restraint in dealing with Vilnius. This position discouraged the more aggressive elements in the Soviet leadership and to that extent was of some help to the Lithuanians.

Nevertheless, the disappointed nationalist leadership correctly concluded that the United States and other Western nations were reluctant to take up the cause of Baltic nationalism. With Gorbachev making extraordinary changes in Soviet foreign and domestic policies, the West did not want to risk strengthening the hand of Communist party conservatives and rivals of Gorbachev who might challenge his leadership if he could not control Lithuania. Moreover, Washington argued, with some plausibility, that the new Lithuanian government had yet to demonstrate the reality of its independence of the Soviet Union. It had no effective control over the country and, therefore, recognition at this juncture was premature. The Bush administration also expressed its desire to avoid the mistake it believed the Eisenhower administration had made in Hungary in 1956, when it led the Hungarian opposition to expect that the United States would help in resistance to Communist rule, but never fulfilled that expectation, even when the Soviets invaded Budapest.

Nor did Lithuania receive strong support from other Baltic republics. While both Estonia and Latvia sympathized with Lithuania, they carefully refrained from imitating its confrontational approach. They took to heart Gorbachev's strong warnings against precipitous efforts to secede from the Soviet Union. They also were sensitive to the absence of effective Western support. They proceeded cautiously on the issue of separation from the Soviet Union and watched events in Lithuania to see how fast they themselves might be able to move toward independence.

The Lithuanian cause was also weak among reformers in the Congress of People's Deputies and the Supreme Soviet, in particular the Interregional Group, which had often sided with deputies from the Baltic republics on issues of economic and political freedom. They voted along with Gorbachevists to declare the republic's secession illegal and invalid. Like Gorbachev, they deplored the Lithuanian Parliament's haste in declaring independence and its apparent unwillingness to consult all the Lithuanian public.

The Lithuanian crisis dramatized for the Kremlin the urgency of addressing the larger problem of reconciling ethnocultural nationalism to Soviet unity. The Supreme Soviet, despite misgivings, approved changes in the Soviet Constitution that created a strong presidential office capable of dealing directly and decisively with threats to unity. It also enacted a new law on union-republic relations that provided for the secession of a republic. The law provided for a complex and therefore difficult process would-be secessionist republics would need to pursue in order to gain independence of the Soviet Union, which made secession practically impossible. According to this law, the secession of a republic could occur only after the holding of a republic-wide referendum in which two-thirds of the voters agreed to secession, after formal approval by the Soviet Congress of People's Deputies and passage of a 5-year period in which issues connected with secession were resolved to the satisfaction of both the central and local authorities, including the payment of resettlement expenses for those who opposed secession and opted to leave the republic that seceded.

Ukrainian Nationalist Activity

Ukraine, the second largest of the union-republics, with a population of 52 million people, a fifth of Soviet industry, and the reputation of being the Soviet Union's breadbasket because it provided one-fifth the Soviet Union's agricultural output, experienced a glasnost-encouraged nationalism. Sources of Ukrainian nationalism were the historic prejudice against the Russians, who obtained control of the region by conquest; economic and social grievances, not least of which were anger at the Chernobyl disaster in 1986 and the new lease on life given the Catholic church, which looked to the Vatican for leadership and recently had been allowed new freedom to function.

In republic-level and local-level government legislative elections in March 1990, candidates favoring independence won seats. These nationalists, many of whom belonged to a popular-front organization known as Rukh, along with many young people, in particular a new anticommunist organization calling itself the Union of Independent Ukrainian Youth, admired and supported the movement toward independence in the Baltic republics. The Rukh issued a declaration urging the conversion of its loose alliance of human-rights activists, environmental activists, and radical Communists into a full-fledged political party. Rukh President Ivan Drach declared that the new party would seek the full sovereignty of Ukraine, which meant, he said, secession from the Soviet Union.

But Ukrainian nationalist politicians were more cautious than their Lithuanian counterparts. They spoke about "eventual" independence, in 5 years or so, and of the importance of laying the groundwork for separation gradually and incrementally. For example, some Ukrainian nationalists said that a start toward independence should be demands on Moscow to allow Ukrainian soldiers to do their military service in Ukraine.

Tatar, Georgian, Moldovan, Armenian, and Azerbaijani Agitation

Forcibly exiled to Central Asia from their homeland on the Crimean peninsula during World War II because of collaboration with Germans by some of their number, the Tatars fought quietly for the first several decades to regain their original homeland. In the summer of 1987 they demonstrated in Red Square and subsequently held rallies and demonstrations for the re-creation of an autonomous republic in the Crimea.

Consistent with glasnost, Soviet authorities reacted with a measure of sympathy and promised in July a hearing with then-Soviet President Andrei Gromyko, who had recently been named to head a commission to examine Tatar complaints. A commission report in October 1987 called for cultural concessions to the Tatars and criticized discrimination against them in matters of housing, employment, and schooling. The Soviets subsequently announced in February 1988 that a limited number of Crimean Tatars would be able to return to the Crimea.

But the commission did not make any significant changes in boundaries, and it officially denied the request of the Crimean Tatars for an autonomous republic. The Gromyko commission argued that the administrative territorial division of the country made it possible to give ethnic groups an independent voice and that the population in the Crimea had trebled in the postwar period and was now overwhelmingly Russian and Ukrainian. These groups would object strongly to the formation of a Tatar republic there.

Georgians also expressed ethnocultural nationalism. They were sensitive about their history and culture, given the fact that for much of their past they had lived under the control of powerful invaders: Greeks, Romans, Turks, Mongols, and now Russians. They were as much the victims of the culture-destroying Russification policies of the late-nineteenth-century czars as other non-Russian peoples conquered and administered by the czars. Religion was an important ingredient of Georgian nationalism. Since the third century A.D. the Georgian people had had their own branch of the Orthodox church, with its own patriarch.

Georgians also were defensive about their language, which belongs to the Caucasian family, is distinct from the Indo-European system and highly inflected, and which they considered threatened by the efforts of the central authorities to promote cultural homogenization. When Moscow tried in 1978 to remove a clause from the Georgian Constitution proclaiming Georgian the official language, thousands of demonstrators poured into the streets, forcing the authorities to back down.

Finally, Moscow had helped, quite inadvertently, to heighten Georgian nationalistic sensitivities by fostering economic growth and development. Moscow brought industry, expanded educational opportunities, groomed a native party and government apparatus, and tolerated a flourishing of Georgian culture, all of which raised aspirations of Georgian autonomy. Moscow also stimulated Georgian eagerness for economic reform, which would allow an expansion of private enterprise and individual initiative, thereby increasing Georgian impatience with economic regimentation.

Georgian nationalists in the late 1980s were divided over the long-range goals of their antigovernment actions. Some would have been satisfied by an extensive autonomy; others favored complete separation from the Soviet Union. The Georgian nationalist movement, consequently, did not develop the kind of unity of purpose and organization characteristic of nationalism in the Baltic republics.

In Moldavia (or Moldova, as it is known today, and called Bessarabia when the area was under Romanian control before World War II), there was also a growing spirit of autonomy. The Moldovans started to campaign for greater popular control over their local economic and political affairs.

This desire for greater autonomy in Moldova was fueled in part by policies of Moscow. In the spirit of glasnost, the Soviet authorities quietly began to undo one of the great cultural hoaxes of the twentieth century—namely, the historic Soviet insistence that Moldovans were a unique ethnic group, independent from the Romanian nationality to which they really belonged. As a consequence, Moldovans were forced to write their Romanian language in the Cyrillic alphabet. In January 1989 the Moldovan party leadership agreed to three demands of intellectuals in the republic: it declared that Romanian and Moldovan tongues were identical; it restored the Latin script; and it established the Moldovan tongue as the official state language of the republic.

These gestures heightened Moldovan sensitivity to their Romanian origins. Informal nationalist-minded political groups sprung up and demanded limits on Russian migration into Moldova, a halt to environmentally harmful industrial projects, and the replacement of leaders considered holdovers from a corrupt and conservative past.

Armenian nationalism came from a strong sense of community based on a shared memory of the 1915 massacre, the influence of the Armenian church, the contribution of Armenians living abroad to a view of Soviet Armenia as a homeland, and the fact that Soviet Armenia was the most ethnically homogeneous of the 15 constituent republics, with more than 90 percent of its population Armenian. Taking advantage of the more tolerant political atmosphere inspired by glasnost as well as by Gorbachev's call for grass-roots political initiative, Armenian nationalism found its voice early in 1988, when a group of Armenian intellectuals raised an old Armenian demand for the return to Armenian control of the autonomous region of Nagorno-Karabakh.

Nagorno-Karabakh, a mountainous enclave situated in the neighboring republic of Azerbaijan, was inhabited predominantly by Armenian people. Historically, this area was under Armenian control. It would have remained so after the Bolshevik Revolution had Stalin not given it to Azerbaijan in 1923. The local Azerbaijani administrative authorities discriminated against the Armenian population living in Nagorno-Karabakh.

At the root of Azerbaijani discrimination were religious and ethnic prejudices. Many Azerbaijani people were Muslims and of Persian or Turkish extraction, while the Armenians were Christians. And in light of their demands for the return of Nagorno-Karabakh to Armenia, the Azerbaijani considered the Armenians land-grabbers.

Azerbaijani discrimination against Armenians in Nagorno-Karabakh took many forms. For example, the local Azerbaijani authorities converted Armenian Christian churches to mosques and curtailed Christian religious training in the state-run school system. And they pursued investment policies that left the region's infrastructure underdeveloped and its Armenian population poverty-stricken.

While the Kremlin was sympathetic to the Armenian position, it steadfastly refused to allow the transfer of Nagorno-Karabakh from Azerbaijan to Armenia. Soviet authorities in Moscow were afraid of provoking the wrath of the Azerbaijani population and of setting a dangerous precedent for boundary changes elsewhere in the Soviet state.

The Armenians resented Moscow's refusal to support the cause of annexation; the Azerbaijanis resented Moscow's perceived pro-Armenian sympathies. And both groups resented the failure of the 19th Communist party Conference in 1988 to disavow Soviet cultural homogenization and Russian assimilationist policies. The Conference offered no solution to the problem of Nagorno-Karabakh beyond acknowledging its seriousness and the existence of interethnic conflict elsewhere in the Soviet Union.

Infuriated by Moscow's unwillingness to sanction the

transfer of Nagorno-Karabakh to the Armenian republic, the Armenians, otherwise sympathetic to Gorbachev's perestroika, now turned against the Soviet leader. A few Armenian activists, representing the intelligentsia and other social groups, created the so-called Karabakh Committee, not only to spearhead annexation of the disputed region to Armenia but also to lobby aggressively with Moscow for increased economic sovereignty, priority for the Armenian language in republic schools and public affairs, and a veto over federal projects in the republic.

This activity in turn provoked the Azerbaijanis to violence against Armenians living not only in Nagorno-Karabakh but elsewhere in Azerbaijan, including Baku, its capital. By the summer of 1989 it seemed as if the two republics were about to go to war—the Armenians to get Nagorno-Karabakh, and the Azerbaijanis to keep it. Each side increased discrimination against the people of the other living under its jurisdiction. In June and July there was a mass exodus of Armenian residents of Nagorno-Karabakh to the Armenian republic. In late 1989 Azerbaijani workers blockaded rail lines carrying food and fuel into Armenia.

Amidst this escalating nationalism was an earthquake on December 7, 1988, in Armenia, killing more than 25,000 Armenian citizens. Armenians blamed the Soviet authorities for taking too long to get necessary equipment to the republic to unearth victims. They also complained that Gorbachev was using the occasion of the disaster to suppress the nationalist protest by arresting nationalist figures, such as the members of the Karabakh Committee.

In early 1989 the Soviet leadership, in the spirit of glasnost and democratization, tried hard to conciliate Armenia. First, it allowed relatively open coverage of the earthquake. Second, it invited foreign help in the pursuit of relief and recovery efforts. Third, it acceded to demands by the Armenians for their increased economic and environmental autonomy of Moscow. Finally, it released interned members of the Karabakh Committee, which subsequently transformed itself into a kind of Armenian popular-front organization.

These Soviet gestures, however, did little to lessen Armenian hostility to Moscow or to Baku. Moreover, Soviet policy seemed to strengthen Azerbaijani nationalism by confirming suspicions of a pro-Armenian bias in Moscow. By late 1989 an Azerbaijani popular-front organization emerged, not only championing the republic's claims to Nagorno-Karabakh but also demanding increased administrative autonomy. Moscow seemed to incline toward the Azerbaijani position on Nagorno-Karabakh, by restoring the region to the control of Baku, an action that heightened Armenian hostility.

Perestroika and the Communist Party

The Soviet Communist Party underwent profound change under perestroika, because Gorbachev believed that the party more than any other institution was responsible for the pre-crisis situation inherited from the Brezhnev era. In his view, the party had to liberalize its highly authoritarian structure, loosen its stranglehold over the Soviet economy and society, and rid itself of a self-interested, unresponsive, and corrupt managerial elite. He was convinced that a successful economic revival depended on party reform in at least three areas: internal organization, party-state relations, and the behavior of individual party members.

Internal Organization

To bring new blood to the party's leadership positions, Gorbachev recommended adoption of new rules for electing leadership on the local and national levels of the party organization. The 19th party Conference in June 1988 agreed to limit terms of first secretaries, who were in effect the bosses of a local party agency, and of the general secretary, who was the leader of the whole party, to two 5-year terms. Gorbachev was excluded from this new ruling. The Conference also agreed to the introduction of multiple candidacies in party elections.

Gorbachev wanted as well to allow more freedom for rank-and-file discussion of critical issues. Party leaders initially were not receptive to this change, fearing that a liberal environment in the party would encourage divisiveness, undermine discipline, and compromise the unity of the party and its ability to act as a cohesive force in leading the country. While there was increased internal party debate, there was no formal agreement to modify democratic centralism.

Party-Government Relations

The 19th party Conference limited the party's involvement in the day-to-day administration of the country. It abolished party departments that duplicated the activities of the government. The work of the party's central apparatus became concentrated in two departments or sectors, each supervised by a secretary: the ideological-propaganda department, and the organization-personnel department. The first department supervised party schooling and promoted the ideological line in primary party organizations and in the country at large. The second department dealt with internal party organization and with personnel matters within both the party and state bureaucracies.

While a great deal of change was implemented, much of the way the party traditionally operated remained the same. The party bureaucracy continued to influence appointments and promotions within the government. Furthermore, to assure continuing party influence over local government, Gorbachev required that party leaders simultaneously run in elections for local government. Gorbachev was extremely sensitive to the way in which incompetent party officials had created the illusion of success while concealing the reality of failure. Enraged by extensive corruption, including embezzlement and bribery, Gorbachev insisted that party bureaucrats change their behavior or risk losing their jobs. He said that party officials had to show humility and undertake periodic self-criticism to identify where they may have gone wrong in the performance of their responsibilities.

In addition, Gorbachev called for scaling down the extraordinary extent of privileges and perquisites that party officials had accumulated over the years. They had special stores, hospitals, and sanatoria and possessed certificate rubles—a special currency that made possible the purchase of goods not available to people with ordinary rubles. Soviet citizens had long been aware of this new class of bureaucrats who lived better than ordinary people and they did not like it, as they made clear under glasnost.

The Party and Glasnost

The party's commitment to glasnost was evident at the 19th party Conference. Delegates, elected for the first time in a relatively free and open manner by the party rank-and-file, openly and on occasion severely criticized past party behavior. The frankness and intensity of the 4-day proceedings startled both the Soviet viewing public, numbered in the tens of millions, and the party delegates who attended and participated in it. One delegate was quoted as saying that he had witnessed a revolution.

What was stunning was not only the dynamic character of discussion but also the participation of ordinary delegates. Many interacted with the party leadership, interrogating and criticizing it in a way that had never been possible at earlier congresses and conferences. The spontaneity of the conference showed how glasnost had changed the party itself.

Under glasnost, new political organizations, called popular fronts, emerged. These offered an alternative to the party, and eventually they opened the way to development of political pluralism and the emergence of a multiparty system. The popular fronts were independent of the party and were committed to an array of political, economic, and cultural reforms. Occasionally they were critical of the Communist party and of its leadership, including Gorbachev.

Glasnost allowed these organizations to demonstrate publicly, to nominate candidates for public office along with the Communist party, and to lobby aggressively for radical change. The most active and influential of the popular fronts appeared in the Baltic republics and Armenia, where they became popular vehicles for expression of ethnocultural nationalism.

Another quasi-political party organization that emerged under glasnost was the Democratic Union (DU), established in 1988. The DU was a truly radical organization of young activists, mostly in their mid-thirties, that called openly for the end of one-party rule and the establishment of a multiparty system. The DU nominated candidates for national public office, held public demonstrations in favor of democratic reform, and displayed distinct anti-Communist tendencies; for example, in March 1989 DU members unfurled the old blue and red flag of Czarist Russia.

The party's tolerance of this new political activism foreshadowed the emergence of competitive political parties. Prominent and influential figures, including Gorbachev, were willing at least to mention and discuss such a radical idea. Articles appeared in the official media in the early months of 1989 severely criticizing the Communist party, charging it with responsibility for helping Stalin create a ruthless police state, a tyrannical bureaucracy, and an enormously inefficient centralized economy. These commentaries were a prelude to an attack on the party's monopoly that led to a decline of party influence and the genesis of other political parties to compete for leadership of the Soviet state.

Finally, glasnost encouraged development of factionalism within the Soviet Communist Party, especially within the top party leadership. From 1988 onward Gorbachev had to confront skepticism, criticism, and sometimes not-so-covert opposition to his reforms from both a left and a right in what seemed to be a serious erosion of democratic centralism. The left wanted the general secretary to go faster in reforming the Soviet system. The most notable representative of this position was Boris Yeltsin, the former head of the Moscow city party organization. The right wanted Gorbachev to move slowly and cautiously and in some areas not at all. Its leading advocate was Yegor Ligachev, a member of the Politburo and of the Secretariat.

The Left and Boris Yeltsin

Yeltsin's position in 1987 and 1988 was that perestroika could not succeed unless Gorbachev broadened and accelerated radical political and economic reforms. He tried to do so in his own district, Moscow. Yeltsin became very popular among the citizens of Moscow for trying to address their complaints about local economic problems and for holding the party responsible for them. He criticized party leaders, including Gorbachev, at a meeting of the Central Committee in October 1988. He was subsequently reprimanded for violating the rules of democratic centralism; eventually, he was replaced as head of the Moscow party organization. Although they did not come to his support, many in the Central Committee, including, perhaps, Gorbachev himself, were sympathetic to his complaints. Moreover, the citizens of Moscow rallied behind him and saw him as a hero against the conservative bureaucrats.

The Right and Yegor Ligachev

Ligachev, the chief spokesperson and defender of the conservative point of view about perestroika in the late 1980s, had the respect of the party apparatus, in which he had served longer and probably enjoyed a higher standing than Gorbachev. He did not break with Gorbachev's policies and, indeed, praised economic restructuring. However, Ligachev urged restraint in the political sphere, criticized the discussion of party privilege, complained about negative news coverage, and warned against a permissiveness toward public dissent.

By the summer of 1989 Ligachev's personal power to challenge Gorbachev had declined. For example, Gorbachev's proposed changes in the traditional agricultural system (in particular the expansion of private leaseholds, tantamount to private ownership of farm land) were diametrically opposed to the collective system which Ligachev staunchly defended. Furthermore, nothing lowered Ligachev's stature so much as the growing popularity and political influence of Yeltsin, whose attacks on Ligachev measurably increased the Moscow chief's public support.

Although Yeltsin called for Ligachev's resignation regularly, and although Gorbachev looked on during these assaults and did not support Ligachev publicly, allowing him to defend himself as best he could, the Soviet leader did not force his ouster or punish him for his criticism. Despite the differences between Gorbachev and Ligachev, there seemed to be an agreed-upon division of labor, in which Gorbachev pressed for change while Ligachev tried to prevent too great a deviation from socialist doctrine and practice.

Perestroika and the Government

Another important aspect of perestroika involved reforms of national and local government called *democratization,* which Gorbachev defined as the need for everybody to participate in shaping society. Democratization was intended to give a sense of common purpose to the Soviet people and to engage them in a process of self-monitoring of their political and economic activity. Gorbachev especially wanted to mobilize people against the all-too-comfortable and conservative bureaucracy. Finally, democratization was supposed to end the alienation of people from government, which was now blamed for the hardships of daily life. Democratization provided mechanisms to allow the regular, nonviolent, popular-based change of leaders to assure their responsiveness to social needs.

Gorbachev's democratization, however, was not the same as Western democracy. It did not involve abandonment of the traditional authoritarian system that had governed since Lenin's time. Democratization did not call for a reduction of the enormous power concentrated in the hands of party and state leaders; or did it provide for all of the individual rights and liberties guaranteed in Western democratic systems.

Democratization initially affected several aspects of the Soviet governmental aparatus, in particular legislative institutions on the national and local levels; the Soviet presidency; the relationship between the republics and the Central government in Moscow; and the criminal justice system, including the KGB, the bureaucracy, and the military. In all these instances, democratization involved either increasing popular influence over state agencies or assuring their responsiveness to popular interests and needs.

Legislative Reform

The Supreme Soviet in December 1988 approved major changes in the Soviet legislative system on both the national and local levels, in order to increase voter influence over legislative behavior. The most important changes were the introduction of multiple candidacies in the nomination and election of members of all legislative bodies and the reinvigoration of the local soviets and the replacement of the old Supreme Soviet with two new bodies, the Congress of Peoples' Deputies and a new, small, bicameral Supreme Soviet.

Multicandidacies were intended to allow the election of mavericks, critics, and dissidents. The Communist party now had to compete with nonparty groups and individuals; the party could no longer monopolize the nomination and election processes.

The reinvigoration of the local soviets, which traditionally did little more than ratify decisions made elsewhere, involved a substantial expansion of their authority. Members of local soviets now were to work full time instead of part time on their legislative duties, thereby strengthening their expertise and eventually their power. The local soviets taxed enterprises within their jurisdiction to provide the revenue they needed to function full time. These bodies assumed responsibilities formerly performed by local party agencies, such as monitoring the performance of farms and factories in their geographic area.

The attempt to reinvigorate the local soviets, however, did not appreciably increase their activities. They had little success in solving problems in agriculture, housing construction, and the environment in their regions. Moreover, they were subject to party influence and control because of Gorbachev's insistence that the first secretary of the local party organization seek leadership of the local legislature. Gorbachev apparently wanted to conciliate the local party apparatus and avoid a dangerous provocation of its already resentful bosses.

The Congress of Peoples' Deputies. The most important change in the Soviet national Legislature was the creation of a new legislative body in Moscow called the Congress of Peoples' Deputies. The Congress was made up of 2,250 members, with 1,500 of them elected from territorial and national districts and 750 from the governing bodies of party, youth, artistic, and other organizations. Elections were to be held once every 5 years. The Congress was to convene yearly to discuss constitutional, political, social, and economic issues. But its real task was to select from its membership a Supreme Soviet—smaller and more influential than the old one—a Constitutional Review Committee, and a chair of the Supreme Soviet, who also would be the president of the Soviet Union. This new chief executive was to preside over the Supreme Soviet, serve as chair of the national Defense Council, the country's highest national-security agency, and have broad authority to shape both domestic and foreign policies. The term of office was limited to two 5-year periods.

The 1989 Elections to the Congress. Elections for membership in the Congress were held on March 26, 1989. They were open and hectic, with much campaigning by candidates of non-party-controlled groups and individuals as well as by party-sponsored people. In that respect, they were unprecedented in recent Soviet political history, with even Soviet voters themselves exhilarated—or befuddled—by the enormous freedom of choice.

In the elections, the Communist party tried, somewhat unsuccessfully, to undermine those whom it disliked, in particular the now very popular party maverick Boris Yeltsin and the political dissident Andrei Sakharov. Eventually both were elected to seats in the Congress and emerged as influential spokespeople for the opposition.

Indeed, despite the efforts of the party to influence the outcome of the nomination and election of candidates for seats in the Congress, the results were a stunning statement of voter opposition to the political establishment. Wherever they could, voters rejected candidates associated with the local party and state administration. Many party candidates rejected by the voters in favor of reformers ultimately lost their jobs within the party, in accordance with Gorbachev's insistence that the party had to be responsive to public will. Still, a majority of the deputies elected, although outspoken reformers, were party members and therefore obliged in their advocacy of reform to adhere to party requirements, under the rules of democratic centralism of loyalty and obedience to the top leadership.

When the Congress of Peoples' Deputies convened for the first time in May 1989, to fulfill its mandate of electing the Soviet president and a new Supreme Soviet, there was an explosion of discussion about complaints against the regime and its leadership, including Gorbachev. Before long there was a demand for Congress itself to become the chief law-making body and to deal directly with key problems like the economy. Indeed, there seemed to be a move among some of the deputies, especially those from Moscow, to draft a new and comprehensive agenda for the Congress that would make it much more than the nominating and oversight body it was originally intended to be.

But the Congress demurred and proceeded to complete the business for which it was charged: it elected both the new, more influential Soviet president and the new Supreme Soviet. The deputies overwhelmingly voted Gorbachev as president of the Soviet Union and elected Anatolyi Lukyanov, as a kind of chief of staff and chief adviser to him, as vice president. It then proceeded to elect the smaller Supreme Soviet.

In its first session, the Congress, in conjunction with the new Supreme Soviet, completed an impressive agenda, including approval of the leasing of farms and factories, the introduction of cost accounting in the Baltic republics as a start toward capitalism, and discussion of many other important issues, such as press freedom, conversion of defense plants to consumer production, and private ownership of property. While there was no action on these issues, the mere discussion of them was noteworthy.

The New Supreme Soviet. In June and July 1989 the newly established Supreme Soviet convened and was asked to approve a slate of ministers submitted by President Gorbachev. Aggressive reformers like Yeltsin and Sakharov worked hard to assure that the new Supreme Soviet would not be like its complaisant and deferential predecessor. The new body, charged with the responsibility of ratifying ministerial appointments, took its business very seriously, perhaps more so than Gorbachev expected.

For example, while the new Legislature approved the reappointment of Premier Nikolai Ryzkhov and Foreign Minister Eduard Shevardnadze without much controversy, its committees cross-examined and vigorously investigated the past record of Ryzkhov's nominees, rejecting eight despite previous party approval of them. The premier ended up dropping six of them; the other two withdrew voluntarily. He subsequently came up with acceptable alternatives—people who were quickly approved by the Legislature.

The Legislature ultimately endorsed the reappointment of Defense Minister Dmitri Yazov, but he had so little support that it was necessary to change the voting rules to allow a simple majority of those present and voting to suffice for endorsement, as opposed to an absolute majority, because Yazov might not have survived a vote by absolute majority. During the debate over his reappointment, critics attacked waste, corruption, and poor living standards in the military and said that the 65-year-old general should make way for a more progressive generation of leadership. Deputies from the Baltic republics had been among the opponents of his reappointment because he fiercely opposed their proposal to let young people from non-Russian republics serve in separate units deployed in their native regions.

The Legislature's assertive behavior in approving the new Council of Ministers was both novel and very significant. The refusal to approve of certain party nominees suggested a historic turning point, a demonstration to the government that in the future it might be dependent on the elected deputies—a situation that would be without precedent in the history of Communist party rule.

The New Soviet Presidency

On March 13, 1990, the Congress of Peoples' Deputies strengthened the presidential office, making the new Soviet president far more powerful than was originally intended. Now the Soviet president was to be elected directly by Soviet citizens. The president had the authority—subject only to notification of the Supreme Soviet and to existing constitutional law—to declare a state of national emergency and to impose martial law. The president could veto enactments of the Supreme Soviet, which could override the veto only by a two-thirds majority.

There was some opposition in the Congress to accommodating Gorbachev's demands for a stronger presidency. Many deputies believed that there were not enough limits and restraints to prevent abuse of power and a possible return to Stalinism. But Gorbachev won the support of the Congress by arguing that the country needed strong national leadership to preserve unity in the face of mounting interethnic conflict and the emergence of secessionist movements. He also argued the need of strong leadership to resolve worsening economic problems and to move forward with perestroika. Moreover, many deputies acknowledged that their fears about the new presidential office did not apply to Gorbachev as much as to his unknown successors.

In deference to Gorbachev and as a sign of its continued backing of his leadership despite reservations about and criticisms of his behavior, the Congress of Peoples' Deputies also agreed that the first presidential election would be held in the old way—namely, the president would be chosen by the Congress. In the latter part of March it elected Gorbachev (who, incidentally, had no opponents) president of the Soviet Union. With his newly strengthened power base in the state apparatus and increased independence of the Communist party, where his critics had been able to undermine and block his policies, Gorbachev accelerated the loosening of the party's still substantial grip over the national economy.

But, in retrospect, Gorbachev's unwillingness to run for president in a direct election was a gross tactical error in his strategy to implement perestroika. In the short term, he did strengthen his leadership authority. In the long term, he was weakened because he lacked the popular base needed to pursue his reformist policies, increasingly challenged by the leaders of the republics who were popularly elected and were able to speak for their constituencies in a much more authoritative way. Had Gorbachev run for the Soviet presidency in a direct election in March 1990, he probably would have won because of enormous popularity with ordinary people who still hoped his perestroika would indeed improve their living conditions. By the following year he had lost that popularity, as people were disillusioned and angry over the perceived failure of perestroika to change daily life for the better.

Reforms of the Criminal-Justice System

Perestroika-inspired reforms of the Soviet government included new criminal and civil codes as well as a new code of legal procedures. The office of public prosecutor was separated from the courts, which were now part of a single institution, the Ministry of Justice. This was intended to give greater independence to the courts and greater rights to the accused.

At the 19th party Conference in June 1988 Gorbachev promised to raise the status of lawyers. But the pledge left details to be filled in by the Ministry of Justice. This secretive organization controlled or at least decisively influenced many of the 100,000 Soviet lawyers, either by directly employing them or through its links with the procuracy and the Supreme Court, which had vast staffs of lawyers. The Ministry at first resisted Gorbachev's ideas but eventually became more receptive to change; and in early 1989 it allowed the establishment, for the first time, of an independent Soviet bar group called the Soviet Advocates' Association.

Other changes in the criminal-justice system aimed at softening treatment of political dissidents. These changes included imposition of shorter terms of detention, curtailment of political interference in court trials of dissidents, a narrowing of the definition of political crimes, and a requirement of fuller proof for conviction. An amendment to the Soviet criminal code replaced a statute that outlawed, with little definition, "anti-Soviet agitation and propaganda" and defamation of the Soviet state or political system.

The Soviet government showed a new determination to eliminate psychiatric abuses, whereby healthy but politically dissident people were locked up in mental hospitals by the KGB for political dissidence. In January 1988 a new corrective statute, passed by the Presidium of the Supreme Soviet, contained legal guarantees against errors and malpractices in psychiatric cases. It provided rules for examination and for the commitment of mental patients to psychiatric hospitals as well as specification that chief psychiatrists of health agencies, rather than doctors working for the police or the KGB, must exercise control over medical treatment of mental patients. The new Presidium order also provided for appeal by patients of a confinement decision and guarantee of legal assistance.

Perestroika and the Bureaucracy

The 19th party Conference acknowledged complaints against the bureaucracy, which Gorbachev considered one of the most important obstacles to perestroika. The Conference formally condemned the bureaucracy's "high-handedness" in the economy and in the social and spiritual spheres, its indifference to the rights and needs of the people, and its disdainful attitude toward public opinion and the social experience of the working people. The Conference called for an end to this behavior, demanding that state and public institutions and party committees become fully accessible to people; that managers refrain from delays and formalism; and that departmental instructions and bureaucratic contrivances cease to encroach upon the legitimate rights of citizens.

Gorbachev replaced top party and government leaders who had condoned bureaucratic abuses and obstructionism. He also used glasnost-inspired public criticism of bureaucrats to make them more responsive and responsible. He expected that recourse to market forces would weaken and eventually supplant bureaucratic managers by ending their stranglehold over the country's economic life.

Perestroika and the Soviet Military

Gorbachev undertook major reforms of the military. Reforms involved almost all aspects of its operation and required it to accept and cooperate with the reforms in other areas of Soviet life. For example, as a result of the new emphasis on improving the quality of life of Soviet consumers, it was necessary to persuade the army to get used to the fact that it would no longer have first claim on national resources and that it would no longer get whatever it said it needed to perform its strategic and security-related functions. Gorbachev made it very clear to the top Soviet military leadership that henceforth, in light of the demands of restructuring in the economic sphere, the army and the navy must make do with less. To achieve this goal, Gorbachev told the military that it had to pay more attention to managerial skills and in particular to improve the traditionally harsh and unpleasant living conditions experienced by recruits.

The military was obliged to accept a new strategic doctrine that emphasized defense rather than offense. Gorbachev reduced the traditionally heavy role of the military in foreign policy-making and excluded its participation, except in an advisory capacity, in decision-making on arms reduction.

Perestroika also required the army to accept with grace growing popular criticism of many aspects of its behavior, from its involvement in Afghanistan to its management of human resources at home. The army was obliged to cooperate with glasnost and to accept a new degree of public scrutiny.

Needless to say, the military leadership was uneasy about perestroika, even though it welcomed economic restructuring, which it believed would ultimately benefit not only the country at large but also the armed forces. To maintain civilian control over the army, in order to assure its cooperation with perestroika, Gorbachev tried to diminish the military's exaggerated stature in Soviet society. For example, he reduced the ceremonial role of the military as seen in the less-conspicuous presence of its leadership in the review of the annual November 7 pageants in Red Square to celebrate the anniversary of the Bolshevik Revolution.

But the most important means of keeping the armed services on a tight leash involved personnel changes at the top. In the spring of 1987 Gorbachev found an opportunity to replace Defense Minister Marshal Sokolovsky, in the flap over the incursion of Soviet air space by a young West German pilot, who had flown his small Cessna aircraft through the Soviet air defense system and landed in the middle of Red Square. To say the least, this incident was terribly embarrassing to the Kremlin. Gorbachev complained about the ineptitude of certain officers and promptly fired Sokolovsky, appointing in his place Dmitry Yazov, at that time a known supporter of Gorbachev's effort to improve management skills in the Soviet military. With Yazov in place, Gorbachev was now in a position—or so he thought, with some justification—to move forward with policies to overhaul the military's inefficient administrative apparatus, to develop new arms-control initiatives, and to reduce Soviet military deployments around the world in order to divert new resources toward domestic development.

PERESTROIKA AND FOREIGN POLICY

Perestroika inspired striking changes in Soviet foreign policy. Gorbachev referred to these changes as "New Thinking" about future Soviet international behavior. Gorbachev and his foreign-policy advisers such as Foreign Minister Shevardnadze, Dobrynin, and Yacovlev rejected the old two-camps theory of ideological conflict between socialist and capitalist countries. Insisting that technology had brought nations closer together and fostered interdependence, Gorbachev argued that national interests could no longer be defined in strictly ideological terms and that nations with different ideological commitments must cooperate to resolve common economic, strategic, and environmental problems.

Because nuclear weapons can obliterate civilization and conventional weapons are almost as destructive, Soviet foreign-policy strategists asserted that war was no longer a rational instrument of policy. They contended that war must be replaced by political and diplomatic instruments such as arms-control agreements, confidence-building measures, and a strengthening of international law and organization. It therefore followed, according to Gorbachev, that the military had to be subordinate to political instruments of foreign policy. Force capabilities had to be reduced to levels of "reasonable sufficiency," and the primary purpose of the military had to be defensive, not offensive.

Gorbachev and his advisers also believed that past emphasis on military strength and excess security had been counterproductive: the costly arms race burdened an already debilitated Soviet economy; suspicion of Soviet intentions prevented good relations with the capitalist West; and Soviet readiness to use massive military power to achieve foreign-policy goals discredited socialism as an attractive alternative to capitalism.

New Thinking affected Soviet foreign policy in many areas. Soviet relations with the West steadily improved; Moscow showed a new leniency and restraint in dealing with its Central/Eastern European allies and included an explicit Soviet renunciation of force in relations with them. The Soviets also began to pull back military involvement in many areas of the Third World. Finally, the Soviets demonstrated new interest in the United Nations as well as other international organizations involved in conflict resolution.

Still, it was also true that New Thinking did not replace traditional Soviet ambitions, interest, and goals in the international community. The Soviet state continued to be extremely security-conscious; it continued to harbor ideological prejudices and suspicious in its dealings with the outside world; it still was not above acting in response to so-called targets of opportunity or to achieve an important goal when the cost of doing so was low and the chances of success great. Furthermore, its policy abroad was still influenced by economic, societal, and military capabilities, which helped to determine objectives as well as limits.

Past Soviet foreign policies would have been altered or reversed starting in the late 1980s, even in the absence of New Thinking, because of their evident weaknesses. Indeed, by the time Gorbachev came to power in March 1985, the Kremlin could not ignore the counterproductive consequences for Soviet well-being of many policies pursued in the 1960s and 1970s.

For example, Soviet military and ideological expansion in the last years of Brezhnev's rule, especially the Soviet invasion of Afghanistan in December 1979, had led to a deterioration of relations with the United States and a denial of much-needed American technology. Soviet heavy-handed interference in Central/Eastern Europe had exacerbated latent anti-Russian feelings and undermined the credibility and legitimacy of socialist regimes, thus compromising the Soviet goal of permanent Soviet security vis-à-vis the West. And Soviet hostility toward China, at its height under Brezhnev, had pushed China closer to Japan and the United States, thereby raising the possibility of a triple entente against Soviet interests in Asia. It had obliged the Soviets to maintain huge and costly deployments of conventional and nuclear forces along the Sino-Soviet frontier in Asia and had complicated the task of protecting the interests of Soviet clients and friends in Asia (North Vietnam, North Korea, Afghanistan, and India).

Relations With the West

Gorbachev gave priority in the late 1980s to improved Soviet relations with the West. He saw many advantages in East-West cooperation, not least of which was an expansion of trade, which would give the Soviet Union access to the financial, economic, and technological resources needed to make perestroika successful. He did not share the view his predecessors had of the West as a threat to Soviet security.

The United States

In Soviet strategy toward the West, relations with the United States assumed central importance. Gorbachev sought a reversal of the deterioration of relations between the superpowers in the late 1970s and early 1980s. The Soviets discussed outstanding issues with the Americans, like regional conflicts in Afghanistan and Angola, arms reduction, human rights, and trade. The conclusion in December 1987 at the Washington, D.C., summit of the Soviet-American treaty eliminating intermediate-range nuclear missiles from Europe and a number of Soviet unilateral reductions in conventional and other nuclear weapons and troop deployments; the Soviet military withdrawal from Afghanistan in February 1989 and support for an end of the civil war in Angola; and the increased tolerance of political dissent and diversity with assurances of further change in human-rights policy sought by the United States—all seemed to confirm a turning point in relations between the two superpowers.

However, many differences remained. The Soviets were upset over the continuing American commitment to the Strategic Defense Initiative (SDI, or Star Wars), the planned U.S. deployment of defense weapons in space. While the Kremlin suspected that the Bush administration would never deploy such sophisticated and expensive weaponry, the Soviets did not dismiss the possibility of SDI becoming a reality. If it did, they would have had to match it with a Soviet equivalent, which would have drained Soviet resources.

Western Europe

Gorbachev aggressively strengthened Soviet relations with the Western European allies. As he gradually diminished the Soviet military presence in Central/Eastern Europe, thereby weakening Soviet security in that region, the importance of good relations with Western Europe increased. At the same time Gorbachev emphasized the commonality of past traditions and current needs between the Soviet Union and Western Europe, referring to their membership in a "common European home."

He intensified past Soviet efforts to encourage disarmament in Europe as a means of enhancing Soviet security without having to invest in a costly military buildup; to decouple the Western European countries from the United States, thereby driving a wedge in NATO; and to increase Soviet access to Western European financial, economic, and technological resources. Gorbachev exploited the growth of neutralist and pacifist tendencies in many Western European societies and especially among the youth; the eagerness of Western European countries, especially West Germany, to encourage perestroika and respond sympathetically to it by expanding trade; and the desire of Western European governments to develop a measure of independence vis-à-vis the United States in relations with the Soviet Union.

Gorbachev's most dramatic and persuasive gestures toward Western Europe involved unilateral concessions on arms reduction. In 1987 the Kremlin agreed to exclude the nuclear defense forces of England and France from coverage in the INF treaty. In 1988 Gorbachev announced a decision to cut Soviet armed forces in Europe by more than 12 percent and to reduce conventional weapons deployed in Central/Eastern Europe. In 1989 the Soviets offered to make cuts in their short-range nuclear missiles deployed in Central/Eastern Europe.

Gorbachev went out of his way to cultivate West Germany and France. Soviet relations with these countries steadily improved as Gorbachev skillfully played on their interest in expanding trade with the Soviet Union and in developing independence in relations with Moscow. They wished ultimately to obtain Soviet support of their own objectives in Europe, especially an expansion of political and economic ties with the Soviet Bloc allies.

Ties With Central/Eastern Europe

Gorbachev introduced major changes in Soviet policy toward Central/Eastern Europe. He accepted (in fact, he actively encouraged) major departures from the Soviet model of socialism. The most important of these departures were increased political pluralism, involving abandonment of the Communist party's monopoly of power, and the expansion of market principles and private entrepreneurialism, leading to a radical reduction of the traditional state control over national economic life. Gorbachev thus presided over the decommunization and desatellization of the Soviet Bloc countries.

Under Gorbachev, the Soviet Union renounced the use of force in the region, thereby repudiating the Brezhnev Doctrine, which was used to justify the 1968 Soviet-led Warsaw Pact intervention in Czechoslovakia. Indeed, the Soviet leadership in late 1989 formally admitted the error of this act and apologized for it.

Gorbachev refrained from interfering with the changes that took place in Poland, Hungary, East Germany, Czechoslovakia, and Romania in late 1989, despite anxiety in the Kremlin over the unanticipated speed and scope of these departures from traditional Soviet Bloc socialism. The Kremlin did not succumb to the temptation to block changes involving the curtailment of Communist party control, on which Soviet power and influence in Central/Eastern Europe had depended since World War II.

Gorbachev's leniency in dealing with the upheaval in Central/Eastern Europe was the result of conditions inside the Soviet Union. The Soviets could no longer afford to spend the money and resources needed to maintain close control of the Soviet Bloc political systems. Heavy troop deployments, never mind a full-scale military invasion, were no longer feasible from an economic point of view. Furthermore, maintaining the close Soviet control utilized by Stalin, Khrushchev, and Brezhnev no longer made sense—a perceived threat from the West, as the Soviets believed existed in the past and used as a justification for demanding Soviet Bloc unity with and subordination to Moscow, had diminished.

The argument that Central/Eastern European departures from the Soviet model would encourage equivalent and unwanted change in the Soviet Union and therefore had to be prevented at all costs (a justification for Soviet suppression of the 1968 Czechoslovak reform program) was no longer valid. Soviet socialism itself was reforming; in fact, Soviet leaders were looking at change in Central/Eastern Europe to see what aspects could be adopted in their own country.

The Gorbachevian leadership was more confident, more flexible, more pragmatic, and more intellectual in its thinking about Soviet-Central/Eastern European relations. Gorbachev and his foreign-policy advisers were quite unlike past Soviet leaders, who always were on the defensive, suspicious, stubborn, and crude in their handling of problems with Soviet Bloc allies.

Conditions in Central/Eastern Europe influenced Gorbachev's departures from past Soviet policies. The socialist dictatorships, which Soviet policy had so assiduously supported, had not served Soviet interests effectively. They had failed to maintain the internal stability necessary to achieve the legitimacy on which their long-term survival—and therefore the survival of Soviet influence and power—depended. They had failed to inculcate a pro-Soviet orientation among peoples who were traditionally hostile to Russia.

Past Soviet policies of intrusion had exacerbated anti-Russian feelings in many Soviet Bloc societies. To that extent, they had weakened and discredited the socialist systems closely linked to Moscow, which were therefore viewed in the public mind as little more than servile agents of a despised national enemy. Certainly past Soviet harshness toward the Soviet Bloc countries did little to help—and, in fact, undermined—the efforts of local Communist party leaders to diminish popular antipathy to the Soviet state.

At the same time pervasive and irresistible pressures for radical change in politics, the economy, and society had been steadily mounting in Soviet Bloc countries. Because the logic of profound change had become as overwhelming in Central/Eastern Europe as it was in the Soviet Union, it would have been foolhardy for the Kremlin to support Soviet Bloc conservatives, with whom the Gorbachevian leadership had little in common in their opposition to change. Gorbachev favored the development of perestroika-like reforms in the Soviet Bloc countries to revive their enfeebled economies, which were closely linked to the Soviet economy and a potential source of help for the Soviet Union's own economic recovery.

Finally, Gorbachev's new approaches to Central/Eastern Europe have to be understood within the context of Soviet relations with the West. The new Soviet restraint was conducive to the strong Soviet ties that Gorbachev wanted with Western Europe and the United States, which sought and encouraged at the very least a softening of the rough edges of the Communist dictatorships and at the most a rollback of Communist and Soviet power.

The well-being of Central/Eastern Europe, compromised, to say the least, by the imposition of Soviet and Communist power after World War II, had always been important to Western Europe, for economic and strategic reasons: Central/Eastern Europe was a potentially large and profitable market for Western industrial and agricultural output and at the same time is important to the security of West Germany and Scandinavia. Thus, as Gorbachev had correctly calculated, the West was bound to respond in a positive way to any Soviet effort to foster the health and stability of Central/Eastern Europe.

The Kremlin understood the inevitability of a severe setback in Soviet relations with the West in the event of a return to the coercive and interventionist policies of the past in Central/Eastern Europe. The resumption of intrusive Soviet policies would surely have compromised any chances the Soviets had of persuading the West to liberalize trade and sell the high technology so desperately needed to reinvigorate as well as reform the Soviet economy and to make possible an improvement in living conditions essential to social stability. It would also have compromised the ongoing process of East-West arms reduction, which Gorbachev wanted in order to reduce defense expenditures.

There were both opportunities and dangers in Gorbachev's shifts away from past Soviet policy in Central/Eastern Europe. By allowing the countries to reject their socialist systems and move toward democracy and capitalism, Gorbachev encouraged new popular sympathy for the Soviet Union. The citizens of most Soviet Bloc countries saw Gorbachev as a hero, perhaps even a savior, who had facilitated their liberation from conservative, hard-line, and corrupt leaders responsible for the dreadful conditions of their daily life. Thus he had a chance of achieving genuine friendship and cooperation between Central/Eastern Europe and the Soviet Union, which had eluded his predecessors.

However, Gorbachev's new policies of leniency and restraint carried liabilities for the enfeebled Soviet Union. As reforms, especially in politics, led to a curtailment of Soviet physical power in Central/Eastern Europe, the Kremlin faced competition for influence with West Germany. Bonn had developed a dense network of human, cultural, and economic ties with individual Soviet Bloc countries. The West German economic presence also seemed to be greater than that of other Western countries. Other aspects of West German influence-building in Central/Eastern Europe involved arms-control policies, such as Bonn's stated reluctance in the spring of 1989 to modernize NATO's nuclear capability, as well as progress toward reunification. West German Chancellor Helmut Kohl in the aftermath of political changes in East Berlin in the fall of 1989 called for closer economic and social relations between the two Germanies as preconditions for reunification.

To offset West German initiatives, Gorbachev looked to France. After years of inactivity, punctuated by occasional denunciations of human-rights violations, President François Mitterrand resolved to make Central/Eastern Europe one of the top foreign-policy priorities of his new term. In December 1988 he visited Czechoslovakia; in January 1989 he visited Bulgaria. The impulse behind the French initiative was partly to recover export markets that, however small, were important for key sectors of the French economy. But the most compelling imperative was, as French diplomats discreetly put it, to accompany West Germany into Central/Eastern Europe as Soviet influence declined. In this effort, Paris may well have had the tacit backing of Moscow.

Gorbachev perceived an increase of American interest in Central/Eastern Europe as he reduced Soviet military power in the region. He noted the ground swell of public support in the United States for an active American role in helping Poland and Hungary to democratize and expressed concern over the apparent readiness of the Bush administration to develop a high American profile in those countries. Gorbachev also was in no rush for the reunification of the two Germanies, although he did not rule it out and eventually accepted it. Indeed, the prospect of a reunified Germany might have provided an incentive to the newly independent Central/Eastern European systems, especially Poland, Hungary, and Czechoslovakia, to support continuation of the Warsaw Pact and good relations with the Soviet Union, as the only effective means of lessening their vulnerability to a powerful united German state. In February 1990, in response to evident anxieties in Moscow about the implications for Soviet security in Europe, Gorbachev insisted that German reunification had to proceed gradually, with due consideration to the interests of Germany's neighbors, especially Poland and the Soviet Union. He eventually retreated from demands that a united German state be neutral, partly in response to the opposition of the United States as well as of Poland, Hungary, and Czechoslovakia. He agreed that a unified Germany could belong to NATO, given that that was what the West as well as most Germans wanted. The Kremlin also supported Poland's insistence on a German guarantee of existing borders and on its participation in any international unification agreement.

The Third World

Gorbachev and his advisers made a fundamental reassessment of past Soviet policy in the Third World. By the early 1980s it had become clear that earlier hopes for strong clients and lasting influence resulting from the promotion of Marxist-Leninist vanguard party-states had not been achieved. By late in that decade the Soviets had realized the flaws of past policy toward Third World countries, acknowledging that the export of their political and economic structures to the Third World had not worked out well.

Although Marxist-Leninist allies had willingly cooperated with Moscow both politically and militarily, they were very poor—even by Third World standards. The introduction of such socialist measures as collectivization of agriculture and wholesale nationalization of foreign and domestic private property had only made them poorer. Moreover, the populations of these leftist countries viewed their Marxist rulers as illegitimate. Several regimes—including those in Angola, Mozambique, Afghanistan, Cambodia, and Nicaragua—faced internal guerrilla insurgencies. As the need for Moscow's assistance grew, the Soviet Third World "empire" became a substantial drain on Soviet resources.

As the Soviets concentrated on perestroika, therefore, they had to redefine their Third World policy. There was new emphasis on technological and economic cooperation; deemphasis of Soviet military assistance; and priority given to the settlement of regional conflicts in such places as Afghanistan, Cambodia, Angola, and Nicaragua.

This shift from military expansion to political diplomacy in policy toward the Third World under Gorbachev can be seen in a number of Soviet initiatives, notably the military withdrawal from Afghanistan and the effort to promote a political settlement in Angola. The Soviets pursued a policy of caution and restraint in the Middle East, with attempts at reconciliation with Israel balanced by support for the Palestinian cause and friendship with the Palestine Liberation Organization (PLO) and Yasir Arafat. They also attempted to balance ties with conservative states, such as Egypt and Jordan, with political and military links to very radical states, like Syria, Iraq, and Iran. Finally, the Soviets attempted to support Cuba and Nicaragua while cultivating good relations with conservative, somewhat pro-American states like Brazil, Mexico, and Argentina.

East Asia

Gorbachev took important steps to improve Soviet relations with China, Japan, and other countries in the Pacific Basin. Moscow wanted legitimacy as a political and economic participant in East Asia; territorial security in the region;

and a lessening of American influence there to prevent a three-way political entente between China, Japan, and the United States, which Gorbachev believed would threaten Soviet strategic interests. Gorbachev's policy was largely economic and diplomatic in order to reverse Moscow's military image, which had been counterproductive. It had not led to an appreciable increase of Soviet political influence. Indeed, it had led the Chinese to do exactly what the Soviets opposed: namely, to draw closer to the United States and Japan and inadvertently to bolster American influence in the region.

China

Gorbachev aggressively pursued reconciliation with China to enable the Soviets to withdraw some of the 53 divisions deployed along the 3,900-mile Sino-Soviet frontier. This would allow a savings in defense costs deeper than any arms-control agreement with the United States might have produced.

To promote this reconciliation, the Kremlin downplayed ideological differences between the two countries and acknowledged similarities between the Chinese and Soviet systems. The Kremlin also paid attention to long-standing Chinese complaints against Soviet policies in Asia: Gorbachev offered to reduce Soviet troop and missile deployments along the Sino-Soviet frontier; he acknowledged the Chinese claim that the border between the two countries ran down the center of the Amur River in its path to the Pacific; he withdrew Soviet military forces from Mongolia and from Afghanistan; and, finally, he interceded successfully with the Soviet Union's Vietnam ally to undertake a political and military disengagement from Cambodia.

In June 1989 the Chinese and Soviet leaders held a summit in Beijing. In a grand gesture of reconciliation, Gorbachev offered the Chinese an apology for the long period of tension in Sino-Soviet relations, expressing regret and acknowledging that to a certain extent "we bear responsibility." The most tangible results of that summit, however, included the signing of agreements on normalization of relations on both party and state levels and the removal of 120,000 Soviet troops from the frontier.

Japan

The Soviets had much to gain from stable relations with Japan. They wanted an expansion of Japanese investment in the exploitation of Siberian mineral deposits and joint ventures with Soviet enterprises, within which the Japanese could provide capital and high technology.

But the Soviets were not as forthcoming with Japan as with China. Some obstacles to close ties included Japan's continuing political and diplomatic intimacy as well as close military cooperation with the United States; its expanding economic ties with China; the interest of the Japanese public in strengthening Japan's military defense; and Japan's persistence in demanding Soviet return of the four islands taken from Japan after World War II.

The dispute over these islands, namely, Kunashir, Shikotan, Etorofu, and the Habomais group, located in the Kurile chain north of the Home islands, was the biggest stumbling block to an improvement of Soviet relations with Japan in the Gorbachev era. The Kremlin was unwilling to give the islands back to Japan, at least at that time, for three reasons: resentment over a perceived Japanese prejudice toward the Soviet Union, the prestige for the Soviet Union of retaining the islands, and their strategic importance to the Soviet military as a result of their proximity to Soviet Navy and Air Force installations headquartered in the Far East. As long as the Kremlin would not accommodate Tokyo on this issue, Tokyo would not expand trade and in other ways improve ties with the Soviet Union.

The United Nations

Under Gorbachev, the Soviet Union showed a renewed interest in the United Nations, in particular in its peace-keeping responsibilities, which in the past the Kremlin had frequently criticized and refused to support. Now UN efforts to reduce tensions and improve the general international environment complemented Soviet policy, especially Soviet efforts to strengthen ties with the United States and China and to wind down regional conflicts.

Gorbachev praised the United Nations for sending military forces to supervise truces or to keep antagonistic forces apart, and he has called for an increase in such UN peace-keeping activities. In his address to the UN General Assembly on September 23, 1987, then-Foreign Minister Shevardnadze called for a UN naval presence in the Persian Gulf to ensure freedom of navigation, saying it should replace the United States and other Western navies there.

Both Gorbachev and Shevardnadze recommended that the United Nations have an army made up of contingents of national armed forces earmarked for international peace-keeping duties. They offered to help develop a new international institute to train troops in peace-keeping duties and to make their own forces available for such duties and to provide logistical support, thereby effectively ending the tradition by which the major powers with permanent Security Council seats do not usually participate in peace-keeping operations.

In addition to expanded peace-keeping activities, Gorbachev suggested that the United Nations could verify compliance with arms-control agreements and peace treaties and investigate acts of international terrorism. He also proposed an increase of UN authority in other areas, such as economic relations and the environment, and he called for enhancing the power of the International Court of Justice to decide international disputes. He said he wanted to see the establishment of international standards on such matters as family reunification and visa regulations. He also indicated interest in expanding the authority of the International Atomic Energy Agency.

The Soviet Union evidenced new support of UN activities on behalf of human rights, reversing earlier opposition to

UN policy in this area. For example, the Soviet experts appointed to the UN Subcommission on Human Rights approved in the summer of 1988 three initiatives that clearly reflected a change of official attitude toward human-rights issues. The first was a draft protocol binding nations that abolished capital punishment not to reintroduce it except in time of war. The second was a draft declaration committing UN members to safeguard the independence of their judiciaries—this was the first such United Nations call. The third initiative was a set of guidelines for the treatment of the mentally ill, drafted in response to accusations that Soviet authorities had been incarcerating political dissidents in mental asylums.

Changes in the Foreign-Policy Machinery

Gorbachev introduced several changes in the foreign-policy-making apparatus, including a reduction of military influence, a strengthening of civilian policymakers, an increase in popular influence over foreign policy-making, and development of a special role for himself. These changes were to make possible departures from policies that Gorbachev considered mistaken and counterproductive.

The reduction of military influence over foreign policy-making took several forms. The minister of Defense under Gorbachev was not a member of the Politburo and thus lacked direct access to the inner circle of top Soviet leaders. Civilian institutions like the Scientific Council on Peace and Disarmament and the various institutes of the Soviet Academy of Science competed with the military academies in doing research on military–technical problems, like arms reduction, connected with foreign policy. Finally, civilian leaders rather than generals and admirals comprised the core of advisers to Gorbachev on foreign policy.

Another change in foreign policy-making involved a strengthening of the national Legislature's role. For example, Shevardnadze referred favorably in his speech at the Foreign Ministry in July 1988 to the idea of having open legislative hearings at which ministers would be required to answer unrehearsed questions from Supreme Soviet deputies. He asserted that the elected organs should supervise the open discussion of military budgets, plans for military development, and the use of Soviet military forces abroad.

THE COLLAPSE OF THE SOVIET UNION

At least five circumstances in 1990 and 1991 marked the collapse of the Soviet political system: 1) agricultural and industrial output declined precipitously; 2) ethnocultural separatism intensified within the republics; 3) a democratic political opposition developed while the Communist party's monopoly of power disintegrated; 4) the August 1991 coup by hard-line Communists failed; and 5) a new self-governing confederation of sovereign republics, the Commonwealth of Independent States, was established.

DECLINE OF OUTPUT

Overall Soviet economic output declined by 4 percent in 1990 and by 10 to 15 percent in the first half of the 1991. In the first 3 quarters of 1991 Soviet national income fell by at least 13 percent, if not more—some Soviet economists suggested it declined between 18 and 25 percent. Here was a phenomenon akin to the West's economic depression of the 1930s.

Decline in Agricultural and Industrial Output

Agricultural output suffered, in part, because of Gorbachev's ultimate failure to upgrade the inefficient collectivized Soviet agricultural system by expanding private entrepreneurialism. Many farmers liked the security of the collective farms and resented those who struck out on their own. If they applied for a piece of land, peasants living on state farms were often threatened with eviction. The few farmers who did farm independently faced insurmountable obstacles. They often got poor land miles from the village, inaccessible to roads and power lines. The collective farms had almost all the livestock and machinery, and their managers refused to rent or sell to private farmers, having found that private farming could wipe out the collective farms. Also, a private farmer who needed extra hands to bring the harvest had to approach the very people who opposed him: the collective farm managers.

The failure of economic restructuring to provide adequate storage and distribution of goods contributed to a decline in agricultural output in 1990 and 1991. There still were not enough grain elevators to store surplus grain and not enough refrigerated railway cars to get perishable goods to market before spoilage began. In early 1992 many collective farms used grain to fatten livestock, in anticipation of promised increases in meat prices. These farms reneged on 1991 contracts with state authorities, expecting that the longer they waited, the higher the prices they would receive for their produce or livestock. State warehouses experienced theft on a grand scale, reckoned by Soviet officials at about 10 to 15 percent of stock.

Steadily diminishing output was also attributable to land degradation. At least 1.5 billion tons of topsoil in the Soviet Union eroded each year, with production losses estimated at $31 billion to $35 billion. Industrial pollution also lowered crop yields. By unhappy coincidence, the major sources of pollution in the former Soviet Union, such as metallurgical centers indiscriminately depositing lead, cobalt, and zinc wastes into the soil, were located in agricultural areas. Inappropriate use of fertilizers and pesticides were another cause of environmental pollution responsible for undermining agricultural productivity. Prices for these agricultural inputs were heavily subsidized, leading farmers to dump more and more of them on the land, regardless of whether they were raising yields commensurately.

Industrial output in 1990 and 1991 declined when the centralized system of allocation of resources broke down.

Factories were unable to obtain supplies and had to shut down. This in turn disrupted the production schedules of other factories. The new, only fitfully functioning system of limited self-management and self-financing had destroyed the chain of command without creating a replacement system for a market-driven exchange of goods and services. Factories had difficulty getting supplies also because trade among the republics throughout 1991 was in chaos. Byelorussia (now called Byelorus), Estonia, and eventually Ukraine and Russia, the largest and wealthiest of the Soviet republics, declared themselves sovereign, took control of their own resources, and proceeded to restrict exports of their products.

Another cause of the decline in industrial output throughout 1990 and 1991 were Gorbachev's difficulties in making state enterprises self-financing. Managers of state enterprises had no idea of costs and earnings. Consequently, when they were told to operate at a profit and threatened with bankruptcy proceedings if they failed, they were thoroughly confused. Production suffered.

The difficulties with privatization contributed to the Soviet economy's decline in 1990 and 1991. Despite the enactment of laws opening the way for privatization, little progress had been made. Most industry was still under state control. The vast state bureaucracy was still attempting to control instead of easing regulation. For example, one new regulation required cooperatives to be "affiliated" with state enterprises in order to engage in business. Affiliation really meant an obligation of the privately owned business to share its profits with a state enterprise. Would-be entrepreneurs also feared that the government might one day reverse free-market policy and make private business firms illegal again.

The Kremlin's failure in the late 1980s to lure foreign investment through its policy of joint ventures also explains the economic problems of 1990 and 1991. Although the Kremlin in 1990 liberalized rules governing foreign investment in the Soviet economy, allowing majority ownership of joint ventures by foreigners, many potential investors stayed away because of uncertainty about earning profits and repatriating them. This was complicated by the fact that the ruble was not freely convertible to dollars or other Western money and that bartering in commodities or settling accounts in convertible currency was almost always illegal. Western banks hesitated to invest because, despite moves toward privatization and away from central planning and control of economic life, there was still no clear Soviet legal concept of ownership.

Finally, the economic slowdown must be blamed on certain cultural characteristics. Apathy, indifference toward work, pessimism about the future, and inertia led many simply to stop working and live by their wits. After years of Communist mismanagement, industriousness, discipline, and efficiency did not rank high with most citizens. Aleksandr Yacovlev, one of Gorbachev's closest and most influential adivsers, believed that psychological dependence on the state nurtured by subsidies of food, housing, education, and medical care had led to a mass inertia, a habit of mind he considered the most serious obstacle to reform. Workers

were being asked to behave in new ways that they did not understand and with which they had little sympathy.

Dramatic evidence of the economic decline was the acute shortages of food, in particular staples such as milk, eggs, cheese, butter, and sausage. Diets moved away from meat and dairy products in short supply to potatoes, cabbages, and wheat porridge. Long lines required shoppers to wait at least 3 hours; workers relied on older retired relatives to do the shopping for them.

Shortages of food and other commodities, especially clothing, provoked a sharp rise in inflation. The currency became almost worthless; bartering became the norm in 1990. The ruble's rate fell to 60 to the dollar—way down from the traditional official value of $1.55 to a ruble in the mid-1980s. Many people in the cities and the rural areas had so little faith in the ruble that they refused to use it as a medium of exchange.

With Soviet gross national product in decline, the state had difficulty in servicing its foreign debt of almost $80 billion. This was complicated by a decline of exports. Natural gas and oil output dropped in 1990, and the decline continued throughout 1991. Meanwhile, imports of consumer goods rose as the state tried to ease shortages resulting from the slack in domestic production. The decline in Soviet GNP also fed unemployment, which, reportedly, increased from 6.8 to 10 percent in 1991.

Other economic problems made life difficult in 1991. The burgeoning budget deficit grew as the Soviet government increased subsidies to try to keep real incomes from falling. The republic governments led by independence-minded nationalist politicians refused to make payments to the central government, depriving it of the revenue necessary to implement its policies. The Soviet military continued to be expensive. Indeed, the expenditure of resources on the military was exorbitant right up to the bitter end of the Soviet state, despite a declining popular and official sympathy for the military. The military probably accounted for some 40 percent of the national budget and consumed 18 percent of GNP in 1990 and 1991.

Last-Minute Remedies

President Gorbachev initially relied upon the exercise of central authority to curb the decline. The Supreme Soviet in September 1990 granted him decree power to force sectors of the economy to comply with previously passed reform laws, meant to force government enterprises to deliver the raw materials and finished goods they had been holding back in order to sell them on the black market.

Since this failed, Gorbachev attempted a liberal approach. He gave tentative backing to the so-called 500 Day Plan, authored by his chief economic advisers Stanislav Shatalin and Nikolai Petrakov. This plan aimed to move the country, in 500 days, to a market-based economy by stabilizing the budget, making the ruble convertible, decontrolling prices, and accelerating the privatization of state-controlled enterprises.

But conservatives in the central government and the Soviet Communist Party, including then-Prime Minister Nikolai Ryzkhov, opposed this plan. Gorbachev also feared moving away too quickly from the old order, with its risks of increasing hardships and provoking social turmoil. In order to strike a balance between the liberals and conservatives, Gorbachev offered in October 1990 his own plan. This kept the central government in Moscow in control of transportation, communication, defense industries, energy, credit, and monetary policy and gave supervision of national economic development to a committee consisting of representatives of the republics. The Gorbachev plan gave the republics broad latitude in setting the pace for price deregulation, privatization of state enterprises, and setting rules governing wages and social security. However, it denied them control over their mineral wealth and extensive autonomy in regulating their economic life, which most of them were now demanding.

Gorbachev's economic plan for a "prudent revolution" was passed by the Supreme Soviet on October 19, 1990. Shatalin and Petrakov were critical and warned that the longer the Soviet president delayed in introducing truly radical change, the worse the economic situation would become. The republics did not like this plan either. The Russian republic said that it would follow the Shatalin plan and dissociate itself from the central government. Ukraine announced a plan to introduce its own crude currency, in the form of special coupons to be used in conjunction with rubles in the purchase of consumer goods. Some republic leaderships, fearful of a popular backlash against reform, increased pensions and wrote off the debts of failing collective farms, thereby enlarging rather than reducing the horrendous budget deficit.

In the spring of 1991, however, Gorbachev again edged toward the left. He cautiously backed a plan by Yevgeni Primakov, a close political adviser, and Grigory Yavlinsky, an economic adviser to Russian President Boris Yeltsin, to ask the Bush administration for massive U.S. assistance, worth about $30 billion annually, to help the Soviet Union move from the centrally planned economy to one based on market forces. The Kremlin would pledge to decontrol prices, privatize state-controlled enterprises, and abandon central planning. This plan, supported by 9 of the then-15 Soviet republics, including Russia, was never adopted because of strenuous conservative opposition.

Following the August 1991 coup attempt, with the hardliners swept from positions of influence, the liberal reformers made several proposals. A plan by Yavlinsky provided for a strong union, with cooperation among the republics on the issues of price decontrol and reduction of expenditures to ease the budget deficit. Yavlinsky's plan won Gorbachev's support because it emphasized a strong center, to which Gorbachev was deeply committed. An economic treaty signed by 8 republics on October 18, 1991, put the plan in place, but it failed because the republics refused to cooperate in the acceptance and implementation of radical change. By the end of 1991 the economy of the Soviet state was in limbo. The Gorbachev leadership seemed to have lost control over the economic destiny of the country. It had no plan to reverse the steady deterioration of the Soviet economy.

INTENSIFICATION OF ETHNOCULTURAL NATIONALISM AND SEPARATISM

A second major cause of the Soviet Union's collapse at the end of 1991 was intense nationalist movements among the large ethnic groups which controlled republic governments and pushed them to seek increased autonomy—and, in some instances, complete independence of the Soviet central government in Moscow. At the same time there were "micro" nationalist movements among the many small ethnocultural groups living in some of the republics that wanted the same autonomy and independence as the large, "macro" nationalist movements. Thus, not only the unity of the Soviet state was threatened but also the unity of republics that had ethnically heterogeneous societies.

Macro Movements

In the 1990 elections for republic legislatures, voters consistently supported candidates who voiced popular historic resentments toward central control. Non-Russian leaderships in particular wanted independence for their republics, an end to Russification, and the establishment of the local tongue as the official language of politics and education. The opposition won power in seven republics. Other republics, still run by Communists, also wanted greater autonomy of Moscow.

The newly elected republic leaders and their parliaments quickly asserted a right to their own political systems and constitutions and to diminish, or even to eradicate, central government control. They laid claim to all the land and property within their borders and to all natural and other resources, including labor, and in some cases the right to their own currency. Republic leaderships also sought control of local police and challenged central authority over border troops, secret police, and intelligence. They demanded the right to direct relations, particularly economic ties, with other countries and insisted that local draftees into the Soviet Army should serve only on their own territory. Some republics began to establish their own armies.

Gorbachev tried with little success to accommodate these demands for autonomy within the framework of a reformed union. In November 1990 he presented a draft treaty providing for greater autonomy for the republics. The powers of the central government were to continue in place. The treaty had no specific method of secession, a point of dispute with the Baltic republics, and did not give the republics control over wealth located inside their boundaries. When only 8 of the 15 republics accepted the draft, Gorbachev, in March 1991, offered a new draft which provided for greater autonomy and a less intrusive central government. The new draft recognized the declarations of state sovereignty passed by all 15 republics; recognized the right of the republics to full diplomatic relations with other countries; provided for the right of secession; and gave the republics a share of control in the defense and energy industries and a role in the writing and adoption of a new Soviet constitution. Because the revised draft still preserved a strong federal union, many independence-minded republics rejected it and called for a very loose confederation to replace the old union.

In mid-March 1991 Gorbachev held a popular referendum throughout the Soviet Union on the issue of the union. Six republics boycotted the referendum, and the outcome of the vote was far from decisive. While the Central Asian republics voted overwhelmingly in favor of preserving the union, voters in other republics approved by only a slim majority. But the Gorbachev leadership spoke of an "impressive majority" in favor of the union and tried to persuade all the republics to accept the revised draft of the union treaty. To get their support, Gorbachev yielded significantly to the demands of the republics for increased power-sharing.

Nine republics, including Russia, agreed in April 1991 to join the central government in producing a confederative union and a new national constitution providing for an extensive decentralization of administrative authority by the Kremlin, as well as the holding of national elections for the new agencies created in the constitution. This Nine Plus One Agreement (nine republics and the central government) gave more to the nine than to the one. The nine republics had the right to secede, significant economic and administrative power, and the promise of a new constitution and genuinely democratic elections throughout the union by 1992. By July 1991 the nine republics that were party to the April agreement had produced a draft treaty which in effect transformed the union into a loose confederation.

But at this point progress toward a reformed union stalled, and the political situation deteriorated over the summer. The explanation for this lay in the internal politics within three key republics: Russia, Lithuania, and Georgia. They reinforced their independence of the central government and complicated Gorbachev's effort to preserve the Soviet Union, even in a confederative form.

Russia

In mid-June 1990 the Russian Parliament declared its sovereignty, including the right to veto any federal law on Russian territory. Russian Communists established their own independent branch of the parent organization that could lobby aggressively with the national party leadership on behalf of Russian interests. These actions strengthened Russian President Yeltsin's administrative authority within the republic. Yeltsin refused to allow the Russian government to transfer any funds to the central government without a strict accounting; he called for a transfer of the bulk of economic decision-making from the center to the republics; and he campaigned for the ouster of conservative Soviet Prime Minister Ryzkhov. Yeltsin also challenged the central government by establishing a Russian-controlled branch of the KGB.

In early April 1991 the Russian Parliament called for the direct election of the republic powers, enabling Yeltsin to continue his challenge to the authority of the center and to Gorbachev's leadership. No progress toward union could occur until after the elections.

Lithuania

The Baltic republics, especially Lithuania, had become increasingly uncompromising about their independence because the Soviet government had treated them so harshly. For example, in mid-January 1991 Soviet troops and armor had taken up key positions in Vilnius in an effort to force the Landsbergis government to retreat from its campaign for independence. The Kremlin hoped that this move would cause Latvia and Estonia to pull back from their own challenges to Soviet authority. But the Landsbergis government refused to reverse course, and a full-blown military confrontation began. Soviet military and Interior Ministry special forces ("Black Berets") invaded Lithuanian government buildings, including those housing the local television station and the press, causing a dozen Lithuanian deaths.

Something of a climax was reached when a bogus provisional government of local conservatives linked to Kremlin hard-liners, calling itself the National Salvation Front, proclaimed itself in control of Lithuania. This failed, but the political consequences for Gorbachev's attempt to preserve the union were serious. Gorbachev's credibility with nationalists and democrats everywhere in the Soviet Union was undermined and provoked an even stronger nationalism among the Baltics.

On February 9, 1991, Lithuanians voted overwhelmingly for independence of the Soviet Union. On March 3, 1991, the peoples of Estonia and Latvia voted overwhelmingly for independence. Ethnic Russians in Latvia supported the republic's independence, giving the Kremlin pause and discouraging ideas for more coercion.

Georgia

The situation in Georgia had developed by April 1991 to the point where its government was reluctant to be part of a confederation. In February 1990 the Georgian Communist Party had called for complete political, economic, and cultural self-determination for the Georgian republic. It supported full sovereignty for all the republics and only a limited role for central government in defense, foreign policy, and for problems most important to the whole country.

On March 9, 1990, the Georgian Parliament declared illegal and invalid agreements of 1921 and 1922 between the Georgian and Soviet Russian governments establishing Soviet control over Georgia after the invasion of Georgian territory by the Soviet Army. This gesture was intended to create a legal basis for independence. In November 1990 the Georgian Parliament terminated the Soviet military draft on Georgian territory and created the equivalent of a republic army, called the Georgian National Guard.

In October 1990 elections for the Georgian republic's Supreme Soviet gave nationalist groups a majority, with Zviad Gamsakhurdia named chair. The Parliament accepted Gamsakhurdia's proposal to create a new post of president of the republic, to be elected directly by the voters, a move that would not only strengthen his bid for Georgian independence of Moscow but also increase his already immense personal authority. Gamsakhurdia, a vehement anti-Communist and champion of Georgian nationalism in the Brezhnev era who had become the spokesperson for the Georgian movement for independence, won the presidency in the May 26, 1991, elections.

The Gamsakhurdia leadership gradually escalated a boycott of the central government by refusing to participate in the meetings of central bodies in which Georgia had a seat. Georgia, like the Baltic republics and Armenia, held its own referendum on independence, on March 31, 1991, as a substitute for Gorbachev's March 17 referendum on preserving a renewed union. Independence was approved by 98 percent of voters. Interestingly, the large Russian, Armenian, and Azerbaijani minorities strongly supported independence. The republic's leadership also repeatedly stated that Georgia would refuse to sign a new union treaty, in any form, and that any such treaties were invalid unless the signatories possessed equal status under international law.

"Micro" Autonomist and Independence Movements

Exacerbating the divisiveness caused by the nationalism of the large ethnic groups in the Soviet state throughout 1990 and 1991 was a resurgence of nationalism among the small ethnic groups in several of the heterogeneous republics, such as Russia, Moldova, and Georgia. These groups demanded increased autonomy of their republic governments and in a few instances complete independence, imitating the assertiveness that the republic governments had shown the central authorities in Moscow.

Bashkir and Chechen-Ingush in Russia

In 1990–1991 some 25 million non-Russians were concentrated in autonomous republics or regions within the Russian republic. These three groups challenged the authority of the Yeltsin government, demanding independence or at least substantially increased autonomy from Moscow. One was the Bashkir autonomous republic. In the center of the highly industrialized Ural Mountains, Bashkir declared its independence from both the Soviet Union and Russia in October 1990, although only 25 percent of the 4 million inhabitants of the republic are Bashkir. The Tatar autonomous republic, perhaps the most restive of the non-Russian minorities within the Russian republic, threatened Russian unity by demanding greater autonomy of Moscow in the fall of 1991.

Finally, the Muslim population of the Chechen-Ingush national area in southwestern Russia near the Caspian Sea demanded independence in November 1991. Yeltsin declared a state of emergency in Grozny, the capital, and wanted to use force against the local nationalists but was restrained by his Parliament. A disturbing aspect of Chechen-Ingush nationalism was the support it sought from neighbors.

Gagauz and Russians in Moldova

In resistance to a law in 1990 making Romanian the republic's official language and requiring people in dozens of jobs, from doctors to hairdressers, to pass Romanian language tests, two small minorities in Moldova, the Gagauz, a group of about 150,000 Turkic Christians living in the southern reaches of the republic, and a larger group of about 300,000 Russians and Ukrainians living in the east near the Dniester River, proclaimed their own Gagauz and Trans-Dniester autonomist republics. Both the former Soviet central government and the Moldovan republic government in Kishinev called these declarations illegal, but the issue is by no means settled.

Abkhazians, South Ossetians, and Meskhetians in Georgia

As Georgia proposed independence of the Soviet Union in 1991, leaders of the Abkhazian and South Ossetian minorities there feared that an independent Georgia would not respect their cultural rights and that they would no longer be able to turn to Moscow for protection. Both groups pushed for secession from Georgia and declared their loyalty to Moscow. Nationalists in both regions boycotted the October 1990 republic elections. In December 1990 Abkhazian and South Ossetian leaders refused to participate in the voting on these issues. South Osseta declared a self-styled "Supreme Soviet of the South Ossetian Soviet Republic," which voted to subordinate the republic directly to the Soviet Union, a move that Moscow, as well as Tbilisi, refused to accept. Gamsakhurdia responded forcefully and suspended Ossetian autonomy, imposing direct rule of Tbilisi. Open warfare between Georgian and Ossetian armed groups broke out despite the presence of Soviet military forces in the region. It continued throughout 1991 as the South Ossetians tried to associate themselves more explicitly and more closely to the rapidly deteriorating Soviet central government in Moscow. And when Moscow hard-liners staged their coup in August 1991, the Abkhazian Communist Party immediately supported their actions, a gesture that provided the Georgian nationalist government with a pretext to shut down the Abkhazian Communist organization.

A wild card in Georgian nationalist politics was the attempt by Meskhetian Turks, exiled to Central Asia by Stalin during World War II, to return to their homeland in the Caucasus. Unwelcome and attacked in Uzbekistan and elsewhere, the Meskhetians want to reclaim their homeland in Georgia. Many Georgians, however, fear that the Meskhetians have lost all ties to Georgia, including knowledge of the Georgian language, and would ultimately want to separate their territory from Georgia and perhaps seek to become part of Turkey. To prevent their return, Georgian officials, reportedly, went to the extreme of faking a landslide on the

Georgian military highway, the only entrance point to Georgia from the northeast. In other key points of entry to the republic, Georgian "volunteers" prevented the return of the Meskhetians. In late 1990 Meskhetian refugees massed on the Georgian border near Sochi and threatened to force their way into Georgia. They eventually relented in hopes of obtaining a negotiated settlement of their claims. Few Meskhetians had succeeded in returning to Georgia by the end of 1991.

Russians and Ukrainians in Central Asia

In Kazakhstan, populated predominantly by Slavs (Russians and Ukrainians), Kazakh people account for only 36 percent of the republic's 17 million people. The Russian population has always thought of the land and its inhabitants as part of Russia, even though it belongs to Kazakhstan; the Russian-dominated Soviet government in Moscow did nothing to discourage such thinking. Once Russians and Ukrainians experience directly the reality of their administrative subordination to the Kazakh Muslim personnel who run the republic government in Alma Ata, there may well be turmoil and political conflict.

There is a potentially explosive situation in Uzbekistan involving the Slavic minority of Russians and Ukrainians, who make up about 8 percent of the population. Uzbeks resented the strong Russian influence in their local Communist party. This was corrected by a gradual process of Uzbekization from 1959 to 1983, resulting in the ascendancy of non-Russians. Now, in the post-Soviet era, many Russians are scared of discrimination and have spoken of an imminent mass exodus back to the Russian republic.

PLURALIZATION OF SOVIET POLITICS AFTER 1989

Another major reason for the collapse of the Soviet Union has to do with the pluralization of Soviet politics during the late 1980s. The many democratic reform groups undermined the historic single-party system that had kept glued together the extraordinarily diverse and conflict-ridden Soviet society.

Rise of Democratic Groups

With glasnost in the late 1980s, radical intellectuals spoke out against the Soviet system. Arguing that Soviet society had been swindled by "seventy years on the road to nowhere," they delegitimized the Soviet system and were a factor in its collapse, especially as the scope and pace of their activities expanded significantly in 1990 and 1991.

This nascent democratic opposition took advantage of the partially open elections allowed by Gorbachev in 1989 to help him create a power base for reform communism. For example, as a result of the March 1989 elections for the Congress of Peoples' Deputies, there emerged independent blocs, such as the Inter-regional Group of Andrei Sakharov,

Gavril Popov, and Anatoly Sobchak, which began to lobby for radical liberalization of the Soviet political system.

These groups eventually went far beyond reform of the system, to outright repudiation of it. Tension mounted between the government and the opposition as the country moved toward local elections set for the spring of 1990. Although the radicals did not publicize their intentions, it became increasingly clear, especially in private conversation, that their goal was to wrest power from the party and to move toward genuine constitutional government, a market economy, and private property.

Throughout 1990 and 1991 the Democrats got a significant lift from Russian President Boris Yeltsin. Dismissed in earlier times as a "maverick populist" with little prospect of mounting an effective challenge to Gorbachev's power and influence, Yeltsin quickly emerged as a central, perhaps decisive figure in the emergence of a vibrant democratic opposition. He strengthened his democratic credentials enormously when, in July 1990, he dramatically resigned from the Communist party during its televised 28th Congress, thus publicly distancing himself from those who were increasingly receiving the blame of the people for the perceived failure of perestroika and the worsening of economic conditions. In August 1990 Yeltsin placed himself firmly in the camp of the radical reformers when he called for Russia's adoption of the economic program of Shatalin. A measure of his extraordinary popularity was the way in which on March 28, 1991, several hundred thousand Muscovites defied a ban on rallies in order to demonstrate their support of Yeltsin against the effort of conservatives in the Russian Parliament to impeach him. This massive explosion of popular wrath was unprecedented in recent Russian history and suggested the kind of power that an alienated citizenry could use to influence the political system. Finally, Yeltsin became a powerful force within the reform movement when, in June 1991, he was elected by an overwhelming popular majority to the presidency of the Russian republic.

Yeltsin was, perhaps, the most influential figure in the democratic movement, having brought real democratic reform to the Russian government through the establishment of a directly elected chief executive. However, he could not bring unity to the democratic forces because of their deep divisions, their lack of experience with party organization other than that of the highly centralized and autocratic Communist party, and their extraordinary diversity of aims and ambitions. Nevertheless, in the beginning of July 1991 the Democrats finally announced the formation of a new political organization, called the Movement of Democratic Reforms, under the leadership of former Soviet Foreign Minister Eduard Shevardnadze. The Democratic Movement was unique in that it included not only outside dissidents but also Communist party members who had been alienated by conservatives in the top party leadership. Although the Movement had a long way to go in mounting an effective challenge to the Communists, its establishment put the Communist party on the defensive and accelerated the decline of its influence and power.

Moreover, with the formation of the Movement, party members like Shevardnadze and Yakovlev, who once had hoped, as Gorbachev still did, that the Communist party could eventually reform itself, now gave up that hope once and for all. Shevardnadze left the party with stinging criticisms of it, calling it intolerant, nostalgic for the discredited past, and doomed to oblivion because of its stubborn conservatism.

Decline and Disintegration of the Communist Party

While the influence of democratic forces increased, that of the Communist party diminished during 1990 and 1991. In this period the party lost power for several reasons. During the February 7, 1990, plenum of the Soviet Communist Party's Central Committee, it voted to end its historic monopoly of power in the Soviet Union. This decision reversed Lenin's policy—adopted following the Bolshevik seizure of power in November 1917—of establishing a single-party state under Marxist leadership. It was an about-face for Gorbachev, who had reaffirmed his support of the party's monopoly of power as late as December 8, 1989. At that time, he declared, "It is essential to maintain the one-party system" during a heated discussion of demands by Andrei Sakharov and other reformers in the Congress of Peoples' Deputies to revoke Article 6 of the Soviet Constitution, which guaranteed the Communist party's supremacy.

Several reasons explain Gorbachev's change of position. His call for the abandonment of the party's monopoly of power was consistent with other steps taken to curtail party influence over the running of the Soviet system in favor of the state apparatus, which became more influential and more powerful in policy-making. Gorbachev benefited personally from a strengthened state apparatus as public criticism of and hostility toward the party increased in consequence of continued deterioriation of economic conditions and interethnic rivalries.

Furthermore, as then-Premier Ryzhkov asserted during the plenum, the Communist party had already lost its political monopoly, because of the de facto existence of pluralism in the form of new political organizations. Mass defections of old and young party members to these new organizations, perceived to have a more promising political future than the Communists, also influenced Gorbachev's new willingness to move faster toward a multiparty system—which, incidentally, he never had explicitly precluded.

The formal termination of the party's political monopoly did not automatically mean the end of its influence and power. The party plenum stopped short of demands for full pluralism in the form of a dialogue with opposition groups, which conceivably could lead to Central/Eastern European-style coalition regimes. Indeed, the party remained the single most well-endowed reservoir of administrative expertise in the country. Thus, the February 7 vote did not mean an immediate emergence of a Western-style pluralistic political system.

The party preserved the bulk of its leadership authority. Despite the fact that the party remained one of the most serious obstacles to the reform and improvement of Soviet life, because of its strong conservative instincts borne out of not only ideology but also the self-interest of its membership, Gorbachev had acknowledged in September 1989 that the Soviet Communist Party "was and remains the main organizing and coordinating force capable of leading the people along the path of . . . Socialist change, of playing an integrating and rallying role in society and, let us be blunt about it, of preventing an undesirable, dramatic turn of events."

Other reasons for the decline and disintegration of the Soviet Communist Party include the March 1989 elections for the Congress of Peoples' Deputies, which put anti-Communists in positions of power for the first time. In some places newly elected noncommunist officials confiscated party property. Seeing the handwriting on the wall, several million party members retired while others joined reformist political groups. Yeltsin showed his power when he banned political organizations in the workplace and effectively ended the long tradition in which party members dominated the inner leadership of offices, factories, and farms.

The party suffered also as Gorbachev tried to transform it into a conventional reformist organization modeled after the Socialist parties in the west. At the end of July 1991, in a plenum of the party's Central Committee, Gorbachev asked the party to give up its Marxist ideology. He supported other reformers and said that the party would lose any claim to participate in the political life of the country if it did not break with the past. In his view, it had lost contact with reality when it set unachievable goals based on "raw ideology" regardless of the concerns of Soviet citizens. Gorbachev also called upon the party to accept power-sharing with noncommunist leaderships and organizations in the republics. The Central Committee eventually endorsed Gorbachev's proposals to transform the party into a broad-based reform organization, effectively abandoning its monopoly of politics.

One consequence was that the Russian branch split into two organizations, one of reformers and the other of hard-liners. Since the Russian branch was the most influential of local organizations, the split tended to undermine further the party's hold on power. Russian Communists were fragmented even more at the beginning of August 1991, when a subbranch of the reform Communists, called the Democratic Party of Russian Communists, emerged, an alternative organization founded by Russian Vice President Aleksandr Rutskoy.

Hard-liners in the party leadership were appalled by the party's decline. They made no secret of their alarm at the decline of centralized authority or their willingness to prevent it. They headed institutions whose power was vested in the old order of state ownership, centralized planning, and the coherence of the union.

On August 19, 1991, Prime Minister Valentin Pavlov, Interior Minister Boris Pugo, KGB Chair Kryuchkov, Defense Minister Yazov, and managers of the military-industrial complex, notably Oleg Baklanov, First Deputy Chair of the Defense Council, called up their resources and tried to force Gorbachev out of power. They believed that the people would support them. Economic conditions had not improved under perestoika. The hard-liners thus had the psychological as well as the political wherewithal to go on the offensive against perestroika and, if necessary, against Gorbachev himself.

The Ascendancy of Hard-line Communists

Gorbachev understood these feelings and may have tried to contain them. As early as December 1990 he had replaced his liberal Interior minister, Vadim Bakatin, with the former KGB General Boris Pugo, and replaced Nikolai Ryzkhov as prime minister with Valentin Pavlov, a command administrative economist deeply hostile to radical reforms.

Hard-liners had gained again at a session of the Congress of Peoples' Deputies, in December 1990, when Gorbachev named a colorless career Communist aparatchik, Gennadi Yanev, to be his Vice President, a move that stunned reformers, including some of his closest supporters like Shevardnadze and Yacovlev. Indeed, Shevardnadze was shocked by the way in which Gorbachev seemed to be allowing the ascendancy of hard-liners who he knew opposed further progress in his reform program. Shevardnadze also was angry that his longtime friend did not defend him against virulent public attacks from the hard-liners who deplored his arms-control initiatives. He eventually resigned as foreign minister in December 1990, predicting a rightist offensive to block the perestroika-inspired transformation of the Soviet Union.

The hard-liners now tried to force Gorbachev to the right on the issue of Lithuanian separatism. They authorized KGB special forces, army paratroopers, and Interior Ministry "black berets" to force Lithuania and Latvia to curtail their campaigns for independence. Although the hard-liners suffered a setback when Gorbachev refused to go to the length of ousting the Landsbergis government by force, Pugo, Pavlov, Kryuchkov, and others renewed their pressure on Gorbachev to pursue a conservative course. Pavlov claimed in January 1991 that Western aid to the Soviet Union was designed to destabilize and destroy Soviet socialism. Obviously Pavlov did not want the West to help Gorbachev move forward with perestroika-inspired reforms. He sought to discredit the West in the eyes of the Soviet public. In another effort to move the country in a conservative direction, Pavlov ordered the confiscation of all ruble bills larger than 50, ostensibly to reduce the monetary excess but, perhaps, to prepare the country for a shift to the right with a command-administrative shock therapy to remedy the country's now desperate economic crisis.

In March 1991 the hard-liners lashed out at Yeltsin after the Russian leader publicly called for a "declaration of war" against Gorbachev for having betrayed perestroika by appointing them. They called for Yeltsin's impeachment. When several hundred thousand Muscovites demonstrated on March 28, and strikes in support of him at the Siberian coal mines occurred, the impeachment failed. Hard-liners felt desperate.

The August 1991 Coup

The hard-liners now turned for the first time on Gorbachev. Infuriated by Gorbachev's support of the so-called Nine Plus One agreement of April 23, 1991, providing for a radical devolution of administrative power from the central government in Moscow to the republics, effectively emasculating the old union, the hard-liners tried to get the Communist party's Central Committee to replace him as general secretary. They proposed Anatoly Lukyanov, a longtime friend of his, for chair of the Supreme Soviet, second in line for the succession.

The hard-liners, however, were checkmated temporarily when Gorbachev beat back their effort against him by threatening to resign from the party if it did not endorse the Nine Plus One agreement. The Central Committee supported Gorbachev, with some misgivings, to avoid a devisive conflict over the succession.

The hard-liners were determined to force Gorbachev to curtail his reforms. They correctly sensed that Gorbachev had been weakened in these battles because the democrats wanted once and for all to stop his shifting between left and right on reform and lead their campaign to democratize and decentralize Soviet political and economic organization.

Grievances of the Military

Among the hard-line faction in the Kremlin in the spring and summer of 1991 was the top Soviet military leadership, in particular Defense Minister Yazov, who deplored Gorbachev's policies of retrenchment internationally, especially in Central/Eastern Europe, a region of prime importance for the security of the Soviet state. He also thought that Gorbachev's decision in 1988 to withdraw Soviet forces from Afghanistan before the achievement of a victory over the Mujahideen was a mistake, not only because it weakened Soviet security in Central Asia but also for reasons of pride. He opposed the shrinking budgets that required severe cutbacks in defense equipment and personnel. And he and other top-ranking Soviet officers were especially resentful of Gorbachev's apparent willingness to tolerate abuse of the military from the new political and national opposition groups and in the public media. They were incensed at the verbal insults and outright theft of military property by lawless gangs of dissidents in places like Georgia, by revelations in a critical press of increased defections, and by charges of brutality in the ranks. They also regretted the downgrading of ideology, which had helped to promote a docile and obedient society.

The Prelude to the Coup

The hard-liners were emboldened when, in June, Pavlov attempted to outmaneuver Gorbachev by asking the Supreme

Soviet for the transfer of decree powers to the prime minister's office to allow it to deal with what was termed the country's imminent collapse. Such a move would have put Pavlov in control of the country. Instead of firing Pavlov and like-minded members of his government for their evident disloyalty to him, Gorbachev skirted this issue, left them in power, and called upon the Parliament simply to reject Pavlov's demands.

Meanwhile, in late July, Yeltsin, eight other republic presidents, and Gorbachev accepted a draft union treaty, which went even further than the Nine Plus One agreement in transforming the union into a confederation of near sovereign constituent republics. This presented a real threat of disintegration, because it involved the breakup of a single economic plan, a single plan for civil rights, a single defense, and a single foreign policy. Under these circumstances, Pavlov insisted, he and his associates had no choice other than to take decisive measures to stop the slide of the country to catastrophe. They decided to force Gorbachev out of power, through a coup.

The chief plotters were Pavlov, Pugo, Kryuchkov, Yazov, Yanev, and Baklanov. Other less well-known plotters were V. A. Starodubstev, chair of the U.S.S.R. Farmers' Union, and A. I. Tizyakov, president of the Association of State Enterprises and Industrial, Construction, Transportation, and Communications Facilities of the Soviet Union. The plotters gave Gorbachev an ultimatum on Sunday, August 18, at his vacation home in the Crimea. They demanded that he reject the latest draft of the union treaty. When he rejected this ultimatum, they put him under house arrest, cut his telephone lines, and proceeded to take control of the administrative offices in Moscow of both the Soviet and Russian governments. They established a Committee on the State of Emergency under Vice President Yanev, who was theoretically in command of the Soviet government and ready to exercise the powers of Gorbachev, who was said to be "incapacitated."

The Failure of the Coup

Beginning on Monday, August 19, the plotters met popular resistance, led by Russian President Yeltsin. Yeltsin called upon hundreds of thousands of Muscovites to surround and defend him and the Russian Parliament buildings. At the same time Ukraine, the second-largest Soviet republic, declared the orders and decrees of the Committee null and void.

Meanwhile, the plotters failed to ensure that the members of a special KGB unit would follow their orders to arrest Yeltsin and other leaders and to take over the Russian Parliament building, which they did not do. Local KGB commanders had mixed feelings about the coup, apparently unknown to Kryuchkov, and refused to go after Yeltsin.

The military also was unreliable, despite its grievances against Gorbachev and eagerness to replace him. Yazov apparently had no stomach for massive civilian bloodshed. Unlike KGB chief Kryuchkov, who was an alarmist, convinced of imminent disaster unless a firm hand took control of the Soviet system and blocked further change, Yazov, whose concerns centered primarily on the perceived negative impact of perestroika on the army, was reluctant to mobilize the army's resources behind the coup.

Moreover, many middle-level military leaders had strong reformist instincts and wanted, rather, to repair the army's image and professionalism. Typical was Air Force Commander-in-Chief Yevgeni Shaposhnikov, who refused to participate in the coup. Shaposhnikov had been very vocal about the need for economic reform, a market economy, and the integration of the Soviet Union into the world economy after 70 years of debilitating and counterproductive isolation.

Conscripts deployed in Moscow, who were uneasy over the role of the army in the attempted seizure of power, went so far as to assure civilians that they would not obey orders to shoot. The plotters also did not have the support of regional commanders, whose willingness to obey orders varied from place to place. In Georgia, for example, the independence-seeking President Zviad Gamsakhurdia persuaded the local commander not to deploy his troops. And Leningrad's Mayor Sobchak persuaded the military commander there to allow mass demonstrations in the center of the city by promising not to call for a strike (which went ahead anyway at several plants). The coupmakers' inability to secure the country's second city was a significant cause of their failure.

Inexplicably, the plotters neglected to call on the independent right-wing group of deputies in the Soviet Legislature. Members of Soyuz were strongly supportive of the traditional Soviet Union and critical of Gorbachev's willingness to decentralize administrative authority and thereby strengthen the power and influence of the Soviet government in Moscow.

The plotters also botched the mobilization of the party out of a desire to exclude the deputy general secretary, Vladimir Ivachoko, who was thought unreliable. This meant that the Central Committee Secretariat did not immediately support the coup after the Emergency Committee's televised press conference. These missteps were catastrophic because they provided Yeltsin with the opportunity to mobilize the Moscow public.

In sharp contrast to the plotters, who had no blueprint for change beyond vague promises to inspire mass support, the loyalists knew exactly how they should act. On Monday, August 19, while the Soviet Cabinet, with only one dissenting voice, endorsed the coup, and while the Soviet Communist Party's Central Committee Secretariat sat in silence, Yeltsin, along with Popov, Sobchak, and others publicly called for resistance. They did not move to take power themselves; they called instead for the restoration of Gorbachev as the legitimate president, both to ensure continuity of state power and to give constitutional legitimacy to their own de facto exercise of that power, a gesture that was useful domestically and internationally in the heat of the crisis.

The beginning of the end of the coup occurred when representatives of Yeltsin went on Wednesday, August 21, to the Crimea, where the hard-liners had kept Gorbachev under house arrest and incommunicado. They brought Gorbachev and his family back to Moscow. Shortly after his arrival the Supreme Soviet formally reinstated him as president. The coup was now officially over.

Movement Toward the Commonwealth

In the weeks following the collapse of the coup and the arrest of its leaders, Yeltsin liberally exploited Gorbachev's legitimacy as well as his new majority in the Russian Parliament to demolish the old Soviet order. He appeared on national television reiterating a series of decrees he had issued during the coup, including one suspending the Communist party and its propaganda instrument, *Pravda*. Dominated by Yeltsin, Gorbachev changed the leadership of the KGB and the army. He appointed Evgeni Shaposhnikov as minister of Defense and Vadim Bakatin, Pugo's liberal-minded predecessor at the Interior Ministry, as head of the KGB. Shaposhnikov and Bakatin began at once an extensive purge of their respective institutions, reducing their size, dissolving existing party cells, and putting them under the control of state authority. Meanwhile, in Russia, Yeltsin systematically rid the Russian government (and ultimately those parts of the Soviet government under Russian control) of the old nomenklatura, replacing them with young, liberal, and modernizing professionals who would drastically reform the economy.

Following his return from the Crimea to Moscow, Gorbachev exhorted the government to avoid a "Yugoslavization" of the Soviet Union's conflict-ridden multinational society and to preserve the union. On September 2, 1991, the Congress of Peoples' Deputies approved a plan essentially similar to the provisions of the Nine Plus One draft threaty. But while Russia favored preservation of the union in a new confederative form, there was now much opposition to it from other republics, in particular the Baltic republics and Ukraine.

The Baltic republics wanted nothing to do with efforts to salvage the Soviet system. Estonia and Latvia had declared their independence on August 20 and 21; and after the coup all three Baltic republics, with support from the West, demanded complete separation from the Soviet Union. On September 6 the Kremlin decreed the complete independence of the Baltic states. Encouraged by this break in the union, separatists in other republics began to plan their own independence.

Ukraine announced on October 17 that it would not sign the new plan, because popular sentiment wanted more autonomy of the Soviet Union than this treaty called for. Indeed, Ukraine was skeptical of a union of any kind, given its fears of a resurgent and powerful Soviet central government. It would wait for the outcome of a referendum, scheduled for December 1, on the issue of independence. On December 1 Ukrainian voters overwhelmingly approved a declaration of independence and elected their nationalist leader Leonid Kravchuk to the Ukrainian presidency.

Support for preserving the Soviet Union in any shape or form was now minimal. When Gorbachev proposed that there should be economic agreement, those who supported the proposal on November 14 insisted on sending it to their respective parliaments for ratification. By this time Russia itself had lost interest in preserving the union, however loose it might be, because Yeltsin believed that Russia could do better alone. In his view, the central government was the biggest obstacle to economic reform. Frustrated by Gorbachev's failure to bring the republics together on issues of unity and economic improvement, Yeltsin now thought that each republic would have to carry through reform on its own, in its own way, and at its own pace.

The Demise of the Soviet Union

On December 8, 1991, the presidents of Russia, Ukraine, and Byelorus, which together controlled 73 percent of the Soviet population and 80 percent of the territory of the Soviet Union, signed an agreement in the Byelorus capital of Minsk to create a new confederation of republics called the Commonwealth of Independent States. They declared the Soviet Union at an end. This agreement was made quite independently of Gorbachev, whom they did not even bother to consult.

In many respects, the powers of the new Commonwealth defined at Minsk resembled those Gorbachev had been seeking for a reformed union with joint control over foreign policy, trade, customs, transportation and communications systems, currency, emigration, the environment, and fighting organized crime. A separate statement at Minsk declared that the preservation and development of close economic ties among the republics were important to the national economy and should continue. Ukraine and Byelorus agreed to follow the lead of Russia in decontrolling prices.

Gorbachev quickly and forcefully denounced the C.I.S. as illegal, denying that the three presidents had the authority to terminate the Soviet state, an action he said could be taken only by the Congress of Peoples' Deputies. Gorbachev predicted that the dissolution of the Soviet Union would lead to chaos and anarchy and eventually to civil war. He clearly was devastated by this irrefutable punctuation of his failure to save the union in which he still had faith as well as by the prospect of his imminent political collapse.

The Slavic presidents ignored Gorbachev. They submitted the Minsk agreement for ratification by their parliaments. The Commonwealth came into being on December 10, 1991. Other republics subsequently sought entry into the C.I.S., and on December 20, 1991, a formal agreement was signed at Alma Ata, in Kazakhstan, by leaders of eight republics. The "Minsk" republics accorded the others the cofounder status they demanded. The Alma Ata signatories recognized one anothers' sovereign independence and agreed to determine shortly the disposition of the Soviet military, with Soviet Defense Minister Shaposhnikov in charge of an interm military command. By December 22, 3 more republics—Armenia, Azerbaijan, and Moldova—joined the Commonwealth, to bring the total membership to 11 former Soviet republics. Only Georgia refrained from seeking admission, because of its civil war as well as its strong urge to have complete independence after the fashion of the Baltic republics.

On December 20 the government of the Russian republic assumed formal jurisdiction over the Soviet Foreign Ministry, the KGB, the Supreme Soviet, and even Gorbachev's presidential office. With a disquieting agressiveness, the Russians took over the Soviet money supply and Soviet trade in oil, gold, diamonds, and foreign currency, fueling suspicion, jealousy, and animosity among the other republics, in particular Ukraine.

With no support among the republics for his leadership, Gorbachev resigned as president of the Soviet state. On December 26 the Supreme Soviet passed a resolution acknowledging the demise of the Soviet Union. Russia subsequently was assigned the Soviet Union's seat in the Security Council of the United Nations, and the former Soviet Union's embassies abroad replaced the Soviet flag with that of the Russian republic.

(Novosti Photo)

Mikhail Gorbachev became general secretary of the Communist Party of the Soviet Union (CPSU) in March 1985. His endorsement by the Politburo was immediate and indicated the power of his influence. Under his administration, the Soviet Communist Party as well as the entire Soviet Union experienced monumental changes. His policies of perestroika (restructuring of the Soviet economy) and glasnost (new openness and candor) brought about changes that would eventually lead to his resignation from office. In August 1991, the hard-liners attempted a coup in an effort to bring back tight Communist control, which was beginning to dissolve. The coup was unsuccessful, and total dissolution of the old U.S.S.R. continued. Gorbachev's Soviet Union officially became a new confederation of republics called the Commonwealth of Independent States on December 8, 1991.

THE C.I.S.: PROBLEMS, POLICIES, AND PROSPECTS

The newly established Commonwealth of Independent States confronts monumental development challenges and problems. The most important of these are: 1) promoting stable, efficient, and popular democratic government; 2) moving toward a market economy; 3) disposing of the former Soviet Union's military establishment; 4) controlling ethnocultural nationalist rivalries; and 5) protecting and furthering the external interests of the republics. We close our discussion with an examination of the chances for survival of the C.I.S.

PROMOTING DEMOCRATIC INSTITUTIONS

Although they rejected Soviet dictatorship, the peoples of the new Commonwealth are still far from embracing Western-style democratic government. Russian President Yeltsin, despite his democratic rhetoric, acted in most undemocratic ways during and after the August 1991 coup. After defying the tanks, Yeltsin issued decrees that exceeded his legal prerogatives, confiscating property, invading the homes of parliamentary deputies, and suppressing a literary association of right-wing writers. Yeltsin hectored Gorbachev after his return from captivity, demonstrating an inability to distinguish between the friends and foes of democracy and forgetting that without Gorbachev's leadership since 1985 there would have been no popularly elected President Yeltsin to symbolize resistance, no Russian Parliament to give him refuge and support, and few if any anticoup protesters in the streets.

The Soviet Communist Party still has its adherents. On August 30, 1991, just 8 days after the coup, Nina Andreeya, the author of the famous 1988 letter defending conservatism in the Soviet Union to party hard-liner Ligachev, declared publicly that the party was not dead, that the decline of the party was a temporary phenomenon, and that it would return to power someday. Alexander Kabanov, vice rector of Moscow's higher Party School, predicted in September 1991 that the party would change its name, break up into several factions, and function through normal political parties. This was historically inevitable, he insisted.

Millions of longtime party members remain important functionaries in the ministries of the different republics, including Russia, that still control about 90 percent of the economy. Former Communist leaders continue to manage factories and farms in Russia and remain in powerful political positions in some of the Central Asian republics. Neither the late Soviet nor current Russian authorities have formally outlawed Communist party groups. Charters have transformed them into conventional political organizations willing to compete in open elections for governmental office. Furthermore, ex-Communists continue to predominate in the legislative and executive bodies of the republics. They are not schooled in democratic ideology and practice; some may not be sympathetic to democracy.

In addition, many recent and current leaders of the republics whose power has rested on a patronage-based network of interpersonal relations are not interested in democratizing their systems. They fear losing their personal political power and inviting an explosion of popular protest and dissent, which could lead to anarchy and revolution. Characteristically, Uzbekistan's President Islam Karimnov said publicly in September 1991 that his republic was not ready for democracy and that he preferred the Chinese model of limited economic reform and a prohibition against popular political manifestations.

Yeltsin himself has expressed some skepticism about moving immediately toward Western-style democracy, resisting pressures to strengthen the Russian Parliament. He said in April 1992 that Russia needed a "presidential government," not a parliamentary democracy. He warned that to move prematurely to democratic government would be "suicide," given the difficult transition when "we still have to deal with a seriously ill society." He spoke of parliamentary democracy as a highly politicized form of politics that would paralyze policy-making. But Yeltsin had another reason for championing "presidential government" in Russia for the next few years. A strengthened Russian Parliament might favor the Communist holdovers elected in 1989, whom Yeltsin would like to push out of power because of their resistance to his economic reforms.

The overwhelming majority of ordinary citizens in the republics are not democratically inclined but, rather, passive or focusing on economic rather than political conditions. Moreover, opinion polls show a popular yearning for a strong government that will improve living conditions. Real opposition to the August 1991 coup came only from several hundred thousand people living primarily in the city areas of Russia. And in the weeks and months following the coup and well into 1992, there were many popular demonstrations in Moscow and elsewhere in Russia calling for a return of the old centralized Soviet state and a restoration of the power and influence of the Soviet Communist Party. Some of these demonstrations reflected a strong anti-Semitic bias, with people blaming the Jews as well as Yeltsin for hard times, a tendency hardly conductive to the development of liberal democracy.

The KGB, even though changed, is hardly a democratic institution. Vadim Bakatin, who replaced the discredited Vladimir Kryuchkov following the coup, was given a mandate to curtail the operations of the KGB; to transform it into a small intelligence-gathering institution; and to shed its responsibilities for border security, executive protection, government communications, and control of dissidence. By December 1991 it looked as if the KGB was becoming little more than a shadow of its old imposing self. But Yeltsin has since fired Bakatin, who acknowledged publicly that the KGB was not really changing. Despite his best efforts, it had not experienced an "ideological perestroika."

In December 1991 Yeltsin issued a presidential decree to create a "super ministry" of internal affairs and public security. This act horrified his liberal supporters, and Russia's new constitutional court rejected it. Next Yeltsin created a new Russian Agency for Federal Security, which has some of the responsibilities of the old KGB, and named Yevgeny Savostyanov to head the Moscow branch. Although the real role of the KGB's successor is by no means clear, Savostyanov indicated that he would like to do "political investigations." There is the possibility of a return in Russia at least to a KGB-like institution, despite widespread popular hostility to the KGB because of its abuses.

TOWARD A MARKET ECONOMY: THE RUSSIAN MODEL

In early 1992 Yeltsin's Russia adopted the radical economic reforms inspired by Shatalin, Yavlinsky, and Yegor Gaidar, director of the Institute of Economic Policy at the Academy of the National Economy in Moscow. Gaidar joined Yeltsin's government as deputy prime minister for Economic Planning. Gaidar advocated a rapid, Polish-style "cold turkey" dismantling of socialism as the only means of expanding output to relieve severe shortages, especially of food, and to raise the standard of living. The Yeltsin-Gaidar program had three general dimensions: decontrol of prices; acceleration of privatization in the agricultural, industrial, and service sectors of the Russian economy; and the transformation of the ruble into a convertible currency.

Decontrol of Prices

Beginning January 2, 1992, Yeltsin allowed prices on most, though not all, consumer goods to rise to their natural levels based upon supply and demand. Producers could set whatever price they pleased on these goods, with distributors allowed to add another 25 percent. Prices on these goods subsequently quadrupled as food producers tried to make the most of the new opportunity for windfall profits. The Russian reformers hoped that by letting prices rise, all producers would soon take their products to market, ease shortages, and bring about lower prices.

Yeltsin tried to soften the impact of the price hikes. Food reserves were made available to people on low fixed pensions and the elderly. Price controls were still in effect for milk, some kinds of bread, sugar, vodka, cooking oil, and medicine. Pensioners, students, and the disabled received help from soup kitchens as well as stipends and special discounts. Regional authorities in Russia could use local money to provide limited subsidies, as some of them in fact did, to ease hardships. The Russians also intended to use Western credits to buy additional goods.

The impact of price deregulation remained brutal. The Moscow Statistical Service announced in January 1992 that an individual now needed 1,944 rubles a month for a bare minimum of subsistence—most Russian workers earned about 400 to 800 rubles a month. The skyrocketing prices for food and fuel provoked angry reactions from ordinary Russian people and also politicians. Ruslan Khasbulatov, the speaker of the Russian Parliament, and many parliamentary deputies wanted a respite from the price reform, calling the program unwise and unrealistic. They argued that price increases before the implementation of privatization of business were premature and provocative. Yeltsin's response also had some merit: he replied that price reforms were being undermined by conservative bureaucrats holding back production of consumer necessities in order to torpedo his policies.

Yeltsin's expectation that, after an initial spurt of inflation, supply would catch up with demand and prices would level off was not fulfilled by the end of the first quarter of 1992. Indeed, scarcity and near hyperinflation continued well into the new year. Production was still dominated by monopolies that were only minimally responsive to supply and demand, and methods of distribution were still either inadequate or inefficient.

This Russian experience explains why the leaders of other republics, in particular Kravchuk of the Ukraine and Nazarbayev of Kazakhstan, were not eager to move quickly to a market economy. They worried about the destabilizing effects of rapid change, the danger of social turmoil, and the inevitability of a threat to their power base by angry consumers. Nevertheless, other republics did decontrol some prices after the fashion of Russia. But by the end of January 1992, in response to loud protests by students and low-paid workers, the leaderships retreated and restored most price controls. In Uzbekistan, for example, there was an explosion of public outrage over price hikes in mid-January, when students, enraged by soaring prices and bread shortages, went on a rampage in Tashkent.

Ukraine, like some other republics, feared a deluge of Russians to pay rubles for goods that were far less expensive than at home. As a temporary preventive measure, the government in Kiev introduced a system of ration coupons which had to be used along with currency for the purchase of Ukrainian goods. In January 1992 Ukraine became the first Commonwealth republic to move toward a local currency— ostensibly, Ukrainian leaders asserted, in response to the Russian central bank's failure to send Ukraine new supplies of rubles. The Kiev government converted the ration coupons into a quasi-medium of exchange. Ukraine paid salaries to workers partly in rubles and partly in coupons, with 1 coupon deemed equal to 1 ruble at the official rate. Prices for food and other items were soon stated in coupons. By mid-February the coupons served as an alternative to the ruble, which slowly disappeared from circulation. The coupons were traded for U.S. dollars, with 16 to the dollar.

Currency Stabilization and Convertibility

In early 1992 the International Monetary Fund requested that the Russian ruble be made internationally convertible, one of several conditions that Russia would have to meet to qualify for financial assistance. This requirement had serious political liabilities for the Yeltsin government. The exchange rate of the ruble had risen in 1991 from 60 rubles to the dollar to

170 rubles by January 1992. With this exchange rate, Russian assets could be purchased cheaply, a dangerous development given latent Russian suspicions and fear of foreigners. In addition, the ruble was unstable. In January there was near hyperinflation, caused by the decontrol of prices and by budget deficits.

The Yeltsin government has tried to meet the budget problem by calling for deep spending cuts, especially in the military sector, where spending already has been reduced to the equivalent of 4.5 percent of GNP, down from about 25 percent under Gorbachev. Yeltsin has planned a tight monetary policy to reduce hyperinflation.

Privatization of Agriculture

Yeltsin has tried to speed up the privatization of agriculture. In November 1991 the Russian Parliament approved an agricultural reform program which set February 1, 1992, as a deadline for local governments to decide on farm sizes and other standards for collective-farm workers to shift to family farming. The law has heavy fines for bureaucrats who drag their feet and interfere with these changes. In late December 1991 Yeltsin also signed an executive order giving collective-farm workers greater rights to buy and sell individual plots and giving nonfarmers small country gardens. Yeltsin so far is way ahead of the Russian Parliament, which is wary of private ownership and the dismantling of the collective-farm system.

Further land privatization in Russia and other Soviet republics in the post-Communist era faces other problems. The lack of land records and assessments of quality variations prevents the easy and equitable distribution of land. There will also be a mismatch of equipment. The massive size of existing collectives means that the heavy tractors designed for them will be unsuitable for the new small farms.

REORGANIZATION OF THE SOVIET MILITARY

Although the republic defense ministers agreed in principle in Moscow, at the end of December 1991, to create a joint armed force and appointed Shaposhnikov to a 2-month term as interim Commonwealth commander, C.I.S. unity of action on military matters was difficult, partly because the republics wanted territorial armies, an inevitable desire given the fragmentation of the former Soviet military along ethnic lines and the much-resented domination of the officer corps by Russians. At their December 1991 meeting the republic leaders agreed that individual members could form separate armies, although strategic weapons would remain under a single command.

Still, Commonwealth leaders do have strong incentives to preserve some kind of central control over the former Soviet military. Many ex-Soviet Army officers oppose the breakup of the army into republic-controlled units and want a unified, if leaner, force under central command. They argue that the security of the republics requires a central military organization, given the reality of a nuclear world and the fact that almost every neighbor of the former Soviet Union is likely to harbor territorial ambitions and be ready to exploit differences among the republics. Former Soviet officers have argued also that republic armies might be able to fight against unarmed peasants but they would be no match for a modern army—indeed, they would be helpless against it.

In a gesture of desperation, 5,000 officers of all ranks from the former Soviet military gathered in the Kremlin on January 17, 1992, to demand of C.I.S. leaders that the Soviet armed forces remain. The gathering was called by local assemblies in all branches of the military. Nothing on the scale of this meeting had ever taken place in the Soviet Union. The officers condemned a perceived civilian hostility toward the army, the murderous weapons raids by armed Georgian bands, and Ukraine's insistence on splitting the army and navy into territorial branches. The officers adopted a resolution expressing concern over the hasty and "unreasonable" division of the army and navy, called on the

(UPI/Bettmann)

Throughout 1990 and 1991 Russian President Boris Yeltsin emerged as a dominant figure in the developing vibrant democratic movement. During and after the coup attempt of August 1991, Yeltsin made decisive moves to thwart the hard-liners. After Gorbachev was returned from house arrest, Yeltsin took him to task over not being able to distinguish friends from foes. As president of the largest of the 11 republics that make up the C.I.S., Yeltsin is generally considered important to the survival of the new Commonwealth. Yeltsin's own political survival also is not certain.

Commonwealth politicians to preserve the army's unity with a single unitary command for a transitional period, and agreed to set up a coordinating council to represent the interests of the armed services.

In mid-February C.I.S. leaders met in Minsk to set up the council. Three republics (Ukraine, Moldova, and Azerbaijan) rejected the idea of a unified military force. Ukrainian President Kravchuk intoned that unified armed forces could logically only exist in a unified state, which the Commonwealth of Independent States had not yet become. Ukraine did not want the C.I.S. to become a quasi-union reminiscent of the late Soviet Union and feared that a Commonwealth army would still be dominated by Russians. Azerbaijan opposed a Commonwealth army because it wanted to have an independent force to deal with Armenian opposition to its administration of Nagorno-Karabakh. It had discovered that Russian troops, the remnants of the Soviet Army, deployed in Nagorno-Karabakh, had been cooperating with the Armenian side.

It certainly appears that the ex-Soviet republics are not likely to adopt any policy regarding the military that impinges on their newly achieved sovereignty. What is more, the military leadership of the former Soviet state has far less influence today than it used to. Its image with politicians and the public suffered substantially from the complicity of its top leadership, in the person of Defense Minister Yazov, in the 1991 coup.

Further complicating the task of reorganizing the former Soviet military are internal divisions. For example, many resent the rapid political changes that have occurred since the coup and deplore the breakup of the Soviet Union, the historical point of their loyalty. Some officers are still loyal to the discredited Communist party, under which they acquired many benefits, and may hope for its resurgence.

Commonwealth leaders face other problems with the former Soviet military. Many ex-Soviet officers complain about living conditions, which have deteriorated sharply for them, underlining the new reality of their loss of prestige in the post-Communist era. In addition, a reduced investment in the military and changes in foreign policy in Afghanistan and Central/Eastern Europe brought home several hundred thousand uniformed personnel to an economy that has little means of supporting them. Soviet forces pouring into Russia, Byelorus, and Ukraine from Central/Eastern Europe have endured severe hardships, especially in the form of cramped living quarters and salaries that have become worthless.

Unless the republics resolve these problems, the armed forces may well be trouble for them, although the officers affirmed in early 1992 their loyalty to the C.I.S. Nevertheless, the military remains the most physically powerful institution in the former Soviet republics, and many officers are impatient with the civilian leadership, which seems unwilling or unable to settle the future of the armed forces in a manner congenial to them. It would be foolish of the republic leaders to underestimate the ability of the military to make a bid for power, especially since they might find support from a large array of alienated groups. Without a unified command, territorial armies will be created. A Russian Army under Russian national control has already been established—something no other republic wanted. Steps toward the Russian Army were taken in March 1992, when the Yeltsin government announced the establishment of a new Russian Ministry of Defense.

CONTROLLING ETHNOCULTURAL NATIONALISTIC RIVALRIES

In the early months of 1992 divisive interrepublic as well as intrarepublic rivalries threatened open conflict in the C.I.S. Russia and Ukraine had serious differences, as did Armenia, Azerbaijan, and Kazakhstan.

Russia and Ukraine

Russia and Ukraine differ over trade, ethnocultural issues, the disposition of the former Soviet government's Black Sea naval fleet, control of the Crimea, and the prospect of Russia's overweening influence in the Commonwealth. Relations between the two republics are strained and compromise the already fragile unity of the C.I.S.

Trade

Ukrainian officials complain about Russia's failure, despite bilateral trade agreements, to fulfill promises of oil deliveries. Ukraine depends on Russia for oil and, with the collapse of the centrally managed Soviet oil industry, supplies have become increasingly haphazard. From Ukraine's point of view, the problem starts at the point of production, namely, in Russia, where distributors demand "extras" such as meat, sugar, and grain before they will ship oil.

The Black Sea Fleet and Other Military Issues

Russia and Ukraine are at odds over the ultimate disposition of the Black Sea fleet of the former Soviet Navy deployed in Ukrainian waters. In early January 1992 Ukraine ordered the entire Black Sea fleet to take an oath of loyalty. Russia is very sensitive about the legendary fleet, for several reasons. It is historically the core of the Russian Imperial Navy, beginning in the eighteenth century; it is responsible for the protection of Commonwealth interests in the Mediterranean, where the U.S. Sixth Fleet is deployed; and half of the Black Sea fleet's ships are capable of carrying nuclear arms. Russians have said that it must remain under the command of the Commonwealth. But Ukraine insisted in the early months of 1992 on its right to command the fleet and to try to enforce the oath of loyalty.

In March another military issue surfaced when Ukrainian President Kravchuk put a halt to further transfers of former Soviet nuclear weapons to Russia. Kravchuk said that he wanted to make sure that they were being destroyed properly and were not being redeployed in Russia. He asked the West for financial and technical assistance in disposing of the weapons on Ukrainian soil. Perhaps he really wanted to strengthen Ukraine's military capabilities vis-à-vis its neighbors, in particular Russia. Although the possibility of an armed conflict with Russia is remote, it is not inconceivable, given the growing differences between Ukraine and Russia over Crimea, over the condition of Russians living in Ukraine, and over the whole question of a dominant Russian influence over the C.I.S.

The Crimea

Closely related to the confrontation between Russia and Ukraine over the Black Sea fleet is control of the Crimea. Russian Vice President Rutskoy, along with other Russian leaders, want the Crimea, which was transferred to Ukrainian jurisdiction in 1954 by then-Soviet Communist Party leader Nikita Khrushchev, returned to Russia. To them the Crimea remains an inseparable part of Russia to which it belonged since the late eighteenth century, when Russian Czarina Catherine II emancipated it from Ottoman Turkish rule. Moreover, the Crimea is inhabited predominantly by Russians. Complicating the issue, at least for the Russian side, is the division of opinion about the Crimea between Rutskoy and Yeltsin. Yeltsin is less eager than is his vice president to provoke the Ukrainians and further complicate Russia's relations with them.

When the Ukrainians rejected Russian claims, Yeltsin backed off and in February 1992 acknowledged Ukraine's sovereignty over the Crimea. The Russian government, however, expressed concern when Ukraine decided to allow the return of the Tatars to their old home in the Crimea. The Russian population in the Crimea has made it plain that it does not welcome the Tatars and looks to Moscow to protect its economic, political, and cultural interests.

Russian Influence in the C.I.S.

Ukraine and other republics have taken issue with Russia's claim to be the equivalent of the legal heir to the Soviet state and, therefore, first among equals in the Commonwealth. In their view, Yeltsin railroaded them into an acceptance of Russian predominance and of Russia's right to the spoils of the Soviet state. Ukraine has assailed Russia for laying claim to all Soviet missions abroad and, in particular, for raising the Russian tricolor to the exclusion of the flags of other republics over those missions.

Ukrainian anxieties about Russia are not without justification. In the period following the August 1991 coup Russia took control of many former Soviet ministries. Russia turned the august Soviet Academy of Sciences into a Russian academy. While the academy had always been headquartered in Moscow, the capital of the Russian heartland, and its members were for the most part Russian, the gesture reinforced fears of Russia's ambitions for cultural hegemony in the Commonwealth.

Armenia and Azerbaijan

The establishment of the Commonwealth in December 1991 coincided with a renewal of violence between Armenians and Azerbaijani in Nagorno-Karabakh. The spark apparently occurred when Armenians allegedly shot down an Azerbaijani helicopter by heat-seeking missiles at the end of January 1992. The intensity of the fighting appeared to mark a new phase in the nearly 4-year-old battle for Nagorno-Karabakh. In response to Armenian requests that the Commonwealth intervene to stop the fighting, Russian Foreign Minister Andrei Kozyrev hosted a conference with Armenian and Azerbaijani leaders in Moscow in late February. The Russian initiative seemed to have some success, because the Armenian and Azerbaijani diplomats agreed to an immediate ceasefire in Nagorno-Karabakh. They agreed to a Russian proposal to set up a negotiating commission consisting of Russian, Armenian, and Azerbaijani representatives. Presumably in response to the Armenian concession in September 1991, in which Yerevan renounced any claims to the territory of Nagorno-Karabakh, the Azerbaijani side agreed to allow participation in the tripartite discussions of representatives of Nagorno-Karabakh. Armenians, with the knowledge, if not support, of the Armenian republic government in Yerevan, attacked Azerbaijani villages in Nagorno-Karabakh. Thus, while officials in Baku and Yerevan might have compromised over the administration of the Armenian minority concentrated in Nagorno-Karabakh, Armenians in the region took matters into their own hands against Azerbaijani villages, when troops of the former Soviet Ministry of the Interior deployed in the disputed area by Gorbachev were evacuated on orders from the Yeltsin government, which was worried about Russians getting caught between the combatants.

Russia wants a resolution of the conflict between Armenia and Azerbaijan because its continuation is likely eventually to involve Iran, which has small minorities of Azerbaijani and Armenian peoples. The Iranian government envisions a crisis that could compromise Iran's stability, security, and reputation in the Islamic world. At the very least, Iran has an interest in mediating between Armenia and Azerbaijan to preclude the interference of Turkey, which also is interested in the development of ethnic nationalism in the Caucasus. The Russian government would like to discourage the intrusion of these outside powers in the internal affairs of Commonwealth republics on Russia's southern border.

But the capacity of the Russians to mediate is limited, given the military resources that would be needed in Nagorno-Karabakh to keep peace. Moreover, there are both economic and political pressures on the Yeltsin government not to get involved. Finally, the dispute between the Azerbaijani and Armenians is so intractable that it requires a Solomon-like settlement which, at least at the moment, eludes the Russian leadership.

Kazakhstan and Russia

Kazakhstan also has problems with Russia, some of them involving national pride. Yeltsin in mid-December 1991 said that eventually all the former Soviet republics would eliminate nuclear weapons—except Russia. Kazak President

Nursultan Nazarbayev responded that Kazakhstan would retain its nuclear missiles as long as Russia did. He said that Kazakhstan was willing to put its nuclear missiles together with those of Russia and the other republics under a unified command of the new C.I.S. but that Kazakhstan would not disarm unilaterally before Russia. Kazakh officials also said that they would eventually seek a seat in the United Nations; they threatened resistance to Russia's assumption of the Soviet seat on the Security Council.

INTERNATIONAL PROBLEMS AND POLICIES

It is still not clear to what extent the leaders of Russia and the other former Soviet republics share the ancient anxieties about powerful neighbors on their frontiers. Some ex-Soviet officers have argued strongly and persuasively that the new independent republics, lacking the unity and cohesion of the old Soviet Union, are indeed fair game for aggressive outsiders.

But the former Soviet republics do share a need for economic, financial, and technical aid from the West in order to ease the transition to a market economy. Some of the republics that have nuclear weapons, notably Russia, Ukraine, Byelorus, and Kazakhstan, must assure the West that the nuclear-weapons arsenal of the former Soviet state will be controlled and will not fall into the possession of foreign countries.

In addressing these and other international problems, the policies of the C.I.S. and its constituent members are likely to follow the principles of New Thinking adopted by the Gorbachev leadership. This means an aversion to the use of force to further international interests and to cooperate with foreign countries in the solution of such cross-national problems as environmental decay. Political diplomacy and reliance on such international organizations as the United Nations and the World Court will protect national interests. Russia and other C.I.S. members will also rely on confidence-building measures designed to improve interstate relations, and on international organizations, starting with the United Nations and including the International Monetary Fund and World Bank.

Having said all of the above, it is also true that in the first half of 1992 it was still too early to identify a "Commonwealth foreign policy." There is no Commonwealth foreign ministry, no Commonwealth foreign minister, and no Commonwealth foreign-policy strategy accepted by all C.I.S. members. Rather, each of the former Soviet republics seems determined to pursue its own foreign-policy goals, based on its self-perceived national interests.

Russian Foreign Policy

The major focal points of the Russian republic's foreign policy in the early months of 1992 were Europe, the United States, and Japan. The Yeltsin leadership seemed willing to continue the spirit as well as the substance of the conciliatory policies of the late Soviet government under Gorbachev.

Europe

Russia will continue to be concerned with the Baltic countries, in particular Finland and Lithuania, with Central/Europe, and with Germany. Yeltsin tried to strengthen Russia's relations with these countries in late 1991 and early 1992 to enhance Russian security and to obtain needed economic help.

Finland. Yeltsin agreed to abandon Finlandization policy, or the neutralization of Finnish international behavior imposed on Helsinki by the Stalinist government after World War II. This attempt to reduce Finish animosity toward Russia, which dates back to the Soviet invasion of Finland in 1939, will set the tone as the Russians develop economic ties with Helsinki.

The Finns will welcome improved relations. Historically, in the trade relationship between Finland and the former Soviet state, the Finns sent 25 percent of their exports to the Soviet Union. Goods ranging from giant icebreakers to tuxedos worn by Soviet musicians went to the Soviet Union in return for Soviet oil and gas. Finland needs Russia perhaps more than Russia needs Finland, judging from the economic dislocation that the Finns have suffered as a result of the collapse of the Soviet state and the ensuing decline in trade. Moreover, because Finland had oriented its export industries toward the Russian market, it has still another incentive to expand trade with Russia.

The Baltic Republics. Post-Communist Russia will carefully and discreetly have to develop relations with the newly independent Baltic republics. The Baltic peoples, especially Lithuanians, are very sensitive about Russia because of the long and harsh Soviet administration. They have been trying to remove all traces of the Soviet presence, notably signs with the Cyrillic alphabet, statues of Lenin, and pictures of the hammer and sickle.

Right now trade is chaotic. Russia no longer sells and therefore no longer buys as it did in the past, causing hardship for the Baltic peoples, who are not yet prepared to buy from and sell to Western markets. Historic patterns of trade with Russia and other former Soviet republics have been completely disrupted.

Other Russo-Baltic problems are territorial. The Yeltsin government wants to continue to administer the Russian city of Kaliningrad, once part of Germany and strategically important to Russia because of its naval base on the Baltic. Kaliningrad, however, is territorially cut off from the rest of Russia by Lithuania and Poland. Also, about 128,000 officers and soldiers of the former Soviet Army are in the Baltic republics. These countries want them withdrawn immediately because of their fear that these troops could jeopardize their independence, say, in supporting a coup against the nationalist governments in Vilnius, Riga, and Tallinn.

There are large Russian minorities in each of the three

Baltic states. Russia worries that they may face discrimination, especially since they were encouraged by successive Soviet leaderships to colonize the Baltic republics and were given privileged economic positions. Now many Russians in the Baltics consider themselves native and want to stay where their children were born. A possible straw in the wind of change for these Russians is the view of Estonian nationalist Tiit Made, a member of the Estonian Parliament in Tallinn, who said that the current 25 deputies representing Russians in the parliament ought to be reduced to 7 or 8.

Despite these strains, Russia would like to strengthen ties with the Baltic republics to further its economic and strategic interests. Some hope—in vain—to bring the Baltic republics into the Commonwealth. In February 1992, in a conciliatory tone, Russia agreed to begin an immediate withdrawal of former Soviet forces from Lithuania and to leave some weapons behind to bolster the Vilnius government.

Central/Eastern Europe. Russia's interests in Central/Eastern Europe parallel those of the late Soviet Union and again center on trade and security. But the former Soviet satellites are hypersensitive to links that in any way would compromise their newly won sovereignty, never mind obstructing their inexorable orientation westward.

Russia and Poland have differed over the speed of Moscow's withdrawal of former Soviet forces from Poland and the rapid decline of Russian trade. While Yeltsin pledged to have all Soviet troops out of Poland by the end of 1992, much earlier than was originally envisaged, the troops were literally stripping the areas they occupied of everything that was removable and leaving the facilities they used in profound disrepair. Polish officials are furious and have presented the Russian government with demands for huge monetary compensation.

The Russian government sharply curtailed the delivery of oil and natural gas to Poland, primarily as a result of a decline of output caused by problems connected with machine maintenance and strikes. The Russian move caused havoc in the already enfeebled Polish economy. Polish factories had to reduce operations, and overall productivity declined. Since the Polish economy has not yet developed new import-export relationships with the West—and is unlikely to do so in the near future—this problem means a crippling setback to Poland's plans for economic recovery.

Western Europe. Russia wants to strengthen ties with the West, to obtain Western technology and financial assistance. Yeltsin insists that the Cold War is over and that Russia is now an ally. Early in 1992 Yeltsin proposed Russian membership in NATO. His eagerness to join the West, so different from the former Soviet state, has confounded Western leaders, who have responded cautiously to his overtures.

Yeltsin has looked to Germany for aid. In November 1991 he went to Germany to meet with political and economic leaders. He strengthened Russo-German relations by signing a statement with Chancellor Helmut Kohl pledging cooperation in a wide range of areas, including arms control, scientific research, and the protection of minorities. Kohl added that Germany was very interested in helping Russia exploit its vast oil and gas reserves and complimented Yeltsin for his stalwart commitment to reform. Yeltsin reciprocated by affirming the end of any hostility between the two nations generated in World War II.

But Yeltsin's effort to deal with the problem of the German minority living in Russia, the so-called Volga Germans, has been difficult. This issue concerns the fate of 2 million ethnic Germans who were deprived by Stalin of their administrative autonomy following the German invasion of the Soviet Union in June 1941. The former Volga German autonomous republic occupied an area straddling the Volga River, in the vicinity of the northwest tip of the Caspian Sea, of about 11,000 square miles. At that time Stalin also moved about 400,000 Volga Germans to Siberia in retaliation for the Nazi invasion. Bonn has asked Yeltsin to honor a pledge he gave Kohl during a meeting in December 1991 to restore an autonomous republic to the 2 million Volga Germans. Bonn expects that restoration of the old Volga republic, with guaranteed rights for Germans, will discourage their mass migration to Germany.

Yeltsin's main problem in accommodating Bonn on this issue is the resistance of Russians who were transplanted in the late 1940s and afterward and who now oppose German administrative control. Yeltsin has said that the boundaries of any autonomous republic for the Volga Germans will include only the territory where 90 percent of the population are German. He has offered an area that is about 1,900 square miles in size. The Volga Germans have rejected this offer and have looked to Bonn for support of their claim to the original size of their republic.

The United States. Yeltsin has gone out of his way to cultivate good relations with Washington. In late January 1992, in a visit to the United Nations in New York, Yeltsin announced that Russia is an ally of the United States, thus officially declaring an end to the Cold War. Washington has responded to Yeltsin's overtures with caution and restraint.

In the weeks and months following the anti-Gorbachev coup and the replacement of the Soviet state with the Commonwealth, the Bush administration let events get ahead of it. The U.S. Congress took the lead, appropriating $100 million for the members of the C.I.S. to dismantle nuclear weapons, to transport emergency supplies of food and medicine, and to catalyze private-sector involvement in the post-Soviet economy.

The Congress certainly did not invest much, considering the mammoth problems of the new Commonwealth. But there is reluctance to undertake an aid program of Marshall Plan dimensions. Critics say that massive aid programs to the former Soviet republics should await the replacement of all authoritarian structures by genuine democracy. Some U.S. economists have argued that massive short-term aid is not what the Soviets need. In their view, technological and managerial assistance to increase the efficiency of the transportation and communications infrastructure are more important than credits to buy American goods. Moreover, they argue, virtually all the resources for restructuring and rebuilding the Russian economy should come from private foreign investors and from the downsizing of the former Soviet military. Because Russia lacks basic institutions such as property rights, a commercial code, and sound money without which markets cannot work, many Western economists believe that money from abroad would be wasted, stolen, or, worse, would dampen the spontaneous growth of the private sector by strengthening the old bureaucracy.

By the end of 1991 the Bush administration was ready to give some help to Russia, but on a far smaller scale than the Marshall Plan and far less than what the Western European countries, especially Germany, wanted the United States to give. To discuss the formation and implementation of a broad-scale multinational aid program to the republics, the United States and other Western nations met in Washington in January 1992. On the eve of this Coordinating Conference, the United States pledged $645 million of economic assistance to the republics. It also endorsed the admission of Russia and several other ex-Soviet republics to the IMF and the World Bank as a means of encouraging their development of market-driven economies.

At the end of the Coordinating Conference, on January 23, 1992, the United States announced further aid. Secretary of State James Baker spoke of plans to send 2,000 American farm volunteers, for periods of up to 3 years, to work directly with farmers. The country also established a fund of $25 million, called the Eurasian Foundation for Democracy, to help strengthen free-market institutions throughout the former Soviet economy.

Washington joined other members of the so-called Group of Seven industrialized nations in establishing a multibillion-dollar fund to help stabilize the ruble. The Bush administration, however, has not been as supportive of this gesture as some of the other members of the Group of Seven. Russia's high inflation rate, its large budget deficit, and the primitive banking system inherited from the Soviet past all suggest that the ruble may not be stabilized for a long time. Washington has linked a permanent U.S. commitment to the fund to Russia's willingness to accept IMF advice on economic discipline. For example, the IMF recommended raising the price of oil domestically and exporting more of it to help reduce the budget deficit.

Another issue in Russian-American relations is how nuclear materials and the know-how of atomic scientists of the former Soviet government will be handled. The old Soviet state exercised a tight and efficient control over the movement of goods and personnel across internal as well as foreign borders, and this meant control over nuclear and other strategic technologies and expertise. To the dismay of U.S. leaders, the Commonwealth seems unable to duplicate this control. Like the former Soviet defense ministries, enterprises involved in special weapons and missile programs face cuts in military funding, and they may well try to stay in business by selling equipment, materials, and services in the international marketplace. According to CIA chief Robert Gates, at the end of December 1991, thousands of Soviet scientists, fleeing starvation wages and slashed research budgets, had already emigrated.

The Bush administration has taken steps to discourage the proliferation of nuclear technology by providing assistance to Russian nuclear scientists to keep them from accepting offers to work in Third World nations. The administration plans to subsidize scientists willing to work on the peaceful uses of nuclear power or to provide expertise in the dismantling of weapons systems. Furthermore, the United States has sent experts to the republics to help them dismantle and disable large chunks of the former Soviet Union's nuclear arsenal. However, the Russians have made it plain to Washington that they have no intention of dismantling their nuclear capability without reciprocal gestures from the United States.

The United States wants Russian cooperation in the negotiation of further reduction in nuclear arsenals. While Yeltsin assured the United States that he and the leaders of the other republics intended to abide by the arms-control treaties signed by Gorbachev, the Bush administration wanted to go further in arms reduction, especially in multiwarhead missiles, which are the core of each country's nuclear capability. On the eve of the president's State of the Union address in January 1992, U.S. Defense Department officials proposed sharp reductions in U.S. land-based, multiple-warhead missiles without any conditions, while other cuts might be offered if the republics act reciprocally. If the republics embrace land-based cuts, the United States might pare warheads and halt weapons-modernization plans for the strategic submarine fleet. The next 2 years will show if this strategy of "first cuts" will pay off.

Japan. In early 1992 Japan still insisted that it could not extend a major economic aid program to Russia without a settlement of the issue of the offshore islands in the northern Pacific (Etoforu, Kunashiri, Shikotan, and the Habomais group). Japan was willing to provide emergency food and medical assistance to Russia and to go forward with a consortium, led by the Mitsui Corporation, to undertake exploration of reserves of oil and gas off Sakhalin Island. Private Japanese investors, however, are reluctant to go into Russia without government guarantees, which will not be forthcoming unless Russia returns the offshore islands to Japanese sovereignty.

A transfer of the islands to Japan is problematical for strategic and nationalistic reasons. The Russian government, like its Soviet predecessor, considers the islands, despite their small size and population and lack of mineral resources, important to the security of Russia, with their proximity to its Pacific missile and naval deployments. At the same time the Russians are experiencing, as is true of the other former Soviet republics, an episode of hypernationalism, which translates into a sensitivity to the loss of any Russian territory. In March 1992, however, there seemed to be a softening in the Russian position. Moscow was willing to split the difference and return two of the four islands, probably in response to its desperate economic situation and the equally desperate need of foreign assistance.

The Central Asian Republics and the Outside World

While committed to good relations with the West and with their rich and powerful Slavic neighbors—Russia and Ukraine—the five Central Asian republics of the former Soviet Union (Kazakhstan, Uzbekistan, Turkmenistan, Tajikistan, and Kyrghyzstan) have focused increasing attention on Central Asia and the Middle East. They have special strategic, economic, and religiocultural interests in India, Pakistan, Iran, Turkey, Saudi Arabia, and Afghanistan.

Relations With Other Islamic Countries

The former Soviet republics in Central Asia have found Islamic countries to be very interested in developing close relations with them. Conservative Islamic countries such as Saudi Arabia and other Persian Gulf members of the Gulf Cooperation Council have begun to channel economic assistance to them with the aim of discouraging their orientation toward countries such as Iran. Indeed, a fierce competition for supremacy in Soviet Central Asia seems to be in the making between Turkey and Iran and between Saudi Arabia and Pakistan.

The governments of the Central Asian Republics have a special interest in Turkey. Its Western orientation and its apparent success as a secular state with an Islamic population with democratic institutions and a free market make it a model. While these considerations appeal to the ex-Soviet elites who are not infatuated with Islamic fundamentalism, ordinary people have shown a sympathy for the Iranian model of a state governed by Islamic law. If Western-inspired economic reforms, especially in the smaller and poorer republics such as Tajikistan and Turkmenistan, fail to improve economic output, a susceptibility to Islamic fundamentalism as an alternative to the secular governments that now rule them is likely to increase. If that happens, Iran will gain an advantage over other Islamic countries in strengthening ties with ex-Soviet republics in Central Asia.

Working against Iranian interests in the Central Asian republics are their secular legacy from the long period of Communist rule and the fact that many of the region's Muslims are Sunni, not Shia (Shi'ite), as in Iran. Kyrghyzstan President Askar Akayev has denounced Islamic fundmentalism and expressed a preference for links with Turkey. The prospect that Iranian fundamentalism will sweep through the former Soviet republics in Central Asia seems unlikely, since Iran has not been such a success story that everyone wants to emulate it. When former Azerbaijani President Mutalibov was asked about the threat of Iranian influence, he dismissed the question as "stupid."

In February 1992 diplomats from Iran, Pakistan, and Turkey met in Teheran to welcome the leaders of the five Central Asian republics and of Muslim Azerbaijan to a regional summit of Central Asian Islamic countries. They revived the long-dormant Economic Cooperation Organization with three of the former Soviet republics: Turkmenistan, Uzbekistan, and Azerbaijan. The ECO had been established in 1963 by Iran, Pakistan, and Turkey. Officials of the other republics were present at a meeting of the ECO as observers, and their formal membership was being considered. In addressing the large summit meeting, Iranian President Rafsanjani emphasized the shared problems of the Central Asian Islamic countries and the need for their cooperation and solidarity.

But cooperation so far remains elusive, with the Turks and Iranians, long rivals, holding different concepts of Islamic solidarity. The Turks want to create an Islamic version of the European Community in Central Asia, while Iran, supported by Pakistan, wants to emphasize the religious and cultural component of the community of Central Asian Islamic states. Nevertheless, discussion of tariff reductions, a common market for agricultural products, and the creation of a common development bank to compete with a Saudi-based Islamic bank already operating in Central Asia comprise the beginning of an Islamic-based cooperation, at least in economic matters.

There is also much interest in and discussion of an EC-type regional confederation, which might be called Turkestan. This would comprise the five Central Asian republics. But the Uzbek nationalist leader and poet Muhammed Salik thinks that this is a dream because the five former Soviet Central Asian republics have more dividing them than bringing them together. Each has acquired a separate national identity which stands in the way of a Turkestani federation. Nevertheless, it is also true, as Salik has said, that the republics cannot live apart from one another. They need one another. When the advantages of unification became evident, union might well occur.

Relations With the United States

The Central Asian republics also want good relations with the United States but, like Russia, have found the Bush administration cautious and ambivalent. In mid-February 1992 Secretary of State Baker toured the five Central Asian Republics and discussed establishment of formal American ties. He made clear U.S. interests. He spoke of the development of democratic government, respect for human rights, and curbs on arms production and deployment. The leaders of the republics were responsive, assuring Baker that their governments would respect human rights and refrain from exporting uranium to other Muslim countries. But it remains to be seen whether the Central Asian leaderships will live up to these assurances. Several of the Central Asian leaders are ex-Communists who have already displayed an intolerance of political opposition. For example, Abdul Rakhman Puklatov, an Uzbek opposition leader, told Baker that the opposition in Uzbekistan still has no democratic freedoms and that total-itarianism is still operating in his country even though it seemed to have been destroyed in Moscow.

Working to the advantage of the Central Asian leaderships in their dealings with the United States is the enormous mineral wealth some of them have, in particular Kazakhstan and Tajikistan, and their susceptibility to Iranian influence, which the Bush administration wants to contain. Washington, therefore, is willing to be cooperative and take the Central Asian leaders at their word on developing liberal and demo-cratic governments.

THE FUTURE OF THE C.I.S.

The chances of the Commonwealth's survival are mixed. On the negative side is a multiplicity of ethnic-based political and cultural nationalisms, which divide the republics against one another and make cooperation among them difficult. Moreover, most of the non-Russian republics of the C.I.S. fear the restoration of a powerful, presumptuous, and Rus-sian-dominated central government like that of the Soviet national government. Ukraine sees the Commonwealth as a temporary phenomenon, nothing more than a "breathing space . . . on the way to full independence." It is, as one high-ranking official observed, likely that Ukraine will stay in the C.I.S. only as long as it takes to stabilize its economy and develop viable government institutions.

Ukraine is not alone in its cautious approach. Leaders of the 11 republics, meeting in Minsk at the end of December 1991 to discuss further development of the Commonwealth, carefully avoided use of the word "union." In their deter-mination to avoid re-creating anything that even faintly resembles the former Soviet state, they spoke of the C.I.S. as neither a state nor a superstate structure. While they had no trouble agreeing to cooperate in a variety of practical matters, ranging from aviation to joint work on cleaning up the fallout from Chernobyl, there were intensely heated exchanges over issues relating to sovereignty of the republics in the area of defense, economic reform, and the future shape and central structures of the C.I.S. In these discussions, Ukraine was again the staunchest in rejecting anything that infringed on its claims to sovereignty. This summit failed to produce a charter, a cohesive plan for economic reform, or agreement on a united military force.

But the forecast is not all bad. The Commonwealth has some strengths. By offering an acceptable framework within which to cooperate and coordinate, the C.I.S. can provide its republics with a basis for the resolution of regional ambitions by nonviolent means. It also offers the republics a chance to start the reform process so desperately needed to reverse economic deterioration.

Despite their strong drives for independence and separate development, most of the C.I.S. is held together by economic interdependencies which go back over several centuries. Members of the Commonwealth are also joined through the irreversible mixture of peoples in different republics, as a result of Soviet policy after World War II of moving ethnic populations across republic borders. Finally, they share a legacy of 70 years of socialist development, which left all the republics impoverished. They need to deal with that legacy collectively rather than individually. Indeed, expanding co-operation among them is inevitable. Most leaders of the republics agreed with Uzbekistan's President Islam Karimov that "today there is no alternative to a Commonwealth of Independent States," and host President Shushkevich of Byelarus noted that at least everybody listened to each other attentively, even if they did a lot of fighting and could agree on very little.

Patterns of Future Development

As the Commonwealth works out its future, there are three kinds of confederative arrangements that it might pursue. One is based on ethnicity. A second is based on economic integration. The third is based on regional cooperation.

Ethnic Union

One kind of development is to have the large ethnic constitu-encies work together instead of against one another. Mem-bers of the C.I.S. need a system that will protect the interests of the small republics against the policies of the large republics. The republics also need enough internal autonomy to run their own affairs. Unfortunately, the prospects for such a model are uncertain. Right now the Russian republic is dominant. Also, there has been an extraordinary prolifera-tion of politically motivated party groups, tending to frag-ment the political environment of individual republics and complicate their participation in the C.I.S. The enormous size of the Commonwealth also is a liability, in the sense that it is difficult for so many republics to allow decisions to be made centrally.

The great complexity of the challenges facing post-Soviet governments—namely, to create market economies, priva-tize, reindustrialize, and alleviate consumer shortages—is not conducive to elite cooperation, especially with the ex-treme ethnic heterogeneity that now prevails in the Common-wealth. The peoples of the C.I.S. lack an overarching political loyalty to a common identity that could mitigate the conflict-producing diversity of its society.

Still another problem for the development of the Com-monwealth into an ethnic union concerns the proliferation of small conflict-ridden minorities inside the heterogeneous republics. Some 65 million people live outside their titular national territory or are members of an ethnic group that has no territorial unit. Approximately 25 million Russians live outside the Russian republic, primarily in Ukraine and Kazakhstan. This Russian diaspora presents one of the most serious challenges to any attempts to link ethnic background to a republic's identity. Yeltsin warned at the end of August 1991 that the borders of Ukraine and Kazakhstan might have to be adjusted if those republics decide to be independent. He

				The beginning of Lenin's New Economic Plan **1921**		The 15th party Congress; the expulsion of Trotsky from the Communist party; Stalin's dominance is affirmed	The beginning of the first 5-year plan to nationalize all industry and collectivize agriculture		
The Bolshevik-Menshevik split in Russian Social Democratic Party (RSDP); the emergence of a separate party, called the Bolsheviks by 1912	Bloody Sunday Massacre; the Revolution of 1905; the October Manifesto	Abdication of Czar Nicholas II; set-up of the provisional government; the Bolshevik Revolution	Founding of the Comintern	The formation of the Soviet Union	Lenin dies			Stalin's purges begin	Pact with Nazi Germany
1902	**1905**	**1917**	**1919**	**1922**	**1924**	**1927**	**1928**	**1934**	**1939**

(United Nations photo)

The Lenin Mausoleum, flanked by the Church of St. Basil on the left and the Kremlin on the right, contains the remains of Lenin in a crystal sarcophagus. Built of granite and completed in 1930, it was the Soviet Union's equivalent of the Washington Monument and Lincoln Memorial.

provoked a sharp response from the leaders of both republics that such attitudes threaten to provoke a civil war.

Economic Union

The C.I.S. might also develop primarily as an economic community based on economic interdependence and mutual self-interest. Steps in this direction had already been taken in the fall of 1991, with the creation of an Interrepublic Economic Committee to coordinate economic relations among the former republics. A draft treaty for a Eurasian Economic Community, drawn up by Yavlinksy and presented to the republics on September 16, 1991, envisioned a common currency and banking system, open trade between republics, free migration of labor, and coordinated tax policies, with each republic allowed to issue its own internal currency but required to use rubles when engaging in interrepublic trade. A further step toward the creation of an

economic community was also taken on September 16, when members of the newly created Soviet State Council agreed on the need to coordinate food aid throughout the winter. In early October representatives of the 12 Soviet republics and Latvia met in Alma Ata to discuss further details of an economic community and to sign an economic agreement.

But nationalist passions have interfered with economic union. Leaders and their bureaucratic lieutenants are under fire by popularly elected parliaments to act on those passions. For example, Ukraine, the second largest, wealthiest, and most populous of the republics, had been critical of Gorbachev's proposal of an economic union in September 1991, because it would have too much of the old union in it and would give rise to a new, powerful, intrusive central government at the expense of newly gained local sovereignty. Ukraine wanted greater control over the spending of funds that it would contribute to the central government and greater freedom to manage Ukraine's share of the Soviet

| Nazi invasion of the Soviet Union **1941** | Formation of CMEA **1949** | Formation of the Warsaw Pact; cultural thaw **1955** | Anti-party crisis; Gromyko becomes the foreign minister **1957** | Khrushchev is ousted; the Brezhnev phase begins **1964** | The Nixon-Brezhnev summit in Moscow **1972** | The new Soviet Constitution; party General Secretary Brezhnev is elected president | SALT II agreements are signed; the Soviets invade Afghanistan **1979** |
| Annexation of the Baltic states **1940** | End of World War II **1945** | Stalin dies; the Khrushchev phase begins **1953** | The 20th party Congress affirms de-Stalinization **1956** | Khrushchev assumes the premiership **1958** | The Soviet invasion of Czechoslovakia **1968** | The Helsinki Accords are signed **1975** | **1977** |

1980s–1990s

Union's $68 billion foreign debt. When it eventually did agree, on November 14, to join the economic union, after the Yeltsin government agreed to take responsibility for 60 percent of the Soviet debt, it did so reluctantly, with grave misgivings. Even in Russia, which would surely dominate any economic union of the former Soviet republics, there is a fear that poorer, less developed republics might drain resources from Russia.

Regional Cooperation

Should the Commonwealth fail, some of its features will remain as it divides into subsets of former republics, possibly in combination with outside states. Two areas in particular have experienced significant regional cooperation: the Baltics and Central Asia. Since early 1990 the Baltic states have held joint sessions of their parliaments and have coordinated economic policies. Some sentiment also exists for integrating the Baltic states into a transnational Scandinavian community. Since 1990 the Central Asian republics also have engaged in efforts to create a regional organization, with the signing that year of a regional cooperation agreement that envisioned broad-based economic cooperation among the five Central Asian republics of Kazakhstan, Uzbekistan, Turkmenistan, Kyrghyzstan, and Tajikistan. Only days before the August 1991 coup, the leaders of these republics had met in Tashkent and established a permanent commission to coordinate implementation of the cooperation agreement. Azerbaijan has expressed interest in joining the group, which some Central Asian observers have begun to call "Greater Turkestan."

Brezhnev-Andropov-Chernenko-Gorbachev successions; Gorbachev implements glasnost and perestroika

Lithuanian, Georgian, and Russian parliaments declare sovereignty

Traumatic explosions of popular discontent in the Baltics, Armenia, and Azerbaijan; the Baltic republics are given large amounts of political and economic autonomy

Communist party conservatives try but fail to halt reform of the Union and oust Gorbachev from power

The Soviet Union allows decommun-ization and desatelli-zation in Central/Eastern Europe

Gorbachev resigns as party chief and Yeltsin suspends Communist party activity in Russia

Leaders of Russia, Byelorus, and Ukraine declare an end of the Soviet Union and the establishment of the Commonwealth of Independent States

Disintegration and collapse of the Soviet Union

The advantages of regionalism within the C.I.S. are several. Regionalism reduces the complexity involved in managing a community by reducing the number of participants. In some cases, it could also provide a cultural cohesion to transnational organizations which, with a larger number of participants, would otherwise be lacking. On the other hand, regionalism is unlikely to be a workable arrangement for all the former Soviet republics. For example, nationalist passions in the Transcaucasus (Armenia vs. Azerbaijan) make regionalism there impractical, and it is not inconceivable that interethnic rivalries among the Islamic peoples of Central Asia may compromise regionalism in that area as well. While Central Asian elites have moved in the direction of cooperation, at the mass level there has been intense nationalist-inspired violence.

DEVELOPMENT

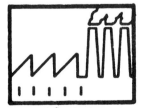

Russia and the other former Soviet republics are following their own separate paths of development away from socialism with Russia moving very quickly and the Central Asian republics moving very slowly. In any event, the economies of all the republics in the C.I.S. still are under extensive central control and experiencing severe hardship.

FREEDOM

Much progress has been made toward parliamentary democracy in most of the C.I.S. republics. Presidential heads of state are now elected directly by the people, prime ministers and their cabinets as well as presidents must respond to public criticism of their administrative leadership, and the overall political environment is more pluralistic than ever.

HEALTH/WELFARE

While the extensive cradle-to-grave health and welfare system inherited from the Soviet Communist past is still in place, historic problems of inadequacy and inefficiency remain and have become worse as a result of economic collapse brought on by moves toward a free-market economy.

ACHIEVEMENTS

In 1992 Russian scientists announced strides in perfecting nuclear-propelled rockets that are twice as energy-efficient as ones that burn chemical fuels, enhancing the prospects for further space travel. The Institute for Marxist-Leninism in Moscow changed its name to the Russian Center for the Study of Documents in Modern History and opened its doors to the public.

Central/Eastern Europe

Sweden

BALTIC SEA

Lithuania

Denmark

Russia

Poland

Berlin

Warsaw

Germany

Byelarus

Ukraine

Prague

Czechoslovakia

Former border
between East
and West Germany

Germany

Austria

• Budapest

Hungary

Moldova

Switzerland

Slovenia

Romania

Croatia

Belgrade

Bucharest

(Yugoslavia)*

Ukraine

Bosnia -
Herzegovina

Serbia

ADRIATIC SEA

Montenegro

Sofia

Italy

Bulgaria

BLACK SEA

Macedonia

Tirana

Albania

TYRRHENIAN SEA

Greece

IONIAN SEA

Turkey

*Yugoslavian state boundaries are graphically interpreted due to continuing disputes.

Central/Eastern Europe: From Dictatorship to Democracy

WHY STUDY CENTRAL/EASTERN EUROPE?

The countries of Central/Eastern Europe—Albania, Bulgaria, Czechoslovakia, the former East Germany (present-day Eastern Germany), Hungary, Poland, Romania, and Yugoslavia—have always been important in world politics. They are the strategic heartland of the great Eurasian landmass that stretches from the Atlantic Ocean in the west to the Ural Mountains in the east. In the past they were the object of intense interest of the large empires on their periphery: Germany, Russia, Austria, and Turkey. Because events in Central/Eastern Europe were at the root of the two world wars in the first half of the twentieth century, political development in Central/Eastern Europe is important to the security of not only Germany, the Scandinavian countries, and the Commonwealth of Independent States, but also of distant outsiders like other countries of Western Europe and the United States.

Central/Eastern Europe is important also because after World War II it came under the rule of Communist parties linked closely to the Soviet Union. In the post–World War II period, most of the Communist party-ruled countries became satellites of Moscow. Satellization meant their acceptance of Soviet political institutions and their subservience to Soviet international policies.

But it is also true—and here is another reason for studying Central/Eastern Europe—that almost all of the countries modified their Soviet-style political systems and developed varying degrees of independence of the Soviet Union. While they shared many characteristics with one another and with the Soviet Union because of their common commitment to communist ideology, they also became differentiated in their domestic and foreign policies.

This diversity contradicted popular notions of sameness among the Central/Eastern Europe countries; of slavish pursuit of a single, Soviet-determined path to socialism and communism; and of abject loyalty and obedience to Soviet foreign policy. Indeed, it was wrong to assume, as many in the West did, Eastern Europe's absolute acceptance of the Soviet path to socialism and communism. Rather, Communist political development in Central/Eastern Europe was polycentric. The countries gradually developed differentiated domestic and foreign policies based on local needs and interests.

Nevertheless, the Central/Eastern European political systems still resembled the Soviet system and were quite subservient to it. Because of their importance to Soviet territorial security and to Soviet global prestige and influence, the Central/Eastern European countries became a sphere of Soviet ideological and strategic predominance.

Finally, it is important to study Central/Eastern Europe because of the extraordinary upheavals that occurred throughout the region in late 1989, leading to rapid decommunization and desatellization. Most Central/Eastern European countries are now in a transitional phase of political development in which they are trying to democratize their national lives. All face severe problems as they move to a new, more liberal political and socioeconomic order; some countries will solve these problems more quickly and effectively than will others.

HOW TO STUDY CENTRAL/EASTERN EUROPE

There are at least two ways to study Central/Eastern Europe. One is a review of the region as a whole. This approach is important because, as compared to other large geographic regions, such as Western Europe, Latin America, and sub-Saharan Africa, the Central/Eastern European region has many commonalities. A second approach, which involves individual country studies, takes into account contrasts among the different countries, their divergence from the Soviet pattern in the era of Communist rule, and their different patterns of democratic development in the post-Communist era. In this book, we look at Central/Eastern Europe in both ways.

THE REGION OF CENTRAL/EASTERN EUROPE

The following review of the Central/Eastern European region consists of nine sections: 1) pre-Communist history; 2) Communist party ascendancy after World War II; 3) Soviet satellization in the late 1940s and early 1950s; 4) conformity with the Soviet model; 5) problems with the Soviet model; 6) divergence from the Soviet model; 7) channels of Soviet influence; 8) causes and consequences of the revolutionary changes that occurred in the region in 1989 and early 1990; and 9) problems in developing political and economic democracy.

PRE-COMMUNIST HISTORY

All of the countries of Central/Eastern Europe are new in comparison with those of Western Europe. They gained political independence only in the last 125 years, after a long period of rule by foreigners. Romania became independent in 1878, Bulgaria in 1908, and Albania in 1912. Poland, Czechoslovakia, and Yugoslavia achieved independence at the end of World War I in 1918. East Germany was carved out of modern Germany by the victorious Allies at the end of World War II.

Foreign Rule
Four great foreign empires occupied most of Central/Eastern Europe for centuries before World War I. The German and Austrian empires partitioned and occupied Poland from the end of the eighteenth century until 1918. The Austrian Empire administered what is now Czechoslovakia, Hungary, and northern Yugoslavia from the fifteenth century until its

demise in World War I. And the Ottoman Turkish Empire, starting in the late fourteenth century, conquered and occupied Romania, Bulgaria, central and southern Yugoslavia, and Albania. The Turks gradually lost control of these areas during the nineteenth century, when there were periodic rebellions against its rule. The empire disintegrated in World War I.

Although all the Central/Eastern European countries had little autonomy while under the rule of foreign empires, some of them fared better than others. Poland, Czechoslovakia, Hungary, and northern Yugoslavia had a limited amount of self-rule; developed some industrialization, which improved the standard of living; and had more contact with Western ideas and institutions than did the southern or Balkan peoples of Romania, Bulgaria, central and southern Yugoslavia, and Albania. These Balkan peoples suffered under Turkish rule, which was oppressive and abusive. They endured religious persecution, onerous taxation, and remained politically and economically underdeveloped well into the twentieth century.

Political Development (1918–1945)
Between World War I and World War II (1918–1939) all the Central/Eastern European countries had at least the appearance of parliamentary and democratic forms of government. But, with the exception of Czechoslovakia, all the countries had become Fascist dictatorships by the end of this 20-year interwar period. The Central/Eastern European peoples could not make democracy work, because they had had little experience with self-rule. They also lacked national leadership that could achieve discipline and unity without undermining popular government. They faced horrendous social and economic problems that burdened their fragile institutions of self-government. After 1933 some ruling groups of Central/Eastern Europe increasingly looked to the Nazi model of totalitarian government to solve these problems and to safeguard society against the spread of communism from the Soviet Union.

In one way or another, the Central/Eastern European countries lost their newly won independence during World War II. Poland, Czechoslovakia, and Yugoslavia were conquered by the Nazis; Romania, Hungary, and Bulgaria became allies and ultimately satellites of the Nazi German state. They were, wittingly or unwittingly, accomplices of Nazi efforts to strengthen German security through political and military control of Central/Eastern Europe and adjacent parts of the Soviet Union.

One explanation for this Central/Eastern European orientation toward Nazi Germany during the 1930s was a strong and long-standing hostility toward the Russians. Most Central/Eastern European peoples disliked the Russians, both for their adoption of communism and for their historic interference in Central/Eastern European affairs. Therefore, on the eve of World War II a number of Central/Eastern

European countries refused to cooperate with the Soviet Union to oppose German expansion.

The Economy
Although there were pockets of industrialization and some urbanization everywhere in Central/Eastern Europe—especially in the north, where there were natural resources for manufacturing, such as coal and iron, and a developed transportation and communications infrastructure—the region as a whole was primarily agricultural and poor. Most of the cultivable land had belonged to a small rural aristocracy. Methods of cultivation remained primitive well into the twentieth century; people and animals continued to do the work that was done by machines in Western Europe. Farming was inefficient not only because of a lack of machines and modern agricultural technology, but also because credit was very difficult to come by and many farms were too small to be economical.

Society
On the eve of the Communist takeover the society of Central/Eastern Europe consisted of four different socioeconomic groups. In addition to a small, affluent landed aristocracy, there was an equally small, new, and well-off entrepreneurial and commercial middle class. This middle class had close ties to the landed aristocracy, out of which it had developed as a result of industrialization. It shared the conservative outlook of the aristocracy, and both classes were political allies. A third class was a small, impoverished, wage-earning proletariat in the cities. This class also was an outgrowth of industrialization.

The largest socioeconomic class was the peasantry. It consisted of two groups: the larger group owned and cultivated small plots of land; other peasants worked on the land of others for a wage.

Most of the societies of the newly independent countries were divided also along ethnocultural lines. The societies of these countries consisted of large and small national groups, many with their own language, religion, and cultural traditions. The new countries inherited multinational societies from the period of foreign rule when large imperial systems administered Central/Eastern Europe and modern boundaries had not yet been drawn.

The largest ethnic groups dominated the political systems of the new countries, because they usually were the most politically advanced and because they had led nationalist movements or political parties in favor of independence and were confirmed in positions of leadership by the Western powers, notably Britain, France, and the United States. In their new countries, the large ethnic groups used their position of dominance to discriminate against minorities, not only politically but also economically and culturally. This discrimination produced interethnic tensions among different ethnic groups within a Central/Eastern European country,

The Kremlin in Moscow. After World War II, despite their historical animosity toward Russians, the Central/Eastern European peoples lived for decades in the shadow of the Soviet Union.

weakening democratic government and increasing its vulnerability to foreign attack.

Czechoslovakia and Yugoslavia had the most serious minorities problems. Obsessed with forging a permanent unity of their multinational societies, in the late 1920s and 1930s Czechoslovak and Yugoslav political leaders strongly resisted the demands of minority groups for administrative decentralization, increased representation in national government, and more equitable distribution of national wealth. Instead, the Czechoslovak and Yugoslav governments went in the opposite direction and tried to promote societal homogenization. Their policies provoked tensions that threatened the stability and ultimately the survival of their countries in the face of Nazi aggression in the late 1930s.

Anti-Semitism

Anti-Semitism was an important aspect of the minorities problem during this pre-Communist period, because Jews were a minority in most of the societies, in particular those of Poland and Romania. Anti-Semitism had existed for centuries and took the form of discrimination against Jews in all aspects of life—in politics, in the economy, and in society. Physical violence against Jews in everyday life, especially in schools, was not unusual.

There were many causes of anti-Semitism in Central/ Eastern Europe. The most important were: the persistence of religious myths about the Jews; their tendency to ghettoize in the major cities like Warsaw, Bucharest, and Budapest; their accumulation of financial wealth and influence through trade and banking; and their determination to preserve their cultural identity, especially language, dress, and values, though many Jews did assimilate the Christian culture in which they lived and worked.

There is little doubt, however, that traditional anti-Semitism in Central/Eastern Europe became very virulent in the 1930s, as a result of the anti-Semitism of Nazi Germany. The national leadership of several Central/Eastern European countries developed close ties with the Nazi government and voluntarily, or under Nazi pressure, made anti-Semitism official policy.

Hostility to Russians

Most of the peoples of Central/Eastern Europe always have had an abiding dislike and fear of Russians. In part, this anti-Russian sentiment is the result of prejudice, of a sense of superiority, and of a belief in the inferiority of Russian civilization.

But anti-Russian feelings are also a response to the historic intrusiveness of Russians in the life of Central/Eastern European societies. Poles and Romanians in particular experienced Russian expansionism in the nineteenth and twentieth centuries. Eastern Poland had been conquered and occupied by Czarist Russia from the end of the eighteenth century until World War I, when the modern state of Poland was reconstituted by the Western powers. The northeastern part of Romania known as Bessarabia had been seized by Czarist Russia in 1878, recovered by Romania after World War I, and then seized again and annexed by the Soviet Union in 1940. Today Bessarabia is known as the Moldova Republic.

The worst nightmare of many Central/Eastern European peoples became a stark reality during and after World War II. The Soviet Union, more powerful than it or its Russian predecessor had ever been in recent history, expanded its political and military power into Central/Eastern Europe, depriving most nations of the region of their newly achieved independence.

COMMUNIST PARTY ASCENDANCY

All the Central/Eastern European countries were involved in World War II, either because they were invaded and occupied by Nazi Germany, as was true of Poland, Czechoslovakia, and Yugoslavia (Albania was invaded and occupied by Fascist Italy); or because they were allies and satellites of the Nazis, as in the case of Hungary, Romania, and Bulgaria. The coming of World War II to Central/Eastern Europe was a prelude to the Communist takeover, because it offered the Soviet Union an opportunity to encourage and to assist local Communist parties directly to expand their political influence, and ultimately to obtain control of the governments of the Central/Eastern European countries in the period immediately after the war.

Toward the end of the war the United States and Britain acknowledged the Soviet Union's special interest in Central/Eastern Europe and agreed that the Soviets should have a major influence in the region. Soviet troops occupied most of the Central/Eastern European countries, where they appeared—at least to themselves—as "liberators." They established close contact with local Communist groups, helping them to expand their influence in national politics.

The Origins of Communist Parties
Although Communist parties developed in all the Central/Eastern European countries following the 1917 Bolshevik Revolution in Russia, they did not acquire popularity and they remained small minority groups. Unlike the Socialist parties before World War I that advocated a nonviolent strategy to achieve economic reforms, the Communists supported revolution and looked to the Russian Marxists for inspiration and guidance. They had little voter support in their countries also because they were too violent and too

pro-Russian. Indeed, they remained small organizations with narrow constituencies throughout the interwar period. In a few instances, Communist parties eventually were outlawed.

Soviet Help
During and after World War II the Soviets helped many of the Central/Eastern European Communist parties to enter the mainstream of politics in their countries. The Soviets wanted to expand Communist influence in an area perceived to be ripe for radical socioeconomic change. After the experience in the 1930s, when several Central/Eastern European states had supported the Nazis or had done little to oppose them, the Soviets also wanted friendly governments in power. They expected the Communists to achieve that objective.

The Soviets enabled Communist parties to acquire cabinet posts in the postwar governments of their countries and to participate in policy-making. This helped the Communists to gain political credibility in their societies, thereby increasing their chances of winning popular support in parliamentary elections.

Communist control of certain ministries also gave the parties significant political power. Control of ministries of agriculture allowed them to put through long-awaited programs of land redistribution. Control over ministries of education gave them influence over the school systems, and control over ministries of the interior allowed them to obtain influence over the local police apparatus.

At all times the Soviet Union stood ready to provide military support of the Communist parties against popular opposition. Soviet forces that expelled the Nazis in 1944 and 1945 remained in most of Central/Eastern Europe long after the war was over.

Communist Party Strategies and Tactics
Following their own political instincts as well as advice from the Soviets, who wanted to avoid provoking Western suspicions of a Communist takeover, the Central/Eastern European parties, in seeking popularity and electoral victories, carefully avoided both revolutionary rhetoric and gestures of subservience to Moscow. They assured voters of their patriotism and of their commitment to the ballot box to gain power. Their advocacy of a moderate socialism had much appeal in the economically difficult period following the end of the war, when there was unemployment, scarcity, and inflation.

To increase their political constituency, the Central/Eastern European Communists recruited any reformist-minded people, whether or not they were Marxist-Leninists. They made a special pitch to workers and infiltrated trade unions. They established links with farmers' parties. And, ultimately, they formed parliamentary coalitions that increased their power in cabinets.

Communist parties also gained much benefit from the war. In resisting fascism, some Communists became national heroes, like Yugoslav Communist leader Joseph Broz Tito, thus making it easy for people to forget for the moment their close links with the Soviet Union.

The local Communists took advantage of the democratic character of the postwar governments in most Central/Eastern European countries. The Communists had an open political arena in which to campaign for power.

Western Policy
All of the Central/Eastern European Communist parties were beneficiaries of the war weariness of the West and in particular the unwillingness of the United States to block Soviet and Communist expansion. Although the Americans protested Communist party gains in Central/Eastern Europe following the end of World War II, they did nothing to counter the advance of Communist political influence. The United States wanted to avoid a dangerous confrontation with the Soviet Union, its ally in the recent war with Germany. Moreover, the American government already had agreed at the Yalta and Potsdam conferences to tolerate substantial Soviet and Communist influence in Central/Eastern Europe.

The focus of American interest and action, rather, was Western Europe, which received enormous amounts of economic assistance. The United States wanted to discourage the kind of social conditions that had benefited Communists in Central/Eastern Europe.

The Takeover
The Communist takeover of Central/Eastern Europe was completed by 1948 or 1949; the precise dates varied from country to country. By that time Communist parties had obtained large pluralities in national parliaments. They dominated cabinets and determined public policy. They used the police power of the state to harass and ultimately to outlaw rival political organizations. They nationalized key sectors of the economy and introduced extensive social-security and welfare programs.

By the end of the 1940s the Communist-controlled governments of Central/Eastern Europe had promulgated new constitutions establishing Soviet-style dictatorships, called in most countries a "people's democracy." These new political systems, while committed to the destruction of capitalism and to the development of socialism, were not considered by Moscow to be equivalents of the more advanced socialism of the Soviet Union.

The Yugoslav Exception
The Communist takeover occurred much more quickly in Yugoslavia than in other countries. When the war ended in the spring of 1945 a Communist-led resistance organization called the Partisans was the dominant political force in the country, and its leader, the Croatian Communist Tito, was a national hero. With the military weapons acquired during the

war, the Partisans seized the administrative apparatus of the country, used force to eliminate political opposition, and established control over their country at least 2 years ahead of the Communists elsewhere in Central/Eastern Europe. They did all of this, incidentally, without much Soviet help.

Indeed, the Yugoslavs were able to keep Soviet influence in their country to a minimum. Tito managed to avoid a Soviet military liberation and occupation of his country at the end of the war by singlehandedly expelling the remnants of Nazi occupation forces, presenting the Kremlin with the fait accompli of Partisan political and military dominance of Yugoslavia. He also excluded from positions of leadership within the Yugoslav Communist Party those known to have special links with Moscow.

Other factors helped Tito to limit Soviet influence in Yugoslavia. The great geographic distance between Yugoslavia and the Soviet Union made it difficult for the Kremlin to threaten Tito. The close political ties Tito had had with the Kremlin in the 1930s weakened during World War II. When the war was over Tito considered himself independent and the equal of Stalin.

By 1947 Tito had established Communist control over local and central administrative authorities in a civil war against political opponents, enabling him to undertake the transformation of Yugoslavia to Soviet-style socialism. This was done despite Soviet advice to the Yugoslav Communists to move slowly lest they arouse Western suspicions and provoke Western interference. Needless to say, Tito ignored this advice.

The Albanian Exception
Albanian Communists, like their Yugoslav counterparts with whom they had developed extensive contacts during the war, had fought the Fascists and emerged from the conflict as the most powerful political group in their country. With help from the Yugoslavs, the Albanian Communists quickly seized power. Although the new Albanian leadership had good relations with the Soviet Union in the late 1940s and received some assistance from the Soviets, Soviet influence in Albanian politics was minimal because of the absence of Soviet occupation forces and because of the great physical distance between the two countries. Albanian imitation of Soviet socialism was voluntary in this early phase of Communist development; it was not the result of direct Soviet involvement.

SOVIET SATELLIZATION

The Soviets had certain expectations of the new Communist-controlled political systems in Central/Eastern Europe. They wanted the Central/Eastern European Communists to imitate their pattern of political development under Stalin and to pursue domestic and foreign policies that were congenial to Soviet national interests. They did not want Central/Eastern

European party leaderships to experiment with the Soviet model, to modify it, and to originate their own national patterns of political development.

Stalin was rigid on Central/Eastern European conformity. He believed that the Soviet model was the only successful way to achieve socialism and communism. Moreover, Central/Eastern European acceptance of Soviet practices reinforced the legitimacy of the Soviet Union's own political system. Conformity also assured the strategic reliability of the new Central/Eastern European systems by strengthening the political, economic, and strategic links they had developed with one another and with the Soviet Union.

Challenges
In the late 1940s some independent-minded Central/Eastern European leaders tried to deviate from the Soviet model. Polish leader Wladyslaw Gomulka, fearing widespread unrest in the Polish countryside, opposed a Soviet-like forced collectivization of Polish agriculture. In addition, both the Polish and Czechoslovak Communist leaderships wanted to draw closer to the West and to accept Marshall Plan aid from the United States to help their countries recover from the devastation of World War II. Yugoslavia's Tito also wanted to go his own way in socialist development. In addition to proceeding more rapidly than other Central/Eastern European Communist parties to establish Communist control over his country, thereby risking an arousal of Western suspicions and possible Western interference, Tito tried to increase Yugoslavia's territory and political influence in Southeast Europe. He sought Trieste from Italy. He also wanted to establish a union of Balkan Communists, which the Bulgarian Communist Party was on the verge of joining.

Especially disturbing to the Kremlin was Tito's insistence on the principle of national independence of the Soviets in the development of socialism in Yugoslavia and in other countries. For this reason, as well as because of his rejection of Soviet advice and his aggressive foreign policies, Tito appeared as a competitor of the Soviet Union and a threat to its influence in the Balkans.

Soviet Responses: The Cominform
The Soviets established the Cominform, a new association of Communist parties. They intended to use the Cominform as a vehicle for disseminating their advice on socialist development and discouraging Central/Eastern European deviation. The Cominform held its inaugural meeting in Poland in September 1947.

Tito defied the Cominform. He did not personally attend the inaugural meeting, and in following months he reaffirmed his independence of the Soviet Union and his determination to pursue a separate national road to socialism. He also argued the right of other Communist parties to chart their own paths to socialism. He encouraged Polish Commu-

nist leader Gomulka to resist the Kremlin's pressure to conform to the Soviet model.

The Soviet Attack on Tito
Stalin was furious over Tito's challenge. He wanted to punish Tito, to weaken him, and to encourage Tito's colleagues to oust him from the party leadership. Stalin also wanted to make an example of Tito to discourage other Central/Eastern European party leaderships from challenging Soviet policy.

Stalin demanded and obtained the support of other Central/Eastern European parties for the expulsion of the Yugoslav party from the Cominform and ostracism of the Yugoslav state in the new socialist community. Central/Eastern European accommodation of the Kremlin in this instance foreshadowed the near total subservience of the new Communist party dictatorships to Soviet will in the next few years.

Soviet Pressure on Other Parties
Clearly, the establishment of the Cominform and the attack on Tito were not enough to induce would-be nationalistic and independent Communist party leaders like those in Poland, Czechoslovakia, and elsewhere to follow slavishly the Soviet line in the mid-1940s. To achieve their subordination, the Kremlin exerted direct pressure on the party leaders. This pressure was primarily political, but there was always an implied threat of military intervention.

One kind of Soviet pressure was Stalin's personal interaction with individual Central/Eastern European Communist leaders in bilateral meetings he held with them in Moscow. In these meetings, Stalin conveyed the Soviet line in domestic and foreign policies that the Central/Eastern European party leaders were expected to follow. While his tone was menacing, Stalin also gave them his support and thereby reinforced their power vis-à-vis colleagues back home, who might have been tempted to question and oppose adoption of Soviet-inspired policies.

Soviet ambassadors were another channel of Soviet influence. They carefully monitored domestic developments in the countries to which they were accredited. They reported to Moscow any signs of deviation or dissent. It was known to the local party leaderships—and this knowledge undoubtedly intimidated them—that the Soviet ambassadors had the authority to call upon Soviet troops stationed in the host countries.

There also were Soviet nationals in key posts within the Central/Eastern European governments. Soviet secret-police operatives circulated throughout Central/Eastern Europe to monitor daily life and report signs of criticism and opposition.

Diplomatic Links
The Soviets concluded defense treaties with the Central/Eastern European countries. These treaties stressed the common threat of Germany and pledged mutual assistance, and also prohibited the signatories from joining organiza-

tions hostile to the interests of the other signatories. They effectively linked the foreign policies of the Central/Eastern European countries to that of the Soviet Union.

The Soviets concluded cultural and economic treaties as well. Bilateral cultural treaties between the Soviet Union and individual Central/Eastern European countries were intended to diminish historic animosities toward the Russians. The economic treaties fostered dependence of the economies of the Central/Eastern European countries on Soviet foreign-trade policies. The Soviets also obliged the Central/Eastern European countries to conclude bilateral treaties with one another.

By 1953 there was a complex network of treaties between the Soviet Union and the Central/Eastern European countries, and between the Central/Eastern European countries themselves. This network effectively limited the foreign policy-making of the Central/Eastern European countries and in still another way helped to convert Central/Eastern Europe into a Soviet sphere of influence.

Newly created multilateral regional organizations reinforced the treaty system and strengthened in still another way Soviet influence in Central/Eastern Europe. The most important of these organizations were the Council for Mutual Economic Assistance (CMEA) and the Warsaw Treaty Organization (otherwise known as the Warsaw Pact).

The CMEA was created in 1949 to promote economic integration and interdependence to draw the socialist countries closer to one another in the critical area of economic planning and output. In its early years, however, the CMEA did little more than set the Soviet ruble as the standard currency for international transactions and reinforce the economic isolation of Yugoslavia following its ouster from the Cominform. Not many CMEA meetings were held during this period, because the Soviet Union wanted to deny the Central/Eastern European countries an opportunity to pressure Moscow for economic assistance to rebuild their dilapidated economies.

The Warsaw Pact was established in 1955, ostensibly in response to West Germany's entry into the North Atlantic Treaty Organization (NATO). But there were other reasons for the Pact. As a collective defense system, it provided a legal justification for the continued deployment of Soviet troops in Central/Eastern Europe. It also linked the defense establishments of the Central/Eastern European countries to one another and to the Soviet Union. The Soviets were able to influence Central/Eastern European defense policies at Pact summit meetings, which were held regularly to discuss political and military matters of common concern; and by Pact maneuvers, which involved the deployment of large numbers of Soviet air, land, and sea forces on the territory of member states.

Satellization Achieved
By 1953 the Kremlin had effectively transformed nearly all of the Central/Eastern European political systems into Soviet satellites. By forcing their adoption of the Soviet model of socialism and their subservience to Soviet foreign policy, the Soviet Union deprived these countries of substantial sovereignty. In this era they were separate and independent states in appearance, not in reality.

Exceptions to Satellization
Yugoslavia escaped satellization. Tito clearly suffered less from Stalin's ostracism of his party and government in 1948 than the Kremlin had expected. Although Yugoslavia temporarily had few dealings with its socialist neighbors in Central/Eastern Europe, it maintained ties with the West. Tito's position in Yugoslavia became stronger as a result of his successful resistance to the Soviet Union. He was now more popular than ever before. He also continued his independence, and in the 1950s he deviated significantly from the Soviet model.

While Albania also evaded satellization, it did become a carbon copy of the Soviet political system, and it aligned closely with Soviet international policies in the late 1940s and early 1950s. The Soviet model was congenial to Albania's underdeveloped society. Moreover, Albania benefited from Soviet hostility to Yugoslavia after 1948 because of a fear that Tito's government might try to seize Albanian territory along the Adriatic, to extend the Yugoslav coastline to the strategically important Strait of Otranto. Albanians also worried that Tito might even annex Albania and join it to the territory in southern Yugoslavia known as Kosovo, which was inhabited primarily by Albanian-speaking people.

INFLUENCE OF THE SOVIET MODEL

As a result of satellization, most of the Central/Eastern European political systems had many characteristics of the Soviet political system in the 1950s and afterward. They all had a monolithic dictatorship by the Communist party, which looked and acted like the Soviet party; a government apparatus that was democratic in appearance but authoritarian in practice; a highly centralized socialist command economy; and a foreign policy based on close relations with one another and with the Soviet Union, opposition to the capitalist West, and support of revolutionary movements and left-wing governments in the Third World.

Dictatorship by the Communist Party
As in the Soviet Union, in the Central/Eastern European countries, the Communist party was the sole source of leadership and policy-making. The existence of other political groups in a national front coalition-type organization, a characteristic of some Central/Eastern European socialist systems, in no way compromised the dominant position of the Communist party. Toleration of these fake political groups, which were allowed little say in policy-making and

(Gamma-Liaison/APN)

Soviet Communist Party leader Leonid Brezhnev (right) months before his death in November 1982, with Polish leader Wojciech Jaruzelski, who was in Moscow for talks about his country's continuing political turmoil.

were prohibited from becoming an opposition, increased the intended illusion of democracy.

The Central/Eastern European Communist parties resembled the Soviet party in the comprehensiveness of their control over not only major institutions, such as the national-front organizations, trade unions, youth and professional associations, and the military, but also over all governmental bureaucracies, from ministers at the top to implementation agencies on local levels of administration. And Central/Eastern European party methods of maintaining this control resembled those of the Soviet party, in particular the so-called interlocking directorate of party and state leaderships, wherein top party figures simultaneously occupied top government posts and the party controlled the appointment of personnel to all important state administrative positions.

The Central/Eastern European parties also resembled the Soviet party in organizational matters. For example, the size of party membership in each country was kept within the range of 6 to 12 percent of the country's population in order to preserve the party's elitist character, which was important for its ideological integrity and internal discipline.

To assure the discipline of its members, the Central/Eastern European parties uniformly practiced the same organizational principles known as democratic centralism that prevailed in the Soviet Union. For example, leaders of the party were co-opted into power rather than elected democratically; in practice, party leaders had unlimited tenure—only a "palace revolt" or death could remove a

party leader from power, which explains why most Communist party leaderships became a gerontocracy; and their accountability to rank-and-file party membership and to the public was minimal. Furthermore, under democratic centralism, rank-and-file members were prohibited from criticizing leadership, from embracing minority points of view and from dividing into factions, and from challenging party policy as defined by the Politburo.

Communist parties in Central/Eastern Europe imitated the Soviet party's insistence on societal conformity with the standard norms of political discipline. Like the Soviet party, they were intolerant of popular dissent and would go to great lengths to suppress it. Their methods, which resembled those in the Soviet Union, included a rigorous censorship of the mass media, a readiness to allow the secret-police apparatus to use terror and coercion against suspected deviants, and an incessant propaganda calling for popular acceptance of and loyalty to Marxism-Leninism.

All the Central/Eastern European parties also were sensitive to the slightest public display of anti-Soviet feeling. They well knew the undercurrent of hostility to the Russians that had always existed in their societies. They also knew that the Kremlin would interfere directly in response to public expressions of anti-Russian sentiment.

Authoritarian Government

Despite the appearance of democratic and parliamentary forms, all the Central/Eastern European governments, like the Soviet government, were autocracies. The Central/Eastern European governments were also highly centralized. Even in Yugoslavia and Czechoslovakia, where there were claims to a federal type of administrative organization in which local authorities supposedly enjoyed a measure of autonomy—similar in some respects to Soviet federalism—public policy-making was concentrated at the center; local government had no real independence.

Central/Eastern European heads of state closely resembled the Soviet head of state in their scope of power. However, they differed somewhat in appearance.

The heads of state of Czechoslovakia and Romania were presidents who in theory were chosen by the legislature, but in practice were determined by the party leadership. The Romanian president most closely resembled the Soviet president, in that he was simultaneously the head of the Communist party. The Romanian presidency, like the Soviet presidency, was a very powerful administrative position.

Other Central/Eastern European countries had a collective chief executive in the form of a state council, as in Poland until 1989, East Germany, Bulgaria, and Hungary; or a collective presidency, as in Yugoslavia. These agencies were most important for their symbolism than for their decision-making authority, which was minimal. Their membership was determined by the Communist party, even though formally elected by the legislature, and their scope of administrative power was limited by what the party allowed them to do.

Day-to-day administrative authority was in the hands of a premier and a council of ministers, who also were theoretically elected by the legislature but in practice were chosen by the top party leadership. Although in theory ministers were answerable for their behavior to the legislature and on occasion were questioned by legislative deputies, they were quite independent of legislative control. They were accountable only to the premier and to the party leadership to which the premier and the ministers of key departments like interior, agriculture, and foreign affairs belonged.

Central/Eastern European legislatures were subservient to executives. While they could debate and discuss executive measures put before them and could even request alteration of items they did not like, they could not condemn, oppose, or reject executive policy.

Nor could they aggressively interpellate and challenge ministerial behavior, after the fashion of Western parliaments. They could raise questions about policy, provided they did so in a controlled and "constructive" manner that did not imply political opposition. Legislatures in Central/Eastern Europe certainly could not oust ministers in a Western-style vote of no-confidence during the years of Soviet dominance.

Thus, while Central/Eastern European legislatures occasionally seemed like they were more active and involved in the process of government, sometimes having longer and livelier debates on government policy than the Soviet Union's Supreme Soviet, they had as little influence over policy-making as did their Soviet counterpart.

Legislatures were weak in Central/Eastern Europe for several reasons. Like the Soviet Legislature, Central/Eastern European legislatures uniformly contained Communist party majorities. Party members who held seats in their legislature were subject to the discipline of the party leadership, in accordance with the rules of democratic centralism. Therefore, members of the legislature who belonged to the Communist party were bound to obey the party and were not free to criticize or oppose policies put before the legislature for its approval, since those policies usually originated in the party.

The Central/Eastern European legislatures generally had very short sessions. Members of legislatures thus never had enough time to obtain the kind of knowledge about the policies they were required to approve that would allow a challenge of them. Nor did members have the opportunity to develop the skills of debate and interpellation generally acquired by members of Western legislatures—skills that are essential to a legislature's exercise of real power.

Finally, even those members of the legislatures who were not card-carrying members of the Communist party were politically reliable and thus unlikely to criticize government policy. These nonparty members were nominated by organizations controlled by the Communist party, which took great care to prevent the nomination of would-be political mavericks or dissidents.

The Central/Eastern European governments resembled one another and the Soviet government also in the frequently inept and occasionally dishonest behavior of their bureaucrats. Like their Soviet counterpart, Central/Eastern European governments frequently gave priority in recruitment of bureaucrats to political loyalty rather than expertise. Moreover, as was true in the Soviet Union, while on the job, Central/Eastern European bureaucratic managers and their subordinates were under constant surveillance, which made them defensive and encouraged their concealment of error. The low wages of government personnel—an age-old problem of bureaucracies in Central/Eastern Europe and the Soviet Union—encouraged petty theft, fraud, and bribe-taking. Finally, many Central/Eastern European bureaucrats, like other citizens, viewed the Communist system for which they worked as alien, forced upon their countries by the Soviets. This feeling undermined loyalty and efficiency.

Bureaucracies in Central/Eastern Europe shared another characteristic of their Soviet counterpart. Despite close party supervision, they exercised a large personal influence over the policies they were to execute. Bureaucrats in Central/Eastern Europe, like bureaucrats anywhere, could drag their feet in carrying out policy and could sabotage policies they did not like, such as reforms that could lead to a curtailment of their responsibilities and perhaps their retrenchment.

(United Nations photo)

The Soviet-style command economy served as the economic model for all the Central/Eastern European countries.

Soviet-Style Command Economies

All the Central/Eastern European countries adopted, in the late 1940s and early 1950s, the highly centralized Soviet economic model. The Soviet model called for a comprehensive and binding national economic plan, nationalization of all industrial activity, complete collectivization of agriculture, and stress on heavy industrial capital-goods production. In line with Soviet practice, Central/Eastern European planners in this era set prices somewhat arbitrarily and determined production goals primarily in quantitative terms, with little reference to market forces of supply and demand. And, like their Soviet counterparts in these years, they paid insufficient attention to the production of consumer goods.

Social Welfare

The Central/Eastern European countries all imitated the Soviet effort—and some exceeded it—to assure citizens a minimum level of material well-being in the areas of health, education, and housing. In the late 1940s and early 1950s the Communist parties introduced comprehensive insurance programs and in many instances established minimum paid-vacation periods to be spent at state-run resorts, where charges were modest.

In 1980 most of the Central/Eastern European countries

(Albania was the exception) spent more money per capita on education than on defense. A few countries, notably Poland and Czechoslovakia, spent more on health than on education. In these areas of public policy, the Central/Eastern European countries outdid the Soviet Union, which spent twice as much on defense as on education and 5 times as much on defense as on health.

Foreign Relations

As a result of satellization, the foreign policies of most Central/Eastern European countries conformed with Soviet dictates. Beginning in the late 1940s, the Central/Eastern European Communist leaderships dutifully followed the lead of the Soviet Union and broke relations with Yugoslavia, echoed Soviet Cold War rhetoric against the capitalist West, and accepted Soviet positions within CMEA, the Warsaw Pact, and the United Nations. When the Soviets moved in the direction of détente in the 1950s and 1960s, so did the Central/Eastern European countries. And on signal from the Kremlin, they became increasingly involved in the Third World in the 1960s, providing economic and military assistance to revolutionary groups and leftist governments courted by the Soviet Union.

One must add, of course, that while their sovereignty in

foreign policy was limited and they were obliged to accommodate the Soviet Union, the Central/Eastern European Communist leaderships derived considerable political, economic, military, and psychological advantages from belonging to a tightly knit bloc of socialist countries guided and protected by Soviet power. Membership in the Soviet Bloc assured domestic stability and external security. It provided new opportunities for economic cooperation and expansion of trade within a diverse and traditionally conflict-ridden region.

PROBLEMS WITH THE SOVIET MODEL

From the mid-1950s onward some Central/Eastern European countries experienced problems with the Soviet model, which was becoming a straitjacket. These problems threatened the stability and legitimacy of Communist party rule. They occurred in four areas: economic mismanagement, environmental deterioration, political repression, and foreign-policy subservience.

Economic Mismanagement
From the mid-1950s onward most Central/Eastern European countries began to suffer from the same ills that afflicted the Soviet economy, in particular scarcity of food and other consumer goods, shoddiness of production, low worker productivity, gross waste of resources, rising prices, and declining growth rates.

The cause of these ills was the same kind of conditions found in the Soviet Union. Chief among these were a disregard of the standards of efficiency and rationality in many sectors of the economy; an excess of manpower and the absence of the high technology used in Western industrial production; a colossal waste of resources; an artificial pricing system that paid little attention to supply and demand; an arbitrary and frequently incentive-diminishing wage scale; and an excessive emphasis on industrial expansion at the expense of agriculture and consumer-goods production.

The severity of economic problems varied from north to south. The economies of the northern countries, notably those of East Germany, Poland, Hungary, and Czechoslovakia, from the beginning of Communist rule had been stronger, with either a highly developed transportation, communications, and education infrastructure and/or substantial industrialization achieved prior to World War II. They suffered less from adoption in the late 1940s of Soviet-style economic organization than did the poorer, underdeveloped countries of the south—Romania, Bulgaria, Yugoslavia, and Albania.

Some Central/Eastern European Communist party leaders, notably those of Yugoslavia, Hungary, Czechoslovakia, and East Germany, acknowledged difficulties in the performance of their Soviet-style command economies. They openly admitted that little if any allowance had been made for local economic and social conditions that differed from those in the Soviet Union and that their countries had suffered chronic economic underperformance as a result of their slavish imitation of the Soviet model. But, with the exception of Yugoslavia's Tito, it took Central/Eastern European leaderships a long time after their recognition of the limits of the Soviet model to devise ways of altering it.

Environmental Deterioration
The lack of attention to environmental deterioration in the Soviet Union in the post-Stalinist era carried over into Central/Eastern Europe, where major pollution problems developed as a result of Soviet-imposed Stalinistic industrialization policies. In addressing these problems, which were occurring at a time of diminishing financial resources, the Central/Eastern European governments received little guidance from the Soviet Union.

The major cause of environmental deterioration in Central/Eastern Europe was physical contamination of air, land, and water resources as a result of inadequate government control of steel, chemical, and energy-producing industries. Lignite-mining and power-generating industries contaminated the panhandle where East Germany, Czechoslovakia, and Poland meet. Industrial debris and sewage clogged the Oder and Vistula rivers. And pollution caused a scarcity of drinking water in Prague and Warsaw.

The Central/Eastern European governments had other problems controlling the environment. Pollution control was expensive. Industrial enterprises could not rely on government support to pay for making their operation safer, but had

(UN photo/Yutaka Nagata)

UN General Assembly President Imre Hollai of Hungary (right) greets Romanian Foreign Minister Stefan Andrei in New York in 1982. The United Nations traditionally acted as a forum from which Central/ Eastern European countries like Romania were able to express foreign-policy independence of the Soviet Union.

to do so themselves at the expense of profit. Moreover, because of political restrictions, ordinary citizens affected by pollution could not lobby aggressively for increased government regulation; all they could do was complain to authorities and hope that they would be responsive.

It was also true that while ordinary people complained about environmental pollution, they were not sympathetic to diverting scarce resources to the task of reducing it. (Central/Eastern European governments were under heavy pressure to give priority to housing and food production and did not even want to enforce the environmental regulations already in place.) Furthermore, pollution across national borders was aggravated by interstate political tensions and the lack of interstate cooperation to correct the problem. Thus, while Poland's polluted environment, especially in the highly industrialized area of Silesia, was the result primarily of Polish industry, it also got 45 percent of its air pollution from Czechoslovakia and East Germany.

Finally, none of the Central/Eastern European countries could expect help from the Soviet Union. Only in the late 1980s did Soviet leaders begin to acknowledge the existence of environmental deterioration; they had little wisdom or resources to share with their allies in this area of socialist development.

Political Repression

In Poland and Czechoslovakia, and to a lesser extent in other Central/Eastern European countries, key groups in society wanted relief from the imposition of Soviet-style societal discipline and the stifling of political expression. These groups included workers, farmers, youths, the scientific and literary intelligentsia, politicians in national legislatures, and the Catholic church. Different groups at different times in different countries sought major political change.

Those seeking change had their own reform and grievance agenda and, therefore, acted independently of one another. Some were interested mainly in achieving political liberalization in the form of a relaxation of censorship and toleration of dissent, open and competitive elections, and a legislature with real power. Other groups wanted redress of economic grievances, such as higher wages, better living conditions, more food, and the establishment of a responsive trade-union organization in contrast to the official party-dominated unions, which did little to protect the interests of workers.

Efforts to obtain change frequently led to political unrest and violence. On some occasions the demand for radical reform caused divisions within the Communist party, in violation of democratic centralism. Invariably, however, the desired reforms did not materialize, and the authorities used coercion to end political turmoil and restore law and order. The Soviet Union invariably had a hand in preserving the status quo against pressures for major alteration of Soviet-style socialism in different Central/Eastern European countries. And the problems that originally caused stress in the society invariably remained to provoke it again at some later time.

Foreign-Policy Subservience

A fourth problem for the Central/Eastern European countries concerned foreign policy. Following in Tito's footsteps, in the 1950s, 1960s, and 1970s several Central/Eastern European leaders questioned the extent of loyalty and cooperation that the Kremlin expected of them on international issues. Indeed, they believed that continuing subservience to Moscow was a cause of economic and political problems. They knew that their servility to Soviet policies contributed to the undercurrent of popular hostility to the Russians and to the possibility of an outbreak of anti-Soviet sentiment.

Central/Eastern European leaderships also were uncomfortable over Soviet-imposed limits on their relations with the West, in particular on efforts to improve political ties and expand trade with Western countries. They wanted to buy from the West industrial goods and technology needed to improve economic performance but not available from either the Soviet Union or from one another. They developed a stake in détente that at times at least seemed, if not in fact was, greater than that of the Soviet Union.

DIVERGENCE FROM THE SOVIET MODEL

A way out of Central/Eastern Europe's problems with the Soviet model of socialism was reform of it. In the years following Stalin's death in 1953 external circumstances as well as internal problems encouraged the Central/Eastern European countries to alter their Soviet-inspired domestic and foreign policies. The scope of divergence from the Soviet model varied from country to country. Eventually, the Kremlin set limits to Central/Eastern European divergence and enforced those limits.

External Circumstances

Certain Soviet behavior following the death of Stalin encouraged some Central/Eastern European countries to modify Soviet practices. Other important events also influenced change. They were the Sino-Soviet dispute, Eurocommunism, East-West détente, and the Roman Catholic church.

Soviet Behavior

In reconciling the Soviet Union with Yugoslavia in 1955 and 1956, Nikita Khrushchev, Stalin's successor as general secretary of the Soviet Communist Party, implied acceptance of Tito's independence of Soviet policy in 1948. Then, at the 20th Congress of the Soviet Communist Party, in 1956, Khrushchev spoke of the legitimacy of "different paths to socialism," implying his country's willingness to tolerate some independence in policy-making by other Central/Eastern European parties. Finally, the Soviet Union's own departure, under Khrushchev's leadership, from several Stalinist policies encouraged some Central/Eastern European party leaders at the time and in succeeding years to assume Soviet approval of their own modifications of Stalinism.

The Sino-Soviet Dispute

The outbreak of a long and bitter dispute between the Soviet Union and China in the early 1960s influenced Central/Eastern Europe. This dispute, which grew out of ideological and strategic differences between the two countries as well as a clash between the personalities of their charismatic and compulsive leaderships, undermined Soviet claims to ideological leadership of Communist parties. Coming as it did after the 1948 conflict with Yugoslavia, the Soviet dispute with China affirmed the inability of the Soviet Union to force all Communist parties, even those on its frontiers, to follow its model of socialism.

Eurocommunism

Eurocommunism was a set of ideas and practices of socialist development advocated in the 1970s by Communist parties in Western Europe, notably those of Italy, France, and Spain. The Eurocommunists envisaged a liberal democratic path to socialism that included respect for political freedom, a multiparty system in which the Communist party would move in and out of power in response to the will of the electorate, and a mixed economy that would allow a substantial amount of free enterprise. Eurocommunists also advocated the sovereignty of Communist parties in the determination of national paths to socialist development. Eurocommunism was at odds with Soviet ideology and practice and it appealed to reformist-minded people in some of the Central/Eastern European countries. Eurocommunism offered an alternative to the Soviet model.

East-West Détente

Beginning with West Germany's *Ostpolitik* (a policy calling for West German reconciliation with Central/Eastern Europe) in the late 1960s, and continuing into the 1970s, the West showed interest in bringing an end to the Cold War and improving political and economic relations with the Central/Eastern European countries. This new Western will to détente, because it offered many advantages to the Central/Eastern European countries, not least of which was an expansion in trade, gave them an incentive to chart their own national paths to socialism. Indeed, through détente the West was able to encourage Central/Eastern Europe to independence of the Soviet Union.

The Roman Catholic Church

The Roman Catholic church also was responsible for Central/Eastern European divergence from the Soviet model. While the church carefully refrained from criticizing individual governments, it continued to denounce the atheism and totalitarianism of socialist countries. Under Pope John Paul

II, the Vatican tried discreetly to encourage Communist party leaderships in Central/Eastern Europe to modify their Soviet-inspired policies against religion. The pope welcomed opportunities to dialogue with Communist leaderships and subtly exploited for this purpose their own interest in interacting with him as another means of legitimizing their rule.

The Scope of Divergence

The extent of divergence from the Soviet model after Stalin's death varied significantly throughout Central/Eastern Europe. Some countries diverged extensively from the Soviet economic model—this was true of Yugoslavia, starting in the 1950s; of Hungary, starting in the late 1960s; and of East Germany, starting in the 1970s. Other countries that attempted substantial divergence in the political sphere, like Poland and Hungary in 1956, Czechoslovakia in 1968, and Poland again in 1980–1981, were less successful, largely because of Soviet opposition.

Other countries, notably Romania, Bulgaria, and Albania, diverged minimally or not at all in the economic and political areas starting in the 1950s. The Communist party leaderships of these countries were very conservative on the issue of domestic reform. They seemed to share the Kremlin's historic fear that change, especially in politics—say, in the form of liberalization—would jeopardize the Communist party's monopoly of power and eventually subvert the national commitment to socialism.

Three countries succeeded in developing a substantial independence of the Soviet Union in their foreign policy: Yugoslavia, Albania, and Romania. Of these, Yugoslavia and Albania displayed the most independence of the Soviet Union; Romania showed the least. While it is true that Romania criticized and opposed Soviet behavior on many occasions, unlike Yugoslavia and Albania it remained closely linked to the socialist community through membership in the Warsaw Pact and CMEA.

The Limits of Divergence

The Soviets under Stalin, Khrushchev, and Brezhnev placed limits on the scope of divergence. Although they never came right out and said as much, they insisted that all of the Central/Eastern European countries remain faithful to three principles of socialist development: 1) a monolithic dictatorship by the Communist party and the party's practice of democratic centralism; 2) socialist control over the means of production; and 3) the preservation of close ties to the socialist community and the Soviet Union through membership in the Warsaw Pact and CMEA.

The Soviets also showed little tolerance of political liberalization. They feared that any weakening of political discipline in a Central/Eastern European country, and especially within the Communist party itself, was a threat to socialism and to that country's closeness to the socialist community. Thus the Soviet Union interfered to end political liberalization in Poland and Hungary in 1956 and in Czechoslovakia in 1968, and it exerted tremendous pressure on the Polish leadership in 1980 and 1981 to suppress a growing political criticism.

On the other hand, the Soviets tolerated departures from their model of socialism in the economic sphere. They appreciated the Polish Communist Party's decision in the mid-1950s to return some farms to private ownership for the sake of increasing incentives to expand agricultural output. They also accepted the Hungarian Communist Party's decentralization of economic decision-making in its New Economic Mechanism of 1968.

The Soviets also appreciated the need for changes in Central/Eastern European economic organization to improve economic conditions as an important means of discouraging outbreaks of social unrest. In the case of Hungary, incidentally, the subsequent success of the 1968 reforms in expanding Hungarian output, which led to a rise in the standard of living, encouraged the Soviet Union to consider its own adoption of a version of those reforms.

The Kremlin also endured Romania's criticisms of the Warsaw Pact and CMEA, neutrality in the Sino-Soviet dispute, and opposition to the Soviet intervention in Czechoslovakia in 1968. The Soviets understood how this independence, inspired by a strong sense of nationalism within Romanian society, strengthened the Romanian leadership. And as long as the Romanian leadership practiced Soviet norms, in particular the Communist party's unchallenged control over society, where they wanted maximum conformity, the Soviets would live with Romania's differences in foreign policy. The Soviet Union was able to do little about the divergence of Yugoslavia and Albania, because they remained beyond its control. The Soviets would have obvious logistical and other difficulties in executing a military intervention in these countries to force their conformity. Moreover, the Soviets knew that they would risk a confrontation with NATO were they to try to limit the independence of Yugoslavia and Albania by military force and thereby disrupt the strategic balance of forces in Europe.

CHANNELS OF SOVIET INFLUENCE

The Soviets wielded extraordinary influence over the development of Central/Eastern Europe until the late 1980s. They maintained substantial influence over most of the countries' political systems. The channels of this influence were political, economic, and military.

Political Channels
The main political channel of Soviet influence in most Central/Eastern European countries was the first or general secretary of each Communist party. But this was true only as long as the process of leadership selection continued to be dominated by a small group of senior party officials and

excluded the influence of a critical and independent-minded rank and file. Moreover, the usefulness of the Central/Eastern European first or general secretaries as agents of the Kremlin depended upon the loyalty and obedience of party members through the enforcement of democratic centralism.

Economic Channels
CMEA provided the Soviets with additional opportunities to influence the behavior of the Central/Eastern European countries. By encouraging economic interdependence among the Central/Eastern European states and the Soviet Union through coordination of economic planning and the development of a division of specialization, the Soviet Union exerted some influence over the states' planning processes and strengthened trade and investment links. The Soviets looked to the East Germans, Poles, Czechoslovaks, and Hungarians to expand industrial output and to Bulgaria and Romania to specialize in the export of raw materials. There was some criticism of this specialization by countries, especially Romania, that wanted to lessen dependence on the Soviet Bloc and expand trade with the West. But no Central/Eastern European country defected from CMEA.

The Soviets had additional economic means of influencing the countries. The Soviet Union remained the chief source of energy for the region. It also was the chief purchaser of Central/Eastern European manufactures. Large Soviet purchases helped the countries to offset the cost of high-priced oil imports. Moreover, in many instances, the Central/Eastern European countries found Soviet goods more attractive than imports from the West, because they were cheaper and could be paid for partly by barter arrangements, which the West rejected.

In the late 1980s the Soviets looked for support within CMEA for the establishment of currency convertibility to expand trade and strengthen intrabloc economic unity. (A *convertible currency* allows a country to use foreign exchange earned in sales to a second country in order to purchase goods in a third country.) Trade within CMEA consisted mostly of bilateral barter transactions, because of the unwillingness of the Central/Eastern European countries to accept one another's currency in payment for exports. But countries like the Soviet Union, Hungary, and Czechoslovakia, which had strong foreign-exchange earning capabilities as a result of competitive export industries, were interested in currency convertibility.

Military Channels
The Warsaw Pact remained an important channel of Soviet influence during the 1980s. The Pact always was under the command of a high-ranking Soviet military officer; no Central/Eastern European military officer headed any top-level Warsaw Pact command. Through the Pact, the Soviets encouraged standardization of weapons and Central/Eastern European dependence upon Soviet sources of procurement.

Warsaw Pact maneuvers in different Central/Eastern European countries served to remind all the countries of the enormous military power that was under Soviet command—power that could be used against the countries to guarantee their loyalty to socialism.

The Soviet-led Warsaw Pact military intervention in Czechoslovakia in August 1968 showed the vulnerability of the Central/Eastern European countries to the collective military might of the Pact, in the event of a deviation from the Soviet model considered dangerous to Soviet security. On that occasion the Soviets laid down a doctrine of intervention, enunciated by Leonid Brezhnev. The Brezhnev Doctrine justified collective military action by socialist countries whenever they were threatened by so-called counterrevolutionary forces. The doctrine meant that the Soviet Union and its Warsaw Pact allies would intervene militarily to prevent any major departures of a Central/Eastern European political system from the single-party dictatorship or any action tantamount to a defection from the alliance system. While Mikhail Gorbachev all but repudiated the Brezhnev Doctrine in a speech on July 6, 1989, to European Community parliamentary deputies in Strasbourg, it would have been foolhardy of Soviet Bloc countries to assume that they were no longer vulnerable to Soviet coercion. The Soviet Union might have revived the Brezhnev Doctrine if Gorbachev were replaced as Soviet party leader by a hard-liner. Or Gorbachev might have been pressured to use force to maintain control by more belligerent Soviet leaders.

The Soviets continued to station troops in East Germany, Poland, Czechoslovakia, and Hungary because these countries were the most highly industrialized and the nearest geographically to NATO and therefore of great importance to Soviet security. Although Soviet military personnel in those countries were subject in certain ways to local jurisdiction, in accordance with status-of-forces agreements the Soviet Union concluded with their governments, the Kremlin had considerable latitude in the use of the troops through secret bilateral agreements with the host authorities. The presence of Soviet troops reinforced the political status quo in these countries, making the threat of a Soviet military intervention possible and therefore credible.

CHALLENGES TO SOVIET INFLUENCE IN THE 1980s

Although most of the Central/Eastern European countries remained closely linked to the Soviet Union, in much the same way they had been since Communist parties achieved power in the late 1940s, developments in the 1980s encouraged some of them—including those that had been most loyal and most deferential to the Soviets in the past—to press for greater autonomy. The most important of these developments were the three Soviet leadership successions in the 1980s, a regionwide slump in economic growth, the sharp deterioration of Soviet-American relations in the aftermath of the Soviet intervention in Afghanistan, the expansion of ties with Western Europe, and perestroika.

The Soviet Leadership Successions

Central/Eastern European Communist leaderships saw uncertainty and ambiguity in the Kremlin in the early 1980s, when there were three leadership successions (from Brezhnev to Andropov in 1982, from Andropov to Chernenko in 1984, and from Chernenko to Gorbachev in 1985). They saw an opportunity in these shifts in the Kremlin to promote their own national interests and ambitions.

For example, in the late summer of 1984 both East Germany and Bulgaria, known for their loyalty and closeness to Moscow, publicized plans of their party leaderships to visit West German Chancellor Helmut Kohl, whose conservative government had just extended a loan of $300 million to East Berlin. Hungary's leadership publicly endorsed this East German policy and encouraged the visit to West Germany.

The Soviets were uneasy, although these initiatives undoubtedly had been cleared in Moscow earlier. (The Kremlin was not unsympathetic to Central/Eastern European countries improving relations with the West to obtain economic help that it was unwilling or unable to provide for its allies.) Moscow did not want its allies to become heavily indebted to the West. The Soviet leadership clearly was uneasy over what looked like a flurry of East German efforts at the end of the summer of 1984 to court West Germany at the expense of ties to the Soviet Union. Thus, it vetoed East German Communist leader Erich Honecker's planned visit to Bonn at the end of September. The Bulgarian visit also did not occur. It was also in the summer of 1984 that Honecker made a conciliatory gesture toward Romania. Relations between the two countries had been correct but cool, because of Romanian party leader Nicolae Ceausescu's frequent disagreements with the Kremlin. Honecker congratulated the Romanian Communists on their country's liberation from Nazi German control 40 years earlier, in August 1944. Moreover, Honecker said nothing—to the dismay of the Soviets—about the new Romanian position that the liberation had occurred prior to the entry of Soviet forces into Romania.

In the spring of 1985, in discussing the renewal of the alliance, Warsaw Pact members raised the issues of national sovereignty and noninterference, in ways that obliquely challenged the legitimacy of the Brezhnev Doctrine. Furthermore, most of the Central/Eastern European countries favored a short period of renewal, in opposition to the Soviets, who wanted a long renewal period. Although the Pact was renewed for 20 years in April 1985, an apparent victory for the Soviets, the Central/Eastern European countries had communicated to the Kremlin their sensitivity to Soviet intrusiveness and their concern with autonomy in domestic and foreign policy-making.

While the Soviets had their way with their allies, they were upset. They did not like the unmistakable tendency of the Central/Eastern European countries to move on their own to improve East-West relations.

Economic Slowdown

The need to remedy an economic slowdown in many parts of Central/Eastern Europe in the early 1980s was another incentive for autonomy. To expand output of consumer goods and of goods exported abroad for hard currency, the countries that were feeling the pinch needed to undertake sweeping reforms toward market-oriented economic structures which would carry them far away from the autarchic Soviet economic model. But they also needed help from the West, in particular Western technology and the financial credit to pay for it. This meant preserving East-West détente when it was being undermined by Soviet-American confrontation.

Because the Central/Eastern European Communist leaderships realized that economic stagnation could lead to political instability, including the kind of unrest Poland experienced, and because they realized the alternative to an expansion of trade with the West was an increased dependency on the Soviet Union, they had a very strong incentive to proceed on their own to keep political and economic ties with the West in good repair. They had a vested interest in diminishing the level of tension between the Soviet Union and the United States.

Soviet-American Relations

It is not an exaggeration to say that the Central/Eastern European countries were worried throughout the early and mid-1980s about the deterioration of Soviet-American relations and the escalation of the arms race in the form of increased superpower missile deployment in Europe. In response to the American deployment of Pershing II and cruise missiles in Western Europe, the Soviets increased deployment of their SS-20 missiles in East Germany and Czechoslovakia. Other deployment sites were in Poland and Bulgaria.

The Central/Eastern European countries conveyed as pointedly as they could to the Kremlin their concern about the tension-ridden Soviet relationship with the United States. The Soviet-American rivalry threatened their own material well-being, endangering their security and compromising efforts to increase their autonomy of the Soviet Union, which tended to become sensitive about diversity within the Warsaw Pact at times of difficulty with the Americans.

Their enthusiasm over the arms-control agreement signed by Soviet party leader Gorbachev and U.S. President Reagan in Washington in December 1987, therefore, was not surprising. They saw the treaty as further evidence of a real improvement in Soviet-American relations. They were grati-

fied by a willingness of the new Soviet leadership to compromise on arms-control issues for the sake of promoting superpower détente. And they were relieved that at last the Kremlin would begin to remove Soviet SS-20 missiles from their territory and thereby lessen the risk of their involvement in a nuclear war with the West.

The United States encouraged the Central/Eastern European countries to move in the direction of greater political and economic freedom. During the economic summit of Western industrialized nations held in July 1989 in Paris, U.S. President George Bush, having just returned from a visit to Poland earlier in the month in which he offered American support and encouragement of Polish reformism, said he believed that, based on his personal contacts with Gorbachev, close American and Western European ties with Central/Eastern Europe were not likely to upset the Kremlin. Thus, Poland and other countries increasingly turned to the United States for economic and financial help to facilitate their reform programs and to cope with economic crises arising out of the transition from controlled centralized economic life to the adoption of market-oriented mechanisms.

However, the United States was reluctant to assume a leading role in fostering change. In July 1989 Bush indicated to the NATO allies that the United States envisaged a multilateral approach to the socialist world. In the American president's view, the European Community would coordinate the West's efforts to help Central/Eastern European countries economically. By this policy, he probably wanted to reassure the Kremlin that the United States was not operating a Western campaign to "decouple" the Warsaw Pact allies from the Soviet Union.

Central/Eastern Europe and Western Europe

In the late 1980s the Central/Eastern European countries actively sought expanded political and economic ties with Western Europe. Good relations with Western Europe could strengthen their independence of Moscow; could help them to acquire high technology unavailable from the Soviet Union for economic expansion; and could provide opportunities for diplomatic settlement of intra-European problems in the areas of environmental control, arms reduction, and mutual security.

The countries tried to draw closer to Western Europe in several ways. One was through bilateral summitry. In 1984 there were meetings between Romanian party leader Ceausescu and West German Chancellor Kohl and between Hungarian party leader Kadar and French President Mitterrand. In 1985 Kadar also met with British Prime Minister Thatcher, and in 1987 East German party leader Honecker met with Kohl. Second, the Central/Eastern European countries negotiated with Western Europe to achieve mutual and balanced force reductions in NATO and the Warsaw Pact. And third, through CMEA, the Central/Eastern European countries worked to develop economic links with the European Community, CMEA's counterpart, and to lessen dependence on the Soviet Union.

While the Western European countries welcomed the interest of Central/Eastern Europeans in strengthening and expanding détente, they were slow with economic and financial aid, perhaps waiting for further developments and afraid of interfering in Soviet Bloc relations and arousing Soviet anxiety. They wanted to avoid actions that appeared to be motivated by the goal of weakening the traditionally close political and economic ties Soviet Bloc countries had with one another and with the Soviet Union within the framework of CMEA and the Warsaw Pact. They took seriously the anxiety not only of Gorbachev but also other Soviet leaders over the future role of the West in Central/Eastern Europe in a period of rapid and profound change that at the very least was weakening Soviet influence and control in the region.

The Impact of Perestroika

By the mid-1980s all the Central/Eastern European countries were in need of some reformism to correct the many deficiencies in their Soviet-style socialist systems. They had failed to provide their citizens with adequate levels of income, housing, consumer supplies and services, social-welfare amenities, education, and job security—the so-called human rights of socialist systems.

The mid-1980s brought evidence of popular unrest provoked by economic crisis. The peoples of Central/Eastern Europe had always tacitly assumed that in return for curtailment of many personal and political freedoms, they would have the material well-being promised by communist ideology and their socialist governments. But by the early 1980s the peoples of Central/Eastern Europe believed that their socialist systems would not perform well and would not deliver on ideological promises.

Official Central/Eastern European reactions between 1985 and 1989 to Soviet perestroika were mixed. While all Soviet Bloc Communist leaders dutifully acknowledged that perestroika in the Soviet Union was a welcome development and that an exchange of experience among the allies was good, some were not ready to introduce it in their own societies. On the other hand, ordinary citizens showed much interest in Soviet reform and in some instances insisted that their governments imitate it, or even go beyond it, to improve local conditions.

Hungary and Poland, and to a lesser extent Bulgaria, reacted positively to Soviet perestroika. Hungary and Poland undertook major reforms to carry them far away from the traditional, orthodox, Soviet-style socialism. Bulgaria also attempted reforms, primarily in the economic sphere; but made little change in its traditional political order.

At the same time, Czechoslovakia, while envisaging substantial change in economic organization, initially adopted little substantive change of traditional policies and priorities and seemed determined to prevent any alteration of its

political structure. East Germany and especially Romania stalwartly refused either to acknowledge performance problems or make policy changes to resolve them.

Yugoslavia and Albania went their separate and independent ways. Yugoslavia continued a conservative pragmatism of its own design until the Civil War started in 1991, when reform efforts came abruptly to an end. Albania remained indifferent and unresponsive to Soviet perestroika, reasserting its commitment to its own brand of neo-Stalinist organization and behavior.

UPHEAVAL IN CENTRAL/EASTERN EUROPE IN 1989

Between October 1 and December 25, 1989, the conservative Communist leaderships of East Germany, Czechoslovakia, Bulgaria, and Romania collapsed. Paradoxically, those countries that at one time had most strongly resisted Gorbachev's call for reform now were in a political revolution that pulled them ahead of the Soviet Union in the development of democratic change.

New political leaderships, composed of pragmatic and reform-minded Communists, succeeded to power in rapid succession in October, November, and December. Responding to the first massive popular demonstrations in 40 years of Communist rule, they were prepared to introduce perestroika-like reforms in their countries and to accommodate other demands for an end to political repression.

The new leaders quickly lifted restrictions on freedom of the press, assembly, speech, and travel. Recognizing the existence of opposition groups, they agreed to share policy-making power with these groups in newly reshuffled coalition-style cabinets. They also consented to the formal liquidation of the Communist party's historic monopoly of power, thereby accepting the principle of political pluralism, and they pledged to hold free elections of new parliaments early in 1990. In these elections, Communists would compete with other political groups for seats. As the new decade began, the old monolithic and Soviet-dominated authoritarian order appeared to be at an end.

In this new political game, the Communist parties tried to hold on to power. They held emergency "soul-searching" conferences which led to changes in name, to the abandonment of their traditional neo-Stalinistic ideological programs, and to the endorsement of political democratization. Reform-minded Communists criticized and attacked their former conservative leaderships, calling for their punishment for incompetence and corruption. Some Communists contemplated disbanding and reconstituting themselves into a totally different political organization to distance themselves further from the "old" discredited policies.

But the scramble of Communists for political survival was a failure. Popular distrust and dislike of them was pervasive, not only because of their mismanagement of society but also because of recent revelations of the deceit and hypocrisy of their dethroned leaderships. While Honecker, Jakes, Zhivkov, and Ceausescu had called for austerity among their citizens and forced them to endure harsh living conditions for the sake of building a better future, these hard-line leaders not only embezzled public wealth for private gain but lived in luxury, enjoying food and other goods that were in many cases unavailable to ordinary citizens and were imported from the West with precious hard currency. As a result, the Communist parties and those associated with their policies—or what was left of them—in most of Central/Eastern Europe lost all credibility. It was unlikely that, even with the new names, new leaders, and new programs adopted by most of them in early 1990 to assure their survival, they would ever enjoy public trust, never mind public support, in a bid to participate once again in national politics.

Roots and Causes

Now that these Communist-controlled systems have fallen so swiftly and dramatically, it is possible to see how fragile the structure was that held them in place. Certainly Gorbachev's clearly stated policy of hands-off regarding the internal politics of the Central/Eastern European countries, along with the model of political reform set by Poland and Hungary earlier in the year, provided the background for the changes in East Germany, Czechoslovakia, Bulgaria, and Romania in the fall and early winter of 1989.

But there were other reasons why these socialist regimes fell so quickly. They had never dug deep roots in their societies. The Central/Eastern Europeans saw their governments as alien, imposed and used by the Kremlin to subject them to Soviet power. Adding to popular dislike of the Communist leaderships was their excessive political repression, at times more harsh than that of the Soviet Union itself and increasingly intolerable in light of the political democratization taking place in Poland and Hungary.

Socialist systems had never obtained legitimacy also because of their failure to provide the material prosperity promised in their communist ideology. Living standards in most of the Central/Eastern European societies had barely improved in the 45-year period of Communist party rule. In some instances, living standards had deteriorated in the late 1980s; and they always had been well below those in the West, with which Central/Eastern Europe citizens increasingly compared themselves. In sum, most people, especially the youth, had become fed up with both the political and economic hardships they had endured for the sake of building a utopian society, which they now realized would never materialize.

Thus, despite the appearance of power, the Communist regimes were in fact weak without Soviet support and therefore unable to suppress forcibly the huge popular demonstrations for democracy—as their conservative leaderships, perhaps tempted by the June 1989 example of the Chinese, initially had been inclined to do. Moreover, the Central/Eastern Europeans were not isolated, as was the Chinese opposition. The societies of East Germany, Czechoslovakia, Bulgaria, and Romania, because of their geographic proximity to other socialist countries going through reform, and because of the influence of the mass media in communicating events elsewhere in the region, were aware of events throughout Eastern Europe, despite the efforts of their repressive governments to interdict the flow of information.

In addition, Gorbachev advocated and welcomed the kind of change taking place in Poland and Hungary in 1988 and early 1989. He urged other allies in Central/Eastern Europe to adopt their own perestroika-style reform programs to remedy a regionwide stagnation, which affected even the most prosperous socialist countries and threatened an unrest dangerous to socialism and to Soviet influence in Central/Eastern Europe. He brushed aside the Central/Eastern European leaders' anxieties about introducing reforms that could and in fact did end by undermining their power and jeopardizing rather than strengthening socialism.

Gorbachev was at least partly responsible for the collapse of Communist party rule in Central/Eastern Europe also because he refused to approve and, indeed, opposed the use of force by East Germany's Honecker, Czechoslovakia's Jakes, Bulgaria's Zhivkov, and Romania's Ceausescu to resist the mounting popular pressures for democracy. In effect, Gorbachev sealed their doom and confirmed what everyone always had believed—namely, that the repressive socialist systems relied on Soviet support for survival. Leaders of the democratic movements in Prague, Leipzig, and Sofia acknowledged that without Gorbachev's policy of leniency and restraint toward Central/Eastern Europe, the political changes that occurred would have been impossible.

Finally, Western European countries, in particular France and West Germany, as well as the United States encouraged and supported the efforts of Soviet Bloc countries to abandon communism. It appeared that they would offer large-scale economic and financial assistance, as West Germany and the United States had to Poland and Hungary, should they move away from Communist rule.

Patterns of Political Change

In their opposition to repressive government, the peoples of East Germany, Czechoslovakia, Bulgaria, and Romania showed similar patterns of response. All had massive anti-government demonstrations in the large urban centers. These were remarkably resilient in the face of the brute physical force. Popular determination to achieve change, even if it meant loss of life, apparently was evenly matched against the deadly weapons used by the authorities. Moreover, in three countries—East Germany, Czechoslovakia, and Bulgaria—the activities of protesting citizens, despite the large numbers of them, were for the most part peaceful, with a minimum of violence and practically no bloodshed. As one commentator observed in Czechoslovakia, "hardly a window was broken." Their example calls into question traditional thinking about the omnipotence of the totalitarian state, in particular its capacity to achieve conformity and obedience for any length of time by coercion.

Romania, however, experienced a very high level of violence in November and December 1989, which culminated with the summary execution of President and party leader Nikolai Ceausescu and his wife, Elena. The violence seemed in proportion to the degree of popular hostility to the regime's political and economic policies in past decades as well as to the stubbornness of its leadership's refusal to heed the writing on the wall, so to speak, in neighboring countries and to respond to the mounting popular pressures, especially among workers, for change. Not surprisingly, in the immediate aftermath of the collapse of the Ceausescu regime, the Romanian people seemed more vengeful in their expression of anti-Communist feelings than were the peoples of other socialist countries.

Whatever the level of violence, though, popular resistance to conservative rule in all four countries during the fall of 1989 cut across class lines. Workers, intellectuals, students, Communist party members, and soldiers cooperated in opposing the leadership of hard-liners. This unprecedented unity of the opposition caught the governments of Honecker, Jakes, Zhivkov, and Ceausescu off guard, unprepared, and more vulnerable than at any time in the past.

In early 1990 the Communist parties rid themselves of their former leaders, who were accused of corruption, dishonesty, and incompetence. The parties changed their names, announced new programs, and agreed to renounce their political monopolies. They also consented to the legalization of multiparty systems, to hold open and competitive elections for parliament before July 1990, and to accept the outcome of these elections, even if doing so meant loss of leadership and exclusion from government. They took these revolutionary steps not only in response to intense popular pressure for an end to Communist dominance but also in the hope that they could salvage some of their political power and play a role in the new democratic order by making timely concessions.

In the immediate postupheaval period, prior to the holding of parliamentary elections in the spring of 1990, the new Communist leaderships also made coalitions with recently formed noncommunist groups and organizations to prepare their countries for the transition to pluralistic democracy. These interim regimes also promised and began, albeit cautiously and haltingly, the dismantling of the command economies inherited from their neo-Stalinistic predecessors. They took the first steps to reduce government control over economic life, to increase private entrepreneurialism, to pay more attention to consumer needs, especially in the area of food, and to expand foreign investment in local enterprises.

POST-COMMUNIST DEVELOPMENT: PROBLEMS, POLICIES, AND PROSPECTS

In the early 1990s all the former socialist political systems of Central/Eastern Europe began to discard their socialist authoritarian systems in favor of Western-style pluralistic and parliamentary governmental systems. By the summer of 1990, six former Soviet satellites had held free elections for new parliaments and had produced new leaderships committed to liberal democracy. Along with efforts to democratize their political systems, the post-Communist political leaderships also began radically to alter or abandon the state-controlled economies that they had been forced to adopt by the Soviet Union. Finally, the former Soviet satellites undertook a reorientation of their foreign policies, shifting their focus of international interest from the East to the West. These major departures from the old socialist order transformed the countries of Central/Eastern Europe into laboratories for the study of political and economic change away from Marxist-Leninist dictatorship toward capitalism and democracy.

Movement Toward Pluralistic and Democratic Government

The newly emancipated Central/Eastern European countries adopted the Western style of parliamentary democracy that involves multiparty systems. Indeed, the unaccustomed openness of the post-Communist political environment encouraged a proliferation of narrowly focused party organizations. The new democratic systems also provided for popularly elected presidential executives endowed with substantial leadership authority, enabling them to determine the broad direction of policy. Another important component taken from the Western European model was ministerial accountability to legislative bodies, which were given the right to vote no-confidence, thereby enabling the legislative bodies to replace ministerial leadership. Most of the new legislatures were elected directly by the voters, sometimes in a complex electoral process involving proportional representation which, while maximizing representation of the popular will, increased the number and competitiveness of the new parties and thereby contributed to a degree of instability that interfered with policy-making, especially the enactment of controversial reforms.

At the same time, however, democracy was developing in Central/Eastern Europe in different ways and at different rates of change, based upon the peculiar national character of individual countries. The sharpest contrast was between the less economically developed and more politically conservative Balkan countries in the south and the economically better-off and somewhat more politically mature countries of the north. For example, throughout 1990 and 1991 Romania, Bulgaria, and Albania moved very slowly in the development of democratic political processes because they lacked a democratic tradition in the pre-Communist era and because under communism their repressive leaderships had destroyed any chances for the emergence of a reformist elite capable of assuming the leadership vacated by the Communists. By contrast, Czechoslovakia, Hungary, and Poland seemed to have more promising futures. They had some experience with democratic ideas before and during the Communist era. In each of these countries, the Communist party leaderships had tolerated democratic dissidents. Although they were harassed and sometimes severely punished by the authorities, they survived to take the place of their persecutors in 1989 and to implement the radical political reform that they had been discussing and writing about for many years. Also favorable to the development of democracy in these northern countries was their achievement under communism of a tolerable standard of living (at least by comparison with their socialist neighbors, including the Soviet Union, if not the West), which provided them with a greater degree of social stability, important to stable democratic government.

But it is also true that democratic institutions established in the former socialist dictatorships since 1989 were extremely fragile and, worse, taxed to the breaking point by potentially destabilizing socioeconomic problems. The most important of these were: 1) ethnocultural rivalries within and among most of the countries in the region; 2) the outbreak of racially as well as economically inspired urban violence; 3) the worsening of environmental degradation, the causes of which had been kept secret by the former Communist party regimes; 4) the revived roles of religion and of divisive religious issues such as abortion, anti-Semitism, and relations between church and state; and 5) the burgeoning corruption resulting from not only past corruption but also the changeover from a state-controlled economy to one based on private enterprise and individual initiative in which, at least in the short term, an aggressive and unscrupulous few tried to exploit the naive and uninformed majority. Trying to solve these problems in the short term sorely tempted the post-Communist leaderships in Central/Eastern Europe in the early 1990s to contemplate authoritarian methods which could jeopardize the new democratic experiments by opening the way for a return to an authoritarianism that would enable them to accommodate popular cravings for stability, if not prosperity. Thus far they have resisted this temptation. It remains to be seen how long they can display this restraint in the face of continuing economic hardships caused by efforts to introduce a market economy in the short term.

Introduction of a Market Economy

Economic reformers in the new post-Communist political systems were eager to introduce a market economy. They argued that, while the state-controlled economic systems of the Communist era had restarted economic life after World War II, they had not led to development of modern economies with high-technology industries, like computers and semiconductors, which depend on innovation and risk-taking. In the view of these economists and the new political leaderships, it will take a market-based, free-enterprise economy to restore economic health, raise living standards, and ultimately assure political stability in the post-Communist era.

Most Central/Eastern European reform economists believe that this transformation will require the privatization of large and small enterprises in industry, agriculture, and such service areas as banking, insurance, and retail sales; the autonomization of remaining state-controlled industries, with freedom of decision-making on prices and wages; and the end of the monopolies and an increase in competitiveness. They are proposing to accept bankruptcies and unemployment, in the belief that these conditions will encourage rationality in management decision-making, improved efficiency, and a reduction of waste. With the termination of centralized control of prices and an end to subsidies to producers and consumers, inefficient industries will go under—and so will distorted prices. The market will determine the real value of what is consumed. To fight the inevitable price inflation when controls are lifted, most governments plan to keep a lid on wages and to use fiscal policy to restrict demand. All the Central/Eastern European countries are in some stage of making their currencies convertible.

There are several obstacles to meeting these goals. Although state control is diminishing, bureaucratic methods of production and allocation persist. Furthermore, most of the countries are in debt to the West. The Central/Eastern Europeans have been especially hard hit by the chaos in relations with their largest trading partner, the former Soviet Union. Trade is now on a hard-currency basis, with both sides short of funds. Thus, the Central/Eastern European countries must pay in hard currency for Soviet oil. Moreover, CMEA is gone, along with its guaranteed markets for even poor-quality manufactured exports. As yet there is no alternative mechanism to facilitate interstate trade and the development of market-based national economies.

There are still other problems in moving toward free enterprise. The only people who have the financial resources to buy or to start up their own businesses are in many instances former Communist party officials, hardly the people most Central/Eastern Europeans want to see succeed. Also, investment banks and stock exchanges are not yet strong enough to finance large businesses. State decontrol of enterprises will continue at a snail's pace, in part because of price distortion, which makes it very difficult for a buyer to determine the value of what is being purchased.

A further obstacle to capitalist development is psychological. Many Central/Eastern European peoples still have a socialist mind-set about the role of the state in safeguarding their well-being. They expect cheap medical care, housing, and education, as well as full-employment policies which guarantee people a job for life. These are expensive expectations which will take time to change. Until this occurs, people are going to view the movement toward a free-enterprise economy with suspicion, hostility, and resistance—especially as thus far they have gotten mostly depressed living standards and increased personal hardships rather than the radical improvement in living standards that they anticipated.

According to the International Monetary Fund, the only way to solvency for the post-Communist governments in Central/Eastern Europe is a harsh austerity, involving a reduction of consumption so that a greater part of gross national product can be earmarked for debt repayment. This approach has required keeping real wages down; closing inefficient centralized industries; and developing efficient, competitive, productive industries. But the costs of such austerity are high, especially for the average consumer/wage earner. Nevertheless, the reformist leaderships of Central/Eastern Europe seem determined to continue austerity in order to facilitate development of a market economy.

Reorientation of Foreign Policies

To help solve the economic and social problems, the new democratic leaderships are looking to the West. They believe that the countries deserve and should receive assistance, most would argue, in Marshall Plan proportions, because they have done what the West has always wanted them to do. They have abandoned socialism and established their independence of Moscow. They argue that if these reforms are to last, they will need aid. They must cushion the traumatic impact of change on the daily lives of their citizens. Replacing paternalistic socialism with a new societal order based on individualism and self-reliance, they point out, needs the full help of the West.

Western Europe, in particular Germany, has been responsive to the needs of the new Central/Eastern European leaderships. They have extended credits, revised export controls to allow purchase of many new high-technology items like computers, civil air navigation, and telecommunication equipment (previously restricted), and encouraged extensive World Bank lending.

In addition, NATO developed new, though modest, links with Central/Eastern Europe to provide a limited security against a return to foreign control. In June 1991 NATO foreign ministers told the former Soviet Bloc countries that NATO would resist coercion against emerging democracies and offered to cooperate in a limited way with Central/Eastern Europe in military matters. NATO acknowledged

the close linkage between the security of Western countries and that of the Central/Eastern countries.

Viewing the stability, prosperity, and friendship of the Central/Eastern European peoples as important to German material well-being, Germany has taken the lead in pressing for a substantial aid program to Central/Eastern Europe. The Bonn government has a sense of moral obligation, now that the Berlin Wall is down, not to abandon the peoples of Central/Eastern Europe and to allow a new economic cooperation to develop between the former socialist societies and the democratic and well-off societies in the West.

But the 12-nation European Community has been ambivalent about admitting the former Soviet satellites to EC membership. Although British Prime Minister John Major argued for broadening the Community to include the new Central/Eastern European democracies "as soon as they are ready politically and economically," he is the exception. French President François Mitterrand thinks differently and has warned that Central/Eastern Europe may be decades away from full membership in the EC. Mitterrand's position derives in part from a concern that the admission of the Central/Eastern European countries would strengthen Germany's already substantial influence in the organization, given existing German political and economic links to the former Communist region. France also has economic reasons for proceeding cautiously on the issue of admitting Central/Eastern European countries to the EC: Paris does not want Western Europe markets flooded with cheap agricultural products from Central/Eastern Europe.

All the EC nations share a certain degree of ambivalence toward the new Central/Eastern Europe because of fear of mass migrations westward to escape economic hardship at home. They feel a need to block such migrations in light of adoption of a single regional market for the EC on January 1, 1993, that will make movement within and between member nations difficult to control.

The United States has responded to the new political situation in Central/Eastern Europe with sympathy and encouragement, but also with caution. While pleased with the abandonment of socialism and with the emancipation from Soviet control, the American government since 1989 has worried about the will and the capacity of the new noncommunist leaderships to adopt capitalism and democracy. Not without some justification, Washington is sensitive to the continuing role of Communists in some countries. American caution also derives from a conviction that it is

Establishment of
the Warsaw
Pact;
Khrushchev
announces
"different paths
to socialism"
1955

A crisis in Polish
and Hungarian
relations with
the Soviet Union
1956

The Soviet-led
Warsaw Pact
intervention in
Czechoslovakia
1968

Communist rule
collapses in
Central/Eastern
Europe

1980s–1990s

The Yugoslavian Civil
War intensifies and
threatens regional
stability

CMEA and the Warsaw
Pact are dissolved

Central/Eastern Europe
debates the potential
effects of the
disintegration of the
Soviet Union

better for those countries in the long term to help themselves rather than to rely on large infusions of foreign capital.

Central/Eastern European relations with the former Soviet Union focused on getting the Soviets to withdraw troops and to consent to the dissolution of the Warsaw Pact and CMEA. Bilateral discussions between Central/Eastern European countries which still had large numbers of Soviet troops deployed on their territory, notably East Germany, Poland, Hungary, and Czechoslovakia, occurred throughout 1990 and were successful in producing agreements on the conditions of final evacuation, which the Kremlin honored. There were some temporary difficulties, reflecting a measure of bitterness on both sides, but these difficulties did not interrupt the withdrawal process. The Kremlin also accommodated demands of the Central/Eastern European countries for the termination of the Warsaw Pact.

At the same time, the Central/Eastern European countries tried to keep their political fences mended with the Kremlin to assure that the end of Communist rule would not be a liability for the Soviet Union. They discreetly lobbied with the West for aid to the Soviet Union while seeking help for themselves, on the assumption that political and economic crises in the Soviet Union endanger their own security and stability. They also proceeded cautiously on the issue of Baltic independence, in which they had a substantial interest. Concerned that they might jeopardize the Soviet troop-withdrawal process, they were careful not to chastise Moscow when it cracked down on Lithuania in early 1991. And in the political crisis of August 1991, they were careful not to take sides, even though they were fearful that if the anti-Gorbachev coup succeeded, they might again be at risk, especially if conservative military leaders who regretted the collapse of Communist rule came to power.

The Central/Eastern European countries also are frightened of the prospect of huge numbers of desperate C.I.S. citizens facing famine and other hardships migrating west-

ward should chaos occur in the new Commonwealth. They have no resources to cope with such an event and do not know how to prevent it except by urging the West to offer food and other help to the Soviet Union in the short term.

One significant means of responding to problems with the former Soviet Union is a new emphasis on regional cooperation. Contacts have increased between Central/Eastern European countries and individual former Soviet republics, such as the Ukraine, especially to consider problems of each country's ethnic minorities. The Central/Eastern European countries also have tried to diminish the historic animosities toward one another and to build a strong foundation for friendship and cooperation in solving shared economic, strategic, and environmental problems. The importance of this initiative is obvious as Central/Eastern Europe confronts what may be the most serious regional problem since the revolutions of 1989: the Yugoslavian Civil War. With the dissolution of the Warsaw Pact in July 1991, the Central/Eastern European countries have had no security apparatus to enable them to deal collectively with the threat to their interests posed by the strife in Yugoslavia. They fear at the very least a spillover of the Yugoslav ethnic strife into their own countries, which are vulnerable because of local inter-ethnic rivalries and disagreements. The organization that aims to ensure peace in Europe, the 35-nation Conference on Security and Cooperation in Europe, does not appear sufficient to provide the region with security; and, to the dismay of the new democratic governments, the Western powers seem unwilling to take a direct hand in promoting peace in Yugoslavia.

Albania

GEOGRAPHY

Area in Square Kilometers (Miles):
28,489 (11,097) (slightly larger than
Maryland)
Capital (Population): Tirana
(310,000)
Climate: varied temperate

PEOPLE

Population
Total: 3,268,000
Annual Growth Rate: 2.9%
Rural/Urban Population Ratio: 65/35
Ethnic Makeup of Population: 96%
Albanian (Geg and Tosk); 4% Greek,
Vlach, Gypsy, and Bulgarian

Health
Life Expectancy at Birth: 67 years
(male); 73 years (female)
Infant Mortality Rate (Ratio):
59/1,000
Average Caloric Intake: 112% of FAO
minimum
Physicians Available (Ratio): 1/574

Religion(s)
70% Muslim; 20% Albanian
Orthodox; 10% Roman Catholic

Education
Adult Literacy Rate: 75%

COMMUNICATION
Telephones: 6,000

Newspapers: 42 dailies; 62,400,000
circulation yearly

TRANSPORTATION
Highways—Kilometers (Miles): 4,989
(3,100)
Railroads—Kilometers (Miles): 417
(258)
Usable Airfields: 10

GOVERNMENT
Type: pluralistic parliamentary
democracy
Independence Date: November 28,
1912
Head of State: President Sali Berisha;
Prime Minister Alexander Meksi
Political Parties: Democrats; Social
Democrats; Republicans; Socialists
(former Communists)
Suffrage: n/a

MILITARY
Number of Armed Forces: 48,000
*Military Expenditures (% of Central
Government Expenditures):* 11.4%
Current Hostilities: internal unrest

ECONOMY
Currency ($ U.S. Equivalent): 5.31
leks = $1
Per Capita Income/GNP: $1,300/$4
billion
Inflation Rate: 30%
Total Foreign Debt: $400 million
Natural Resources: oil; gas; coal;
chromium
Agriculture: wheat; corn; potatoes;
sugar beets; cotton; tobacco
Industry: textiles; lumber; fuels;
semiprocessed minerals

FOREIGN TRADE
Exports: $428 million
Imports: $363 million

BITTER LEGACY

For Albanians, 1991 was a banner year. They successfully challenged the
Communist regime, bringing to an end 40 years of brutal rule. But their
euphoria was short-lived, because the Communist party leaders, for all
their pompous pledges of building a socialist utopia, had bequeathed an
economically destitute society to their successors. The new parliamentary democracy in Tirana now faces the challenge of feeding the people.
In mid-1991 dairy shops and bakeries had empty shelves and 50,000
people were unemployed, provoking in the summer a cruel exodus to
Italy of more than 100,000 people, mostly youth, to find food and work
and the means of survival.

ALBANIA

Since its independence from Turkey in 1912, Albania has been threatened by foreign enemies seeking to partition and annex it. Albania is vulnerable because of its small size; its lack of natural resources needed for an effective military defense; and the sharp differences between the country's largest social groups, the Gegs and the Tosks. Moreover, its strategically significant location astride the Strait of Otranto, which links the Adriatic Sea to the Mediterranean, has made Albania a tempting target of its powerful neighbors, Italy and Yugoslavia.

Albania's existence was threatened only 3 years after gaining independence from the Turkish Empire. In 1915 the Allied powers concluded a secret agreement—which they never executed—to partition Albania at the end of World War I. In the 1920s and 1930s Benito Mussolini's Italy had designs on Albania; Italy expanded its political influence in Tirana, the Albanian capital, until in 1939 it finally invaded and occupied the country. And when Albania regained its independence, after Italy left the war in 1943, a new threat came from the Yugoslav Communists who helped the newly formed Albanian Communist Party to take over the country at the end of World War II.

The Albanian Communist Party, founded in 1941, understandably had an obsession with security that bordered on paranoia. The worry about security explains the speed with which the Communists adopted the Soviet-style political dictatorship, which would assure the unity and defense of Albania. By 1953 the Albanian Communists had transformed their country into a socialist police state.

Although the Albanian Communists were on very good terms with the Soviets, who already had begun to expand their influence in Tirana, Albania never became a Soviet satellite. It was too geographically distant from the Soviet Union for the Kremlin to coerce and control. Albania was never occupied by Soviet forces. The Albanian Communists preserved their independence from Moscow.

ECONOMIC BACKWARDNESS AND POLITICAL REPRESSION

Albania, predominantly agrarian, is still the most economically backward of the Central/Eastern European countries. It has the lowest standard of living in the region.

When other Central/Eastern European countries began experimenting with and diverging from the Soviet model after

1953, Albania continued to be rigidly conformist. It never veered away from the police-state character it acquired in the late 1940s, nor did it diminish in any significant way the highly centralized Soviet-style command economy also developed during that period.

Indeed, the Soviet Union's own departures from Stalinism and the growing diversity among socialist countries in Central/Eastern Europe frightened the conservative Albanian leadership. In the 1960s, inspired partly by Chinese policies at that time, Albania pursued a minicultural revolution to reinforce Stalinist norms of socialist behavior. There were ruthless purges of political moderates both in and out of the Communist party; people living in the cities were moved to the countryside; and there was a campaign to obliterate foreign influence of any kind, especially printed materials. Much emphasis was placed on ideological conformity and political obedience. While the country eventually abandoned some of the more extravagant efforts to achieve a Maoist-like egalitarianism and conformity, it remained a repressive dictatorship.

FOREIGN-POLICY EXTREMES

There was a tendency toward extremes also in the area of foreign policy. After World War II the Albanian Communist leadership gradually weaned itself away from its Yugoslav patrons, fearing an eventual Yugoslav takeover of the country. Albanian leaders were comforted by Stalin's anger with Joseph Broz Tito, Yugoslavia's Communist Party leader, and looked to the Soviet Union for protection.

There was a radical change in Albania's relations with the Soviet Union, however, following Joseph Stalin's death, largely in consequence of the Kremlin's decision to reconcile with Tito. Albanian Communist leader Enver Hoxha and Premier Mehmet Shehu were afraid that this improvement in relations with the Soviets would encourage Tito to expand Yugoslav influence over Albania. Although Albanian fears about Yugoslavia proved groundless, the Albanian Communists were still upset with the Soviets.

At the same time there was an expansion of Albanian ties with China. Despite the huge geographic distance between the countries, they gravitated diplomatically toward each other because of several strategic and sociopolitical commonalities. Both countries had a dislike of Soviet criticisms of Stalinism, to which they were committed for similar reasons: both Albania and China were awash in conflict, economically underdeveloped, and inse-

cure because of perceived threats by powerful outsiders. Both wanted mutual cooperation. Albania needed Chinese economic assistance and was willing to provide in return a base from which China could expand its influence in Central/Eastern Europe.

Thus, during the 1960s and early 1970s there was a Sino-Albanian entente. But it never developed into an alliance, and it collapsed shortly after Mao Zedong's death in 1976; the relationship ended 2 years later when the Chinese government announced a termination of economic aid to Albania. The Albanians once again were isolated.

NEW DIRECTIONS IN THE 1980s

In the next phase of Albanian foreign relations, beginning in the late 1970s, the Albanian leadership tried to diminish its isolation in world affairs for reasons of economic expediency as well as security. Albania needed outside help to survive, let alone prosper. It needed friends to help strengthen its security. The Albanians moved in a variety of directions: toward Yugoslavia and Greece, the capitalist West, and the Soviet Union.

Yugoslavia and Greece

Premier Shehu apparently was sympathetic to the idea of a reconciliation with Yugoslavia, but he was opposed by party leader Hoxha, who was vehemently anti-Yugoslav and feared a resurgence of Yugoslav influence over the Albanian Communist Party. Hoxha feared especially the spread of Yugoslav ideas on administrative decentralization to Albania, which needed national unity for the development of Albanian socialism. Another obstacle to an Albanian-Yugoslav reconciliation was Yugoslavia's alleged discrimination against the Albanian-speaking people of its Kosovo autonomous republic.

In the conflict over the issue of reconciliation with Yugoslavia within the top Albanian leadership, Shehu lost out to Hoxha, and no reconciliation between the two countries materialized. Shehu died under mysterious circumstances in 1981. Although the official explanation for his death was suicide, there were suspicions that Hoxha, who tried to discredit Shehu after his death (he called the former premier a spy for the United States, the Soviet Union, and Yugoslavia), had him executed.

Albania also sought to improve relations with its southern neighbor, Greece, which renounced claims on Albanian territory in 1984. But a major obstacle to any effort to improve relations with Greece was the Greek government's concern about the living conditions of the Greek minority in Albania, though the Greek minority lived no worse than the Albanians. While Greece's left-leaning Papandreou government continued to be interested in an improvement in relations, it was unlikely to move closer toward Albania without some satisfaction on this issue.

Albania and the West

Albania also expressed some interest in developing ties with other Western nations, notably Canada, but was restrained. The Albanian approach to international affairs was very ideological, and the traditional suspicion of outsiders remained. The Albanian leadership still feared and disliked Western capitalism and had not developed the pragmatism needed to transcend those prejudices. Nor was it ready to forgive the British and Americans for trying to overthrow Communist rule in the early 1950s.

Albania's foreign-policy initiatives in the 1980s did not diminish its isolation in the world community. Albania was the only socialist country in Central/Eastern Europe—or anywhere else—to have no close ties with any other socialist country or with the West.

THE END OF THE HOXHA ERA

Hoxha's death, on April 11, 1985, did not lead to any major change in the country's domestic and foreign policies. His successor, Ramiz Alia, reiterated the policy of isolation. The Albanian leadership rejected all Soviet overtures for a reconciliation.

Nor were there any improvements in Albanian relations with the United States, which Alia condemned for trying to involve Europe in Ronald Reagan's Strategic Defense Initiative ("Star Wars"). The Albanians also denounced the 1986 U.S. bombing of Libya and called for the withdrawal of all American military power from the Mediterranean. On the other hand, other kinds of contacts between Albania and the United States, which could have some positive political significance for the future, increased. Notable among these were Albanian exports to the United States and visits to Albania by U.S. citizens of Albanian ancestry.

In the domestic sphere, the Albanian regime remained one of the most repressive in Europe and, according to the UN Commission on Human Rights, a "gross violator" of the rights of individuals. Religious persecution and political oppression did not abate under Ramiz Alia. The Alia regime also continued Hoxha's policy of forceful assimilation of non-Albanian-speaking minorities, in particular Greek-speaking Albanians.

The regime faced problems, however, that eventually changed its neo-Stalinistic character. Albanian youth had become restive—they sought a relaxation of political control and a let-up of emphasis on behaviorial conformity. Three circumstances underlay this discontent: sharp generation conflict (one-third of the Albanian population were under 15, and the median age of Albanians was 25); the influence of Western radio and television broadcasts; and the inability of the Albanian economy to absorb new workers.

To promote economic growth, the Albanian leadership emphasized incentives, in particular increased remuneration of highly productive or "model" workers to stimulate greater worker productivity. It allowed a limited open criticism of bureaucratism, corruption, and nepotism and began to reexamine the role of privately owned plots of land and livestock. There also was administrative decentralization and some wage differentials. One large incentive for this departure from orthodox Stalinist economic organization and behavior was desperation: still Europe's poorest country, Albania was plagued by shortages of basic foods like milk and was confronted with Europe's highest population growth (2.9% per year).

In an unusual acknowledgment of Albania's economic difficulties, Premier Adil Carcani in 1986 spoke of shortages of energy and imported raw materials and condemned mismanagement of economic enterprises. While he insisted on an increase of control everywhere and over everything to increase efficiency, he also called for an emphasis on enterprise profitability and an increase in foreign trade to earn foreign exchange. In 1987 Alia echoed these sentiments, criticizing poor planning and control by enterprise managers. He complained about a serious decline of output in the chrome industry, a source of hard-currency earnings, and accused the Ministry of Industry and Mines of poor planning and poor management.

Not surprisingly, given the country's economic malaise, the Albanian leadership continued to diminish—albeit only modestly and very gradually—its traditional xenophobia-inspired isolation. Greece apparently helped to bring Albania to a Balkan summit in 1988. Indeed, former Greek Premier Andreas Papandreou's government responded rather generously to Albanian signals of interest in developing relations between the two countries, even though Albania continued to discriminate against its Greek-speaking minority in southern Albania. Greece in 1988 aban-

doned claims to the territory inhabited by Albania's Greek minority, known in the past as northern Epirus, and formally terminated a technical state of war that had existed since Italy struck at Greece from Albania in 1940—this despite Tirana's continuing refusal to allow its citizens of Greek origin to practice their religion publicly.

There were also efforts to strengthen ties with the West. In 1987 Albania normalized relations with West Germany, despite Bonn's refusal to accommodate Tirana's longstanding request for war reparations. But in November 1987, during a visit to Tirana, Franz Joseph Strauss, then head of the Bavarian state government, gave the Albanian regime an outright gift of 6 million marks to spend on anything it wanted in West Germany except weapons and police vehicles.

THE BEGINNINGS OF DOMESTIC REFORM

Evidence of interest in domestic reform existed, even if it was difficult to assess. Some Albanian party members openly discussed the need to introduce reforms—provided that Communist party dominance and control of Albanian society continued. For example, Foto Cami, a member of the Communist party Politburo and of the Secretariat, observed in 1987 that Gorbachev's perestroika policies had relevance for Albania, which must introduce some changes of its own. Other influential Albanian officials also spoke in this spirit, such as Professor Hamid Beqeja, a psychologist at the University of Tirana, who criticized the national education system for emphasizing rote memorization, which discouraged critical thinking and student capacity to innovate.

Another reason for movement toward real reform had to do with Albanian youth, who were becoming increasingly impatient with social and economic conditions in their country. Albanian authorities acknowledged difficulties with the country's young people, especially with their "anti-social" tendencies, such as disinterest in the study of Marxism-Leninism and their growing interest in religious activity. They also complained about other kinds of aberrant behavior, such as willful destruction of socialist property and violent behavior on the streets. The mere discussion of these problems suggested the beginning of a reassessment of national life that could provide the justification for reform at a later date.

Albania's reaction to the political upheaval in the rest of Central/Eastern Europe in the summer and fall of 1989 initially was defensive and negative. President Alia declared on January 1, 1990, that the uprisings that had ended Communist control in most Central/Eastern European countries would not affect Albania. He pledged to continue the policies of the past, which, he insisted, had served the country well.

Nevertheless, at the 9th plenum of the Albanian Communist Party's Central Committee, in January 1990, Alia outlined a number of changes that have been called a democratization of the country's political, economic, and social changes. Alia seemed to be suggesting two reasons for change. One was preservation of the essence of socialism—or, to put it another way, to reform and thereby reinvigorate an administrative system that had become obsolete and illogical and contributed to economic stagnation and latent social tensions, especially among the country's youth. Another reason was a determination to avoid a replication in Albania of the revolutions against Communist party rule in Central/Eastern Europe.

Meaningful change in Albania, however, was slow in coming. President Alia enacted some of the reforms discussed in the January 1990 Central Committee plenum: he decontrolled prices for some consumer goods and allowed private enterprise, mostly in the service area. The government also allowed farmers, who make up 60 percent of the total population, to cultivate private plots and sell their produce in open markets. But Alia proceeded very slowly in other areas of national life. Despite the collapse of Communist rule throughout Central/Eastern Europe, the Albanian leadership had no interest in relinquishing the Communist party's monopoly of power in Albania for a system of political pluralism. In recognition of the changing times, however, the government said that it would allow freedom of religion, of movement, and of speech. But there would be no political opposition, forbidden under Albania's Stalinist Constitution.

Alia had to deal with a large and influential conservative constituency, mostly in the bureaucracy, which wanted a traditional Stalinist system for its own self-interest rather than for ideology. Thousands of bureaucrats, at all levels of society, resisted change. Despite a new more liberal emigration policy, the bureaucracy grudgingly processed requests for passports by citizens seeking to travel abroad. Xheli Gjonj, a prominent spokesperson for the conservative point of view and a candidate member of the party Politburo, severely condemned Albanians seeking to emigrate, calling them enemies of their country.

A WEAKENING
OF COMMUNIST RULE

Events soon went beyond Alia's cautious change. A loosening of the regime's iron grip precipitated revolution. The country's small intelligentsia began to speak out critically about the Communist government's repression, lamenting its frequent violations of human rights. They advocated genuine political change. Albanian youth shared these sentiments and voted with their feet against the regime. As soon as it was possible to obtain travel visas, during the summer of 1990, more than 4,000 Albanians tried to leave. Alia responded in early July 1990 with promises of more reforms. He announced the imminent enactment of a law on parliamentary elections and reminded Albanians that they were free to travel abroad wherever they wanted and therefore there was no reason for so many to be in a rush to seek entry to foreign countries.

But these reforms were still not enough, and popular pressure for radical political change mounted. By the latter part of 1990 many Albanians, especially in the large urban centers like Tirana, were aware of the profound changes that had taken place throughout Central/Eastern Europe. They wanted equivalent change in their own country. Some even discussed the possibility of having to imitate the bloody Romanian revolution against Ceausescu to achieve the decommunization of Albania.

Although lower-level Communist party officials deplored this new political assertiveness, the top leadership was cautiously sympathetic. In a major speech to the Albanian Parliament on November 13, 1990, Alia declared that the Constitution would be revised to guarantee human rights, permit foreign investments, and allow the government to accept foreign credits. He also said that the party would give up its constitutionally guaranteed monopoly of power. Furthermore, the Parliament subsequently approved a law allowing mass organizations to field their own candidates in parliamentary elections.

Again, however, there were limits to these changes. As 1990 drew to an end, people attacked the symbols of dictatorship, such as monuments and buildings illustrative of the Stalinist era and of the late Enver Hoxha, including even the headquarters of the Communist party. In December dissident students led anti-government demonstrations in Tirana, Shkoder, Albasan, and Durres. These events reached a climax with the formation of Albania's first opposition party under Communist rule, the Democratic

Party. One of its founders was economics professor Gramoz Pashko, a self-styled "dissident," who declared the Democratic Party's committment to a multiparty system, protection of human rights, a free-market economy, good relations between Albania and her neighbors, and integration with Europe. The national trade union declared its independence of the Communists in the last week of December, asserting that it would no longer act as a party lever, and promised to fight for higher pay and better conditions for workers.

Demanding a role in parliamentary elections, scheduled for February 10, 1991, the new political organizations sought a postponment of election day for at least a month and a half in order to give them an opportunity to cultivate voter support. The Alia government agreed and provided the opposition parties (there were now several, although they still were quite small) with space for campaign headquarters, some telephones, and some automobiles. Moreover, on the eve of the elections Alia said that the Communist party would accept defeat if that were the will of the people.

THE PARLIAMENTARY
ELECTIONS

Parliamentary elections, held on March 31, 1991, were the first contested elections Albania had had since 1923. The two major contenders were the Communist and Democratic parties. To the dismay of voters in the large urban centers, who voted overwhelmingly for the candidates of the Democratic Party, the Communists won a comfortable majority of 162 out of 250. Albanians living in the countryside had voted overwhelmingly for the Communists because they were used to Communist rule and feared an outbreak of lawlessness and anarchy if reformers were elected to lead the country. Indeed, Alia lost his seat in Parliament to the hard-liner Gjonj. The Communists had also benefited from the enormous resources at their disposal: they had run a well-coordinated campaign against the opposition, and they had exploited their tight control over radio, television, and printed media. They had made it very difficult, by virtue of the government's control over the distribution of newsprint supplies, for the opposition to publish its organs, *Rilindja Demoktatie* and *Republika*. The Communists also used the old electoral trick of bribing voters in the countryside to win their support; on the eve of the elections the regime announced decisions to allow enlarged private farms and unlimited ownership of livestock.

Furthermore, the opposition Democrats had not had enough time to develop a rural constituency, nor to develop their electoral organization. Rural voters, who made up a majority of the electorate, knew little if anything about the noncommunist organizations challenging the Communist party in the election. According to Dr. Sali Berisha, now the leader of the Democrats, the Communists had cheated. He told members of the U.S. Congress in May 1991 that there had been killings and beatings of opposition candidates as well as severe restrictions on opposition access to news outlets.

The election intensified the split between town and country, creating rifts between parents and children, between officers and ordinary soldiers, and between the northern and southern parts of the country, which were inhabited by Gegs and Tosks, respectively. The elections did, however, tend to confirm what was already evident: a steady and seemingly irreversible Albanian movement away from communism. Although the conservative Gjonj intoned that the election results showed that Albanians still had faith in Marxism-Leninism, the opposite was more true, given the fact that the Democratic Party, only 4 months old and hamstrung in so many ways by the Communists, had been able to win 38 percent of the popular vote.

Hard-liners inside the party made a last desperate effort, following the March 1991 elections, to block further departures from the old order. Gjonj was elevated from candidate to full membership in the party Politburo in April. The hard-liners published in the party's *Zeri i Popullit* an editorial hailing the late Enver Hoxha as a great leader and saying that there was no need for the party to apologize to the Albanian people, since it had done its job.

THE END OF COMMUNIST RULE

Reformers pressed on, and finally even Gjonj was prepared for compromise. In the hope of being elected leader of the Communist party at its 10th Congress, in June 1991, Gjonj, in the keynote address, criticized Hoxha's leadership and promised further reform. This political about-face did not fool the reformers, who succeeded in electing former Prime Minister Fatos Nano as the new chair. The Congress criticized the Politburo and replaced it with a 15-member party presidency. It also changed the name of the party. Henceforth it was to be known as the Socialist Party, with no reference to communism. Subsequently *Zeri i Popullit* dropped the hammer and sickle insignia

from its masthead and published startling criticisms of Hoxha and his family.

In early July 1991, following post-Communist political patterns in other Central/ Eastern European countries, the former Albanian Communists affirmed their break with Marxism-Leninism. A new party program formally abandoned the goal of creating a communist society. It also called for a market economy with a safety net that would minimize the hardships of the new system. While advocating privatization, the Socialists favored preservation of agricultural cooperatives and retention of state control over vital industries, such as those involving national defense.

Chosen president of the republic by the newly elected Parliament, Alia accepted the job and resigned as head of the Communist party. The Parliament approved a Law on Constitutional Powers, which temporarily superseded the existing Constitution until a new one could be written. The Law on Constitutional Powers endorsed political pluralism and the establishment of a multiparty political system, and it guaranteed human rights and the equality of all forms of private ownership—state, collective, and private. Finally, the Law on Constitutional Powers explicitly banned party activity in the government ministries of Defense, Internal Affairs, Justice, and Foreign Affairs.

Alia took the lead in this evident effort to dismantle the old socialist order. He called for an Albanian version of democracy in national life. This would involve freely contested elections for managers of industrial enterprises, farms, and Parliament; public debate on changes in higher education; and economic decentralization, in order to give more policy-making authority to district authorities. Alia also intended to ease conservative bureaucrats out of power through the introduction of elections with multiple candidates and a secret ballot for municipal councils, Parliament, and internal party positions. He wanted limits of 10 years on terms of office in the government, with a fifth-year review of performance and the possibility of dismissal by peers, and limits of 5 years for holding party office. But strikes and street demonstrations in Tirana against the government forced the resignation of Prime Minister Nano in June 1991. Alia replaced him with Ylli Bufi, a nonpartisan, nonideological economist. Bufi formed a coalition Cabinet in which half the 24 ministers were drawn from newly formed opposition groups and half from the Communists.

The final collapse of Communist rule occurred in late March 1992, when Alba-

nians voted to elect a new Parliament. Berisha's Democratic Party won an overwhelming majority of the popular vote. While support for the Democrats in the city areas was expected, because they were strongholds of reform, support for them in the countryside, which had voted for the Communists in the last parliamentary elections, came as a pleasant surprise. People in the small towns and villages of rural Albania were disappointed by the failure of the Communists to improve conditions while they put through major reforms, such as decollectivization. Albanian farmers said they were disgusted, now that they had their own land, over their inability to cultivate it—they complained about the lack of tools, fertilizer, and seed. Other reasons for the nationwide support for the Democrats included the hope that they would once and for all end Albania's international isolation and open up the country to European ideas and values; Berisha's recent visits to Western countries, in particular the United States, had been publicized on the national radio and television. Albanians hoped that with new ties to the West, their country might receive much-needed economic and financial help. Whether Berisha's Democrats could do better than their Communist predecessors remained to be seen.

ECONOMIC PROBLEMS

As Alia and the Albanian government, with a factionalized democratic opposition, moved toward pluralism and other internal reforms, they faced terrific obstacles. The economy was severely debilitated. Albania is the poorest country in Europe. Most Albanians live with ox- and donkey-drawn carts, grimy steam-powered factories, and threshers dating back to the 1950s. Towns and villages have few shops, and workers either walk to their jobs or travel on rickety buses.

A drought forced factories to close down for several months for lack of spare parts, raw materials, and power, causing increased unemployment. This in turn drained the state treasury, because of the government's obligation to pay idled workers 80 percent of their normal wages. Albania ended up having to import 70 percent of its energy supplies at high prices because of the Persian Gulf crisis. Inflation rose to 30 percent and agricultural production fell into slump, with food reserves dangerously low. (In July 1991 many peasants seized land and livestock in a veritable revolution against the old collectivist order.) Making matters worse was a brain drain through emigra-

Independence 1912	Formation of the Albanian Communist Party; Hoxha becomes the head 1941	The Albanian Communists take power with the help of Yugoslav Communists 1944	Communist leader Hoxha becomes the head of government 1945	Albanian Communists break with Yugoslav Communists 1948	Albania joins the Warsaw Pact 1955	Albanian-Soviet relations are broken; Albania strengthens ties with China 1961	Albania ends participation in the CMEA 1962	Albania withdraws from the Warsaw Pact 1968	All Chinese military and economic ties with Albania are severed 1978

1980s–1990

Shehu dies under mysterious circumstances; Hoxha dies and is succeeded by Alia

Party Congress rejects ties with the Soviet Union, the United States, and Yugoslavia

Communist rule collapses; Albania begins economic and political liberalization.

tion, depriving the country of valuable technical and managerial expertise. There was also a drastic decline in revenue from hard-currency exports such as oil, electricity, and chromium; and the foreign debt, which previously was nonexistent, climbed to the equivalent of $400 million.

Waves of impoverished unemployed Albanian young people tried to emigrate to Italy, beginning in the summer of 1990. In March 1991, some 24,000 Albanians went to Italy, and in the summer another 10,000 Albanians in desperate straits sought refuge in Italy, in the hope of finding work and better living condtions.

Nevertheless, Albanian reformers were ready to accept the prospect of shock treatment. In the summer of 1991 they proposed to move forward with plans for a market economy. Bufi also proposed an immediate and extensive reduction of government expenditures for administration, the military, and price subsidies and an acceleration of privatization of small- and medium-size enterprises. And in September 1991 the government announced preparations for a reform of the banking and currency systems.

THE END OF ALBANIA'S ISOLATION

To help facilitate reform of the country's dilapidated economy—in particular to obtain much needed foreign investment—the

Alia leadership initiated a dramatic foreign-policy shift. In June 1990 it asked to join the European Conference on Security and Cooperation and said that it would adopt the principles of the 1975 Helsinki Accords on which the ECSC is based. Other incentives to expand ties with neighboring countries were the collapse of Communist regimes throughout Central/Eastern Europe in 1989 and the efforts of the new governments to draw closer to the West, thereby accentuating Albania's psychological as well as diplomatic isolation in Europe.

Alia was especially interested in improving relations with the United States. In April 1990 the government opened negotiations with Washington, and in March 1991 Washington announced a restoration of ties between the two countries. When U.S. Secretary of State James Baker visited Tirana in June 1991, an estimated 300,000 Albanians gathered in central Tirana to welcome him, a display, incidentally, that was not only anti-Communist but also a strong expression of faith that somehow the United States could and would help Albania. Baker offered a modest program of economic aid, worth about $6 million—not the aid of Marshall Plan dimensions that the Albanians said they needed to implement their reform program. Baker also cautioned the Alia leadership that the future of Albanian–U.S. relations would depend on its continued

pursuit of political and economic liberalization.

THE YUGOSLAV CIVIL WAR

Albania faces problems on its borders as well as at home. The Albanian minority in the Yugoslav province of Kosovo is subject to Serb repression. In mid-1991 Serb Republic President Slobodan Milosevic reduced Albanians to second-class citizens by abolishing their autonomy, dissolving their local parliament, and closing down Albanian-language radio, television, and newspaper publications. Following the invasion of Croatia by the Serb-dominated Federal Army, Serbia intensified its repression in Kosovo. The Albanian government responded in the summer of 1991 by accusing Serbia of planning genocide. Alia appealed for intervention to the European Community, the UN Security Council, and the Conference on Security and Cooperation in Europe. Although Albania is ill-prepared for a military confrontation with Yugoslavia, the outbreak of an armed conflict in Kosovo would in all probability involve Albania.

DEVELOPMENT

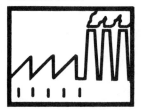

The country is predominantly agrarian and depends more on human than mechanical labor to produce food. What technology does exist was imported from the Soviet Union in the 1950s or from China in the 1960s and 1970s. Oxcarts, donkeys, and broken-down Czechoslovak trucks are the main means of transportation. People in cities rely on bicycles to get around, because private cars are banned.

FREEDOM

Albania has had two open, free, and competitive parliamentary elections since 1989, which led to the final collapse of Communist party rule. Albanians are now free to criticize, oppose, and replace government officials as the result of their bloodless revolution against 40 years of brutal authoritarian rule.

HEALTH/WELFARE

Clothing is simple and drab, and there are shortages of many consumer necessities. Nevertheless, thanks to improved health care, the population has trebled since World War II, and average life expectancy has risen from 38 to 72 years.

ACHIEVEMENTS

The illiteracy rate has dropped from 80% in 1945 to 25% today, and other quality-of-life indicators have also improved. Albania's economic and political isolation has diminished somewhat.

Bulgaria

GEOGRAPHY

Area in Square Kilometers (Miles):
110,994 (42,855) (slightly larger than
Ohio)
Capital (Population): Sofia
(1,200,000)
Climate: dry, hot summers and damp,
cold winters, but with strong regional
variations

PEOPLE

Population
Total: 8,978,000
Annual Growth Rate: 0.06%
Rural/Urban Population Ratio: 33/67
Ethnic Makeup of Population: 85%
Bulgarian; 9% Turk; 6% Gypsy,
Macedonian, Armenian, Russian, and
others

Health
Life Expectancy at Birth: 68 years
(male), 74 years (female)
Infant Mortality Rate (Ratio):
18/1,000
Average Caloric Intake: 146% of FAO
minimum
Physicians Available (Ratio): 1/319

Religion(s)
85% Bulgarian Orthodox; 13%
Muslim; 2% Jewish, Roman Catholic,
Protestant, and others

Education
Adult Literacy Rate: 98% (estimate)

COMMUNICATION
Telephones: 2,228,680
Newspapers: 17 dailies; 2,200,000
circulation

CULTURAL LIFE

Bulgaria is moving slowly but steadily away from its socialist past.
Although Bulgarian citizens were able to vote directly for president for
the first time in 40 years in January 1992, ex-Communists are still in
control of many government ministries. Most ordinary Bulgarian citizens miss the paternalism of the past as the government gradually
diminishes state control of the economy. One reason for Bulgarians to be
optimistic about their future, however, may be its prime minister, Filip
Dimitrov: at 36, he is the youngest leader in Central/Eastern Europe.

TRANSPORTATION
Highways—Kilometers (Miles):
36,908 (22,030)
Railroads—Kilometers (Miles): 4,294
(2,662)
Usable Airfields: 380

GOVERNMENT
Type: pluralistic parliamentary
democracy
Independence Date: October 5, 1908
Head of State: President Zhelyu
Zhelev
Political Parties: Socialists (former
Communists); Union of Democratic
Forces; Bulgarian Agrarian Party;
Turkish Rights Movement; Bulgarian
Green Party
Suffrage: n/a

MILITARY
Number of Armed Forces: 127,000
*Military Expenditures (% of Central
Government Expenditures):* 6.0%
Current Hostilities: none

ECONOMY
Currency ($ U.S. Equivalent): 2.89
levas = $1
Per Capita Income/GNP:
$5,660/$50.8 billion
Inflation Rate: over 30%
Total Foreign Debt: 10.6 billion
Natural Resources: bauxite; copper;
lead; zinc; coal; lignite; lumber
Agriculture: grain; tobacco; fruits;
vegetables; sheep; hogs; poultry;
cheese; sunflower seeds
Industry: food processing; machinery;
chemicals; metallurgical products;
electronics; textiles; clothing

FOREIGN TRADE
Exports: $16.8 billion
Imports: $16.9 billion

BULGARIA

Bulgarian Communists were in a hurry to come to power and right the wrongs of a conservative and despotic past. During World War II they made common cause with other anti-Fascist elements in the so-called Fatherland Front, which fought against the Bulgarian monarch and his German ally. When the war was over, the Bulgarian Communists controlled the Front and used it as a stepping-stone to power.

The first postwar leader of the Bulgarian Communist Party (BCP) was Georgi Dimitrov, who had had a long career in the world communist movement before the war. He was extremely loyal to the Soviet Union, which had obtained his release from a Bulgarian prison in the early 1920s and helped him to become secretary general of the Comintern from 1935 until 1943. His only apparent sin—but it was a major one in Soviet eyes—was his willingness to cooperate with Yugoslavia's Tito in the proposed establishment of a Balkan union of Communist parties, which the Soviets successfully blocked.

Dimitrov's successors to the leadership of the BCP, Vassil Kolarov in 1949 and Vulko Chervenkov from 1949 to 1954, followed in his footsteps. They loyally pursued Soviet-inspired policies in their transformation of Bulgaria into a socialist state. By 1953 the new People's Republic of Bulgaria, which had replaced the monarchy, was a replica of the Soviet dictatorship and a loyal Soviet ally. Chervenkov's successor, Todor Zhivkov, who led the BCP until 1989, continued the conservative and loyalist traditions of his predecessors.

AUTHORITARIAN SOCIALISM

Soviet-style political authoritarianism was unchallenged in Bulgarian society. In the era of Communist rule after 1946, Bulgaria had a very small intelligentsia and virtually no dissent. Bulgarian society had little experience with Western-style political liberalism, partly because of the autocratic monarchs who ruled the country from 1878 until 1946.

The economy was another dimension of Bulgaria's Soviet-inspired authoritarian socialism—but it did experience some modest yet promising reform. In the 1950s and 1960s Bulgaria's economic organization conformed very closely to the Soviet model, in its highly centralized decision-making, its expansion of heavy industry, and its achievement of almost 100 percent collectivization of agriculture.

Beginning in the 1970s, however, the Bulgarian Communist leadership introduced changes in industry and agriculture

that, while not identical, did resemble in some respects the Hungarian reforms of that era. The Bulgarian leadership established its own "New Economic Mechanism," which provided for some decentralization of managerial decision-making. It also moved certain industries with small physical needs out of the large urban centers. The Bulgarian government later offered foreign capitalists willing to invest in Bulgaria part ownership of state enterprises and partial receipt of profits from them.

The Bulgarians also undertook some reforms in agriculture. In the 1970s the government created huge agro-industrial complexes which integrated the growing, processing, and marketing of food products. In addition to increasing the mechanization of agriculture, the Bulgarians expanded the amount of cultivable land to be set aside for private use. Farmers could not own this land; they could only cultivate it. But what they grew was theirs to sell to state purchasing agencies or in public markets. The result of this incentive-generating reform was a surge of food output.

FOREIGN POLICY

The most conspicuous aspect of Bulgarian foreign policy in the era of Communist party rule was closeness—indeed, subservience—to the Soviet Union. Still, Bulgaria had other, compelling international interests that became increasingly important in the determination of Bulgarian foreign policy.

Closeness to the Soviet Union
Bulgaria was the least questioning and most subservient satellite of the Soviet Union. It almost always sided with the Soviets at international meetings of Communist parties and consistently endorsed Soviet policy. Bulgaria approved the 1968 Soviet intervention in Czechoslovakia; it echoed and sometimes outdid (with Kremlin approval, of course) harsh Soviet rhetoric toward the West.

Bulgarian closeness to the Soviet Union existed for several reasons. The two countries shared common cultural characteristics, such as the use of the Cyrillic alphabet and the prevalence of the Orthodox faith. The Bulgarians also remembered how the Russian Czarist government helped Bulgaria to emancipate itself from Turkish rule in 1878; although the Russians were sometimes overbearing in their relations with the new monarchy in Sofia, they were not threatening. In addition, after World War II the Kremlin acknowledged that, unlike Hungary and Romania,

Bulgaria did not participate in the German military invasion of the Soviet Union in June 1941.

The Bulgarian Communist leadership also identified with the Russian revolutionary tradition. Like the Marxists in prerevolutionary Russia, Bulgarian Communists were faced with a brutal authoritarian regime and endorsed violence to overthrow it.

In addition, Bulgaria was close to the Soviet Union out of gratitude. Bulgaria received much Soviet economic assistance, in particular in the development of its electronics industry. It is not an exaggeration to say that Bulgaria's relative economic well-being could be attributed largely to help given by the Soviet Union.

Bulgaria and the Balkans
Bulgaria has had much in common with other countries in the Balkans—Yugoslavia, Albania, Romania, Greece, and Turkey. These countries have had similar economic problems: all agrarian, economically underdeveloped, and dependent upon foreign sources for manufactured necessities. They also have shared a common political past: they have all been governed at one time or another by the Turks.

At the same time, Bulgaria under the Communists saw an opportunity in the Balkans to play an important international role that gratified national sentiment. Despite their intimacy with the Soviet Union, Bulgaria's Communist leaders showed a continuing interest in cooperating with other Balkan countries, both socialist and capitalist, to solve political and socioeconomic problems that the countries of the region shared. Their shared interests included the creation of a nuclear-free zone; the establishment of a regional parliament and other devices for regular discussion of regional problems; and the acceptance of a declaration of respect for territorial integrity, noninterference in internal affairs, and renunciation of the use or threat of force. But the Soviets limited Bulgaria's development of a Balkan policy. The Kremlin did not want its Balkan allies to develop multilateral relations between themselves and the nonsocialist countries of the region, viewing such independent diplomacy as a challenge to Soviet influence and power in Central/Eastern Europe. Thus, Bulgarian leaders stressed—as the Kremlin wanted them to do—bilateral relations as the best way to address regional problems. (But in the future, in response to Bulgarian national sentiment and patriotism, the Bulgarian leadership may seek to expand Bulgaria's role in the Balkans.)

Other limits on Bulgaria's role in the Balkans have concerned problems with particular countries, such as Yugoslavia, Greece, and Turkey. These problems are historic and continue to be a source of antagonism between Bulgaria and its neighbors. They discourage development of real friendship, mutual understanding, and effective regional cooperation.

Yugoslavia and Greece

Bulgarian relations with Yugoslavia and Greece have been strained because of differences over Macedonia, most of which is currently part of Greece. However, other, smaller portions of Macedonia that are in contention belong to Yugoslavia and Bulgaria and are a cause of controversy between them. Bulgaria rejects a Yugoslav claim that Macedonians living in Bulgaria's Pirin district are a distinct ethnic minority entitled to cultural autonomy; Bulgaria argues that so-called Macedonians are ethnic Bulgarians.

Macedonia is an issue in Bulgarian-Greek relations primarily because of the Sofia government's concern about the well-being of a Bulgarian-speaking minority living in the part of Macedonia ruled by Greece. Moreover, in the nineteenth and early twentieth centuries Bulgaria sought control of this region because of its location on the Aegean Sea. Possession of Macedonia could have provided Bulgaria with an alternative to the Russian-dominated Black Sea outlet to the Mediterranean. In 1941 Bulgaria temporarily occupied and annexed Macedonia in conjunction with the German invasion of Greece.

Turkey

Bulgaria's difficulties with Turkey resulted in part from alleged efforts of the Sofia regime to obliterate the ethnic identity of its Turkish minority, nearly 800,000 people. The BCP asserted that there were no Turkish people in Bulgaria, only "pure Bulgarians," some of whom were converted to Turkish culture when Bulgaria was part of the Ottoman Turkish Empire.

To the dismay of Sofia, the Turkish leadership championed the rights of people in Bulgaria said to have Turkish blood. The Turks invited their kin in Bulgaria to return "home," where they were promised a hospitable reception. But Bulgaria refused to allow emigration. Bulgaria's curtailment of support for Turkish-language broadcasts and other pressures to acculturate Bulgarians of Turkish origin contributed to the continuing strain in Bulgarian-Turkish relations.

Bulgaria and the West

The Bulgarian Communists demonstrated an interest in expanding trade with the West. While they did not trade as much as they would have liked with the United States, because they had not been given most-favored-nation treatment, their trade with Germany increased to the point where Germany is now Bulgaria's largest trading partner in the West.

Out of a desire to avoid prejudicing their relations with the West, the Bulgarians maintained a careful neutrality in the growing East-West confrontation over arms control. While Czechoslovakia went out of its way to support the Soviets against the West, the Bulgarians showed restraint. Their official press refrained from the harsh propaganda against the West that was published by the Czechoslovaks. Thus, while Bulgaria certainly remained most loyal to its Soviet ally, there were subtle distinctions in its foreign-policy behavior. Significantly, the Bulgarians now say that they retain the "right to pursue their own interests."

THE PLOT TO ASSASSINATE THE POPE

In the early 1980s Bulgaria encountered a new international problem—one of image—that compromised its relations with the West. This problem stemmed from charges that Bulgaria was complicitous in the attempted assassination of Pope John Paul II in 1981. It has been said that Bulgarian officials acted as intermediaries between the Turkish gunman Mehmet Ali Agca and the Soviet Union's KGB, which was reputed to be the inspiration of the plot. It has been speculated that the Soviets wanted to kill the pope because of his sympathy for and encouragement of political opponents of the socialist regime of his Polish homeland and that they used their servile Bulgarian ally in this effort.

It may be a long time before the truth about any Bulgarian complicity in the plot is known. But in the 1980s people in the West were willing to believe the worst about the Bulgarians. This was true because of the long-standing closeness of the Bulgarian leadership to the Kremlin and because of Soviet fears about the pope's support of the political opposition in Poland through his repeated statements of concern about events in his homeland and especially about the threat of Soviet military intervention in Poland.

BULGARIA AND PERESTROIKA

Bulgaria seemed to be embracing a form of Gorbachev's glasnost and perestroika,

though with mixed success. While the Bulgarian leadership acknowledged a Soviet view of the need to be more open and candid about problems of socialist development, it continued to limit the scope of permitted criticism and dissent, allowing public expression only of general complaints about corruption, the importance of reducing consumption of alcohol, and the need for everybody to work harder.

Moreover, Bulgaria's narrow definition of glasnost was evident in the renewal of its aggressive cultural-assimilation policies toward the Turkish minority. Worried that the country might be overwhelmed in the next decade by a Turkish minority—now about 15 percent of the total population—whose birth rate had increased at a time when that of ethnic Bulgaria had remained static, the Bulgarian authorities seemed determined to prevent people of Islamic and Turkish culture from becoming a factor in Bulgarian society. They especially did not want the Turkish minority to gain the power to influence the government (which could conceivably happen in the future as their percentage of the total Bulgarian population increases).

As the leadership in Sofia intensified its policies of forced assimilation of its Turkish-speaking citizens, it met resistance. In May 1989 the villagers of Razgrad and Shumen, east of Sofia, demonstrated against the government, presumably to attract the attention of the East-West Conference on Human Rights meeting at that time in Paris. The authorities responded with overwhelming force. Using helicopters and tanks against civilian protesters, they ruthlessly suppressed the demonstration and deported many of the Turkish activists.

This repression provoked an unexpected exodus from Bulgaria to Turkey in June and July 1989 of about 150,000 ethnic Turks. The emigrants vacated key jobs in the Bulgarian economy, crippling factories, mines, and agriculture, in particular undercutting the production of tobacco, a cash export crop that earned desperately needed hard currency.

Nevertheless, rather than retreat from its policies of cultural homogenization, the Communist regime in Sofia seemed reconciled to the permanent loss of its ethnic Turkish people and replaced them with imported Vietnamese labor. Willing to work at very low wages, these workers, numbering about 17,000, were intensely disliked by the local population.

In the economic sphere, however, there were both logic and justification for reform. This was recognized by the leadership, some of whom called for Gorbachev-style administrative reform to correct flaws in the highly centralized Stalinist administrative mechanism, with its emphasis on heavy industrial output. They wanted to emphasize the production of consumer goods and to improve the standard of living.

Incentives to undertake economic reform included the acute energy shortage in 1985, which led to darkened and unheated apartments and disrupted the manufacture and distribution of industrial goods. And in 1986 there was a significant lag in the production of housing and foodstuffs; there were complaints in the media that enterprises were ignoring consumer needs, deceptively passing on price increases to consumers, and showing little imagination or initiative in the production process.

Changes outlined by party leader Zhivkov in 1987 included the introduction of self-management throughout the Bulgarian economy. While some central planning would continue, industrial enterprises would be free to make their own adjustments to assure profitable levels of quality and quantity. Industries would raise capital through newly created investment banks, determine their own management, and use income as they wished for wages or reinvestment and expansion. Other planned changes would affect the political sphere and involve a reduction of adminis-

tration by merging some central ministries, abolishing several state planning agencies, and eliminating the jobs of numerous state functionaries.

Whether these measures to alter Bulgaria's highly centralized economic administration will ever remedy the country's growth problems and improve its output still remains to be seen. For the moment at least, the Bulgarian economy has outgrown the reforms of the 1970s and consequently faces a stagnation that could be a potential source of popular discontent.

UPHEAVAL IN THE FALL OF 1989

Encouraged by the popular attacks on Communist party rule in East Germany and Czechoslovakia—two conservatively ruled socialist states that in this respect had much in common with Bulgaria—large numbers of Bulgarian citizens staged antigovernment demonstrations in November 1989, calling for democratization in Sofia. Zhivkov responded in a somewhat conciliatory fashion, no doubt influenced in this regard by the fate of Honecker and Jakes. Zhivkov acknowledged what he termed the positive role of nongovernment groups and pledged extensive change in all areas of Bulgarian life, including politics. The demonstra-

tions, however, continued. Unwilling to use force, and in the absence of any Soviet support, Zhivkov resigned as party leader on November 9. He was quickly succeeded by Petar Mladenov, a less-well-known party official with close links to Gorbachev. In April 1990 the Bulgarian Parliament elected Mladenov president of the republic.

The new party leadership introduced many changes in an effort to forestall a frontal attack against its rule. It quickly rid itself of the most conservative elements in the top leadership and renewed a pledge to enact substantive political reforms which would lead to democratization of Bulgarian life. It was, however, careful to avoid saying or doing anything that would compromise its leadership role, at least for the time being. It did promise political pluralism and a greatly reduced party role in Bulgarian life. And in the face of continuing antigovernment demonstrations in Sofia and other Bulgarian cities in November that blamed the former party leader for gross mismanagement of the Bulgarian economy during his 35-year rule, the party expelled Zhivkov and ultimately approved a government arrest warrant against him.

Limits on how far Bulgaria would go in liberalizing its repressive political order,

(UN photo/Doranne Jacobson)

Bulgaria has much in common with other countries in the Balkans—Yugoslavia, Albania, Romania, Greece, and Turkey—they are all agrarian, economically underdeveloped, and dependent upon foreign sources for manufactured necessities. The couple above is a common sight.

however, were apparent from the outset of the changes. It is true that the party leadership eased censorship to enable the media to focus attention on the flaws and abuses of the old regime. It also did nothing to prevent the continuation of massive popular demonstrations; and it began consultation with new, hastily formed opposition groups to involve them in governmental policy-making. But it did little to initiate extensive political changes, as the leaders in East Germany and Czechoslovakia had done. Thus, in December 1990 the National Assembly delayed enactment of a constitutional amendment that would have stripped the Bulgarian Communist Party of its monopoly of power. It tried to distract public attention from the issue by publicizing the wrongs of Zhivkov and his associates. The readiness of Bulgarian society for democratization seemed in doubt when, as a result of the government's decision to restore some cultural privileges to Bulgaria's large Turkish-speaking minority, there was an explosion of popular opposition, which was embarrassing to liberals advocating equality and protection of minority rights.

TRANSITION TO DEMOCRACY

In the early months of 1990 Bulgaria seemed to be following Gorbachev's perestroika model. The Bulgarian Communist Party continued to dominate both Cabinet and Parliament while making changes in leadership, policies, and institutions intended to effect a thorough democratization of Bulgarian political life. At the head of the new leadership which took power at the end of 1989 were two Gorbachev-style reformers, Mladenov and the premier, Andrei Lukanov. One suspects, however, that their commitment to democratization was partly motivated by an attempt to preserve the BCP's dominant position in the transition and post-transition eras, in which Bulgaria was moving away from its repressive past toward a new liberal and pluralistic political order.

Among the changes that occurred in Bulgaria in early 1990 were the Bulgarian Communist Party's adoption of a new name, the Bulgarian Socialist Party, the abandonment of all vestiges of Stalinism, and a call for coalition government, which the newly formed noncommunist parties ignored, because they did not want to prejudice their chances of defeating the Communists in the parliamentary elections scheduled for the spring of 1990 by cooperation with the Communists. The new Communist leadership also produced a draft constitution which contained a detailed bill of rights and provisions for a

powerful legislature. Opinion polls in early April seemed to suggest that the Communists were making progress in strengthening their credibility with Bulgarian voters: their party was given a lead in public support over the opposition groups—this despite new revelations of excesses by the Zhivkov regime in its early years, when it had established Nazi-style concentration camps where prisoners were tortured and killed.

PROBLEMS OF DEMOCRATIC DEVELOPMENT

While Bulgaria was spared the turmoil that other former Soviet satellites experienced in their efforts to develop a new democratic order, it will be a long time before Bulgaria becomes a stable and prosperous democracy. Severe political and economic obstacles must be overcome by the new post–Communist leadership in successfully negotiating the transition away from socialism.

Parliamentary Elections in June 1990

Parliamentary elections were held in early June 1990. They gave the former Bulgarian Communist Party, now the Bulgarian Socialist Party, a decisive victory. Although the Bulgarian Communists had shed their old name and eased their grip on economic and political life by abandoning their claim to a monopoly of power; by reducing their control of factories, farms, the military, and the police; and by adopting the rhetoric of liberal democracy, their victory set a precedent in Central/Eastern Europe in 1990: it was the first time that a ruling Marxist party in the region had competed in multiparty elections and won without recourse to the quasi-legal shennanigans that had enabled them to obtain large voter majorities in the late 1940s. Moreover, the final days of the campaign passed peaceably and without violence, in striking contrast to elections in neighboring Romania.

The success of the Bulgarian Communists was partly the result of a strong conservative tendency in the countryside. Farmers had a sense that Bulgaria had not done badly, even if it had not thrived, under Communist rule. Moreover, as one influential member of the Socialists explained, the party was victorious because its policies still corresponded to the interests of a majority of Bulgarian voters. Those interests remained security of work, income, and well-being, through continuation of the state-administered comprehensive welfare program, which guaranteed medical care and education. But it was also true that the former Com-

munists had been successful because of their continued stranglehold over local political life. Local Communist authorities took advantage of their control over jobs, housing, and other necessities in the small towns and villages of rural Bulgaria to persuade voters to support Socialist Party candidates. It was impossible for outside observers supervising the elections to prove that this intimidation—indirect and oblique—was happening. Finally, the Bulgarian Socialist Party benefited from the fact that, unlike the Communist parties in other Central/Eastern European countries, the Bulgarian party had its own integrity and was not viewed as a stooge of the Kremlin. And, in any event, anti-Soviet and anti-Russian feelings had never been as strong in Bulgaria as elsewhere in Central/Eastern Europe. The euphoria of the Socialists, however, was short-lived. They tried to form a coalition with the opposition parties but failed, weakening their power to govern, never mind to implement controversial reform measures.

Economic Crisis

People were angry over a deepening economic crisis: sooty and crumbling facades of buildings, giant potholes in streets and highways, road tunnels closed indefinitely for repairs. They endured hours-long waits at gas stations, frequent power cuts, and production shortages with the rationing of such essentials as butter, cheese, sugar, eggs, and detergents. The economic structure still favored production of capital and industrial goods at the expense of consumer goods. Unfavorable weather contributed to economic hardship: a continuing drought dried out the food-producing countryside north and east of Sofia, which looked yellowish when it should have been green. Bulgarian farmers began to withhold livestock from government slaughterhouses toward the end of 1990, in anticipation of vastly higher prices when price controls should be lifted.

And, like in other former Soviet Bloc nations, there was a downward trend in both exports and imports. Bulgaria had to stop arms shipments to the Middle East. It also had to cope with reduced oil supplies from the Soviet Union, its principal supplier of petroleum products, partly because Moscow wanted to be paid in hard currency. In other respects, trade with the Soviet Union, which had been Bulgaria's largest trading partner, was disrupted as a result of production slowdowns caused by political turmoil. Moreover, Bulgarian hopes for replacement deliveries of oil from Iraq to pay back the latter's approximately $2.6 billion debt were dashed by the international trade embargo imposed after Iraq's August 2, 1990, invasion of Kuwait. In the meantime, the government further depressed Bulgarian foreign trade by forbidding the export of scarce agricultural commodities and by suspending payments on its $10.6 billion foreign debt, thereby cutting itself off from trade credits and other forms of overseas help.

Leadership Problems

The Socialists were divided in their leadership of the country. Membership of the party in the Parliament was split between moderates, who sought rapid, radical reform, after the fashion of Poland, and conservatives, who advocated a very slow pace of change. The moderates were youthful, energetic, and outspoken in their advocacy of change, but the conservatives were more influential, because they still controlled the levers of power in the party, as evidenced by their success in reelecting Lilov as party leader at a Congress in the summer of 1990.

Furthermore, the party was distracted in its management of the country by its ongoing effort to bring former leader Todor Zhivkov to trial, on charges of corruption and the commission of illegal actions. Unfortunately for the Socialists, Zhivkov fought back and insisted that he was innocent. He defended his record by condemning the Soviet invasion of Prague in August 1968, saying that he and Bulgaria had been forced by the Kremlin to participate in "this foreign occupation" of Czechoslovakia. He also denied any responsibility for the plot to assassinate Pope John Paul II. His resistance to his party's effort to use him as a scapegoat turned out to be a time-consuming, energy-wasting exercise in futility which prevented the Socialists from focusing on the real economic problems facing the country in its new era. Worse, Zhivkov threatened that if persecution of him continued, he would make startling revelations that would implicate many influential members of the Socialist Party.

Antigovernment demonstrations erupted in Sofia in the latter part of 1990. The Union of Democratic Forces, which supported the demonstrations, was predicting the downfall of the Socialists. It pressed for another election for Parliament and called for a confidence vote. It also refused to back a government economic plan to turn over state enterprises to private hands, end price controls on most goods, and expand foreign trade until the resignation of the prime minister. Angry workers, especially miners, backed the Union and seemed ready to man the barricades, so to speak, to force the former

Communists out of power. The frustrated Lukyanov resigned on November 29, 1990, taking his 5-month-old Socialist government with him.

Leaders of the largest of the many Bulgarian parties agreed to establish a coalition in which the Socialists would participate, but without Kukyanov. His successor was Dimitar Popov, a lawyer without party affiliation. Although the coalition was made up of the three largest parties plus five independents, the Socialists remained in a dominant position, by virtue of their majority in the Parliament. Ironically, this new government was very similar to what Lukyanov had been seeking since the June 1990 elections: a multiparty coalition with the Socialists dominating it. But all parties agreed that the country's new leadership would last only until the next set of parliamentary elections, tentatively scheduled for 1991.

Without waiting for new elections, Prime Minister Popov announced in January 1991 a major long-term shake-up of the Bulgarian economy. It involved substantial austerity to halt the decline in output and to reduce the country's foreign debt. It abandoned subsidies on many basic goods and utilities as part of an overall effort to create a market economy. Anticipating increases in the price of heating, public services, and many food items, the government struck a deal in advance with trade unions to allow a modest increase in wages and a hike in the minimum wage, to soften the blow of change for already strapped wage earners.

Popov's economic changes met with immediate opposition. In mid-August 1991, about 21,000 Bulgarian miners in 81 of the country's 90 mines again struck, ostensibly for wage increases, better working conditions, and a government guarantee that mines would not be closed as part of the austerity program. The strike threatened to interrupt the supply of coal to plants producing more than a third of the country's electricity.

But miners are unlikely to find themselves better off very soon, despite the government's best efforts. Working against success are powerful external factors, most signficantly Bulgaria's enormous foreign debt and its inability to trade with hard-currency countries. Its goods cannot compete on the open market; they lack the minimum of quality that would make them attractive in the West. For too long the Bulgarian economy was insulated from genuine competition by virtue of its close commercial relationship with the Soviet Bloc nations, which accounted for 80 percent of Bulgarian trade. Indeed, the future of Bulgarian trade, at least until the econ-

omy is successfully overhauled and made competitive with that of hard-currency areas, is likely to lie in sales of computers at cut-rate prices to the soft-currency countries of the Third World. And, although Bulgaria joined the International Monetary Fund and the World Bank in the fall of 1990, swift help was not forthcoming. Finally, the inefficient and dilapidated production and distribution systems remain obstacles to substantial foreign investment in the Bulgarian economy.

Renewal of Hostility
Toward the Turkish Minority

Complicating Popov's problems was a renewal of anti-Turk chauvinism among ultra-nationalist groups like the Fatherland Labor Party. The Socialists were annoyed that Turkish-speaking voters had elected 23 of 400 deputies to Parliament in the June 1990 elections; they were afraid that this development might cause an erosion of Slavic dominance in Bulgaria or become a secessionist movement that could compromise the country's territorial integrity. But hostility toward the Turkish minority also had a narrow economic motive: the Socialists' anxiety over the loss of jobs to small ethnic groups. Bulgarian nationalists wanted the government in Sofia to enact job quotas in areas where Bulgarians are outnumbered by ethnic Turks, and at the very least to guarantee a continuation of the practice, followed by the Zhivkov regime, of excluding ethnic Turks from managerial positions in state-owned industrial enterprises. In late July, in places with large concentrations of people of Turkish cultural origin, the nationalists staged protests against the Turks by blocking their access to municipal buildings, closing down factories, blocking roads, and preventing people from shopping.

THE END OF COMMUNIST RULE

The final collapse of Communist power in Bulgaria came with the parliamentary elections in October 1991. The Union of Democratic Forces bested the Socialists, though by only a hair's-breadth margin (the party won a plurality of 34.4 percent, less than half a percent more than the runner-up Socialist Party). Nevertheless, the results of the elections formally terminated 40 years of Communist party rule. And the new government, headed by Prime Minister Filip Dimitrov, pledged quick privatization of state-owned businesses, changes in laws on land ownership to encourage private entrepreneurialism in agriculture, and stimulation of foreign investment to accelerate Bulgaria's move

Independence
1908

Bulgaria joins
the Rome-Berlin
Axis
1941

Soviet troops
enter Bulgaria;
Dimitrov returns
to Bulgaria from
the Soviet Union
to head the BCP
1945

Dimitrov dies;
"nativist"
Bulgarian
Communists
succeed to
leadership of
the party
1949

Zhivkov
becomes the
first secretary
1954

The new
Constitution
reaffirms
Bulgarian
commitment to
Soviet-style
socialism
1971

Bulgaria
supports the
Soviet invasion
of Afghanistan
1979

1980s–1990s

150,000
Bulgarian Turks
flee to Turkey

50,000
Bulgarians
participate in
the country's
first mass
protest in 40
years

The final
collapse of
Communist
power; the
Turkish minority
gains a pivotal
role in national
politics

toward a free-market economy. The Union also promised to start confiscation of property illegitimately held by Communists, a move intended to assuage a growing popular resentment over the way in which many former party members had taken advantage of their skills and wealth to exploit the denationalization of industrial property.

There were, however, problematical aspects to this election. To begin with, with 33 percent of the popular vote, the Socialists remained influential in the new Parliament and in a position to complicate implementation of Dimitrov's program of rapid reform, given their commitment to gradualism in the transition away from socialism. Second, the Movement for Rights and Freedom, the party of the Turkish minority, won 7 percent of the popular vote and therefore became a factor in Bulgarian national politics for the first time ever. It was now in a position to sell its support to the party that was the most sensitive to the needs of the Turkish minority. Third, the multiplicity of party groups that emerged during the campaign and the failure of any party to get more than one-third of the vote were not conducive to the development of political stability in the democratic era. At the very least, the new Cabinet had to be based on a coalition of the Union and other, much smaller democratic parties, including the Movement, which has as a primary concern the betterment of the Turkish minority. Yet any party that tilts too much toward the Turks is likely to be severely criticized by a good proportion of the public, which remains sensitive to the growing political influence of the Turkish minority.

Prospects of Stability

There are two reasons to be optimistic about the prospects of Bulgaria's political and economic stability in the early 1990s. One is the defeat of the Socialist Party in the parliamentary elections of October 1991, representing the final collapse of Communist power in Bulgaria.

Another reason has to do with the United States. In January 1991, after having refused to offer Bulgaria an assistance program comparable to what had been given Poland, Hungary, and Czechoslovakia, because of alleged Bulgarian Communist cheating in the June 1990 elections, the Bush administration, convinced that Bulgaria was nevertheless making progress in the transition to democratic rule, cleared the way for lifting of restrictions on U.S. trade with Bulgaria. It affirmed that Sofia, by allowing unrestricted emigration, had qualified for most-favored-nation treatment. With the new trading status, Bulgaria became eligible for loan guarantees from the Export-Import Bank and participation in Overseas Investment Corporation programs.

Undoubtedly to encourage this and other Western initiatives to help the Bulgarian economy, Sofia voluntarily undertook in the spring of 1991 a sweeping investigation of long-standing international accusations of Bulgaria's complicity in the plot to assassinate Pope John Paul II in 1981. Despite the reticence of senior Bulgarian police and intelligence officials, who were reluctant to compromise colleagues and apparently had tried to destroy incriminating documents, the Bulgarian government released more than 127 volumes of secret police documents in May 1991. President Zhely Zhelev offered to provide whatever additional relevant documents came to light. At the very least this gesture of candor was intended to increase the credibility of Bulgaria's stated commitment to break completely with the past.

While Bulgaria is moving more slowly than other Central/Eastern European countries toward a liberalization of the political environment, it is also true that it is moving away from the old order without the violence and trauma that have characterized change in Romania. Nor has there been the kind of massive vote of no-confidence on the part of the Bulgarian people in their government, as was taken by the peoples of East Germany and Romania. Bulgaria remains what it has always been in the recent past: a conservative country whose society for the most part is unsympathetic to radical change.

DEVELOPMENT

The leadership has begun to dismantle the socialist economy and to move the country toward free enterprise and a market economy. Progress has been slow and painful, with unemployment running at 25%, the inflation rate over 30%, and a foreign debt of $10.6 billion.

FREEDOM

Bulgaria adopted a pluralistic party system in October 1991 with the holding of parliamentary elections in which 60 different political organizations fielded candidates for parliamentary seats. Other evidence of Bulgaria's moves toward democratization was the very high turnout—about 60% of the 6.5 million eligible Bulgarian electorate voted.

HEALTH/WELFARE

In 1989 Bulgarians demanded improved social-security benefits and wage increases for low-paid workers as a means of halting a perceived decline in living standards. Since 1987 the government has identified over 22 carriers of the AIDS virus and has waged an intensive campaign to ease popular but exaggerated fears of an AIDS epidemic.

ACHIEVEMENTS

Food stocks have begun to appear in shops, albeit at prohibitively high prices. The semblance of a market economy appears to be emerging, with Bulgarians comparing prices and buying only what is immediately needed. The U.S. dollar remains a preferred currency, but Bulgarians are showing new confidence in their own lei.

Czechoslovakia

GEOGRAPHY

Area in Square Kilometers (Miles):
127,870 (49,371) (about the size of
New York State)
Capital (Population): Prague
(1,139,000)
Climate: temperate

PEOPLE

Population
Total: 15,695,000
Annual Growth Rate: 0.2%
Rural/Urban Population Ratio: 27/73
Ethnic Makeup of Population: 65%
Czechoslovak; 30% Slovak; 4%
Hungarian; 1% German, Polish,
Ukrainian, and others

Health
Life Expectancy at Birth: 68 years
(male); 75 years (female)
Infant Mortality Rate (Ratio):
13/1,000
Average Caloric Intake: 141% of FAO
minimum
Physicians Available (Ratio): 1/312

Religion(s)
77% Roman Catholic; 20%
Protestant; 2% Orthodox; 1% other

Education
Adult Literacy Rate: 99%

COMMUNICATION
Telephones: 4,000,000
Newspapers: 30

THREATENING DIVISIONS
Czechoslovakia has always had a strong liberal spirit. Alone among all
the nations of Central/Eastern Europe, Czechoslovakia preserved democracy until it was invaded by Nazi Germany. Even in the harsh
repression that followed Soviet suppression during the Prague Spring of
1968, the notion of democracy was kept alive by people such as Vaclav
Havel, now the president of the republic.

In today's post-Communist era Czechoslovak liberalism is again
challenged, this time by divisive ethnocultural nationalistic rivalries
between Czechoslovaks and Slovaks that threaten to tear the country
apart. Citizens today, happy to be free, may nonetheless ask, "Will there
always be a Czechoslovakia?"

TRANSPORTATION

Highways—Kilometers (Miles): 73,881
(45,910)
Railroads—Kilometers (Miles): 13,142
(8,167)
Usable Airfields: 130

GOVERNMENT

Type: pluralistic parliamentary
democracy
Independence Date: October 18, 1918
Head of State: President Vaclav Havel
Political Parties: Socialist Party;
Civic Forum; Public Against
Violence; Christian Democratic
Movement
Suffrage: universal over 18

MILITARY

Number of Armed Forces: 193,400
*Military Expenditures (% of Central
Government Expenditures):* 7.5%
Current Hostilities: none

ECONOMY

Currency ($ U.S. Equivalent): 27.09
koronas = $1
Per Capita Income/GNP: $7,870/$123
billion
Inflation Rate: 0.7%
Total Foreign Debt: n/a
Natural Resources: Coal; coke;
timber; lignite; uranium; magnesite
Agriculture: wheat; rye; oats; corn;
barley; potatoes; sugar beets; hogs;
cattle; horses
Industry: iron and steel; machinery
and equipment; cement; sheet glass;
motor vehicles; armaments;
chemicals; ceramics; wood; paper
products

FOREIGN TRADE

Exports: $11.8 billion
Imports: $13.7 billion

CZECHOSLOVAKIA

Already one of the most industrialized countries in Central/Eastern Europe at the time of the Communist takeover, Czechoslovakia accommodated the Communist party's Soviet-inspired transformation to socialism with far less stress than other Central/Eastern European countries did. By the early 1950s Czechoslovakia had become a Soviet-style socialist dictatorship and a loyal ally of the Soviet Union.

In the early years of Communist party rule the Czechoslovak people, unlike most other Central/Eastern European peoples, had no deep-seated hostility toward the Russians. They did not seem to blame the Soviet Union for not helping them to de-fend their territory against Nazi aggression in 1938 and 1939. In fact, after World War II Czechoslovakia viewed the Soviet Union as the only country able to assure its security and survival. The Czechoslovaks had little faith in the West—even if culturally they were closer to it than to the Soviet Union—because of the way in which the great Western powers (Britain and France) had appeased the Nazis in the pre-World War II era and thereby contributed to the invasion and partition of Czechoslovakia in 1939.

When the Czechoslovak Communist Party (KSC) gained power after World War II it enjoyed substantial popularity, in contrast to the Communist parties of other Central/Eastern European countries. The Czechoslovak Communists had participated in the parliamentary system of the 1930s, had fought the Nazi occupiers in the 1940s, and were active partners with other Czechoslovak parties in the coalition governments following the war. The KSC thus had credibility with many voters, as seen in the first national elections after the war, when the Communists won more than one-third of the popular vote.

ORTHODOXY IN THE 1950s

In the years following Stalin's death in 1953, when its neighbors Poland and Hungary were experiencing political turmoil, Czechoslovakia remained the ideal Soviet satellite. It had a tight Stalin-like dictatorship under KSC leader Antonin Novotny; it slavishly imitated the Soviet model of socialist development in other ways, especially in the economic sphere; and it remained closely linked to the Soviet Union and the Warsaw Pact.

PRESSURES FOR CHANGE IN THE 1960s

The appearance of stability belied the reality of developing problems in Czechoslovak society. In the 1960s influential people both within and without the KSC discussed the need for significant divergence from Soviet practices in order to improve economic performance and raise the standard of living. Some also favored political liberalization and an expansion of trade with the West. There was enough support for sweeping change to replace Novotny, the symbol of Czechoslovakia's subservience to the Soviet model. In January 1968 he was succeeded as general secretary of the KSC by Alexander Dubcek, the leader of the Communist Party of Slovakia.

THE PRAGUE SPRING

When Dubcek tried to introduce political liberalization, in the form of a relaxation of censorship and to permit open discussion and debate of national problems, in the spring of 1968, the Kremlin became alarmed. In the summer of 1968 the Soviet leadership was afraid that Dubcek would allow massive change in Czechoslovakia that would lead to an erosion of socialism and to a westward orientation of foreign policy subversive of Czechoslovakia's links with the Warsaw Pact. It decided that the reform program under Dubcek's leadership must be stopped at once.

The Soviet Intervention

Accordingly, the Soviets led a Warsaw Pact invasion of Czechoslovakia. Pact

(Gamma-Liaison/Gilles Caron)

The Prague Spring, the Soviet invasion of Czechoslovakia in August 1968.

forces occupied Prague in August 1968. The Soviets ultimately forced the ouster of Dubcek. They approved his replacement by Gustav Husak, another Slovak but a conservative willing to lead Czechoslovakia exactly as the Soviets wanted.

The Soviets imposed on the Czechoslovak state what they termed "normalization." Soviet normalization meant the reversal of Dubcek reformism, the imposition of a strict political discipline throughout society, Czechoslovakia's explicit reaffirmation of its loyalty to the Warsaw Pact, and Czechoslovakia's acceptance of the supposedly temporary stationing on its soil of an unspecified number of Soviet troops. Soviet troops were to be withdrawn "as soon as the threat to socialism in Czechoslovakia and to the security of the Socialist community had passed."

Charter 77

While the Soviet intervention restored stability in Czechoslovak society, it also provoked an undercurrent of opposition. A major challenge to the Husak regime's political repression and servility to Moscow occurred in January 1977, when 300 Czechoslovak intellectuals from different sectors of national life signed a document called Charter 77. The charter contained a detailed condemnation of the government's political repression, accusing it of a systematic discrimination in education, in employment, and elsewhere in society against citizens critical of its policies.

The Charter 77 movement was quickly and ruthlessly suppressed. The regime continued in succeeding years to persecute and harass any who were associated with the charter. Although the signatories tried to show resilience in succeeding years by holding parties commemorating the signing of the charter, the fact remained that they had been silenced and their complaints largely ignored.

THE ROMAN CATHOLIC CHURCH

A recent challenge to the stability and conformity imposed by the Soviets was the Czechoslovak Roman Catholic church, for a long time politically quiescent in the face of official atheism and efforts to undermine traditional religion. There was an increase in church attendance in eastern Slovakia, where people had always been deeply religious and seemingly impervious to the KSC's antireligion policies. Even more striking was a new expression of interest in religion and in the church by youth in the large urban centers. There was also substantial clandestine religious activity in the home.

Several factors helped to account for the resurgence of interest in the church. One was the resilience of the church itself. It was one of the few surviving noncommunist institutions in Czechoslovak life. Because the socialist regime was neither willing nor able to attack the church in the same compulsive and brutal way it attacked political dissidents, the Czechoslovak people found that they could express their inner hostility toward the regime—albeit in an oblique way—by association with the church and through the pursuit of permitted religious activity. The Czechoslovak Catholic church, like its Polish counterpart, also benefited from its ties with the Vatican and gained strength from the leadership of the activist Pope John Paul II.

FOREIGN RELATIONS

In the area of foreign policy, the Husak regime displayed consistent servility to the Soviet Union. The party leadership dutifully accepted the deployment of additional Soviet SS-20 missiles on Czechoslovak territory. It strongly supported the Soviet position in East-West arms negotiations. Its official press even outdid the Soviet press in its denunciation of Western policies and in its placing blame for the collapse of the arms-control dialogue on the United States. It also condemned Poland's Solidarity movement and in other ways reinforced Soviet policy toward the Polish political crisis of the early 1980s.

Czechoslovakia was supportive of Soviet policy in Poland, however, not only out of loyalty to the Kremlin but also for reasons of national self-interest. Both the Czechoslovak people and their party leadership were critical of Solidarity's confrontation with the Warsaw authorities in 1980 and 1981. Unlike the Poles, the Czechoslovaks were not given to street demonstrations and the use of violence to protest government policies. The Czechoslovaks also believed that the Poles themselves, as much as their Soviet-style system, were to blame for their country's economic and social problems. The Czechoslovaks, with their high regard for the authority of the state, also believed that the Poles were too political for their own good and too cynical and rebellious in their relations with the state.

While the Czechoslovaks had misgivings about Soviet pressures on the Poles and understood Polish resentment toward the repressive Jaruzelski regime, they were not especially upset by the declaration of martial law and the suppression of Solidarity. They seem to have appreciated the concern of their leadership that if the unrest in Poland continued and spread to Czechoslovakia, it could invite further Soviet interference.

ECONOMIC POLICY

Finally, with all that was wrong with the Soviet economic model—not much was done by the Husak regime to modify it to resolve problems of underperformance—the Czechoslovak economy still provided its society with an adequate standard of living. The standard of living was not as high as it might have been under capitalism or with a major overhaul of the highly centralized administrative apparatus, but it was better than that of most other socialist economies. However, the regime's excessive conformity with the traditional Soviet model, in particular its commitment to a highly centralized decision-making apparatus and its stress on heavy-industrial output, especially armaments, at the expense of consumer goods, was a serious liability for future economic growth and political stability.

FROM HUSAK TO JAKES

Despite the appearance of affluence, there were serious problems threatening Czechoslovak economic health and social stability. These problems disturbed the Kremlin as well as the Czechoslovak party leadership (and led eventually to Husak's resignation as head of the party). Czechoslovakia's relative well-being in the Soviet Bloc was not the result of positive conditions such as an up-to-date, competitive, and in other ways healthy economy, but of a serious aberration: a flourishing nonsocialist underground economy in which a very high percentage of the people produced and consumed outside the official, centralized, command economic structure. The official economy was doing very poorly in terms of modernizing its antiquated and inefficient industrial facilities, checking pollution, protecting health, keeping pace in science and technology, and innovating to enable its exports to gain greater access to Western markets.

Making the Czechoslovak economy and society permanently healthy, however, required doses of glasnost and perestroika, to which Husak was disinclined. He and other party officials worried that economic reform would generate political pressures like those in the Prague Spring of 1968 for a radical liberalization of society, in particular individual freedom and human rights.

Indeed, there was no let-up in the regime's emphasis on a repressive political conformity. It opposed the revival of interest in religion, a growing popular interest in Western music, and the development of peace movements among the youth as well as dissident groups like Charter 77 and the Vons (an acronym that stood for Committee for the Defense of Unjustly Persecuted People).

Mikhail Gorbachev seemed in no hurry to push the Czechoslovak party leadership toward change, because of the fear Czechoslovak leaders themselves had that Soviet-style glasnost and perestroika in their country might unleash forces detrimental to the country's socialist system and its ties to the Soviet Bloc. However, the Kremlin was concerned that Husak's conservatism could turn out to be a dangerous threat to the long-term stability of Czechoslovak socialism, which had yet to achieve the legitimization essential for its survival. During his April 1987 visit to Czechoslovakia (where, interestingly, there was much public enthusiasm for him) Gorbachev called for "dynamic development," a possible allusion to the economic liberalization he was trying to pursue in his own country. In December 1987 Husak was replaced as Czechoslovak Communist Party leader by Milos Jakes—a move approved, and possibly encouraged, by the Kremlin. Husak remained as president of the republic, a far less powerful post than that of party leader.

JAKES AND PERESTROIKA

In many respects, the Jakes regime continued the spirit, if not the letter, of its predecessor's conservative policies in the political and cultural spheres. Like Husak, Jakes showed little interest in Gorbachev's glasnost and democratization policies, which he adamantly refused to introduce in Czechoslovakia.

Cultural Conservatism
Under Jakes, the regime reacted strongly to the revival of popular interest in religious activity. Jakes asserted that while the church was legal and free, some people used it for political purposes, in the form of church-supported demonstrations. These, Jakes argued, had nothing to do with religious services and served only to undermine social stability.

The Czechoslovak regime therefore moved in the opposite direction of the Soviet Union in its policy toward religion and the church. For example, in February 1988 the official Czechoslovak media criticized Cardinal Frantisek Tomasek for supporting a 31-point petition calling for increased religious freedom. The media charged that much of the petition had been propagated by church radicals concerned not with religious freedom but with political objectives and the disruption of Czechoslovakia's communist society.

In March 1988 the government disrupted and dispersed a demonstration in favor of religious freedom in Bratislava. This use of force against the peaceful protestors provoked an angry reaction in the West, which denounced the action as "appalling," as a violation of solemn promises made by the Czechoslovak government in the Helsinki Final Act, and as damage to détente. But the Czechoslovak government did not respond to this pressure, possibly because it feared the church's potential for disruption.

Political Conservatism
The regime also remained conservative in the political sphere under Jakes. For example, the leadership could barely conceal its dismay over Gorbachev's closing speech at the 19th Conference of the Soviet Communist Party, in Moscow in June 1988, in which he spoke of "the human image of socialism," a phrase associated with reforms of the Prague Spring of 1968 and the political turmoil that led eventually to a Soviet invasion and the restoration of a neo-Stalinist repression.

Hard-liners in the Czechoslovak political leadership gained more power when, in October 1988, Premier Lubomir Strougal was replaced by Ladislav Ademec, a pragmatic economist but also a political loyalist who was expected to support Jakes's conservative strategies. Jakes used the opportunity of Strougal's removal to warn against hurried solutions to economic difficulties and underlined his belief in centralized control. And party ideology chief Jan Fojtik spoke against radical political and economic changes, advocated cautious reform, and emphasized the party's leadership role in any policy changes.

Repression of dissent intensified in late 1988 and early 1989. On November 11, 1988, the authorities broke up a meeting in Prague that had been called by Charter 77 to discuss recent Czechoslovak history. Charter 77 members wanted to know about the facts surrounding the founding of the republic in 1918, the Munich agreement to hand over parts of Czechoslovakia to Germany in 1938, the seizure of power by the Communists in 1948, and the Soviet-led invasion of 1968, especially Soviet motives and the Soviet argument that Czechoslovak officials had asked for outside military intervention in Prague.

A major confrontation between dissidents and the regime occurred in early 1989, coincidental with the government's signing of a newly strengthened Helsinki agreement on human rights. In January thousands of Czechoslovak and Slovak youth held rallies in Wenceslas Square in Prague to commemorate the 1969 death of Jan Palach, a student who set fire to himself to protest the Soviet invasion.

The government responded forcefully. Among other actions, it detained the noted writer Vaclav Havel, a leading signatory of Charter 77, while he was trying to lay flowers at the place where Palach set himself on fire. This behavior in turn provoked a counterresponse in the form of a petition by 1,000 people in theater, the arts, and television demanding Havel's release; as well as a letter from Cardinal Tomasek to Premier Adamec warning that "the justified yearning of citizens to live in a free environment, something which has become a matter of course in the twentieth century, cannot be stifled by crude violence."

PRESSURES FOR CHANGE IN THE 1980s

Pressure mounted on the Communist regime to alter its conservative course. Much of this pressure came from within the country, but socialist neighbors, in particular the Soviet Union, Poland, and Hungary, also contributed.

Soviet Pressure
Gorbachev made no secret of his dislike of Czechoslovak conservatism in politics and culture. The Czechoslovak crackdown on dissidents, including the imprisonment of Havel, was a burden for Soviet efforts to strengthen ties with the West through a more liberal policy toward human rights. Furthermore, the Kremlin worried that this conservatism would eventually destabilize Czechoslovak society and endanger its socialism.

In November 1988 Soviet Politburo member and Gorbachev adviser Aleksandr Yacovlev journeyed to Prague to urge a more tolerant approach to political dissent. The Kremlin led the Czechoslovak leadership to expect sometime in the near future a Soviet reassessment of the 1968 invasion of Prague, perhaps including an exoneration of Dubcek. Such a Soviet move would weaken the credibility and authority of conservative elements in the Czechoslovak party and, possibly, encourage increased tolerance of political dissent. Indeed, many in the Czechoslovak opposition were confident that continuing Soviet pressure on Prague eventually would force the regime to embrace a reformism similar to, if not identical to, perestroika.

(Reuters/Bettmann newsphotos/Jaroslav Koran)

Vaclav Havel, the noted playwright, was arrested in 1988 in response to his representing the younger, more pragmatic politicians in the Politburo. By the end of 1989 the conservative hard-liners were forced to relinquish power, and by December Havel had become the president of Czechoslovakia. He had received enormous support from both the Parliament and Western nations.

Pressure from Poland and Hungary

External pressure on Prague to ease up on political discipline came also from its neighbors, Poland and Hungary. These countries, which used to be reticent about the internal politics of their allies, began to speak out publicly against the repressive policies of the Prague regime. During the month between the eruption of anti-government demonstrations in Prague in January 1989 and the trial of Havel and other leading Czechoslovak dissidents in February, the Polish and Hungarian party leaderships met with Jakes to urge leniency.

Internal Pressure

Internal pressure to liberalize the political environment came especially from the youth. The regime's agreement with the public—a sort of social contract whereby the population remained politically passive so long as there was economic stability—crumbled as a younger generation of students and workers, untainted by the fear and defeatism that followed 1968, grew increasingly impatient for the change the Gorbachev era appeared to promise. Although their organization was weak and their political strategy almost nonexistent, their aspirations for change were vocal and persistent.

THE BEGINNINGS OF REFORM

In late 1988 there was evidence that the Jakes regime was loosening up. The conservative leadership promoted younger and more pragmatic elements to the Politburo, and conservative figures departed. The leadership also showed some restraint in dealing with political dissent. For example, although the authorities had arrested Havel, they did not stop a public demonstration in Prague in early December commemorating the 40th anniversary of the signing of the universal declaration of human rights. The government also ceased jamming Radio Free Europe broadcasts and authorized the publication of the works of Franz Kafka after a 20-year ban imposed in the aftermath of the Prague Spring. The leadership also accepted the resignation of long-time conservative spokesperson Vasil Bilak, the party's toughest arbiter of orthodoxy, from the Czechoslovak Politburo–Presidium and other party posts.

The regime also treated Havel gingerly, for all its frustration over his dissident activity. Eventually his sentence was reduced to 8 months. He was released in May 1989, after he had served 4 months.

This slight shift in politics was accompanied by a gradual implementation of

modest economic reforms. State companies were made more independent of central planning and accountable for their profits and losses. The government called for the setting up of workers' self-management councils in all factories, divided the state bank into several autonomous commercial banks, revised industrial pricing, and encouraged joint ventures with Western companies. Official economists suggested, however, that change would be slow. They wondered whether popular pressure for reform extended beyond the youth who thronged to demonstrations. For nearly 2 decades, so it was argued, Czechoslovaks had enjoyed a "happy stagnation," a relatively comfortable consumer economy that trailed increasingly behind the West but made few demands on the workers. Thus, so the argument went, while ordinary people complained about problems, many were not ready to take the necessary steps for a real reform, fearful of what it would bring.

UPHEAVAL IN THE FALL OF 1989

Events, however, had a momentum of their own. After the sudden and unexpected collapse of conservative rule in East Germany in early October 1989 and in Bulgaria in early November, as well as the subsequent relaxation of political control in Czechoslovakia itself, Czechoslovaks started to organize and demonstrate for swifter change in their own country. The Jakes regime initially tried to resist this pressure, using force to disperse demonstrators. On November 12 it warned that the party would not tolerate dissent and would not diminish control.

But public pressure on the regime intensified, and on November 24, 300,000 people demonstrated in Prague in favor of political reform, an unprecedented gesture of massive protest and dissent. This time the regime capitulated, probably because the only alternative was the use of massive force with unpredictable consequences. Jakes resigned as party leader in favor of Karel Urbanek, and power shifted to the moderate and reform-minded Premier Adamec.

Subsequently, other hard-liners resigned from the party leadership or were ousted. In December Husak resigned as president and was succeeded by Havel, who had the overwhelming backing of the Parliament as well as tremendous support among Western nations. Dubcek was named presiding officer of the Parliament. Before long even Adamec was obliged to resign because of popular dissatisfaction with the slowness of his reform program—opposition leaders were angry over his hesitation to assign to them a substantial share of Cabinet seats. He was succeeded as premier by an obscure Czechoslovak Communist leader, Marian Calfa.

Under mounting pressure, the party eventually met the demands of the newly formed coalition of opposition groups, called Civic Forum, and agreed to share power with noncommunist organizations. It also agreed to relinquish its monopoly of power by accepting the establishment of a multiparty system, and it consented to free and open parliamentary elections in 1990. And in January 1990 it agreed, albeit grudgingly, to give up 100 seats it had held in the Federal Assembly. It was also about this time that Premier Calfa announced his withdrawal from the Communist party.

The Soviet Union played a neutral role that benefited and encouraged the reformers. The Kremlin refused to support the Jakes regime. The ease with which the regime fell affirmed the obvious: namely, that survival of the Czechoslovak Communist regime had depended not on Soviet backing but on popular loyalty and support.

As the country looked forward in early 1990 to the parliamentary elections scheduled for the middle of the year, a number of important events marked the progress of Czechoslovakia's decommunization

and desatellization in the aftermath of the November upheaval. In response to demands by the Czechoslovak government for the departure of all Soviet troops by the end of 1990, the Soviets agreed to start the withdrawal process by bringing home approximately 18,000 of the 73,500 troops deployed in Czechoslovakia since the 1968 invasion. The Czechoslovak government also terminated all course work and academic programs in Marxist-Leninist studies in the nation's universities and dismissed those faculty who had participated in and benefited personally from the purge of instructors and administrators carried out by the newly installed Husak regime 20 years earlier. Finally, Prague prepared to take major steps in desocializing the economy by expanding private entrepreneurialism.

THE END OF
THE COMMUNIST ERA

Czechoslovakia held its first free national parliamentary elections since the end of World War II on June 8 and 9, 1990. Twenty-two parties fielded candidates for seats in the two houses of the federal Parliament and for seats in the Czechoslovak and Slovak provincial parliaments, but only three groups had substantial popular backing. The Civic Forum and its co-movement in Slovakia, the Public Against Violence, reflecting their leading role in toppling the Communists and the popularity of their leader, President Havel, received the overwhelming majority of votes on both the federal and provincial levels. The Christian Democratic Bloc, a bloc of parties somewhat to the right of Civic Forum and less eager than the Forum to proceed with a rapid purge of Communists from the central administrative apparatus, received the next-largest number of votes. The Communists, discredited by their past leadership of the country and by recent public revelations of the degree of secrecy with which they had ruled, received 13 percent of the votes, somewhat more than the 10 percent they had been expected to win. None of the other 19 parties, many of which were committed primarily to local interests, obtained more than 4 percent of the electorate.

Following the elections Havel promptly reappointed Calfa as premier and charged him with the formation of Czechoslovakia's first democratic government in more than 40 years. On July 5, 1990, the federal Parliament duly elected Havel president of the republic, by a strong majority. He became Czechoslovakia's first noncommunist president since 1948.

PROBLEMS AND PROSPECTS OF DEMOCRATIC DEVELOPMENT

While most of the important positions in the Czechoslovak federal government are filled by Charter 77 activists, who are strongly committed to democratic principles, making democracy work in Czechoslovakia is not easy. The country faces factionalism within Havel's own party, the Forum. One cause of division is the question of what to do with the old Communist elite who are in positions of administrative responsibility. Havel wants to avoid a witch-hunt, if only because in many instances ex-Communists are the only people with the technical skills needed to manage the bureaucracy. Moreover, more than half the signatories of Charter 77 who founded Civic Form are themselves former Communists, even if they were disciplined by the Husak leadership after 1969 for their reformist instincts and their involvement in the Prague Spring reforms. Havel's support for utilizing Communist experience has met opposition from many in the Forum who suffered persecution under the former regime and want now to expel former Communists.

Forum leaders also have disagreed on economic reforms. Federal Finance Minister Vaclav Kraus supported rapid movement to a free-market system with a minimum of restrictions on the development of capitalism and free enterprise. Havel wanted this but with safeguards to protect people from hardship. While Kraus spoke for the farmers and other entrepreneurs located in the countryside, Havel spoke for the wage-earning groups in the densely populated urban centers who were worried about job security and adequacy of wages. Toward the end of 1990 Kraus started a campaign to pack the Forum with people who shared his views. In response, Havel, Foreign Minister Jiri Dienstbier, and other close supporters of the president created a dissident faction within the Forum, called the Liberal Club. Liberal Club supporters accused Kraus and his followers of being little more than heartless technocrats, oblivious to the misery of the poor and the displaced caused by the gradual termination of the security and protection of the socialist welfare state.

Economic Reform
Beyond Havel's caution, there were other reasons why Czechoslovakia moved slowly toward the market economy, and by the end of 1990 most industries were still state-owned, most stores still offered only a narrow, drab supply of items, and legislation providing for privatization was still

stalled. Many people in Czechoslovakia had little if any spare capital to purchase newly privatized industries. Czechoslovakia also lacked any kind of entrepreneurial experience.

Beginning in January 1991, with Kraus pushing for change, the Prague government took major steps to accelerate the "desocialization" of the economy. The government removed price controls on 85 percent of goods sold, initiated the closure of inefficient state-owned enterprises and the privatization of thousands of shops, and restricted the money supply and took other measures to make Czechoslovak currency convertible.

Nevertheless, in 1992 Czechoslovakia still faced serious problems in making the transition from socialism to a market-based economy. Scarce hard currency had to be spent on the purchase of oil rather than on modernization of industry. Outdated machinery was keeping costs of production high and preventing Czechoslovakia's exports from becoming competitive on the world market, stunting growth, pushing up consumer prices, and depressing the standard of living for average Czechoslovak wage earners. Federal authorities tried to control the effects of high costs of food and energy production by establishing price ceilings in retail outlets, which offered desperate consumers an alternative to the private shops whose high prices kept necessities beyond reach.

The government tried some imaginative ways to facilitate privatization in its capital-starved society. They began auctioning state-run stores to the highest bidders, who paid much less than market value for what they were buying. But citizens were angry that those among them who had the money to take advantage of the auctions were ex-Communist officials, money-changers, swindlers, and black marketeers; they also were concerned about Germans and Austrians coming into their country to exploit the cheap prices.

There were special problems involved in privatizing agriculture. There was little knowledge on how to run a private farm, as a result of the completeness of collectivization by the Stalinist leadership of the country in the late 1940s and early '50s, as well as a lack of will to do the endless work that private farming entails. Furthermore, large cooperatives, which control 80 percent of Czechoslovak farmland, had proved to be more efficient than the tiny family farms they replaced. This efficiency was the result of the autonomy that farm managers had enjoyed in the recent past, which had allowed them to become imaginative and innovative, plus the practice of distributing the cooperative's

profits to its workers, who consequently had more incentive than workers in factories to excel in the quality and quantity of their output.

But Prague wanted to put agriculture back into private hands. In May 1991 the federal Parliament passed a bill returning all land confiscated by the Communists to their original owners, on the assumption that clearly defined property titles are fundamental for prosperity. This law was not likely to affect the farm cooperative system adversely, because most of those people who regained land were expected, at least initially, to rent it back to the cooperatives.

Czechoslovakia's Polluted Environment

Czechoslovakia has one of the most polluted environments in Central/Eastern Europe. According to a study by Civic Forum, 25 metric tons of pollutants fall every year on every square kilometer of Czechoslovak territory, as compared to less than 1 metric ton in Sweden. More than 30 percent of Czechoslovak territory, including Prague, is ecologically devastated. Prague is frequently darkened during the day by a foul smog which endangers both the health and spirit of people living there and causes many of them to flee the city when the smog sets in.

The town of Most, at the edge of the Erzgebirge Mountains, is a symbol of the tragedy of the entire region. The town was literally swallowed up by pollution resulting from the use of lignite, a low-quality coal used to fuel factories throughout Central/Eastern Europe that has high sulphur and ash content. Factories and plants using lignite surround Most and caused the government literally to depopulate it, in order to prevent an epidemic of chronic-pollution–caused illnesses.

Although Havel has made environmental protection a top priority of his government, there are almost insurmountable problems because of the cost and complexity of remedial policies. As is true of other Central/Eastern European countries, there is a lack of funding for the environment, requiring the country's political leadership to look outside Czechoslovakia for help, notably to Germany and the United States. In Czechoslovakia, the Green party focuses mainly on the solution of environmental problems, but it lacks the experienced and talented leadership and organizational unity needed to lobby effectively for environmental cleanup programs. Finally, an effective cleanup program depends on the cooperation of Czechoslovakia's neighbors, eastern Ger-

many, Poland, and Hungary. A large cause of Czechoslovakia's polluted environment is the emissions from polluted industrial plants in the Katowice-Krakow region of southern Poland, and cooperation between the two countries in solving environmental problems is only beginning.

Resurgence of Interethnic Conflict

Since the end of Communist rule in 1989 and the subsequent liberalization of the political environment, there has been a renewal of Slovak demands for separation from the Czechoslovak federation. While Slovaks are more resentful than ever before of Czechoslovak dominance of the federation (Czechoslovaks constitute 65 percent of the population, control an equal percentage of federation territory, and exert a dominant influence over the national economy), the Public Against Violence Party, which represents the majority of Slovak people, considers separation impractical and lobbies for autonomy in local government. The party wants a new federal constitution that will give Slovaks their own central bank, labor market, and eventually taxation rights and customs control. They also want to enter the European Community as an equal and independent partner of the Czechoslovaks. They have sought control of railroads and the national pipeline network located in their territory.

Another cause of Slovak separatism has to do with economic conditions in Slovakia, especially unemployment (8.7 percent by October 1991, as compared to 3.4 percent for the Czechoslovak republic), and with other hardships resulting from the transition to a market economy pursued by the central government in Prague. Moderate Slovak politicians worry that further economic deterioration will lead to Slovak demands for complete independence. Slovakia is vulnerable to worsening economic conditions because it is the home to giant smelting, chemical, and weapons industries built by the Husak regime after 1968. These are unprofitable and require huge amounts of costly energy while polluting the atmosphere, and therefore are prime candidates for closure. Finally, Slovaks worry about being left out of the huge programs of Western economic and technological assistance to the Czechoslovak part of the federation; they complain that of 3,000 joint ventures with Western companies, only 600 had located in Slovakia by the fall of 1991.

President Havel adopted a conciliatory approach. He chose as premier a Slovak, Marian Calfa; he agreed to call Czechoslovakia the "Federation of Czechs and Slovaks"; and he began to explore ways of granting the Slovaks the substantial autonomy that they wanted. In November 1990 the federal government and the governments of the Czechoslovak and Slovak republics drew up a compromise on power-sharing. But the Czechoslovak federal Parliament made changes requiring a restoration of federal control over the post office and the central bank and assumption of responsibility for the protection of minority rights, instead of placing that responsibility in the hands of the republics. In late November the Slovak Parliament in Bratislava threatened to declare its laws to be paramount over those of the federal government. Havel responded by asking the federal Parliament to grant him emergency powers to preserve the unity of the country and worked to meet Slovak demands, but Slovak anger mounted.

By the end of 1991, however, it was clear that Slovaks were not unanimously in support of secession from the Czechoslovak state. While nationalists harassed advocates of moderation and demanded secession, other Slovaks called for less radical solutions to the problem of Slovak self-determination. For example, the Slovak Parliament in October 1991 failed to pass a motion providing for consideration of a declaration of sovereignty. Moderate Slovaks were worried about the negative consequences of Slovak independence and argued in favor of a reduction of central authority in Prague. This would allow Slovakia a much greater control over its local administration and a larger role in the distribution of investment capital, which could be used to soften the impact of economic reforms. Secession from Czechoslovakia would entail the interruption of critical economic links between the east and west of the country and might also contribute to a revival of nationalist sentiments among Slovakia's 600,000 Hungarians, who might themselves demand autonomy in a Slovak state or even union with the Hungarian republic.

Right-Wing Violence

As Czechoslovak-Slovak relations became quarrelsome, so too did the national temper. Post-Communist Czechoslovakia, which prided itself on the nonviolent character of its political transition to independence, in what has frequently been Zreferred to as the "velvet revolution," began to experience a new and disquieting phenomenon of street violence. Right-wing gangs of young people in their late teens and early twenties, trapped by high unemployment and social dislocation, went on a rampage. They attacked migrating Gypsies and Vietnamese workers brought to Czechoslovakia by the former

Communist leadership. In the industrial city of Teplice, northwest of Prague, gangs of several hundred youths on October 5, 1991, overturned a car carrying two Gypsies and beat the driver so badly that he required hospitalization. The attackers, wearing arm bands with swastikas, chanted Nazi and xenophobic slogans.

Prague authorities worried that this unrest would worsen if economic problems, in particular unemployment, did not soon abate. Moreover, they expected an increase in the population in Czechoslovakia of Gypsies, fleeing hardship in Romania (Germany and Hungary have closed their borders to them). On a deeper, psychological level, the behavior of the Czechoslovak youths toward the Gypsies, Vietnamese, and other foreigners was disquieting. It reflected a racist-inspired intolerance incompatible with the liberal democratic political system that Havel and other leaders want to build. In response to Gypsy demands for Czechoslovak protection of their human rights, in October 1991 Havel established a commission to examine the new outbreak of violence and recommend ways of curbing it.

NEW FOREIGN-POLICY INITIATIVES

The Prague government wants Czechoslovakia to be the bridge between East and West. (In this policy, the government reflects the thinking of the late Eduard Benes, the last president before the Communist takeover.) To facilitate this role, President Havel and Foreign Minister Jiri Dienstbier have sought a resumption of Czechoslovakia's traditional closeness to the West, to which they believe it belongs, while maintaining close relations with the rest of Europe and especially with the Commonwealth of Independent States.

The United States

The government and residents in Prague enthusiastically received U.S. Secretary of State James Baker when he visited in February 1990. Baker's visit offered Prague the hope of American material assistance and symbolized an end to Czechoslovakia's isolation from the West. When President Havel visited Washington at the end of that month, he received a warm welcome from the White House, a standing ovation from Congress, and promises of investment from members of the business and banking community. In October 1991, during another visit to Washington, Havel assured Americans willing to invest in Czechoslovakia that they could

return their profits to the United States and freely exchange currencies.

The Bush administration was responsive to Czechoslovakia's interest in restoring good relations with the United States and was forthcoming with praise and encouragement, but it did not offer much financial support. Washington wanted to foster, but not bankroll, economic reform and development in Czechoslovakia. Still, the United States did much to help the country through the transition from socialism to democracy. In April 1990 a trade agreement between Prague and Washington reduced tariffs on Czechoslovak imports into the United States. The Overseas Private Investment Corporation, which provides insurance for American business firms interested in foreign investment, began operation in Czechoslovakia. The U.S. government supported Czechoslovakia's request to join the International Monetary Fund, which would make Prague eligible for lending programs; and it also supported a European Development Bank location in Prague (the bank was established to aid Central/Eastern European countries in reconstruction). Washington planned to reopen the American consulate in Bratislava, which had been closed in 1948. Also proposed were the opening of American cultural centers in Bratislava and Prague, an increase in cultural and educational exchanges, the start of a Peace Corps program for English-language instruction, and a joint study of Czechoslovakia's air-pollution problem, the worst in Europe.

Yet economic progress was slow. Potential U.S. investors were wary of sinking capital in Central/Eastern Europe. Havel's efforts were hampered by the possibility, however remote, that the country might experience a severe ethnic-based turmoil. Moreover, American investors were put off by the slowness of Czechoslovakia's dismantling of the state-controlled economy and Prague's focus on the creation of small private businesses while leaving the major industrial giants, where foreign investment was most needed, under state control.

A final aspect of relations with the United States concerned American policy toward the Commonwealth of Independent States and Yugoslavia. In his address to a joint House-Senate meeting of Congress during his February 1990 visit to Washington, Havel asked the United States to help the then-Soviet Union navigate the "immensely complicated" road to political and economic democracy, this despite the fact that his country had for so long been a victim of Soviet aggrandizement. He argued that the sooner and the more peacefully the Soviet Union moved

| Independence 1918 | Nazi Germany conquers and partitions Czechoslovakia, annexing Bohemia, 1939 | establishing a protectorate over Moravia, and giving Slovakia its independence | Czechoslovak Communists obtain control over the national government in Prague 1948 | Pro-Soviet and Stalinist Novotny becomes leader of the KSC 1953 | Dubcek replaces Novotny; Soviet military intervention in Prague 1968 | Husak replaces Dubcek 1969 | Czechoslovak dissidents sign Charter 77 1977 | 1980s-19 |

Jakes replaces Husak as leader of the KSC; he later resigns in favor of Urbanek

Massive public demonstrations force political liberalization

Playwright Vaclav Havel is arrested, imprisoned, and released in 1989; later he is named president of the republic

toward political pluralism and a market economy, the better for not only Czechoslovakia but also all the other new democratic governments in Central/Eastern Europe. His advice struck a very responsive chord among the American legislators. His advice also may have had an impact on the Bush administration's thinking about an American response to the departures from traditional socialism occurring in the Soviet Union. During his visit to Washington in October 1991 Havel also emphasized the negative impact on Czechoslovakia of the growing Soviet economic and political crises in the previous year.

Germany

Havel has gracefully accepted German reunification and has established good relations between Czechoslovakia and Germany. In late 1989, shortly after being elected president by the Czechoslovak Parliament, Havel declared that Czechoslovakia must apologize to 3.2 million Germans who were expelled from their homes in the Sudetenland when, after World War II, Czechoslovakia recovered that region, which had been annexed by Nazi Germany on October 1, 1939. To underscore the importance of good relations in the new post-Communist era, Havel also chose the two Germanies, rather than the United States or the Soviet Union, for his first official visit abroad as Czechoslovakia's chief executive, in January 1990. While his discussions with German leaders focused on practical matters like border crossings and protection of the

environment, their real importance was in their symbolism: they punctuated the Czechoslovak state's determination to begin a new chapter in relations between the two countries and not allow the past to poison the present and the future.

The Soviet Union

While seeking to develop strong links to the West, Czechoslovakia also tried to reassure the Soviet Union of its friendship and readiness for cooperation in many areas, especially trade, on which the Czechoslovaks had long depended for their material well-being. But there were problems between post-Communist Czechoslovakia and the Gorbachev Kremlin.

The most serious of these problems involved the withdrawal of about 80,000 Soviet troops stationed in Czechoslovakia since August 1968. Moscow agreed to a joint Czechoslovak-Soviet commission of military and civilian officials to examine all aspects of the Soviet military presence. But a speedy Soviet military withdrawal was problematic, if only because it had moved so slowly on previous troop withdrawals and because the Soviet leadership was distracted by so much turmoil at home. Moreover, as was the case with Soviet troop withdrawals from other Central/Eastern European countries, the Kremlin had a problem of housing, feeding, and employing its returning military personnel.

The Czechoslovak Foreign Ministry publicly accused the Soviets of foot-dragging on the withdrawal issue; its spokesperson added on another occasion that the

Soviet forces deployed in Czechoslovakia had broken many agreements and had violated the UN Charter. He declared that Soviet reluctance to start the troop withdrawal had provoked tension among the Czechoslovak public, as seen in demonstrations in Prague and other cities.

The strong language to the Soviets may have helped to speed up their efforts at withdrawal. In February 1990 they signed a formal agreement to begin an immediate withdrawal of 18,500 soldiers and equipment, with the remainder to be withdrawn by July 1991. Despite logistical and political problems, involving the dissatisfaction of high-ranking Soviet officials with the precipitous disengagement of the Soviet Union from Central/Eastern Europe, the Soviets lived up to this agreement.

DEVELOPMENT

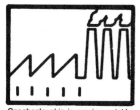

Czechoslovakia is moving quickly to capitalism. In late 1991 a plan went into effect to give ordinary people the chance to buy stock in big state-owned industries which will gradually come under private ownership. Popular interest was so great in subsequent months that government offices selling stock coupons were forced to extend their work hours.

FREEDOM

In March 1990 the Czechoslovak Parliament voted to eliminate the word "Socialist" from the name of the republic. In June 1990 Czechoslovakia held its first truly free and competitive parliamentary elections since the Communist takeover in 1948. They voted overwhelmingly for democratic parties and against the Communists, bringing to an end 44 years of Communist rule.

HEALTH/WELFARE

Immense power-plant construction involving the use of smog-causing brown coal along the Danube River frontier with Hungary has led to the pollution of one of Bratislava's most beautiful regions and to a cleanup campaign that is costing the regional government $2 billion dollars a year. Crime is a major social problem.

ACHIEVEMENTS

A breakthrough in cultural liberalization occurred with the publication in early 1989 of Franz Kafka's principal writings, 20 years after the famous Czechoslovak author's works were denounced and suppressed following the Prague Spring. Czechoslovak citizens may now travel freely into neighboring countries.

Eastern Germany*

GEOGRAPHY

Area in Square Kilometers (Miles): 356,945 (137,780) (about twice the size of Oklahoma)
Capital (Population): Berlin (3,410,000) after reunification the seat of government remained at Bonn (279,700)
Climate: cool and temperate

PEOPLE

Population

Total: 79,070,000
Annual Growth Rate: n/a
Rural/Urban Population Ratio: 14/86
Ethnic Makeup of Population: more than 99% German; less than 1% Slavic and others

Health

Life Expectancy at Birth: 71 years (male); 73 years (female)
Infant Mortality Rate (Ratio): 6/1,000
Average Caloric Intake: 144% of FAO minimum
Physicians Available (Ratio): 1/357

Religion(s)

47% Roman Catholic; 44% Protestant; 9% unaffiliated or others

Education

Adult Literacy Rate: 99%

COMMUNICATION

Telephones: 47,076,844
Newspapers: 395 dailies; 31,630,000 circulation

DISCOURAGING LEGACY

Outwardly one of the most efficient and productive socialist systems, Eastern Germany, with its blackened factories, soaring unemployment, and block after grey block of dreary and depressing buildings in almost all its towns and cities, is not unlike other former Communist party-ruled countries in Central/Eastern Europe. Most former East German citizens are saying—or at least believing—what other Central/Eastern Europeans have said: "Goodbye, communism, and good riddance!"

TRANSPORTATION

Highways—Kilometers (Miles): 220,855 (136,930)
Railroads—Kilometers (Miles): 43,879 (27,205)
Usable Airfields: n/a

GOVERNMENT

Type: federal republic
Independence Date: October 3, 1990 (reunification date)
Head of State: President Richard von Weizsäcker; Chancellor Helmut Kohl
Political Parties: Christian Democratic; Christian Socialists; Free Democrats; Democratic Socialists (former CED—East German Communists); others
Suffrage: universal at age 18

MILITARY

Number of Armed Forces: 488,400
Military Expenditures (% of Central Government Expenditures): n/a
Current Hostilities: none

ECONOMY

Currency ($ U.S. Equivalent): .609 dmarks = $1
Per Capita Income/GNP: $19,000/$1,208 billion
Inflation Rate: n/a
Total Foreign Debt: n/a
Natural Resources: lignite coal; potash; uranium
Agriculture: grains; potatoes; sugar beets; meat and dairy products
Industry: steel; chemicals; machinery; electrical and precision engineering products; fishing vessels

FOREIGN TRADE

Exports: $398 billion
Imports: $342 billion

*Note: These statistics are for the reunited Germany; accurate figures reflecting the current situation in Eastern Germany are not yet available.

*Seat of government after reunification

THE FORMER
EAST GERMAN STATE

East Germany, officially known as the German Democratic Republic (G.D.R.), was established in 1949 during the Cold War. It consisted of German territory occupied by the Soviet Union following World War II and included Berlin, the capital of the defeated German state.

With Soviet help, East German Communists, who called themselves the Socialist Unity Party (SED) because of their merger with Social Democrats and other reformist politicians in 1949, quickly acquired control of the East German government and proceeded in the early 1950s to introduce Soviet-style socialism. Under the leadership of Walther Ulbricht, the SED transformed East Germany, which was mostly agricultural, into a highly industrialized state. By 1953 East Germany was a loyal, conformist Soviet satellite.

SOURCES OF UNREST

While East Germany had conformed to the Soviet model since Stalin's death in 1953, it is also true that there were popular pressures for political and economic change. East Germany was the first Central/Eastern European country to experience unrest after Stalin's death.

Economic Austerity

Unrest occurred in 1953 because East Germany had been obliged to endure a brutal austerity in the early 1950s as the price of industrializing an essentially agrarian society. Heavy industrial production was given priority over consumer goods. Wages were kept low in order to sustain high investment in the expansion of plants as well as to control inflation in an era of consumer-goods scarcity.

Like their counterparts in other socialist countries, East German workers had no effective trade-union organization to lobby their causes with the regime. The official union to which the East German workers belonged was controlled by the SED and was unresponsive to workers' complaints.

Strikes and Emigration

In June 1953 industrial workers in East Berlin struck for higher wages, the release of political prisoners, and free elections. While the regime did raise wages, although not by very much, it refused to grant political concessions. Subsequently, many East Germans expressed opposition by emigrating to affluent and liberal West Germany. In 1961 the East German government built the infamous Berlin Wall, which reduced emigration to a trickle.

Political Dissent

In the 1970s East Germany also experienced political dissent. Influential German intellectuals like Wolf Biermann, a musician, and Rudolph Bahro, a writer and journalist, criticized the East German regime's political repression. They advocated liberalization. Bahro acknowledged openly his sympathy for Eurocommunism. In the early 1980s a new source of dissent appeared. Antinuclear peace groups condemned the arms race and called for nuclear disarmament. They also protested a militarization of German life in the form of incessant parades, flag-waving, and the proliferation of war toys. In 1983 and 1984 they opposed the Soviet decision to increase deployment of SS-20 missiles in Central/Eastern Europe, in response to the North Atlantic Treaty Organization's deployment of Pershing II missiles in Western Europe. The peace groups found support from the East German Evangelical church, which endorsed and worked with the independent peace movement.

(Gamma-Liaison/Patrick Piel)
The Berlin Wall, which the East German government began to dismantle in 1989.

POLITICAL STABILITY

Despite complaints from workers, farmers, intellectuals, and youth about dictatorship and harsh living conditions, East German society experienced a high degree of internal political stability as compared to other socialist countries. In part, this stability was the result of the SED leadership's conscious effort to avoid extremes. Other reasons for the relative tranquillity of East Germany had to do with economic conditions and foreign relations.

Avoidance of Extremes

The East German regime was always sensitive about the country's Nazi past. It refrained from Stalin-like purges and excessive political repressiveness in order to avoid arousing memories of the Hitlerian past. It thus did not provoke the kind of pervasive, organized, and violence-prone political opposition that Poland experienced.

The SED also abandoned atheistic propaganda. It had recognized the right of the Evangelical church, which had deep historical roots in East German society, to speak out critically on major public issues like détente and inter-German relations. In 1983 the East German government celebrated the 500th anniversary of the birth of Martin Luther. As Reverend Heino Falke, a pastor in the city of Erfurt, put it, the integration of Luther in contemporary East German society was "a sign of inner stability." At the very least, the regime's gesture toward the church, along with the easing of restrictions on religious life and the construction of new churches, contributed substantially to the country's social peace and tranquillity.

Culture was another area in which the East German regime eschewed extremes. While it insisted that artists select "socially useful" themes and stress "party mindedness" in their forms of expression, it refrained from setting mandatory rules on content and form. The SED looked to art forms, in particular literature, to obtain clearer views of social problems, and it viewed art as a source of national self-enlightenment that could strengthen the party's role in society.

Economic Conditions

Although the East German economy was highly centralized, it provided East German citizens with the highest standard of living in Central/Eastern Europe. This achievement was the result of several developments during the 1970s and 1980s, including: 1) limited but nevertheless effective reforms providing for some administrative decentralization and an increase in workers' incentives, sometimes called East Germany's "New Economic System"; 2) the admission of so-called technocrats into top-level economic decision-making positions; 3) the rationalization of industrial output by automated production processes like robotics; 4) rational utilization of scarce imported petroleum; 5) the existence of an extraordinary degree of labor discipline; and 6) the infusion of large amounts of capital from West Germany. The relatively high level of East German economic well-being was another source of the country's social and political stability.

Foreign Policy

Another reason for East German political stability had to do with its foreign policy. While it was true that on balance East Germany remained a loyal ally of the Soviet Union, in the mid-1980s the SED leadership began to show strong autonomist tendencies in a critical area: relations with West Germany. The East German regime continued to maintain a dialogue with Bonn, regardless of the ups and downs of East-West relations. East Germany derived much material benefit from remaining on good terms with West Germany. In return for modest concessions in the area of travel and communication between the two Germanies, East Germany received generous amounts of interest-free credit to finance its imports.

The former East German Communist leader Erich Honecker's nationalistic single-mindedness in the area of inter-German relations, which aroused suspicions in 1984 that the two Germanies were moving to solidify relations with each other independently of their powerful allies, strengthened his regime, even if it disturbed the Kremlin. The East German people were encouraged to look forward to greater contact with West Germany.

Of course, there was a limit to how far Honecker could go in pursuing East Germany's national interests. He depended on Soviet support because his regime was not popular in East Germany. The Soviets had no interest in allowing Honecker to develop policies that would increase his popularity and ultimately encourage his independence of the Soviet Union and a possible movement toward reunification of the two Germanies. The maneuverability the Soviets allowed him was just enough to assure the stability of the socialist regime, not its independence or unification with West Germany. For this reason, the Kremlin campaigned against closer links between East Germany and West Germany in the summer of 1984 and

vetoed Honecker's plan to visit West German Chancellor Helmut Kohl in September 1984.

But Honecker and Kohl did meet, albeit briefly, in Moscow in March 1985, during the funeral of Soviet party leader Chernenko. All that came of the meeting was an innocuous communique pledging the two German leaders to work for détente. On the other hand, the very fact that a meeting of the two German leaders had been held signified to the Soviets that inter-German relations had a momentum of their own.

ECONOMIC PROBLEMS

The seemingly healthy East German economy, touted by the SED leadership as the best in the Soviet Bloc, began to experience a slowdown in 1987. The reasons for the slowdown, which threatened to produce new social unrest, were primarily systemic. The regime adhered to the priorities and processes of the Stalinist economic model, tinkerings and adjustments of recent years notwithstanding. Thus, while the regime reduced waste and excessive use of manpower, energy, capital allocations, and valuable raw materials, it did little to develop the flexible economic-management structures and motivational environment within which real technological innovation and intensive growth could take place. Furthermore, continued central control of pricing complicated the gearing of production for profit, denying factories sufficient autonomy to expand productivity.

The Stalinist administrative system also undermined the country's economic growth, because it overemphasized self-sufficiency, causing the country to produce too wide a range of goods. In addition, the bureaucracy blocked the rapid application of the results of research and development. Moreover, the government heavily subsidized consumer prices. About 20 percent of East Germany's total budget was spent on subsidies to keep consumer prices, especially for housing, at an artificially low level.

Although the price subsidies drained precious capital from investment, the Honecker regime wanted to continue them, because they helped to promote political stability. The East Germans increasingly compared their standard of living with capitalist West Germany and would resist a lowering of that standard.

International conditions may have slowed growth. East Germany's export trade had been hurt by competition, most notably from the economic emergence of East Asian nations. While the economy per-

formed fairly well in the first half of the 1980s, raising exports while conserving raw materials, in the second half of the decade, when the demand shifted to higher-quality technological products, the system simply did not work. And East Germany worried about a further deterioration in its foreign-trade situation with the European Community introduction of a single, borderless market by the end of 1992.

Finally, the East German economy was less healthy than was claimed by its administrators because it depended heavily on West German financial assistance and commercial concessions. East Germany was never considered a foreign country by West Germany; it received preferential treatment in trade. Sixty percent of East Germany's trade with the West went to and came from West Germany, and East Germany relied on imports of West German technology.

Moreover, East Germany had an external reservoir of capital, unparalleled elsewhere in the Soviet Bloc, that spared it from the kind of indebtedness other socialist countries had to incur. For example, it received interest-free loans from West Germany, more than $1 billion a year, in the form of private remittances from relatives in the West and payments for services rendered to West Berlin.

Slow growth severely compromised the consumer economy and threatened social unrest. The average East German industrial worker had to put in 300 hours more a year than a West German counterpart in order to earn an equivalent salary. Waiting time for an automobile averaged 13 years. There were acute shortages of staple items, and the quality of most of them was very poor. Private consumption was about half the level of West Germany's. Furthermore, there was a problem with housing. East German homes built since 1945 were usually smaller than those in Western states and poorly equipped, many with no indoor toilet. Most were made of prefabricated concrete blocks and were part of sprawling complexes vulnerable to crime.

Not surprisingly, East Germans began to vote with their feet against the shortcomings of their government. In the summer of 1989 there was an exodus of East German citizens into Austria and Hungary, seeking asylum and ultimate transit rights to West Germany. In July alone, 11,707 East Germans emigrated to West Germany. The exodus involved 55,970 East Germans in the first 6 months of 1989, as compared to a total of 39,832 emigrants to West Germany in all of 1988.

The exodus continued throughout the fall of 1989 and the winter of 1990. Many

East German citizens were willing to do anything to escape economic hardship. Also, many seemed to think that when change did take place, it would occur very gradually, over a long period of time, and they did not want to wait through the transition. At the very least, the exodus was testimony to the growing popular dissatisfaction with the Honecker regime and helped to facilitate in the fall a modification of—indeed, the termination of—East Germany's conservative anti-perestroika orientation.

EAST GERMANY AND SOVIET PERESTROIKA

Party leader Honecker resisted undertaking perestroika-like policies in any sphere of contemporary East German socialism in the late 1980s. He showed little interest in any major alteration of the neo-Stalinistic character of East Germany's political system.

Many reasons explain this conservatism. Honecker argued with some truth that the country was doing very well and therefore its economy did not need any radical overhaul. Moreover, the East German government believed it had already instituted sweeping economic reforms. It pointed to the creation of industrial combines, in which factories in related branches of the economy were grouped together and were responsible for everything from research and design to foreign trade. The government also pointed to regional agricultural cooperatives, in which a grain farm and two to three animal farms coordinated production and feed supply among themselves.

Furthermore, East Germany appeared to be making the traditional Stalinist-style socialist system work to promote a moderate standard of living, not as high as in the West but much higher than in other socialist countries. East Germany had become the most important exporter of machine tools and other advanced manufactured items to the Soviet Bloc. Considering East Germany's lack of access to advanced technology and the restraints of a centralized economy, its relative economic success was truly impressive.

This achievement was attributable to qualities of East German society that had not been present to the same degree in other socialist societies, including the Soviet Union. Those qualities included a tendency to value work as a virtue in itself, discipline and obedience to authority, and a gift for organization. Calls for voluntary cooperation for the national good were met with responses from a disciplined population that could not be expected in most other societies.

The East German government also was aware that reform inside the Soviet Union had brought no tangible success and, in fact, economic conditions there had actually worsened. East German officials were aware of the destabilizing unemployment that resulted from restructuring policies in the Soviet Union and Hungary. It declared that socialism and unemployment were incompatible.

Finally, the East German leadership's refusal to adopt perestroika-inspired economic changes must be attributed to its desire—stronger than had been suspected in the past—to be autonomous of the Soviet Union in the development of domestic and foreign policy, at least in appearance if not in practice. The East Germans were uncertain about the future of Gorbachev and his programs, given the sharp differences within the Soviet leadership over the scope and pace of reform. They feared the possibility of a reversal of reformism in the Soviet Union and a consequent reversal of Soviet policy in Central/Eastern Europe, which now encouraged reform.

The East German leadership showed little interest in glasnost and democratization. It did not want to strengthen the influence of existing dissident elements in East German society or to generate a national enthusiasm for change which the regime might not be able to control.

Soviet policy may have been responsible for East German resistance to glasnost. While the Soviets would clearly have preferred that the SED be more accepting of glasnost, they refrained from the kind of strictures used against the Ceausescu regime in Romania. The Kremlin's unwillingness to press hard on the East Germans may have been attributed to its economic successes, which were of primary importance to the Soviets, who were eager to exploit the East German economy for their own benefit.

Consequently, as glasnost and democratization proceeded apace in other Soviet Bloc countries, the East German regime preserved the conservative status quo. For example, in 1988 the regime criticized the Soviet Union for its discussions of social and political problems. The regime tried to deny East German citizens access to information about Soviet reformism, especially the new official tolerance of criticism and dissent in the Soviet media. When the Soviet Union acknowledged the 1939 pact with Germany, the East Germans suppressed the information and continued to propagate the myth that communism had always been the enemy of Naziism.

At the same time East Germany welcomed and took advantage of an apparent shift in Soviet policy on inter-German relations under Gorbachev. In 1987 the Soviets lifted their veto of a summit meeting between Honecker and Kohl and thus made possible a meeting between the two German leaders in Bonn, in September 1987. Honecker was the first East German party leader to make an official visit to West Germany.

This inter-German summit had few tangible results beyond the conclusion of two agreements providing for more scientific and technical cooperation, cooperation on environmental protection and nuclear-reactor safety, and measures to make travel and communication between the Germanies a bit easier. However, it was of enormous symbolic significance, especially for Honecker, who received the recognition he had been seeking for so long and promises of more financial help from West Germany. And he obtained these gains without having to offer much in return: he made no concessions on the Berlin Wall, which was to continue to stand; or on the issue of unification, which he again dismissed, calling it a "fireside dream."

UPHEAVAL IN THE FALL OF 1989

The continued exodus of East German citizens in the fall of 1989 was an ominous message of trouble to the Honecker regime. The loss of several hundred thousand people, many with valuable work skills, was beginning to undermine the economy as well as to embarrass the regime at a moment of great vulnerability: during the October 1989 celebrations of its 40th anniversary. Those East Germans who stayed behind because they could not or did not want to emigrate demanded change in massive antigovernment demonstrations, first in Leipzig and eventually in Dresden and East Berlin.

Honecker initially seemed ready to react with force. In early October he authorized the use of police force against the demonstrators in Leipzig. His orders, however, were countermanded by Security chief Egon Krenz, after consultation with Gorbachev, who was opposed to a crackdown. Isolated in the Politburo and unsupported by his Soviet ally, Honecker, along with Premier Willy Stoph, resigned. For the moment, leadership of the party went to Krenz and the premiership of the government to Hans Modrow, a reformer who had been critical of past opposition to perestroika.

Krenz immediately announced a limited political relaxation. He allowed the demonstrations to continue without official interference; he eased restrictions on travel to the West, especially West Berlin and West Germany; and on November 9, 1989, he officially opened the Berlin Wall. He subsequently promised free and open elections for a new parliament in March 1990. But his days of leadership were numbered, because popular pressure for radical change increased in November, as hundreds of thousands of East Germans crossed the border into West Berlin. A

freer press reported the existence of pervasive corruption within the party elite. East Germans learned for the first time of Wandlitz, not far from the capital, where the top party leadership had secretly been living a scandalously luxurious existence. Wandlitz had been furnished with many scarce and expensive items imported from the West and not generally available to the rest of the country. Wandlitz undoubtedly diminished further the already weakened credibility of the East German Commu-

nist Party and that of its new leader. Krenz ultimately resigned on December 19 in favor of Gregor Geysi, a less well-known, but pragmatic and reform-oriented, high party official.

The party was weakened in other ways. As the Politburo and Central Committee lost most of their old membership associated with the Honecker regime, political power shifted to the state apparatus and to Premier Modrow. In response to pressure from the opposition, Modrow agreed to

(Reuters/Bettmann/Bill Creighton)

The Christian Democratic Union won a decisive victory in the March 1990 parliamentary elections, with 40.5 percent of the vote. Chancellor Helmut Kohl, the head of the CDU, was rewarded for his aggressive advocacy of reunification.

broaden the political complexion of his Cabinet. He began consultations with New Forum, a large coalition of opposition groups seeking to share power with the Communists and to expand East German economic, social, and cultural ties with West Germany, to which all East Germans were now free to travel. As 1990 began, pressure steadily increased on Modrow to move further away from the old political order and, in particular, to reduce the party's political role.

THE END OF COMMUNIST RULE

As East Germany prepared for the March 1990 parliamentary elections, Modrow's battle to salvage the leadership of the Communist party seemed lost, despite its effort to break with the past by changing its name to the Party of Democratic Socialism and despite its appeal to East German voters with misgivings about reunification. The party was in favor of a very gradual amalgamation of the two Germanies, fearing, as many East Germans did, that in a reunified German state, East German society would be controlled by a dictatorship of big business, would lose the extensive social umbrella the Marxist regime had developed in its 40 years of rule, and would impoverish most East Germans. But the party was running against the tide on the reunification issue—most East Germans favored reunification and a complete break with the past.

The Communists were overshadowed in the campaign by the East German Christian Democratic Union and Social Democratic Party. These parties captured the news headlines and aroused the most interest of the East German electorate. Leading West German politicians like Chancellor Helmut Kohl, the head of the CDU and an aggressive advocate of reunification, and Willy Brandt, the chair of the SPD, campaigned in East Germany as if it already was a part of West Germany.

The parliamentary elections, held on March 18, were a triumph for the Kohl-sponsored Christian Democrats, who won 40.5 percent of the vote and 162 of 400 seats in the new Parliament, known as the Volkskammer. Along with their small-party allies, the German Social Union and the Democratic Awakening, they ended up controlling 193 seats. The election results confirmed that a large plurality of East German voters favored not only reunification but also a rejection of socialism and a rapid transition to free-market capitalism.

While the Communists lost decisively, they were not annihilated, as many people

in and outside of East Germany had expected. The new Party of Social Democracy came in third, with about 16 percent of the popular vote. Another casualty of the election was the newly formed East German New Forum, which had played a leading role in the overthrow of the Honecker regime. The New Forum lacked leadership of the stature and appeal of Kohl and Brandt, who were immensely popular in East Germany. Moreover, it had also soft-pedaled the reunification issue, which was very popular in the cities, especially East Berlin.

It was now up to Lothair deMaiziere, the leader of the East German CDU, to negotiate a coalition to obtain the majority needed for a Cabinet. It took deMaiziere 10 days of discussions with other political parties, including the Social Democrats, who at first were in opposition. Eventually the Social Democrats agreed to enter a Grand Coalition under deMaiziere's leadership, and on April 9, the Volkskammer formally elected deMaiziere's Cabinet.

The new East German government, the first noncommunist leadership of East Germany in the post–World War II era, made an auspicious beginning. The Volkskammer voted to acknowledge and to apologize for the genocide carried out by Hitler's Germany against Jews throughout Europe and expressed willingness to establish ties with and pay reparations to Israel; to affirm the inviolability of Poland's western border; to condemn East Germany's participation in the 1969 Warsaw Pact invasion of Czechoslovakia; and to announce the new government's primary task of expediting union with West Germany.

REUNIFICATION

In the 4-month period between the collapse of the Honecker regime in November 1989 and the establishment of East Germany's first freely elected noncommunist government in March 1990, popular sentiment for reunification with West Germany steadily increased. Many East Germans favored unification, primarily for economic reasons, although other considerations were important, such as national pride and a deep resentment of the Communist past. East Germans viewed reunification as a means of rapidly improving their depressed and depressing economy and society and achieving a standard of living on a par with that in the West.

Kohl's conservative government of West Germany welcomed the prospect of reunification. Kohl saw himself as a second

Bismarck, the architect of a reconstituted German state. His role in promoting reunification would not only assure him of a large place in modern German history but would also bring political benefit in the short term by enhancing his party's chances of victory in the next Bundestag elections. At the same time Kohl saw reunification as a permanent solution to a growing problem for West Germany: the continued flow of East German citizens into West Germany through the late winter of 1990 and the difficulty of absorbing these newcomers into West German society, in particular finding jobs and homes for them.

But many in West Germany had misgivings about a rapid pace of reunification. Willy Brandt, former Chancellor Helmut Schmidt, and other Social Democrats advised caution and an evolutionary process. Schmidt warned against any West German action that appeared as an annexation of East Germany. Much time would be required to mesh the entirely different systems of law, medicine, taxation, and even traffic. Ordinary West German citizens began to worry about the cost and the prospect of higher taxes.

Furthermore, West German business firms began to wonder how much benefit they would get from reunification. Some months after the beginning of the migration of young East Germans to West Germany in the summer of 1989, West German employers were finding problems with their new East German employees, many of whom had a lax attitude toward work, an attitude developed in the more permissive and casual work environment of East Germany and other socialist countries. West German employers found that many East German employees did not adjust well to the more hectic work schedule in West Germany and had to dismiss them.

East German unemployment rose steadily throughout 1990, reaching 350,000 by the end of August, with some economists saying that the number of unemployed was in fact much higher, at about 1.7 million workers. By March 1991 about 40 percent of the area's 8.5 million workers were either unemployed or underemployed, some reporting to work just to collect part of their wages. This unemployment threatened to be chronic, because would-be West German and other foreign investors in the East German economy were discouraged by a lack of understanding among East German managers of free-market pricing. Also, most East German firms had dilapidated plants, inept management, outmoded products, heavy debts, and redundant employees. Furthermore, East German consumers no longer wanted to buy goods manufactured locally and preferred, despite higher costs, products from West Germany. Finally, privatization of state-owned enterprises, being implemented by the Treuhand, a giant privatization agency established in West Germany, contributed to unemployment, because new owners frequently discharged hundreds of workers in an effort to cut costs and raise efficiency.

Indeed, the progress of German reunification depends more fully on the Treuhand than on any other agency. The governments in other former Soviet Bloc countries are watching its progress carefully. The Treuhand has a threefold mandate: it sells companies, restructures those not attractive enough to be sold, and shuts down any deemed unsalvageable. When the Treuhand was created, in 1990, it assumed ownership of 22,000 small businesses, 8,000 industrial companies, and vast amounts of real estate, including 28 percent of East Germany's farmland and

two-thirds of its forest land.

The scale on which the Treuhand operates dwarfs that of any other privatization agency in the world. Nearly all the small businesses—among them shops, cafés, restaurants, cinemas, and pharmacies—as well as about 3,400 of the larger companies had been sold by 1992. Many of the companies it still owns, which employ about 2 million workers, have been broken into smaller units to make them more attractive for sale. Although the govern-

(Metin Yilmaz/Zenit Bildagentur/Photoreporters)

The full extent of the repression and surveillance conducted by the East German secret police (Stasi) came as a painful surprise to many. These East Germans are members of the "People's Committee," going through the enormous collection of papers at the Stasi's headquarters in Leipzig to see for themselves just how insidious the Stasi's accumulated files were.

ment has provided huge subsidies for unemployment compensation to ease the shock of job loss, and although the Treuhand favors buyers of former state-controlled enterprises who promise to keep workers working, many Eastern Germans despise the Treuhand for upsetting their lives. Their only consolation is the knowledge that their local economy had been in such disarray on the eve of reunification that nothing less than the draconian privatization efforts of the Treuhand were sufficient to restore economic health to the region.

There are grounds for optimism in the transition of the former East German socialist system to free enterprise. Throughout 1991 an economic rebirth in the former East Germany was evident, largely in consequence of massive West German investment, a situation without parallel in any other Central/Eastern European country. The Bonn government poured about $20 billion into Eastern Germany in 1991 and was expected to invest an equal amount in 1992. Much investment capital has gone into the repair of the communications and transportation infrastructure and into export industries that will sell to other former Soviet Bloc countries. The impact is already apparent: since late 1990 more than 200,000 new telephones have been installed in Eastern Germany, and the Eastern German road system is approaching the level of quality and quantity of the West German *autobahn* system. The effects of unemployment have been somewhat mitigated by generous pension awards and guarantees of free medical care. The most gratifying aspect of economic regeneration in Eastern Germany, however, may well turn out to be psychocultural, in the sense that Eastern Germans are getting used to and enjoying new economic freedom. In mid-1991, a poll showed that a majority of people living in Eastern Germany were optimistic about the future.

As an incentive to East Germans to remain in their country and help in the reshaping of its political and economic institutions, as well as to begin steps toward reunification, accelerate economic reform in the East, and facilitate economic integration, Kohl proposed a monetary union with East Germany. According to the Kohl plan, West Germany would exchange the nearly worthless East German mark for the strong West German mark. But determining the rate of exchange was both complex and controversial: what was good for one side was bad for the other. If West Germany exchanged soft East German marks for its own hard marks at a rate unfavorable to East Germans, the exchange would harm East German citizens.

In April 1990 the West German government agreed to a compromise exchange of West German marks for East German currency at a rate of 1 for 1 on wages, pensions, and some savings. East Germans could exchange up to 4,000 of their marks per person, with higher amounts at the less favorable rate of 2 for 1. West Germany also agreed to bring East German pensions up to West German levels, a boon to the 2.7 million East German retirees then receiving approximately 420 East German marks, as compared to the 1,100 West German marks collected by the West German retirees.

Another problem complicating eventual integration of the two Germanies concerned abortion, a hotly debated issue during much of 1990. In East Germany, there had been few restrictions on having an abortion; while in West Germany, an abortion required permission from a panel of doctors on the grounds of medical risk or social hardship, such as poverty or emotional instability. Behind these different legal situations were conflicting philosophical positions and sociological conditions in each of the Germanies. According to the East German Independent Women's Association, "every woman has a right to decide what will happen with her body." The West German Catholic Council of Bishops argued against abortion on the grounds that life had to be saved from the moment of conception. The conflict over abortion also was a reflection of the differing status of women in each Germany: about 90 percent of East German women were wage earners doing work outside the family vs. less than 50 percent of West German women. In East Germany, day-care facilities had been extensive and state supported; day care in West Germany was hard to find. Furthermore, while 80 percent of East German men claimed to do at least some housework, this was true for only about 20 percent of men in West Germany. Consequently, political leaders of the two Germanies reached a compromise on abortion rights after formal integration of the two Germanies: women living in what was formerly East Germany would be able to receive an abortion on demand up to the 12th week of pregnancy for a 2-year period; but to seek an abortion in Western Germany, they would have to obtain permission or else risk criminal prosecution.

This concession to women in East Germany was not likely to mitigate what otherwise was and will continue to be very difficult conditions for women living in the eastern part of the country. Women in Eastern Germany are likely to face increasingly hard times as they are forced out of the workplace as a result of rising unemployment caused by the transformation of the old socialist economy to one based on market forces and private enterprises.

There also was an international dimension to the reunification issue. Germany's neighbors to the East and West, notably the Soviet Union, Poland, Czechoslovakia, and France, approved reunification. But behind their public declarations were anxieties arising out of the memory of German aggression against them in World War II and the knowledge that a united German state of more than 80 million people was bound to be dominant, perhaps uncontrollable, and therefore possibly dangerous in Europe in the next century. Poland in particular expressed anxiety, demanding a say in how the two Germanies went about reunification, a guarantee of its border with Germany, and a formal disavowal of claims on Polish territory obtained from Germany after World War II.

Everybody in the West contended that reunification could and should proceed, but that it should be gradual and should involve an anchoring of the new unified German state to Western Europe to assure its good behavior toward neighbors. This meant that the West expected a unified Germany to be part of the European Community and NATO. The Soviet Union, however, opposed a reunified Germany's membership in the Western alliance, but it eventually backed down on this issue to avoid confrontation with the West as well as with the Germans, who wanted to be part of Western Europe. The Kremlin expected that the new Germany would continue its predecessor's links with the Warsaw Pact and that, at least for the time being, Soviet troops would remain in the old East Germany.

THE END OF "EAST GERMANY"

After weeks of discussion and debate, representatives of the two Germanies signed a treaty on August 31, 1990, of almost 1,000 pages detailing the mechanics of reunification, scheduled for October 3. The document covered all aspects of unification and codified agreements previously reached on such matters as the monetary union and abortion. Among other things, the treaty resolved questions of property in Eastern Germany (it recognized the land reforms of 1945 and 1949, which had broken up the large estates of the now-defunct "junker" aristocracy), established incentives for foreign investment in the East, and called for

Eastern German repayment of state indebtedness temporarily assumed by the Western German government. On October 4 the former East German *Volkskanner* and the West German *Bundestag* met as a united Parliament in the old Reichstag building, located in what was the former Communist eastern sector of Berlin.

Lingering Problems

Several large socioeconomic problems, a legacy of the Communist era, have the potential for political destabilization in the eastern part of the new reunified Germany. They are the continuation in positions of economic power of former Communists, an intensely polluted environment, the all-too-abrupt and flaw-ridden decommunization of Eastern German schools, the appearance of an ultra-conservative and neo-Nazi youth cult, sometimes referred to as "skinheads," and revelations of Stasi outrages.

Old Bosses With New Power

Ordinary citizens in Eastern Germany have discovered that many of the owners of the newly privatized enterprises are Communists. More than any other group in Eastern Germany, it was Communist party members who had accumulated the capital needed to buy out formerly state-controlled property. People are incensed by this but acknowledge that half the people who ran the country were Communists and they can't completely be gotten rid of. It is also true that the Communists who used to manage enterprises that they have now purchased seem to find the complex procedures easier to understand and deal with than ordinary people. However, this apparent advantage is likely to be only temporary, because popular resentment is forcing authorities to limit the ability of former party officials to exploit the move toward free enterprise.

Although some former Communists have indeed prospered, their party has lost all credibility, despite changes in name and platform. The new all-German government continued to seek prosecution of former Communist leaders, including Erich Honecker, who fled Germany for refuge in the then-Soviet Union. And in October 1990 the party, still under the leadership of Gregor Geysi, was caught illegally transferring huge sums of money for safekeeping to the Soviet Union. Although it still has a following, as demonstrated in state elections in October 1990, in which its candidates obtained 10 percent of the vote (most of which, incidentally, went to Kohl's Christian Democratic Union), the chances of revival of the Communists are slim.

Pollution in Bitterfeld

Typical of the environmental decay bequeathed by the late Communist regime is the extensive pollution in Bitterfeld, on the west bank of the Elbe River southwest of Berlin. Bitterfeld is the home of a huge chemical complex of 80 separate factories which produced basic chemicals, aluminum, pesticides, dyes, and plastics. The complex spewed out coal dust, which fouled the air, caked the buildings of Bitterfeld with black grime, poisoned the air until it stung the eyes, and transformed brook water into muddy syrup. In 1990 investigation revealed that Bitterfeld and its environs were poisoned deliberately by the East German government in a scheme to raise money. East Berlin had taxed the enterprises for pollution control and then refused to honor requests by the management for funds to build antipollution control devices, using the money collected from the fines to spend elsewhere. This revelation suggests that the East German Communist leadership was far more callous and cynical about the health of East German workers than was ever suspected. It had added insult to injury by having declared environmental statistics to be a state secret. Now, even though some of the factories are being closed and a massive cleaning operation is planned, trouble continues: German environmentalists say it will take years to restore environmental health to Bitterfeld.

Decommunization of Schools

In the former East Germany, the new government abruptly removed old and publicly revered symbols of 45 years of socialism. Communist youth organizations, like the Young Pioneers and Free German Youth, once the sole centers of extracurricular activity, disappeared; red flags and portraits of Communist heroes vanished. Schools will have a difficult time, therefore, to make an objective inquiry into the Communist era. How will they address the question of how a people can be blinded twice in a generation, first by the Nazis and then by the Communists? Moreover, this is the second time since World War II that Eastern Germans have been subjected to an official policy of national forgetfulness. Some people, including teachers, wonder whether a society can bear such "forgetfulness" twice within such a short period and worry about the moral confusion likely to result among impressionable East German youth.

A New Racism: The Skinheads

A dangerous signal of the difficulty of socializing youth and, perhaps, sections of the adult population as well in the princi-

ples of democracy was the emergence in 1990 of a virulent nationalistic and anti-Semitic racism. At least 30,000 people, most of them youths, have become involved in militant chauvinistic politics in Eastern Germany. They have weapons purchased from the 300,000 Soviet soldiers deployed in Eastern Germany who wanted hard currency to take back to the Soviet Union. In public rallies, they shout Nazi slogans and make Nazi salutes. They have attacked foreigners and displayed intense hostility to Jews, writing anti-Jewish epithets on walls and tombstones. In 1991 they seemed to be proliferating in cities like Dresden and Leipzig, where they attacked the gathering places of homosexuals. They have also launched attacks against new centers of pornography started up in Dresden by West German criminals; in this activity, they have gained a measure of sympathy from people who oppose the spread of the West German criminal underworld to Eastern Germany.

Many of the youths involved in this activity are known as skinheads. Mostly factory workers, they speak against anybody whom they consider to be "un-German." Their behavior seems to be a reaction to the years of strict punishments meted out to right-wing radicals by the Communist government. A conflict between generations may also explain the skinhead phenomenon, since many of the young people involved in the violence against minorities and the revival of Nazi sentiments are children of former Communist secret police personnel. Their behavior is dangerous because Eastern German society, under Communist rule, never learned about democracy and therefore is vulnerable to the appeal of anti-democratic ideas, especially given the poverty of the region and the interest in simple solutions to complicated problems, a trait inherent in Fascist-oriented thinking.

The Stasi Revelations

A final problem in the decommunization of Eastern Germany concerns the way in which many Eastern Germans are finding out that, in the Communist era, friends and relatives had spied on them as informers for the East German secret police, or *Stasi*. These revelations are causing great personal anguish and trauma.

Under a law approved by the German Parliament at the end of 1991, any German citizen was given the right to examine his or her Stasi file. Most of these files contained reports about the person's private life and political views, submitted by informers under code names. Special librarians at the Stasi archives can usually

The Soviet zone
of military occu-
pation in eastern
Germany be-
comes East
Germany
1949

A strike by
industrial
workers in East
Berlin is
suppressed by
the regime
1953

Construction of
the Berlin Wall
1961

Honecker
succeeds
Ulbricht as SED
chairman
1971

East Germany
joins the United
Nations
1973

1980s–19

Erich Honecker resigns as SED party chief and is succeeded by Egon Krenz; Stoph resigns as prime minister and is succeeded by pary reformer Hans Modrow

The Berlin Wall is officially opened; parliamentary elections result in a defeat for the Communists; currency union between East Germany and West Germany

East Germany and West Germany sign reunification agreements; East Germany is formally reunified with West Germany

identify the informer. Many Stasi victims who have seen their files have discovered that some of their friends, coworkers, and even relatives were informers for the secret police. These revelations have left former Stasi informers deeply embarrassed and, in some cases, overwhelmed with guilt. The law opening the Stasi files also empowered government agencies to request background checks on their employees, which have resulted in the dismissal of thousands of judges, police officers, schoolteachers, and other public employees living and working in the former East German state. Stasi files have shaken the German sports world, revealing how certain prominent Olympic champions had been informers. These people, along with many others, stand discredited, with their professional ambitions severely compromised. All Germany has become transfixed by what the German weekly *Der Spiegel* calls "the horror files."

When researchers from anti-Stasi groups began analyzing files in Berlin and other cities, their first shock was at the sheer volume of paper facing them: Stasi files filled 125 miles of shelf space, with each mile containing about 17 million sheets of paper and weighing nearly 50 tons. After German unification, in October 1990, members of the new all-German Parliament disagreed over what to do with all this information.

Some politicians warned that the files were too explosive ever to be read; they proposed burning them. Others wanted the files sealed for a number of years or opened only selectively. But members of

the Budestag from the new constituencies in Eastern Germany insisted that the files be opened to those on whom they were kept. Fleeing Stasi agents managed to destroy some of their most incriminating files, such as those documenting their support for West Germany's murderous Red Army Faction and other terrorist groups. Nevertheless, the files are remarkably complete and reveal the Stasi's voracious appetite for even the most trivial information about suspected individuals, including their bathroom and sex habits, reflecting how the former East German Communist regime considered almost all its citizens potentially subversive.

Today people in Eastern Germany on whom files had been kept and on whom close friends and relatives had informed are in shock and cannot understand the behavior of these informers whom they had trusted. Nevertheless, they all seem to agree that knowing what happened, confronting informers, and seeking some retribution, even if they know none will be forthcoming—the democratic state has no way to compensate them for what they have suffered—are all necessary actions that must be taken, for the sake of not only psychological consolation but also for justice and morality and in the hope that the painful revelations of past outrages may somehow prevent a recurrence of them in the future. At the very least, however, the effects of the revelations about the Stasi files have had a profoundly disruptive effect on the society of the former East German state.

PROSPECTS OF A LASTING DEMOCRATIZATION

Preparing the society of Eastern Germany for democracy is likely to take a long time. In the interim, Eastern Germans are in a sort of developmental limbo. It is difficult for them to reject the authoritarian order under which they lived for a long time, and it is almost as difficult for them to adjust to the liberal and democratic one with which they have had little experience. While the Bonn government is trying very hard—and at great cost to the society of Western Germany—to ease the transition in Eastern Germany from the old to the new, there will be political instability and even trauma before the transition is complete.

DEVELOPMENT

Although times remain hard for most people in Eastern Germany, recent public opinion shows that most Eastern Germans are optimistic about the future. The all-German government poured about $83 billion into Eastern Germany in 1991 to facilitate economic growth. As a result, the economy of Eastern Germany was expected to grow by 10% in 1992.

FREEDOM

Now that Eastern Germans are part of a new all-German parliamentary democracy, they enjoy the full array of Western-style freedoms and civil rights. Especially important is the openness of the government in allowing Eastern Germans unfettered access to files about their behavior maintained by the former East German secret police, or Stasi.

HEALTH/WELFARE

Social conditions in Eastern Germany have deteriorated temporarily as the region moves through the transition from socialism to capitalism. While the health and welfare system in West Germany has been extended to cover Eastern Germans, it is not as thorough as the one developed by the Communists in the former German Democratic Republic.

ACHIEVEMENTS

Although Eastern Germany's economic revival is still a long way off, there are some modest achievements that augur well for a successful recovery from the economic mismanagement by the Communists. For example, there is a "din of renewal" in East Berlin, as five once-crumbling buildings in the city's *Raabestrasse* are undergoing renovation.

Hungary

GEOGRAPHY

Area in Square Kilometers (Miles):
92,980 (35,900) (slightly smaller than Indiana)
Capital (Population): Budapest (2,115,000)
Climate: temperate

PEOPLE

Population
Total: 10,546,000
Annual Growth Rate: −0.2%
Rural/Urban Population Ratio: 38/62
Ethnic Makeup of Population: 96% Hungarian; 4% German, Slovak, and others

Health
Life Expectancy at Birth: 65 years (male); 73 years (female)
Infant Mortality Rate (Ratio): 20.2/1,000
Average Caloric Intake: 134% of FAO minimum
Physicians Available (Ratio): 1/343

Religion(s)
67% Roman Catholic; 20% Calvinist; 5% Lutheran; 8% Jewish, atheist, and others

Education
Adult Literacy Rate: 98%

COMMUNICATION
Telephones: 858,200
Newspapers: 29

GENEROSITY UNDER DURESS

Prime Minister Jozsef Antall's repeated assertion that in his heart he is the leader not only of more than 10.5 million people in Hungary but several million more reflects the awareness of most Hungarians that their small country represents only a fraction of what it once was: more than 3 million ethnic Hungarians live in 5 countries bordering Hungary. Sad though they may be about the loss of past glory, and distracted, as most other Central/Eastern European peoples are, by the hardships of moving away from socialism to capitalism and democracy, Hungarians are still a generous people and have opened their hearts and home to refugees fleeing the Civil War in Yugoslavia. They share willingly their scarce and costly necessities, especially food.

TRANSPORTATION
Highways—Kilometers (Miles): 29,701 (18,414)
Railroads—Kilometers (Miles): 7,766 (4,815)
Usable Airfields: 80

GOVERNMENT
Type: pluralistic parliamentary democracy
Independence Date: April 4, 1919
Head of State: President Arpád Göncz
Political Parties: Hungarian Socialist Party; Hungarian Socialist Workers' Party; Alliance of Free Democrats; Democratic Forum; Independent Smallholders Party; Federation of Young Christians; Christian Democratic People's Party
Suffrage: universal over 18

MILITARY
Number of Armed Forces: 94,500
Military Expenditures (% of Central Government Expenditures): 5%
Current Hostilities: none

ECONOMY
Currency ($ U.S. Equivalent): 75 forints = $1
Per Capita Income/GNP: $6,100/$64.5 billion
Inflation Rate: 23%
Total Foreign Debt: $20.6 billion
Natural Resources: fertile land; bauxite; brown coal
Agriculture: corn; wheat; potatoes; sugar beets; wine grapes; vegetables; fruits
Industry: precision and measuring equipment; mining; pharmaceuticals; textiles; food processing; transportation equipment

FOREIGN TRADE
Exports: $9.5 billion
Imports: $8.6 billion

HUNGARY

Soviet troops liberated Hungary from Nazi control in the spring of 1945 and helped Hungarian Communists, who formed a new party called the Hungarian Socialist Workers Party (HSWP), to expand their influence in the postwar Hungarian government. There were two groups of Hungarian Communist leaders: conservatives, who were loyal to Moscow and ready to imitate Soviet policies in the development of Hungarian socialism; and pragmatists, who favored deviations from the Soviet model to make socialism fit the characteristics of the Hungarian environment. Metyas Rakosi, a conservative, was HSWP first secretary from 1945 until 1956. Under Rakosi, party pragmatists and reformers like Imre Nagy were ousted from positions of power in the late 1940s. By 1953 Rakosi and the conservatives had replicated the Soviet model of socialism and had transformed Hungary into a Soviet satellite.

THE OCTOBER 1956 CRISIS

In the aftermath of Stalin's death in 1953, people from all sectors of Hungarian society—workers, farmers, students, intellectuals, and bureaucrats—wanted major reforms. Some wanted a Western-style pluralistic social democracy, others an end to collectivization of agriculture and an adjustment in investment priorities away from the Soviet-inspired emphasis on capital-goods expansion. They wanted production of more consumer goods. Many would have liked to expand ties with the West.

Reformist elements in the Hungarian party leadership who had kept silent in the Stalinist years were emboldened after Stalin's death to elevate one of their own, Imre Nagy, to the premiership of the government. Rakosi stayed on as party leader.

Nagy promised reforms, but few occurred. By 1955 the conservatives, who still controlled the party and opposed reform, ousted Nagy. In the next year intense popular pressure for change mounted, reaching a climax with antigovernment demonstrations in Budapest in October 1956. University students and dissident intellectuals, meeting in recently formed discussion clubs, demanded political liberalization. There was unrest also in the countryside, where farmers demanded a return to private ownership of farm property. The country seemed on the threshold of revolt.

In response to demonstrations for sweeping reform in Budapest during the last days of October, the Hungarian party leadership returned Nagy to the premiership and replaced Erno Gero, who had succeeded Rakosi in April, with Jänos Kadar as party first secretary, with a mandate to achieve some reforms in the political and economic spheres. But when, on November 1, Nagy announced over Hungarian radio a restoration of the multiparty system, the appointment to his Cabinet of members of noncommunist parties long since banned in Hungary, and Hungary's withdrawal from the Warsaw Pact, the Soviets became alarmed and prepared for a military intervention.

Soviet Intervention

On November 4, 1956, the Soviets intervened with massive military force. Soviet tanks patrolled the streets of Budapest, and Soviet armor quickly overwhelmed popular resistance. The Soviets ended Nagy's reform efforts and insisted upon his ouster from power. Nagy was executed in 1958. The Soviets obliged party leader Kadar to restore public order, to guarantee Hungary's conformity with Soviet-style socialism and to assure its loyalty to the Warsaw Pact alliance system.

With Soviet backing, Kadar suppressed political opposition in Hungary. He rebuilt the Hungarian Communist Party, ridding it of reformers and deviants. In the 1960s he presided over a tightly disciplined, conformist, and loyal Hungary.

KADAR'S MIDDLE-OF-THE-ROAD SOCIALISM

Determined to avoid the extremes of his predecessors, Kadar remained a moderate. He supported neither the radical democratization that Nagy had tried to put through nor the reactionary Stalinism practiced by the conservative Rakosi. During the 1960s Hungary developed into what might be called a middle-of-the-road socialist system. And, under Kadar's leadership, Hungarian society became stable and comparatively well-off.

The New Economic Mechanism

The hallmark of Hungarian socialism was its success in the economic sphere, achieved partly through deft reforms starting in 1968 and called the "New Economic Mechanism." The reforms were intended to correct some of the flaws of the Soviet model. They provided factory managers with much autonomy in plant operation, in particular in the setting of wages, the procurement of raw materials from foreign sources, and the renewal of equipment. Efficiency and profitability were to determine the sizes of industries. Firms unable to sell their products and make a profit were to be liquidated. The New Economic Mechanism led to a reduction in the size of enterprises, making it easier for them to adjust production to accommodate changes in demand. Other reforms included the establishment of a flexible pricing system whereby some prices were to be determined by supply and demand, the creation of a sphere of individual activity free of state central planning that involved small-scale commerce and crafts shops, and permission for workers to organize themselves into teams and offer their labor to a factory at premium wage rates.

An important aspect of the reform program involved agriculture. There was a significant departure from Soviet-style collectivization. Farm families had fewer centrally imposed quotas to meet, more control over the use of their time and labor, and lucrative remuneration. Productive farmers were rewarded by permission to use state-owned land as if it were their own property. Farm families also were encouraged to establish cooperatives which enjoyed a substantial independence of the central planners in Budapest.

The result of these reforms was an astounding increase of agricultural output during the 1970s and early 1980s, producing enough for domestic needs and also for export. Hungary's success in agriculture could be gauged by the extraordinary quantity and quality of food commodities in the markets and grocery stores of the country's urban centers as compared to what was available in nearby Poland and Romania.

Political Stability

After 1956 there was very little political dissent and no mass antigovernment demonstrations in Hungary. Hungarians seemed willing to tolerate the political dictatorship of the Communist party, partly because of what it had achieved in the economic area. Hungarians were inclined to remain silent about the regime's much-resented insistence upon political discipline.

The absence of any massive unrest in Hungary must be attributed also to Kadar's willingness to tolerate some public discussion of controversial issues and to allow some—albeit gentle—criticism of regime policies. Kadar did this to diffuse tension as well as to provide channels of communication essential to rational policy-making.

Relations with the Soviet Union

Hungary was close to the Soviet Union in terms of foreign policy. It was usually supportive of Soviet international positions. Thus, despite reservations, Hungary participated in the Soviet-led Warsaw Pact intervention in Czechoslovakia in 1968. And in the 1970s, although he echoed Eurocommunist advocacies of Communist party autonomy, Kadar carefully refrained from endorsing the Eurocommunist position on a liberal path to socialism, which the Soviets had strongly criticized.

In the Afghanistan crisis, however, Hungary was only mildly supportive of the Soviet position, because of Hungarian sensitivity to Soviet interventionist behavior anywhere. But Kadar stood by the Kremlin in its resistance to the Carter administration's retaliation. For example, Hungary dutifully supported Soviet opposition to the U.S. boycott of the Olympic Games held in the Soviet Union in the summer of 1980.

In sum, one might characterize Kadar's behavior toward the Soviet Union as autonomous without having aroused the Kremlin's animosity. Indeed, Kadar's loyalty to the Soviets won their indulgence of a substantial Hungarian autonomy in domestic policy-making. But he was still sufficiently independent in foreign affairs to avoid arousing his people's resentment over Hungary's deference to Soviet foreign policy.

HUNGARY AND PERESTROIKA

Hungary began to embrace perestroika in the late 1980s, with plans to go beyond the scope of reforms that Gorbachev was introducing in the Soviet Union to remedy serious economic and social problems. The severity of these problems caused widespread demoralization, a sense of hopelessness about the future, and political alienation and popular distrust of the Communist party. Eventually, there developed support everywhere in Hungarian society—including the leadership of the party—for radical and immediate change in all spheres of Hungarian life.

Economic Problems
In the mid-1980s Hungary's buoyant economy turned sour. State-owned smokestack industries like steel and coal mining were bleeding the economy dry with their losses. The Hungarian government heavily taxed the private and more productive areas of the industrial sector to subsidize these enterprises.

The country had difficulties with the Council of Mutual Economic Assistance. For example, a Soviet demand for products that were already outmoded by Western standards at unreasonably low prices forced Hungary to maintain inefficient, out-of-date industries and discouraged

production of advanced goods at world-market prices. Hungary also had to invest in the Soviet infrastructure, for example in the Yamburg oil fields, or in Soviet-designed development projects inside Hungary that were not cost-efficient. Moreover, CMEA trade reportedly resulted in the conversion of dollar imports into transferable ruble exports at a rate that was highly unfavorable to Hungary.

Additionally, as a result of decisions made at the beginning of the 1980s to finance growth through Western loans and to import about one-half of Hungary's energy requirements for hard currency, the country's net foreign debt rose from $6 billion to $12 billion between 1981 and 1988. Between 65 and 70 percent of convertible export earnings was spent on debt service. Because hard-currency growth had not kept pace with imports, Hungary had an increasingly difficult time repaying its debt and finding new credit.

Finally, Hungary's economic malaise was attributable to the inadequacy of existing reforms. For example, some of the reforms already on the books, such as the bankruptcy law, had not been fully enforced, because of the authorities' fear that strict application would affect about 30 percent of Hungarian industrial enterprises and cause massive unemployment. Moreover, liquidation proceedings had not been enforced against bankrupt enterprises, partly because self-interested bureaucrats did not want to preside over the dissolution of the traditional Stalinist economic infrastructure, which was the source of their power and privilege in Hungarian society.

Social Problems
Economic stagnation aggravated social ills. There was, for example, a frightening deterioration in the delivery of medical services, because of decreasing expenditures for public health. Approximately 90 percent of the entire population suffered from poor nutrition, smoking, alcoholism, or chronic nervous strain. Hungary's life expectancy at birth was among the lowest in 33 developed countries examined by the World Health Organization. As a result, Hungary's population was no longer reproducing itself. During the second half of the 1980s the country's net population decreased by 125,000.

A chronic housing shortage also worsened the people's physical and mental health. The state simply failed to continue redistribution of existing housing, and not enough was invested in the construction of new housing. Assistance to those who wanted to build their own residences by the offer of loans at reasonable rates bene-

fited only the well-to-do. The vast majority of people still lived in substandard housing.

A pervasive and visible poverty induced by an unrelenting inflation led to pessimism about the future and a popular disgust with political system and with its Communist leadership. By the end of the 1980s there was a truly national constituency in support of advanced reform that would open up the political system and restore economic health.

RENEWAL OF REFORM

The government's response to these problems included short- and long-term economic strategies. In June 1987 Kadar appointed Karolyi Grosz as premier. Grosz was personally committed to economic reform. He had criticized the inept handling of the economy by the Kadarists and also had publicly castigated Hungary's workers for their low productivity. When Grosz took over, he made important changes in top government and party posts to strengthen the hand of those who shared his commitment to achieving a revitalization of the Hungarian economy.

Short-Term Strategies
Grosz's strategy started with an austerity program, which included a reduction in deficit spending and foreign borrowing. On July 19, 1987, prices were increased by 10 to 20 percent in four categories of products: bread, gasoline, cigarettes, and household energy. The price hikes drastically reduced consumers' purchasing power, and the aged and disadvantaged, especially in rural areas, suffered. This upward adjustment of prices, however, was little more than a quick fix for the economy, because no steps were taken to expand output or to reform the deficit-ridden industrial sector.

The new program also called for further decentralization of the economy. Enterprises were allowed more independence; central control over operations was diminished. Emphasis was placed on increasing profits and exports for hard currency. Enterprises that were consistently losing money were to be liquidated. In September 1987 a law was passed that specifically provided for the winding down of nonviable enterprises and for their liquidation. However, this law was not aggressively implemented, for political reasons—the liquidation of all of Hungary's inefficient enterprises would have created horrendous unemployment.

Long-Term Strategies

The Hungarian government's long-term strategy sought to expand economic output and make Hungarian exports competitive in the world market. It involved an expansion of private entrepreneurialism in agriculture, the service industries, and retail trade; substantial wage differentiation to increase workers' incentives; and the introduction of a two-tier banking system, consisting of a central bank and a series of commercial and specialized banks. Hungarian reformers also wanted to curtail uneconomic projects imposed on Hungary as a result of its membership in the Soviet Bloc.

Some of the economic changes in 1987 were quite innovative and unique, especially those in the area of monetary and fiscal policy. The new banks made short-term loans to enterprises, issued bonds to raise capital that would make possible larger loans for longer periods to more extensive and ambitious enterprises, and gradually developed a substantial autonomy of—although not complete independence from—the Hungarian national bank, which continued to be the chief source of investment capital for very large industrial enterprises and showed no sign of relinquishing its hold over the investment area.

In the fiscal area, the government introduced Western-style personal-income and value-added taxes while reducing taxes on enterprises, thus departing from the traditional socialist emphasis on collective responsibility for funding public policy. The hope was that by shifting the tax burden to the individual, there would be increased popular pressure on the bureaucracy to use public money judiciously and discreetly to improve economic efficiency, while enterprises would be encouraged with additional discretionary funds to improve production and maximize output.

The regime introduced more radical economic reform in October 1988 to diminish still further state control of the economy and expand the free market. The Parliament unanimously passed a new law that opened the way for full foreign ownership of Hungarian companies and provided that joint ventures with less than 50 percent foreign participation no longer needed official registration. It also allowed Hungarians to trade shares in private companies (previously, Hungarians could own shares, but their holdings were restricted to the companies where they worked) and employ up to 500 citizens for private profit. Indeed, the law created a framework for a Western-style capital market and revived types of companies not seen in Hungary since before the

Communist takeover in the late 1940s. The law also abolished a number of rules governing state and private enterprises, leaving regulation mainly to financial means.

MOVEMENT TOWARD DEMOCRACY

Pressure had been mounting both inside the Communist party and throughout the society as a whole for a radical alteration of the political system, in the belief that economic improvement depended on political change. Much like Poland, but in contrast with the Soviet Union, the impetus for change came as much from outside the party leadership as from within it.

Beginning in 1987 there was an increase of popular interest in democratic reform. In September 1987 Hungarian intellectuals established a new umbrella-type organization of political advocacy, the Democratic Forum, which invited all Hungarians interested in solving the nation's economic, social, and political problems to join its ranks. It called for open and uncensored debates in periodicals.

In May 1988, some 200 Hungarian journalists applied to the government to establish a glasnost club. They wanted to provide ordinary citizens with information about important issues in the reform movement neglected in the official media. They also wanted to publicize violations of citizens' rights. The journalists' application was carefully worded to stress the authors' positive evaluation of Soviet leader Mikhail Gorbachev's pronouncements and of the club's intention to work alongside rather than against the official journalists' association.

Also in May 1988, workers and academics formed Hungary's first independent labor union since the Communist takeover. The Democratic Union of Scientific and Academic Workers (TDDSZ) consisted of academic and nonacademic university personnel in Budapest and pledged to protect the professional interests of its members. The creation of TDDSZ apparently inspired similar initiatives by other special-interest groups.

THE END OF KADAR'S RULE

Because Grosz could not make great strides as long as the Kadarist conservatives dominated the top party and state organs, he decided to challenge the conservatives at a special party conference. To prepare for this conference, he imitated Gorbachev's strategy, calling upon the party rank-and-file to discuss intensively what was wrong with the country and

what the party could do about it, in the context of selecting delegates.

To Grosz's satisfaction, the party rank-and-file for the most part wanted substantial political change. Apart from wanting to replace Kadar, who was personally blamed for much of what had gone wrong in the country during the 1980s, many in the party apparatus were critical of democratic centralism, which had left excessive control over decisions in the hands of the Politburo at the expense of the Central Committee. They argued that personal as well as collective responsibility for party behavior was essential to more efficient policy-making and to a restoration of popular confidence in the party's leadership of the country.

In May 1988 the special party conference formally endorsed major political reforms, starting with the replacement of Kadar as party first secretary with Grosz. Imre Pozsgay, one of the founders of and chief spokesperson for the Democratic Forum, and Reszo Nyers, another prominent advocate of reform, were elevated to the Politburo. While Pozsgay had sought radical political change, Nyers wanted a further extension of economic reform. He was among the leaders who initiated the first phase of Hungary's economic reforms in 1968.

The final conference statement, adopted on May 22, called for greater intraparty democracy, involving increased participation of local party organs in national-policy decision-making; direct election of at least some of the party's national leadership by local organs, which should have the power to recall those elected; and personal political responsibility of those involved in formulating and implementing policy. The conference also endorsed an expansion of political pluralism outside the party and emphasized the exclusiveness of National Assembly jurisdiction over lawmaking.

POLITICAL LIBERALIZATION

The Grosz regime soon came under intense pressure of reformers like Pozsgay to move ahead with political liberalization, in particular preparations for the reinstitution of a multiparty system and free parliamentary elections. Grosz somewhat grudgingly acknowledged that the multiparty system and the holding of free parliamentary elections might be possible as the only means of achieving the openness needed to facilitate economic improvement. Yet he called for sharp limits on party proliferation, insisting that if there were to be a transition to multiparty pluralism, it must be gradual to avoid destabilization. In any event, he insisted that parties allowed to compete in parliamentary elections in 1990 would have to respect the constitutional provision mandating socialism for Hungary and to accept the Communist party's continued preeminence in the government into the mid-1990s.

Plans for a New Constitution

In the spring of 1989 the party leadership reviewed the draft of a new constitution, which would retain public ownership of industry and reaffirm Hungary's existing alliances with the Soviet Union and other Warsaw Pact countries but which also would include radical changes in the governmental system. It would create a new, powerful, popularly elected president who would not simultaneously hold high office in either the Communist party or any other party. A new, powerful constitutional tribunal would be empowered to accept or reject applications of new political parties, after examining their programs to determine if they were congruent with socialism.

Under the constitution, the party leadership would expect the opposition groups to allow a Communist to occupy the presidential office and to guarantee a certain proportion of seats in the Parliament to the Communist party. The party itself also would control the ministries of Foreign Affairs, Interior, and Defense during a transition period. And while new political parties would slowly build their strength and become accustomed to operating in Parliament, the Communist party would use the transition period for a radical transformation of its role from one of security and economic administration to grass-roots electioneering.

Ascendancy of the Radical Reformers

While this proposed constitution was being reviewed, reformers in the party leadership moved forward with their own agenda. In May 1989 they ousted Kadar from the Central Committee, thus limiting even further the power of conservatives. Advocates of radical reform within the Politburo also weakened Grosz, who differed with Pozsgay and Nyers in the belief that political reform should preserve the socialist regime. Thus, for Grosz, the multiparty system, a mechanism of governmental checks and balances, and other reforms were not the end in themselves but the means to another end: prosperity. Moreover, he also had made clear that he did not intend to preside over a loosening of his party's hold over the country by allowing reforms to develop into a transfer of power to a nonsocialist government.

In June 1989 Pozsgay, Nyers, and other reform-minded party leaders, along with many others in the Party's Central Committee, mobilized a majority in the Committee in favor of replacing Grosz as first secretary with Nyers, who assumed the new title and post of president of the party. The Central Committee also created a new leadership quartet of Nyers; Pozsgay, who was nominated to be president of the republic (a post introduced early in 1990); Nemeth; and Grosz, whose membership in the new executive body indicated some continuing support for caution and restraint.

In October 1989 the reform-oriented leadership accelerated Hungary's move toward political democracy but also tried to safeguard the Communist party's role in Hungarian politics in this new era, when it would have to compete for leadership with other, noncommunist groups. It agreed to hold free elections for Parliament in March 1990, 3 months ahead of the original date of June. The Communists also changed their name to the Socialist Party and officially abandoned orthodox Marxist ideology.

The Communists' strategy to keep power in the new decade, however, suffered a setback in November, when, under pressure from the democratic opposition, they were obliged to hold a national referendum to allow the public to decide whether elections for the presidency of the republic should be held before or after parliamentary elections. The referendum, which was the first really free electoral experience Hungarians had had in 42 years of Communist rule, was significant also because of its outcome. Hungarians voted to hold presidential elections after the parliamentary elections. Since the Communist party was expected to lose its majority in the parliamentary elections and thus lose control of the government, it would be severely handicapped in the presidential elections. As the new decade began, the former Hungarian Communist Party was trying to retain some influence over the country's political future.

THE END OF COMMUNIST RULE

In early 1990 Hungary made further strides toward pluralistic democracy. For example, at the end of January Parliament passed a law establishing freedom of conscience and religion that marked a final break with past policies of atheism and repression of the churches. But the most dramatic development was the campaign for parliamentary elections, held on March 25 and April 7, 1990, which brought to an end almost 45 years of Communist totalitarian rule in Hungary. Not surprisingly, the former Communists suffered a decisive defeat in the elections. Victory went to the parties of the center right, in particular the Democratic Forum. Three factors explained the success of the Democratic Forum in winning more than 50 percent of the seats in the new Parliament. First was a pervasive popular aversion to the former Communists, including those who had spearheaded reform and laid the groundwork for the democratization of Hungarian politics, because of revelations about scandals in the mishandling of state property and continued abuses of the secret police and because of the memory of Communist party repression, incompetence, and subservience to Moscow. It was impossible for the Communists to regain credibility with Hungarian voters, changes in name, program, and leadership notwithstanding. Second, the Forum offered a moderate, confidence-inspiring program that called for a careful transition from socialism to a free-market economy, the creation of a convertible currency, and integration with Western Europe. The Forum also expressed concern about the treatment of Hungarian minorities abroad. Third was the weakness of other parties, in particular the Forum's nearest competitor and rival, the Alliance of Free Democrats. The Free Democrats lacked a dynamic leadership at the top, an equivalent of the Forum's charismatic Josef Antall. And the Independent Smallholders, a reincarnation of the farmers' party which had been suppressed by the Communists after having won 58 percent of the popular vote in parliamentary elections in 1945, was now too small and too new, although it clearly had the promise of becoming more popular in the near future.

POLITICS AFTER COMMUNISM

Hungary faced serious problems as it developed democracy. In the first place, the new democratic political system sometimes functioned more like an oligarchy. For example, following the parliamentary elections, leaders of the two large parties, the Forum and the Free Democrats, secretly agreed among themselves on a wide range of issues concerning the style and content of policy-making in the new government. They did this without consulting their own party colleagues, never mind other political groups supporting them in the Parliament.

Forum and Free Democratic leaders agreed that the president of Hungary would be Arpád Goncz, the noted Free Democrat. They also decided on the staffing of the 10 permanent and 5 Special Committees of the Parliament. They agreed to establish an independent body to supervise radio and television and to require a two-thirds majority in Parliament for the adoption of amendments to the Constitution. They chose Josef Antall, leader of the Forum, the plurality party, as prime minister.

While it is true that the Forum and the Free Democrats have had little experience with this new political system or democratic decision-making based upon compromise, their tendency to make deals rather than engage in debate and seek a compromise with various constituencies is unfortunate. It works against representative and responsible government.

Hungary's democracy needs the support of its people. But the July 1990 referendum on electing the president of the republic directly brought out only 14 percent of the vote, indicative of a pervasive political apathy suggesting either disinterest in or depression over national politics. When this referendum was declared invalid because of the small turnout, conservative politicians in Budapest, who fear a popular demagogic political leader, were relieved because 85 percent of those who did vote wanted a directly elected chief executive.

Economic Deterioration

In addition to the problems of setting up democratic government, Hungarians have to struggle with economic problems inherited from the Communist past. In 1990, the first year of post-Communist government, the country was in the third straight year of recession. The annual rate of inflation was 23 percent, and 75 percent of the money in cash or bank accounts belonged to only 25 percent of the population, while 2 million people—20 percent of the total population—lived below the poverty level. Hungary also had and still has the highest per capita foreign debt in Central/Eastern Europe. To complete this somber picture was the significant decline in trade with the Soviet Union, because Moscow held back the payment of almost 1 billion rubles for the buses, machinery, and other Hungarian products that it imported in 1989.

Some of the new economic initiatives set in motion in 1990 have not worked out. For example, in 1990 the government of Prime Minister Antall set up a new stock exchange, but it has had hardly any business, largely because most enterprises remain under state control and no one has spare cash to spend on stock in enterprises that have been privatized. Moreover, many Hungarians are suspicious of the

stock exchange, which they view as little more than a capitalist gambling table. In addition, they hardly know what securities are, never mind how they are valued. After all, stock exchanges represent values and attitudes that the Communist government criticized throughout its rule.

To stem the economic decline, the Hungarian government has tried to cultivate foreign investment. It has offered attractive joint ventures with tax breaks and liberal rules for foreign investors who create jobs in Hungary to repatriate their profits. It points to an efficient labor force willing to work for far less than workers in the West. This strategy is working to some degree. Many U.S. firms see in the Hungarian market a stepping-stone to the huge Russian market and to the markets of other Central/Eastern European countries.

Social Problems

On top of the political and economic problems are social problems. Poverty is severe and much more obvious than under communism. Homeless people live in the railway stations of Budapest. Now that it is no longer a crime, as it was under Communist rule, people hang out in public places. The situation is made worse by Budapest's chronic housing shortage and the migration of people to Hungary from countries like Romania, where living conditions are even more intolerable. Indeed, with the Romanians living illegally in Hungary numbering over 100,000, almost half of the homeless people sleeping in the railway stations are Romanians.

In coping with the homeless, the Hungarians have come up against problems familiar to social agencies elsewhere, including the "not in my backyard" phenomenon. When the Budapest City Council considered in late 1990 turning an empty military barracks into a shelter for the homeless, residents of the district protested, causing the city to back down temporarily. And in Hungary, where the private sector will be struggling for a long time to get started, private charity is in no position to be of much help. Both the Red Cross and the Roman Catholic Church sponsor shelters, but they are dependent on state aid, which has been modest.

Another major social problem in post-Communist Hungarian society is an apparent resurgence of anti-Semitism. Sometimes anti-Semitic expressions are oblique; but at other times they are obvious and blatant, as when a small weekly publication in the provincial city of Debrecen openly blamed Jews for the calamities of the Communist era, which were described as the revenge of the Jews for

the Nazi horrors. The paper accused the Jews of responsibility for a range of problems, from Hungary's rising crime rate to liberal abortion policies.

Hungarian Jews say that these expressions of anti-Semitism are isolated and that the vast majority of Hungarians are not anti-Semitic. But it is also true that Hungary has a tradition of anti-Semitism, which reached a climax in World War II, when the Hungarian government joined the Axis alliance and cooperated with German policy to exterminate the Jews by sending 500,000 Hungarian Jews to death camps.

Hungarians are also dissatisfied with how the democratic leadership has dealt with former Communists. Certainly the Communist government of the late János Kadar was the least inefficient of the Central/Eastern European socialist governments, but it too was guilty of abuses and excesses. But the country cannot afford a witch hunt, which might well divide and demoralize people just as they are being asked to show tolerance of difficult circumstances. It is also true that the new democratic order has to rely on the help of former Communists to provide much-needed administrative experience.

The new government, however, has agreed in many instances to a restoration of property or some kind of cash indemnification for those hurt under communism. But it has also stonewalled some demands, especially when they involve searching for past records to identify guilty parties or to determine the fate of victims, some of whom disappeared without a trace. Today's officials simply do not want to open old wounds. Indeed, some members of the Hungarian Parliament have suggested destroying old files of the Communist secret police. That is not likely to happen, but neither is it likely that the Hungarian government will be able to satisfy Hungarians seeking retribution. With priority given to stability, justice will be served only when it does not cause more problems than it solves.

REFORM AND FOREIGN POLICY

Change in both the political and economic spheres in the late 1980s depended on the external environment—in particular, Hungary's relations with the Soviet Union and with the West. Indeed, East-West détente as well as Hungary's relations with the superpowers were essential to the success of its reforms.

The Soviet Union

Gorbachev viewed the Hungarian reform program as an experiment in socialist change important to the development of Soviet perestroika. The Kremlin valued the enthusiastic Hungarian support of Soviet perestroika and the Hungarian potential for encouraging reformism in other Soviet Bloc countries that were resisting it, such as Romania, Czechoslovakia, and East Germany.

Thus, the Kremlin accepted the removal of Kadar, the ascendancy of radical reformers like Pozsgay and Nyers, and the prospect that Hungary would adopt political pluralism and substantially reduce the role and power of the Communist party in the foreseeable future. The Soviets did not pressure the Hungarian regime to close its frontiers to the East German citizens seeking refuge in West Germany, but did privately advise the Hungarian Communists to diminish tensions with their Soviet Bloc neighbors.

Finally, the Kremlin punctuated its acceptance of Hungary's rapid democratization by agreeing in January 1990 to begin discussion of a withdrawal of Soviet forces deployed in Hungary since the 1956 invasion of Budapest. The Kremlin accepted the argument of Premier Nemeth in talks with Soviet Premier Ryzkhov that Hungary's strategic position in Central/Eastern Europe—Hungary has no borders with NATO countries—made the Soviet withdrawal logical and risk-free. The Kremlin decided to accommodate Hungarian demands for an end to the Soviet military presence in Hungary, which had become a political issue in the campaign for the parliamentary elections in March that worked against the former Communists, also to strengthen Nemeth's position and help the cause of his reelection. In any event, the Soviet decision to withdraw its 48,000 troops from Hungary by mid-1991 effectively completed the desatellization of Hungary and the restoration of Hungary's full independence of Moscow.

Although the new democratic leadership was concerned about the Kremlin's anxieties over the loss of Soviet power in Central/Eastern Europe at the end of 1989, it moved to dissolve the Warsaw Pact. In June 1990 the Hungarian Parliament voted unanimously to withdraw Hungary from the Warsaw Pact by the end of 1991. The government also asked for the evacuation of the 50,000 Soviet troops on Hungarian territory. In March 1990 the Soviets agreed, albeit grudgingly, to the short timetable. The last Soviet troops departed Hungary on June 16, 1991.

Hungary also sought to protect itself against a possible reassertion of Soviet influence and to give itself maximum diplomatic flexibility in negotiations in April 1991 over a new bilateral treaty with the Soviet Union. Hungary resisted language that would have banned either country from joining any alliance that could be considered hostile to the other country. Concerned that Hungary might prejudice its chances of eventually joining the European Community or NATO, Prime Minister Antall said that Hungary wanted a treaty with Moscow guaranteeing Hungary's right to join groups and alliances of its own choosing.

While seeking to protect the country's independence in foreign policy, the Hungarian government muted its tone in dealing with Moscow, avoiding anything in the nature of anti-Soviet rhetoric. It discreetly turned to the Soviet republics that were declaring their independence of the Soviet center, notably Russia and the Ukraine, which together accounted for 90 percent of Hungarian-Soviet trade. The Hungarians found the individual Soviet republics eager to establish bilateral trade relationships which they, as well as Hungary, desperately needed. For example, Hungary's search for adequate quantities of oil since the Soviet central government could no longer guarantee delivery (Moscow indicated that in 1991 it would sell Hungary only 20 percent of the oil previously sold to it) led to oil purchases from individual Soviet oil-producing regions, such as the Bashkir and Tatar autonomous republics.

Hungary and the West

Hungary's relations with the West, in particular West Germany and the United States, had been good and thus an asset for reform. Grosz had spoken of Hungary's closeness to other European countries and said that from its beginnings in the ninth century, the Hungarian nation had been able to survive and develop only by remaining open to European scientific development and cultural values. He emphasized Hungary's intention of relying even more on international economic relations and of opening its doors even wider to all foreign partners, including West German firms willing to take part in modernizing the Hungarian economy, on the basis of mutual benefit. Pozsgay and Nyers shared this interest in promoting Hungarian ties with the West. The new democratic leadership of President Göncz and Prime Minister Antall emphasized this goal.

Since early 1990 Hungary has strengthened its ties with the West. As part of its desire for stability, it particularly wants to be linked with NATO, perhaps through NATO's political consultative committees such as the North Atlantic Assembly.

West Germany

The Hungarian Communist leadership in the late 1980s found in West Germany strong support of the commitment to perestroika, especially economic restructuring and modernization. The leadership, especially Grosz, deftly exploited West Germany's strong interest in not wanting the Hungarian reform effort to flounder, because of its importance to similar reforms elsewhere in Central/Eastern Europe. Grosz visited Bonn in October 1987, where he concluded five different agreements on economic, scientific and technological, and cultural matters, the most important involving a government guaranteed credit of 1 billion marks. The two leaderships also endorsed the pending Soviet-American agreement over nuclear missiles and stressed their interest in the continuation of the Helskini process.

Kohl commended Hungary for the liberalization of travel restrictions, for Hungary's persistent diplomacy of dialogue with the West, and for its equitable treatment of the small German minority living within its borders, which was especially important for Bonn because of the implications for the well-being of German minorities in Poland, Romania, and the Soviet Union.

The United States

Hungary also sought good relations with the United States, for economic as well as political reasons. The Hungarians wanted American companies to participate in Hungarian enterprises, as a means of injecting new technology and investment capital into the Hungarian economy, especially the consumer sector. But Hungary's interest in developing good relations with Washington was also part of its strategy of doing its part to strengthen East-West détente and to protect Hungary's links with the West against possible difficulties between the superpowers.

In July 1988 Grosz came to the United States for a meeting with then-President Ronald Reagan and a visit to several U.S. cities to promote investment in Hungarian industry. He was given a very warm reception by Reagan, who extended to him the same courtesies given to Gorbachev, to a degree that signified American recognition of Hungarian reformism as well as the expectation that it would continue to go forward.

Grosz obtained a joint-venture agreement worth $115 million between Guardian Industries of Northville, Michigan, and a glassworks enterprise in southeastern Hungary that will transform it into a modern manufacturer of glass products to be sold in Western Europe. Grosz also discussed the expansion of an educational exchange program between Hungarian and American secondary and higher education institutions in which Hungarian high school and college students would come to study in the United States.

U.S. President George Bush's visit to Hungary in July 1989 punctuated the good feelings Washington had developed toward the Hungarian reform movement. Bush announced in Budapest unlimited access to U.S. markets and a token $25 million aid package to encourage Hungary's free-enterprise system.

Israel

In recent years the Hungarian regime sought ways to improve the condition of Jewish culture in the country. It was the only Soviet Bloc socialist state to have a rabbinical seminary. In the fall of 1988 the Hungarian government established a Center for Jewish Studies at Budapest University. The director of the new center, a non-Jew, Professor Geza Komocraczy, an expert on Assyria, was given complete freedom to run the center and in particular to bring in Israeli scholars.

At the same time Hungary moved closer toward the resumption of formal diplomatic ties with Israel. In September 1988 Grosz met with Israeli Premier Yitzak Shamir in Budapest. Grosz agreed to meet an Israeli request to act as intermediary between Israel and the Soviet Union to urge on Gorbachev an improvement of the conditions of Soviet Jews, especially a lifting of restrictions on their emigration to Israel. On September 18, 1989, Hungary and Israel formally restored diplomatic ties with each other.

Austria

Hungary also improved relations with Austria, to which it is bound by centuries of cultural and political tradition. Since the beginning of 1988 Hungarians have been free to travel to Austria. On June 27, 1989, Hungarian officials cut the barbed wire at the border at Sopron. There has since been a flood of citizens from each country to the other. Indeed, Austria may turn out to be a valuable lever for Hungary's eventual integration into Western Europe. Anticipating a move by Austria to join the European Community, Hungarian authorities are studying the possibility of applying for membership in the European Free Trade Association, which groups Austria with Sweden, Switzerland, and other neutral Western European countries. Such a step could give Hungary indirect access to the European market after 1992.

(UN photo/Interfoto)

Margaret Bridge and Margaret Island on the Danube River in Budapest, Hungary.

Hungary and Central/Eastern Europe

Hungary's reformism had complicated its relations with the late Ceausescu's Romania. Hungarian citizens openly called for an end to Romanian discrimination against people of Hungarian extraction living in Transylvania. In August 1988 Hungarians demonstrated at the Romanian Embassy in Budapest and persuaded the Hungarian leadership to accept an invitation from Ceausescu to discuss the nationalities issue. At the end of that month Grosz met Ceausescu in the Romanian city of Arad, near the frontier with Hungary. Grosz wanted Ceausescu to agree to four points: 1) Romanian recognition that Hungary had a legitimate interest in the fate of its ethnic minority; 2) concessions on Romania's program of consolidating rural communities by eliminating thousands of villages historically inhabited by Hungarian-speaking peasants: 3) reopening of the Hungarian consulate in Cluj, the capital of formerly Hungarian Transylvania, which was ordered closed by Romania in June; and 4) establishment of a Hungarian cultural center in Bucharest.

To the dismay of his party colleagues and the anger of the Hungarian population, Grosz came back from his meeting with Ceausescu virtually empty-handed.

Worse yet, he had accepted a joint communique stressing mutual goodwill that clearly was not achieved in the talks between the two leaders. Ceausescu had refused to reopen the consulates, and he had refused to alter his sweeping plan of consolidating rural districts.

Relations had taken another turn for the worse when the Hungarian government in 1989 honored Imre Nagy, by exhuming his remains from the unmarked grave into which they had been deposited by the Kadar regime in 1958 and reburying them in a public ceremony. In a statement handed to the Hungarian ambassador in Bucharest by the Romanian Foreign Ministry, the Romanian government said the funeral service betrayed "anti-Socialist, anti-Romanian, nationalist-chauvinistic, and revisionist manifestations."

The angry Romanian reaction had to be understood in the light of not only the dispute over the long-simmering ethnic issue. Ceausescu also disliked the political liberalization program going on in Hungary, fearing that the Romanian people would soon demand similar reforms in their country—which indeed they did in the fall of 1989, leading to Ceausescu's execution.

The honoring of Nagy also provoked the Czechoslovak Communist leadership,

Independence 1919	Soviet troops liberate Hungary from Nazi control; Rakosi becomes the leader of the Hungarian Communists 1943	Nagy becomes the premier 1953	Nagy is ousted by Rakosi because of his reformist orientation of independence from the Soviet Union 1955	Antigovernment demonstrations in Budapest; Nagy is restored to the premiership 1956	The Soviets intervene militarily to block liberalization and Hungarian withdrawal from the Warsaw Pact	The Soviets support Kadar's election to the leadership of the Hungarian Communist Party 1956	The Kadar regime announces the New Economic Mechanism 1968	Economic relations with the United States are normalized; Hungary receives most-favored-nation treatment 1978	Hungary allows 7,000 East Germans to emigrate to the West; new freedoms of travel and emigration

1980s–1990s

Steady economic and political liberalization	The Soviets withdraw their troops from Hungarian soil	The Hungarian Communist Party changes its name to the Socialist Party, ousts Kadar, and abandons Soviet-style Marxist ideology

which shared at least some of the skepticism and dislike of Hungary's radical reform program displayed by the Romanians. The conservative Czechoslovak leadership feared an equivalent evaluation of Alexander Dubcek and criticism of the strict orthodox dictatorship imposed by the Kremlin in 1968.

Hungary's rapid movement away from orthodox socialism also strained relations with the former East Germany. The East Berlin regime was not happy that in the summer of 1989 thousands of East German citizens, professing themselves tourists, emigrated through Hungary to West Germany. The refusal of Hungary to close its frontier to the East German refugees violated past agreements among Warsaw Pact countries not to allow one another's citizens transit rights to the West without official approval of the home country. It also contributed to a difficult and increasingly embarrassing political problem for the East Berlin regime, which was hard put to stem the flow of its citizens westward.

The Hungarian leadership faced a dilemma in its decision to allow the East Germans to travel through Hungary without visas. On the one hand, Hungarian leaders knew that they would provoke neighboring East Germany and probably the Kremlin as well, further isolating Hungary in the Soviet Bloc as the pariah of reform. At the same time, however, the new leadership in Budapest wanted to strengthen its credibility with both its own people and the West and therefore was unwilling to turn back the East Germans.

Moreover, the Hungarian regime was under considerable pressure from West Germany to treat the East German refugees tolerantly. Since Hungary desperately needed West German economic assistance, there was a strong practical incentive for the Hungarian leadership to accommodate Bonn.

In the post-Communist era Hungary remains vulnerable to political instability not only in Romania but also in Czechoslovakia and Yugoslavia. For example, with growing friction between Czechoslovaks and Slovaks and with a large Hungarian minority of some 600,000 people living in eastern Slovakia, the Hungarian government fears that the Slovaks might endanger the Hungarians if they pursue cultural homogenization policies.

Hungary also has problems with Czechoslovakia over the opening of a large hydroelectric dam and power plant at Gabrcikovo, on the Danube River. The Hungarian government vehemently opposes construction and operation of the dam, warning that it will alter the flow of the Danube and pollute one of Central/Eastern Europe's largest aquifers supplying drinking water for several million people in Hungary and the Slovak portion of Czechoslovakia. In addition, the Danube's inland delta, a unique wetlands habitat, may die out as water from the Danube is diverted to turn the eight large turbines at the dam. The Hungarians first threatened to block all river and truck traffic bound for Czechoslovakia if Prague went ahead and put the dam into operation. But when the Czechoslovaks, who already had

made an enormous capital investment, refused to consider abandoning the project, the Hungarians withdrew their threats to block surface traffic into Czechoslovakia. The Czechoslovaks expressed appreciation for Hungary's concerns, and both sides agreed to discuss ways of minimizing environmental damage. One plan is to build a system of dikes and reservoirs to lessen the impact once the dam starts to operate and sends strong surges downriver.

Equally disturbing is the explosion of ethnic conflict and civil war in Yugoslavia. Hungarians feel some solicitude for the Croats, who were governed by Budapest before World War I and with whom they have familial links. And they also worry that the fighting in Croatia will cut off Hungary's access to the Adriatic oil pipeline, a problem for the strained Hungarian economy. Moreover, Yugoslav federal airplanes have violated Hungarian air space on several occasions and have caused some minor damage to Hungarian border villages. In addition, fighting has spilled over from northern Yugoslavia into southern Hungary. With 35,000 refugees from the fighting in Yugoslavia, Hungary has to provide food and shelter from its own limited resources.

DEVELOPMENT

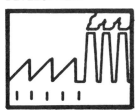

Capitalism and foreign investment are coming to Hungary with a vengeance, and in comparison to other countries in the region, Hungarians are not doing badly: the quantity, quality, and variety of goods are the envy of the country's strapped neighbors. But sharply higher food and clothing prices put the good life beyond the reach of many working people.

FREEDOM

In a country where attitudes toward politics range from indifference to contempt, democracy seems to be flourishing. Communists have been voted out of control in local and national elections. With the disappearance of cultural control in the form of censorship, artistic expression is now unhampered.

HEALTH/WELFARE

Despite outward signs of prosperity, a fifth of the population live below the poverty line. The country still has the highest suicide rate in the world, drug and alcohol abuse remains a serious problem, and crime against public property has increased significantly.

ACHIEVEMENTS

Budapest University inaugurated the first Institution for Jewish Studies in the Soviet Bloc. Hungary set another precedent in 1989 by allowing foreigners for the first time to buy shares in Hungarian enterprises and to own up to 100% of some private and public businesses. Also in 1989, Hungary became the first Central/Eastern European country to restore full diplomatic relations with Israel, severed in 1967.

Poland

GEOGRAPHY

Area in Square Kilometers (Miles):
312,612 (120,700) (smaller than New
Mexico)
Capital (Population): Warsaw
(1,649,000)
Climate: temperate

PEOPLE

Population
Total: 38,363,000
Annual Growth Rate: 0.5%
Rural/Urban Population Ratio: 40/60
Ethnic Makeup of Population: 99%
Polish; 1% Ukrainian, Byelorussian,
and others

Health
Life Expectancy at Birth: 66 years
(male); 74 years (female)
Infant Mortality Rate (Ratio):
21/1,000
Average Caloric Intake: 123% of FAO
minimum
Physicians Available (Ratio): 1/480

Religion(s)
95% Roman Catholic; 5% Uniate,
Greek Orthodox, Protestant, and
Jewish

Education
Adult Literacy Rate: 98%

COMMUNICATION
Telephones: 3,648,000
Newspapers: 99 dailies; 9,630,000
circulation

TRANSPORTATION
Highways—Kilometers (Miles):
159,000 (98,580) (161,359)
Railroads—Kilometers (Miles): 24,287
(15,058)
Usable Airfields: 140

A NEW ROLE MODEL

Poland is entering the third year of wrenching economic changes from
socialism to capitalism and democracy. The positive effects are evident:
the private sector has grown and there are signs of an economic rebirth.
But negative side effects have been severe: prices are sky-high and
unemployment has soared; people are confused and demoralized. Nevertheless, in the scope and pace of its reform, Poland is the leader of the
region's decommunization and a role model for other former socialist
countries. What has happened in Poland already has affected its neighbors, including the Russian Federation and its president, Boris Yeltsin,
whose government is watching events in Polish society and shaping its
policy on the basis of the Polish experience.

GOVERNMENT
Type: pluralistic parliamentary
democracy
Independence Date: July 22, 1918
Head of State: President Lech Walesa
Political Parties: Social Democracy
of the Republic of Poland (formerly
the Polish Communist Party, officially
known as the Polish United Workers'
Party); Solidarity Movement (a quasi-
party); Peasants Party; Christian
National Union; Center Alliance;
Confederation for an Independent
Poland; Liberal Democratic Congress
Suffrage: universal and compulsory
over 18

MILITARY
Number of Armed Forces: 312,800
including frontier and security forces
*Military Expenditures (% of Central
Government Expenditures):* 7.7%
Current Hostilities: none

ECONOMY
Currency ($ U.S. Equivalent): 9,512
zlotys = $1
Per Capita Income/GNP: $2,000/$172
billion
Inflation Rate: 40%
Total Foreign Debt: $45.5 billion
Natural Resources: coal; sulfur;
copper; natural gas; silver
Agriculture: grains; sugar beets;
oilseed; potatoes; hogs; other
livestock
Industry: machine building; iron and
steel; extractive industries; chemicals;
shipbuilding; food processing

FOREIGN TRADE
Exports: $13.5 billion
Imports: $8.2 billion

POLAND

After World War II the Polish Communists, under the leadership of Boleslaw Bierut and Wladyslaw Gomulka, established a new party called the Polish United Workers' Party (PUWP). The PUWP acquired power in the late 1940s. But there were differences between Bierut and Gomulka over how much of the Soviet model should be replicated in the development of Polish socialism. Bierut was a conformist; he favored complete adherence to the Soviet line, whereas Gomulka wanted to make adjustments where imitation of the Soviet pattern would cause unrest in Polish society. With Soviet support, Bierut ousted Gomulka, who was subsequently brought to trial, convicted, and imprisoned for his will to deviate. In the meantime the PUWP, under Bierut's leadership, created the Polish People's Republic, a Soviet-style socialist dictatorship, and transformed Poland into a Soviet satellite.

THE OCTOBER 1956 CRISIS

The first outbreak of protest and dissent in Poland reached a climax in 1956. There were popular demands for an end to the excesses of Stalinist policies of the late 1940s and early 1950s. People wanted a higher standard of living, the establishment of political freedoms, democratization of the Polish government, and independence from the Soviet Union.

Following Stalin's death, moderates in the party Politburo, having voted to oust conservatives subservient to the Kremlin, including Bierut himself, tried to accommodate popular pressures for reform. They released Gomulka from prison and returned him to power, relaxed censorship, and halted persecution of the Roman Catholic church. They allowed resumption of religious instruction in the schools and lessened interference in church appointments. They also permitted private ownership of some farms to stimulate agricultural output.

The Kremlin was uncomfortable over these changes, especially as they had led to the appearance in the Polish media of anti-Soviet sentiment. In October 1956, fearful of a nationalist-inspired move to weaken Poland's ties with the Soviet Union, Soviet Communist Party leader Nikita Khrushchev and other members of the Soviet Politburo paid a surprise visit to Warsaw to discuss the Polish internal situation with Gomulka. The Soviet leadership apparently told Gomulka of its willingness to allow Poland a limited amount of autonomy in the economic sec-

tor, provided that Gomulka restore political discipline, curtail the influence of the church, suppress anti-Soviet sentiment, and assure Poland's loyalty to the Warsaw Pact.

Although Gomulka's leadership in the early 1960s provided Poland with a measure of stability, it became repressive. His efforts to assure political discipline provoked popular opposition. In 1968 there was an outbreak of strikes by students and workers. A significant aspect of the political scene at that time was the appearance of anti-Semitism. Party leaders blamed certain Jewish students and professors for stirring up criticism of the government's authoritarianism, even though at that time the influence of Jews was minimal in Polish life and almost nonexistent within the Communist hierarchy.

THE DECEMBER 1970 CRISIS

There was a great deal of popular dissatisfaction with Gomulka's neo-Stalinistic leadership. A crisis occurred in December 1970, when the government announced a decision to raise food prices. Agricultural output had not kept up with demand, and by the end of the 1960s government subsidization of food prices was becoming an intolerable burden. When the authorities used force to suppress protests against the increased prices, the workers struck. By the end of December antigovernment demonstrations and violent confrontations between angry citizens and the authorities were occurring throughout the country. The government now retreated and rescinded the price increases. Under great pressure from flustered colleagues, Gomulka resigned in early 1971.

The party leadership changed from Gomulka to Edward Gierek, who promised more food and higher wages and increased popular participation in factory management. But workers struck again in 1976, ostensibly because of another regime decision to increase food prices but also because Gierek's promises of 1971 had not been fulfilled. For the first time, dissident intellectuals showed some interest in the complaints of workers. They expressed willingness to help those workers whose protests had gotten them into trouble with the regime, while restating their own criticisms of the regime's political repression and persistent calls for "ideological orthodoxy" in Polish society. Even the Catholic church became vocal in the mid-1970s, demanding the regime's acknowledgment of the church's moral leadership in Poland and of its right to speak out on public-policy matters.

THE AUGUST 1980 CRISIS

Once again it seemed as if the Polish Communist regime had learned nothing from the past. In the summer of 1980 there was another explosion of strikes and antigovernment demonstrations, more violent and more prolonged than similar events in the 1970s. Workers in shipyards of the Baltic Sea port of Gdansk struck for more food, higher wages, new fringe benefits, and a democratization of Polish society, including real workers' participation in factory management and freedom for the Catholic church.

Polish workers had lost confidence in the official, party-controlled trade-union organization, which they considered unresponsive. They thus insisted upon the Polish government's acceptance of a new federation of factory unions independent of the party, called Solidarity, and the legal right to strike to obtain redress of grievances. After a month of strike actions that spread beyond Gdansk, the Polish workers, led by one of their own, Lech Walesa, obliged the Polish government to agree to approve the establishment of Solidarity, in the so-called Gdansk Agreement between the workers and the government on August 31, 1980. In this unprecedented action—no other Central/Eastern European country had allowed an independent trade-union organization—the Polish workers had the support of the dissident intelligentsia and the Catholic church.

In the latter half of 1980 and during most of 1981, prominent members of the dissident intelligentsia, like Jacek Kuron and Adam Michnik, came out in support of the workers. They and other intellectuals helped with the establishment of Solidarity and with the workers' efforts to get the government to accept the union. They also repeated their own demands for a sweeping liberalization of the Polish political system, including foreign-policy independence of the Soviet Union.

The Catholic church also became politically active in this new crisis. While it avoided open confrontation with the regime, it restated its past criticisms of official atheism and its condemnation of the regime's harassment of the clergy, destruction of personal freedoms, and subservience to Moscow.

ROOTS OF POLISH PROTEST AND DISSENT

Periodic expressions of protest and dissent in Polish society since the death of Stalin, especially the crisis that began in August 1980, had many roots. The more important of them were the unrelenting and excessive political repression by the Polish Communist leadership of a traditionally politically active society; the leadership's inept management of the economy, especially in agriculture and industry; its offensive servility to the Soviet Union; and the increasing political activism of the Catholic church, which enjoyed strong and dynamic leadership in both Poland and the Vatican.

Excessive Political Repression

Regime political repression involved the persecution of critics and opponents of the regime, insistence upon Poles' acceptance of Soviet-inspired norms of political discipline and ideological orthodoxy, and other offensive gestures. Poles complained about the Communist party's refusal to share information about conditions in the country. They believed that the party treated them as children, expecting blind obedience while denying them any real say in the management of their political affairs. There were also complaints about corruption in the party and state bureaucracies and about the misuse of privileges.

Inept Economic Management

Although the government, beginning in the mid-1950s, retreated from collectivization to increase incentives of farmers to expand output, the production of food did not keep pace with demand and food shortages continued. While it is true that Polish farmers lacked modern machinery

and labor-saving technology, especially in the area of fertilizers, an equally important explanation of the party's failure to expand agricultural output was its conscious discrimination against the private farmers it had created.

Polish authorities made it very difficult for these farmers to acquire credit and supplies, thus impoverishing and demoralizing them. In the 1960s and 1970s the regime apparently had ideologically inspired, and perhaps Soviet-encouraged, second thoughts about having allowed the departure from collectivization.

During the 1970s the Polish Communists made serious errors in their extensive investment in so-called turnkey industries, in an effort to upgrade rapidly the quality and quantity of Polish industrial output. They purchased entire industries from the West and transplanted them to Poland. But these industries, paid for by substantial advances of credit from the West, did not function well, because Polish labor lacked the proper technology. Industrial output did not expand, and matters were made worse by the international recession which followed the 1973 Arab oil embargo. Increased ability to earn foreign exchange did not materialize. By the end of the 1970s the country was deeply in debt to the West.

Servility to Moscow

The conspicuous servility of the Polish leadership to Moscow galled the Poles,

not only because of their historic dislike of Russians but also because of a belief that most of what was wrong with Poland since World War II was attributable to the Soviet Union. Especially provocative to Poles was the regime's insistence on including in the draft of a new Constitution in 1975 a statement about Poland's closeness to the Soviet Union. It caused such an uproar in the Polish Parliament (Sejm) and elsewhere in society that the regime agreed to alter the wording.

Polish intellectual and church leaders persistently called for independence from the Soviet Union and for closer relations with the West. Mounting Polish hostility toward the Soviet Union peaked in the summer of 1981, when there was a visible outbreak of anti-Soviet sentiment throughout the country that took such ugly forms as the desecration of the graves of Soviet soldiers killed in Poland in World War II.

Strong Leadership of the Church

In the 1970s the Polish Catholic church boldly reminded the Communist authorities in Warsaw that it was an ancient Polish institution that had survived many regimes and undoubtedly would survive them. The church insisted that Polish Communists recognize its role as the moral guardian of Polish society and its right to speak out on Polish national affairs. The church benefited from the election in 1978 of the Polish-born Pope John Paul II. The pope encouraged the church

(Katalin Arkell/Spooner/Gamma)

Poland under Wojciech Jaruzelski saw the rise of the black market as commodities became scarce. These people lined up for food at a shop in Warsaw.

to resist Communist atheism and Communist efforts to deny the church's legitimate influence in Polish life. Pope John Paul II has been a great source of strength to the Polish Catholic church and an important catalyst of popular political activism in Poland.

SOVIET RESPONSES TO THE AUGUST 1980 CRISIS

The Soviets were alarmed by the apparent unwillingness or inability of the Polish Communist Party to restore public order to Polish society during the autumn of 1980. The Soviets suspected that some in the party leadership, including First Secretary Stanislaw Kania, who succeeded Gierek in September, favored major departures from Soviet-style socialism and from Poland's closeness to the Warsaw Pact and the Soviet Union.

The Soviets also were appalled by divisions within the Polish Communist Party over how to cope with the crisis. There were those who favored conciliating the workers and tolerating Solidarity; others wanted a severe crackdown on opposition to the regime. These divisions were forbidden by the rules of democratic centralism, and the Soviets were concerned that they would weaken the party in its confrontation with groups that were aggressively seeking wide reforms.

Toward the end of 1980 the Soviets considered a military intervention in Poland to help the Polish party restore order. They ultimately decided in December against an intervention for several reasons, not least of which was the possibility of meeting fierce popular resistance, which could have led to a full-scale war.

The Soviets also had to take into account the strongly expressed opposition of the West, in particular the United States, which threatened retaliation. There is also reason to believe that the Soviets were not militarily prepared for the deployment of massive military forces in Central/Eastern Europe, because of mobilization problems. Finally, a number of the Soviet Union's allies, in particular Romania and Hungary, opposed an intervention. At a meeting in Moscow on December 5, 1980, all of the Warsaw Pact countries expressed a preference for a political solution to Poland's continuing turmoil and unanimously agreed to allow the Polish party to put its house in order without outside interference.

During most of 1981 the Kremlin exerted intense political pressure on the Polish leadership, demanding that it take a firm line against the opposition. A climax of Soviet pressure occurred in the summer of 1981, during the PUWP's 9th Congress in Warsaw. The Soviets were disturbed by the party's decision to increase its responsiveness to popular will—which risked a diminution of responsiveness to the Kremlin—by democratizing its leadership-selection process and in other ways departing from democratic centralism.

In the fall of 1981 the Soviets sought the replacement of Polish leader Kania. Because the Polish Communist Party's Politburo agreed with the Kremlin that Kania had failed to restore order in the past year, thus provoking the Soviets and increasing the risk of their interfering in Poland, it removed him from the position of first secretary and elected Premier and Defense Minister Wojciech Jaruzelski.

Jaruzelski's Ascendancy

Although Jaruzelski was not their first choice, partly because of his military background, the Soviets approved of his selection as PUWP first secretary and agreed to support him. Jaruzelski did not disappoint the Soviets, at least in the short term. He quickly took steps to restore order in Poland. In December 1981 he declared martial law. The following year he banned and arrested the leaders of Solidarity and other independent union organizations that had sprung up, like Rural Solidarity, which had been formed by independent farmers. Subsequently Jaruzelski harassed, persecuted, and silenced most of the dissident intellectuals. He also denied the Catholic church the influence over public policy-making it had been seeking. The official Polish press mercilessly attacked the church, accusing it of "expanded sponsorship of underground culture" and of inculcating the youth with a hatred of socialism.

But Jaruzelski also tried to avoid excesses he knew would provoke a new outbreak of unrest and pursued his own policy of normalization. He allowed former Solidarity leader Lech Walesa to continue to express his views, which were often critical of the regime. He continued to dialogue with Cardinal Joseph Glemp, the Catholic primate of Poland, and he consented, despite the political risks, to allow the pope to visit Poland in 1983. While it is true that Jaruzelski tried to restrict the church's influence in the spring of 1984 by calling for the removal of crucifixes from public places, this was an ephemeral gesture that did not interfere with the ongoing church-state dialogue. Jaruzelski also tried to increase worker participation in management of factories and to address the complaints about unresponsive trade unionism by the creation of new union organizations, which were,

however, still under party control. And in 1985 he encouraged independent candidates in parliamentary elections.

ECONOMIC STAGNATION AND DECLINE

The Polish economy steadily deteriorated during the 1980s. Economic underperformance, which caused shortages of everything—especially consumer necessities like food, clothing, and housing—was partly the result of public apathy, inspired by a pervasive hostility toward the Communist regime and by pessimism about the prospects of economic improvement. But the Polish economy also still suffered from outdated industrial practices and obsolete machinery, which were difficult to replace because of Poland's already staggering foreign debt and the low quality of its exports.

Polish agriculture in particular was badly off; it was unable to feed the population. Output was inadequate because of the low priority the Polish government assigned to the agricultural sector, which received about one-fifth of total investment capital. Also, the regime failed to earmark an increase of industrial production to agriculture in order to accommodate the need for modern farm machinery, and it still discriminated against the private farms, which now produced 80 percent of all foodstuffs and were 13 percent more productive than state farms.

The regime attempted to improve output in industry as well as in agriculture, in three ways. The first, a reform program initiated in 1981, guaranteed self-management and some autonomy of central control to state enterprises to set wage rates and reinvest profits. It failed because the party leadership imposed restrictions on certain heavy industries, amounting to a recentralization of government control and effectively depriving workers of independent action, initiative, and responsibility in their operation.

The second Jaruzelski scheme was to allow the Catholic church to channel funds from the West into the private sector of Polish agriculture in order to purchase badly needed machinery, spare parts, and fertilizers. This scheme led nowhere, as a result of party opposition to an increase of church influence.

The third Jaruzelski plan involved Poland's readmission to the International Monetary Fund, enabling Poland to obtain new sources of Western credit for economic rehabilitation, provided it pursued austerity measures to curtail consumption and limit inflation. It was hoped that access to new credit and the economic belt-tightening program mandated by the IMF would faciliate Poland's economic recovery.

The Polish government tried to improve the country's economic health also by reducing the gap between the real value of goods and what was charged for them. In 1987 the regime announced a 40 percent increase in food prices and asked for popular backing of this move. But in a referendum held to approve the price increase, Polish voters responded with a resounding "No!" Jaruzelski thereupon had to retreat: the government announced a scaled-down price increase to be introduced gradually.

THE FRAGILITY OF COMMUNIST RULE IN POLAND

The Jaruzelski regime itself admitted—albeit in secret—its chief weaknesses. A 25-page confidential report, issued in numbered copies to the Polish Council of Ministers in March 1984, described the perceived threats to the regime's efforts to expand its influence over Polish society.

The document, which was surprisingly candid, singled out credibility as the Jaruzelski government's major problem. The report spoke of "insufficient growth of confidence in the regime and its credibility" and of the "relatively low . . . effectiveness with which [its] voiced declarations are implemented."

The credibility problem persisted because the conditions that originally gave rise to the unrest in the summer of 1980 remained unresolved. These conditions included economic stagnation, in particular shortages of food and other consumer necessities; the stubborn, insensitive, and generally unpopular rule of the Communist party; and continuing subservience of the Polish Communist leadership to the Soviet Union.

The Jaruzelski regime tried to bolster its credibility with the Polish public by several conciliatory actions in 1986 and 1987 designed to curry popular support. For example, the official media acknowledged the pluralistic character of Polish society and the permissability of a diversity of popular views. The media recognized that the system could be questioned, though they rejected the concept of pluralism advocated by Solidarity and continued to insist that there were limits on tolerable debate of national questions.

Jaruzelski tried to increase popular acceptance of his regime by strengthening ties with the Catholic church. He met twice with Pope John Paul II in 1987 to normalize relations with the Vatican. But on both occasions the pope put pressure on Jaruzelski to liberalize, saying that

normalization of church-state relations must await the end of the regime's interference with the work of his bishops in promoting Polish political freedom.

The pope used Jaruzelski's eagerness for normalization of relations to encourage his departure from Soviet-inspired policies of atheism and repression. In June 1987, in the most direct attack on Poland's socialist system he had yet made, Pope John Paul called upon Polish Catholics "to rethink communism" and to consider major changes in the country's political, socioeconomic, and cultural life.

POLAND AND PERESTROIKA

In the late 1980s Poland was faced with an enormous economic and political crisis, which ultimately forced the Communist leadership to adopt many of the reforms Soviet leader Mikhail Gorbachev had addressed in speeches on perestroika. During these years, the Polish economy became bankrupt: there were shortages of everything, especially the daily necessities of life, including food and clothing. Coupled with the repressive policies of the Jaruzelski regime, the economic hardship became intolerable.

In the spring of 1988, when workers in the steel mills and coal mines of the highly industrialized Silesian region of southern Poland called for strikes for higher wages to offset galloping inflation, strike actions quickly spread to other industries. By the end of the summer workers were calling not only for higher wages but also for the legalization of Solidarity. Church leaders stated that the principal cause of the social disorder was the regime's violation of the rights and dignity of working people.

Newly appointed Premier Mieczyslav Rakowski called for a limited pluralism, the legalization of some noncommunist clubs and organizations, the broadening of ministerial leadership to include noncommunists, and negotiation with the outlawed Solidarity to obtain the trade union's help in resolving the economic crisis, especially the paralytic strikes. In continuing talks between government and party leaders, Solidarity demanded legalization and political democratization involving a reduction of Communist party control of the government. The regime at first refused to accommodate these demands, hoping for Solidarity's cooperation with minimum concessions required of the government.

The Communist authorities were betting that older Polish workers would soon weary of the strikes. They also thought that most workers would not support radical economic changes, which would be

required if economic reform were to take place. These would include wage differentiation, factory closings, and other economic hardships.

The authorities tried to undermine Solidarity's bargaining position. For example, in November 1988 the government decided to close the Lenin Shipyards in Gdansk—Solidarity's home, the symbol of its defiance, and the focal point of popular loyalty to it. The government artfully defended the decision on economic grounds—namely, that the yard had been losing money, that it was a drain on precious economic resources, and that foreign demand for Polish ships had declined, all of which were true.

But the continuation of strikes and political protests through December and January, despite the government's repressive measures, ultimately proved that its assumptions about dealing with Solidarity on the cheap, so to speak, were counterproductive. Its refusal to agree to the legalization of the trade union enhanced Lech Walesa's already substantial popular charisma and contributed to the soaring percentage of Poles who favored Solidarity's legalization.

In early January 1989 Jaruzelski sought, with several concessions to Solidarity, to break a deadlock in the talks. He decided to approve Solidarity's legalization and to introduce democratic changes in the Polish political system. The dialogue between the union and the government resumed in earnest and in April produced an agreement that satisfied both sides. In return for a government pledge to legalize Solidarity, Walesa agreed to certain conditions: Solidarity renounced strikes for 2 years, accepted the Communist system, and rejected links with groups calling for the abandonment of communism.

The agreement provided for the creation of a second chamber for the national Parliament, to be called the Senate. Members of the Senate were to be elected in a free and open way with no restrictions on who could run for seats or on who could be elected. The agreement also said that in the other, lower house of the national Parliament, the Sejm, independent groups not under the control of the Communist party could compete for seats, provided that Communist party candidates and candidates of parties in alliance with the Communist party held a majority. The two houses would elect a head of state, called the president of the republic, who would have substantial policy-making authority in both domestic and international affairs. The president would be commander-in-chief of the nation's military forces and would have the authority to select a premier who, in consultation with the president, would appoint a Cabinet. The choice of premier and the Cabinet would need the approval of Parliament. Both sides also agreed that implementation of the agreement would be immediate, starting with the legalization of Solidarity, to be followed by the holding of elections for the Sejm and the Senate, which would then elect a president and ratify a new government.

Under the new arrangements, the Communists would still maintain their grip on the administration of the country, through understandings that provided for party control of a majority in the Sejm, for party leadership of the defense and police establishments, and for the election of Jaruzelski as the first president. But Solidarity and other noncommunist groups gained substantial political advantages, and the way was now open for a progressive weakening of communism in Poland. Following the agreement, political events moved very quickly. In fact, the scope and pace of change far exceeded the expectations of either the party or Solidarity.

The Parliamentary Elections
Elections for a new bicameral Parliament began on June 3, 1989. Despite the complexity of the balloting, which was designed to assure a Communist majority, the elections resulted in Solidarity's winning 99 of the 100 seats in the Senate and every possible seat in the Sejm. Polish voters had used every opportunity to express their opposition to the party's candidates. Solidarity now had more political strength than ever.

The Presidential Election
The next step in the implementation of the April agreement was the new Parliament's election of the president. Although Jaruzelski had been ready to run as the Communist party's candidate, there was now a chance that he might not get elected. Many Solidarity-affiliated members of both houses of Parliament opposed him. The two small parties that had loyally worked with Communists over the past 40 years wavered in their support as well, no doubt a real prospect that Solidarity might someday rule Poland and because of a fear that they would be shut out of power because of their close association with the Communists.

However, Jaruzelski decided to run when the small parties agreed to back him and when Walesa also indicated his support. He was elected president on July 19, by the slimmest of majorities. It was clear that his election was by no means a strong

mandate or a statement of popular preference for him.

Appointment of a Noncommunist Premier
In the formation of a new government, President Jaruzelski immediately ruled out the possibility of a noncommunist premier, saying that Poland's socialist neighbors, East Germany and Czechoslovakia, would oppose such an unprecedented move. He thus appointed as premier former Interior Minister Kisczack. But Kisczack's appointment provoked an immediate and angry reaction from Solidarity deputies in Parliament. They said they would refuse to endorse him because, like Jaruzelski, he had been instrumental in the campaign to destroy the trade union. The fate of the appointment, however, was sealed by the decision of the two small Communist parties once and for all to join the Solidarity opposition. Consequently, the Communists, without their allies and with the determined opposition of Solidarity deputies in both houses of Parliament, lacked the majority needed to gain parliamentary approval. Kisczack withdrew on August 14.

Eventually Jaruzelski turned to Solidarity to propose a premier. Although many wanted Walesa, the Solidarity leader demurred, pleading the priority of his interest in dealing with large organizational and policy problems confronting the trade union. There was speculation that he preferred to run for the presidency in the 1990s and thought it best to remain aloof from the premiership.

The Solidarity leadership, in consultation with leaders of the Peasant and Democratic parties and Jaruzelski, put forward Tadeusz Mazowiecki, a less politically prominent but politically active member of Solidarity's leadership with close connections to the church. On August 19 Parliament formally endorsed, by majority vote, Mazowiecki's appointment by the president.

Formation of a Cabinet
Solidarity assumed policy-making responsibility, but the Communist party still held police power of the state and controlled the economy. Moreover, hard-liners in the Politburo were reeling over the new situation of noncommunist control of the Cabinet. On August 20, 1989, the party's Central Committee announced in militant tones that membership of the Cabinet that Premier Mazowiecki was now forming "must correspond to [the Communist party's] political and state potential." In other words, the Communists should have

the lion's share of ministerial posts, including the Ministry of Foreign Affairs.

But the party quickly backed down, not only because the Solidarity leadership had no intention of accepting a Communist monopoly of the Cabinet but also because the trade union was willing to allow the party four ministries, including Defense and Interior. It accepted this concession and gave up claims to the Foreign Affairs Ministry. Gorbachev's personal intervention may have been instrumental in the party's retreat. He called Jaruzelski to urge the new party leader to pursue a conciliatory approach.

POLITICAL DEMOCRATIZATION

The Polish leadership also took important steps in moving the country closer toward political democracy. In December 1989 the Polish Legislature formally amended the national Constitution to eliminate reference to the leading role of the Communist party, thereby officially ending its historic monopoly of power and legalizing the already extensive political pluralism. The Cabinet also sought to schedule local elections in the spring of 1990 rather than later in the year, to give voters an opportunity to vote Communists out of power on the municipal level, where they were able to block reforms lessening state control and expanding private entrepreneurialism.

As a practical matter, the Poles were steadily moving toward a return to political pluralism as individuals and groups became increasingly active in public criticism of government policies. Solidarity deputies in the Polish Parliament no longer showed the same unity they had in the summer and were faction-ridden over the issue of how far and how fast to go in dismantling Communist rule.

At the end of January 1990 the Polish Communist Party, at a Congress in Warsaw, formally dissolved itself and created a new organization called the Social Democracy of the Republic of Poland. By trying to distance themselves from those discredited, the Polish Communist elite acknowledged the former party's loss of popularity and its failure to lead. The new organization, which seemed to be using the socialist parties of France, Spain, and Italy as models, presumably was trying to offer itself as an alternative to Solidarity. Miezyslaw Rakowski, the head of the old Communist party, became the new party's leader. Whether this tactic will work remains to be seen.

Jaruzelski's Resignation
In December 1990 President Jaruzelski resigned, with 4 years remaining in his term of office. He was the last of Europe's old-guard Communist leaders to relinquish power and, quite unlike any of them, he did so with some grace. People probably will be arguing for a long time about what kind of leader he was—Soviet puppet or national patriot. As the instrument of martial law and a brutal repression in the 1980s, he clearly followed the Brezhnevian Kremlin; but it also is true that he helped along the radical political reform that restored democracy to Poland and therefore must be viewed in a more favorable light.

The 1990 Presidential Elections
The presidential elections on November 25 and December 9, 1990, brought about a reduction in Communist influence. Three candidates were quite different from one another. Prime Minister Mazowiecki, representing the intelligentsia and professional groups, advocated gradualism in the movement, away from socialism to a market-based economy, good working relations with the Soviet Union, and the avoidance of an anti-Communist witch-hunt design. Solidarity leader Lech Walesa favored a rapid acceleration of economic reform accompanied by policies to ease the hardships of ordinary Polish citizens, the immediate removal of Communists from whatever authority they still had, and restrictions on Communists' acquisition of newly privatized enterprises. Joseph Tyminski, a Canadian citizen of Polish origin, promised to apply the economic principles that had led to his own business success. Tyminski, a somewhat bizarre candidate given that he was a foreigner with no political experience in Poland, appealed to disaffected workers whose industries were hardest hit by Mazowiecki's reforms. He was especially popular with young workers, who were willing to overlook his political inexperience, his abusive criticism of opponents, and the inconsistencies of his arguments. His appeal to Polish frustrations and phobias struck a responsive cord throughout Polish society, and the fact that he was a self-made millionaire gave him a lot of credibility with ordinary Polish citizens, who have always admired successful emigrants. Tyminski also was a beneficiary of public disillusionment over the bribery, fraud, and corruption that accompanied the transition away from socialism. He capitalized on public anger over the continued influence of former Communists.

In the first ballot, on November 25, none of the candidates obtained the 50 percent-plus of popular votes needed to win: Walewsa won a 40 percent plurality, Tyminski came in second, and Mazowiecki was a weak third. Mazowiecki, shocked by the lack of popular support for his leadership and by the vote for Tyminski, withdrew from the race and resigned the premiership. In the run-off election, on December 9, Walewsa ran against Tyminski and won by a 3-to-1 margin.

New Political Cleavages and Conflicts
The elections showed how fractured Poland's political leadership had become. The intelligentsia, including former dissident Adam Michnik, editor of *Gazeta Wyborcza*, the Solidarity daily, questioned Walesa's fitness for national leadership, viewing him as a radical populist and would-be strong leader who might sacrifice democratic principles for the sake of policy-making expediency. They thought that Walesa lacked the education and intellectual sophistication needed to manage power effectively and humanely; they also were envious of the elevation to power in neighboring countries such as Czechoslovakia of rather sophisticated, even cosmopolitan, political leaders. Walesa, backed by industrial workers, was convinced that the Mazowiecki group was insufficiently sensitive to the hardships endured by ordinary Polish people in the move toward a market-based economy.

A wild card remains the voting bloc of Polish farmers, who constitute 35 percent of the population, represent a relative homogeneous economic and social constituency, and are bound by their shared sense of historical oppression under the Communists. They are dissatisfied with attempts to foster a market economy by streamlining the distribution system. This system has increased the food supply and brought an end to long lines and hoarding, but farmers are now producing more than they can sell and must destroy some of their surpluses. Moreover, Polish farmers have lost the Soviet market, since the former Soviet Union cannot pay for Polish food. In addition, Polish farmers must compete with the European Community, which has dumped some of its heavily subsidized agricultural products on the Polish market.

Governmental Stalemate
In early December 1990, President Walesa appointed as prime minister an economist with a background in private business, Jan Krzysztof Bielecki, charging him to expedite the move toward a free-market economy. Both he and Walesa wanted the fastest possible privatization of the economy. Walesa also asked for new parliamentary elections, hoping to rid the government of the Communist hangers-on who had been guaranteed a majority in the Sejm by the terms of the agreement between the Solidarity and Communist leaderships in April 1989. These Communists wanted to prolong their privileged economic situation. They had obstructed implementation of a sweeping privatization bill, passed in July 1990, designed to privatize 7,600 state enterprises making up 80 percent of the economy. The slowness of this process was politically and socially damaging; it also jeopardized the government's effort to obtain debt relief from Western creditors. In June 1991 Walesa asked the Polish Parliament to empower the Cabinet to rewrite the nation's economic laws—he wanted Prime Minister Bielecki to be able to issue decrees with the force of law to break the logjam. But the Legislature eventually refused to accommodate the president: on September 14 the Sejm rejected the government's request for extraordinary powers.

The October 1991 Parliamentary Elections
The parliamentary elections of October 1991 confused rather than clarified the political situation. Only 40 percent of eligible voters participated in the elections, while 60 percent of Polish voters abstained to show their dissatisfaction with politics as well as perhaps their apathy. Nor did any single party win a majority of the 40 percent of popular votes. More than 25 parties, none holding more than 1 percent of the total vote, were now in the Sejm. The Democratic Union, led by former Prime Minister Mazowiecki, and the former Polish Communists, who now called themselves the Democratic Left Alliance, each won about 12 percent of the popular vote, and each received 24 out of 460 seats. But Mazowiecki wanted nothing to do with the Communists, and the Communists had no enthusiasm for cooperating with Mazowiecki.

Walesa had to form a Cabinet coalition from these divergent groups, recognizing that any such coalition would be extremely fragile, compromising his ability to continue implementation of controversial reforms. His response to this confusing political situation was immediate, striking, and, in character with himself and with Polish history: he offered to serve as his own prime minister. This move would have greatly strengthened his personal political power and called to mind the behavior of Josef Pilsudski, the

Polish president of the 1920s who emasculated democracy and became an autocratic leader for the sake of assuring discipline and stability in the conflict-ridden society of that era. Poles wondered whether Walesa's offer reflected the beginnings of autocracy or whether Walesa was simply trying to goad the different factions to find some common ground, producing a working alliance that would allow a prompt resumption of policy-making.

In any event, Walesa continued the search for a new prime minister capable of forming a coalition Cabinet. He eventually selected in early November 1991 Jan Olszewski, a former Solidarity lawyer who had the support of a center-right coalition of parties, including the Christian National Union, the Center Alliance, the Confederation for an Independent Poland, the Peasants' Party, and the Liberal Democratic Congress. Olszewski was critical of the rapid pace of free-market reforms and, therefore, at odds with Walesa, but he was the only political figure of stature who could muster a near majority of support in the Sejm. As 1992 began Olszewski faced monumental problems of governance, not the least being the weakness of his coalition.

Walesa, now more than ever, was convinced of the need to strengthen the presidency by allowing it to appoint a Cabinet without having to obtain the approval of the Sejm and by endowing the chief executive with the power to implement policy by decree. Bielecki, now the former prime minister, observed that a return to authoritarianism would not work because the spirit of individualism in Poland is too strong. Poles cannot be threatened very easily, he said. The only alternative for Poland's reformers is to continue using political democracy, however unpredictable, to achieve the economic democracy needed to restore Poland's economic health.

ECONOMIC REFORMS

Former Premier Mazowiecki announced in September 1989 his intention to introduce capitalist practices to revive Polish economic life. He found the going tough, for at least two reasons. First, he had to reduce party control over economic enterprises. Communist party members threatened with losing their privileges and perquisites could be expected to resist change. Indeed, in anticipation of losing their power over the economy, party managers of various enterprises were actually buying them as personal property, under the guise of cooperating with government calls for privatization, a practice that infuriated many in Solidarity. Second, as state control ended and private entrepreneurialism was introduced, ordinary Polish people were going to suffer even more: prices based on supply and demand would remain prohibitively high for most, and production would not increase substantially right away.

Furthermore, the success of domestic reforms depended partly on debt relief. Poland needed outside help in easing its enormous debt burden. In the summer of 1989 it owed Western creditors about $39 billion and the Soviet Union $6.5 billion. The new government sought help, in the form of a major rescheduling of debt payments, new loans, and increased foreign investment. It looked for help to the IMF and the World Bank as well as to West Germany and the United States. By the end of 1989 both the Sejm and the Senate had approved a program of radical reform which put Poland in the forefront of the movement toward capitalism in Central/Eastern Europe. In addition to ending price subsidies, this new law terminated price controls, transferred many state-owned companies to private ownership, and allowed employers to dismiss redundant employees to cut costs and increase efficiency. The law also provided for bankruptcy proceedings in the case of firms unable to make a profit. This program made Polish currency convertible, was supposed to promote financial accountability in industrial management, and laid the groundwork for an expansion of both industrial and agricultural output.

Problems Promoting Privatization

Privatization has proceeded very slowly. People do not have the resources to buy the large industries that the government wants to sell. Most Poles, with an average per capita income of $2,000, have barely enough cash to buy food, never mind stock. The government also has difficulty assessing the real value of the enterprises to be sold, often overvaluing them—or, more often, undervaluing them, thereby encouraging the people who do have spare capital, namely former Communists, to buy them at bargain-basement prices. Poland also lacks an effective banking system to provide the credit to finance purchases and operate enterprises. Poland lacks computer systems, so it often takes banks weeks, not hours or days, to cash checks and transfer funds from one geographic location to another. Privatization is hamstrung also because of the lack of an adequate communications infrastructure, essential for a complex capitalist economy. (Lacking in particular is a modern telephone system to replace the old one, inherited from the Communist era, in which all lines had to go through Warsaw for political reasons: the regime wanted to be able to interrupt service to any part of the country in a crisis.) Finally, Poland lacks people with Western-style managerial skills capable of running the large, complex enterprises that it wants to privatize. Nor does Poland have business schools and other educational institutions to provide a reservoir of trained executives for the management of private firms. Finally, many of the large enterprises that the government wants to unload are so inefficient that no one wants them. They are obsolete, or paternalistic in the Communist sense, using income for expensive recreational and housing facilities for workers.

In June 1991 the Polish government introduced an imaginative program to increase the reservoir of potential buyers of state concerns. All of Poland's 27 million adults will receive vouchers in the form of what is called National Wealth Management Funds. These are to be the Polish equivalent of U.S.-style mutual funds, with each citizen owning about $9,000 worth of shares. Under the plan, 60 percent of each enterprise's shares will go to the Funds for distribution to the general public, while the remaining 40 percent will go to the employees of the enterprise and to the central government in Warsaw. A lead shareholding of 33 percent should go to one fund, with the remaining 27 percent distributed equally among other funds, with the idea that one investment group will take primary responsibility for overhauling a particular enterprise. Fund managers are not to be allowed to own shares, except to the extent that fees paid to them may be in shares as opposed to cash. The Polish government hopes that this program, scheduled for implementation in 1992, not only will allow privatization of about 7,000 enterprises by the end of 1994 but also will have some positive political fallout, in the sense of involving as many people as possible in the ongoing process of economic transformation.

The High Social Cost of Other Economic Reforms

Other reforms to move the country toward a free-market capitalist economy included slashing inflation to 40 percent, a far cry from the 2,000 percent rate, or hyperinflation, that the country had at the end of 1989; making food lines a thing of the past—it was now possible to buy anything in Warsaw for a price; and stabilizing the Polish currency, which at long last was made convertible. Its value against Western hard currencies steadily rose in the 2-year period of intensive reform, and the black market in currency virtually faded away.

But these reforms caused enormous hardship for Polish citizens, who could not afford to buy even simple necessities. With wages restrained, they suffered from the loss of purchasing power. To make matters worse, production plunged by more than 25 percent in 1990, partly because of economic turmoil in the Soviet Union. Poland also needed to pay for expensive energy imports at world-market prices. Finally, the disruption of old patterns of trade within the region, which had been run by the now inoperative Council for Mutual Economic Assistance, had not yet been replaced by new ones, and so the government had little capital to soften the blow of economic dislocation.

A possibility of renewed social turmoil threatened Polish economic reform in early 1992. The country had suffered a 10 percent decline in industrial outlook and a sharp rise in unemployment throughout 1991. Making matters worse for the national economy and Olszewski's leadership was a Russian decision to interrupt deliveries of natural gas to Poland to allow Russian producers to sell more of their output to buyers with hard currency. The Russian action, which violated a previously signed trade agreement, caused the shutdown of Polish industry from the Gdansk shipyards to the Galician metalworks and paralyzed the already enfeebled national economy.

Prime Minister Olszewski wanted to ease the hardships of ordinary Polish citizens by guaranteeing prices for farmers, providing financial help to potentially profitable state enterprises as an alternative to privatizing, lowering interest rates, and printing more money. But President Walesa opposed this conservative approach, insisting that Poland should stay the course in its rapid transition to the free market and echoed the IMF demand that Poland accept a harsh stabilization program as the prerequisite for receiving Fund credits and the forgiveness of half of Poland's enormous foreign debt. Eventually, Olszewski opted for a continuation of the "shock-treatment" approach, despite its political risks.

By the end of the first quarter of 1992 one could point to significant, if modest, achievements of reform: real wages had risen in 1991 by 3 percent and a private-sector boom had occurred that promised more and better jobs and an eventual easing of inflation. Furthermore, large Western investment was coming to Poland: at the end of February 1992 General

Motors Europe agreed to a $75 million joint venture, in one of the largest external investment deals in Poland since the collapse of Communist rule. Finally, the IMF had signaled its willingness to resume payment to Poland of a $2.5 billion credit package.

CONTROVERSIES SURROUNDING THE CATHOLIC CHURCH

The Polish Catholic church has long had enormous credibility with the Polish people because of its outspoken opposition to the Communists. It has tried to expand this influence over the country's overwhelming Roman Catholic population with the help of the Vatican. The church is working to make Poland a role model for Catholicism in post-Communist Central/Eastern Europe. In 1990 Poland's bishops won a big victory with Parliament's approval of a return of religious education to the schools.

Behind this ambitious agenda is the church's worry that it might lose the loyalty of the young people as a democratic and capitalist society opens itself up to materialistic values and attitudes. Sure enough, the new policy has sparked controversy, with the Protestant minority complaining that the return of religion to the classroom will foster division among students and even encourage intolerance and acts of discrimination.

With the pope's aggressive advocacy, the Polish church has also supported restrictions on abortion. But most Polish people, although they personally abhor abortion, also oppose restrictions on it. In 1990, to the dismay of the pope, the Polish Sejm refused to pass a restrictive abortion bill endorsed by the pope.

The Polish government, and in particular President Walesa, who is very loyal to the church, are in a quandary. While the Warsaw government does not want to antagonize the Vatican, it also cannot ignore popular misgivings about the church's effort to influence how Poles live. Leading politicians have responded with silence to demands from the church for the rewriting of the Polish Constitution to omit clauses that guarantee the separation of church and state. The Parliament also has not supported the church's desire to limit the number of divorce courts. Despite evidence that its political efforts are losing popular support, the Polish church is trying to strengthen its political influence by urging the faithful to vote for candidates, in particular those of the Catholic Action Committee, who espouse Christian values and oppose abortion.

Muddying the situation is the perception of an oblique linkage of the church to a resurgence of anti-Semitism in Poland. Anti-Semitism is bizarre in Poland because most Polish Jews died in the Holocaust. Of those Jews remaining after the war, most emigrated when the Communists took power after World War II. But the church aroused anti-Semitic feelings when, in 1990, Cardinal Glemp entered a dispute over the location in 1984 of a convent at the site of the Auschwitz death camp. Jews objected to this convent dedicated to Catholic values, in the light of the special significance of Auschwitz for Jews. In fact, the church had signed an agreement to remove the convent. But Glemp angrily declared that Jews were attacking Polish feelings and national sovereignty and were using the "Jewish controlled" Western media to promote their views. Glemp not only provoked an angry outcry from Jewish groups in the West but also embarrassed the new noncommunist government, which wanted the friendship and support of Western countries. The government considered Glemp's remarks very damaging to the world prestige of Poland as well as to the harmony, unity, and peace of an already deeply conflict-ridden Polish society. Nudged by an embarrassed Vatican to take a more conciliatory stand on the issue, Glemp retreated, albeit reluctantly, saying ultimately that Catholics in Poland knew too little of the sentiments of the Jews and the wounds that remained from the Holocaust. Although eventually the dispute wound down, Cardinal Glemp's criticism of the Jews and the perceived slowness of the Vatican's effort to avoid a confrontation aroused the suspicion of many inside as well as outside of Poland of the church's own prejudices and its readiness to appeal to the prejudices of the Polish people.

RECENT POLISH FOREIGN POLICY

Reform in the domestic sphere in the late 1980s influenced Polish foreign policy, because the Polish political leadership looked to both East and West for support of its version of perestroika. But there were problems that caused tensions in Polish-Soviet relations; and while relations with the West, in particular West Germany and the United States, steadily improved, there were difficulties with these countries, too.

The Soviet Union
Polish relations with the Soviet Union were very good in the late '80s. Jaruzelski looked to Gorbachev for friendship and

support in his efforts—ultimately futile, of course—to stabilize and legitimize socialist rule in Poland in the face of mounting popular opposition to it. Jaruzelski scored points with Gorbachev in 1988 and 1989 for having enthusiastically supported Soviet perestroika, in contrast to the stubborn resistance to it of the East German, Czechoslovak, and Romanian leaderships, and for having taken care in the transition to noncommunist government in the summer of 1989 to protect the instruments of Communist party power in Poland and to guarantee Poland's continuing commitment to the Warsaw Pact, the CMEA, and close ties to Moscow.

Gorbachev reciprocated, backing all Jaruzelski's decisions to loosen Communist party control of Poland in 1989. The Soviet leader approved, albeit reluctantly, the April 1989 agreement between the Warsaw authorities and Solidarity that legalized the union and provided for radical changes in electoral rules for June 1989, which allowed Solidarity to obtain control of the Senate. He also raised no objection to Jaruzelski's appointment of a noncommunist prime minister in August 1989. Thus, Soviet policy toward Poland had significantly changed from what it had been under Brezhnev, who would have fiercely resisted the weakening of Communist influence in Poland that Gorbachev was willing to accept in the expectation that liberalization would strengthen, not weaken, the chances for survival of the socialist system.

The Soviets also accommodated the Poles on a more difficult issue: the Kremlin's candor in Polish-Soviet relations. Reform-minded Polish leaders wanted the Soviets to acknowledge responsibility for its actions during World War II, which were suppressed by the Communists in the past but which most of Polish society knew about. These blank spots included the Soviet-German Non-Aggression Pact of August 1939, which led to the invasion of Poland; the mass deportation of Poles from Soviet-occupied Poland between 1939 and 1941; and the Katyn Forest massacre in 1940, when the Soviets killed about 10,000 interned Polish officers and enlisted men. In early 1989 the Polish government issued a formal charge of Soviet responsibility for the massacre, specifically indicting Stalin's secret-police establishment, the NKVD.

The Kremlin initially refused to acknowledge responsibility for Katyn. A Polish-Soviet commission formed in 1987 had investigated the massacre for more than 2 years but had not issued a formal report, despite intense pressure from the Polish side. All that the Kremlin had been willing to allow, because of its acute sensitivity to the Katyn issue, was discussion. For more than 40 years successive Soviet leaderships had denied Soviet responsibility and had blamed the Nazis for the killings. But in April 1990 the Kremlin finally stopped lying about Katyn and acknowledged Soviet responsibility for the tragedy. Gorbachev personally delivered to Jaruzelski, during a meeting in Moscow, documents that made clear that the NKVD, Stalin's secret-police apparatus, had killed thousands of Polish officers in the Katyn forest. TASS immediately published an official Soviet expression of regret for the tragedy.

The Kremlin was also forthcoming in regard to the Soviet-German Non-Aggression Pact. It acknowledged that there were secret protocols which provided for the partition of Poland and which led very shortly afterward on September 1, 1939, to the German invasion of western Poland. This Soviet gesture provided Warsaw with at least a moral if not a legal basis for demanding of the Soviet Union at some future time the return of deported Poles now scattered throughout the Soviet Union and for making other claims, such as for war reparations.

There were several reasons for this Soviet candor. First was Gorbachev's sympathy for Jaruzelski and his interest in doing what he could to strengthen the Polish leader's political situation in Warsaw. Second was his commitment to glasnost, which extended to foreign as well as domestic Soviet behavior. Finally, there was a strategic consideration. Gorbachev wanted to strengthen Polish-Soviet relations in an era when Poland would be under noncommunist rule and both countries will need to cooperate to meet the challenge of a powerful united German state.

The number-one issue in post-Communist Poland's relations with the Soviet Union was the withdrawal of 50,000 Soviet troops from Polish territory. The withdrawal issue was political as well as strategic. The continued presence of Soviet troops heightened Poland's sense of vulnerability to the Soviets. Moreover, with guarantees of its western border from Germany, it no longer considered itself mortgaged to the Soviet Union for defense.

But the Soviets were slow to leave. The reason was partly logistical. The Soviet military's links to its much larger contingent of troops in what was formerly East Germany ran through Poland, and Moscow said that it would take at least through 1993 to complete the Soviet military withdrawal from Eastern Germany. But it was also true that the Soviet military was dragging its feet for reasons of pride and prestige. Legal, financial, and property issues also had to be settled: Moscow wanted compensation from the Polish government for military housing built in Poland, and Warsaw filed a counterclaim demanding that the Kremlin pay for the damage done to its environment by the long Soviet military presence. Behind this rhetoric was the Soviet military leadership's general discomfort over the way in which it had severely to curtail Soviet military strength in an area of historic importance for Soviet security.

However, after the failed August 1991 coup attempt in the Soviet Union, troop withdrawals accelerated. In October 1991 the Kremlin agreed to withdraw the remaining 45,000 Soviet troops by the end of 1992, ending 2 months of especially tense negotiations between the countries. The Kremlin apparently abandoned all efforts to use a definitive agreement on troop withdrawal as leverage to get the Poles to accept a bilateral political agreement with a provision barring Poland from joining NATO or any other alliance regarded as hostile. The Poles had balked at making such a deal, rightly seeing it as an attempt on the part of the Soviet Union to recoup some of the influence it had lost with the demise of the regime in Warsaw in 1989.

The West

Poland desperately needed Western economic, technological, and financial assistance. In the short term, it needed help to relieve immediate emergencies like the scarcity of food. Jaruzelski asked the Western powers at their summit in Paris in July 1989 for a multibillion-dollar emergency aid package over the next 2 years, with $1 billion allocated for food, $2 billion to support the economy through 1992, a rescheduling of the Polish debt by Poland's Western creditors, and a series of measures to enhance Poland's export capabilities. Jaruzelski also sought assistance in Poland's privatization of the economy. He wanted help with several projects in fields such as mining, telecommunications, and banking; with private foreign investment in Poland; and with the modernization of the agricultural infrastructure.

The Polish regime's high expectations of the West were not unreasonable. For years the West had let it be understood that any serious help for Poland's devastated economy and $39 billion of debt to the West was contingent on the regime's agreeing to legalize Solidarity and move toward democracy. Now that that had happened, the Polish government expected help.

The two Western countries to which the Poles now looked were the United States and Germany. While Bonn and Washington expressed satisfaction over the extensive political changes about to take place in Poland, they reacted with caution and restraint.

The United States
Since coming to power in August 1989, the noncommunist leadership has looked to the United States for support. The United States, after all, had urged Poland to stand up to the Soviet Union. The Poles have sought an American aid program of Marshall Plan dimensions. Poland, moreover, needs and wants close ties with the United States to counterbalance the growing, if somewhat benign, economic influence of Germany throughout Central/Eastern Europe and especially in Poland.

But so far the United States has provided limited help, nowhere near the scope sought by President Walesa. The Bush administration, taken by surprise when Communist party rule in Central/Eastern Europe abruptly collapsed in 1989, has been reluctant to give large amounts of financial assistance without a planned program of aid that clearly defines goals and methods. U.S. officials also want to be sure that Poland really wants a free-market economy. Aware of the slowness of privatization in Poland and the continued power, by whatever label, of Communists in top managerial positions, the Bush administration is determined to wait before considering large grants of aid. The administration also prefers to have the Central/Eastern Europeans help themselves rather than provide massive support. It is also true that in light of its own economic recession, the United States has had "more will than wallet," as Bush himself has said. Nevertheless, partly in response to much support in Congress and among the voters, especially those of Polish-American origin, the Bush administration has made several, if comparatively modest, gestures of financial support to Poland. It has supported loans to Poland by the IMF and the World Bank. And in March 1991, during Walesa's visit to Washington, the Bush administration agreed to erase 70 percent of Poland's $3.8 billion debt to the United States.

Poland and Germany
The Mazowiecki government watched with anxiety the unexpected progress that West Germany and the newly emancipated East Germany made toward reunification in 1990. The Polish people and their new leadership worried about Poland's strategic vulnerability to a united Germany with the political unity, economic power, and diplomatic will to lead and influence Europe in the next century. This worry was rooted, of course, in the brutal German treatment of Poland during World War II, when the Hitler regime attempted to go beyond mere conquest of Poland to achieve the systematic destruction of the country's national identity. Poles can forgive but can never forget the war with Germany and therefore have difficulty being at ease with a powerful German neighbor.

Contributing also to Polish anxiety about German reunification was the border question. One part of this question concerned the region known as western Pomerania, which consists of territory in northwestern Poland including Szcezin (in German, Stettin) and along the Baltic coast. Poland acquired this territory from a defeated Germany after World War II as compensation for the loss of the eastern part of Poland, including the city of Lvov, to the Soviet Union. The Polish leadership was afraid that a powerful unified Germany someday would demand the return of the lost territory, because many of its inhabitants are ethnic Germans and some at least would prefer German to Polish rule.

When in early 1990 Premier Mazowiecki asked West German Chancellor Kohl, an ardent champion and facilitator of German reunification, to guarantee Poland's western frontier with Germany, the German leader demurred. Kohl said that the kind of guarantee Poland wanted could come only from the government of a unified German state. In any event, he said, German government had pledged such a guarantee in the early 1970s. Kohl's position disturbed not only the people of Poland and West Germany but also the governments of other Western European countries and the United States.

Before long, Kohl offered a compromise: West Germany would guarantee the Polish border if Poland agreed to give up any claims to reparations from Germany for the damage done to Poland during World War II and if it pledged fair, equitable, and tolerant treatment of the German-speaking minorities in Poland. Kohl's plan was met with suspicion about the real German intent with regard to the border. The Bush administration, as well as the Kremlin, put tremendous pressure on Kohl to back down, and in March Kohl agreed to propose that both German parliaments adopt matching pledges on the sanctity of the frontier. On March 8, 1990, the West German Parliament agreed that a united Germany should honor Poland's current boundary.

There was also a potential problem for Warsaw in Silesia, a highly industrialized coal-rich area in southwestern Poland that borders Germany and Czechoslovakia. This region, inhabited by 600,000 to 800,000 people of ethnic German origin, was part of Germany before World War II. In these Silesians of German origin there seemed to be a certain nostalgia for German rule, when life was easier and better than under Polish Communist rule. Contributing to this nostalgia was resentment among the German-speaking Silesians over Polish policy after the war, when Warsaw forced them to adopt Polish culture or be deported, and subsequently encouraged the migration of Polish citizens from other parts of the country to settle in Silesia and facilitate the imposition of Polish ways on the region. Especially disturbing was an apparent resurgence of Naziism in Silesia among some of the residents of the area whose only memory of German rule was the Hitlerian state. The current Polish leadership, therefore, had good reason to worry about the future of Silesia and about its relationship to a powerful unified Germany.

The border question led the Mazowiecki government, which was not completely satisfied with matching pledges from the two Germanies on the Poland's western boundary, to demand a role for Poland in the international discussions of German reunification among the Four Great Allies (the Soviet Union, France, Britain, and the United States) begun in Ottawa in March 1990. In Ottawa, the Allies agreed on the two-plus-four formula, which involved discussions by the two Germanies on technical details of reunification and discussions by the four wartime Allies on the acceptability of these details to all of Europe. Poland demanded that the constitution of a united German state should contain a provision guaranteeing the existing Polish-German frontier in perpetuity. At the opening of reunification discussions among representatives of the two Germanies and the four World War II Allies, an agreement was reached to include Poland in discussions about borders of the new state.

Yet in early 1990 Chancellor Kohl refused to make the guarantees sought by the Poles, saying that only a united Germany could put the border issue to rest. In his view, guarantees sought by Poland should await action by an all-German government. In addition, he was responding to pressure from a powerful lobby of

Independence
1918

Poland is
invaded,
partitioned, and
occupied by
Nazi Germany
and the Soviet
Union
1939

Polish Commu-
nists and like-
minded political
groups coalesce
to form the Polish
United Workers
Party
1947

German "expellees," people settled in West Germany but originally from Silesia, Pomerania, East Prussia, and the Sudetenland, who hoped someday that these areas would again be German. He may also have been concerned with the fate of people of German cultural background living in the Silesian and Pomeranian districts of western Poland, who complained, not without some justification, of occasional discrimination by the Warsaw authorities. In the past these ethnic Germans were forbidden to speak German, to practice religion in their own way, or to preserve their folk traditions and cultural dances.

On March 6, 1990, however, responding to intense pressures from the United States, the Soviet Union, and Western Europe, as well as from members of his own government, Kohl moved to accommodate Poland. He proposed that both Germanies adopt identical resolutions renouncing any territorial claims to Poland and that a new unified Germany would reaffirm such resolutions. And in July 1990 Germany agreed to remove from a new all-German Constitution language in the Bonn Basic Law that offended Poland because it provided for German acquisition of Polish territory to complete its reunification.

On November 14, 1990, the border issue was formally put to rest with the signing of a Polish-German agreement, which recognized the Oder-Neisse line as the permanent border between Poland and Germany. In addition, Foreign Minister Genscher pledged that Germany would help Poland and other Central/Eastern European countries to rebuild their economies to assure, as he put it, that "the frontier [between Germany and Poland] does not become a watershed between rich and poor." Genscher also announced Germany's intention to lift visa requirements for Polish citizens, allowing them for the first time since World War II to have easy access to a country within the European Community.

Finally, in June 1991, the issue of German reparations to Poland was settled in a manner somewhat favorable to Poland. Bowing to intense Polish pressure on Bonn to make restitution to Poles forced to work in Nazi labor camps during World War II, Chancellor Kohl announced that a

new German-Polish friendship treaty, designed to mend the wounds caused by Germany's invasion and occupation of Poland beginning in 1939, contained a provision for German compensation. This treaty, which also pledged German financial help for Poland's economic reforms and assistance to Poland in gaining entry into the EC trading bloc, reaffirmed the German commitment before and after reunification to develop strong, close German-Polish relations.

Poland has always had close cultural and political links to Lithuania, which had been united with Poland in a confederation from 1386 until 1569. Lithuania remained an integral part of Poland until the partitions at the end of the eighteenth century. Conflict broke out between the two peoples in the late nineteenth century and persisted with increasing intensity in the period between the two world wars. A Lithuanian national movement arose in opposition to Polish culture in the late nineteenth century and in the immediate aftermath of World War I, when Lithuania became independent, along with Poland. The two countries fought over possession of Vilnius, which ended up as part of Poland in the interwar period. Many Poles regard Vilnius, originally called Vilna, as a Polish city and remember Vilnius as the home of some of their nation's greatest poets and politicians; some would like to see Vilnius returned to Poland.

In any event, Poland did try to encourage and help Lithuania toward emancipation of the Soviet Union at the risk of straining relations with Moscow; at one point the Soviets complained that Poland was interfering in the internal affairs of the Soviet Union. For example, in June 1990 Mazowiecki received Lithuanian Prime Minister Kasmiera Prunskiene in Warsaw and toward the end of the year Poland advocated observer status for Lithuania, Latvia, and Estonia at the Conference for Security and Cooperation in Europe. The Polish government under Walesa reacted strongly to the renewal of Soviet pressure on Lithuania in January 1991, when Soviet forces assaulted the Lithuanian state television studio.

Despite popular sentiment in favor of an early Polish recognition of Lithuania's independence, however, the Warsaw gov-

ernment was inclined to proceed cautiously in 1990. While Poland had a lot at stake in avoiding actions that might antagonize Moscow and provoke retaliation, say, in the form of foot-dragging on the issue of the Soviet troop withdrawal, it was also true that an independent Lithuania posed special problems for Poland. One had to do with the Polish minority of 300,000 people living in the countryside surrounding Vilnius. The other had to do with the uncertainties surrounding Poland's boundary with Lithuania.

The Polish Minority in Lithuania
The Polish leadership remained uneasy over the excessive chauvinism of the Landsbergis government, afraid that it would try to homogenize Lithuanian society at the expense of its minorities. Poles in Lithuania felt discriminated against by the Lithuanian government, especially since the surge of Lithuanian nationalism at the end of the 1980s. Polish regions reportedly received 50 percent less funding from the Vilnius government than Lithuanian ones, and ethnic Poles claimed that their region had the lowest per capita number of doctors, hospitals, schools, and telephones in Lithuania. Adding to interethnic antagonism were class-based distinctions between Poles and Lithuanians: Poles in Lithuania were mainly workers and peasants without a local intelligentsia that could act as intermediaries for the Polish community with the Lithuanian leadership. Lithuanian nationalists were annoyed by the preference of Poles, who entered higher education, for the study of Russian, which was close to their own language, rather than Lithuanian, on the assumption that fluency in Russian would be more useful than fluency in a language spoken by only a very small minority in the Soviet system. The Polish minority strongly resented Lithuanian language laws of 1988 and 1989 that established Lithuanian as the official state language and made no concession to districts in Lithuania that were predominantly Polish. Finally, more than half of the Polish minority, fearful of its status under a nationalist leadership, opposed Lithuania's independence and supported preservation of the Union to which Lithuania technically still belonged until the independence

GLOBAL STUDIES: THE COMMONWEALTH OF INDEPENDENT STATES AND CENTRAL/EASTERN EUROPE

Polish industrial workers strike in Poznan for economic and political concessions 1956	A crisis in Polish-Soviet relations	Students' and workers' strikes in Warsaw against regime repressiveness 1968	The regime's announcement of increased food prices provokes industrial strikes and demonstrations 1970	Gierek replaces Gomulka as PUWP first secretary 1971	Another announcement of increased food prices provokes a wave of industrial strikes 1976	Polish-born Pope John Paul II visits his homeland 1979

1980s–19

Industrial unrest spreads quickly throughout Poland; establishment of Solidarity; martial law; Solidarity is banned; Pope John Paul II pays a second visit to Poland and talks with Jaruzelski	Martial law is lifted; Lech Walesa, former Solidarity leader, is awarded the Nobel Peace Prize; the West agrees to favorable rescheduling of Polish debt; the United States lifts sanctions against Poland	Political, economic, and social liberalization move briskly forward, stunning the world; Walesa becomes president

decrees of Moscow following the abortive anti-Gorbachev coup in August 1991.

While Warsaw was concerned about the fate of the Polish-speaking minority in Lithuania, it did little to encourage its achievement of increased autonomy of Vilnius. The Polish government did not want to antagonize the government in Vilnius, which certainly would have taken umbrage over any Polish effort to champion the cause of autonomy for the Poles living permanently in Lithuania. Nor did Poland want to raise the hopes for autonomy of the small Polish minorities living in Byelorussia and the Ukraine or, worse, arouse fear in the governments of these republics of the prospect of Polish territorial claims against them in the future. Also the post-Communist Mazowiecki leadership had a bit less sympathy for the Polish minority in Lithuania than one might have expected because, frankly, Polish government officials with roots in the Polish intelligentsia were more interested in contacts with their Lithuanian counterparts in the Vilnius administration than they were with Polish-speaking Lithuanians, who had little in common with them intellectually. In sum, there was some mistrust between Poles in Poland and the Polish minority in Lithuania. The government in Warsaw hopes that the government in Vilnius will take care to avoid blatant acts of discrimination that might force a reluctant Warsaw to champion the rights of Lithuanian Poles.

Nevertheless, the Polish government did speak out strongly against the Vilnius government decision on September 4, 1991, to dissolve the two self-governing Polish regional councils and to impose direct rule on the areas inhabited primarily by people of Polish culture. According to the Lithuanian side, the action was the result of the alleged support by Polish Lithuanan citizens of the failed anti-Gorbachev coup as well as their boycott of the 1990 referendum on independence, which had been approved overwhelmingly by ethnic Lithuanian voters.

The Polish Boundary With Lithuania
Another major issue in Polish-Lithuanian relations had to do with the border between the two countries. As a consequence of the August 1939 Molotov-Ribbentrop Pact and related agreements, Lithuania gained territories that had belonged to Poland in the interwar period. According to the secret protocols of the pact, Lithuania and eastern Poland were to fall within the Soviet sphere of influence. After the Soviet Union's conquest of eastern Poland in September 1939, Stalin gave Vilnius to Lithuania. In the fall of 1940, after Lithuania was annexed by the Soviet Union, Lithuania received additional Polish territories which Stalin had originally **given to Byelorussia. The postwar Polish-**Soviet border, which was imposed on Poland by Stalin, was confirmed in an August 16, 1945, Polish-Soviet treaty. In declaring their independence in March 1990, the Lithuanians repudiated the Molotov-Ribbentrop Pact once and for all, but they did not reject the territorial changes brought about by the pact—changes that worked to Lithuania's advantage. The Lithuanians

now fear that Poland might in the future attempt to reclaim territories, especially Vilnius.

Poland, however, is unlikely to make border claims against Lithuania or any other of its eastern neighbors, because any such demands would encourage German groups, if not the German government itself, to call for a reassessment of the November 1990 German-Polish treaty of guarantee confirming Poland's post–World War II western border. Moreover, any territorial claims by Poland would impede its progress back to Europe. Polish leaders have given oral assurances of their country's disinterest in reclaiming lost land and have acknowledged that Vilnius is now a Lithuanian city. But, just as oral assurances by German leaders on the permanence of the German-Polish frontier had not been sufficient for Poles, so Polish oral assurances on the Polish-Lithuanian border will not be sufficient to quiet Lithuanian anxieties. The border remains a hidden issue in Poland's relations with the new Lithuania.

DEVELOPMENT

Burdened by a massive foreign debt, Poland suffers from clumsy centralized planning which has kept productivity low. There are acute shortages of everything—materials, machinery, capital—causing scarcities of virtually all consumer goods.

FREEDOM

Polish society is at last truly democratic and pluralistic. In the parliamentary elections of October 1991, more than 100 different political party groups competed for seats in a free-for-all electoral competition. Poland's president is also elected directly by voters. There is complete freedom of thought and expression in Polish society.

HEALTH/WELFARE

Poles who work in important professions can go to high-quality clinics serviced and supported by their employers; the rest of the population must go to public clinics, which lack adequate facilities and therefore cannot give quick and efficient treatment. The country continues to wage a war on drug addiction, which is growing and bringing with it a familiar pathology of crime and prostitution.

ACHIEVEMENTS

The initial phase of the economic shock-therapy program launched on January 1, 1990, Central/Eastern Europe's first and boldest plan for abandoning the Communist economic system in favor of a free-enterprise, market-driven economy has brought fast and impressive results. Prices have been freed from control, borders opened to imports, and consumer goods of all kinds have become available.

Romania

GEOGRAPHY

Area in Square Kilometers (Miles):
237,499 (91,699) (slightly smaller
than Oregon)
Capital (Population): Bucharest
(1,976,000)
Climate: moderate

PEOPLE

Population

Total: 23,269,000
Annual Growth Rate: 0.4%
Rural/Urban Population Ratio: 49/51
Ethnic Makeup of Population: 88%
Romanian; 12% Magyar, German,
Ukrainian, Serb, Croat, Russian,
Turk, Gypsy, and others

Health

Life Expectancy at Birth: 67 years
(male); 73 years (female)
Infant Mortality Rate (Ratio):
25/1,000
Average Caloric Intake: 126% of FAO
minimum
Physicians Available (Ratio): 1/559

Religion(s)

80% Romanian Orthodox; 6% Roman
Catholic; 4% Calvinist, Lutheran,
Jewish, and Baptist; 10% other

Education

Adult Literacy Rate: 98%

COMMUNICATION

Telephones: 1,960,000
Newspapers: 60

TRANSPORTATION

Highways—Kilometers (Miles): 14,666
(9,093)
Railroads—Kilometers (Miles): 11,110
(6,904)
Usable Airfields: 160

GOVERNMENT

Type: pluralistic parliamentary
democracy
Independence Date: August 23, 1878
Head of State: President Ion Iliescu
Political Parties: The National
Salvation Front; Romanian National
Unity Party; Democratic Left Party;
The Democratic Convention (a union
of 14 antigovernment parties);
Democratic Union of Hungarians in
Romania; Ecologists Party
Suffrage: universal and compulsory
over 18

MILITARY

Number of Armed Forces: 163,000
*Military Expenditures (% of Central
Government Expenditures):* 2.6%
Current Hostilities: none

ECONOMY

Currency ($ U.S. Equivalent): 35.6
lei = $1
Per Capita Income/GNP:
$3,445/$79.8 billion
Inflation Rate: n/a
Total Foreign Debt: $500 million
Natural Resources: oil; timber;
natural gas; coal
Agriculture: corn; wheat; oilseed;
potatoes; livestock
Industry: mining; forestry;
construction materials; metal
production and processing; chemicals;
machine building; food processing

FOREIGN TRADE

Exports: $14.2 billion
Imports: $9.7 billion

SLOW TO CHANGE

In postrevolutionary Romania, there have been political and economic
changes: people can speak out against the government, and the country
is beginning to develop a small private sector. But in other respects not
much has changed. Many so-called democratic leaders, including President Ion Iliescu, are ex-Communists whose behavior sometimes calls to
mind the excesses and abuses of the totalitarian past; while daily life for
the overwhelming majority of Romanians is still miserable, or, as some
have said, "as bad as it was under Ceausescu," with little food, few
amenities, and a lot of pessimism about the future.

ROMANIA

Romania paid a heavy price for its support of the Nazi invasion of the Soviet Union in June 1941. When World War II was over the Romanians had to cede Bessarabia to the Soviet Union, pay reparations to the Soviets and other Central/Eastern European countries invaded by the Nazis, and, worst of all from the point of view of Romania's King Michael, allow Communists to participate in the national government. And that was only the beginning. With Soviet support, the Romanian Communists, who formed with other reformist elements the Romanian Workers' Party (RWP) in 1947, expanded their influence throughout Romanian society and ultimately forced the king's abdication in December 1947. The RWP converted Romania into a republic and in 1948 proceeded to eliminate political opposition and to establish state control over industry, agriculture, and foreign trade.

In the late 1940s the RWP leadership was divided into so-called nativist and Muscovite groupings, the former having spent the war years in Romania, and the latter having stayed in the Soviet Union in continuous contact with the Soviet leadership. But the RWP leadership was in agreement on fundamentals: it was committed to imposing the Soviet socialist model on Romania and to remaining loyal to Soviet foreign policy. By 1953 Romania had become a Soviet satellite.

MONARCHICAL SOCIALISM

Under the leadership of Gheorghe Gheorghiu-Dej and his successor, Nicolae Ceausescu, who became RWP first secretary in 1965 and president of the republic in 1974, Romania remained faithful to the Soviet model. Gheorghiu-Dej and Ceausescu tolerated no challenges to democratic centralism inside the party and no expression of political criticism among the Romanian people. They were also very sensitive to the slightest expression of hostility toward the Soviet Union.

Another dimension of the regime's repressiveness was the personality cult around Ceausescu to compensate for the regime's waning popular support, legitimacy, and authority. Ceausescu's birthday had become a national event in which journalists and public figures tried to outdo one another in praising him. His home village of Cornicesti contained a memorial house and a museum and had become a national pilgrimage site with almost religious overtones.

The Ceausescu personality cult included a vicious nepotism. He gave close

relatives enormous political influence. His wife, Elena, was a full member of the Political Executive Committee (PEC), the Romanian Communist Party's equivalent of the Soviet Politburo. She was also first deputy prime minister and head of the party's cadre commission, which oversaw all personnel matters. Ceausescu's youngest son, Nicu, was an alternate member of the PEC and a leader of the Communist youth organization. Other members of Ceausescu's family also held key party and government positions.

In addition to relying heavily on family members, Ceausescu continued the practice of rotating individuals in and out of party and government positions. According to a Yugoslav source, between 1985 and 1987 there were more than 20 government reshufflings, including changes in the key departments of Defense, Finance, Foreign Trade, and Foreign Affairs. While Ceausescu defended this procedure as normal and a sign of appreciation and an expression of confidence, the real reason for it was to prevent party officials from establishing a solid geographic or organizational base from which to challenge the incumbent party leader.

For the most part, the RWP's political authoritarianism was acceptable to the Romanian people. Liberal and democratic ideas never took deep root in Romanian society. Even when Romania had parliamentary institutions in the 1920s and 1930s, the political system was democratic only in appearance. Romanian political life for most of that era, especially in the late 1930s, was dominated by a powerful and paternalistic monarchical despotism.

The Romanian people historically have admired charismatic leadership. This tendency toward hero worship influenced Ceausescu's behavior. He acted like a king even though he was a president. He presided over the government as a monarch over a court. He placed relatives in positions of influence. His picture hung everywhere and his birthday was the occasion of a national celebration. He imparted to the Romanian autocracy a personal quality important to its acceptance by the Romanian people and thus to its authority and legitimacy.

Romanian economic conditions also made authoritarian government expedient. When the Communists came to power in the late 1940s Romania was predominantly agricultural and underdeveloped, and its people had one of the lowest standards of living in Central/Eastern Europe. To modernize the economy, in particular to accelerate industrialization and expand overall economic output,

the Romanian Communists insisted upon social discipline and absolute obedience to party rule. Faced with the task of modernizing and socializing the backward economy, the RWP leadership never had any qualms in the post-Stalinist era about continuing a repressive political dictatorship. The party was convinced that it was the only way to achieve socialism.

NONCONFORMITY IN FOREIGN POLICY

Although Romania conformed to the Soviet model in the domestic sphere, the RWP leadership showed some independence in foreign policy. This independence was inspired by a nationalism born of a strong and longstanding hostility toward the Russians. Since Romania's political independence in 1878, the Czarist government and its Soviet successor had threatened Romanian territorial integrity. Romanians rightly feared the Russians and believed that they intended someday to dismember and annex Romanian territory.

Reinforcing Romanian nationalism was the pride of the Romanian people and their leaders in the country's long history, which goes back to Roman times and thus predates the establishment of state systems elsewhere in Central/Eastern Europe and even in Russia itself. Gheorghiu-Dej and Ceausescu cultivated this pride as a means of legitimizing their regimes.

The groundwork for Romania's independence of the Soviet Union in foreign policy was laid shrewdly by Gheorghiu-Dej during his leadership of the RWP in the late 1940s and early 1950s. By convincing Moscow of his own personal loyalty, he was able to obtain its approval of changes in the RWP leadership, in which he gradually removed Muscovites. Gheorghiu-Dej thus nationalized the Romanian party in much the same way that Tito had nationalized the Yugoslav party in the late 1940s.

The Soviets hardly noticed, until it was too late, their loss of influence over RWP decision-making. The Kremlin's influence was further eroded when in 1958 it removed Soviet troops from Romania. The Sino-Soviet dispute in the 1960s also diminished Soviet influence over the Romanians by demonstrating to them the limits of Soviet capability to oppose the independence of other socialist countries with which it had disagreements.

The first expression of Romanian independence of the Soviet Union was Gheorghiu-Dej's 1957 announcement of a decision to accelerate industrialization of the country. This decision ran counter to a Soviet-inspired policy of the Council for Mutual Economic Assistance, which sought to have Romania concentrate on agricultural expansion and to export primary products to the already industrialized socialist countries in the north.

In the 1960s and 1970s the Romanians differed with the Soviets on many international issues. They refused to support Soviet efforts to isolate China in the world communist movement. Indeed, they maintained party and state ties with China despite its dispute with the Soviet Union. Romania also insisted on Soviet respect for the principles of Communist party autonomy and noninterference in the internal affairs of other parties. The Romanians thus opposed the Soviet intervention in Czechoslovakia in August 1968, despite a dislike of Czechoslovak leader Dubcek's liberalization policies, and endorsed the advocacies of autonomy by the Eurocommunist parties in the 1970s, despite opposition to their liberal ideas.

Romania also proceeded independently of the Soviets in its relations with the West. It was the first Central/Eastern European country to respond to West Germany's Ostpolitik (the policy of good relations with socialist countries in the Soviet Bloc) and to restore relations with Bonn in 1968. Romania also sought an expansion of trade with the West, especially West Germany, France, and the United States.

Romania gave special attention to relations with the United States, because it was a good source of desperately needed industrial technology. In 1969 Ceausescu gave U.S. President Richard Nixon a hospitable reception in Bucharest, despite Nixon's vehement opposition to communism. In succeeding years Ceausescu paid several visits to Washington, seeking more trade and the credit needed to finance Romanian industrial expansion. In 1975 U.S. President Gerald Ford visited Bucharest.

Romanian policy toward the United States paid off. The Communist leadership was more successful than some other Central/Eastern European leaderships in obtaining American trade concessions, including most-favored-nation status.

Another example of Romanian independence was criticism of the Warsaw Pact and CMEA. Although Romania remained a member of those organizations, it called them instruments of Soviet influence. The Romanians advocated the abolition of military pacts in Europe like the Warsaw Pact and the North Atlantic Treaty Organization. On occasion the Romanians refused to participate in Warsaw Pact maneuvers. They consistently opposed the Soviet pol-

icy in CMEA that encouraged economic specialization, because it infringed on the freedom of member states and ran counter to Romania's domestic policies.

Another example of Romania's foreign-policy independence was opposition to a Warsaw Pact proposal to increase defense spending. Ceausescu instead reduced Romanian defense expenditures, to allow increases in spending on social welfare. He supported multilateral nuclear disarmament in Europe and called for the withdrawal of Soviet troops from Afghanistan. He also defied the Soviet boycott of the 1984 Summer Olympics in Los Angeles.

The Romanians reaffirmed their misgivings about membership in CMEA and the Warsaw Pact. In 1985 Foreign Minister Stefan Andrei questioned the benefits of belonging to CMEA while simultaneously trying to improve Romania's relations with the European Community. And in 1986 Ceausescu called upon his Warsaw Pact allies to follow the Romanian example of reducing defense expenditures for 1987.

Soviet Toleration

The Kremlin tolerated Romanian independence in foreign policy, mainly because of its conformity in domestic policy. The Soviets appreciated Romania's commitment to such key aspects of the Soviet model as political dictatorship and economic centralization. The Soviets were willing to indulge Ceausescu's challenges also because they understood how this behavior, the result of nationalism, strengthened his control over the country and its commitment to socialism.

Additionally, the Kremlin's toleration was the result of an awareness that Romania had not threatened Soviet power in Central/Eastern Europe—it had not disturbed the strategic balance of forces between East and West. It had not compromised Soviet or Soviet Bloc security. On the contrary, Romania was a loyal ally of the Soviet Union.

Indeed, a former U.S. ambassador to Romania, David Funderburk, insisted that Romania's so-called independence of the Soviet Union was greatly exaggerated in the West. Funderburk argued that Romania's ties with the Soviet Union were closer and more extensive than the U.S. leadership cared to believe, and he called for a revision of past U.S. trade concessions to Bucharest, which were given to encourage its independence of Moscow. Events in 1986 and 1987 vindicated to some extent Funderburk's assessment. Romania's need of Soviet energy supplies and raw materials limited its capacity

to proceed independently of the Soviet Union in the international arena.

Romania's independence of the Soviet Union in foreign policy seemed to have eroded somewhat in the late 1980s and may have been of diminishing importance to U.S. strategy, as Funderburk suggested. By turning to the Soviets for oil, Ceausescu weakened Romania's unique position in the Arab world, which had enabled it to help arrange the Arab-Israeli peace talks a decade earlier. Furthermore, when Poland upgraded its ties with Israel in 1986, Romania's relations with Israel automatically became less strategically significant for the United States. And with the visits of East German and Polish party leaders to China in 1986, the significance of Romania's having been the only Warsaw Pact member to maintain links with China during its long dispute with the Soviet Union diminished.

ETHNIC PROBLEMS

Although Romanian society is made up principally (88 percent) of ethnic Romanians, there are several minority groups. Of these, Hungarians and Jews have attracted attention in the West, because of their complaints of official discrimination. The egalitarian principles of Marxist socialism did not seem to have applied to these peoples, despite special provisions for minority groups in the Constitution.

Discrimination Against Hungarians and Jews

Approximately 1.7 million Hungarian-speaking people live in the Transylvanian region of Romania, which was part of Hungary before World War I. Romania's Hungarian-speaking citizens complained of discrimination in education and employment and accused the authorities in Bucharest of trying to Romanianize them by making fluency in the Romanian language obligatory for jobs and even to obtain food in state stores. These complaints were taken up by the Hungarian government; but when protests were made to Bucharest, the official response was that Hungarian-speaking citizens received the same treatment as Romanians. Therefore, there was "no discrimination."

Hungarian-speaking citizens tried to emigrate to Hungary. But when they did, they confronted obstacles in the form of overelaborate bureaucratic procedures for getting exit visas and the payment of an obligatory tax (although eventually this was lifted in response to complaints and threats of retaliation from the United States). The Hungarian minority living in Romania was virtually marooned; and there was little prospect of change, because of the hypernationalism of the leadership and a historic ill will toward Hungary, due to its alleged mistreatment of Romanians living in Transylvania prior to World War I.

Tensions between the two countries reached an all-time high in the spring of 1987. The Hungarians charged that Romania was steadily diminishing the rights of the Hungarian-speaking population in Transylvania and was destroying their cultural identity by preventing the circulation of Hungarian newspapers and confiscating Hungarian-language books. The Romanians countered with accusations of Hungarian atrocities against Romanian-speaking people in the region when it was under Hungarian control during World War II. Hungarian officials did not deny the Romanian revelations, but they did condemn them as a propaganda maneuver.

Both sides were warned by the Soviets to keep a lid on this dispute and to work to resolve it by themselves. Although the Kremlin did not want to get involved, it was concerned about the heightened tensions between its allies, whose reliability in the Warsaw Pact could be affected adversely by this persistent discord. During his visit to Romania in May 1987, Soviet party leader Mikhail Gorbachev pointedly reminded his hosts of Vladimir Lenin's view that issues like the treatment of national minorities in a socialist society must be handled with "delicacy and care."

Romania also came under substantial pressure from outside the socialist community to alter its policy toward its Hungarian-speaking citizens. A human-rights monitoring group, the U.S.-based Helsinki Watch Committee, affirmed in February 1989 that Romania's Hungarian minority was the victim of a government campaign to destroy its separate cultural identity. The report encouraged the United Nations Human Rights Commission to investigate accusations of widespread human-rights abuses in Romania. Although previous attempts to get Romania investigated had been blocked by the Soviet Union, this time, given the Kremlin's dissatisfaction over Ceausescu's opposition to perestroika and in particular to glasnost, there was reason to believe the investigation would go forward.

Another minority problem involved Romania's Jews, who were convinced that the historic anti-Semitism of Romanian society persisted and that there was discrimination against them everywhere. The Jewish population of Romania, drastically reduced as a result of official persecution during World War II, when Romania was

an ally of Nazi Germany, had diminished even further in recent times.

Romanian Jews began to speak out against their government's perceived discrimination in the 1970s. People with Jewish names, they said, did not get the same treatment as others. There were few Jews in the upper echelons of the Romanian Communist Party, and none was in the top leadership close to President Ceausescu. And when Jews tried to emigrate, they encountered difficulties. A prominent Jewish writer for Romanian television was told by officials that a refusal to publish a book of hers was based solely on the fact of her Jewish name. When she tried to emigrate, she was denied permission, fired from her job, and obliged to make her living as a nurse.

The Ceausescu regime in Bucharest pleaded innocent to charges of discrimination against Jews. Romanian officials pointed to synagogues and kosher butchers to prove their point. They reminded others that Romania was the only country in Central/Eastern Europe to maintain relations with Israel after the 1967 Six-Day War.

Only outside pressure, in particular from the United States, seemed to make a difference for the Jews, albeit a modest one. When the Romanian government curtailed Jewish emigration in the 1970s and imposed an emigration tax at the end of 1982, the United States warned that Romania would lose the newly acquired trade advantages that it had been seeking for so long. This warning had an influence on Romanian policy. The Romanians relented. They allowed a substantial number of Jews to emigrate and in 1983 rescinded the emigration tax.

While the regime seemed to accommodate the United States on the issue of its alleged discrimination against Romanian Jews, however, it continued to mistreat members of other religions, such as Evangelical Christians, Seventh-Day Adventists, Pentecostals, and Baptists. As a result, relations between Romania and the United States deteriorated steadily in the late 1980s. In January 1987 the U.S. government removed Romania from the duty-generalized system of preferences—an action that may have cost Romania about $150 million in exports to the United States in 1988. A second setback was the bipartisan action of the U.S. Congress to suspend most-favored-nation status for 6 months or longer, because of Romanian human-rights violations.

Although the loss of trade with the United States, estimated by the U.S. Commerce Department to be in the neighborhood of $300 million a year, was

especially difficult for Romania, given its campaign to reduce foreign indebtedness, the Ceausescu regime did not curtail its repressive policies. Indeed, in an act of defiance, in 1988 it renounced most-favored-nation privileges with the United States.

ECONOMIC PROBLEMS

Romania continued throughout the 1980s to have one of the lowest standards of living in Central/Eastern Europe. There were chronic shortages of everything the consumer needed or wanted—especially food, much of which was exported to offset the country's indebtedness to the West incurred for the sake of industrial development. But food shortages were also the result of poor labor productivity, attributable in part to the absence of incentives, as Romanian agriculture still followed the Soviet model of collectivization. The Romanians also lacked modern agricultural machinery. A shortage of energy was especially painful to Romanians. It increased their dependence on Soviet oil and imposed an unpleasant austerity. They were obliged to curtail consumer use of electricity by turning it off at home early in the evening and spending the rest of the night in a chilly gloom. Yet the Ceausescu regime's immediate response to these problems was only the slightest adjustments of the economic system.

The continuing harshness of the daily life of ordinary Romanian citizens provoked a renewal of social unrest in November 1987, when thousands of workers in Brazov went into the streets to demonstrate against severe pay cuts, against increasingly extreme shortages (bread was rationed to 300 grams a day, and other staples were either unavailable or unaffordable), and against the prospect of continuing hardship. The catalyst for this action was a presidential decree which had gone into effect on November 10, reducing domestic consumption of electricity and heating gas by an additional 30 percent from a level already deemed inhumanely low. This protest in Brazov, a model industrial city whose work force was supposed to be the elite of the Romanian proletariat, was indicative of the depth of popular discontent.

Dismissing the country's shortages and other economic hardships as inconveniences that did not justify further reform along Soviet lines, the Ceausescu regime exhorted workers to expand productivity, threatened them with further wage cuts if they did not fulfill quotas, and called for "increased revolutionary awareness" among the people. It blamed the country's economic woes on inadequate loyalty and reliability of party leaders and accused them of not fully implementing party and state decisions in the workplace.

Instead of looking to systemic reform to resolve these problems, Ceausescu opted for a diversion of resources from the military to the civilian sector. The leadership announced a unilateral 5 percent reduction in military spending for 1987 and even held a nationwide referendum in November of that year "to consult the people" on the decision. (The voter turnout was 99.9 percent, with 100 percent voting in favor.) Ceausescu asserted that nearly 50 percent of the Romanian Army had been diverted to economic activity. He even proposed the use of tanks to transport water on cooperative farms.

POLITICAL PROBLEMS

Prospects of change in Romania in the late 1980s seemed slim, despite changes taking place almost everywhere in Central/Eastern Europe. Egoism or stupidity, or both, made the Romanian party leader stubbornly oblivious to the flaws and failures of his Stalinist-inspired policies. He was determined to transform Romania from a backward, agricultural society into a socialist industrial nation, much like the one Stalin had tried to build in the Soviet Union. As late as November 26, 1989, addressing a party Congress meeting in Bucharest, Ceausescu vowed not to follow other countries in the region that he accused of "blocking socialism" and insisted with an unaccustomed stridency that the old order would continue. He thereby dashed the hopes of workers, intellectuals, and some party pragmatists on lower levels of the party hierarchy that there might be some change.

Dissatisfaction with his leadership had been growing not only among hard-pressed workers but also among former high-ranking party officials, like George Apostol, Alexandru Birladeanu, and Constantin Pirvulescu, who had been disgraced for having revealed their disillusionment and disagreement with Ceausescu. In March 1989 they and others had sent a letter to the Romanian leader attacking his hardline policies, accusing him of violating human-rights agreements and condemning him for a gross mismanagement of Romania's economy. The letter also criticized and called for the abandonment of Ceausescu's plan to eliminate villages and move peasants to new urban centers, and it took issue with an unpublished but widely feared law banning Romanians from talking to foreigners. Although this criticism, coming as it did from former influential Politburo members and political loyalists, was a significant challenge to Ceausescu's leadership, it had little impact on his offending policies, which remained intact.

As late as November 1989, after the ouster of conservative leaders in East Germany, Czechoslovakia, and Bulgaria, the likelihood of change seemed slight. People feared the extraordinarily efficient and ubiquitous state security police, the Securitate. They lacked organization and had nothing comparable to Czechoslovakia's Charter 77 group. Also, leaders at the top of the party hierarchy seemed unified; there appeared to be no faction within the inner core of the party leadership willing to exploit the popular dissatisfaction with Ceausescu.

In addition, the Soviets were reluctant to do anything about Ceausescu, despite their intense dislike of his policies, especially his opposition to perestroika. Gorbachev was determined to refrain from interfering in Romanian internal affairs and to allow the Romanians themselves to deal with Ceausescu as best they could. He may have expected the Romanian leader, who was in his early seventies and reputed to be ill, to resign and be succeeded by more flexible and pragmatic leadership. This is not to say that the Kremlin lacked leverage with the Romanians—the Soviet Union was Romania's largest supplier of energy and chief trade partner. And while the price of Soviet oil had been increasing, the Soviet Union continued to purchase Romanian food exports and poor-quality manufactured goods that could not be sold outside the Soviet Bloc. Still, Gorbachev was unwilling to exert economic pressure on the Romanian regime to induce a change in policy.

ROMANIA'S REVOLUTION IN DECEMBER 1989

Thus, the sudden collapse of the Ceausescu regime in December 1989 came as a shock to everybody, including the Romanian people themselves, who were surprised by the spontaneity and success of their sudden explosion of resistance.

The beginning of the end of Ceausescu's rule occurred in Timosoara, in west-central Romania, where in early December security forces were carrying out orders to deport a dissident cleric of Hungarian background, Laszlo Toekes of the Reform Church of Timosoara, who was being protected by local citizens. With massive and brutal military force, killing hundreds of people, the Securitate attacked these people and others who were demonstrating in support of the belea-guered priest. To the shock of the police, the demonstrations not only continued, but they spread to other Romanian cities as news of the brutality spread.

By the third week in December elements of the national army joined the insurgents in what was fast becoming a national insurgency against the regime, spontaneous in its origins but furious in its opposition to the old order. The army hated the regime because of its establishment and lavish support of the Securitate, a rival military organization favored by Ceausescu over the army, as well as because of its policies of reducing investment in the conventional military establishment and channeling these funds to the police. Eventually, with the help of the army, the insurgents captured Ceausescu and his wife and executed them on December 25. The trial and punishment had occurred more quickly than most had expected, because it was necessary to undercut the morale of the Securitate forces to discourage their continued fighting.

Meanwhile, with Ceausescu gone, power passed into the hands of the Council of National Salvation, which consisted of a variety of Ceausescu's political opponents, including members of the Romanian Communist Party. The new administration of Romania quickly took steps in early 1990 to introduce political relaxation. There was in the next few weeks a deluge of new policies. These included the lifting of censorship; the acceptance of new, noncommunist political organizations demanding a share of power in the government of Romania; the formal abolition of the Romanian Communist Party's political monopoly; and the toleration of new freedoms of speech, assembly, and travel. Romanians were no longer required to register their typewriters, to address one another as "Comrade," and to submit to laws against abortion and the use of birth-control devices. The new government also announced the immediate cancellation of Ceausescu's rural modernization program, which involved the destruction of many villages and the annihilation of much of the country's traditional village life. The new regime also abruptly ended Ceausescu's intolerable program of economic austerity and made available food that had been destined for export. Many food items that had not been seen by Romanian consumers in many years because they were exported abroad, such as fresh fruits and vegetables and high-quality cuts of meat, were diverted and appeared suddenly in grocery stores and butcher shops throughout the country.

In the aftermath of this revolution, there seemed to be three sources of political power. One was the insurgency, a mixture of dissident elements with different ideas about what to do next, ranging from the complete destruction of the old socialist and authoritarian order to less extreme alternatives, which included a role for the Romanian Communist Party, albeit a totally reformed one under a pragmatic leadership sympathetic to a thorough perestroika-like overhaul of the Romanian system.

A second source of political power was the party, or what was left of it following the removal of a large number of officials closely associated with Ceausescu. The party was totally discredited in the eyes of most Romanians. They began calling for its dissolution, because of the excesses of its former leader. These calls intensified as a result of new revelations of the shocking personal corruption of the Ceausescu family, who apparently lived in a grotesque luxury while the rest of the country suffered miserably from acute and persistent shortages of everything. The party, nevertheless, angled to preserve some role in the future governance of Romania. It had a reasonable chance of achieving this goal, because of its experience and the lack of any real alternative to it.

Third, there was the army, now the most powerful physical force in the country. For the time being it supported the Council of National Salvation and a program of radical reform of the Ceausescu order. However, it would not stand idly by if law and order broke down and the country sunk into anarchy because of the Council's lack of authority. A military dictatorship that conceivably might lead eventually to a monarchical restoration was always possible—King Michael, the last sovereign of Romania, who left the county in 1948, even offered to return home to lead his people.

The timing of Ceausescu's collapse was partly the result of Gorbachev's policy of noninterference. But other, equally important, determinants of the rapidity of change in Romania in December 1989 concerned the internal situation. In no other Soviet Bloc country was the socialist regime more irrationally oppressive than in Romania. As a result of the excesses of the Ceausescu regime, there was a latent popular desperation, perhaps unequaled in its depth and severity elsewhere in Central/Eastern Europe. Consequently, the regime had almost no margin for error: one slip was all that was needed to provoke an explosion of popular wrath capable of destroying the system, despite its impressive defense mechanisms. Finally, there was the logical but unanticipated role of the Romanian Army, bent on retribution

for the discriminatory policies of the Ceausescu regime; it called to mind the efforts of German officers in July 1944 to get rid of Hitler, because of a pent-up desperation over his irrational policies and of the favoritism he showed the SS, the Nazi equivalent of the Securitate.

GROPING FOR DEMOCRACY

Many Romanians distrusted and disliked the National Salvation Front and its chief executive, President Ion Iliescu. In mid-January 1990 Bucharest crowds demanded the resignation of both Iliescu and the prime minister as well as the immediate banning of the Romanian Communist Party. The NSF Council voted to ban the party but spoke of a Romanian "brand" of democratic development different from that of "outmoded Western democracies." Maintaining a strong grip over the mass media, the NSF obstructed free and vigorous political criticism. Independent newspapers and magazines had difficulty in getting newsprint supplies and making distribution arrangements. Opposition parties also had problems: they could not get office equipment or space. Some opposition politicians complained of harassment by security forces.

But in the face of the almost daily antigovernment demonstrations in Bucharest, the Iliescu leadership consented to share power with other opposition groups in a coalition. The NSF Council of 145 members was replaced by a new Council for National Unity of 180, representing the NSF and the 30-odd opposition groups. The NSF itself split into two sections, one concerned with administration and made up of the Council leaders governing the country, and another concerned with developing a new political party with candidates in the upcoming parliamentary elections, scheduled for the spring of 1990.

The May 1990 Parliamentary Elections

Popular hostility to the Iliescu regime did not abate. At the end of April some 40,000 people in Timisoara, the cradle of the anti-Ceausescu revolution, demanded Iliescu's resignation, accusing him of seeking to reestablish some form of communism in Romania. As the election drew near the mood became bitter and divisive. The central issue in the elections—the first free elections in 40 years—was the credibility of the NSF and its leadership. Romanian voters were split between those who supported the Front, mainly industrial workers, miners, and similar wage-earning groups, and those who opposed

the Front, from the same sectors of society as well as from the student and professional intelligentsia.

The outcome of the elections was a disappointment for reformers. The Front won about two-thirds of the vote, a strong showing, even allowing for some high-handed, quasi-legal pressure tactics by the NSF to get out the vote in support of it. Perhaps the vote also reflected a greater popular concern for stability than for democracy and the success of the Front as well as Iliescu in exploiting a strong anti-intellectual bias among working-class Romanians. Ordinary people, Iliescu said, should keep the intelligentsia from power, because these privileged city people were rich and educated and unjustly looked down on them. This rhetoric called up the kind of radical-populist appeal made by Fascists in Romania in the pre–World War II period. Many wondered if Romania, despite its Marxist interlude, had ever lost its Fascist orientation.

Explosions of popular wrath continued after the elections. Many Romanians were furious over what appeared to many to be an artful manipulation of the new political system by Communists. It was now common knowledge that the Front's list of parliamentary candidates for the recent election had included many of the former regime's regional Communist party bosses and several former close associates of the late Ceausescu. In what was, perhaps, the worst episode of repression since taking office, the Iliescu regime called miners in northern Romania to Bucharest to help the government put down the demonstrations. About 7,000 miners, among the most hard-pressed of economic groups in Romanian society and most supportive of Iliescu, whom they hoped would do something to improve their lot, mercilessly beat down and bloodied the demonstrators, bringing what seemed to be an incipient coup d'etat against Iliescu to an end.

Prospects for Democratic Development

Opposition groups in Romania eventually began to grasp the weakness of their situation: they had been continually bested in their confrontation with Iliescu, especially in the elections, because of deep internal divisions which deprived them of leadership, cohesion, and unity. The opposition seemed willing to compromise and unify around one party, the Civic Alliance (PCA), which, in July 1991, pledged to transform itself into a national political party to challenge the Front in the next parliamentary elections, tentatively slated for June 1992.

The Alliance claims several million backers and is supported by the largest-selling antigovernment daily, *Romana Libera*. The Alliance in fact may signal a watershed in the political development of post-Communist Romania. Its leadership is drawn from the intelligentsia and consists of university rectors, medical doctors, trade-union leaders, lawyers, student activists, and artists. The young age of the leadership is indicative of the PCA's determination to represent young Romanians. And the party leader, Nicolae Manolescu, seems to have no ties to the discredited Communist party past. Furthermore, the Alliance supports ties to the Western democracies and the protection of minorities and thus rejects the racist nationalism that seems to inspire other Romanian political groups, including the Front. It favors an independent media and strict control over the secret police. It champions a free-market economy and substantial investment in the service industries.

Meanwhile, popular opposition to the NSF government persisted throughout 1991. In September 1991 aggrieved miners were back in Bucharest. This time they opposed the regime, blaming Iliescu and Prime Minister Roman for the persistence of inflation, food shortages, and unemployment. Despite sharp class differences between the miners and the residents of Bucharest, there was an apparent solidarity between the two constituencies. This time the din was so loud, the demands so compelling, and the violence so threatening of anarchy—thousands of protesters of all persuasions and backgrounds penetrated the Parliament and firebombed the main television center—that Roman at last agreed to step down. He was succeeded by Theodor Stolojan, a former Finance minister who announced in early October that he intended to continue Roman's economic-reform program but would try to make adjustments to quiet social discontent. He indicated his determination to stay with his predecessor's price hikes but said that he would allow some wage increments.

The miners have now become a visible and vigorous political force in the country. Their political impulse comes from a notion that the country owes them a debt for the harshness of their daily existence and from their view that life is no better now than it was under Ceausescu, despite all the promises of improvement. They seem to have little understanding of or interest in democracy. Indeed, they see the myriad of political parties that Romania adopted after Ceausescu as little more than anarchy. The miners want relief from the austerity policies that accompanied the introduction of a market-driven economy; some frankly acknowledged that all they had demonstrated for was some additional pay to improve their living standard, rather than the fall of Roman. Not surprisingly, therefore, economics as much as politics continues to destabilize post-Communist Romania.

ECONOMIC REFORM

The Romanian economy remains in desperate straits. Ordinary Romanian citizens live in hardship. There is no poultry, no wine, no beer, little bread, and not very much meat in the stores. Sugar rationing limits each citizen to 2.2 pounds a month, while gasoline lines for scarce automobiles can stretch for 2 miles. There are shortages of other commodities, from shoelaces to matches. In farmers' markets, prices are sky-high. There are hardly any light bulbs in Bucharest, which means that at night homes and stores are almost dark, adding to the city's general dinginess and contributing to the pervasive mental depression.

The Iliescu regime has made a reluctant decision to introduce market forces and private enterprise, changes that in the short term have tended to worsen rather than improve living conditions. In February 1990 the regime allowed private businesses with up to 20 employees. Then it opted for a completely free economic system, on the assumption that a centralized sector could not coexist with a free sector and that economic life had to be in one camp or another. But privatization has led to an increase of prices without an adequate expansion of supply, because, as Roman pointed out in October 1990, private enterprise in Romania has remained small, with investors starting up businesses simply to exploit shortages to earn quick profits, after which they close down and liquidate.

Private enterprise in agriculture, however, has been a bit more successful than in the manufacture and retailing of durable goods. In 1990 the regime distributed leaseholds to farmers amounting to almost one-third of the country's arable land, a stunning departure from the nearly 100 percent collectivized agricultural system left by Ceausescu. Romanian farmers showed some initiative and persistence and managed to increase the supply of meat and fresh produce in the unregulated farmers' markets. But prices of commodities in private markets were much higher than in state stores, which remain almost empty because of pent-up demand. Indeed, the sharp increase in prices for staples like bread, eggs, and meat led the regime, beginning in April 1991, to provide compensatory cash handouts and to allow wage increases. By the beginning of 1992, a year after the reform law redistributing land had been in effect, however, there were serious problems in Romanian agriculture. Although agricultural cooperatives ceased to exist as of January 1, 1992, the overwhelming part of Romanian agriculture was unaffected, with most farmers still landless, still only employees of the former collective farms, now called "agricultural associations," and still under management that consisted primarily of ex-Communists who were enriching themselves at everybody else's expense. The government had failed to provide the farmers with the wherewithal not only to buy but also to cultivate the land they were supposed to obtain. There was no farm machinery for them—what there was belonged to the associations—and no gasoline to run the machinery, even if the would-be free farmers had had such machinery. In sum, the reform turned out to be only a beginning of private farming, with little of the follow-up needed to develop an efficient farm sector capable of feeding the country.

SEVERE SOCIAL PROBLEMS

In the post-Communist era Romania confronts serious social problems inherited from the Ceausescu era, when they were all but swept under the rug by a socialist society that said it was perfect, or, at least, superior to the societies of the capitalist world. Primary social problems have to do with ethnic minorities and AIDS.

Renewed Conflict Between Hungarians and Romanians

Ethnic conflict is quite serious. Romanians in Transylvania distrust the Hungarian majority there. In the immediate aftermath of the December 1989 Revolution, the Romanians in Transylvania mobilized for resistance to demands of the region's Hungarian population for cultural autonomy. They set up an organization, called Vatra Romaneascea, or Romanian Hearth, committed to the perpetuation of Romanian cultural hegemony in Transylvania. The organization is highly nationalistic, somewhat right-wing in its political thinking, and reminiscent of the chauvinistic and Fascist groups that sprung up in Romania on the eve of World War II. The danger in this organization lies in its ability to encourage and support physical violence by ethnic Romanians against their Hungarian neighbors. Evi-

Independence 1878	Romania joins the Nazi invasion of Soviet Union and recovers Bessarabia 1941	Romania loses Bessarabia to the Soviet Union and pays war reparations 1944	Soviet troops enter Bucharest to force King Michael to include Communists in his government 1945	The Soviets withdraw their occupation forces from Romania 1958

dence of their disruptive power occurred in late March 1990 in Tirgu Mures. Crowds of angry Romanian peasants attacked Hungarians with clubs and sticks, sending many to the hospital, and shattered the windows of stores owned by people with Hungarian names. The conflict shows no signs of abating, and many Hungarians hope for an eventual union of their region with Hungary.

Resurgent Hostility Toward Jews and Gypsies
Anti-Semitism is also on the rise. A gutter press spews hatred against all minorities, especially Jews. When, in what should have been a redemptive gesture, Romania dedicated in the early summer of 1991 a memorial in Bucharest to the 400,000 Jews who fell victim to the local Fascist regime during World War II, people commenced with an ugly taunting of Elie Wiesel, a Nobel laureate who survived the pogroms in Transylvania. Meanwhile, the Romanian Parliament rehabilitated Ion Antonescu, the Romanian ally of the Nazis who initiated the mass killings of Romanian Jews in the World War II era. While the rehabilitation of Antonescu, who was executed on orders of the Soviets at the end of the war, may have been intended as a gesture of independence of Moscow by the new Romanian leadership, it is also possible that Parliament showed its lingering antipathy toward Jews in Romanian society. The Iliescu regime took no steps publicly to condemn Antonescu's Fascist beliefs or his blatant anti-Semitism.

Worse off than the Jews in Romania today is the very small minority of Gypsies. Romanians have accused the Gypsies of black marketeering, saying that this is causing the shortages and high prices in Bucharest. Anti-Gypsy sentiment has erupted in pogroms, characterized by collective attacks by ethnic Romanians on rural communities inhabited by Gypsies. Local administrative authorities do little to punish the aggressors, thereby encouraging them. The failure to provide security of life and property to the Gypsy population may have a sinister motive: to make living in the country as uncomfortable as possible, thereby to encourage the emigration of Gypsies to other countries and to preserve "racial purity."

The AIDS Epidemic
Of all the legacies of the Ceausescu era, the epidemic of AIDS among newly born Romanian children may be the most grim. According to statistics gathered by Romanian virologists and confirmed by French doctors, Romania has a pediatric epidemic of AIDS, concentrated in crowded orphanages and clinics, which was spread by an old-fashioned practice of giving blood transfusions to newborn infants. This was compounded by poor equipment, bad medical practices, and large numbers of abandoned children born as a consequence of the prohibition of birth-control devices and of abortion by the Ceausescu regime, which had been eager to swell the population of Romania. Hard evidence about AIDS among Romanian children was first reported only in June 1989, as a result of random testing for other viruses. When the investigating doctors reported their findings to the central Ministry of Health in Bucharest, they were told bluntly to stop testing. They ignored this instruction and continued their investigation at different hospitals in the country; eventually they discovered that children with untreatable AIDS-related infections were everywhere in the hospital system. The new post-Communist leadership of Romania, hampered by a continuing shortage of equipment and a sluggish bureaucracy, never mind chronic instability and severe economic stagnation, has made scant progress in fighting AIDS.

FOREIGN RELATIONS IN THE POST-COMMUNIST ERA

The new Romanian leadership looked to the Soviet Union for security and stability. Although relations with the Soviets had been poor, they improved as soon as the Ceausescu leadership, long an object of Soviet contempt and embarrassment, was deposed. In January 1990 then-Soviet Foreign Minister Eduard Shevardnadze said that he found the new atmosphere in Bucharest "absolutely purifying," and he pledged Moscow's support of any political system that the Romanians should choose. "Whatever political groups lead Romania is the business of Romanians themselves," he said. Nothing has changed since this declaration: the new Commonwealth of Independent States has shown no interest in resuming Soviet-era

influence over Bucharest and seems to want a normal relationship with Romania based on mutual trust and advantage.

But there are problems. One concerns the republic of Moldova. Largely inhabited by people of Romanian culture, Moldova was known historically as Bessarabia and was a part of Romania before 1878, and from 1918 until 1940, when it was ceded under duress to the Soviet Union. The future of Soviet Moldova became an issue with the advent of glasnost and a gradual opening of Moldova's frontier with Romania after Ceausescu's overthrow. For the moment the open border, which has led to free movement of peoples between Moldova and Romania, has been peaceful. But, although in August 1991, following the abortive anti-Gorbachev coup in Moscow, Moldova declared its independence of the Soviet Union, it has not yet raised the issue of a possible transfer of Moldova to Romania, perhaps because of the hardship and misery in Romania. While emotional ties to the Romanian motherland are strong, and while their visits to Romania have been welcome, Moldovans are not yet ready to seek annexation to Romania. Ordinary Moldovans criticize the Romanian government for its communist tendencies, its antidemocratic policies, and its delay in reform. Moldovan Jews are wary of calls for Moldova's reunification with Romania. Moldovan President Mircea Snegur observed that he did not know when a unification with Romania might take place.

Romania is more worried about its economy than about an annexation of Moldova. Romania is dependent on imports of oil and natural gas from the former Soviet Union. In early 1990 the Kremlin pledged to ship 390,000 tons of oil and 22 million cubic meters of natural gas daily to Romania, to support its industrial base and meet the energy needs of its newly expanding consumer market. The Kremlin also agreed at that time that Romania might limit exports of meat and dairy products to the Soviet Union because of its desperate need of these commodities at home.

Romania and the West
In 1990–1991 Romanian relations with the West, especially with the United States,

| Gheorghiu-Dej dies; Ceausescu succeeds **1965** | Romania restores relations with West Germany **1968** | Romania opposes Soviet military intervention in Czechoslovakia **1968** | Ceausescu receives Nixon in Bucharest **1969** | Romania condemns the Soviet invasion of Afghanistan **1979** | Ceausescu opposes Warsaw Pact military intervention in Poland | **1980s–1990s** |

ACHIEVEMENTS

The U.S. Congress votes to suspend most-favored-nation treatment for Romanian trade; Romania later breaks those ties; they are renewed in 1992

In a massive popular and army uprising, the Ceausescu regime is deposed; Ceausescu and his wife are executed

Romania embarks on a new, hopefully better, economic, social, and political path

were strained as a result of the Iliescu government's repressive policies, of its evident Communist background, and of its slowness in moving away from the old socialist political and economic order toward pluralistic democracy and free-enterprise capitalism. The Western powers suspended major aid and cooperation with Romania, and the United States shunned the inauguration of President Iliescu in June 1990, to protest his use of the miners to break up an antigovernment demonstration in Bucharest. In early 1991 Western Europe and the United States brought Romania into an aid program, set up a year earlier, which provided a total of $38 billion in assistance to Romania.

The United States, however, remained skeptical of Romania's commitment to a real break with the Communist past and was reluctant to replicate for Bucharest the assistance programs it had formulated for Poland, Hungary, and Czechoslovakia. Indeed, the apparent shift in Washington's attitude toward Romania in early 1991 may have been merely a one-time reciprocation of Romania's support of the Allies in the Gulf War. While the United States would have liked to have helped Romania develop and maintain independence, Washington declined to offer Bucharest large assistance programs until it made more progress toward democracy, free enterprise, and equitable treatment of its ethnocultural minorities.

In the spring of 1992, however, the official American position on Romania seemed to soften somewhat, partly as a result of local elections held at the end of

February. These were the first free local elections since the Communist takeover after World War II; they resulted in a setback for the ruling NSF. Although NSF candidates won most of the 1,340 mayoral races, candidates of democratic opposition parties won local government posts in the major Romanian cities, including Bucharest, confirming the extensive popular disillusionment with the NSF national leadership, which, to the surprise of Washington and other Western capitals, had done little to prevent the democratic ascendancy. The only negative feature of the elections, from the U.S. point of view, was the success of the extreme right-wing Romanian National Unity Party in the Transylvanian city of Cluj, which is inhabited by a large Hungarian ethnic minority, because it favors a tough national response to the Hungarian minority's demands for increased cultural autonomy.

Washington acknowledged at the end of March that progress had been made in Romania toward the development of democratic government. The Americans also commended Prime Minister Stolojan for his role in guiding Romania toward a market economy. They were cautiously hoepful that Romania soon would adopt real political pluralism and eventually reject the authoritarian NSF, still dominated by former Communists.

Washington officials were still concerned in early 1992 about lingering vestiges of the old authoritarian order. These were the government's monopoly over television; the absence of parliamentary control over the intelligence service,

which had replaced the Ceausescu's Securitate, had reported directly to President Iliescu, and had been suspected of maintaining a domestic political surveillance program; and continuing violations of human rights, in particular a perceived official tolerance of anti-Semitism.

Nevertheless, U.S. President George Bush and Secretary of State James Baker were inclined to reward and to encourage the new liberal tendencies in Romanian life. The Bush administration therefore agreed to sign a new trade agreement with Romania, again granting it most-favored-nation trade status.

DEVELOPMENT

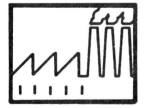

Although the current Romanian government has accelerated economic reform, insisting on financial accountability of state enterprises, the economy is still inefficient and has barely grown since the revolution of 1989. In spite of a 1991 land reform act returning land to dispossessed farmers, little has changed in the countryside.

FREEDOM

Romanians are now free to protest against their government, although their political leaders, especially President Iliescu, remain sensitive to criticism and ready to ban political activity, with force, if necessary. Disgruntled coal miners are becoming an assertive political force in the new, more open political environment.

HEALTH/WELFARE

Despite the extensive system of social welfare, the daily life of average people is miserable. Food stores have empty shelves. In winter the heating goes on only a few hours of the day and all year-round use of lights and other electrical appliances is greatly restricted.

ACHIEVEMENTS

In March 1992 Romanian health-care professionals completed a workshop in management skills at Case Western Reserve University to help them get the Romanian government to upgrade the dilapidated health-care system.

Yugoslavia

GEOGRAPHY

Area in Square Kilometers (Miles):
256,409 (99,000) (about the size of
Wyoming)
Capital (Population): Belgrade
(1,300,000)
Climate: coast: hot in summer, rainy
and mild in winter; inland: warm in
summer, cold in winter

PEOPLE

Population
Total: 23,864,000
Annual Growth Rate: 0.6%
Rural/Urban Population Ratio: 50/50
Ethnic Makeup of Population: 36%
Serb; 20% Croat; 9% Bosnian
Muslim; 8% Slovene; 8% Albanian;
6% Macedonian; 6% Yugoslav; 3%
Montenegrin Serb; 2% Hungarian and
Turk; 2% others

Health
Life Expectancy at Birth: 69 years
(male); 75 years (female)
Infant Mortality Rate (Ratio):
25/1,000

WHITHER YUGOSLAVIA?

The Yugoslav Civil War, which started in the summer of 1991 with federal
military action to suppress separatist movements in Slovenia, Croatia, and, in
the spring of 1992, Bosnia-Herzegovina, has killed more than 10,000 soldiers
and civilians, wrecked one of Central/Eastern Europe's most promising
economies, created a half-million refugees, and stirred enough interethnic
hatred to incite generations of future conflict.

Virtually no one in Yugoslavia believes that Yugoslavia still exists. Citizens,
soldiers, and officials across the country describe national disintegration as
complete. Separate transportation, financial, and communication systems are
beginning to rise from the ruins of the old Yugoslav state. Citizens and
officials alike now frequently refer to "the former Yugoslavia" in their
discussions.

Average Caloric Intake: 144% of FAO
minimum
Physicians Available (Ratio): 1/534

Religion(s)
50% Eastern Orthodox; 30% Roman
Catholic; 10% Muslim; 10% others

Education
Adult Literacy Rate: 90.5%

COMMUNICATION

Telephones: 4,550,000

Newspapers: 28 dailies; 2,100,000
circulation

TRANSPORTATION

Highways—Kilometers (Miles):
73,527 (45,587)
Railroads—Kilometers (Miles): 9,567
(5,981)
Usable Airfields: 184

GOVERNMENT

Type: federated parliamentary
democracy
Independence Date: November 29,
1918
Head of State: Acting President
Branko Kostic
Political Parties: the national political
organizations have given way to many
local, republic-based parties
Suffrage: universal over 18 (16 if
employed)

MILITARY

Number of Armed Forces: 180,000
*Military Expenditures (% of Central
Government Expenditures):* 4.7%
Current Hostilities: internal strife

ECONOMY

Currency ($ U.S. Equivalent): 22.21
new dinars = $1
Per Capita Income/GNP: $2,490/$159
billion
Inflation Rate: 70%
Total Foreign Debt: n/a
Natural Resources: coal; copper;
bauxite; timber; iron; antimony;
chromium; lead; zinc; asbestos;
mercury
Agriculture: corn; wheat; tobacco;
sugar beets; sunflowers; livestock
Industry: metallurgy; machinery and
equipment; chemicals; textiles; oil
refining; wood processing; food
processing

FOREIGN TRADE

Exports: $14.6 billion
Imports: $19.1 billion

*graphic interpretation as of this writing

YUGOSLAVIA

Yugoslavia, a federation of the south Slavic peoples created in 1918, was invaded and occupied by German and Italian forces during World War II. The Yugoslav monarch went into exile, never to return to his country. When the war was over the Yugoslav Communists, under the leadership of Joseph Broz Tito, had achieved military and political dominance. Tito refused to allow a monarchical restoration. Yugoslavia became a republic in 1946.

Unlike most other Central/Eastern European Communist parties, the Yugoslav Communists were a popular political force, because of their resistance to the Fascist enemy during the war. This popularity helped them to sweep the monarch aside, eliminate political opposition, and establish a Soviet-style dictatorship by 1947.

Tito's biggest problem in the immediate postwar period—a problem that still characterizes Yugoslavia—was assuring the loyalty of the different ethnic groups that comprise Yugoslavia's multinational society. In the early years of Communist rule, however, Tito's personal popularity, which had been reinforced by his successful resistance to Soviet pressures, was sufficient to guarantee a national unity needed to begin the transformation of the country to socialism. By 1953 Yugoslavia was a socialist dictatorship that in many ways resembled, but was in no way subservient to, the Soviet Union. It was not a Soviet satellite.

Yugoslav socialism tried to achieve three objectives: to foster societal harmony and national unity; to expand agricultural and industrial output in order to raise the standard of living of Yugoslav society; and to maintain ties with, but independence of, the Soviet and Western blocs. The achievement of these objectives was essential to the long-term stability and legitimacy of socialist regimes in Yugoslavia.

INTERETHNIC TENSIONS

The Yugoslav Communists inherited from their conservative monarchical predecessor a deeply divided, conflict-ridden multinational society. The dimensions of this ethnocultural and linguistic diversity were impressive. In the northern part of Yugoslavia were the Croats and the Slovenes, who belonged to the old Austro-Hungarian Empire that collapsed in World War I. They were the most economically developed of all the Yugoslav peoples and were predominantly Catholic. In the cen-

ter of the country were Serbs, the first Balkan people to emancipate themselves from Turkish rule, in 1828. The Serbs were the largest ethnic group in Yugoslavia, the most politically experienced of the Yugoslav peoples, and nominally of the Eastern Orthodox faith. In the south were other, smaller ethnic groups, Bosnians, Macedonians, Montenegrins, and Albanians, who were among the last to achieve independence of the Turks and who were less economically developed than the peoples in the north.

Conflict among these groups was historic and continued through World War II. It seemed to subside in the early years of Tito's leadership, because of his national popularity. But in the 1960s and 1970s there was a resurgence of interethnic hostility. This was largely in consequence of the sharp disparity in levels of material well-being among the different national groups. In the north, the Croats and Slovenes and some Serbs were—and remain—much better off than the peoples in the south, many of whom were dreadfully poor.

The Albanians living in Kosovo, a self-governing province in the Serbian republic, were another source of interethnic tension. The Albanians, 75 percent of Kosovo's population, lobbied aggressively for the status of self-governing republic, like that of the Serbs. The Albanians also resented other, smaller ethnic groups in Kosovo, a resentment fueled by economic poverty—Kosovo had the highest unemployment rate, the lowest per capita income, and the highest birth rate of all the regions in Yugoslavia.

The Albanians used violence against Serb and Montenegrin minorities living in Kosovo, who in turn carried out their own counterprotests and demanded additional protection by the local authorities, who were predominantly Albanian. The Albanians seemed bent on forcing the Serbs and other non-Albanian groups to leave the province and to get republic status within the Yugoslav federation. While they did not appear interested in joining their cousins in the neighboring Albanian republic, which covertly encouraged the ferment in Kosovo, Yugoslavia's Albanian minority shared much in common with the independent Albanian state, in its political conservatism, economic backwardness, and cultural parochialism.

Yugoslav authorities in Belgrade worried that the bitter ethnic feuding in Kosovo would eventually lead to the emigration of all non-Albanian peoples from the province. Since 1981 more than 10 percent of the Serb population of Kosovo have emigrated.

In 1988 and 1989 there were new outbreaks of ethnocultural conflict between Albanians and Serbs in Kosovo, because of a depressed standard of living; and because of a campaign by the Albanian majority to harass Serb residents, especially in Pristina, the capital of the province, as well as in the surrounding countryside, by acts of terrorism intended to force their flight from the province. Indeed, the local Albanian law-enforcement authorities in Kosovo did little to protect the Serbs, and the Serb republic authorities in Belgrade could not interfere with the province's autonomy.

Under these circumstances, Serb resentment of the Albanians in Kosovo steadily mounted. The Serb minority looked for help to the Serb party and state authorities and to their charismatic leader, Slobadan Milosevic, an aggressive exponent of Serb nationalism. He expressed concern over the plight of Serbs living among the Albanian population in Kosovo and encouraged huge pro-Serb, anti-Albanian rallies throughout the Serb republic. He supported a change in the Serb Constitution to increase the republic government's authority over the autonomous provinces of Kosovo and Vojvodina, and he replaced local political leaders in Kosovo and elsewhere in Serbia opposed to his policies. He wanted to establish Serb control of the police, court system, and civil defense of both Kosovo and Vojvodina, thereby lessening their autonomy; and in the case of Kosovo to prevent the provincial Albanian authorities from condoning the violence against the Serb minority.

In March 1989, in response to these efforts, there was an explosion of Albanian wrath. Tens of thousands of Albanians struck in Pristina, and other Albanians went on a rampage against Serbs, wreaking havoc by murder, rape, theft, and wanton vandalism. This episode turned out to be a personal political boon for Milosevic, increasing his popularity and the appeal of his calls for reform. By the summer of 1989 he had become the most powerful republic-level politician in Yugoslavia and an obvious candidate for national leadership.

Still another dimension of the nationalities problem in Yugoslavia involved the wealthy republic of Slovenia, which had the highest standard of living in the country and resented having to share its wealth with the much less developed southern republics, notably Bosnia-Herzegovina, Macedonia, and Montenegro. Slovenes make up only 8 percent of the Yugoslav population, but their republic produces 18 percent of Yugoslav gross national product and 25 percent of the country's exports that earn hard currency in the West.

While they did not immediately advocate separatism, the Slovenes wanted more independence of the central authorities in Belgrade, less official interference in the economic life of the country, and the opportunity to keep within Slovenia the wealth it generated—in short, a Yugoslav version of Soviet perestroika. These Slovenian ambitions illustrated in still another way how the rich-poor split of republics in Yugoslavia not only undermined its fragile national unity but also challenged its orthodox socialist system.

EFFORTS TO ACHIEVE SOCIAL HARMONY AND POLITICAL UNITY

To maintain the loyalty of Yugoslavia's ethnic groups to the socialist system and thereby assure political stability and administrative unity once he was gone, Tito and his successors modified the central government in Belgrade in the 1970s and early 1980s. The objectives were to provide equitable representation of the major ethnic groups and adequate means of reconciling policy differences among them.

The changes included a new head of state consisting of nine persons, one from each of the country's six constituent republics and the two autonomous provinces, and one *ex-officio* member. A chair of this executive was to be elected annually on a rotational basis.

Ministerial leadership continued to be in the hands of the Federal Executive Council, or Cabinet. This body was the real source of day-to-day governmental administration of the country, rather than the presidency, which was concerned primarily with ceremonial responsibilities. The Federal Executive Council was constructed to assure equitable representation of the different ethnic groups.

The Yugoslav national Legislature as well was organized to provide equitable representation of the national groups. Its upper house, called the Chamber of the Republics, consisted of members of the legislatures of the various republics and autonomous provinces.

Tito also made changes in the Yugoslav Communist Party. In 1952 the party was renamed the League of Yugoslav Communists, to stress its federative and collective character and to assure members of different ethnic backgrounds that the party would not try to destroy their cultural identities. Along with the change in name was a decentralization of authority. Leaders of republic-level party agencies dominated the central organs of the party in Bel-

grade. Representation in those central organs was apportioned equitably among the ethnic groups of Yugoslavia.

While these changes contributed to the development of some interethnic harmony in state and party agencies at the center, they at the same time contributed to divisiveness and conflict, especially within the party. The diffusion of power worked against cohesiveness in the party and encouraged competitiveness between republic-level party leaders, thereby weakening the party's leadership role in Yugoslav society.

ATTEMPTS AT PARTICIPATORY DEMOCRACY

The post-Tito leadership tried in the 1980s to increase participatory democracy in Yugoslavia without inducing pluralism and a threat to the Communist party's monopoly of power. A new and complex process of electing members of the Federal Assembly in Belgrade was supposed to stimulate popular interest in self-government. The process started with ordinary voters nominating delegates to communal assemblies, who nominated members of republic-level assemblies, who in turn selected the membership of the Federal Assembly.

Yugoslav voters showed little interest in this cumbersome procedure. The system still left them little choice in the determination of candidates, who continued to be hand-picked and approved by Communist authorities. At the same time the Assembly lacked the kind of authority in policy-making enjoyed by legislatures in Western democracies and therefore did not inspire much popular interest.

The Yugoslav national leadership continued to insist on political conformity and severely limited expression of criticism, protest, and dissent. Milovan Djilas, an eminent and perennial regime critic, was still in some ways treated as a nonperson (he did, however, receive a passport in 1987), and the leadership still feared the ideas he had presented in his *New Class* more than 30 years ago. Indeed, the establishment of Western-style political freedoms and of a multiparty system were forbidden topics of public discussion in the late 1980s, even in places like Slovenia, which was more politically tolerant than the other republics.

The elevation to the federal prime ministership in 1987 of Branko Mikulic, a hard-liner known for his criticism of internal dissidence, affirmed the Communist party's determination to enforce a somewhat neo-Stalinistic political conformity throughout Yugoslav society. The conser-

vatism of past Yugoslav leaders on the issue of political expression—which was at odds with their efforts to generate popular interest in government elections—was a result of the country's ethnic diversity, of a fear that toleration of pluralism would encourage ethnic particularism and national disunity, and of the problem of containing pressures for political liberalization that could challenge the Communist party's control of the country.

ECONOMIC REFORMS

Starting in the 1950s Tito introduced substantial decentralization and democratization of the Yugoslav economy in order to increase productivity. The Communist leadership returned some farms to private ownership. Today the private sector predominates in Yugoslav agriculture. Private farms eventually had 83 percent of the country's cultivable land and 88 percent of its livestock.

In the 1960s the Yugoslav leadership reformed industrial management by increasing the autonomy of plant-level managers and diminishing the power of central administrators and planners. Yugoslav industrial production also took into account market forces, and prices were responsive to supply and demand. While there was a state planning agency in Belgrade that continued to draw up a national plan, production goals were determined by republic-level planning agencies, with the national agency serving primarily as a coordinator. These changes had a drastic impact on Yugoslav economic and social life, beginning in the late 1950s and early 1960s. Enterprises produced what would sell and improved the quality of their output. The economy became more consumer-oriented.

The establishment of Workers' Councils was the most controversial of Yugoslav economic reforms. The councils gave workers an opportunity to participate in managerial decision-making and to share responsibility for running factories. In theory, at least, workers were entitled to help determine wages, plant renewal, and production rules.

A growing indebtedness to the West, beginning in the 1970s, and the appearance of recession in the early 1980s made it difficult to judge the effectiveness of the economic reforms. There were no startling increases in Yugoslav agricultural and industrial output. At the same time unemployment climbed, while prices rose, partly because of low labor productivity and the increase in energy costs.

While the concept of the Workers' Councils was very attractive, because it

((Un photo/Philip Teuscher)

The Yugoslav economy confronts many necessary changes that stretch the limits of the socialist economic system. Many Yugoslav officials are considering the value of private enterprise in order to stimulate personal initiative as a means of increasing national productivity. These farmers selling their produce at a market in Sarajevo typify this movement.

derived from Marxist ideas of direct worker ownership of the means of production, it remained controversial. It was criticized inside Yugoslavia on the grounds that it fostered individualism, competed with and undermined party rule, and increased anarchy in an already conflict-ridden society. Worse, it contributed to the development of a privileged class in a society that was supposed to be working to eliminate such distinctions.

Moreover, it became clear that self-managed enterprises had not worked as they were supposed to. They were unable to cut wages to the minimum to increase profit and had difficulty liquidating themselves, as required by law, when they were on the verge of bankruptcy. It would appear also that some workers in managerial positions often were not good decision-makers.

By the late 1980s inflation had become the country's number-one problem. In 1987 the Yugoslav economy had $21 billion of debt to the West; inflation was running at more than 200 percent; and 1 million, or 15 percent of Yugoslav working people, were unemployed. Yugoslavia was suffering from the same kind of slow-down that afflicted almost all other Soviet Bloc countries in the 1980s. It was attributable to a stagnant economy which desperately needed restructuring of the kind started by the Soviet Union, Poland, and Hungary in the late 1980s.

The galloping inflation seemed to defy economic solutions and forced the conclusion among party officials that the cause lay in the system of Yugoslav socialism itself. In the system, Workers' Councils voted wage increases at the expense of investment. In addition, the monopoly status of many firms enabled them to fix prices at artificially high levels to justify the wage hikes voted by workers. Finally, cost-cutting measures to increase profitability, such as layoffs of unneeded and uneconomic labor, were unacceptable, because Yugoslav socialism was committed to full employment. A draconian program of quick-fix wage and price controls in November 1987 hardly made a dent in the inflationary spiral.

In May 1988 the central authorities in Belgrade adopted another austerity plan on the prodding of the International Monetary Fund as a precondition for a $430 million loan. They imposed new wage ceilings and spending cuts while allowing prices to float upward. Living conditions for many Yugoslav citizens sharply deteriorated as earning capacity declined. Food shortages became so severe by October that the Belgrade government finally eased the austerity program and agreed to import emergency food.

While official economists, political leaders, and Yugoslavia's Western creditors all agreed that it was necessary to expand output by reliance on market forces, to close many unprofitable concerns, and to reduce substantially state control over the economic life of the country, the central leadership of the Communist party, despite much discussion in 1988 and early 1989, were unable to agree on any decisive action. They could not depart from traditional orthodox socialist practices and were unable to goad a conservative bureaucracy to implement changes that inevitably would lead to a loss of jobs and a lessening of its influence and power over the country's economic life.

The country's leaders also feared the destabilizing effects of strict application of laws providing for bankruptcy and the closing of unprofitable enterprises. Like Communist authorities elsewhere in Central/Eastern Europe, Yugoslav officials hesitated to put an uneconomic enterprise out of business and cause the dismissal of thousands of workers.

The new Yugoslav premier, Ante Markovic, in a televised address in January 1989, acknowledged the failure of socialism in its approach to the market and promised substantial curtailment of state interference in business. He promised to allow currency, prices, wages, and interest rates to move freely. And he spoke about opening the Yugoslav market to competition from imports and of inviting new foreign investment. Even Serbian leader Milosevic supported the application of market forces to Yugoslavia, allying him with many of his detractors, including the Slovene leadership.

But by the end of 1989 the Yugoslav economy confronted four major problems that hampered growth and the achievement of improved living conditions: 1) the need to spend 44 percent of precious foreign currency to service a staggering foreign debt; 2) rising inflation and declining exports, which complicated debt repayment; 3) a 14 percent unemployment rate; and 4) the continuing and unequitable division of the country into two economic spheres—one developed and relatively well off (in the north), and the other underdeveloped and poor (in the south). Having reached the outer limits of change in the Yugoslav socialist economy, some Yugoslav officials wondered whether the time had come to introduce a substantial private enterprise and lessen party and state control of the economy in order to stimulate personal initiative as a means of increasing national productivity.

FOREIGN POLICY

Perhaps the most important foreign-policy objective of the Yugoslav state since World War II was independence of the Soviet Union. Throughout his period of leadership, Tito successfully resisted Soviet efforts to limit his independent foreign policy. A conflict with Stalin in 1948 merely strengthened Tito's resolve to go his own way in domestic and foreign policy. He opposed Soviet efforts in the early 1960s to isolate China and to force other socialist countries, notably Czechoslovakia in 1968, to follow the Soviet line. Tito steadfastly refused to bring Yugoslavia into the Warsaw Pact and the CMEA, although in 1964 he sought and received for Yugoslavia affiliated status with the CMEA in order to facilitate trade with its members.

In the 1970s Yugoslavia diverged sharply from the Soviets on several matters. Following Mao's death in 1976, Tito undertook an improvement in relations with China. The Yugoslav leadership condemned the Soviet invasion of Afghanistan in 1979 and opposed the Soviets intervening in Poland in 1980 and 1981.

Yugoslav relations with the Soviet Union improved substantially in the late 1980s, mainly because Mikhail Gorbachev favored the autonomy of socialist countries. In March 1988 Gorbachev went to Dubrovnik, on Yugoslavia's Adriatic coast, to conclude a joint declaration in effect ruling out future Soviet interventions in Central/Eastern Europe. The declaration, intended to reaffirm Soviet adherence to agreements concluded in 1955 and 1956 establishing Yugoslavia's independence of Moscow, said that the two Communist party-ruled countries had no pretensions of imposing their concepts of socialist development on anyone.

Although the Yugoslavs had not sought this declaration, which was the result of Soviet initiative, they did benefit from accommodating Gorbachev's request for it. By specifically acknowledging and thereby endorsing Yugoslav self-management policies—which, incidentally, the Soviets were beginning to copy—the declaration removed from the sphere of interstate relations an aspect of the Yugoslav reform program of which the Kremlin had been skeptical. The declaration seemed to imply that henceforth the Kremlin would not make an issue in diplomatic relations with Belgrade of advanced Yugoslav domestic reforms or radical foreign-policy initiatives.

Yugoslavia also pursued a separate and independent policy toward the Third World. While sharing Soviet sympathy for revolutionary movements and left-leaning governments, it supported the policies of neutralism and nonalignment of Third World countries.

The Yugoslavs, however, began to reassess their leadership role in the nonaligned movement with the decline of the East-West rivalry. At the meeting of the nonaligned countries in Belgrade in September 1989, the Yugoslav delegates were somewhat embarrassed over the West-bashing of delegates from Libya and Cuba. Yugoslavia increasingly looked to the West for stronger economic and political ties and therefore was no longer as interested in occupying a middle position.

Yugoslavia also wanted to improve ties with Israel as a means of broadening its influence in the Middle East. Yugoslav and Israeli officials met in 1986, and Belgrade reportedly hosted secret Palestine Liberation Organization–Israeli meetings. Perhaps Yugoslavia planned to assume the role of peacemaker in the Middle East and in that way strengthen its influence with wealthy Arab states, which could provide some economic assistance.

Yugoslavia avoided the harsh and often belligerent anti-West rhetoric of the Soviet Union and its Warsaw Pact allies and, rather, worked to improve political and economic ties with Western countries. The Belgrade government showed an interest in joining the European Community.

Major issues in the late 1980s in Yugoslavia's relations with the West were a rescheduling of the country's huge debt and an expansion of joint ventures. The Yugoslav government desperately needed help from the West. As mentioned earlier, it worked closely with the IMF in 1988 to meet its stiff demands of internal spending cuts and other austerity measures in return for a loan.

Yugoslavia and the United States

The Yugoslav leadership went out of its way to cultivate good relations with the United States. Yugoslav leaders saw political ties with the United States as a counterweight to Soviet efforts to move Yugoslavia into the Warsaw Pact. Good relations with the United States were important to Yugoslavia's continuing independence of Moscow and its Central/Eastern European allies.

An equally important objective of Yugoslav policy toward the United States was American economic assistance. In recent years Yugoslav leaders had found Washington sympathetic to their requests for help and willing to make generous offers of financial aid, despite ideological differences between the two countries.

The United States wanted to encourage Yugoslav independence, not only because of its importance to the security of Yugoslavia's noncommunist neighbors, Italy and Greece, but also because it contributed to the peace and tranquillity of the entire Mediterranean region. Moreover, a weakening and ultimate subversion of Yugoslavia by the Kremlin, never mind the disintegration of the Yugoslav state in consequence of civil war or economic collapse, would upset the strategic balance in Europe, to the detriment of NATO and American security.

The Impact of the Central/Eastern European Upheavals in 1989

The collapse of Communist party rule elsewhere in Central/Eastern Europe, as well as Lithuania's movement toward independence of the Soviet Union in late 1989 and early 1990, contributed to a restiveness in Yugoslavia's northern republics of Croatia and Slovenia, where there had been much internal pressure for liberalization and independence. The Slovenes in particular were more eager than ever before to abandon communism; to achieve sovereignty over their national life; and to strengthen political, economic, and cultural ties with Western Europe. Slovenian citizens complained that their wealth was being drained by the demands of the impoverished south of the country. (In 1989 the annual per capita income in Slovenia was the equivalent of $5,700, vs. $2,500 for Yugoslavia as a whole and $750 for the province of Kosovo.) They resented the loss of 11 percent of their total earnings to the central government in Belgrade for economic policies they opposed and for an army that defended the communist way of life, which they disliked and sought to reject.

Slovenia, always more tolerant than the other republics of political discussion and

criticism, allowed in February 1989 the establishment of two new political organizations that contested the Communist party's monopoly of power in Slovenia. In December 1989 Croatia expressed support of a pluralist system. Addressing the Croatian party Congress in Zagreb, party leader Stanko Stojecevic called for freedom of expression and association and early elections for a new federal Parliament. There was a strong Slovenian-Croatian entente in support of democratization of the Yugoslav national government in Belgrade as the only real way of assuring the continued unity of the country.

Serbia, too, showed some interest in political liberalization. In 1987 a Serb presidential commission, under the direction of Milosevic, proposed changes in the Yugoslav Constitution limiting the Communist party's monopoly of power, although not providing for the establishment of opposition parties. The proposals called for a transformation of the Communist party-dominated socialist alliance into a pluralistic entity that would welcome all shades of opinion, for an end to party control of nominations of candidates in elections to legislative bodies, and for the institution of direct and secret elections. The Commission also urged abolition of restrictions on speech and on political criticism throughout Yugoslavia as well as guarantees of freedom of thought and association.

The Serb proposals, however, were less radical than they appeared. The commission did not recommend a multiparty system; it reaffirmed the country's commitment to socialism; and it supported Communist party rule. The commission insisted that the Communist party play a necessary integrative role in what were described as the conditions of political and economic disintegration of society existing in Yugoslavia.

In early 1990 Croatia and Slovenia accused the conservative Serb leadership of seeking to destroy Yugoslavia by its perceived political conservatism, which was running against the tide of change elsewhere in Central/Eastern Europe—the Serbs wanted to preserve the Communist party's leadership monopoly to control the federation. In response, the Serb republic government broke off all economic relations with Slovenia. However, it was unable to block the national party leadership's approval of a recommendation in January 1990 to the upcoming party Congress to allow other political parties to compete in parliamentary elections.

On January 20, 1990, the Yugoslav League of Communists met for the 14th Congress in Belgrade to address the new

shape of Yugoslav government. Trouble began when the Congress opposed a transition from the old Yugoslav federal and socialist system to a federative, pluralistic, and democratic version. Serbia wanted to preserve the old Union of the Tito era; Slovenia and Croatia preferred a loose confederation, with the constituent republics and provinces largely autonomous in fiscal, monetary, and defense matters. In addition, liberals from Slovenia wanted the establishment of political pluralism and democracy in both the federal government and in party organizations; while conservatives, led by Serb party leader and President Milosevic, opposed liberalization. Milosevic believed that centralism could revitalize the party. He also had in mind his own elevation to the party leadership, with the support of the Serb republic delegation and the delegations from Vojvodina, Kosovo, and Montenegro to unify the country and restore a measure of discipline to Yugoslav society. This bid to preserve Communist power failed, and the Congress rejected Milosevic's schemes for an internal strengthening of the party under his leadership. Indeed, the Congress voted to end the party's monopoly of power. Nothing else was resolved because, when it failed to get an agreement on the confederative type of union or democratization, the Slovene delegation walked out of the Congress, forcing its adjournment and destroying any chances the Yugoslav Communists might have of reforming the Yugoslav political system.

Slovenia and Croatia Move Toward Autonomy and Independence

On the eve of the republic-level presidential and parliamentary elections held in April 1990, Slovene voters and politicians were comparing themselves to Lithuanians, saying the Slovenes shared the feelings Lithuanians had of being a foreign element in their own country.

Although a conservative separatist-oriented coalition of political groups, known as Demos, won a majority in the lower house of the Slovenian Parliament, there was no evidence of a Slovenian intention to adopt a Lithuanian-style unilateral declaration of independence. Unlike Lithuania, which was annexed by the Soviet Union, Slovenia joined the Yugoslav federation in 1918 voluntarily. Moreover, while Lithuania could exert little economic influence on the Soviet Union, that was not the case with Slovenia, which was critical to the economic well-being of the Yugoslav state and provided the republic with some leverage in dealing with Belgrade. It was possible that the Slovenes might now work more arduously for a substantial loosening of the federation to allow the republics maximum control over their internal affairs and to look to secession only as a last resort.

On the other hand, the defeat of the Communist party in the Slovenian parliamentary elections (a Communist party reformer won the republic's presidency), despite the party's reformist orientation and despite its role in sponsoring democratic reforms in Slovenia, including the republic's right to secede, confirmed the electorate's unequivocal hostility to Marxist-Leninism. It also confirmed Slovenia's eagerness to embrace Western-style political and economic institutions.

The results of the Slovenian elections troubled federal Premier Markovic, who was trying to unite the Yugoslav peoples in support of his belt-tightening economic policies. For example, the new Slovenian government refused to support his proposal to amend the federal Constitution to give the national government in Belgrade taxation and monetary powers at the expense of the republics.

The anti-Communist and pro-independence movement in Slovenia also affected Croatia, which shared Slovenia's yearning for democratization and increased autonomy. On May 6, 1990, Croatia held republic-wide elections for a new Parliament. The Croatian Democratic Union, led by Franjo Tudjman, won two-thirds of the seats in the Zagreb Legislature, while the Communists won only 18 seats. The results showed that there was strong public sympathy for a transformation of the Yugoslav state into a confederation of autonomous republics.

But, unlike Slovenia, Croatia had a problem in the pursuit of autonomy—namely, the aspirations of the Serb minority of about 600,000 people in the southern parts of Croatia bordering the Serb republic in the east and along the Adriatic in the west. Leaders of the Serb minority demanded cultural, political, and territorial autonomy within Croatia. Intimidated by the new forceful expression of Croat nationalism in the April 1990 elections and the subsequent Croat declaration of sovereignty in July, the Serbs were afraid that if Yugoslavia became a confederation, an independent Croatian republic, inspired by old prejudices dating back at least to World War II, when Croats fought Serbs, would try to obliterate Serb cultural distinctions for the sake of homogeneity-inducing unity.

The new democratic Croatian government was sympathetic to the demands of its Serb minority for cultural autonomy.

But it firmly rejected any kind of administrative autonomy. It called a demand of the Serb minority for a referendum on administrative autonomy unconstitutional, insisting that the republic's Constitution protected the rights of minorities in the republic. The leadership in Zagreb accused Serbia's President Milosevic of stirring up the Serb population in Croatia with a view to encouraging its union with Serbia. In any event, the referendum was held in August 1990, and 99 percent of Serb voters endorsed political autonomy of Zagreb. On October 1, 1990, the Serb National Council, a local political party speaking for all Serbs living in Croatia, declared the territory inhabited predominantly by Serbs autonomous of the Croatian republic government. In the following weeks and months, extreme Serb nationalists in Croatia formed parmilitary organizations, their weapons and ammunition seized from local police stations and from depots belonging to Yugoslav federal forces stationed within Croatia. Croat authorities responded by sending police to Serb-inhabited areas to seize weapons.

Meanwhile, in a plebiscite held in Slovenia on December 23, 1990, 88 percent of voters opted for an independent and sovereign Slovenia. The Slovenian government in Ljubljana said that a confederation pact modeled on the European Community must be formed in 6 months or Slovenia would secede from Yugoslavia. To emphasize its independence, Slovenia occupied federal posts on the republic's frontier with Austria and began collecting customs duties. In June 1991 both the Slovenian and Croatian parliaments declared the formal independence of their republics of Yugoslavia, although they would agree to remain in a very loosely structured Yugoslav federation. These declarations of independence by Slovenia and Croatia brought the old Yugoslav system a step closer to disintegration.

BEGINNINGS OF THE CIVIL WAR

The federal government tried to reverse Slovania's control over the frontier posts and the collection of customs duties in the spring of 1991, but it could not evict Slovenian forces. Despite their overall numerical and weapons superiority, federal forces could not prevail against the united Slovenian republic. In Croatia, by contrast, the Serb minority was in a position to cooperate with and strengthen the federal military should it try to force a change in Croatian policy.

Not surprisingly, the federal army turned to Croatia, where the conflict be-

tween Croats and Serbs had been escalating in the spring of 1991. In July federal army forces crossed the Serb frontier into Croatia and, with the help of armed Serb guerrillas living in Croatia, fought Croatian paramilitary forces in Glina. Within several weeks fighting between federal and Serb groups and Croat forces spread to Vukovar and Vinkovici along the Sava River, in a northerly and westerly direction toward the Kraijina region and the Croatian capital of Zagreb. This effectively removed about 20 percent of Croatian territory from Zagreb's control.

What were the federal army's objectives in Croatia? Was the army fighting for Yugoslavia and under the authority of the federal presidency, or was it fighting for the interests of the Serb republic and following instructions from Serb President Milosevic? Or, given the predominance of Serbs in the army's officer corps and the fact that the army seemed to be seeking control over those parts of Croatian territory inhabited by Serbs, did the army have its own agenda?

Although the army leadership insisted that it would not act without authorization of the federal presidency, eventually the army on its own expanded into Croatia and extended the civil war. The federal presidency was paralyzed. Four republics opposed the use of force in Croatia (Slovenia, Croatia, Bosnia-Herzegovina, and Macedonia). Two republics (Serbia and Montenegro) and two autonomous provinces under Serb influence (Kosovo and Vojvodina) favored force. President Stipe Mesic, a Croat and the chair of the collective presidency, had legal control over the Yugoslav armed forces. He ordered federal forces in Croatia to return to barracks to avoid violence in dealing with Croatian independence moves. The army ignored him.

In this response, the army was protecting its own interests, among other things. The army wanted the kind of Yugoslav state bequeathed by Tito. In Tito's unified country, the army had enjoyed a special place of honor and had been amply rewarded for its loyalty with very high wages and generous pensions. Were the Yugoslav state to disintegrate or to lose control over the two wealthy northern republics, the army's privileged economic situation would have been severely compromised.

Most significant was the fact that the army's officer corps was composed largely of Serbs; it was more sensitive to the aspirations of the Serb republic and its president, and of Serbs living in Croatia, than it was to Yugoslav national interests. Its relentless efforts to control Croatian territory inhabited by Serb minorities left little doubt that it was under the influence of Serb President Milosevic and that it shared his commitment to the creation of a "greater Serbia," a term that meant an extension of the Serb republic's jurisdiction over Croatian areas with Serb minorities.

The Role of Serbia

Apart from its dedication to preserving the old Yugoslav union, the Milosevic leadership was fighting to preserve the old Communist system. Serbia still had a centrally controlled economy and a monolithic political system. In January 1991 Milosevic arrested a number of opposition politicians, while authorities in other republics were moving their societies toward pluralistic democracy. The Milosevic regime's crackdown provoked turmoil in Belgrade, especially after the arrest of the popular and charismatic Vuk Draskovic, head of the anti-Communist Serbian Renewal Movement. Furthermore, in September 1991 the Communist-dominated Serb Parliament adopted a new Constitution which greatly strengthened the presidency. Despite more liberal provisions, such as the legalization of political pluralism and the acceptance of a mixed economy involving private ownership, the Constitution indirectly strengthened Communist influence by taking almost all autonomy from the Serb provinces of Vojvodina and Kosovo.

Serbia still repressed its Albanian minority in Kosovo, which further deepened the crisis in Yugoslavia. Popular demonstrations against Serb control took place in Pristina, the capital of Kosovo; and an Albanian antigovernment opposition group, called the League of Democrats of Kosovo, under Ibrahim Rugova, an Albanian intellectual, developed. A major political association, with 300,000 supporters, including former members of the Kosovo branch of the Yugoslav Communist Party, the League called for a multiparty system and an independent judiciary. Most Serbs in Kosovo as well as the republic government in Belgrade were suspicious of the League, viewing it as a camouflage for a nationalist grouping with separatist tendencies.

Milosevic fought back. He encouraged the formation of vigilante groups, made up of radical Serb nationalists, to go into Kosovo and engage in hand-to-hand combat with the Albanians. He also financed the return of Serb citizens to Kosovo who, in past years, had left when Albanians trying to achieve ethnic homogenization of their province had discriminated against Serbs.

This conflict between Serbs and Albanians, along with the Serb-Croat conflict, polarized the country as different ethnic groups chose to be pro- or anti-Serb. The efforts of Serb republic authorities to centralize administrative control aroused fears in other republics of Serb nationalism, affirming deeply held suspicions of Croats and Slovenes—for example, of Milosevic's ambition to build a greater Serbia out of the Yugoslav state. Indeed, Kosovo became a code word for Serb aggrandizement at the expense of non-Serb minorities; and Croats and Slovenes, who never had had a high regard for their Albanian compatriots, were now very sympathetic.

ECONOMIC DETERIORATION

Economic chaos accompanied civil war. The central banking system collapsed, with republic banks issuing money through credits and promissory notes independently of the Yugoslav national bank in Belgrade. A debilitating trade war developed between Slovenia and Serbia. Belgrade stores refused to sell televisions and other consumer appliances manufactured in Slovenia; Slovenes were depicted as clever exploiters taking the artificially low-priced energy, food, and minerals from Serbia and other regions and selling manufactured goods at inflated prices.

Wage earners suffered. With industry at a standstill and the movement toward a market economy erratic, hundreds of thousands of Yugoslav workers were out of work or had not been paid for several months. Many more received only minimum wages. Also, because of the economic and political turmoil in the country, Yugoslav workers abroad were reluctant to send money home. The Yugoslav tourist industry, always a lucrative source of foreign hard currency, disappeared as the war intensified.

In 1990 then-Yugoslav federal Prime Minister Markovic put in place a belt-tightening reform program, starting with a devaluation of the Yugoslav dinar. He opened the country to almost unlimited foreign investment by permitting 100 percent foreign ownership of business, 99 percent foreign ownership of banks, and liberalization of rules for imports and the repatriation of profits. He also sought but had to abandon wage controls and currency convertibility to stimulate Yugoslav exports to hard-currency countries.

Impeding his efforts to stimulate output and expand exports were not only the persistence of inefficient management inherited from the Communist past but also the unwillingness of the republics to coop-

erate with the federal reform program. Thus, the leaderships of Croatia and Slovenia, the two most well-off republics, raised wages to gain political popularity with workers, although in so doing they contributed to an expansion of inflation, which the federal prime minister had successfully controlled since coming to power. Serbia's President Milosevic opposed a market-based economy in Yugoslavia, for ideological reasons: he was skeptical about the efficacy of privatization and preferred policies that would keep people at work. Finally, making matters worse for Markovic was the failure of the republics to pay federal taxes while helping themselves, without authorization, to money from the national banking system. In 1990 Serbia took $1.8 billion, by far the largest amount.

THE YUGOSLAV CRISIS AND THE WEST

Fearful that a breakup of Yugoslavia in 1991 could lead to violence and spread instability throughout the Balkans, the 12-nation European Community and the 34-nation Conference on Security and Cooperation in Europe initially opposed moves of Slovenia and Croatia toward independence. But there were serious differences among Western countries. For example, Germany and Austria, with strong historical and cultural links to Slovenia and Croatia, adopted a more flexible attitude regarding their aspirations toward independence, suggesting that these republics conceivably might receive recognition if they could demonstrate effective control over their territories. In the late summer of 1991 the Germans warned federal army leaders against the conquest of Croatia, saying that they should respect the right of republics to self-determination and threatening economic sanctions if the army did not show restraint. At the same time France and Spain tended to favor preservation of a united Yugoslav state, if only to avoid setting a precedent. With regional identities in these and other countries of Western Europe strong, there was evidence of growing regional particularism, which conceivably could be strengthened by a successful separatism in Yugoslavia.

In Western Europe and in the United States, there were soon misgivings about the costs of opposing self-determination of Croats and Slovenes, especially in light of Serbian aggression, which the West opposed. The West responded to the civil war by escalating its protests against Serbia's behavior. It proposed conferences and ceasefires and, when these led nowhere, the EC countries made recourse to sanctions. They froze arm sales and financial aid to Yugoslavia, in the hope that the combatants would stop fighting once they ran out of ammunition. One official observed that the combatants intended to fight each other indefinitely; and once they had run out of guns and bullets, they would use knives to kill each other; and if they had no knives, they would use their teeth!

Fourteen ceasefire agreements between Croatian and Yugoslav federal forces in the 6 months of war preceded the UN-sponsored ceasefire, concluded in Sarajevo on January 2, 1992. Former U.S. Secretary of State Cyrus R. Vance, the UN special envoy to Yugoslavia, used shuttle diplomacy between Zagreb and Belgrade to get the Serb-led Yugoslav Army and Croat military forces to lay down their arms and make way for the deployment of a UN peacekeeping force in the Krajina and other disputed areas of Croatia. The UN presence was intended to lay the groundwork for a permanent political settlement. By the end of 1991, according to Vance, both Croat and Serb republic leaders welcomed the prospect of a winding-down of the war. Both sides were worn out. There had been more than 10,000 casualties, a terrible toll on the physical environment, and the refugee problem had burgeoned. The Western trade embargo on Serbia had contributed to shortages, especially of gasoline, and the Serb government's fevered printing of money to pay for the war had ignited debilitating hyperinflation. An economist at Belgrade University estimated that the civil war had cost the Serb republic $6.5 billion in lost trade and production. Many ordinary Serb citizens also were beginning to criticize the conflict with Croatia, saying that Serbs living outside of Serbia were dragging the republic into a dangerous war. At the same time the Croatians, who originally preferred European mediation because of the sympathy of the EC for the independence policies of the republics, now welcomed the prospect of a United Nations intercession. This, they hoped, would eventually restore Croatian authority to areas of the republic seized and controlled by the Yugoslav Army.

But many in Western Europe as well as in the war zone were skeptical of the ceasefire. Serbs in Croatia feared the evacuation of Yugoslav forces, who were protecting them from Croat retaliation. In February and March 1992 local Serb extremists blew up some Croatian homes. Croats retaliated, destroying vacant Serb homes. Eventually, however, Serb moderates in Croatia accepted the UN presence in their territory. Croat leaders agreed that

rebel Serb governments set up in the disputed areas overrun by Yugoslav forces could remain until a general political solution was worked out; the leaders were, however, determined to prevent the Serb minority from cemeting its control over disputed areas and discouraging the return of Croat refugees who had fled to Zagreb months earlier. Inside the Serb republic was a growing siege mentality, with many people quite prepared to take on the whole world, so to speak, to protect the republic's interests in the rapidly disintegrating Yugoslav state.

In April 1992 UN peacekeeping forces finally arrived. But the obstacles to a peaceful settlement in Serb-dominated areas in Crotia such as the Krajina are enormous. UN officials fear that extremists on both sides are opposed to a negotiated settlement and want to wreck the peacekeeping operation. While Serbia's Milosevic and Croatia's Tudjman still support a negotiated political settlement, it is by no means clear that the Serb minorities in Croatia will accept anything less than their complete independence of Zagreb or their annexation to Serbia.

THE END OF YUGOSLAVIA

One might argue that the beginning of the end of the Yugoslav state occurred when, in mid-January 1992, the European Community, under strong pressure from Germany, recognized the independence of Slovenia and Croatia. German policy reflected a conviction that recognition was in the interest of promoting democracy and stability in the Balkans but also the influence in domestic German politics of powerful Catholic politicians who wanted to protect the largely Catholic populations of Slovenia and Croatia.

At first the Bush administration withheld recognition, in the hope that the old Yugoslav state somehow might survive, but the administration became increasingly critical as Serbia continued to try to acquire control of territory in neighboring republics inhabited by Serb minorities. Washington attempted to pressure the Serb government in Belgrade to curtail its interference in the ethnic conflicts of its neighbors. However, it eventually abandoned hope for the survival of a unified Yugoslavia and, in April 1992, formally recognized not only Slovenia and Croatia but also Bosnia-Herzegovina.

Conflict in Bosnia-Herzegovina
After the United States recognized the independence of Bosnia-Herzegovina, the Serb minority there tried to seize control

of the areas they inhabited. These Bosnian Serbs, who make up about one-third of Bosnia's population and live in the region along the Bosnian frontier with Croatia, from Kupres to Bosanzki Brod, also resisted the independence efforts of the non-Serb majorities that governed them. They did not want an international frontier separating them from Serbia. The other 60 percent of the republic's population, consisting of Muslim Slavs and Croats led by Bosnian President Izetbegovic, a Muslim Slav, were bent on achieving independence.

Izetbegovic had good reason to fear Serb domination if his republic did not get independence. The Yugoslav minister of Defense in early January 1992 was General Blagoje Adzic, a pro-Serb hardliner. Furthermore, Serbia and Montenegro have a constitution for a new Yugoslav state that will unite them and thus considerably enhance Serb influence. Serb minorities in Croatia and Bosnia are understandably eager to join such a Serb-dominated Yugoslav state.

The Bosnian president also has strong support for his stand on independence. In late February Bosnia-Herzegovina held a referendum on independence, with Croat and Slav voters overwhelmingly supporting independence. Izetbegovic then appealed to the West for recognition of the republic's independence. On April 5 the European Community decided to recognize the independence of Bosnia-Herzegovina, hoping that this move would help reduce the interethnic conflict in the republic and head off a possible partition of the republic by Serbia and Croatia.

Bosnian Serbs have since been on the offensive to wrest the areas they inhabit—approximately 60 percent of the republic's territory—from Bosnian control. The Serbs seem to have the backing of the Yugoslav Army and of the Serb republic government in Belgrade. The Serb Volunteer Guard, a paramilitary organization responsible for an attack on the town of Bijelina, is reportedly under the command of a Belgrade gangster wanted for bank robbery and other crimes in Western Europe and supported clandestinely by Serb republic officials. And Yugoslav forces officered by Serbs and fighting side by side with Serbs in Bosnian towns like Sarajevo have forced non-Serb peoples to flee their villages and towns, in an effort to create purely Serbian enclaves which, presumably, will seek annexation to the Serb republic. With 100,000 troops stationed in Bosnia-Herzegovina, the army has a vast advantage over Croat and Muslim Slav militiamen. The Yugoslav Air Force has control of Bosnian airspace and has bombed and strafed areas inhabited

Independence 1918	Nazi Germany invades Yugoslavia 1941	Yugoslav Communists acquire control of the government 1946	Tito's independence of the Soviet Union is condemned 1948	Yugoslavia begins decollectivization of agriculture 1953	Tito calls for the dissolution of NATO 1957	Yugoslavia condemns the Soviet intervention in Czechoslovakia 1968	Yugoslavia condemns the Soviet invasion of Afghanistan 1979	Tito dies; explosions of Albanian discontent in Kosovo

1980s–1990s

The Yugoslav party Central Committee endorses political pluralism and by implication a restoration of the multiparty system; Slovenia and Croatia end Communist party rule

Civil war begins; Slovenia, Croatia, and Bosnia-Herzegovina receive international recognition as independent states

Macedonia seeks recognition as an independent state; Serbia and Montenegro promote a new Yugoslav state

predominantly by Muslim Slavs and Croats. Croat President Tudjman, meanwhile, has indicated that his republic will protect the Croatian minority living in Bosnia. Thus, by the end of April 1992, while a fragile truce seemed to be holding in Croatia itself, the Yugoslav Civil War threatened to engulf Bosnia-Herzegovina and provoke a bloodbath among its diverse and antagonistic ethnic groups.

Macedonian Moves
Toward Independence

If the situation in Bosnia-Herzegovina seems confused, that in Macedonia is even more so. It has an ethnically diverse society. It seems to have more to gain than other republics in the preservation of a unified Yugoslav state, which could provide much-needed economic help to improve its poor living conditions. Moreover, Macedonian Communists and the Reform Party of then-federal Prime Minister Markovic shared a common interest in keeping Macedonia within a unified Yugoslavia; they had the support of Macedonian intellectuals, business executives, and others. Markovic saw the Yugoslav federal union as the only means of restoring economic health and improving living conditions in the less well-off central and southern republics. Futhermore, as an independent state, Macedonia might well become prey to ethnic-based territorial ambitions of its neighbors Bulgaria and Greece. These two countries have their own Macedonian minorities and might in the future claim the allegiance of Yugoslav Macedonians. Indeed, the domi-

nant language of Yugoslav Macedonia is a dialect of Bulgarian, while the northern part of Greece, from Thessaloniki to the Turkish frontier, is inhabited by people of Macedonian extraction who trace their history back to the pre-Christian era of the Macedonian empire-building King Alexander the Great.

There were also strong reasons for Macedonian independence. Many people in Yugoslavia's Macedonia cherished the hope of a reunification of Macedonians throughout the southern Balkan region in a "greater Macedonia." A referendum on the issue of independence, on September 9, 1991, showed voters overwhelmingly in favor of separation unless the Yugoslav state could be transformed into a loose confederation.

In early 1992 Macedonia tried to get Western recognition of its independence. Greece opposed its independence, on the grounds that an independent Macedonia would eventually lay claim to Greek territory on the frontier with Bulgaria that is also known as Macedonia. Greek fears are based upon alleged efforts of Macedonian Communist leaders in the recent past to undermine the sovereignty of Greece over *its* Macedonia, which they called "Aegean Macedonia" and characterized as "occupied" territory.

The NATO allies, including the United States, decided to accommodate Greece on this issue, at least for the moment. No doubt they considered the vulnerability of an independent Macedonia to the territorial pretensions of its Balkan neighbors and the possibility that it could become a

new object of contention among these countries. They might also want to protect the Albanian minority in Macedonia, which constitutes about 40 percent of Macedonia's population and has been systematically underrepresented in the republic's Parliament. The two political parties committed to Albanian interests urged the EC not to recognize Macedonia's independence because of its perceived failure to meet the Community's human- and civil-rights standards for recognition. The Macedonians are afraid that their Albanian minority might someday seek to join their kin in the Kosovo province of Serbia and ultimately become part of a greater Albanian state on the Adriatic.

From its creation in 1918 the Yugoslavia national idea was artificial, contrived for reasons of expediency by the victorious great powers in World War I. Most so-called Yugoslav people always identified themselves first by their regional culture and secondarily, if at all, by their citizenship in a Yugoslav state. When the current conflict is over the post-1918 Yugoslavia will have disappeared. What will replace it is by no means clear.

DEVELOPMENT

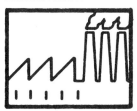

The Yugoslav economy is problem-ridden: there is hyperinflation, massive unemployment, and a daunting foreign debt. Workers, especially in the poorer southern republics, protested against low wages by fomenting illegal strikes.

FREEDOM

Free, open, and competitive parliamentary elections have been held in many of the Yugoslav republics. Only in Serbia has a quasi-authoritarian political system continued in place, under the autocratic leadership of Serb President Milosevic.

HEALTH/WELFARE

Living standards in many parts of Yugoslavia continue to decline. The cost of food has been steadily outpacing wages of workers in industries unable to increase pay because they are not making profits. Low-paid workers eat people's bread, a cheap, dark bread that bakeries must produce for the poor and that sells at a subsidized price.

ACHIEVEMENTS

Slovenia, Croatia, and Bosnia-Herzegovina have been recognized as independent states by the EC and the United States. Macedonia declared its independence and is seeking international recognition.

Articles from the World Press

CENTRAL/EASTERN EUROPE

Topic Guide to Articles

TOPIC AREA	TREATED AS AN ISSUE IN:	TOPIC AREA	TREATED AS AN ISSUE IN:
Peasants		**Social Reform**	
C.I.S.	9. Soviet Muslims: Seeking Reform	*C.I.S.*	9. Soviet Muslims: Seeking Reform
		C/E Europe	15. The Eastern Bloc Two Years Later
Politics			21. Bulgaria Starts Down Hard Road
C.I.S.	1. The Soviet State		25. Post-Communist Nationalism
	2. The Return to History		
	5. The Yeltsin Revolution	**Standard of Living**	
	6. The Four Lives of Mikhail Sergeiyevich	*C.I.S.*	11. Moscow's Market Movers
	7. The Tragedy of Gorbachev	*C/E Europe*	15. The Eastern Bloc Two Years Later
C/E Europe	2. The Return to History		
	15. The Eastern Bloc Two Years Later	**Trade**	
	16. Democracy in Eastern Europe	*C/E Europe*	20. Going to Market
	17. Eastern Europe's Past		
	21. Bulgaria Starts Down Hard Road	**Underground Economy**	
	24. Poland's Leap to Democracy	*C.I.S.*	10. The Moment of Truth
Religion			
C.I.S.	12. The Revival of Religion	**Women's Rights**	
		C.I.S.	14. Left Behind in the Rush to Freedom
Revolution			
C.I.S.	5. The Yeltsin Revolution		
Roots			
C.I.S.	2. The Return to History		
	4. International Boundaries		
	9. Soviet Muslims: Seeking Reform		
	12. The Revival of Religion		
	14. Left Behind in the Rush to Freedom		
C/E Europe	4. International Boundaries		
	26. The Massacre of Yugoslavia		

The Commonwealth of Independent States: Articles

Article 1

THE NEW YORK TIMES **INTERNATIONAL**
THURSDAY, DECEMBER 26, 1991

The Soviet State, Born of a Dream, Dies

Serge Schmemann

Special to The New York Times

MOSCOW, Dec. 25—The Soviet state, marked throughout its brief but tumultuous history by great achievement and terrible suffering, died today after a long and painful decline. It was 74 years old.

Conceived in utopian promise and born in the violent upheavals of the "Great October Revolution of 1917," the union heaved its last in the dreary darkness of late December 1991, stripped of ideology, dismembered, bankrupt and hungry—but awe-inspiring even in its fall.

The end of the Soviet Union came with the resignation of Mikhail S. Gorbachev to make way for a new "Commonwealth of Independent States." At 7:32 P.M., shortly after the conclusion of his televised address, the red flag with hammer-and-sickle was lowered over the Kremlin and the white-blue-red Russian flag rose in its stead.

No Ceremony, Only Chimes

There was no ceremony, only the tolling of chimes from the Spassky Gate, cheers from a handful of surprised foreigners and an angry tirade from a lone war veteran.

Reactions to the death varied widely, according to Pravda, the former mouthpiece of the empire: "Some joyfully exclaim, 'Finita la comedia!' Others, heaping ash on their heads, raise their hands to the sky in horror and ask, what will be?"

The reaction depended somewhat on whether one listened to the ominous gunfire from Georgia, or watched spellbound the bitter if dignified surrender of power by the last leader of the Union of Soviet Socialist Republics, Mr. Gorbachev.

Most people vacillated. The taboos and chains were gone, but so was the food. The Soviet Union had given them pitifully little, but there was no guarantee that the strange-sounding "Commonwealth of Independent States" would do any better.

As for Mr. Gorbachev, public opinion polls indicated a virtually universal agreement that it was time for him to move on—not because he had failed, but because there was nothing more he could do.

It was perhaps a paradox that the ruler who presided over the collapse of the Soviet Union was the only one of its ill-starred leaders to leave office with a measure of dignity intact. It was possible that history would reach a different verdict, but among many thoughtful Russians, it was to his undying credit that he lifted the chains of totalitarian dictatorship. Whether he could also have saved the economy was another question.

"Gorbachev was unable to change the living standards of the people, but he changed the people," Komsomolskaya Pravda wrote in a sympathetic farewell that seemed to capture the dominant mood. He didn't know how to make sausage, but he did know how to give freedom. And if someone believes that the former is more important than the latter, he is likely never to have either."

Another man might have done things differently. But it was difficult to conceive that any of those then available—

the conservative Yegor K. Ligachev, the rough-hewn Boris N. Yeltsin, the bureaucratic Nikolai I. Ryzhkov or the scholarly Eduard A. Shevardnadze—possessed just that blend of reformer and ideologue, of naïveté and ruthlessness, that enabled Mr. Gorbachev to lead the Communists to the edge of the cliff.

"Gorbachev was a true instrument of fate," declared Viktor Yerofeyev, a writer and literary critic. "He had just enough intelligence to change everything, but not enough to see that everything would be destroyed. He was bold enough to challenge his party, and cautious enough to let the party live until it lost its power. He had enough faith in Communism to be named its head, but enough doubts about it to destroy it. If he had seen everything clearly, he would not have changed Russia."

Mr. Gorbachev struggled to the end, and beyond it, to keep the union alive. But in the end, it was by letting the union die and by stepping aside that he gave a new lease on life to the great Eurasian entity, whatever its name.

The Union
EPIC ACHIEVEMENT AND EPIC FAILURE

Measured against is own ambitions, the U.S.S.R. died a monumental failure.

It had promised no less than the creation of a "Soviet new man," imbued with selfless devotion to the common good, and it ended up all but crushing the initiative and spirit of the people, making many devoted only to vodka. It had proclaimed a new humanitarian ideology, and in its name butchered 10 million of its own. It envisioned a planned economy in which nothing was left to chance, and it created an elephantine bureaucracy that finally smothered the economy. Promising peace and freedom, it created the world's most militarized and ruthless police state.

Promising a people's culture, it created an anti-culture in which

mediocrity was glorified and talent was ruthlessly persecuted. An entire department of the K.G.B. existed to wrestle with art, trying first to co-opt any rising talent "to the service of the state" and if that failed, to muzzle or exile it. The roll-call of repressed or exiled artists is a stunning indictment: Mandelstam, Malevich, Pasternak, Solzhenitsyn, Rostropovich, Brodsky, and so many more.

In the end, promising a new life, it created an unspeakably bleak society—polluted, chronically short of everything, stripped of initiative and spirituality. While the bulk of the nation stood in line or guzzled rot-gut vodka, the Communist elite raised corruption to new heights: The likes of Leonid I. Brezhnev and his cronies pinned endless medals on one another and surrounded themselves with a peasant's notion of luxury—grandiose candelabras, massive cars, vast hunting estates, armies of sycophants, secret hospitals filled with the latest Western technology.

And yet the Soviet Union was also an indisputable superpower, a state and a people that achieved epic feats in science, warfare, even culture.

Perhaps all this was achieved despite Communism, not because of it. Yet by some combination of force and inspiration, the system begun by Lenin and carried out by Stalin unleashed a potent national energy that made possible the rapid industrialization of the 1930's, the defeat of Nazi Germany in the 1940's, the launching of the first Sputnik in the 1950's, the creation of a nuclear arsenal in the 1960's and 1970's. Even now, for all the chaos in the land, two astronauts, Aleksandr A. Volkov and Sergei Krikalev, continue to circle the globe.

In culture too, both the "thaw" of Nikita S. Khrushchev in the 1960's and the "glasnost" of Mr. Gorbachev offered testimony that the enormous creativity of the nation was as tenacious as the people.

And in sport, the tangle of Olympic medals and international victories were a tacit source of national pride even among the staunchest critics of the Communist regime.

The Dream
A UTOPIAN ILLUSION SURVIVED INJUSTICE

It is easy now, gazing over the smoldering ruins of the Soviet empire, to enumerate the fatal illusions of the Marxist system. Yet the irresistible utopian dream fired generations of reformers, revolutionaries and radicals here and abroad, helping spread Soviet influence to the far corners of the globe.

Until recently, rare was the third world leader who did not espouse some modified Marxist doctrine, who did not make a regular pilgrimage to Moscow to join in the ritual denunciations of the "imperialists."

Much of it was opportunism, of course. In the Soviet Union as in the third world, Communism offered a handy justification for stomping on democracy and keeping one party and one dictator in power.

Yet it was also a faith, one strong enough to survive all the injustices done in its name. Lev Kopelev, a prominent intellectual now living in Germany, recalled in his memoirs how prisoners emerged from the gulag after Stalin's death firmly believing that at last they could start redressing the "errors" of Stalinism and truly building Communism.

And only last March, Mr. Gorbachev would still declare in Minsk, "I am not ashamed to say that I am a Communist and adhere to the Communist idea, and with this I will leave for the other world."

The tenacity of the faith testified to the scope of the experiment. It was a monumental failure, but it had been a grand attempt, an experiment on a scale the world had never known before.

Perhaps it was the height of folly and presumption that Russia, a country then only at the dawn of industrialization and without a bourgeoisie or proletariat to speak of, would have been the one to proclaim itself the pioneer of a radically new world order.

Two Worlds
'WESTERNIZERS' vs. 'SLAVOPHILES'

But Russians have always had a weakness for the broad gesture. The greatest czars—Ivan the Terrible, Peter the Great—were those with the grandest schemes. The greatest writers, Dostoyevsky and Tolstoy, explored ultimate themes in immense novels. The Russian Orthodox Church embroidered its churches and its liturgy in the most elaborate gilding and ceremony.

Nothing happened small in the Soviet era, either. Twenty million died in the war, 10 million more in the gulag. And the pride of place was always given to grandiose construction projects—the world's biggest hydroelectric plant at Bratsk, the world's biggest truck factory at Kamaz, the trans-Siberian railroad.

The czarist merchant wrapped in coats of gold and sable racing in his sleigh through wretched muzhiks in birch-bark shoes translated into the ham-fisted party boss tearing through Moscow in his long black limousine.

Many theories have been put forward to explain these traits. There is the sheer expanse of a country that spans 11 time zones. There is the climate, which imposed a rhythm of long, inactive winters punctuated by brief summers of intense labor. Some posited the absence of a Renaissance, which stunted the development of an individual consciousness and sustained a spirit of collectivism.

Above all it was a nation straddling two continents and two cultures, forever torn and forever fired by the creative clash at the faultline of East and West.

Russians have ever split into "Westernizers" and "Slavophiles," and the death of the Soviet Union had everything to do with the struggle between the "Westernizing" democrats and free-marketeers and the anti-Western champions of powerful statehood and strong center.

The West has always been deemed both attractive and dangerous to Russia. Peter the Great campaigned desperately to open his nation to the West, but Westerners remained suspect and isolated. Communism found nourishing soil in the Russian spirit of collectivism, but its Western materialism proved alien.

Western democracy is foundering here on the same ambivalence. The Soviets plunged whole-heartedly into the plethora of new councils and parliaments inaugurated by Mr. Gorbachev. But their endless debate and inability to organize into cohesive interest groups soon diminished public attention, and at the end the parliaments readily transferred most of their powers to Mr. Gorbachev, Mr. Yeltsin and other powerful men.

"What remains after the Soviet Union is this Eurasian essence, this unique interplay of Europe and Asia, which will continue to amaze the world with its culture and totally unexpected actions," Mr. Yerofeyev said.

"What was imported in Western Marxism will vanish," he continued. "But Communism will not disappear, inasmuch as the spirit of collectivism is at the heart of this nation. The nation will always say 'we' rather than the Anglo-Saxon 'I'.

"This was Lenin's deftness, that he realized Russia was ready to accept Communism, but needed only 'class struggle' for everything to fall into place. As soon as it had an enemy, the collective consciousness became dynamic."

Contrasts
IMPRESSIVE FEATS, AWESOME LITTER

That spirit was forever captured in the revolutionary posters, with their capitalists in top hats dripping workers' blood, or the muscular young Communists crushing bourgeois vipers.

Lenin's successors understood this equally well, that it was easier to fire Soviets to enormous feats and extraordinary sacrifice than to organize them for sustained work and steady growth.

The capacity for suffering and sacrifice, whether in the war or in the endless lines today, is something that still awes foreigners. The ability to focus enormous talent and energy on a grand project is equally impressive, and from this came the great achievements in science, weaponry and construction.

Yet the sloppiness and inefficiency of everyday life make an even stronger impression on visitors. The shoddiness of even the newest apartment block or hotel is shocking. Old houses seem to list precariously in the mud. Wreckage litters every yard. Cars come off the assembly lines half broken.

The planned economy served only to intensify the squalor. It made volume, not quality or inventiveness, the primary measure of production, and it put a premium on huge factories over flexibility or distribution.

The system also gave consumer goods the lowest possible priority, thus institutionalizing shortages and reducing ordinary people to a permanent state of dependence on the state and rude salespeople.

Icons
THE CULTS END IN STATE'S DOTAGE

Whether Lenin would have built the Soviet state this way is not certain. Three years before his death, in 1921, he replaced "War Communism" with what became known as the "New Economic Policy," but was in fact a return to a measure of old laissez-faire. The national income rose to pre-revolutionary levels, but that failed to dissuade Stalin from starting the first Five-Year Plan.

Nonetheless, it was Lenin who became the first deity of the new order. He was a convenient hero: He had died while still enormously popular, and he left behind enough writings on every topic to support whatever position his successors chose to take.

Thus his goateed visage soon became the mandatory icon in every official building or every town square, and his words became scripture. All the powers of science were summoned to preserve his remains forever, and his mausoleum became the spiritual heart of the new empire. His name became an adjective denoting orthodoxy, as in "the Leninist way." Plaques were raised at every building he stayed in, and an enormous temple was built over his childhood home.

The cult seemed only to gain strength with the passing years, as his successors denounced one another and struggled to portray themselves as the one true interpreter of Lenin. Stalin set the trend, killing most of Lenin's comrades as he perfected the machinery of repression, all the while claiming to act in the name of the great founder.

Next, Khrushchev dismantled the Stalin cult and halted the worst of the terror in the name of restoring "true Leninism," only to be overthrown himself. Before long, Brezhnev was the sole heir, and Khrushchev's "voluntarism" joined Stalin's "personality cult" among the heresies of Leninism.

With Brezhnev, the Soviet state passed visibly into dotage. As he grew bloated and incoherent, so did the state. Production fell while an uncontrolled military machine devoured ever-larger portions of the national product. Foreign policy sank into a pattern of stagnant coexistence and fierce military competition with the West, while at home the political police steadily put down the small but brave dissident movement inspired by the brief Khrushchevian thaw.

After 18 years in power, Brezhnev was succeeded by two other old and sick men, Yuri V. Andropov and Kon-

stantin U. Chernenko, and by the time Mr. Gorbachev took the helm in 1985, it was obvious to all that the state was in radical need of help.

Mr. Gorbachev, at 54 the youngest Soviet leader since Stalin, electrified the land almost immediately with the introduction of "glasnost," or openness. Suddenly the people could talk and think freely, taboos began to crumble, East-West hostilities evaporated, and dissidents emerged from labor camps and exile. The sweet perfume of hope scented the air.

But Mr. Gorbachev's parallel attempts to reform the economy perished on the same shoals as all previous reforms—the thick and privileged Communist party apparat. The more glasnost flourished, the more it became evident that perestroika was foundering, and everything Mr. Gorbachev did seemed to be too little or too late.

Floundering in the end, he lurched first to the left, ordering a radical "500 day" reform plan in the summer of 1989, then to the right, rejecting the plan and encircling himself with party stalwarts and letting them use force, then back to the left last spring, opening negotiations with the republics on a new Union Treaty.

By then it was too late. The rejected right-wingers tried to seize power by force in the August coup, and with their defeat, the republics had no more need for or faith in Mr. Gorbachev or the remnants of his union.

On Dec. 8, the leaders of Russia, Ukraine and Byelorussia pulled the plug, proclaiming a new Commonwealth of Independent States, and after that it was only a question of time before the breathing stopped.

Afterlife
PROBLEMS SURVIVE BUT WILL PRIDE?

The union was dead. But the great Eurasian entity on which it fed remained very much alive—as Russia, as a new Commonwealth of 11 republics, as a culture and a worldview, as a formidable nuclear arsenal, as a broad range of unresolved crises.

The gunfire in Georgia, the long lines across the land, the closed airports and the myriad unanswered questions about the new Commonwealth—would it confer citizenship? would it remain a single military and economic entity? would it manage transport and communications?—made clear that the legacy of the union would long survive.

Mr. Gorbachev had given people a new freedom. But the Soviet Union had also given them something tangible—the pride of superpower. Whatever their problems and shortages, they had been one of the two arbiters of global destinies, a nation that nobody could intimidate or bully.

Now that was being taken away, too, and how the humiliation would play out, especially in conditions of hunger and poverty, was among the troubling questions for the future.

"The parting with the Union of Soviet Socialist Republics will be long and difficult," Izvestia warned. "We must acknowledge that many will not believe or agree to the end of their days with the death warrant written in Minsk and confirmed in Alma-Ata. The idea of superpower has a force equal to nationalism, and in certain conditions it is also capable of uniting millions of fanatic supporters."

Article 2

THE BROOKINGS REVIEW
SPRING 1992

THE RETURN TO HISTORY

THE BREAKUP OF THE SOVIET UNION

SHLOMO AVINERI

SINCE 1989

events in Central and Eastern Europe have given rise to a number of questions—and false hopes—about the alternatives to communism in countries that have been ruled by Marxist-Leninist governments for many decades. The dissolution of communist regimes in the former Warsaw Pact countries and the disintegration of the former Soviet Union make the question of the alternatives into a central issue of current international politics. They also pose some tough challenges for political analysts about the limits of their own professional expertise.

It is obvious that the defeat of communism is primarily seen in the West through an ideological prism. It is equally obvious that such a prism may sometimes impose triumphalist distortions on the interpretive faculties of the observer. Thus in the rush of the initial enthusiasm over the demise of communism, some Western analysts went so far as to announce the End of History. Finally—so they argued—liberal democracy, with the free market as its mainstay, had won its ultimate victory. After defeating fascism and Nazism in World War II, Western liberalism had triumphed over the other alternative ideology confronting it, communism. No other system or ideology could ever successfully challenge it. The Sons of Light had finally vanquished the Sons of Darkness. Gloria in excelsis.

Actual developments in Eastern Europe and the currently unfolding drama in the former Soviet Union itself, however, advise caution. Although there is no doubt that the communist system as such—a one-party dictatorship coupled with a planned command economy—is dead and buried in Central and Eastern Europe (China, Vietnam, and North Korea may be a

different story), it becomes less and less clear whether the emerging alternative is a democratic and free-market society. Even in the brief period since the autumn of 1989, clear differences in developments in several postcommunist societies suggest that not all these societies are traveling on the same tracks or even necessarily moving in the same direction. Czechoslovakia and Romania, for example, show completely different patterns of development.

If one begins to look more carefully at these differences, as well as at the vastly different course taken by the various former Soviet republics, it becomes clear that the most pronounced determinants in these different developments are historical factors. Far from seeing an end of history, Eastern Europe now goes through a massive return of history and to history. Past structures and ideologies become a more reliable guide to the general contour of things to come than any other indicator, just as pre-1914 atlases give a better picture of the tangled conflicts emerging in postcommunist societies (for example, Yugoslavia) than recent atlases. Paradoxically, they are more up to date precisely because they are older. And anyone who has studied the Balkan wars of the 1910s is better equipped to understand the current developments in Yugoslavia than anyone conversant only with recent GNP or other indicators of these societies.

Taking the Long View

In assessing the meaning of this return to history, it is helpful to try to fit the developments of the past few years into a broader historical perspective. Otherwise, the picture is fragmented, and the fragments do not make much sense, nor are they helpful in trying to formulate policies for the future. What we are witnessing is, in historical terms, much more encompassing and complex than the mere disintegration of communism.

In the wake of World War I, three centuries-old continental empires collapsed: the Ottoman, the Austro-Hungarian, and the Russian.

While the collapse of the first two empires was final, the reverberations of the collapse are still very much with us in the form of lingering regional conflicts. In the Middle East, the Israeli-Palestinian conflict, the civil war in Lebanon, the Greek-Turkish conflict in and over Cyprus, and even some aspects of the Iraqi-Kuwaiti dispute are, in essence, disputes between successor states of the Ottoman Empire over the heritage left by it. Similarly, in Central and Eastern Europe, tension between Hungary and Romania over questions connected with Transylvania, the current war in former Yugoslavia, even the possibility of the breakup of the Czechoslovak federation all stem from the unfinished business of carving up the defunct Austro-Hungarian Empire.

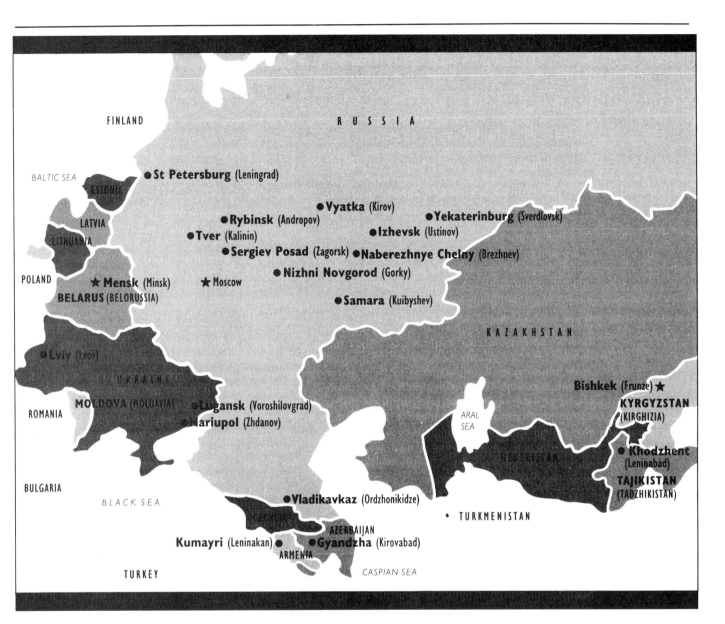

Changing Place Names in the Commonwealth of Independent States, 1992

That the breakup of these two continental empires has continued to haunt the successor states for more than 70 years now (with no end yet in sight) should be a cautionary note for anyone expecting a quick fix to the collapse of the Soviet Union and the Warsaw Pact.

For the collapse of the old Russian Empire in 1917 was more complex than that of the Ottoman or Austro-Hungarian systems. On coming to power in November 1917, Lenin and the Bolsheviks recognized and announced the right of the non-Russian nations within the old czarist empire to secede and form their own states. As a consequence, Finland and the Baltic states attained their independence with Soviet blessing. The Russian part of Poland aligned itself with the Polish areas under German and Austrian rule to establish the independent Polish republic. The Ukraine declared its independence, as did the Transcaucasian nations of Georgia and Armenia and other regions in the Central Asian parts of the old czarist empire.

The policy of self-determination, however, was reversed during the ensuing civil war and Western anti-communist interventions, when some of the seceding republics became involved in the war against communist rule in Russia. Eventually, central authority was reestablished by force in most of the seceding areas, mainly in the Ukraine and the Transcaucasus. Up to a point, the old Russian Empire was reestablished, this time with a revolutionary, internationalist ideology. During and after World War II this old-new Russian-Soviet empire was able to re-annex the Baltic republics and some other areas in Eastern Poland and Northern Romania. And with the Soviet victory over Nazi Germany in World War II, the Soviet army was instrumental in imposing communist rule over Poland, Czechoslovakia, Hungary, Romania, Bulgaria, and East Germany (Yugoslavia was a different story)—thus adding an unprecedented outer rim to Russian-Soviet domination.

189

Not by Arms Alone

It would, however, be a mistake to attribute the existence of this extended empire to force alone. It was held together by a powerful combination of force and ideology—a messianic vision of communism as the harbinger of a New World Order of equality, social justice, and solidarity. Flawed as communist society was, one can never understand its staying power only in terms of its coercive instruments of repression. There was always the vision—the vision that made it possible for people in Moscow and Kiev, Riga and Tashkent, Yerevan and Tbilisi to believe that despite their differences in language and customs, religious background and national origin, culture and race, they were still united in an unprecedented effort to create a new world and a new man.

Indeed, for many, *homo sovieticus* was seen to arise out of the debris of the old world. Some of the best and the brightest of the Eastern European intelligentsia believed that given the history of the region's economic backwardness, social conservatism, ethnic strife, and fascist or near-fascist governments, only the promise of communism could deliver these societies and lead them to a new, bright, and peaceful future. The dream might have been naive, but it was born out of the noblest sentiments, and the nobility of the vision makes the abyss of Stalinist horrors even more tragic, as so poignantly shown in Arthur Koestler's *Darkness at Noon*. Only those who understand the attraction of communism for Eastern European intellectuals can understand the depth of the catastrophe brought upon that dream by Stalinism and its aftermath.

Today, the two pillars of communism—force and ideology—have both crumbled. The repressive system has disintegrated, and so has the dream. Nobody believes any more in the redemptive potential of communism. The void is almost fathomless, and frightening.

What will replace this dream and the political structures erected by it? Those who, in their early enthusiasm, naively saw communism as being inevitably replaced by democracy and a market economy are beginning to realize that the countries of Central and Eastern Europe lack the social building blocks—the network of voluntary associations, modes of thinking, traditions, and institutions—cultural, economic, and religious—that make democracy, and the market, possible. The fact of the matter is that before the advent of communism only one country in Eastern Europe—Czechoslovakia—had a viable democratic system coupled with a thriving market economy, and even that was encumbered by grave problems of ethnic minorities (Sudeten Germans, Slovaks, Ruthenians, and Hungarians). Poland did try, between the two World Wars, to achieve a democratic structure, but the nobility of its intention was not matched by the reality of its politics and economics. Parliamentary fragmentation and the fact that almost a third of its population consisted of non-Polish ethnic minorities (Ukrainians,

Germans, Jews) undercut its fledgling democratic structures. Hungary, Romania, Bulgaria, Yugoslavia, and the Baltic States developed, between 1918 and 1939, a variety of authoritarian regimes, with various degrees of xenophobic repression and semi-fascist tendencies. And last and not least, Russia itself, despite the historical yearnings of many of its poets and scholars, never had a viable democratic tradition of self-government, pluralism, civil society, tolerance, and individualism. For all the best intentions in the world, postcommunist societies find themselves, in most cases, lacking the building stones of democracy that made the West European and North American experience of freedom possible.

The Past as Prologue

Events since 1989 suggest that the best predictive indicator of a country's postcommunist future is—its past. Not that the past is about to be repeated. Heraclitus knew long ago that you cannot step twice into the same river. But the past does, to a large degree, circumscribe the contours of the future political discourse—and its potentialities.

Thus Czechoslovakia, with its liberal, secular, Western-oriented traditions, has made the most successful attempt to develop along democratic lines. Even so, the success has been greater in the Czech lands than in Slovakia, whose historical tradition is much more lacking in these ingredients and which went through an autochthonous fascist phase (the Slovak fascist independent state between 1938 and 1945). Poland and Hungary are able to draw with some success on historical resources and traditions to which representative government was not wholly foreign. But countries like Romania and Bulgaria, let alone Albania, with hardly any democratic or civil society tradition, show how difficult the transition is. And in Yugoslavia, two parallel throw-backs to history are discernible: the historical enmities, mainly between Serbs and Croats, are coming back in all their ferocity, and in the vortex of this ethnic conflict, both independent Croatia and the Serb-dominated rump Yugoslavia show clear signs of developing along the historical authoritarian lines of their past traditions. Only Slovenia, with a history of relative tolerance and decency (mainly under benevolent Habsburg rule) may yet escape the slide into ethnocentric authoritarianism of various stripes now engulfing the former communist attempt to bridge those centuries-old conflicts.

The return to historical patterns is also exemplified by the unification of Germany. Few thought the two Germanies would come together so quickly when the Berlin Wall came down on November 9, 1989. But once the wall was down, and the communist system in East Germany was being transformed, there was no *raison d'etre* for a separate existence of the German Democratic Republic, and the forces of national unity and historical memory very quickly turned the battle

---

Today, the two pillars of communism, force and ideology, have both crumbled.

cry of East German dissenters *Wir sind das Volk* (We are the people) to *Wir sind ein Volk* (We are one people).

What once seemed Soviet permafrost blanketing Central and Eastern Europe is now melting. And all the grass and all the dirt are coming back. Fifty or seventy-five years of communism appear to be a hiatus in time, and postcommunist societies go back to the political discourse of pre-1917 or pre-1945, respectively.

In the former Soviet Union, with the disappearance of communism as an ideology and a system of power, the disintegration of the world's second-strongest superpower into its national components appears complete. Even Russia itself is being challenged by some of the smaller nations incorporated into it by the czars and commissars alike (Tartars, Chenens—and the list will grow). Erstwhile communist leaders become overnight champions of nationalism—so Leonid Kravthuk in the Ukraine, Nursultan Nazarbayev in Kazakhstan. Georgia and Armenia emerge as separate nation states, with at least the former showing some rather repressive features. Russia itself, while possessing a leadership hailing democracy and the market, lamentably lacks the infrastructure for both, and the dangers for an authoritarian, populist regime are evident. That 25 million ethnic Russians live outside the borders of the Russian Republic (11 million of them in the Ukraine) suggests enormous potentialities for Yugoslav-like problems. The breakup of the old Russian empire—postponed for 75 years by Soviet power—appears to be now final.

The return to history is nowhere more evident than in the return to the old names of streets, squares—and cities: so Leningrad becomes Saint Petersburg again; Kalinin, Tver; Sverdlovsk, Yekaterinburg; Ordzhonikidze, Vladikavkaz (the last one, a nice czarist triumphalist name: 'the conqueror of the Caucasus').

A Return to Religion

And with the return to history and historical memory comes a return to religion, which in Eastern Europe is closely intertwined with ethnicity and national consciousness. The void left by the demise of communism in the belief system of Eastern European societies is being replaced by a revival (sometimes uncritical) of religiosity and religious symbolism. During the days of Solidarity's fight against communism in Poland, the Church was both a system of beliefs and a helpful alternative organizational structure. But the phenomenon is much wider. Not only Czestechowa, but also Zagorsk and many other shrines in Eastern Europe now enjoy a place in the public realm that few comparable religious sites can claim in the West.

Out of the communist experience many societies may emerge as being more religiously devout than most contemporary Western societies—but also more devout than these societies were themselves before the advent of communism. In Soviet Central Asia, fundamentalist Islam may become a strong political force in

the processes of replacing communist structures. Similarly, many Jews in Russia who saw communism (with all its repressive anti-Jewish policies) as a passport into general society are now discovering that with the demise of Soviet Man and the reassertion of Russian, Ukrainian (or Uzbek) nationalism, often coupled with religious connotations, they have to redefine the problems of their own identity. No longer can they claim to be Soviet citizens "of Jewish origin." It is this, as much as economic hardships and the ravings of some marginal anti-Semites, that drives so many (former) Soviet Jews to seek a new homeland in Israel.

History at the Heart of Social Science

This return to history, with all its accompanying dangers, also poses a question to social scientists. After all, social science was not very successful in grasping, let alone predicting, the dramatic processes that brought about the disintegration of communism.

The lesson in this for social scientists, and it can be touched on only briefly here, is a need for more humility with regard to the usefulness of quantitative data, for more reverence for historical contexts—that is, for the role of human consciousness in human affairs. History is not an ontological entity, existing outside human consciousness. Ultimately, it is the totality of choices human beings make about what they remember and transmit to their next generations. As Hegel once remarked, all revolutions are preceded by a quiet and lengthy revolution in human consciousness, "a revolution not visible to every eye, especially imperceptible to contemporaries, and as hard to discern as to describe in words." And "it is the lack of acquaintance with this spiritual revolution which makes the resulting changes astonishing."

Changes in the core of human thinking cannot be captured through diagrams or observed from a distance through digests of official statements and press cuttings (usually in translation). They can be glimpsed in the way human beings express themselves and behave—in their language, their literature, their concrete human discourse. Two examples suffice. In 1974, on Assumption Day in Zagorsk, thousands of young female pilgrims, none of whom was even born when the communist revolution broke out, gathered at the shrine. And in 1986 Moscow intellectuals were preoccupied with whether local street names should be changed to their prerevolutionary names to preserve the meaning of 19th-century Russian literature. It is fair to guess that these two foreshadowings of the dramatic events of the past several years were never documented in the voluminous files kept by professional Western observers of the Soviet Union.

Some humility, then, is in order. If we are to understand in the future the momentous events connected with the decline and fall of communism and the Soviet empire, we must be guided by humility before the obdurate nature of human consciousness.

Article 3

SOCIAL EDUCATION February 1992

Changes 1988-1991

Created by :
R.R. DONNELLEY CARTOGRAPHIC SERVICES
Lancaster, Pennsylvania

Incorporated into Soviet Union[1]	Republic	Declaration of Sovereignty[2]	Declaration of Independence[2,3]	Signatory to new "Commonwealth" agreement[3]	Recognition of Independent Status[3]
1940	ESTONIA	16 Nov. 1988	A 21 Aug. 1991		F 6 Sept. 1991
1940	LITHUANIA	18 May 1989	11 March 1990		F 6 Sept. 1991
1940	LATVIA	28 July 1989	B 21 Aug. 1991		F 6 Sept. 1991
1922	AZERBAIJAN	23 Sept. 1989	30 Aug. 1991	21 Dec. 1991	G 25 Dec. 1991
1922	GEORGIA	9 March 1990	9 April 1991		G 25 Dec. 1991
1922	RUSSIA	12 June 1990	C	D 8 Dec. 1991	G 25 Dec. 1991
1924	UZBEKISTAN	20 June 1990	29 Aug. 1991	21 Dec. 1991	G 25 Dec. 1991
1940	MOLDOVA	23 June 1990	27 Aug. 1991	21 Dec. 1991	G 25 Dec. 1991
1922	UKRAINE	16 July 1990	24 Aug. 1991	E 8 Dec. 1991	G 25 Dec. 1991
1922	BYELARUS	27 July 1990	25 Aug. 1991	E 8 Dec. 1991	G 25 Dec. 1991
1924	TURKMENISTAN	22 Aug. 1990	27 Oct. 1991	21 Dec. 1991	G 25 Dec. 1991
1922	ARMENIA	23 Aug. 1990	23 Sept. 1991	21 Dec. 1991	G 25 Dec. 1991
1929	TAJIKISTAN	24 Aug. 1990	9 Sept. 1991	21 Dec. 1991	G 25 Dec. 1991
1936	KAZAKHSTAN	26 Oct. 1990	16 Dec. 1991	21 Dec. 1991	G 25 Dec. 1991
1936	KYRGYZSTAN	12 Dec. 1990	31 Aug. 1991	21 Dec. 1991	G 25 Dec. 1991

Sources: 1. The Statesman's Yearbook (1991-92)
2. U.S. Department of State
3. News Media

© 1991 R.R. Donnelley & Sons Company

Notes: A. Transition to independence declared March 30, 1990.
B. Transition to independence declared May 4, 1990.
C. No formal declaration. In effect declared independence by signing commonwealth agreement, and asking for international recognition as an independent state.
D. Ratified by parliament on December 12, 1991.

E. Ratified by parliaments on December 10, 1991.
F. Independence formally recognized by Soviet Union.
G. Widespread international recognition began on December 25, following the resignation of Mikhail S. Gorbachev as President of the Soviet Union formally marking the point at which the U.S.S.R. ceased to exist.

Recent* city name changes in the former USSR

*Information as of December, 1991

RUSSIA

BYELARUS

•St. Petersburg

Tver'
•Rybinsk
•Sergiyev Posad

MOLDOVA   UKRAINE   •Nizhniy Novgorod

Zmiyev,   Liski

Bulgar,   •Izhevsk

Mariupol'   •Lugansk   Naberezhnyye   •Yekaterinburg
Chelny

Samara

RUSSIA

Sharypovo

Martvili   Khoni
Senaki   Kharagauli
Ozurgeti   •Vladikavkaz
Bagdadi   GEORGIA
Kumayri

ARMENIA

•Gyandzha

KAZAKHSTAN

AZERBAIJAN

UZBEKISTAN

TURKMENISTAN   •Bishkek
Khudzhand,   Issyk-Kul'•
KYRGYZSTAN

TAJIKISTAN

N

| 0 | | .400 | | 800 Mi. |
| 0 | 400 | 800 Km. | | |

New Name[1]	Former Name	Location[3]
Bagdadi	Mayakovskiy	GEORGIA
Bishkek[2]	Frunze	KYRGYZSTAN
Bulgar	Kuybyshev	RUSSIA (Tatarskaya ASSR)
Gyandzha	Kirovabad	AZERBAIJAN
Issyk-Kul'	Rybach'ye	KYRGYZSTAN
Izhevsk	Ustinov	RUSSIA
Kharagauli	Ordzhonikidze	GEORGIA
Khoni	Tsulukidze	GEORGIA
Khudzhand	Leninabad	TAJIKISTAN
Kumayri	Leninakan	ARMENIA
Liski	Georgiu-Dezh	RUSSIA
Lugansk	Voroshilovgrad	UKRAINE
Mariupol'	Zhdanov	UKRAINE
Martvili	Gegechkori	GEORGIA
Naberezhnyye Chelny	Brezhnev	RUSSIA
Nizhniy Novgorod	Gor'kiy	RUSSIA
Ozurgeti	Makharadze	GEORGIA
Rybinsk	Andropov	RUSSIA
St. Petersburg	Leningrad	RUSSIA
Samara	Kuybyshev	RUSSIA
Senaki	Mikha Tskhakaya	GEORGIA
Sergiyev Posad	Zagorsk	RUSSIA
Sharypovo	Chernenko	RUSSIA
Tver'	Kalinin	RUSSIA
Vladikavkaz	Ordzhonikidze	RUSSIA
Yekaterinburg	Sverdlovsk	RUSSIA
Zmiyev	Gotval'd	UKRAINE

1. Spellings as approved by the U.S. Board on Geographic Names.

2. Capital city.

3. The former republic of Byelorussia has recently changed its name to *Byelarus* (translation as approved by the U.S. Board on Geographic Names). Moldavia, in 1990, changed its name to *Moldova*.

Created by :
R.R. DONNELLEY CARTOGRAPHIC SERVICES
Lancaster, Pennsylvania

Article 4

THE WORLD TODAY
MARCH 1992

International boundaries: ex-Soviet Union and Eastern Europe

In these times of recession, one group of people you do not have to feel sorry for are the cartographers. They are being kept busy. The map of Europe, set in stone for so long, is having to be redrawn all the time as countries are born, reborn or disappear.

In fact, the question of international boundaries is dominating politics throughout Europe, but in contrasting ways in East and West. In the West, a massive effort has been under way to reduce the borders between EC countries almost to insignificance, in the effort to create a frontier-free internal market and eventually (if the federalists have their way) a United States of Europe.

The old physical boundaries between East and West have come crashing down too: in Budapest you can buy pieces of the Iron Curtain from the border between Hungary and Austria, in Berlin there is little sign of the Berlin Wall save for the bits touted by street traders. But farther still to the East, new frontier posts and barbed-wire borders are busily being erected, as Yugoslavia and the Soviet Union break up. Here lies a frightening potential for conflict - and a great challenge for diplomacy.

For years, borders in the East did not seem to matter. Not that they were really uncontroversial. Far from it. It was just that any border disputes were frozen under Communist rule. Communist leaders, Stalin especially, altered borders and transported whole tribes from their homelands almost at whim. The result has been to create a time bomb that is now ready to explode (and in Yugoslavia, has already exploded): scores of border questions that suddenly have to be resolved, some of them no doubt bloodily.

A few figures illustrate the scale of the problem. They are based on research at the Russian Academy of Sciences Institute of Geography. Of the 23 borders between the republics of the former Soviet Union, only three are not contested at all (the three are those between Latvia and Lithuania, between Latvia and Byelorussia, and between Byelorussia and Russia). In all, the researchers had by December 1991 counted more than 160 border disputes in the former Soviet Union. Since 1921 there have been at least 90 changes in Soviet borders. Most happened in the early years of Soviet rule (45 in 1921-30, 26 in 1931-40, and no more than 7 in any subsequent decade), when the Communists were not in full control of the country, since when the status quo was fixed by repression. Now the repression has gone, and the old border tussles are ready to resume.

One immediate result of this is that diplomats, journalists and any other interested observers have to scurry back to their history, geography and ethnography books. Suddenly there is a need to know about the difference between the Chechen and the Ingush, about the history of places like Nagorno-Karabakh and Dagestan, about the ethnic mix in would-be independent Tatarstan or Bashkiria (as it happens, Bashkirs 22 per cent, Tatars 28 per cent, Russians 39 per cent), about the conflicts over Bucovina and Transdniestria, about the grievances of South Ossetians, Abkhazians, Adjars, Meskhetians and so on.

To begin to bring some order into this potential chaos, the disputes in the East can be categorised in various ways. One way might be according to the type of border change envisaged. Thus there is:

● Secession. Attempts to turn 'internal' boundaries into external ones (e.g., Slovenia, Croatia, Latvia, Lithuania), or to secede from one country to another (e.g., Nagorno-Karabakh).

● Revision. May accompany, or be a response to, secession (e.g., Serbia's attempt to carve out 'Greater Serbia'). Could apply to countries arguing over control of particular border areas (e.g., Russia and Ukraine over the Crimea).

● Deletion. Happens when one country merges with its neighbour (e.g., German unification, possibly Romania and Moldova).

● Creation. The push for new enclaves to accommodate minorities (e.g., the demands for a German republic in Russia).

● Restoration. The re-introduction of a frontier that had been abolished (e.g., attempts to restore the border between the self-proclaimed independent republic of Chechenya and Ingushetia that disappeared when Stalin merged the two autonomous *oblasts* in 1934).

● Partition. A specific form of the creation of new frontiers or restoration of old ones, when a country is divided into two or more pieces, possibly by a rather arbitrary new border (e.g., the attempt by Bosnian Serbs to partition Bosnia to give Serbs a separate area; possibly, eventually, a division of Kazakhstan into Russian and Kazakh parts).

Alternatively, border disputes can be classified according to their degree of immediacy. A useful scale might run as follows:

● Dead (e.g., with luck, the dispute over the Oder-Neisse line as the border between Germany and Poland).

● Dormant (e.g., Transylvania, potential Finnish claims on the parts of Karelia lost to Russia). Most disputes in the ex-Soviet Union were in this category until the Gorbachev reforms.

● Awakening (e.g., the Crimea, Kosovo). Many disputes in the ex-Soviet Union have now moved up into this category.

● Wide awake (e.g., the Kuriles, Tatarstan, Bashkiria, Czechoslovakia). A growing number of disputes are graduating into this category.

● Hyperactive (e.g., Yugoslavia, Nagorno-Karabakh, South Ossetia, Checheno-Ingushetia).

It is pointless in this space to attempt to list all the actual or potential disputes in Eastern Europe and the ex-Soviet Union. But a look at three examples gives a flavour of what can be involved, and their potential to create havoc.

First, the most immediate current example: *Yugoslavia*. The details and complexities of the Serb-Croat conflict are by now common knowledge thanks to exhaustive news reporting. Less attention has been paid to the potential for trouble to spread beyond the current war zone (or, with luck, cease-fire zone) of Croatia. The Kosovo province in Serbia, 90 per cent inhabited by ethnic Albanians, is a flash-point still waiting to explode; leaders of crisis-ridden Albania proper may be tempted to play the 'national card' and make a claim to Kosovo. The prospect of Macedonia's independence alarms Greece. And ethnically mixed Bosnia will have to sort itself out.

Second, there is a potential conflict with perhaps the best chance of leading to a war with wider ramifications: the looming dispute between *Ukraine and Romania/Moldova* over Northern Bucovina. It could develop like this. Sooner or later, Romania and Moldova are likely to re-unite. A row could then flare up over Northern Bucovina, which used to be part of Romania but which Stalin gave to Ukraine when the Soviet republic of Moldavia was formed from what used to be Bessarabia. The Romanians will want Bucovina back. The issue could fan Romanian nationalism (already a potent force), and that in turn could increase tensions with the Hungarian minority in Transylvania, which could in turn stir up anti-Romanian passion in Hungary proper.

Third, consider the case that could potentially cause the biggest explosion: *the Crimea*. This was part of Russia until it was casually handed to Ukraine by Nikita Khrushchev in 1954 as a gift to commemorate the 300th anniversary of the 'fraternal union' between the Ukrainian and Russian peoples. Now Ukraine has exploited the fact that Crimea is part of its newly independent country to claim the whole of the Black Sea Fleet, based at Sebastopol in the Crimea. Russians outnumber Ukrainians in the area, though there was (just) a majority for Ukrainian independence in the December 1991 referendum. If local Russian dissatisfaction rises, and if the political leaders in Moscow succumb to the urge to claim back arbitrarily lost territory, Crimea could easily become the cause of conflict between the two big new (and nuclear) Slav states.

One prominent Russian nationalist is Vladimir Zhirinovsky, a far-right fanatic who won 6m votes in last year's election for Russian president. He illustrates the potential for conflict over the 25m or so Russians who live outside Russia proper. Once in power, he said recently that he would invade Afghanistan and turn it into a Russian 'province'; sell off western Ukraine to Poland and take the rest for Russia; and 'bury radioactive waste along the Lithuanian border and buy powerful fans and blow the stuff across the border at night. They'll get radiation sickness and die of it. When they either die or get down on their knees, then I'll stop it. I'm a dictator. What I am going to do is bad, but it is good for Russia.'

But just pointing to dangers is easy. Scare-mongering about the East is a popular new sport. What is needed is a realistic assessment of the risks (which suggests a third possible categorisation of disputes, ranging from localised and low-key to international and urgent), and ideas on how to respond to them. Exactly how serious is the potential for conflict? What lessons can be drawn from the Yugoslav experience? What can outsiders do to limit the dangers or help resolve disputes? Are there any useful rules or guidelines that might help policy-makers?

It is still too soon to draw confident conclusions from the war in Yugoslavia, but compared with early fears the verdict may in the end prove rather reassuring. The nightmare has been that the conflict would spread, like previous Balkan wars, and that Serbia would grab the bits of territory it wanted with relative impunity, showing that might is right. In fact, the war has remained contained, so far anyway. And it is beginning to look as though the Serb-dominated federal army is going to have to move back from Croatia, showing that aggression does not pay after all. Encouragingly, therefore, it may well be that others in the East will be unable to conclude, looking at the Yugoslav example, that they should simply take coveted territory by force and expect to get away with it.

Nor will would-be secessionists conclude that a bid for independence is a simple and costless venture that can be undertaken lightly. That does not mean that the Yugoslav disaster is cause for complacency. On the contrary, Yugoslavia has also shown that third-party mediation is helpful and necessary, but that the mediation should come much earlier and be more imaginative than was managed in Yugoslavia. Foreign governments, too attached to the status quo and with no special interest in seeing Yugoslavia come unstuck, naively failed to appreciate that the force of old ethnic conflicts is something that cannot be wished away. Even in late twentieth-century Europe, it has to be adjusted to, carefully managed and accommodated.

Western governments are in a position to influence developments in a number of ways: for example, through the carrot of diplomatic recognition and aid, or the stick of economic and political sanctions. In deciding how to respond, it would be convenient if governments could follow a ready set of rules or principles. Prominent in any rule book might be the following:

● Encourage economic integration. The European Community is the best model available of how age-old national antagonisms can be contained and overcome. It has been based on a concerted effort at mutual economic openness. This should be encouraged in the East (and the growing temptation to construct customs barriers resisted).

● Encourage respect for borders. Let 'Helsinki rules' apply to all borders, whether internal or international: they should not be changed by force, only if at all by negotiation. Encouragingly, in a protocol at the December meeting in Alma Ata that set up the new Commonwealth of Independent States, the 11 members recognised each others' borders. Maybe many of the borders in the ex-Soviet Union are unfair or irrational, but then so are the arbitrary straight-line borders in Africa. Tampering with them or with the previously internal borders of Yugoslavia is to open, as it were, a Pandora's Bosnia.

● Encourage respect for minority rights. Proper attention to the culture, language, self-government and other needs of ethnic minorities may be the best way of containing many disputes. New or would-be countries should be pressed to accept rules of the Conference on Security and Cooperation in Europe (CSCE) and other tests of good behaviour, much as the European Community has made recognition of ex-Yugoslav republics conditional on their satisfying a number of criteria (including acceptance of UN, Helsinki Act and Paris Charter commitments on the rule of law, democracy and human rights and acceptance of the inviolability of all frontiers).

● Respect the principle of self-determination. If a region really wants to secede, and has voted democratically to do so, the right to go its own way should be respected.

● Insist on adherence to security treaties. For example, do not grant recognition to ex-Soviet republics planning to ignore the START (strategic arms limitation) or CFE (conventional forces reduction) treaties.

● Beware of involvement in a country's 'internal affairs'. The West should not just barge in everywhere. It should beware of doing more harm than good. Sometimes the best policy will be to do nothing.

The trouble is that none of these rules can be neatly applied. Each case is complicated. It is all very well to encourage economic integration, but both the Soviet Union and Yugoslavia were single-currency areas with highly interdependent economies; that did not prevent break-up.

The case against any forced border changes is strong. There should be an extreme prejudice against any tampering. But should border changes never be imposed by outsiders? What about the extreme case where the alternative to a border change is heavy bloodshed? An alternative (or accompaniment) to shifting borders might be the organised transfer of populations.

Minority rights are all very well, as far as they go. But can Western tests of good behaviour really be strictly enforced? Political pressures and interests have weighed heavily, for example, in the EC's decisions on whether or not individual ex-Yugoslav republics pass the test. Besides, minority rights (including the right to self-determination) can clash with majority rights. It would patently be unfair if any rich bit of any country were able to secede and thus leave the rest of the country in the lurch. That is why Russia has a good case in resisting the independence of a number of oil sheikhdoms or diamond kingdoms, whose secession would leave the Russians without some of their most valuable natural resources. A greedy few would in effect be impoverishing the majority.

So additional rules for secession have to be brought in. For example, it might be deemed essential that a seceding area must have some sort of 'historical identity'; that financial or other compensation must be negotiated for the assets and future revenues forgone by the country being seceded from; that special needs and demands - such as access to ports or renunciation of nuclear weapons - be set down in new treaties. But those extra rules are problematic too: the question of historical identity may be highly disputed (Macedonia is a case in point), and arguments over who exploited whom economically and by how much may often be insoluble. The most explosive current argument over assets is that between Russia and Ukraine over the Black Sea Fleet - which also shows how easily military hardware can become part of a power tussle that pays little heed to the security concerns of the West.

As for non-interference in countries' 'internal affairs', this will often look an absurd principle. In Yugoslavia, part of the whole issue has been whether the affair was 'internal' (i.e., Yugoslavia still exists) or international (i.e., Slovenia and Croatia are independent states). The West was drawn in willy-nilly.

The unhappy conclusion is that the situation in Eastern Europe and the ex-Soviet Union is unusually messy. In response, foreign diplomacy will have to be flexible, creative, quick off the mark, sometimes thrusting, sometimes restrained.

The formula sounds rather like the recipe for a successful service industry. Imagine the creation of a thing called Western Border Solutions plc (WBS for short). This would be a joint venture between the Western governments and various organisations whose services are likely to prove useful: the European Community, the UN, the CSCE. According to the needs arising, WBS would be able to call on various specialist subsidiaries: General Mediation Offices; Human Rights Advisory Partners; Justice B. Dunne Legal Services: Sanctions Unlimited; Blue Helmet Security Amalgamated. One thing is sadly sure: over the next few years, it is going to be a growth industry.

DANIEL FRANKLIN

Article 5   FEBRUARY 10, 1992 THE NEW REPUBLIC

THE YELTSIN REVOLUTION

By Martin Malia

Over the last five years, it has become clear that the process of communism's disintegration is as revolutionary as the process that established it in power. And this second revolution, a revolution against the heritage of the first revolution, has just as clearly not yet run its course. So far this new revolution has known three phases. The first was Gorbachev's perestroika, which one of his idea men, Fedor Burlatsky, now characterizes as "a revolution of the dilettantes," an impossible wager to reform the system without abandoning its socialist foundations. The second was the actual demise of communism, when the wager ended in the total collapse of the system: the fall of Eastern Europe in 1989, which demonstrated that the "conquests of socialism" were reversible, and hence the system everywhere was mortal; then the coup de grace in the heart of the system, Russia, last year. At present Boris Yeltsin and the Russian democrats are launching a third phase, that of building a post-Communist order, or as they would put it, of "returning Russia to Europe" by creating a "normal society." The great question now is whether this, too, will turn out to be an impossible wager.

Clearly no one in the West takes Yeltsin for a miracle worker, as some once did Gorbachev, and there is no Western cult of his personality. Quite the contrary, his government is regarded with suspicion, if not hostility. At best he is accorded grudging support in the interests of post-Soviet stability. The lack of a positive Western response to the Yeltsin wager could weigh against its chances of success. This is a government, after all, that aims at integration into the world community.

But the principal factor governing the prospects for Yeltsin's reform is the legacy of Soviet failure, including perestroika. The scope of the Soviet collapse is unprecedented in modern, indeed world, history. This point

MARTIN MALIA is professor of Russian history at the University of California, Berkeley. His book *The Soviet Tragedy* is forthcoming from Free Press.

bears emphasis because mainline American Sovietologists have long misconstrued the Soviet system, making it appear much more of a success than it really was. They argued that the USSR was no longer totalitarian but had developed into an "institutional pluralism," and was thus capable of a "transition" to some sort of social democracy. Their processing of flawed Soviet data through Western models for calculating the GNP produced an economic success story that augured well for an evolution to democracy and that also informed the CIA's absurd belief that the Soviet economy was some 60 percent of the American.

Thus we were presented with a maturing Soviet society quite prepared to make the wager of perestroika a success. And so such authorities as Professors Jerry Hough and Stephen Cohen, for five years, regularly assured us. But the exit from communism, when it came, was not a transition or an evolution. It was a brusque collapse, a total implosion, of a sort unheard of in history: a great state abolished itself utterly—in a matter of weeks—and right from under its president. The reason this happened is that the Soviet Union, *pace* most Western Sovietology, was in fact a total society, with all aspects of life linked in what one scholar called a "mono-organization" whole. At its core was the Party to which all aspects of life were subordinated: the economy, government, culture, private life itself. This total society logically ended in a total collapse of all its interrelated parts at once. Thus we now have in the midst of the resulting rubble a total problem embracing every aspect of life.

What is Yeltsin's program for coping with this universal crisis? Indeed, does Russia's first democratic government have a coherent program at all? And how do its policies relate to Russian nationalism, the matter that seems to worry the West most about post-Sovietism? The bedrock of the Russian democratic program since 1989 is to undo everything that communism has done since 1917, including Gorbachev. As such, the program is truly revolutionary, its notion of "democracy" a post-Communist and revolutionary notion. Yeltsin and the democrats have too often been presented in the West simply as populist rivals of Gorbachev, out for power. But all Yeltsin's statements, from his June presidential campaign through his recent New Year's address, show that he seeks to effect the "rebirth of Russia" by "liberating" her from the "destructive disaster of communism." This aim should be taken quite seriously, and literally.

Thus, Russian democracy means, first, refusal of the Communist monopoly of political power, which translates as the principle of a multiparty order. Democracy means, second, refusal of the Communist monopoly of economic power, which translates as the principle of private property. And the rule of law derives logically from the first two principles. Finally, at the end of the process of challenging the Communist order came the challenge to still another Party monopoly of power—that of state authority—which translates as the dissolution of the pseudo-federation, or Union.

The history of this program's development bears repeating, since it was generated by a series of shocks, of collisions with Party authority. The first came at the Congress of People's Deputies in May-June 1989. Even though Gorbachev had an overwhelming, and in the words of Yuri Afanasiev, "aggressively submissive" majority, a liberal minority of the Congress spoke out, on national TV, against the appalling ills of the system. The result was a "demystification" of communism from which it never recovered. At the same time these liberals, largely from the *Moscow Tribune* group, became convinced that Gorbachev in no way contemplated power-sharing and must be openly opposed. They formed the Interregional Group of Deputies, under Andrei Sakharov and Yeltsin, which brought together all the future stars of Russian democracy, from Gavriil Popov and Sergei Stankevich to Anatoli Sobchak. Russian "civil society," as all groups independent of the state now came to be known, thereby received a political expression; and its program was the end of the Party's "leading role" in all spheres of life.

At first the heretical right to private property was mentioned only sotto voce by the democrats. But with the collapse of Eastern European communism in the fall of 1989 this issue, together with its corollary—the market, now came to the fore. By spring 1990 the example of Poland's "big bang" transition to the market led the Soviet government to draft plans for transition to a "regulated market," another self-defeating half-measure. But they were soon forced to go further when a new front against the Party-state was opened up in June 1990 by the movement for the sovereignty of the Union republics. Launched by Russia, following the Baltic example, this movement by the end of the summer had spread throughout the Union. The very existence of the "center" was now called into question.

Because of this weakening of the center, it became possible for the democrats to force the issue of private property. The result was the "500-Day Plan" associated with Stanislav Shatalin and Grigori Yavlinsky. This plan was not exactly "shock therapy," because the shift to the market was spread over a year and a half, but it had revolutionary implications. A political as much as an economic document, it emanated from a group of younger economists under Yavlinsky who wanted simply to finish with the system. They planned to do this by establishing republic, or local, control in moving to the market, an approach that would automatically undermine the Party-state's "center." Yeltsin quickly espoused this plan, and then prevailed on Gorbachev to accept it also. But in September Gorbachev suddenly drew back, as he and the rest of the establishment realized the political threat this economic program entailed.

From the fall of 1990 to the spring of 1991 Gorbachev moved to the "right," back to the Party, police, army, and military-industrial hierarchies. The Yeltsin democrats, sensing they could soon be eliminated, fought back with demonstrations and strikes. As a result, Gorbachev in April flipped again to the left, giving way to Yeltsin and the republics on most points in a new, more flexible Union treaty. But this capitulation appeared to the old guard as the death sentence of the Party-state. Just before the new treaty's signing on August 19, this group declared their president to be incapacitated and took over, as a prelude to quashing the democrats by force.

Two things about this famous "coup" require emphasis, because both are prudishly ignored in the Western press. First, this "coup" was in fact no coup at all, because the "coup plotters," as they are quaintly called, were none other than the Soviet government: the vice president, the prime minister, the ministers of defense and interior, the head of the KGB, the chairman of the Supreme Soviet, and the chief of staff of Gorbachev's personal Cabinet. They were quite simply the whole Communist establishment; their aim was to depose a chief whose indecision they believed, correctly, was leading the system to catastrophe. If Gorbachev did not know that these close collaborators, all of whom he had appointed, were working toward a state of emergency, then he was incompetent, which is as bad as complicit.

The second notable thing about the August coup is that Yeltsin and the democrats were ready not only to resist it, but also to escalate this resistance into a counter-coup against the Party-state. Once the junta's military thrust had been thwarted, Yeltsin suspended the Communist Party, took over the KGB and army command, appointed an economic committee under Yavlinsky, and began measures to decommunize and professionalize public functions. All of this was done by a cascade of decrees previously prepared in the Russian Council of Ministers. Thus, although all constitutional forms were preserved by restoring Gorbachev to power, and indeed using him to validate the new decrees, in fact a counter-coup had been carried out disestablishing the Communist system. This behavior was criticized abroad at the time as "autocratic." But there could be no democracy in Russia without first dismantling the Leninist system. It would have been absurd to try to pass Yeltsin's measures through the "due process" of a Communist legislature. The only feasible course was to seize the opportunity provided by the post-coup vacuum and to act swiftly, while the momentum of victory was still strong.

So began the third and most radical stage of what had become an open revolution against Leninism. And this third stage will be the most difficult in the exit from communism. For getting rid, at last, of the system also means provoking the final collapse of all its components: the economy, the administrative system, the state structure itself. Nor were the democrats ready for these problems. Their clear adversary, the Party, had evaporated. Thrust into power far sooner than they had anticipated, the new government floundered in its first six weeks, eroding the trust of a public bewildered by Yeltsin's lack of follow-through and panicked as full realization of the economic disaster at last hit them. The president disappeared to the Crimea for two weeks, whether to recuperate after a grueling year or to let his contentious followers sort themselves out back in Moscow, it is still not clear. For there was—and still is—a real problem of the coherence of the Yeltsin coalition.

Who constitutes this coalition? Among Yeltsin's supporters there is first the Democratic Russia Movement, whose president is Afanasiev, an alliance of various parties and lobbies going back to March 1990, which put Yeltsin, Sobchak, Popov, and other democrats into office. But this is a broad movement, like Solidarity, not a cohesive political party; and once *the* Party was no longer in the field, "Dem Russia" began to splinter, just as Solidarity did. Second, there is the Interregional Group of Deputies, which has given Yeltsin crucial members of his Advisory Council, such as Stankevich and the radical democrat Galina Staravoitova. Quite different is the Urals group of old Yeltsin aides, prominent among whom is his de facto prime minister, Gennadi Burbulis, a 45-year-old ex-professor of "scientific communism." These men are provincials, often from the old apparat and with links to the military-industrial complex so dominant in the Urals, though they are now fiercely anti-Communist.

Then there are the liberal deputies of the Russian Parliament, associated with that body's chairman, Ruslan Khasbulatov, who is, however, still a defender of social-

ism. Yeltsin acquired this dubious ally for his first election as president in 1990, and Khasbulatov, as well as most of the Parliament, is now opposing Yeltsin's liberalization by refusing to name a new, non-Communist director of the State Bank. Beyond this circle, there is General Alexander Rutskoi, Afghan War hero, leader of "Communists for Democracy," and vice president. This ally Yeltsin acquired in March 1991 in order to split the Communist majority in Parliament, so as to survive impeachment by Gorbachev's Communists, and he took him in June as vice president. Rutskoi is also outspoken against liberalization, so there is a growing chance of constitutional conflict between Yeltsin and Parliament. Then there is Yeltsin's still solid clientele in the army, which voted heavily for him in June, led by Marshal Shaposhnikov; and with these, most of the intelligentsia of Moscow and St. Petersburg, who abandoned Gorbachev for Yeltsin. Such a heterogeneous group obviously could not live in harmony for long after August: choices both of policy and of personnel would have to be made. It was only in late October that these choices began to emerge, and it was not until late November that a new government was formed to implement them.

After August two great issues faced the new government: how to effect the unavoidable shift to the market and private property, and what to do about the "Union." And these two were closely linked: economic reform within the Union as a whole could only be based on compromise and hence would be by steps; economic reform in Russia alone would mean a sharp plunge, and hence meant destroying the Union framework. On both issues the radical option was finally chosen—but only after four months of struggle within the democratic coalition, and between Russia and the other republics.

In August a special committee under the Russian prime minister, Ivan Silayev, and Yavlinsky was put in charge of the economy and made into a Union body. This approach led by October 1 to the signing of an economic Union at a meeting of most of the republics in Alma-Ata. A month after Alma-Ata, however, further talks failed to give life to the new economic Union because of a deep divergence of Russia's interests from the other republics'. The conflict was due above all to the fact that Russia—unlike all the others except the Baltic states and Caucasian republics—had made an anti-Communist revolution. In Ukraine, Belarus, Kazakhstan, and Central Asia, the Party of Leonid Kravchuk, Ivan Shushkevich, and Nursultan Nazarbayev is still in power. All had behaved ambiguously during the coup. Most were neither ready nor eager for rapid marketization.

In late October the Yeltsin government therefore opted for a radical "Russia first" program, which the republics could follow as they might. In an address on October 28, Yeltsin announced that most prices would be freed by year's end, without wage indexation; privatization would also begin. He also called for accompanying emergency political measures. First, he had elections suspended for a year. Public opinion surveys made by the government had shown that if elections were held, the democrats would be in trouble. The Russians had also noted that recent elections to the Polish Sejm had returned a fragmented, unmanageable legislature. Yeltsin thus received power to rule by decree, subject to some parliamentary supervision. Finally, he assumed direct responsibility by taking the post of premier himself. He declared that if his new government did not begin to produce results within a year, he would step down.

When things had shaken down by November, it turned out that the August government of Prime Minister Silayev, and yesteryear's economic innovator, Yavlinsky, who advocated an all-Union, phased approach, had lost out to a more junior group of economists, mostly under 35, led by Yegor Gaidar, who favored a "Russia first" program of shock therapy. It is Burbulis, the allegedly benighted professor of scientific communism, who persuaded Yeltsin (obviously no expert in economics) to adopt this radical program, and to form the new ministry around the "Young Turks," or the "Boys in Reeboks," as they are known.

Accordingly, at the end of November Burbulis became first deputy prime minister, Gaidar deputy prime minister for the economy and finances, and Alexander Shokhin deputy prime minister for labor and employment. In the words of Mikhail Berger, the highly regarded economic expert of *Izvestia*, these men and their colleagues are the first group of real economists ever to be put in charge of the Russian economy. Basically pragmatic, they have also worked with the International Monetary Fund and the World Bank to make sure their program meets international standards, and with such Western economists as Jeffrey Sachs of Harvard and Anders Aslund, the Swedish economist and Soviet expert, who have been given offices near the Kremlin and have worked actively in preparing Gaidar's reform.

This reform proposes the most far-reaching change since Stalin built socialism. In December the country was opened to almost unrestricted foreign investment, with a right to repatriate profits. On January 2 came the liberation of prices except for basic food staples, energy, and transportation, where prices are to be increased three- or fourfold. Still to come are control of the budget deficit and inflation, stabilization of the currency, and internal convertibility of the ruble. Privatization of 70 percent of retail commerce and services has been targeted for the end of 1992. At the same time, measures of "social defense" have been adopted by Labor Minister Shokhin to tide the country over what can only be a painful transition for the majority of the population, some 50 percent of which lives below the official poverty line.

In addition, major decisions have at long last been made about agriculture, the greatest scandal of the Soviet economy. At the end of the year Yeltsin decreed that land would be given to peasants as private property, with resale subject only to minimal restrictions. This measure was to take effect immediately to permit results before spring sowing. Moreover, Russia's state and collective farms are to be dissolved. Gorbachev never contemplated anything more than long-term leasing of land to peasants, a precarious tenure they were never willing to accept. Yeltsin's decision is truly revolutionary, the surest sign that the new government is in earnest. Though many criticisms can be made of this program, Russia at last *has* a program, and Yeltsin must act while he still enjoys public confidence. The program is risky, but it is less risky than doing nothing.

This choice of a radical economic program was also a major factor in condemning the Union. Gaidar and his "boys" had always wished to get rid of the dead weight of the republics and their conservatism. When in December the latter tried to postpone the date of price liberalization from December 15 to late January, Russia unilaterally fixed the date at January 2. Most of the republics followed. If the former empire is to modernize its economy rapidly, clearly Russia will have to be the locomotive of the transformation.

Other forces worked to condemn the Union. Nationalism is one of these, but it acts in a special way under Soviet conditions. Most of the fifteen former republics are not real nations. With the exception of Georgia, Armenia, and the Baltic states, none has existed as a historic nation within its present borders or ever had an independent state. These republics were administrative subdivisions, created by the "center" to neutralize national feeling and, in Asia, Islamic internationalism, by giving them a purely formal statehood. Russia is a case apart, because it is a real historic nation with a genuine state. But it was never simply a *russkii*, national state. It was a *rossiiskii*, imperial state, that included other nations as protected, if not equal, subjects of the czar. The USSR was not a Russian national state either, though it used the Russian language and culture to cement the empire. The Soviet empire was a Party-empire, in which Communist, not national, loyalty was what counted.

Moreover, neither under the old regime nor under the new had the present Russian Federation existed as a separate entity; like all the other republics, it was a Soviet administrative creation. And, strange as it may seem to foreigners, the Russians have long considered themselves to be especially oppressed by Sovietism. Their standard of living was lower than that of the other republics. Their republic had been accorded none of the external trappings of nationhood, such as a separate Communist Party or Academy of Sciences. Rather, their culture was expropriated by the "center" for socialist purposes, and Russian values denigrated as reactionary. Hence, Russian nationalism could be even more virulently anti-Soviet than that of the non-Russian republics.

When the Union's crash came last year, it was propelled by two forces: ethnic nationalism and a strong movement for local control against the Party-center. This drive for local power explains why even Russian areas of the Federation, from St. Petersburg to the Far East, and even districts within the city of Moscow, sought autonomy. And it explains the iconoclastic passion with which all Bolshevik symbols, from the name of Leningrad to the Red Flag itself, have been repudiated. Finally, it tells why the apparently reasonable device of the federal Union framework, so convenient to foreign powers and so potentially handy for negotiating the transition to democracy, could not in the end be preserved.

What emerged was Yeltsin's Commonwealth, no analogue to the European Community, and no body capable of coordinating the ex-Soviet "economic space." But neither is it simply a device for creating a new Russian hegemony in the East: Yeltsin's sponsorship of Baltic independence and his willingness to let the Asian republics go show he is no traditional "Great Russian chauvinist." What the Commonwealth comes down to is the best available compromise to keep Russia and the republics cooperating, to negotiate their real and many conflicts of interest.

For Russia, the first of these interests is the 25 million nationals beyond its frontiers, especially in Ukraine and Kazakhstan. The members of this diaspora are Yeltsin's constituents; they are, after the Armenians, the ethnic group most threatened by violence; and the Russians at home expect their government to protect those now abroad. And Ukraine, though wary of Russia's intentions, has in fact taken account of these concerns by extending citizenship to all who live on Ukrainian territory, recognizing the official use of Russian where its speakers are the majority, and reassuring the Jewish population that their rights will be respected. So far, that permanent diplomatic conference that is the Commonwealth—and the caution of its leaders—has kept the former Soviet Union from going the way of Yugoslavia.

Moreover, the Russian nationalism that we have so far seen is a positive one. The horrors of World War II have given national sentiment such a bad name that it is now often considered the antichamber of fascism—except in the Third World. This is a shallow judgment: a sense of communal cohesion, of common values, all founded on a minimally "usable past"—in short, of patriotism—is

necessary for the healthy functioning of any nation. And humanity does come in national units.

The nationalism of Yeltsin and the Russian democrats is in the lineage of the national democrats of the European revolutions of 1848. Moreover, it is not so much directed against other ex-Soviet peoples as against the spurious internationalism of communism. In its most dignified and cultural form it is represented by the medieval historian Dmitri Likhachev, advocating the return to traditional spiritual values. In its more practical and predominant form, as represented by Yeltsin and his Young Turks, it is a "Westernizing" nationalism, in the tradition of Peter the Great or the reformist prime minister of 1906–11, Piotr Stolypin. Its aim is to modernize Russia along European, and especially American, lines so as to realize her national potential.

So what can we in the West reasonably expect as the outcome of this revolution? It would be wholly misplaced to assess the Yeltsinian wager through the prism of our own Jeffersonian democracy. Attaining such standards is not in the cards; insisting on them would simply play into the hands of the many losers, East and West, of the August revolution, who have a vested interest in its failure, so as to salvage belief in the allegedly unrealized potential of the Soviet experiment. For what the Yeltsin democrats are building now in Russia is capitalism, and building capitalism is not a goal that inspires lyrical engagement, or one that people of generosity readily take to. Yet it is only if Russia succeeds in building a market economy that the higher refinements of democracy will eventually be added onto it. Thus Yeltsin's economic effort is far more important than the attempt to contract a Commonwealth. Yeltsin and his partisans also know that they have only the narrowest margin of error, and that if they fail, some rougher modernizer, on the model of General Pinochet, will take over and resort to much more brutal methods.

What we will have for at least one more year, therefore, will be an emergency executive government trying, from one crisis and improvisation to another, to navigate its way out of what is the most appalling national collapse in history. This crisis is often described as a deeper version of the Great Depression in America. In fact, the ex-Soviet Union is in much worse condition, nearer to that of post-World War II Germany and Japan. Its infrastructure is crumbling. Aeroflot no longer has adequate fuel, its planes decrepit and disintegrating; the collapse of the railroads is not far off; the oil industry is a similar shambles. At the same time, factories now function mainly through barter. This is a situation that in any country leads to emergency government. We should not forget that Franklin Roosevelt in 1933 governed largely by decree, and with the aid of Young Turks known as a "braintrust," or that the Mother of the Parliaments in 1940 suspended elections during the war, with the result that Britain went ten years without a vote. Lincoln's Emancipation Proclamation was an executive decree. Perhaps we should be prepared to allow "Czar" Boris a similar leeway, as well as the margin to make a number of mistakes.

For the task in Russia now is difficult beyond anything the privileged West has ever known. Not only must a modern society be built out of the unprecedented wreckage of the late Soviet economy and polity, but this building must be done by a population that until 1991 was molded and deformed by the Leninist lie. As the matter was put, on the day the Union died, by one longtime Party member who always knew the system was a fraud: "And we must now try to produce good out of all that evil."

Article 6

GUARDIAN WEEKLY, January 5, 1992

The four lives of Mikhail Sergeiyevich

By Michel Tatu

THE EXIT isn't glorious, but basically it was necessary for rounding out the work he has accomplished. For while Mikhail Gorbachev will go down in history as the revolutionary who helped Russia and its former dependencies to catch up at last with world civilisation and the 21st century, he will not, and could not, have been the midwife of the society which is about to emerge.

It is to his credit that he destroyed the old system, and that is already a major accomplishment. He has done as much as and even more than Lenin who, while he destroyed the regime of the tsars and left — yes, he too — his country in a parlous state, will never have been anything but the midwife of totalitarianism. As he waits for a possible "fifth life" as his country's prophet of gloom and doom, a more or less embittered "opponent" and a habitué of the international lecture circuit, Mikhail Gorbachev has already had the opportunity to ponder on a very rich career, both before and after making it to the Kremlin, a life that can be divided into four sections of very unequal length.

His first life is the one carried in the official iconography of the period "before", the life of the obedient Komsomol member, the meritorious student and the model party man who in 30 years was to work his way up from his home village of Provolnoye near Stavropol to the pinnacle of power in Moscow. Even a careful search does not turn up much about this period. Up to this day glasnost has not touched this area. Besides there still appears to be a blank on the subject of Stavropol and the area around it, a place where nothing ever happens.

That said, the young Misha's life was to be marked by three important events — the German occupation of his region for six months in 1942; Stalin's death in 1953 when the young man had already been a communist for just about a year; and, finally, the 22nd Congress of the Communist Party of the Soviet Union in 1961, an anti-Stalinist high mass organised by Khrushchev.

If the father of perestroika has still said nothng about the first event and little about the second, he has been much more prolix about the last, which was his first big political event in Moscow (he was the leader of his regional Komsomol and took part as a delegate in the congress).

Like most of his future partners in perestroika, he proclaimed himself "a child of the 20th Congress" and the first thaw. A thaw which offered him, among other advantages, a chance to travel extensively under Brezhnev. He discovered the French masses as early as 1966 (he was 39 then) and Czechoslovakia in 1969 when it was just about "normalised".

There still remain many mysteries, but the key to the unstoppable ascension which was to follow is to be sought in the skill Gorbachev had in winning the favours of powerful patrons. There was first Fedor Kulakov, head of the party in Stavropol, who completed his regional career and then nominated Gorbachev as his successor. Next, Yuri Andropov, a native of the same region, who propelled him into the forefront in the early '80s. Probably also Mikhail Suslov, the Kremlin's eminence grise, who was anxious to keep at least one young hopeful in reserve in view of all the geriatric cases crowding the Politburo. And finally Leonid Brezhnev himself, a man well-known for promoting his kith and kin. But the general secretary of the "stagnation" suspected nothing when he let this agricultural expert propel himself into the upper reaches of power in the wake of his favoured protégé, Konstantin Chernenko, a man who was 20 years his senior.

Andrei Gromyko, was another eminent party man who was caught nodding. Becoming chief king-maker, it was he who in March 1985 tilted the balance in Gorbachev's favour as Chernenko's successor, in the face of competition from Brezhnev's candidate Grishin and the Leningrad boss Grigori Romanov. Gromyko, the last survivor of Yalta died in July 1989 just in time not to see the Berlin Wall come down and the collapse of the Warsaw Pact, but late enough to have observed the ravages of the "new thinking" in the Soviet empire, the concessions made to the United States on disarmament and the withdrawal from Afghanistan (Gromyko approved its invasion in person in 1979).

The new general secretary did not however hide his hand from everybody. In the early '80s he told his wife Raisa: "Things can't go on like this." He said this also to Eduard Shevardnadze, his former Georgian "neighbour" whom he made foreign minister in 1985, and to Alexander Yakovlev, the man who was to become the ideologue of perestroika whom he had met in Canada in 1983 and whom he called back to Moscow the same year.

Yet the "second life" which began in 1985 opened on an ambivalent note. For these two genuine liberals became increasingly isolated in a team which had quite a different idea of perestroika. The former wanted to change the system of society, whereas the latter — the majority — merely wanted to make a few small changes to it to make it more efficient. The Rizhkovs, Ligachevs, Zaikovs, all brought in by Andropov because they were opposed to Brezhnev's clique, and a little later the Yazovs, Kriuchkovs and Pugos hired by Gorbachev himself were all agreeable to combating corruption and rationalising the economy, but not to go any further. Their criticism was to be concentrated mostly on the past, slightly on the present but not at all on "socialism".

It is very difficult to say to which side the general secretary tilted. Besides it was not very important at this stage. First, because Gorbachev had to take the political balances into account and couldn't do everything at once. Secondly, because any lifting of the lid on the Brezhnevian system brought in a welcome draught of fresh air.

The period of triumphant perestroika lasted until the summer of 1989. It was marked by two landmark achievements. The first was glasnost, partially inaugurated in the spring of 1986 after the Chernobyl disaster, but extended as from 1987 to policy decisions beginning with the criticism of the past. History was gradually liberated and the effect it produced was tremendous after decades of silence. The press rushed into the breach, winning 14 million new readers in 1987 alone.

The second was free and open debate. Politics became lively first inside the Communist Party, then spreading to elections. Parliamentarianism was born, and the trend was not to be stopped.

It might seem going too far to characterise the next two years as a period of stagnation. But a new and important fact appeared at this stage of Gorbachev's career. Up to now the changes had very clearly been the result of his initiatives. From now on they were increasingly to look as if they were happening against his will.

It was Andrei Sakharov who right up to his death in December 1989 kept insisting that Article 6 of the constitution, giving the country's leading role to the Communist Party rather than to its general secretary, be abrogated. It was Boris Yeltsin who now appeared to be the champion of radical reforms much more than a rather distraught Soviet president whose speeches had become flabby and who was reduced to resorting to pointless manoeuvring and lashing out all around with warnings.

Party politics made their appearance in a big way in 1990, but it was only reluctantly that Gorbachev went along with the trend.

He criticised the "politicking" which he claimed was preventing real "politicians" from doing their work properly (the subject was to crop up again in his last public addresses in 1991). The leader's popularity was in free fall in his own country as he kept hemming and hawing over perestroika.

Gorbachev was bound to pay the price for missing out on the four big opportunities of his perestroika. The first was the economic setback. He advocated radical reforms in 1987, but did nothing serious about it while at the same time introducing political reforms that shook up the entire "command economy" without replacing it with anything else. Economic ruin and mass discontent were the end result.

The second was the powerlessness to tackle the "nationalities issue" in good time. It was now the turn for blame to be shared by the whole of the Communist Party's perestroika leadership, which was more Slav than at any other time since Lenin. The rejection of Moscow's orders manifested itself from the end of 1986 in Kazakhstan, the Nagorno-Karabakh conflict erupted in 1988, and Baltic separatists began agitating the same year before going on to win power in the national parliaments the next year. Gorbachev was to fight tooth and nail to prevent the break-up of the empire, but he was always just a shade too late. The "union treaty" he was trying to negotiate right up to the very last was within his grasp until 1989. After that it was too late.

The last two opportunities he passed up were even more political. He would undoubtedly have been returned to office with a triumphant majority if he had agreed to go directly to the country. Instead of that, he chose to remain loyal to his Politburo and got himself elected cheaply on a locked slate presented by the Communist Party. He thus left the field wide open for Yeltsin, whose legitimacy was accordingly to become incomparably superior to Gorbachev's. This prevented him from getting down to a job that had been neglected for too long — purging the party and its executive bodies.

Yegor Ligachev, his N° 2 man at the time, today admits that perestroika blew off course in 1988 and he struggled against it, but the general secretary "did not have a majority in the central committee to oust me". He simply diminished the bases of his power by making questionable adjustments. Nor did he have a majority to call a regular congress for renewing the party parliament. This took place only in the summer of 1990, once again too late.

For meanwhile the hardline communists had become reorganised pretty well everywhere, both in the state machinery and the party. In August 1990, under pressure from his prime minister Nikolai Ryzhkov, Gorbachev shelved Stanislav Shatalin's plan for economic reforms.

December saw the promotion of two bureaucrats to the top ranks of the state and administration, Gennadi Yanayev and Valentin Pavlov, who were found leading the putsch the next year. In January 1991 Gorbachev did not react to the killings perpetrated in Vilnius by the interior ministry's Omon troops and went even so far as to consider restoring press censorship.

After the August 19 putsch, he found himself even more isolated than ever. His fourth career which now began was to be the shortest and the most painful, one in which the survival of the man was identified with the continuation of a doomed system.

Gorbachev inherited many of the apparatchik's faults, like "double think" and authoritarian habits. But the authoritarianism was almost always verbal. The man can be credited with a sincere abhorrence of the use of force. He showed that when he refused to intervene against the revolutions in Eastern Europe, even when they overran the bounds—probably against his wishes—of simple Gorbachevian perestroika. He followed the same rule at home, ceaselessly pleading, despite many hiccups, for a return to dialogue and democratic methods.

But history will give him credit for having begun the work. Well may we say that Brezhnev's USSR was slowly lapsing into underdevelopment, that things "could not go on this way", but we can bet on it that the system would still be in place today if its leader had touched nothing.

(December 26)

Article 7

SOVIET
CRACKUP

NEWSWEEK : SEPTEMBER 9, 1991

The Tragedy of Gorbachev

The former foreign minister says his boss was deaf and blind

BY EDUARD SHEVARDNADZE

During the past two years, my sense that an explosion was imminent grew ever stronger. One word came increasingly to mind: "dictatorship." Finally, at dawn on Aug. 19, I was awakened by the voice of an announcer declaring a state of emergency. Everything that I'd feared and that I'd warned about had come to pass.

Today I am writing in Moscow to the sound of funeral marches for the three young men who died defending Russia's White House. The evolution of the reform process culminated in a revolution, and a personal revolution for me as well.

I knew the signatories to the document issued by the "State Committee for the State of Emergency," from Baklanov to Yazov. With some exceptions, I had already counted them among our enemies. But mistrust and speculation about the possibility of a looming dictatorship is one thing; it is another to have precise and irrefutable proof. I didn't have such proof until the coup. Still, a politician is justified in guiding himself by his intuitions. He must reveal his fears to his colleagues, his society and indeed to the whole world. This I had done.

But what had I left undone? [Two weeks ago] there was no time to think about that. I went to our Democratic Reform Movement headquarters to cheer on the Organizing Committee. Astonishingly, I was able to drive right up to the building. It was clear which way Moscow itself was

going to vote. The mass of people that had become a nation had already jammed the tank treads.

We gleaned information from the reports of the station Moscow Echo. The publications banned by the junta joined forces to put out a so-called "collective newspaper." Workers from Izvestia's printing fa-

Everything I'd feared and warned about came to pass

cility copied various Russian government documents with a manual press. With its courage, its inventiveness and its contempt for the conspirators, this independent journalism illustrated the triumph of ideas long stifled by the system: freedom of information is an inalienable aspect of freedom and democracy. Praised be information technology! Praised be CNN. Anyone who owned a parabolic antenna able to receive this network's transmissions had a complete picture of what was happening. Meanwhile, Leonid Kravchenko's servile television broadcasts emitted murky waves of lies and disinformation.

I have never lived through anything like what I would experience in those hours. At the approaches to the White House, soldiers let us pass unhindered. A young fellow in a khaki uniform embraced me and whispered, "We will defend you!" A colonel shouted after us, "Tell Yeltsin we won't let them storm the White House!" Young men who had linked arms pushed a path for us through the heavy crowds. Some women wiped the rain off my forehead with their kerchiefs.

My reflections inevitably lead back to Mikhail Sergeyevich Gorbachev, his destiny and odyssey. Who is to blame that our paths diverged? No matter how sternly I judge myself, I cannot find any guilt in myself. I did everything I could.

More than a year ago, I shared with him my conjectures that ultrareactionary forces were consolidating, clearly gravitating toward a reactionary suppression of *perestroika*. All through 1990, I had been warning him. Had I not spoken out from the podium of the Congress of People's Deputies, after exhausting all private opportunities and resources, in order to say that a dictatorship was coming?

I did speak out, but what of it? I should have stated that the president is deaf and blind, he cannot see or hear anything. I already knew very well that Mikhail Gorbachev is extremely choosy in his response to things that happen without his knowledge or agreement. With some he may be unusually patient or indulgent; with others, intolerant or irritable. Some destroy his life achievement virtually before his eyes, and he seems not even to notice. Others attempt to save this achievement, but run up against his lack of understanding.

Excerpted from "The Future Belongs to Freedom" by Eduard Shevardnadze, Будущее принадлежит свободе, to be published Sept. 23 by the Free Press, a division of Macmillan, Inc., a Maxwell Macmillan Company. Copyright 1991. Translation by Catherine A. Fitzpatrick and Joel Golb.

In my case, he said that he saw absolutely no threat of dictatorship.

I recall Oct. 15, 1990, the day the announcement was made that Gorbachev had won the Nobel Peace Prize. In the hours when Gorbachev was accepting congratulations, his foreign minister was in the Supreme Soviet, fending off attacks from the Soyuz group which accused him of the very same things that had led the Nobel Committee to award Gorbachev the prize. The next day, I called Gorbachev and congratulated him on the prize. He thanked me and said that I shared it with him. I had no need of this private recognition or any public tribute to my real or imagined merits. The only thing I needed, wanted and expected from the president was a clear delineation of his position, a direct rebuff to the right-wingers, and an open defense of our common position.

I waited in vain.

On July 23, 1991, the newspaper Sovetskaya Rossiya carried an article with the headline A WORD TO THE PEOPLE, which in my view was a call to rebellion. Among those who signed this incendiary manifesto I found the names of all those who had for many years overtly or covertly acted against the legitimate government, organized smear campaigns against us, slowed down the execution of the decisions we had made, and had called Gorbachev, Yakovlev and myself "the Knights of Malta" [a reference to the U.S.-Soviet summit in Malta, where Gorbachev made compromises disliked by the conservatives]. Heroes of the Soviet Union and Heroes of Socialist Labor, generals from the infantry and from literature proposed a plan of action. The article even mentioned people who were willing and able to take the helm of power. Two of those who signed this piece wound up in the lists of dictators, and a third went to Gorbachev in the Crimea with an ultimatum.

Despite the increasingly visible right-wing reactionary front, what did the president do? He went on vacation. What did we do, his former friends and comrades in arms who did not want to cover for the actions of the "gang" surrounding him?

Everything, even resigning from the team, was in vain. The president always remained deaf to the advice of the people genuinely loyal to him. Thus in June 1991, I felt I had to call for the unification of the country's democratic forces, for the creation of a legal opposition. I was motivated by the thought that an organized democratic opposition should become a bulwark to those few reformers who still remained in the leadership. The elbow

with which the president tried to prop himself up on the right was obviously slipping out from under him.

How did he reply to me and my friends? How did the leadership of the Communist Party respond? With threats of a party inquisition and punishment. New insults and insinuations. Persecution of the most prominent party members devoted to democracy. But the Democratic Reform Movement, which we had founded in spite of the president's wishes—and even with his obvious opposition—did not weaken, but grew and spread. And the right-wingers, seeing a threat to themselves, concentrated their fire on its initiators and leaders.

We were attacked, but Gorbachev was silent. Yes, he was busy with the drafting of the new Union Treaty. Yes, he himself suffered attacks and humiliations, but even so, with amazing stubbornness, he refused to see that the ring of the coup was closing in on him.

Did he not see it? Or did he not want to see it? Or was it something else? I don't know.

As a man and as his former comrade in arms, I agonized through the 72-hour nightmare of Gorbachev's confinement in the comfortable palace jail of Foros. He was a prisoner of the junta. But when he returned and spoke at the press conference, I saw that he was still a prisoner—of his own nature, his conceptions, and his way of thinking and acting. And now I am convinced that none other than Gorbachev himself had been spoon-feeding the junta with his indecisiveness, his inclination to back and fill, his fellow-traveling, his poor judgment of people, his indifference toward his true comrades, his

When Gorbachev returned, he was still a prisoner— of his own nature

distrust of the democratic forces and his disbelief in the bulwark whose name is the people, the very same people who had become different thanks to the perestroika he had begun.

That is the enormous personal tragedy of Mikhail Gorbachev, and no matter how much I empathize with him, I cannot help saying that his tragedy almost led to a national tragedy.

In the final analysis, the people who defended Gorbachev were those he had betrayed, mistrusted or seen as enemies: Boris Yeltsin, the people of Russia and Moscow, the democratic movements and parties, his former comrades. And I take enormous satisfaction in this, despite the tragedy of the situation, because the outcome confirmed the rightness of my chief principle: only the policy that is morally correct is victorious; only the idea based on the highest value of human life will triumph.

The coup plotters took many things into account, except the most important: the years of perestroika had rid us of fear, and we were different people now. And since we were different and they had remained the same, they could not conquer us. I am certain that the end of the military coup will be the beginning of a new country, a new community of proud, strong and free people and a new world community. During those days I was convinced anew how many of us there are, and how we are united in the thirst for honor, dignity and truth.

We cannot succumb to euphoria. Everything may still turn out differently. Anything is possible in the hours and days of the death throes of a system pitched in its final battle. And eight conspirators are not the whole conspiracy. They are not the entire dictatorship. They could not have succeeded in launching their dark intention if they had not relied on a fair number of their supporters. I am not calling for a witch hunt, the settling of political scores or political revenge, but only for justice. "Mercy to the defeated" has been a component of a moral policy. But we have no right to forget how many "defeated" there still are among us. Only then will the politics of conspiracies be doomed, just as its champions and adherents are doomed.

I'd like to think that Mikhail Gorbachev has also become a different person. It cannot be otherwise. He endured a hard trial—standing at the edge of death, betrayed by his colleagues, and fortuitously saved. Such events leave their traces—and they must do so.

The danger is great. The conspirators brought about a chaotic, irrational development of events; they've set a fateful pendulum in motion. They must be stopped at any cost, so that the country and the world can be saved and further human suffering avoided. Law must speak, not arbitrary will. We cannot take the enemies of democracy as our models. I wouldn't want my prophecies to be confirmed yet again.

Article 8

THE CHRISTIAN SCIENCE MONITOR
Thursday, September 5, 1991

THE NEW SOVIET UNION

Republics Ill-Prepared for Solo Economies

As the Soviet Union's 15 republics move toward political sovereignty, decades of central planning have ensured that they are interdependent in every economic sphere, from energy to industry

By Amy Kaslow

Staff writer of the Christian Science Monitor

WASHINGTON

AMBITIOUS in their political aspirations for independence, the breakaway Soviet republics are reluctantly recognizing the economic limitations to full autonomy.

As the once all-powerful Soviet center dissolves, local leaders have been trying to literally capitalize on the long-repressed republic pride. Soviet President Mikhail Gorbachev's desperate pleas for some semblance of an economic union have been met by local leaders' calls for their own national currencies.

Management over every aspect of the economy once held by the tight-fisted central government in Moscow – including budgets, money supply, trade, production and natural resources – is up for grabs by leaders in all 15 republics.

Both Soviet and Western economists warn that a total break now from the giant, if tottering, Soviet economy would only leave individual republics scrambling for survival. Decades of Moscow's central planning have ensured that the republics are interdependent in every economic sphere: energy, food, consumer goods, light and heavy industry.

The ailing Soviet economy would collapse without at least a central clearinghouse for production and distribution by republics, says Leonid Grigoriev, Soviet economist at Moscow's Institute of World Economy and International Relations. Mr. Grigoriev has spent the past several years doing economic plans for local republic leaders as well as for Mr. Gorbachev. He was a co-author of the controversial 500-day plan for Soviet economic reform announced last fall.

Not one of the individual republics, no matter how mineral-rich or industrialized, can afford such a collapse of the larger economy as it embarks on its own, he says. The collapse of the Council for Mutual Economic Assistance (Comecon), which coordinated trade with former Soviet satellites in Eastern Europe, has made inter-republic barter trade even more crucial.

Because Soviet agricultural and industrial production has been largely region-specific, individual republics are poorly diversified. With the exception of the food industry and machine-building and metalworking sectors – each present in almost all geographical areas – regions tend to be dominated by clusters of specialized manufacturing plants geared to the national market.

Regional interdependence

Uzbekistan, for example, is the principal supplier of cotton to the Soviet Union. This so-called "cotton monoculture" leaves the republic vulnerable to blight and incapable of feeding, clothing, or housing itself.

Opportunities for entering the global marketplace are few. Aside from certain raw materials, such as oil and natural gas, there is little that republics can now export internationally. Soviet manu-

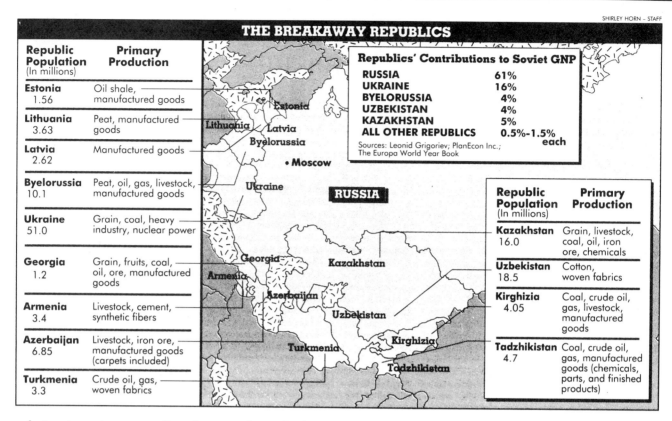

SHIRLEY HORN – STAFF

THE BREAKAWAY REPUBLICS

Republic Population (In millions)	Primary Production
Estonia 1.56	Oil shale, manufactured goods
Lithuania 3.63	Peat, manufactured goods
Latvia 2.62	Manufactured goods
Byelorussia 10.1	Peat, oil, gas, livestock, manufactured goods
Ukraine 51.0	Grain, coal, heavy industry, nuclear power
Georgia 1.2	Grain, fruits, coal, oil, ore, manufactured goods
Armenia 3.4	Livestock, cement, synthetic fibers
Azerbaijan 6.85	Livestock, iron ore, manufactured goods (carpets included)
Turkmenia 3.3	Crude oil, gas, woven fabrics

Republics' Contributions to Soviet GNP

RUSSIA	61%
UKRAINE	16%
BYELORUSSIA	4%
UZBEKISTAN	4%
KAZAKHSTAN	5%
ALL OTHER REPUBLICS	0.5%-1.5% each

Sources: Leonid Grigoriev; PlanEcon Inc.; The Europa World Year Book

Republic Population (In millions)	Primary Production
Kazakhstan 16.0	Grain, livestock, coal, oil, iron ore, chemicals
Uzbekistan 18.5	Cotton, woven fabrics
Kirghizia 4.05	Coal, crude oil, gas, livestock, manufactured goods
Tadzhikistan 4.7	Coal, crude oil, gas, manufactured goods (chemicals, parts, and finished products)

factured goods are mostly substandard and probable losers in the highly competitive world market. Except for natural gas, the energy sector is degenerating.

Severing links now means that the republics would be cut off from their automatic markets and suppliers. This would exacerbate economic troubles, says Matthew Sagers, senior economist at PlanEcon Inc. in Washington.

Dr. Sagers says political changes in recent weeks will give economic restructuring a jump-start on the local republic level, but republics will need each other. Local leaders recognize the folly in now venturing out on their own and abandoning all former Soviet commercial ties.

Highly indebted and cash-poor, these republics are now incapable of sustained self-sufficiency or financing economic reforms by themselves.

"No one has any choice but to join an economic union of some sort," Mr. Grigoriev says.

Last week there was an ironic twist in the union's disintegration. As the richest republics were busy forging new relationships with each other, the poorest declared their independence. Russia and the Ukraine, the two most populous and productive Soviet republics, agreed to establish new ties. Kazakhstan and Russia, the two largest republics in terms of territory, also pressed for a new economic union. The heavily subsidized Central Asian republics of Uzbekistan and Kirghizia announced their secession as a way of jockeying for a better economic position with the economically dominant Russian republic, Grigoriev says.

"Republics, totally unprepared for economic independence, are taking advantage of the collapse of the center," agrees Jonathan Halperin, president of FYI Information Resources, based in Washington. Mr. Halperin's advisory firm is involved in the community of 500,000 independently operated businesses (not state-run) in the Soviet Union.

Nationalist divisions

But links that bond the republics may be very difficult to forge, Grigoriev says. Political obstacles remain, including mistrust along ethnic and nationalist lines. "They remember who ate whose cow 500 years ago," he says.

Grigoriev warns of strife in republics that have sizable Russian populations. "The Russians will go from being first-class citizens in a huge country to second-class status in a small country. They will not take that well."

Among the first to suffer from the union's ongoing political breakdown will be the Central Asian republics, says Grigoriev. The predominantly Muslim and rural region, including Kazakhstan, Turkmenia, Uzbekistan, Kirghizia, and Tadzhikistan, received subsidies from Moscow-center at the expense of wealthier republics.

Moscow's role as collector of national earnings and distributor of incomes has abruptly ended. Russia, the Ukraine, Georgia, Armenia, the Baltics, and other relatively well-heeled republics whose incomes were partly distributed to the nation's fund for Central Asian subsidies have ceased to be a ready source. "There will be a huge economic crisis for republics who received subsidies," Grigoriev says.

If the breakaway republics defy economic cooperation, large portions of the Soviet landscape will turn from poorly diversified to dangerously deprived. Northern Russia and Siberia boast heavy industry, for example, but are almost wholly dependent on imports of consumer goods from other parts of the vast Russian territory and from other republics. If trade agreements are abrogated and the already unreliable transportation and communication links are weakened by the breakup, economic calamity will ensue, Grigoriev says.

Who'll pay the debts?

Should the republics' separatists ultimately reject a union bound by a financial center, the collective liabilities of the 15 republics remain. In recent days Gorbachev pledged to calculate each republic's portion of the national budget in order to transfer the sums to the local level.

Meanwhile, republics are demanding their fair share of the center's gold reserves. The amount of reserves – long a state secret – will soon be told.

As important as doling out assets is the far more difficult task of apportioning the national hard-currency debt, estimated at $65 billion. "The distribution will be very complicated," Grigoriev says. The country's debts are spread among many kinds of creditors. "One country [republic] will owe debts to France and own assets in Ethiopia."

The dire straits of the Soviet economy point to the republics' need to bond together. According to PlanEcon estimates, the Soviet gross national product fell by one tenth during the first half of this year, and foreign trade plummeted by 37 percent. Soviet oil and coal mining industries are atrophying due to the high cost and inefficiency of extracting oil and coal. The country's grain harvest is down by more than half.

Ukraine battered

The most robust republics are in peril. The Ukraine, once called "the breadbasket of Europe," and "an economic powerhouse" has been reduced to a third-rate producer due to low worker incentive, agricultural inefficiencies, inadequate storage facilities, and poor transportation.

Even without economic restructuring, high unemployment will soon occur, says Jay Mitchell, a PlanEcon economist. Inefficient factories will not survive without subsidies. Local political opposition can slow down the closure of the major employer in a town, he says, and delay reform. "The state-owned enterprises won't die so quickly because they have a lot of resources. Many giants live longer than they should because they have supplies, equipment, and money stashed away."

If there is no safety net prepared for the unemployed, tensions will ignite, says Adrian Karatnycky of the AFL-CIO's international department in Washington.

> 'After a period of trial and error, the republics will cede back power to a central body which can better coordinate' trade and financial relationships.
>
> – *Jonathan Halperin, President, FYI Information Resources*

The Federation of Russian Independent Trade Unions, representing roughly 90 percent of the work force, or some 60 million workers, has long been in the communist grip. Hardliners will try to appeal to disenchanted workers, says Mr. Karatnycky, whose organization supports the independent Federation of Free Trade Union workers, with 60,000 members in the Soviet Union. The latter, he says "totally distrusts the center."

In terms of wresting control from Moscow over local natural resources, the Russian and Ukrainian coal miners are the bedrock of the worker's reform movement. After a wave of carefully orchestrated and economically debilitating strikes, the coal miners won the transfer of mines from the center to the republics. The AFL-CIO promotes democratization of unionized labor there.

Workers have found important common ground with independently operated enterprises, say Karatnycky and Halperin. Karatnycky says the unions have received financial contributions from the business community.

"Historically, trade unions have been the mechanisms of control, not the voice of the workers," says Halperin. "The miners' strikes were an effective means of making a political statement – for more local control, freedom and rights, and management of local affairs. These are the same objectives of independent businesses – greater economic autonomy instead of politically dictated goals." As large manufacturing facilities go private, often at the urging of the workers, the two groups could form a powerful merger, Halperin says.

Banking system needed

Before much more can develop on the local level, there need to be banks where "people can go for mortgages and companies for funds," Mr. Mitchell says. Without a viable banking system, "you almost put a noose around economic restructuring."

Halperin says banking and other goals and instruments of reform will ultimately be coordinated among republics.

"After a period of trial and error, the republics will cede back power to a central body which can better coordinate" the intricate trade and financial relationships, he says.

Article 9

THE WORLD & I
OCTOBER 1991

Soviet Muslims: Seeking Reform, Not Revolution

by Marat Akchurin

Not long ago people in the West were accustomed to calling the Soviet empire Russia, and they considered all of its population Russian. By now even nonspecialists have discovered that the Soviet Union consists of approximately 100 ethnic groups and nationalities who do not consider themselves one nation, and the relationships among them are, alas, far from idyllic. However, while Americans are aware of Lithuania (1 percent of the Soviet population) and Armenia (2 percent of the population), few people here know even the names of the rest of the Soviet republics. But there is bloodshed and violence there as well.

It appears that westerners have only hazy notions about the so-called Muslim republics of the USSR. This is not particularly surprising since even in the Soviet Union the central government sees the Central Asian colonies in much the same light as Americans imagined Khomeini's Iran

in the early 1980s. Later we will discuss who in the Soviet Union benefits most from this image. Meanwhile we will turn our attention to a very strange issue. How is it that the Muslim republics of the USSR have turned out to be Moscow's only non-Slavic allies within its crumbling empire? Why are the small Christian nations of Georgia, Armenia, Lithuania, Latvia, Estonia, and Moldavia violently breaking away, while the leaders of the mysterious Muslim republics, with a total population of more than 50 million people, have never so much as mentioned seceding from the Soviet Union? And why does the Bolshevik Kremlin frighten the West with talk about the growth of pan-Islamism in the southern USSR and bend over backward to look like some kind of bulwark in the eyes of the Western world, shielding Christian civilization from the Muslim threat coming from the East!

Nevertheless, you must judge for yourself: of the 14 union

republics, all formally part of the USSR, only 9 have confirmed their intention of remaining a part of it. On the one hand, there are the Russian Federation, the Ukraine, and Belorussia, all three populated primarily by Russian Orthodox Slavs. On the other hand there are Uzbekistan, Kazakhstan, Azerbaijan, Tadzhikistan, Kirghizia, and Turkmenia, the majority of whose populations (with the exception of Tadzhikistan) are Turkic peoples and traditionally consider themselves Muslims.

THE ISLAMIC VIEW

First, we must precisely define the term *Muslims*. Most people in the United States are probably not aware that the concept of "Muslim," as applied to the majority of the Central Asian and Transcaucasian peoples of the USSR, fundamentally differs from the concept as applied to the people of the Middle East, North Africa, or Pakistan.

Arabs who have visited Soviet Central Asia and the Transcaucasus have often expressed bewilderment and even disappointment concerning the extremely vague conception the local inhabitants have about the religion they profess. It was not quite clear to the visitors how it was possible for these people to consider themselves true Muslims while not fulfilling the main precepts of Islam.

Indeed, of the 70 million Soviet citizens who, according to Moscow's scenario, should be perceived in the West as bearers of the "Muslim threat," the overwhelming majority cannot even name the five major rules, the so-called pillars of Islam. However, the strict fulfillment of these principles is precisely what makes a person a Muslim. (For the non-Muslim reader, they are as follows. First and foremost is the belief in one God: "There is no God but Allah, and Muhammad is his prophet," followed by the five daily prayers, annual fast during the month of Ramadan, giving of alms to the needy, and the pilgrimage to the holy places in Mecca, which a believer, given the means to do so, is obliged to complete at least once.)

Anyone who has lived in or even visited the Central Asian republics will likely confirm that virtually no one among the local population knows how to read the Koran, the sacred book of Islam, since it is written in the classical Arabic language that is known only by people who have received a religious education. It has obviously not been easy under Soviet power to obtain such an education, mostly because you can count the Muslim educational institutions on the fingers of one hand. Imagine a Christian who had never read the Bible! Given this situation, why do the majority of Cen-

tral Asians and many inhabitants of the Transcaucasus, the Caucasus, and the Volga region continue to call themselves Muslims?

The foregoing suggests that the Soviet variant of Islam long ago evolved from a purely religious doctrine into one of the elements of a national secular lifestyle. It became simply a means of ethnic self-expression and self-affirmation, directed against the long-term efforts of the communist central bureaucracy (the "center") to deprive its colonies of their ethnic identity. And if the communists' 70-year experiment in melding the citizens of the multinational Soviet empire into a "new historical community—the united Soviet nation"—has collapsed, one of the reasons for this lack of success in the southern republics is the stability of national traditions and customs, which are based on Muslim heritage.

What about mosques? How many are there in these republics? you ask. There are some mosques. In 1930 there were about 5,000, of which about 250 remain. That is approximately one for every 200,000 people. Ponder these figures.

WHO'S THE BOSS IN THE MUSLIM REPUBLICS?

This question would simply evoke laughter among the inhabitants of these republics. "Of course, the local communists!" they will answer. And it is 100 percent true.

The "Muslim" republics are considered the most conservative and politically rigid region of the USSR at present. Here, unlike the relatively "Christian" republics of the Soviet Union, the power of the communist apparatus has not weakened; on the contrary, it has been enhanced. Why this paradox?

In the first place, keep in mind that the ruling communist parties of the Central Asian and Transcaucasian puppet republics of the USSR have never borne any resemblance to what is understood in the West as parties or communists. Nor have they had anything in common with dogmatic Chinese or North Korean communism. They have long been functioning simply as ruling mafia clans, depending upon the corrupted state structures and the organized crime world. However, while they previously had to observe specific political rituals in order to maintain the semblance of ideological societies, the rules of the political game have changed.

Certainly, the local party clans demonstrate, as before, their loyalty to the center. Unlike the democratically elected leaderships in the Baltic states, Armenia, or Georgia, the communist leaders of the Muslim republics were seated on the throne by the administrative command system in Moscow. Following Gorbachev's example, they simply declared themselves presidents of their own republics, although they remained essentially the same party apparatchiks that they were under Brezhnev. Moreover, many of them were even in the highest ranks of the party nomenklatura before perestroika and therefore to some degree involved in the regime's political, economic, or ecological crimes against its citizens.

The local communist parties still have complete control over the press, radio, and television. They deny all democratic publishers even the right to register. In several republics such as Turkmenia, for example, even Central Moscow television broadcasts critical of the Communist Party of the Soviet Union (CPSU) are be-

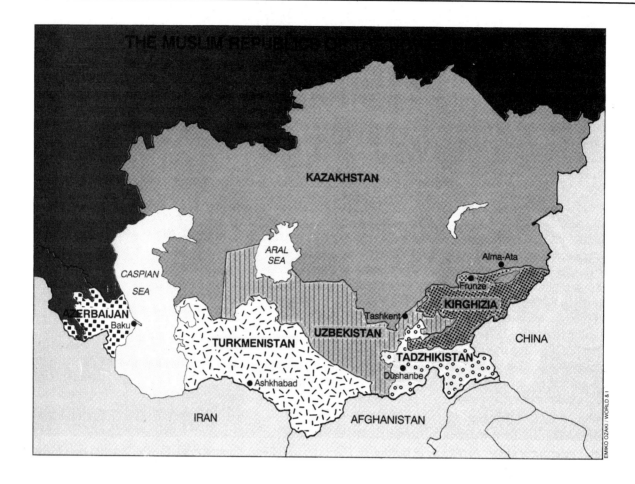

ing refused transmission. Under the pretext of a campaign against disorder, all meetings and gatherings in virtually all the Muslim republics are being banned. In Tashkent, not long ago, the municipal authorities denied registration to the democratic party on the grounds that "in connection with Uzbekistan's proclamation of sovereignty, no parties except the communist party may exist in the republic."

The communist leaders in Kirghizia and especially in Kazakhstan are more liberal, but in any case, the issue is one of repair of the exterior facade, not construction of a new building. The primary effect of Gorbachev's perestroika for the Muslim republics is not reform of the political system but replacement of generations of communist rulers.

Indeed, the republic leaders are not the former puppets of the center, who just a few years ago could not conceive of themselves as being outside the current politi-

---

The local communist partocrats have just as much interest in preserving the empire as the center does.

---

cal system. Their political lexicon is now sprinkled with expressions like "economic sovereignty," "national consciousness," the "right to dispose of the national wealth." What is meant by this is that the national partocracy (high-ranking party bosses) is going to continue to control the republics it has managed to ruin.

The leaders are sure of their political prospects partly because in the East, in accordance with centuries-long traditions, the institution of power itself is the object of esteem. The rulers and the majority of the population are minimally concerned with the ideology of authority. Perhaps this is why no spontaneous anticommunism has been observed here, unlike other regions of the empire. It is hard for a Muscovite to believe, but in Tadzhikistan or, for example, Turkmenia, Orwellian slogans are still in evi-

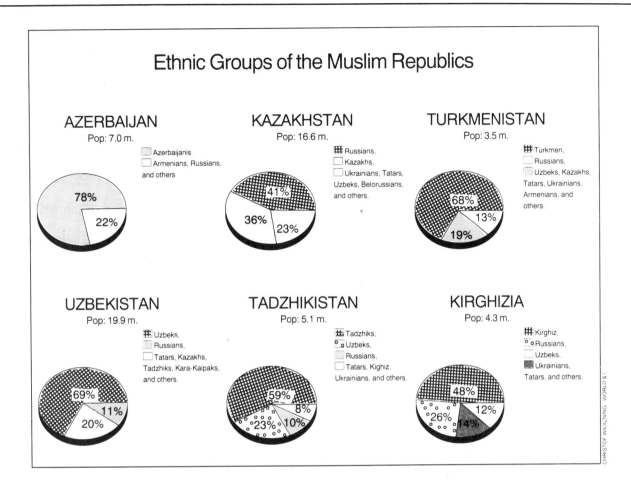

Ethnic Groups of the Muslim Republics

AZERBAIJAN
Pop: 7.0 m.

- Azerbaijanis
- Armenians, Russians, and others

78%
22%

KAZAKHSTAN
Pop: 16.6 m.

- Russians,
- Kazakhs,
- Ukrainians, Tatars, Uzbeks, Belorussians, and others.

41%
36%
23%

TURKMENISTAN
Pop: 3.5 m.

- Turkmen,
- Russians,
- Uzbeks, Kazakhs, Tatars, Ukrainians, Armenians, and others.

68%
13%
19%

UZBEKISTAN
Pop: 19.9 m.

- Uzbeks,
- Russians,
- Tatars, Kazakhs, Tadzhiks, Kara-Kaipaks, and others.

69%
11%
20%

TADZHIKISTAN
Pop: 5.1 m.

- Tadzhiks,
- Uzbeks,
- Russians,
- Tatars, Kighiz, Ukrainians, and others.

59%
8%
23%
10%

KIRGHIZIA
Pop: 4.3 m.

- Kirghiz,
- Russians,
- Uzbeks,
- Ukrainians, Tatars, and others.

48%
12%
26%
14%

CHRISTOF WILKENING WORLD & I

dence everywhere: The people and the party are one! Or simply, Glory to the CPSU!

A RIVAL TO TAKE SERIOUSLY

However, at the end of the 1980s a democratic opposition emerged from the milieu of the national intelligentsia. For a short time it organized mass movements of the people's front type. In Uzbekistan the opposition was called Birlik (Unity), in Tadzhikistan Rastokhez (Rebirth), in Kazakhstan Azat (Freedom). In Kirghizia, it was Kirghistan; in Azerbaijan, it was the People's Front of Azerbaijan. The example of Lithuania and Estonia, who have enjoyed the sympathy and support of neighboring European countries and the United States, has played an important role in stimulating this process.

The fact that new democratic movements emerged in the Muslim republics was itself a direct challenge to the existing order. For the local communist parties it represented unexpected and undesirable competitors encroaching upon the "holy of holies": state power. For the center it was an uncontrollable political force, whose accession to power would threaten the imperial command with deprivation of the rich natural resources of its colonies. This was absolutely obvious, since these democratic activists, unlike the local partocrats, were not obligated to the center in any way and have loudly declared their aspiration for both economic and political independence.

It was at this precise moment that the notorious "Islamic

threat" card was played. To compromise the young and politically naive opposition by accusing it of pan-Islamism and nationalism was fairly simple. Members of the republic intelligentsia, advancing new claimants to power from within its ranks, had in fact originally taken up the banner of Turkic and Muslim unity. It is likely that the KGB deserves the credit for this. It had been acting through agents and informers introduced in great numbers into the ranks of the opposition.

The scenario of later events in all the Muslim republics was virtually identical. First, as if on command, interethnic conflicts and pogroms began to flare up, responsibility for which was, of course, placed on the democratic opposition. Then to "restore order," the center was "forced" to bring in troops and declare a state of emergency. This was the sequence of events in Azerbaijan, Tadzhikistan, Kirghizia, Uzbekistan, and Kazakhstan.

Particular alarm in the West was evoked by fantasies, inspired by the partocrats, about the possible future fate of nuclear weapons. They hinted that the weapons could turn up in the hands of "irresponsible separatist nationalists." In fact, neither extremist nationalist organizations (as a rule, up to half of the members were KGB provocateurs), nor any democratic people's front groups had even thought about possessing nuclear weapons. All talk of their own military was limited to plans for their own police and border guards. Moreover, after the Chernobyl disaster, every republic, regardless of whether it planned to secede from the Soviet Union or not, dreamed of one thing: to become a nuclear-free zone as soon as possible.

After confronting stern political reality, the democratic forces quickly realized how improbable it was that their initial beautiful ideas concerning Turkic unity could be implemented. But the first skirmish had already been lost on all fronts. The Western countries believed that in the south of the USSR a monster had arisen by the name of "Islamic fundamentalism." It has not occurred to anyone that the communist Dr. Jekyll and the pan-Islamic Mr. Hyde are one and the same.

DISSIDENT IN PRISON

His name is Almaz Estekov. In 1985 he was sentenced for three and a half years for his human rights activity. In December 1990 he was deprived of his Soviet citizenship and exiled from the USSR. For what offense, you may ask, could a Soviet citizen possibly be deported from his native land in the era of glasnost and perestroika?

It may be astonishing, but Almaz Estekov's "crime" consisted in the fact that he was actively working for the democratic union of Turkic peoples and Slavs against "Islamic fundamentalism" and radical nationalism. Another paradox? No, a sober and realistic policy of the communist-dominated bureaucracy. "Islamic fundamentalism" and radical nationalism, entailing bloodshed and violence at the southern borders of the empire, were promoted by the center to ensure that Western democracy would turn away with disgust from the peoples of the Muslim republics. Homemade pan-Islamism with puppet fanatics in these republics was much more useful to the Kremlin than democratic movements and groups that could conduct an independent dialogue with the West. But what use is a dialogue if, after events in Iran and Lebanon, the very word *Muslim* causes an allergy in the West! It is this situation that permits Moscow to close off Turkestan (the five Muslim republics east of the Caspian Sea) with a barrier much sturdier than the Berlin Wall. Therefore, anyone who, like Almaz Estekov, attempts to break it down could expect to be proclaimed *persona non grata* in his homeland.

We should not deceive ourselves. Both during and after perestroika, the Soviet Union has remained an imperial state. After a long struggle, the Communist-dominated bureaucracy is finally willing to concede some authority to new political forces. But the imperial mentality is here to stay.

The local communist partocrats have just as much interest in preserving the empire as the center does. Naturally, they insist upon one condition: They must keep the requisite amount of political and economic independence to guarantee the absolute inviolability of their power.

Complete political independence, if it is understood as the withdrawal of each republic from the USSR, will most likely lead to a new union of former Soviet republics, only then at a regional level. This would mean absolute political obscurity for the local partocrats. Is it not safer for them to preserve the status quo under subjugation to the Kremlin?

GREAT EXPECTATIONS

Obviously, the interests of the center and the local partocracy will not always coincide. Presumably, any complications in the relationships among the Central Asian republics, including conflicts among the ruling clans, would directly serve the interests of the center in that region. Unfortunately, lack of space prevents me from analyzing in detail each instance of interethnic conflicts that has occurred in the Muslim republics in the last five years. I have given more details in my forthcoming book, *Red Highways*. But at least three incidents could be highlighted, which were virtually ignored by Western observers.

First, notwithstanding popular opinion, the interethnic conflicts in the Muslim republics are not of a religious nature. Fratricidal pogroms have killed thousands of Kirghizians and Uzbeks, Kazakhs and Chechens, Tadzhiks, Meskhetian Turks, and Uzbeks—coreligionists who consider themselves Sunni Muslims.

Second, the partisan war between Armenia and Azerbaijan that, with Moscow's assistance, was portrayed by the American mass media as a war between Christians and Muslims, was in fact a territorial conflict that originated at the beginning of the nineteenth century. Indicative of this was the fact that when asked whether the conflict [between Armenia and Azerbaijan] was religious in nature, the presidents of the warring republics answered with a decisive No (see their interview in the Soviet weekly *Argumenty i fakty* [Arguments and facts] no. 18, May 1991).

Third, Russians (who make up from 10 percent of the population in Tadzhikistan to 41 percent in Kazakhstan) were not the target of violence in any of these tragic situations. However, the KGB spread rumors among the Russian population about alleged forthcoming anti-Russian pogroms, which caused a panic resulting in a partial exodus of the population to Russia in the form of refugees. As a result, the partocracy succeeded in provoking persistent hostility among the Russians, both in the colonies and in Russia, toward the local democratic movements, which were held responsible for all the accumulated problems.

After succeeding in compromising the opposition (who had no access to the mass media either within the country or abroad and could not generate counter-propaganda), the ruling clans of the local communist parties are now the most stable political force in the region. Despite their demagogic arguments about tran-

sition to a market, it is unlikely the communist leaders of the Muslim republics are truly interested in this process. Why should they promote market relations if, acting on behalf of the state, they are thus sole owners of all the major means of production (with the exception of the factories of the military-industrial complex). The system of collective farms and state farms gives them complete ownership of all the land and its harvests. Of course, the lion's share of natural resources and fossil fuels, as well as industrial and agricultural production, must be given to the center, but this is the usual price of power.

In any event, the dissension between the center and the local partocracies has intensified recently. The government of Premier Pavlov has attempted to return to the old administrative command methods of tightly controlled central planning and distribution in his relations with the colonies. Meanwhile, the communist leadership of the Muslim republics is more loudly demanding independence in foreign trade and even foreign affairs with the free world.

What about the West? Its position in relation to the noncommunist republics of the Soviet Union is more or less clear: to support reforms that do not encourage separatism. How will the West react to the curtsies of the communist bosses of the Turkic republics of the USSR?

As long as three years ago, at the height of universal hopes for rapid democratic changes, it was easy to say, "Don't have anything to do with communists; they are

obviously a political mafia. They hold their power only through violence and deception."

But now it is too late to speak thus. The indecisiveness and inconsistency of Gorbachev's reforms have sent the Soviet economy into convulsions. The majority of the population of the Muslim republics has slipped below the official poverty level during the era of perestroika. The people are close to despair, and at any moment they may turn into an enraged mob. Without outside assistance, an explosion of violence is inevitable. This outburst would bury all hopes of peaceful and bloodless reforms under a mound of debris.

Meanwhile, the democratic opposition has not managed to become a real alternative for the "Muslim" partocracy. Therefore, the patient West apparently has to continue to deal with communist regimes in this region. Consequently, it is doing business with terrorists who have taken hostages—only this time, the "hostages" are the 50 million inhabitants of the Muslim republics of the USSR. In order not to sink into despair, they must sense the support of the West. For the time being, the people are hoping they can avoid bloodshed. They need reforms, not revolution.■

Marat Akchurin is a free-lance writer and lecturer based in Pacific Grove, California. He has published books, major anthologies, and more than 300 articles and short stories in Soviet magazines and newspapers. His most recent book is Red Highways *(HarperCollins, forthcoming in 1992).*

Article 10

U.S.NEWS & WORLD REPORT, DECEMBER 23, 1991

■ WORLD REPORT

AFTER THE EMPIRE

The moment of truth

The economic choice is now between strong medicine and disaster

Will the new year in the new commonwealth of former Soviet republics start off with a "Big Bang"—a burst of sweeping economic reforms like those Poland adopted in January 1990? Or will it begin with a whimper as the commonwealth's leaders, like Mikhail Gorbachev before them, slink away from the necessity of moving toward a market economy? Bowing to requests from Ukraine and Byelorussia, Russian President Boris Yeltsin has agreed to delay until January 2 a bold reform plan that his republic was to have begun this month. Yet once more, efforts to create a market economy have reached a critical pass. Come January, either Russia will pull other reluctant republics along or more temporizing will deepen the economic disaster.

The former Soviet republics must act quickly and collectively to break a dangerous cycle of deficit spending, price controls and inflation that has even further distorted the doomed command economy. A drastic drop in tax revenues has helped to widen the old union's budget deficit, prompting authorities to print billions of extra rubles to paper over the gaps. As a result, the ruble stock has grown a whopping 75 percent this year, while America's basic money supply rose about 3 percent. Meanwhile, price controls reduce the incentive to produce more, and too much money chasing too few goods has spurred inflation in black markets, which now is estimated to be at least 250 percent per year.

Worthless rubles. With the value of rubles deteriorating daily, no one wants to hold them; currency is quickly exchanged for goods, worsening widespread hoarding. Fixed prices for products such as food and oil only encourage the trend: At free-market exchange rates—which have tumbled from about 20 rubles to the dollar to about 100 rubles to the dollar this year—oil now sells for the equivalent of about $1 a ton, notes Baylor University economist Stephen Gardner. And the huge government subsidies paid to producers to keep such prices low are further widening the budget deficits.

The commonwealth republics agreed to tackle this mess together, vowing to keep the ruble as their common currency while coordinating efforts to slash their own budget deficits and halt the ruble printing presses. Those steps must now coincide with the gradual decontrol of fixed prices for many goods that is set to begin in January. According to plans made by Russian officials, prices for "critical" goods such as milk and vodka will remain fixed for the time being.

Prices for most other goods will be allowed to float freely—while those for still other commodities, such as oil, will be raised sharply at the outset. As in Poland, these higher prices should quickly put a halt to hoarding and help coax scarce goods back into stores. At the same time, inflation will probably skyrocket to an annual rate of about 1,000 percent for at least several months.

But the inflationary shock could be multiplied many times if too many rubles continue pouring onto the market. "We're dealing with the possibility of another Weimar Republic, with hyperinflation and seething resentment [creating a] fertile ground for fascism," says Robert Hormats of Goldman, Sachs & Co.

The danger only underscores the need for the republics to cooperate on economic reforms, yet it is not clear whether they will. Ukraine may carry out plans to create its own national currency, complicating the task of forging a coherent monetary policy. Then there's the matter of dismantling what's left of the old central economic apparatus. Keith Savard, senior economist of the Washington-based Institute of International Finance, visited Moscow two weeks ago, after Yeltsin had nominally taken control of the old union central bank, Gosbank. He found the printing presses still rolling and Gosbank officials still in command. With the union dead, that could all change. "But right now," says Savard, "it's day by day."

The West's role. The impetus for a Big Bang may soon get a boost from stepped-up Western assistance. Even though none of the former Soviet republics is yet a member, institutions such as the International Monetary Fund and the World Bank are laying the groundwork for supporting their reforms. At next month's coordinating conference, moreover, Western officials may discuss both granting additional trade credits to help the republics compensate for inadequate hard-currency reserves and creating a vast hard-currency "stabilization fund" so the new commonwealth could buy up rubles, if necessary, to create confidence in the currency. But first, the republics will have to convince the world that they're serious about economic reform. Like their still-suffering neighbors in Eastern Europe, they have no choice but to start down the grim road ahead. ■

BY SUSAN DENTZER

Article 11

U.S.NEWS & WORLD REPORT, SEPTEMBER 9, 1991

Moscow's market movers

Feisty capitalists in Russia struggle to build their futures

Entrepreneurs in Moscow are one of Boris Yeltsin's most loyal constituencies, and not just because the Russian president stared down the hard-liners' coup. In recent months, Yeltsin's republic has moved boldly to remove a host of restraints on commerce. Entrepreneurs still complain about the recalcitrant, corrupt bureaucracy, but they applaud the easing of corporate taxes and the creation of new laws that protect private enterprise.

When the Soviet right wing launched its putsch, Yeltsin's pro-business leanings enabled him to marshal the support of Moscow's feisty small-business owners. Hundreds of enterprises sent equipment that might prove helpful—mobile phones, copying machines, computers and printers—to Yeltsin's headquarters in Russia's White House. The Congress of Russian Business Interests sent 10 trucks and five cars loaded with food, medicine and firewood to the demonstrators arrayed around the building. The private detective agency Alex dispatched about 80 of its trained guards to help defend the barricades. With the exception of Yeltsin's 12 personal bodyguards, it was Alex's sole responsibility to combat the military assault that many were expecting at the time.

According to business leaders, this aggressive response reflected the ardent commitment of the private sector to democratic change—and its experience with pushing for reform. "Businesses here in the Soviet Union are used to activism," explains Mikhail Moruhov, vice president of the U.S.S.R. Association of Chief Executives. "Entrepreneurs have had to track down legislators and simply demand that laws be created."

It should come as no surprise, then, that the mood among business leaders in the aftermath of the thwarted takeover is as buoyant as it was during the early days of *perestroika*. Entrepreneurs widely welcome the demise of the conservative Communist Party and cheer what they believe is the rise of pragmatic politics. "The power of people with money is bigger," says Nicolai Tyrin, general director of TIMP, an enterprise that manufactures such diverse items as electric space heaters, pots and pans and tin soldiers. When asked what his company makes, one TIMP worker responds simply: "Everything."

At a mere 33 years of age, Tyrin and his business are flourishing. He works long, hard hours and watches American basketball on television. His other hobby is penning aphorisms. Tyrin recently published a proverb that reflects his country's burgeoning capitalist spirit and indicates that many in Russia now recognize what free marketeers in the West have known for a long time: Time is money. "Russians say you measure seven times, then cut," says Tyrin, "but I wrote: 'While you are measuring seven times, the others will cut it.'"

Tyrin's influence, and that of the Soviet Union's growing business elite, has extended well beyond the marketplace. "Businessmen are more and more the ones in a position to order the music," says the entrepreneur, using a Russian expression that means to call the shots. This jaunty confidence is well deserved. In 1988, Tyrin had a chance to buy a bankrupt state-run enterprise that was slated to close. It took six months of official stamps, special signatures and numerous "favors," but he finally was able to close a deal that put him and his partners in control of TIMP.

Tyrin and his syndicate lost no time rebuilding the company, using a straightforward strategy. They received two bank loans, invested in new machinery, fired the "drunks and loafers," doubled salaries and offered their workers *zakazy*, special food supplies, as incentives to increase productivity. Sur-

'Entrepreneurs have had to track down legislators and simply demand that laws be created.'

———

prisingly, the company was turning a profit within a year. "One mustn't be afraid of using the word *discipline*," advises Tyrin. TIMP obviously has its finger on the pulse of the emerging Soviet marketplace. Thousands of product-hungry consumers have flocked to buy the company's wares. And in another sure-to-please business move, Tyrin's company is planning to produce toasters, which are not currently made anywhere in the Soviet Union.

But even though Soviet consumers eagerly purchase Tyrin's products, they continue to have mixed feelings about wealthy entrepreneurs like him. The leaders of the aborted coup, in fact, tried to exploit feelings of anger and frustration among the salaried public, describing the owners of cooperatives and other private businesses as greedy capitalists.

That sort of propaganda undoubtedly strikes a responsive chord among many average Soviet citizens. But there are a growing number of workers who would rather join the free market than fight it. At Moscow's Labor Exchange, the central clearinghouse for jobs in the city, the number of openings in the private sector is rising by about 10 percent every month.

Warming up. "The situation is changing," says Anatoly Byizyakin, the deputy director of Krosno, a company that manufactures satellite dishes. "Three years ago, the cooperative owner was hated by 99 percent of the population,

but now this negative attitude toward representatives of the new economy may be held by 50 percent. Now that there are more private enterprises, it is different. The state structures are even more warm toward us."

The gradual acceptance of entrepreneurs among the Soviet people isn't the only positive change flowing through Moscow's marketplace. For Krosno, the recent gains are dramatic: Just one year after taking over the 1905 Revolution

---

COMMENTARY

Can the Soviets fire up trade?

Until now, the unraveling of the Soviet empire has had limited impact on the world economy because liberated countries like Hungary and Poland are too small and too poor to make much of a dent in international markets. The sudden collapse of communism in the Soviet Union changes all that. The capitalist world has gained a potentially huge new market—and some global industries may have acquired new competition.

Many people think of the Soviet Union as an economic midget because of the turmoil that has gripped its economy in recent years. But this perception is wrong. Although production is grossly inefficient and the standard of living has always been miserable, the Soviet Union was until recently the world's second largest economy.

Under Mikhail Gorbachev, the Soviet Union fell apart because political reforms undermined the command economy. Gorbachev was unwilling—or unable—to replace central planning with a true market economy. Today, the way is clear for radical reform. It will take many years before that reform produces a Western standard of living, but the Soviet republics will eventually regain economic ground lost during the Gorbachev era.

Boosting exports. In the past, the Soviet Union tried to be self-sufficient, either producing goods for itself or bartering with its satellites. The result was limited world trade. But now, in the wake of the recent countercoup, the Soviet Union will become a player in the global marketplace. The most dramatic changes will take place in foreign trade—not in the domestic

economy. Even if there is absolutely no economic growth in the Soviet Union over the next five years, the republics could well increase their annual exports to, and imports from, the West by $200 billion. Experience tells us that this increase in trade will come quickly. When Poland introduced its economic reforms in early 1990, for example, its exports to the West grew 20 percent in less than a year, and they have continued to expand rapidly.

Over the next decade, the Soviets could dramatically increase their exports of unsophisticated manufactured goods such as steel, bulk chemicals and plywood. With a huge military budget and an emphasis on heavy industry, the Soviet Union was for many years the world's largest steel producer. But chaos in the U.S.S.R. has destroyed this domestic market, leaving the republics with tremendous excess capacity. This will force them to sell their steel products abroad at very competitive prices—the same strategy that enabled South Korea and Brazil to become successful exporters in this area.

As they move into the global marketplace, the Soviets must make sure that their goods meet minimum global quality standards. They will also have to come to grips with worldwide overcapacity and protectionism in many of the markets they wish to enter. The key question is whether the West will raise these barriers to keep the Soviets out. It may be that the excommunists are about to test our belief in free markets.

By Paul R. Krugman
Professor of Economics at the
Massachusetts Institute of Technology.

Plant, the joint stock company produced in one month what it used to make in one year under the old central command-and-control economy. Krosno's new owners continue to manufacture the factory's traditional line of low-voltage electrical goods, but they have added several new products, including satellite dishes. Just a few years ago, owning a dish was punishable by law in the Soviet Union.

Manufacturing electrical equipment is complicated by the nonconvertibility of the ruble, says Byizyakin. Krosno needs high-quality, low-noise transistors to make its satellite dishes, and these components are not yet produced in the Soviet Union. Byizyakin says his company orders from abroad and is forced to pay for imports with expensive hard currency. The ability to purchase parts with rubles, he adds, would be a big relief. At TIMP, Tyrin's company, tin soldiers are painstakingly produced, but to maintain craftsmanship the company must work with high-quality Western paints. "We are the country of Fabergé," says Tyrin wistfully.

Pent-up demand. The next step for struggling Soviet entrepreneurs is to secure long-term capital commitments that will help them to expand their fledgling businesses and thus meet the huge pent-up demand of Soviet consumers. To achieve this goal, Russia's commercial movers and shakers keep chipping away at the system. They seek banking reform, because very few institutions are capable of providing the credit they need. They also want completely free pricing as soon as possible. "Economic life can be compared to the life of a human being," says Krosno's Byizyakin. "Artificial barriers aren't proper. It's like blocking the blood vessels in the human body."

And at detective agency Alex, managers express a simple but essential wish — for reduced government regulation. The company is hoping that a new law will be enacted that will allow its employees to carry weapons. If Alex's men had been forced into action at the Russian White House, they would have been fighting the hard-liners' tanks with mace guns, the only weapon they are currently permitted to carry. ∎

BY VICTORIA POPE IN MOSCOW

Article 12

CURRENT HISTORY
OCTOBER 1991

The Revival of Religion

BY DAVID E. POWELL

DAVID E. POWELL *is a fellow of the Harvard University Russian Research Center. He has written widely on political, economic, and social problems in the Soviet Union. Among his publications is* Antireligious Propaganda in the Soviet Union *(Cambridge: Massachusetts Institute of Technology Press, 1975). He is also a co-editor of* Soviet Social Problems *(Boulder, Col.: Westview Press, 1991) and* Soviet Update *(Boulder, Col.: Westview Press, 1991).*

From the beginning of the Soviet regime until recently, Lenin and his successors demonstrated fear of and contempt for "the opiate of the people." Concerned about the political and economic influence of the church, and fearful of any alternative belief system challenging the primacy of the Communist party, the leaders of the Soviet Union worked to limit religion's role in society. Their unremitting pressure (except during World War II), including the threat or use of terror and pervasive anti-religious propaganda, transformed churches and believers alike into little more than "vestiges of the past."

The first few years of President Mikhail Gorbachev's reign witnessed continued assaults against Russian Orthodoxy, Islam, and other denominations in the Soviet Union. Anti-religious propagandists were encouraged to pursue their work energetically (even though it was largely ineffectual), and each year the authorities closed a few hundred more churches. In 1988, however—the year of the millennium of Christianity in Kievan Rus—public policy began to change, and since then there has been a dramatic improvement in church-state relations.

HISTORIC CHANGES

On April 29, 1988, Gorbachev met with Patriarch Pimen and members of the Holy Synod (the assembly of leading hierarchs of the Russian Orthodox Church). The Soviet leader expressed regret about the treatment of the Russian Orthodox Church during Stalin's reign and promised that there would be genuine "freedom of conscience" in the future. Since the meeting with the Patriarch, "scientific-atheist propaganda" has been sharply curtailed and its earlier excesses denounced. Copies of the Bible and the Koran have been made more readily available than ever before, and the number of Jews allowed to emigrate and Muslims allowed to make the pilgrimage to Mecca has increased sharply. Church bells once again may be rung in the Soviet Union, and religious organizations have once again been authorized to carry out charitable work.[1]

Many churches, mosques, and prayer houses, as well as cathedrals, monasteries, seminaries, and other religious buildings, have been reopened, and new ones have been built or are currently under construction. By the summer of 1988 almost 100 more Russian Orthodox

Church parishes existed than had been the case one year earlier, and by the end of the year several hundred additional churches had been opened. In mid-1990 it was announced that about 5,500 parishes (4,100 of them Russian Orthodox) had been established or reactivated in a period of a little more than five years, increasing the total by almost 50 percent.

Perhaps the most striking development is that many clergymen have sought election as "people's deputies" to the country's legislative bodies. One of these individuals, Metropolitan Aleksii of Leningrad and Novgorod (who later was chosen to succeed Pimen as Patriarch), said in his election platform in 1989 that he thought it "inconceivable that a genuine renaissance of our society [could] take place without the inclusion of the Christian element." In elections held in March 1990 approximately 300 clergymen, including 190 from the Russian Orthodox Church, were chosen to serve as deputies to the soviets (councils).

A variety of motives seem to be driving Gorbachev's rapprochement with organized religion—a quest for legitimacy, a "need" for popular support in carrying out the policies of glasnost and perestroika, a desire for allies in combating the country's social problems, perhaps even the idea of unleashing the creative energies of those alienated by decades of restrictions on religious belief and conduct. Gorbachev is taking a risk in seeking détente, perhaps even an entente, with organized religion, and his efforts have not been uniformly successful. But his opening of the country to religion is a quintessentially democratic act that has generated considerable enthusiasm among the people.

ALLOWING CHURCHES A SOCIAL MISSION

Many religious groups have begun to experiment with assistance programs, and although their proportions are still exceedingly modest such programs are playing a role in humanizing Soviet society. The Russian Orthodox Church, the Catholic Church, Evangelical Christian Baptists, Seventh-Day Adventists, Pentecostals, and several other so-called sects have been especially active. They have focused on assisting hospital patients, elderly people living at home, and mentally handicapped children, and on visiting labor camp inmates.

Churches in some parts of the country have "adopted" local hospitals, day-care centers, or orphanages—occasionally at the request of local government officials. Members of the congregation carry out repairs, decorate the premises, purchase furniture and appliances, set up clubs and workshops, and take children from shelters into their homes. Metropolitan Filaret of Kiev and Galicia has even made the extraordinary suggestion that, if cooperation between the Orthodox

Church and public health authorities were legalized, medical training could be provided in convents so that nuns would be better qualified to tend the sick.

All the available evidence suggests a strong commitment to such action on the part of religious leaders and ordinary believers, but a good deal of ambivalence on the part of the government to this extension of church involvement and influence. Until 1990 Soviet law did not allow churches a "social mission." Church bodies were prohibited from engaging in charitable work, and most volunteer efforts were clearly illegal. But the 1990 Law on Freedom of Conscience and Religious Organizations radically altered this state of affairs; its Article 23 authorizes religious groups to engage in charitable and philanthropic activities on their own and through foundations.[2] In view of the parlous state of the country's finances, intensified efforts by churches to help people in need will be doubly important.

SACRED TEXTS AND SUNDAY SCHOOLS

In 1988 the government authorized various Western religious organizations to send one million Bibles to the Soviet Union; other organizations have since added to the total. In late 1988 the journal *V mire knig* began to serialize the New Testament in an edition of 105,700 copies. This represented the first time since the Bolshevik Revolution that a state publishing house had made religious materials available to readers.[3] Current plans call for the publication of the Bible in Russian and in other languages of the country, making it, as advocated by *Pravda*, "truly accessible to believers and atheists [alike]."

Secular authorities have also granted permission to the Saudi Arabian government to ship one million copies of the Koran to Muslims in the Soviet Union, and have allowed domestic publishing houses to print Uzbek, Kazakh, and Russian translations of the book. The Russian-language literary journal *Pamir*, the organ of the Tajikistan Writers' Union, last year began printing the Muslim holy scriptures. Religious newspapers are now appearing even in Central Asia. *Islam nuri* (Ray of Islam), published in Tashkent, explains the tenets of the Muslim faith for readers, describes how to perform various rituals and ceremonies, provides information about Muslims in other countries, and tells the faithful to fight for religious purity.

The decision to make copies of the Bible and the Koran available may turn out to have been one of the most revolutionary acts of glasnost. Having been denied access to the most basic sources of religious belief and tradition, both urban sophisticates and simple peasants had a very limited understanding of their heritage.[4] Finally given a chance to read the Old and New Testaments, many atheists and agnostics experienced a genuine spiritual awakening. Here are the words of one man from Novosibirsk, writing to *Ogonyok* in 1989:

> Now that I have turned the last page of the great book, I cannot get over the feeling of gratitude and joyful shock.... [But] why only now, why so late?
>
> At the age of 30, I have read the Gospels for the first time.... the text gripped me: I was impressed by the austere power of the words, the elegance of the finely tuned aphorisms, the subtle poetic quality of the images.... [G]radually I became very angry: what a treasure they have been hiding from me! Who decided, and on what basis, that this was bad for me—and why?... I did not run off to church... I simply understood that I never was and never will be an atheist.[5]

This is vivid testimony to the power of Gorbachev's "revolution from above." But whether exposure to the Gospels or other religious literature will bring about a renaissance of faith among the Soviet people remains to be seen.

Beginning in 1989 the Soviet government also granted churches and (in some areas) schools permission to organize religious instruction. Latvia was the first republic to offer some form of religious education; the first Orthodox Sunday school opened in Vilnius in November 1989. (Authorities in Vilnius also granted Jewish children permission to study Hebrew and Yiddish.) By year's end, scores of church Sunday schools were operating in Moscow, Leningrad, the Baltic states, and elsewhere, serving thousands of children. In addition, several state schools began to offer optional courses on the history of religion, some of them taught by priests.

JEWS AND THE NEW REFORMS

Greater freedom of religion has been accompanied by increasingly open expressions of anti-Semitism by members of various extremist organizations. In early 1989, for example, Pamyat (Memory) and other reactionary groups staged a rally at one of Moscow's largest sports arenas. Participants enthusiastically applauded speeches condemning the Jews for having committed numerous "crimes" against the Russian people and for their alleged lack of loyalty to the Soviet Union. Many carried posters with anti-Jewish slogans or caricatures. One banner, proclaiming, "No to Rootless Cosmopolitans" (a Stalin-era anti-Semitic term), showed St. George slaying various "serpents"—most prominently Leon Trotsky, Yakov Sverdlov, and Lazar Kaganovich, as well as several of Gorbachev's closest advisers

(many of them Jewish or presented as caricatures of Jews).*

In addition, the myth of a Jewish-Masonic conspiracy has been resuscitated, the anti-Semitic *Protocols of the Elders of Zion* has again appeared in print, and Jews have been accused of an astounding array of evil acts. These range from the forced collectivization of agriculture and repressions of the Stalin era to the corruption of Russian culture and the destruction of the environment.

At the same time, the Soviet government, elements of the media, and concerned citizens, both Jewish and non-Jewish, have spoken out against the resurgence of anti-Semitism. Major newspapers denounced the "anti-Zionist" propaganda that had served as an oblique expression of contempt for the Jews. Journalists and scholars pointed out the many parallels between such writings and those of the pre-revolutionary anti-Semitic "Black Hundreds" in Russia and Nazi propagandists in Germany.

The government has also relaxed its restrictions on expressions of Jewish identity and Jewish culture. Since 1987 the ban on teaching Hebrew has been lifted (indeed, a union of Hebrew teachers was established); a yeshiva, a Jewish cultural center, and a Jewish youth center have begun operations; facilities for the ritual slaughtering of animals, as well as bakeries for producing matzoh, have been made available; and a kosher restaurant has opened in Moscow.

Synagogues have been opened or reopened: between January 1, 1985, and July 1, 1990, the number of functioning synagogues in the Soviet Union rose from 91 to 106. Finally, record numbers of Soviet Jews have been permitted to emigrate to Israel, the United States, and Western Europe. Formerly, the peak year of Jewish emigration from the Soviet Union was 1979, when 51,320 Jews were allowed to leave. In 1989, 71,217 Jews emigrated, and the figure for 1990 was an astonishing 186,115.[6]

RELIGION'S TROUBLE SPOTS

Official policy toward Islam has also undergone a major change. Media attacks directed against Muslim leaders and the faith in general occur less and less frequently, and the authorities have allowed considerably greater freedom of worship. Throughout Central

---

*Editor's note: Trotsky competed with Stalin for control of the party after Lenin's death; Sverdlov was secretary of the Central Committee, chairman of the all-Russian Executive Committee of Soviets (the titular head of state), and the person who apparently gave the order to kill Czar Nicholas II and his family; and Kaganovich was deputy chairman of the Council of Ministers and one of Stalin's henchmen, one of the few Jews to survive Stalin's purges.

Asia, Azerbaijan, and other areas with large Muslim populations, local groups have been permitted to open new mosques or to repair and reopen places of worship that had been shut during the Stalin, Khrushchev, and Brezhnev years. Between 1985 and 1990 the number of "working" mosques in the country rose from 392 to 1,103, an increase of nearly 300 percent.

Why has the government adopted a more conciliatory stance? Looking at the Central Asian republic of Uzbekistan, James Critchlow sees "a desperate striving on the part of the Uzbek establishment to bolster the sagging regime with new sources of legitimacy." With the Communist party "discredited by the failures and revelations of recent years," he continues, "espousal of Islam is clearly a bid for the support of traditional religious and national-minded forces in society." It is also, he concludes, part of "an attempt to fill the vacuum in society caused by the decline of secular authority—a vacuum reflected in soaring crime rates, drug abuse, etc."[7] His hypotheses make a great deal of sense; indeed, they can be applied, by extension, to Soviet policy toward religion in general.

Of course, a policy of increased tolerance for Islam is laden with risk for the Soviet regime. For example, the Islamic Revival party, established in 1990, has pledged "to revive [the religion] in areas from which it has been driven out and to spread it to regions where it is altogether unknown or where people have a distorted notion of it." Furthermore, the party professes highly conservative beliefs, including the idea that "women must, above all, be keepers of the home and rearers of children." Thus its leadership is dismayed at some of the changes introduced under Soviet rule. To quote one official, "The emancipation introduced in our country… has had the result of estranging women from the family and home."[8]

According to Muslim leaders in Central Asia, the Islamic Revival party represents a grave social and political danger; its members are determined, they say, "to overthrow the socialist system and set up a theocratic regime."[9] In view of the new party's militancy, some analysts in the Soviet Union have expressed serious concern about "separatist tendencies" within Islam, pointing with particular alarm to calls for a Muslim state in Central Asia.

The most complex and contrary developments affecting religion in the Soviet Union are taking place in the Ukraine, where changing church-state relations are accompanied by widening divisions and growing friction among denominations. Adherents of the Ukrainian Catholic Church (also known as the Greek Catholic or Uniate Church), which was dissolved and forcibly incorporated into the Russian Orthodox Church by Stalin in 1946, have been trying to secure legal status for it. Ukrainian members of the Orthodox faith who resented being part of the Russian Orthodox Church have successfully campaigned for independence from it. Since October 1990 they have been permitted to function as the Ukrainian Autocephalous Orthodox Church. They even have their own leader, Patriarch Mystyslav of Kiev and the Ukraine.

The principal area of religious controversy in the Ukraine is the Uniates' struggle for acceptance by the state—and by the Russian Orthodox Church. The latter task appears to be more difficult. According to one estimate there were approximately 5,700 Orthodox parishes in the Ukraine in the summer of 1989; of these, more than half, located primarily in western Ukraine, were Uniate. Virtually all of these were acquired in 1946 when Stalin united the Uniate Church with the Russian Orthodox. To legalize Ukrainian Catholicism and return to it properties taken 45 years ago would be to reduce substantially the wealth and power of the Russian Church—which is already under siege from the Ukrainian Autocephalous Orthodox Church.

During 1989 and 1990 significant numbers of churches were turned over to—or appropriated by—the Uniates. One recent report put the figure for Ukrainian Catholic churches at 1,737, with another 74 churches under construction. According to some Russian Orthodox clergy the takeovers are illegal acts by extremist Uniates; Ukrainian Catholics, by contrast, believe that they are simply taking back what belongs to them. Although attempts have been made to resolve the conflict through negotiation, measures taken by the two sides continue to be confrontational. Indeed, the differences between the Uniate and Orthodox churches may well be insurmountable.

BARRIERS TO FREEDOM OF RELIGION

Party, Komsomol (Communist Youth League), and government agencies in some localities resist the more permissive attitude toward religious self-expression adopted under perestroika. There are frequent reports of recalcitrant officials who refuse to acknowledge the rights of the faithful: Party activists or the chairmen of local soviet executive committees in places as diverse as Kirov, Brest, Kerch, Leningrad, Donetsk, Novgorod, and Tambov oblasts illegally obstruct groups attempting to register as a religious community, to reopen or carry out repairs on a church, and so on.

Obstructionism is prevalent partly because the shift from militant atheism to a policy that is supposed to respect a plurality of views and behaviors is difficult to make for bureaucrats who have spent their career harassing believers and religious groups. But a second factor appears to be at work as well. People in positions of authority, it seems, "yearn to show believers that whatever may be written in the law, their word is stronger," and that they still know what is best for the Soviet Union.[10]

Izvestia in 1989 recounted the story of a group of teachers in a small town in Riazan oblast who had organized a church choir and been subsequently reprimanded by the head of the district Communist party organization for their lack of ideological fervor. A teacher, this party official declared, "is responsible for new and progressive ideas"; to sing hymns in a church was to engage in "the propaganda of religion"—an "unacceptable" practice in the Soviet Union, in his view. "Such people," he added, "cannot be entrusted with the education of children." (The only Communist among the teachers was expelled, as were two Komsomol members.)[11]

In the village of Chernianka in Belgorod oblast, the local priest, attempting to regain control over a dilapidated Orthodox church, was told: "How can a new church be opened practically on the main street? That is ideologically incorrect, even anti-atheistic." In yet another example of "old thinking," a group of Baptists in the Siberian city of Krasnoyarsk was given permission to construct a prayer hall—but only on the outskirts of town, on a site that had been used as a dump.

These are not isolated incidents. Official attitudes and conduct, formed over many decades, are difficult to change—and many officials, especially those with responsibilities in the sphere of ideology, find it particularly difficult to "restructure" their own thinking. As the writer Aleksandr Nezhny has noted, "The contemptuous and dismissive attitude toward anything connected with the church, which has been drummed into us over decades, still controls our consciousness."[12]

A different kind of barrier to genuine religious freedom is the conservative character of many religious functionaries, especially the leading figures in the Russian Orthodox Church (and, to a lesser degree, Islam). One Western specialist on Russian Orthodoxy has spoken of the "Stalinist-Brezhnevian ecclesiastical nomenklatura that [has] ruled the Church since 1943."[13] Similarly, the British historian Geoffrey Hosking has written that "decades of active persecution alternating with contemptuous manipulation have left it not only numerically reduced but spiritually debilitated.... Enfeebled by subservience to an atheist state, the Church is no longer fit to act as [a] vehicle for [a] religious revival or to promote social solidarity."[14]

In early 1990 the Holy Synod stated publicly that the government had been interfering in church appointments and in the administration of parishes for many years. Indeed, some have raised the question of whether the new Patriarch might not have cooperated too closely with the state in the past. Even if the public continues to regard Orthodoxy itself and Jesus Christ himself with reverence, the Church will not be able to exercise a full measure of influence until a new generation assumes leadership positions within it.[15]

[1]Since the 1988 meeting, religious data for the Soviet Union have been collected and released. A major study published in 1990 concluded that more than 90 million Soviet citizens of various faiths, or one-third of the population, consider themselves believers. See *Argumenty i fakty*, no. 6 (1990). Approximately 50 million of these are adherents of the Russian Orthodox Church, according to Metropolitan Filaret of Kiev and Galicia. Commenting on another poll carried out in March 1990, the youth newspaper *Komsomolskaya pravda* pointed out that "there are many more [believers] who were not counted, since, no matter how much is written and spoken about it, this subject remains very private." Cited in Oxana Antic, "Statistics on Religion Speak a Language of Their Own," Radio Liberty, *Report on the USSR* (hereafter cited as *Report*), vol. 3, no. 2 (January 11, 1991), p. 9.

[2]*Pravda*, October 9, 1990.

[3]See Oxana Antic, "One Million Bibles for the Soviet Union," *Report*, vol. 1, no. 10 (March 10, 1989), p. 17.

[4]In the past, atheist activists urged that copies of the Bible and the Koran be made available in order to help students become "politically conscious Marxists" and more effective anti-religious propagandists. See, e.g., *Komsomolskaya pravda*, May 13, 1988. In Khrushchev's time, a "humorous Bible" mocking the original was published in an edition of 255,000 copies. See Leo Taksil, *Zabavnaya bibliya* (Moscow: Izdatelstvo politicheskoi literatury, 1964).

[5]Christopher Cerf and Marina Albee, eds., *Small Fires* (New York: Summit Books, 1990), p. 82. For evidence of concern among professional atheists that religious literature is now too readily available, see *Sovetskaya kultura*, March 12, 1988.

[6]National Conference on Soviet Jewry, "Jewish Emigration from the USSR" (New York: Soviet Jewry Research Bureau, 1991), p. 1.

[7]James Critchlow, "Islam in Public Life: Can This Be 'Soviet' Uzbekistan?" *Report*, vol. 2, no. 11 (March 16, 1990), p. 25.

[8]*Izvestia*, January 8, 1991. This official claimed a party membership of 10,000, primarily in Central Asia and the North Caucasus. Another source puts the figure at 20,000. See *Literaturnaya gazeta*, March 8, 1991.

[9]*Komsomolskaya pravda*, April 3, 1991; see also *Soyuz*, no. 2 (1991), p. 11.

[10]"Believers' Right to Register," *Soviet Analyst*, vol. 17, no. 9 (May 4, 1988), p. 5.

[11]*Izvestia*, September 28 and 29, 1989.

[12]"Church Gains from the Millennium?" *Soviet Analyst*, vol. 17, no. 12 (June 15, 1988), pp. 6–7.

[13]Vladimir Moss, "Russian Orthodoxy and the Future of the Soviet Union," *Report*, vol. 3, no. 24 (June 14, 1991), pp. 3, 5.

[14]Geoffrey Hosking, *The Awakening of the Soviet Union* (Cambridge: Harvard University Press, 1990), pp. 113, 115.

[15]For survey data underscoring the popularity of the Church, as well as the pervasive and intense feeling of admiration for Christ, see *Moskovskiye novosti*, nos. 21, 22, and 49 (1990).

Article 13

U.S. NEWS & WORLD REPORT, APRIL 13, 1992

TOXIC WASTELAND

In the former Soviet Union, economic growth was worth any price.
The price is enormous.

In satellite photos of the Eurasian land-mass at night, the brightest pools of light do not emanate from London, Paris or Rome. The largest glow, covering hundreds of thousands of acres and dwarfing every other light source from the Atlantic to the Pacific, can be found in the northern wilderness of Siberia, near the Arctic Circle. It comes from thousands of gas flares that burn day and night in the Tyumen oil fields, sending clouds of black smoke rolling across the Siberian forest. During the past two decades, the steady plume of noxious sulfur dioxide has helped to ruin more than 1,500 square miles of timber, an area that is half again as large as Rhode Island.

Siberia's acid rains are just one more environmental catastrophe in a land where man has run roughshod over nature and is now facing the deadly consequences. The former U.S.S.R. had no monopoly on pollution and environmental neglect, as residents of Minamata, Mexico City and Love Canal can testify. But Soviet communism's unchecked power and its obsessions with heavy industry, economic growth, national security and secrecy all combined to produce an environmental catastrophe of unrivaled proportions.

"When historians finally conduct an autopsy on Soviet communism, they may reach the verdict of death by ecocide," write Murray Feshbach, a Soviet expert at Georgetown University and Alfred Friendly Jr. in the new book, "Ecocide in the U.S.S.R." (Basic Books, $24). "No other great industrial civilization so systematically and so long poisoned its air, land, water and people. None so loudly proclaiming its efforts to improve public health and protect na-

ture so degraded both. And no advanced society faced such a bleak political and economic reckoning with so few resources to invest toward recovery."

In the name of progress. Communism has left the 290 million people of the former Soviet Union to breathe poisoned air, eat poisoned food, drink poisoned water and, all too often, to bury their frail, poisoned children without knowing what killed them. Even now, as the Russians and the other peoples of the former U.S.S.R. discover what was done to them in the name of socialist progress, there is little they can do to reverse the calamity: Communism also has left Russia and the other republics too poor to rebuild their economies and repair the ecological damage at the same time, too disorganized to mount a collective war on pollution and sometimes too cynical even to try. Even when the energy and the resources needed to attack this ecological disaster do materialize, the damage is so widespread that cleaning it up will take decades. Among the horrors:

■ Some 70 million out of 190 million Russians and others living in 103 cities breathe air that is polluted with at least five times the allowed limit of dangerous chemicals.

■ A radiation map, which has never been released to the public but which was made available to *U.S. News,* pinpoints more than 130 nuclear explosions, mostly in European Russia. They were conducted for geophysical investigations, to create underground pressure in oil and gas fields or simply to move earth for building dams. No one knows how much they have contaminated the land, water, people and wild-

life, but the damage is almost certainly enormous. Red triangles on the map mark spots off the two large islands of Novaya Zemlya where nuclear reactors and other radioactive waste were dumped into the sea. Tapping one location, Alexei Yablokov, science adviser to Russian President Boris Yeltsin, says a nuclear submarine sank there 10 years ago, its reactor now all but forgotten. "Out of sight, out of mind," he says with disgust.

■ Some 920,000 barrels of oil—roughly 1 out of every 10 barrels produced—are spilled every day in Russia, claims Yablokov. That is nearly the equivalent of one Exxon Valdez spill every six hours. To speed up construction of oil pipelines, builders were permitted to install cutoff valves every 30 miles instead of every 3, so a break dumps up to 30 miles worth of oil onto the ground. One pool of spilled oil in Siberia is 6 feet deep, 4 miles wide and 7 miles long.

■ According to Yablokov, the Siberian forests that absorb much of the world's carbon dioxide are disappearing at a rate of 5 million acres a year, posing a bigger threat to the world environment than the destruction of the Brazilian rain forests. Most of the damage is caused by pollution and by indiscriminate clear-cutting, mostly by foreign companies, in soil that can't tolerate such practices.

■ Because the rivers that feed it were diverted, the Aral Sea is evaporating, altering rainfall patterns, raising local temperatures as much as 3 degrees and releasing so much salt and dust that the level of particulate matter in Earth's atmosphere has risen more than 5 percent.

■ Officials in Ukraine have buried 400 tons of beef contaminated by radiation

Thirty Percent of All Foods Contain Hazardous Pesticides

from the Chernobyl nuclear accident. An additional 920 tons will be buried in June.

A confidential report prepared by the Russian (formerly Soviet) Environment Ministry for presentation at the Earth Summit in Rio de Janeiro this summer blames the country's unparalleled ecological disaster primarily on a policy of forced industrialization dating back to the 1920s. The report, a copy of which was obtained by *U.S. News,* notes the "frenetic pace" that accompanied the relocation of plants and equipment to the Urals and Siberia during World War II and their rapid return to European Russia after the war. This, the report says, created a "growth-at-any-cost mentality."

The communist state's unchallenged power also was reflected in its obsession with gigantism and in its ability to twist science into a tool of politics. The late Soviet President Leonid Brezhnev planned to reverse the flow of the Irtysh River, which flows north, in order to irrigate parts of arid Central Asia for rice and corn growing. But to redirect 6.6 trillion gallons of water each year would have required building a 1,500-mile canal. Critics warned that the project would alter world weather patterns, but Soviet officials gave up only after spending billions of rubles on the plan. "Soviet science became a kind of sorcerer's apprentice," write Feshbach and Friendly.

Unexplained anthrax. Not surprisingly in a nation obsessed with national security and secrecy, another culprit was the military-industrial complex, which the Environment Ministry's report says, "has operated outside any environmental controls." In 1979, some 60 people died in a mysterious outbreak of anthrax near a defense institute in Sverdlovsk (now renamed Ekaterinburg). After years of Soviet denials of any link with defense matters, the Presidium of the Supreme Soviet voted in late March to compensate the victims of the incident and conceded that it was linked to "military activity."

At the same time, the report says, communism's reliance on central planning and all-powerful monopolies produced an "administrative mind-set" that created huge industrial complexes that

overtaxed local environments. The report says the emphasis on production over efficiency has led to some 20 percent of all metal production being dumped—unused—into landfills. Nor did Soviet industries, shielded from competition, feel any need to improve efficiency or switch to cleaner, more modern technology.

Worse, it became virtually impossible to shut down even the worst offenders, because doing so could wipe out virtually an entire industry. In Estonia, for example, the Kohtla-Jarve chemical plant, a major polluter, squeezes 2.2 million barrels of oil a year from shale and provides 90 percent of the energy for the newly independent country. Environment Minister Tanis Kaasik says flatly that it is "impossible" to shut down production.

Terrible secrets. A pervasive secret police force, meanwhile, ensured that the people seldom found out about the horrors visited on them in the name of progress and that, if they did, they were powerless to stop them. It took Soviet officials more than 30 years to admit that an explosion had occurred at a nuclear storage site near Chelyabinsk in 1957. The blast sent some 80 tons of radioactive waste into the air and forced the evacuation of more than 10,000 people. Even with *glasnost,* a cult of silence within the bureaucracy continues to suppress information on radiation leaks and other hazards. Indeed, the No. 1 environmental problem remains "lack of information," says former Environment Minister Nikolai Vorontsov.

Even now, with the fall of the Communist Party and the rise of more-democratic leaders, there is no assurance that communism's mess will get cleaned up. Its dual legacy of poverty and environmental degradation has left the new political leaders to face rising demands for jobs and consumer goods, growing consternation about the costs of pollution and too few resources to attack either problem, let alone both at once.

Although 270 malfunctions were recorded at nuclear facilities last year,

Two Kindergartens in Estonia Were Built on a Radioactive Waste Dump

Six Million Acres of Productive Farmland Were Lost to Erosion

economic pressure will make it difficult to shut down aging Soviet nuclear power plants. In March, radioactive iodine escaped from a Chernobyl-style plant near St. Petersburg, prompting calls from German officials for a shutdown of the most vulnerable reactors. Yeltsin adviser Yablokov warns that "every nuclear power station is in no-good condition, a lot of leaks." In the short term, Russia has little choice but to stick with nuclear power, which provides 60 percent of the electricity in some regions.

Environmental consciousness has permeated only a small fraction of society, and rousing the rest will require breaking the vicious circle of social fatalism. "We haven't got any ecological culture," says Dalia Zukiene, a Lithuanian official. Russian aerosols still contain chlorofluorocarbons, though Russia has now banned them, but if a Russian is lucky enough to find a deodorant or mosquito repellent, he will grab it—regardless of the consequences to the ozone layer. "We still bear the stamp of *Homo sovieticus*—we're not interested in the world around us, only in our own business," says Zukiene. Adds Alla Pozhidayeva, an environmental writer in Tyumen, in the oil fields of western Siberia: "Sausage is in the first place in people's minds."

Despite the mounting toll, the environmental activists who rushed to the barricades in the early days of *glasnost* have largely disappeared. When the Social Ecological Union recently tried to update its list of environmental groups, it found that more than half of them had disbanded in the past year. "If people go to a meeting at all, it isn't for the sake of ecology," says Vladimir Loginov, an editor of *Tyumen Vedomosti,* a newspaper in the Tyumen oil region. "They have to eat."

In fact, the crisis of leadership afflicting much of the former Soviet Union poses a whole new set of threats to the environment. The loosening of political control from Moscow already has turned the provinces—especially Siberia—into the Wild West. Local authorities, particularly in the Far East, have extended vast timber-cutting rights to foreign companies, especially Japanese and South Korean, without either imposing strict controls on their methods or requiring reforestation. "The economic chaos here presents enormous opportunities for local administration, without any government control, to cut forest, to sell it abroad and to receive some clothes, cars, video equipment," says Yeltsin adviser Yablokov. "If you visit the Far East forest enterprises, you will be surprised how many Japanese cars you will find."

The breakup of the Soviet Union is adding to the tensions. Despite Chernobyl, Ukraine, facing an energy crisis as the price of the oil it imports from other regions rises to world levels, is quietly contemplating building new nuclear power plants. But a stepped-up Ukrainian nuclear power program would create its own problems: Krasnoyarsk, the traditional dumping ground in Russia for nuclear waste, is refusing to accept Ukraine's spent reactor fuel because Ukraine is demanding hard currency for its sugar and vegetable oil.

In the mountainous Altai region of Russia, which recently declared itself autonomous and elected its own parliament, newly elected officials are trying to revive a controversial hydroelectric project on the Katun River. Victor Danilov-Danilyan, the Russian minister of ecology and natural resources, says local officials in Altai, many of whom are former Communist Party leaders, are now trying to cast the battle over the project as a nationalist issue. He says local authorities have deliberately ignored the danger of increased toxic wastes in the water and intentionally underestimated both how much the project will cost and how long it will take to build. "They're just deceiving people," Danilov-Danilyan charges. "They just want to grab as much as they can while they're in power, to build *dachas* for themselves."

Still, there are some glimmers of progress, including the recent creation of three new national parks in Russia. In February, President Yeltsin signed a

Scientists Recently Found 11 More Areas Poisoned By Chernobyl

new environmental law that empowers local officials or even individuals to sue an offending enterprise and demand its immediate closure. It also holds polluters, not some distant ministry, responsible for their actions. The new law further permits aggrieved parties to sue for damages, not just fines. The environmental ministry's report notes that over the years, "few ministries, if any, chose to clean up their act and didn't go beyond paying lip service to the need to protect the environment." In most cases, polluters got off with small fines or escaped punishment altogether by passing the buck to government ministries.

But Vladislav Petrov, a law professor at Moscow State University and the main author of the new legislation, says that if it is strictly enforced, the law would shut down 80 percent of the country's factories overnight. In the sooty steel town of Magnitogorsk, in the Urals, an independent radio journalist says he will try to force the Lenin Steel Mill, which employs 64,000 people, to close. He doubts he will succeed.

Growth industry. Moreover, while the new, 10,000-word statute has teeth, only a handful of lawyers, and ever fewer judges, are familiar with environmental law. Petrov says the courts are ill-equipped to handle claims from individuals and would be overwhelmed if

The Soviets, With 10% of America's Cars, Had 67% of U.S. Auto Pollution

people tried to collect damages from polluters. "In order for this article of the law to be effective, the whole court system should be changed," he says.

Still, environmentalism is a growth industry in the former Soviet Union. Many scientists in fields such as nuclear physics hope to recast themselves as ecologists. Mindful that the Russian government does not have the funds for large projects, they are looking for foreign partners to join them in cleanup projects. So far, most Western groups have offered advice but not much money.

Some Western input may be necessary, however, to prevent the environmental effort from succumbing to its own form of gigantism. One Central Asian academic's plan for saving the Aral Sea, for example, calls for building a 270-mile canal from the Caspian Sea to divert water into the depleted Aral. But because the Caspian Sea is lower than the Aral, the water could have to be pumped into the canal, and that would require considerable electricity. The proposed solution: Build a network of solar power stations.

The spreading ecological disaster may yet force change on an impoverished and cynical people. "We have a Russian saying: 'The worse, the better,'" says Yablokov. "This situation has now become so obvious for all people that I feel that a lot of decision makers began to turn their minds in this direction." The Stalinist idea, he says, was to build socialism at any cost because afterward there would be no more problems. "It was an unhealthy ideology," he says. "Now I feel that my people are coming to understand the depths of this tragedy."

By Douglas Stanglin with Victoria Pope in Moscow, Robin Knight in Tyumen, Peter Green in Tallinn, Chrystia Freeland in Kiev and Julie Corwin

Article 14

WORLD MONITOR
APRIL 1992

PEOPLE · RUTH DANILOFF

Left Behind in the Rush to Freedom

In a far corner of Yeltsin's domain the lot of women worsens amid ethnic turmoil.

I n Dagestan no man will marry a girl who isn't a virgin," said Aminat, adjusting the white scarf she always wore over her head and turning to her friend Zaira for confirmation. Zaira nodded, but Nina their Russian friend rolled her eyes and said, "That's why I'll never marry a Dagestani man." I wasn't sure if she was flaunting her sophistication or trying to tell me that the 200,000 Russians who settled in this Muslim region were culturally more advanced than the 1.8 million natives. Here, as in other Muslim regions of what was until recently the USSR, the role of women will become an increasingly thorny issue as the people struggle to survive the chaos created by the disintegration of the Soviet empire.

Our conversation took place in Koubachi, a village high in the northern Caucasus, which I reached after a five-hour ride in a bone-rattling bus. I'd always wanted to visit this part of the world, which has captured the imaginations and pens of Russian writers such as Tolstoy, Pushkin, and Lermontov. They were not alone. Either to escape gambling, the boredom of St. Petersburg, or exile to Siberia, the cream of 19th-century Russia's nobility volunteered to fight the Muslim tribes among these snow-capped peaks.

My three young companions, two of them descendants of those tribal Dagestanis, were English-language students from the university in Makhachkala, Dagestan's capital. They had been sent by the local tourist bureau to practice their English and learn how to act with foreigners. In the company of men the two Dagestani girls became silent, lowering their eyes, but once the men left they lit up, bombarding me with questions about the lives of American women and being touchingly honest about their own.

As we mounted a steep path, Nina's blue jeans and Zaira's short uncovered hair drew a disapproving look from an old woman carrying a huge metal pitcher full of water. Over her head and shoulders she wore a white gauze shawl, embroidered with gold threads, similar to those worn in this ancient village for more than 600 years. Back in the dusty square, three old men sitting on a stone bench interrupted their conversation about the current food shortages to examine this Westerner and the three city girls.

Many Dagestanis—and not just religious conservatives—insist that traditions are undermined when a woman goes out in public without a head scarf, wears make-up or trousers, rejects the man the family has selected for her to marry, or pursues higher education or a career. And they argue that traditions must be strengthened for Dagestan to survive the current turbulence and avoid the ethnic bloodshed that has shattered neighboring Armenia, Georgia, and Azerbaijan.

For example, Regina, a fourth-year student at the university, said her father now objects to her wearing lipstick and jeans. "He has started to learn Arabic, so he can read the Koran in the original," she said, "and it isn't because he is religious, it's because he thinks Islam is the only way to save Dagestan."

Paradoxically, just when the region is enjoying unprecedented freedoms, women's horizons are narrowing. Dagestan is one of the 16 autonomous republics in Boris Yeltsin's Russia. Not unexpectedly, the abortive coup last August, the establishment of the new Commonwealth of Independent States, and all the other changes have rekindled an age-old debate: whether Dagestan should (1) remain under Russian rule, (2) become an independent democratic state, or (3) become an Islamic state. So far the Islamic fundamentalists are in the minority, largely because Dagestanis are Sunni Muslims rather than the more radical Shiites. Still, educated women like Aminat and Zaira worry that, as the religious revival gathers momentum—fueled by Iran, which is shipping Korans and mullahs into Muslim-dominated former Soviet republics—they could become the losers, though what they have now is far from liberation by Western standards.

Not surprisingly some of the most tenacious traditions in Dagestan govern sexual roles. Dagestani ethnographers offer two main explanations for the old customs remaining so strong here.

One is the geographic isolation. Even today 75% of the population lives in villages, some of them stacked so high on the rock faces that outsiders need a helicopter to visit. The other explanation is that 33 unassimilated nationalities—each with its own language—live in Dagestan, all struggling to maintain ethnic identities. In fact, this tiny region is a microcosm of the former Soviet Union. Now that Mikhail Gorbachev is no longer in power, Boris Yeltsin will be regarded as the enemy in Moscow by autonomous republics seeking independence.

Although women may move to the cities for education and work, and thus gain some independence, they continue, like everyone else in Dagestan, to have strong ties to their native villages. There the lives of women are governed by a set of traditions as unchangeable as the seasons.

"Traditionally, the woman must be educated in domestic matters," says Dr. Magomedkhan Magomedkhanov, an ethnographer with the Dagestan Branch of the Academy of Sciences in Moscow. "At home her diploma is of no interest to anyone, even if she has 20 degrees."

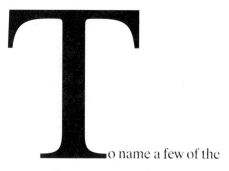

To name a few of the customs: A woman cooks—unless it is outside over a fire, the only time cooking is the man's job. Women serve the men but do not eat with them. However, a woman cannot serve guests. Under Islam's highly developed sense of hospitality, that's the host's job. A woman weaves carpets, but she cannot sell them. Bargaining at the bazaar is a man's job, though ritual requires that he receive the weaver's OK before finalizing a deal on a rug, in recognition of the many months she worked at the loom. Cows are women's business. A man wouldn't be caught dead milking one. Carrying water is a woman's work. Anything to do with machinery is a man's.

Women don't drink. Men do, as I discovered the first time I stayed in a village home. Tradition demanded that I, as the honored guest, sit with the host through endless toasts. Finally one evening when my host, a retired militia chief from Makhachkala, had listed all Gorbachev's failures for the fifth time, I excused myself and joined the women in the kitchen. There the conversation was far more interesting and certainly less repetitive.

One of the host's nieces was a schoolteacher, the other a local pediatrician concerned with the health of children in large families, which are common in Dagestan. "When a woman has had 10 children she is so worn out she can't give them what they need, especially now, when buying the basic necessities is so difficult," the pediatrician told me as we sat around the table drinking tea.

Having babies is, of course, a Dagestani woman's most important role, the more the better and preferably boys. In the ancient city of Derbent, which recently celebrated 5,000 years of history, I accompanied Zuleika to the Forty Martyrs Cemetery, which contains a special shrine for women.

"We have three daughters but no son," she confided sadly. Her husband, Rafik, was in charge of food supplies for a trade union—a job that with the current shortages made him a powerful figure in the city. The family owned a large dacha with swimming pool on the Caspian and was building a three-story mansion.

It was clear from the way Zuleika was greeted by the aged women who guarded the shrine that this was not her first visit. Behind the walls of the small open enclosures the lilacs were in bloom, but the purple blossoms were almost invisible beneath thousands of cloth strips, which had been tied to the branches as offerings from women with problems similar to Zuleika's. One crone led her to a wall and she placed her head inside an alcove, said a brief prayer, and made her wish.

Zuleika was a pianist, but her husband wanted her to stop working as soon as they could afford it. She expressed no regrets, "because it is impossible to do everything for the girls and Rafik and work as well." Earlier, she had shown me the glass, silver, and china they'd been collecting for the dowries of their three daughters. Already, a boy had been selected for the 14-year-old to marry when she got older.

In Dagestan marriage outside the ethnic group or with a Russian is rare, especially for women. Marriages are arranged between the families, as they still are in many places around the world. They should take place, at the very latest, by the time the girl is 21. When I told Minayet, my hostess in the village of Akhty, that my 28-year-old daughter wasn't married, she looked at me sadly.

"Is gold very expensive in America?" she asked, as if it were just a question of raising money for the dowry.

The family starts preparing her dowry almost as soon as a girl is born. In most of the homes where I stayed, the hostess took great pride in showing me the special room where the things were displayed. Although the dowry varies slightly from nationality to nationality, the basics are three carpets for the wall and two for the floor, bedroom furniture, kitchen equipment, and various items of gold jewelry.

For Zaira, her dowry was a problem because her father had died several years before and her mother couldn't raise the money. Zaira wanted to become a lawyer but said she would have to start working after graduating from university so she could earn the money for her dowry.

At the moment it doesn't look as though increased freedom is on the agenda for Dagestani women. The instability and economic hardship created by the political collapse of the Soviet Union are fertile ground for religious or political fanaticism, especially in the Muslim republics. The Soviet war in Afghanistan and expanding contacts with the outside Muslim world have resulted in an attraction to Islamic fundamentalism. Islam, many say, is the only weapon for fighting increasing social ills such as alcoholism, drugs, crime, and corruption, not to mention the damage to Dagestani self-esteem caused by communist propaganda, which continually made Dagestanis feel their native culture is backward and inferior.

"Mikhail Gorbachev"—as I discovered when several small boys started throwing stones at the bus as it maneuvered a particularly dangerous hairpin bend on a mountain road—has become a curse word in Dagestan as in many other places.

If anyone is a hero in Dagestan these days, it is Shamil, a 19th-century imam who declared a holy war against the czar and kept the czar's soldiers busy fighting in the mountains for almost 30 years. As Dagestanis are rediscovering their past, thanks to the years of glasnost, a cult is building around this legendary warrior who swept down from the mountains, the reins of his horse between his teeth.

Then there is Stalin. Stalin symbolizes the law and order that Dagestanis so desperately desire as everything else seems to be falling apart. "*Vot shto muzhik* (There's a man for you)," said Vagid, the son of my hostess in Akhty, a village near the Azerbaijan border. He pointed to a bust of the late dictator on top of the television set. "Things were better under him, and at least there was something in the stores." Vagid also had a soft spot for Saddam Hussein, whom he admired for taking on the Western giants led by George Bush.

As I talked to the women, it became clear that, despite the economic hardships, they were more supportive of Gorbachev's political reforms than the men. It was, after all, largely thanks to the Russians that Dagestani women had any

higher education at all. Russian and Soviet domination created untold devastation in Dagestan—the destruction of villages and crops under the czars; then of mosques, priceless manuscripts, and books under Stalin; horses under Khrushchev; and vineyards under Gorbachev. But this domination did produce two important things: a common language, which allows Dagestan's 33 ethnic groups to communicate with one another, and education, however much it was loaded with communist propaganda.

Soon after the 1917 Revolution, when the Soviet leaders established control over Central Asia and the Caucasus, they realized that the Muslims, if united, could be a serious threat to Moscow's power. As a result, the leaders launched a brutal antireligious campaign, eliminating Dagestan's clerics and destroying the religious schools and all but 28 of its 2,000 mosques.

Religious practice may have been banned, but way up in the mountains people continued to enjoy a Muslim way of life. Birth, circumcision, marriages, and funerals were observed much as they had been for centuries, except without mosques or the participation of the mullahs. Then in the late 1980s, when Gor-

Education was viewed as a tool to combat religious superstition, especially the education of women, who were considered the main upholders of belief in Allah.

The attempt to stamp out Islam in Dagestan didn't succeed any better in the 20th century than it did in the 19th, when Shamil and a few fanatic tribesmen kept one of the largest armies in Europe jumping for three decades. Over the centuries fighting for freedom has been a way of life for these fiercely independent mountain people living at the crossroads between Asia and Europe, where Islam and Christianity meet and clash.

bachev proclaimed freedom of worship, religion burst into flower like a tree in spring, almost as if the suppression had been fertilizing it all the time. Within two years more than 200 mosques were rebuilt from private donations, with more going up all the time. Already a site has been earmarked for a Grand Mosque in Makhachkala.

Although Aminat, Zaira, and their friends fear the excesses of Islamic fundamentalism, they do not appear to be beaten down or angry, like so many Russian women I encountered in Moscow. Maybe they have yet to learn how oppressed they really are, compared to their sisters in the West, or even in Russia. Or maybe they enjoy some inner security knowing their place in the society. As I answered their questions about the freedoms American women enjoy, I often wondered if I wasn't sowing the seeds of their discontent.

Women work harder than men in Dagestan, as in most other Islamic societies. As I watched them hauling water, making rugs, working in the fields, I concluded that if everyone in the new Commonwealth were that industrious, the economy would turn around overnight.

Aminat and Zaira were far too respectful of men to criticize them directly,

though they did venture a few negative comments when aided and abetted by Nina, the Russian, who had no such inhibitions. "Our men are not very serious," volunteered Zaira, as we watched a young man rev up his motorcycle, then ride it at top speed down the narrow streets between the houses, frightening the chickens and dogs. Because of this all three girls said they preferred to spend their time together rather than with boys.

Whatever happens in Russia, whether Dagestan chooses the path of Islamic fundamentalism or Western-style democracy, the lives of Aminat, Zaira, and their friends will undoubtedly change dramatically over the next few years. It will not

be easy to juggle the new freedoms with the demands of a religious revival. Sadly, it will be a long time before they have the kind of freedoms I enjoy.

RUTH DANILOFF lived in the Soviet Union during the early 1960s and again between 1981 and '86, when her husband, US News & World Report correspondent Nick Daniloff, was expelled for "spying" (WM, February). She has written for many publications, including The Christian Science Monitor, Washington Post, Los Angeles Times, and Discover and London Observer magazines.

Central/Eastern Europe: Articles

Article 15

Europe, March 1992

The Eastern Bloc Two Years Later

Barry Wood

Barry Wood is an economics correspondent based in Washington, D.C.

Color is returning to eastern Europe. The dreary grays and browns of neglect are being discarded. The enforced drabness that stretched from the Baltic to the Balkans has lifted.

It is as if for survival and sanity people had retreated beneath rocks. Pale and subdued from 40 years of austerity, cautiously at first, they crept out into the sunlight. Then, convinced the change was real, they rushed out into the open. A venerable Czech journalist escorts a visitor to his central Prague apartment in a building that was probably elegant in the 19th century. Apologizing for the peeling stucco, the unlit vestibule, and primitive plumbing, he laughs, "We didn't live in these flats, we slept in them." If you seek symbols for freedom's triumph in Old Europe, think of paint brushes and fluorescent light bulbs.

Thanks to the 1989 revolutions we now have a clearer sense of geography. Central Europe, as an entity and concept, has been resurrected. This now

identifiable region includes Czechoslovakia, Hungary, and Poland, and is anchored by Germany and Austria. Aware that the word "eastern" connotes poverty, other former East Bloc lands—particularly Romania, but also the Baltics and Ukraine—aspire to be "central." Alas, geography is not on their side.

Useful for journalists, and others comfortable with neat categories, it is the three central Europeans—Hungarians, Czechoslovaks, and Poles (in that order)—who are well in the lead in the race to build democracy and free markets. Regrettably, Klaus Friedrich, the incoming chief economist at Dresdner Bank, is right. "Economically and politically," he says, "it get worse the further east you go."

Looking back to 1990, it was the joy of freedom and the hope for better lives, that sustained people in these emerging democracies through the first difficult months of electoral politics and economic shock therapy. That exhilaration and optimism are still alive but being severely tested. The fruits of reform are not ripening as fast as promised. But as a Prague housewife observes, "Yes, it is hard. But we are free. And what is most important, our children have a future."

How long can hope be sustained? With growth in

the European Community slowing, 1992 will be another down year in Central and Eastern Europe. Only Hungary and Czechoslovakia are on the launch pad for economic take-off. For the region as a whole living standards continue to erode from an already low base. Industrial output is off 20 percent, trade with what was the Soviet Union has all but collapsed, privatization—with the notable exception of Czechoslovakia—has hardly begun, and long suppressed ethnic animosities have sprung to the surface, revealing weak and fragile political structures.

POLAND

It was Poland that boldly stepped forward to be first in attempting to build democratic institutions atop the rubble of a failed social experiment. It was here in the region's most populous country where the 1980's freedom struggle was waged most vigorously. By mid-1989—before the wall was breached—there were partially free elections and there was a non-Communist prime minister. By 1990 the Solidarity trade union ran the government and radical free market reforms were launched. Lech Walesa, electrician and recently imprisoned trade union activist, was elected president.

Poland held its breath when prices were freed, trade liberalized, and the currency stabilized beginning in January 1990. Long absent consumer goods returned to the shelves. Many private businesses flourished, but the slam on the monetary brakes triggered a deep recession.

Last October, during a year in which the economy declined a further 7 percent, Poland held its first truly free elections in over 60 years. Apathy and political gridlock, however, seemed to emerge the winners. Retread Communists did surprisingly well. The strongest party got less than 14 percent of the vote and 29 parties gained parliamentary seats. A dejected Lech Walesa observed, "Poles do not yet know how to use their newly won liberty."

Poland, long the model student for western free market academics and technocrats, is suffering adjustment fatigue. Leszek Balcerowicz, the finance minister who presided over the economic shock therapy, has been dismissed. Foreign investment continues to lag and unemployment is still rising. Once ambitious privatization plans have been modified and delayed. Poland appears to have lost its once impressive momentum.

CZECHOSLOVAKIA

Along with neighboring Hungary, Czechoslovakia is best placed—geographically, culturally, and economi-

cally—to succeed. Historically, a kind of adjunct to Germany and wedged close to traditional western markets, Czechoslovakia seems only to have overcome its own relatively brief but fractious history. The fragmentation and disintegration of Yugoslavia bear grim warning of the consequences if Czechs and Slovaks are unable to resolve their differences and establish a consensus in favor of a federal structure.

The best hope for Czechoslovakia may be its president, playwright Vaclav Havel. He is a man of moral authority, untarnished both by the Communist past and ethnic nationalism. Elected president in the afterglow of the 1989 Velvet Revolution, Havel's vision of a unified country will be tested in nationwide elections this June.

Unique to the region is the Government's enduring commitment to market based reform, Vaclav Klaus, Finance Minister, party leader, and a Milton Friedman free market disciple, pursues reform with a steadfastness that makes Poland's reformers look weak-kneed by comparison.

A centerpiece of the Klaus reforms is voucher privatization, a controversial method in which for nominal costs (10 days wages, on average) citizens can obtain ownership shares in their choice of hundreds of large state enterprises that are being readied for sale. This attempt to make every Czech and Slovak an instant capitalist is fraught with dangers. Upon its outcome—to be determined in the next few months—Klaus will emerge either a hero or villain.

The Klaus reforms began in January 1991. For the year as whole Czechoslovak output declined by up to 16 percent. A recovery would be a 4 percent decline this year.

HUNGARY

Hungary proves that gradualism can work—if you began in 1968. When Hungary's parliamentary elections were held two years ago, the victorious coalition appeared weak and some predicted its early demise. Fortunately for Hungarians the opposite seems to be the case. The country's 60-year-old, self-effacing prime minister Jozsef Antall, is the least known central European leader, but he is arguably the most effective. Having already traveled some distance along the free market path by 1989, Hungary has been able to avoid the big bang shock treatment that so traumatized Czechoslovakia and Poland.

Under Antall's resolute guidance, Hungary stands head and shoulders ahead thus far in the economic sweepstakes. It has attracted fully two-thirds of all new foreign investment to the region. A unique combination of direct investment and part-ownership has succeeded in privatizing several thousand Hungarian firms.

But success is relative. The economy declined 6 percent last year and is expected to be flat this year. Conceding that the obstacles to economic transformation are immense, Hungary's central bank chief, Akos Bod, explains that full privatization can't occur without a commercial banking system. Hungary, he says, boasts 35 banks with 500 offices—by far the most extensive network in what was the Eastern Bloc. But that, he says, is grossly inadequate and well behind the poorest west European country. "We are," he says, "from five to 20 years behind."

THE OTHERS: ROMANIA, BULGARIA, ALBANIA AND THE YUGOSLAV REPUBLICS

A lesson of the past two years is that market-based reform stands a chance of success only if the reformers enjoy political legitimacy. That means free elections, something that hasn't yet happened in Romania and Albania and only occurred in Bulgaria in January. Yugoslavia, destroyed by civil war, is a special case.

Romania, which after Poland has the region's largest population, embarked on rigorous economic reforms in 1990. Regrettably, they have failed to win popular support and most potential investors are staying away

to see how the political situation evolves. Local elections were held in February, but international human rights groups complained they were neither free nor fair. At the national level the ruling National Salvation Front is comprised of former Communists. Romania's industrial production plummeted by 17 percent in 1991.

Bulgaria, with only nine million people, is a sleeper and a candidate for eventual success. Zhelyu Zhelev, a 56-year-old reformer, won January's presidential election over a former Communist. Zhelev's Union of Democratic Forces, which won 34 percent of the votes in earlier parliamentary elections, formed Bulgaria's first non-Communist government only three months ago. Bulgaria has a considerable distance to travel just to regain the economic losses of the past two years. In 1991, Bulgaria's Soviet dependent economy declined by a shocking 22 percent. That followed a 12 percent decline in 1990.

Albania, where Communists retain power, is by far the poorest country in Europe. In the best case scenario, Bulgaria will provide a model for Albania, whose economy is flat on its back. New elections are being planned, but economic prospects are dim for the next 12 months. Albania will be powerfully affected by what happens in the neighboring Yugoslav republic of Macedonia and Serbian-administered Kosovo province, which is inhabited by ethnic Albanians.

Article 16

THE ECONOMIST FEBRUARY 1ST 1992

Democracy in Eastern Europe

In a region that before 1945 had mostly authoritarian rule, removing communism will not alone bring democracy

MANY historians, reflecting in 1989 on the French Revolution 200 years earlier, concluded that its significance had been overdone. What struck them most were the continuities between France before and after the revolution. The notion that complex societies can ever be turned upside down in one peacetime convulsion was, these historians suggested, a myth. Societies do change, but only slowly.

Until 1989 most people in the West thought much the same

about Eastern Europe. From the left it was argued that, grim as they were, East European societies had a certain stability. On the right it was explained that communism was unlike the authoritarian regimes in Eastern Europe's past. Communist parties had monopolised not only the economy but schools, unions, newspapers, churches. Once in power, they would never give up.

In 1989 one East European communist regime after another loosened its grip on one-party power: Hungary (February), Po-

land (June), Bulgaria, East Germany and Czechoslovakia (November), Romania (December). By January 1992 every East European country had freely and fairly elected governments. All were non-communist, though in Romania and Albania ex-communists kept much power.

Even war-wracked Yugoslavia, at least to start with, fitted the pattern. Its six republics held elections (1990). Nationalist democrats seeking independence won in Croatia and Slovenia. Nationalist communists pre-

vailed in Serbia. The ensuing conflict between them tore the Yugoslav federation apart.

Decline and fall

With hindsight, this European revolution looks so natural that it seems pointless to ask why it happened. Given a chance to escape from Soviet-imposed communism with its one-party corruption, bullying of dissenters and bread queues, any country would take it. Yet almost nobody in the West dreamed of so swift a break. Was communism's strength in Eastern Europe misjudged? Or does its sudden fall need a deeper explanation?

The commonest answer is that revolution came from outside. Communism had been imported in 1945 by Soviet armies freeing Eastern Europe from the Nazis. When East Germans (1953), Hungarians and Poles (1956) and Czechoslovaks (1968) had tried to break its grip, Soviet force prevented them. By the late 1980s Soviet leaders were unable or unwilling to do this. Eastern Europe rolled free like a ball from an open palm.

This answer is true as far as it goes. But East Europeans' own struggle for change also counted. This included open dissent from anti-communists—Lech Walesa, Bronislaw Geremek and Jacek Kuron in Poland; Vaclav Havel and Jiri Dienstbier in Czechoslovakia—as well as sapping from within by reform-minded communists. The motives of such communists were mixed: to abolish the system, to save it by timely fixes, to protect their perks. Whatever its cause, their apostasy had dire results for the old regime.

By 1989 bargaining was under way in Hungary and Poland similar to the postwar "Sovietization" of Eastern Europe, only in reverse: communists (in 1945 it was democrats) eager for change or too demoralised to resist gradually gave in to democrats (after the war, to communists).

Czechoslovakia was rather different. Its Communist Party, purged of reformers after 1968, had almost no leaders able to see, let alone accept, the inevitable. Refusing compromise, they left no choice but to fight or fold—and fighting without Soviet support was unthinkable.

The pressures on the old regime were political, economic and patriotic. People were better educated than 20 or 30 years previously. More and more thought for themselves and had jobs they did not expect to be bossed about in. The old distinction between "workers" and "intellectuals" looked ever more artificial. It became easier for dissent to spread through the system. A classic example was Poland's Solidarity movement, an anti-communist

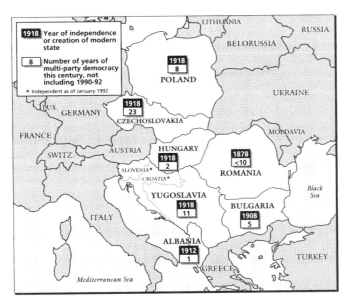

1918 Year of independence or creation of modern state
8 Number of years of multi-party democracy this century, not including 1990-92
* Independent as of January 1992

No longer just constitutional niceties

	Type of state and date of constitution	Presidential term and powers	Type of parliament	Most recent elections		Government
				Parliamentary % of vote (seats in lower house)	Presidential % of popular vote	Pr=president Pm=prime minister (party in brackets)
Bulgaria	Republic 1991	Popular, two-round election for five-year term; non-executive	Single-chamber, five-year parliament with 240 seats; proportional representation with 4% threshold	October 1991 Union of Democratic Forces: 35% (111); Ex-communists: 33% (106); Turkish party:7% (23)	January 1992 Zhelyu Zhelev (UDF):53.5% Velko Vulkanov (Ex-communist): 46.3%	Pr: Zhelyu Zhelev (UDF) Pm: Filip Dimitrov (UDF)
Czechoslovakia	Federal republic 1960 (amended 1990)	Chosen by parliament for two-year term; non-executive; powers in dispute	Two-chamber federal parliament: Chamber of People (Czech Lands:101 seats; Slovakia: 49 seats); Chamber of Nations (75 seats each)	June 1990 Civic Forum: 47% (87); Communists:14% (23); Christian Democrats: 12% (20)		Pr: Vaclav Havel (CF) Pm: Marian Calfa (CF ally)
Hungary	Republic 1949 (amended 1990)	Chosen by parliament for four-year term; non-executive	Single-chamber, four-year parliament with 386 seats; part proportional, part constituency	March-April 1990 Democratic Forum: 25% (165); Free Democrats: 21% (92); Smallholders: 12% (43)		Pr: Arpad Goncz (FD) Pm: Jozsef Antall (DF)
Poland	Republic 1952 (amended 1990)	Popular, two-round election for five-year term; non-executive; powers in dispute	Two-chamber, four-year parliament: Sejm (460 seats); senate (100 seats); both proportional	October 1991 Fragmented parliament of more than 20 parties, none with more than 13% of vote	December 1990 Lech Walesa (Centre-right): 74% Jan Tyminski (Party X): 26%	Pr: Lech Walesa (Centre-right) Pm: Jan Olszewski (Centre-right)
Romania	Republic 1991	Popular, two-round election for four-year term; executive	Two-chamber, four-year parliament: Chamber of Deputies (260 seats plus seats for minorities); senate (130 seats); both proportional	May 1990 National Salvation Front: 66% (233); Hungarian party: 7% (29); Liberals: 6% (29)	May 1990 Ion Iliescu (NSF): 85%	Pr: Ion Iliescu (NSF) Pm: Theodor Stolojan (NSF)

Yugoslavia is, or was, a federation of six republics and two autonomous provinces. Under the much amended 1974 constitution, each had a seat on an eight-man collective presidency. A federal government was responsible to the Skupstina or Yugoslav parliament. Real power lay with the republics. As the old Yugoslavia broke up in late 1991, its federal bodies became defunct.
Albania held a multi-party election in April 1991. The ex-communist Albanian Party of Labour won 68% of the votes and 169 seats in the single-chamber, 250-member People's Assembly.

alliance of Gdansk ship workers and Warsaw dons.

In the 1980s the gap between communist economies and capitalist ones in the West became a gulf. There were local variations on the Soviet model. Poles had private farms. Small businesses existed in Hungary. Though the most heavily nationalised, Czechoslovakia's economy was the stablest and had the fewest queues, perhaps because it was also the richest before communism. Yet economic growth was everywhere slow, technology backward and shortages chronic.

In the Soviet Union, dissenters and reform-minded communists diagnosed the same disease. Soviet self-doubt emboldened Eastern Europe. Turmoil there fed back into the Soviet Union, further weakening faith in the old regime. The distinction between a revolution from outside and one from within turns out, on closer inspection, to be too neat: each fuelled the other.

A third source of pressure was present in Eastern Europe and missing, or at least delayed, in the Soviet Union: national pride, long battered not just by communist but by pre-war failure.

No past to be proud of

Except for Czechoslovakia, communism's fall in Eastern Europe did not restore democracy. As independent nations, the other countries of the region had never really been democratic (see map). Poland had a brief parliamentary free-for-all until 1926, when Marshal Pilsudski imposed authoritarian rule. Another strongman, Admiral Horthy, dominated interwar Hungary.

The parliaments of coup-prone Bulgaria and Romania (both monarchies) were corrupt and unstable. Tensions among Czechs, Slovaks and ethnic Germans—patiently exploited by

Hitler—weakened and eventually helped to do away with democracy in Czechoslovakia.

Anti-Semitism was everywhere strong. Some places, notably Slovakia and Croatia, welcomed Nazism. Even anti-German governments seized on the chaos brought by growing German power and war to settle old territorial grievances at their neighbours' expense. Add 4½ decades of communism. Is it any surprise that East Europeans should hanker for a modern past to be proud of?

In 1989, they won it. But this heroic time of national unity was short, as anti-communist movements broke up into governments and oppositions.

The anti-communist phase of democracy took four forms. In Hungary and Poland change was gradual. In Czechoslovakia the Communist Party crumpled like an empty eggshell. Bulgaria's communists went in two steps. Reform-minded communists won a first democratic election in June 1990. But then, as trouble overwhelmed them, they lost a second election in October 1991 to the Union of Democratic Forces, a combined anti-communist opposition. This may soon be the story in Albania, where ex-communists won a multi-party election in April 1991 but hold power shakily.

The fourth model is Romania. There the break with the old regime was more ambiguous. In December 1989 the communist dictator, Nicolae Ceausescu, was overthrown and put to death with his wife. An umbrella group called the National Salvation Front took over. This was undoubtedly anti-Ceausescu. How democratic it was is still disputed. Its leader, Ion Iliescu, won 85% of the presidential vote in May 1990. Opposition parties are intimidated by gangs.

Democracy's second phase

With exceptions, Eastern Europe is already well into a second phase of democracy: forming new parties and writing or adapting constitutions.

It is normal to see in the new party systems of Eastern Europe first chaos, then order, and, on a third look, chaos. Each country has, on paper, numerous parties. Most are no more than names.

The ones that matter look familiar. They can be arranged from left to right on the conventional spectrum. A few ex-communists, usually called Socialists, and a few social democrats sit in most parliaments. Then comes the centre-left: the Free Democrats and Young Democrats (Hungary), the Democratic Union (Poland), the left of the Civic Forum (Czechoslovakia). To the centre-right belong the Democratic Forum (Hungary), the Centre Alliance (Poland) and the right of Civic Forum (Czechoslovakia). Both groups are for capitalism. The centre-left favours welfare and civil liberties. The centre-right, which includes Christian parties, is more tradition-conscious.

But "left" and "right" are treacherous terms. Some right-wing parties want more state intervention, some left-wing ones sound like free-market radicals. "Conservative" often means old-time communist. Many parties cannot be placed on the left-right line at all: Bulgaria's Turkish party, Hungary's Freeholders (farmers wanting nationalised land back), Romania's Hungarian party, Slovakia's nationalists.

In any constitution, it matters how power is divided between president and parliament and how the rights of minorities are protected. If one thinks of Eastern Europe's past, both of these are especially important.

The first means piloting between parliamentary chaos and one-man rule. Romania has anchored power in the presidency, Hungary in the parliament. Poland's parliament has over 20 parties, none with more than 13% of the vote. President Walesa wants the right (now the parliament's) to name the prime minister, and for that person to have more decree-power. President Havel is seeking more powers to prevent tension between the Czech Lands (Bohemia and Moravia) and Slovakia from breaking up the federal government.

As for protecting minorities, there is an ambiguity. Does it mean protecting individual rights by punishing discrimination? Or the active promotion of the rights of, say, ethnic groups? Must minority schoolchildren be taught in their own language? Should, as in Romania, seats be kept in parliament for ethnic minorities? To name another sort of minority, ought former Bolsheviks be punished or left alone?

These were fundamental questions that faced the new democracies of Eastern Europe 70 years ago. None, save possibly Czechoslovakia, tackled them well. Is Eastern Europe then back at the beginning? Problems look familiar. But the starting-point is different. East Europeans are better educated and more self-reliant; they have nationalist lessons of the past (and, in Yugoslavia, of the present) to avoid; to their West is not a war-prone continent but a democratic E.C.

Communism's fall surprised the West because it was less monolithic than usually thought. Yet even in victory the shoots of initiative and dissent that communism did allow were tender. The hard work of building democracy (and a market economy, the topic of a later brief) remains to be done.

Article 17   *The Economist, February 1-7, 1992*

EASTERN EUROPE'S PAST
The complexities of justice

What should be done about those who served communism in Eastern Europe? It is not a simple question for the new democracies. Issues of law, of morality and of political and economic expediency are intertwined

IN A SESSION of parliament lasting almost three days, the deputies, by an overwhelming majority, convicted their former ruler of conspiring with foreign enemies and trying to flee the country. A motion to put the judgment to a referendum failed. The exhausted deputies then voted, closely this time, for the death sentence. Two attempts to suspend it were defeated. On January 21st 1793 citizen Louis Capet—Louis XVI—went to the guillotine.

With the gruesome exception of Romania, Eastern Europe's anti-communist revolutions were notably bloodless. The death penalty has, for practical purposes, disappeared in the region. Yet, the method of punishment aside, the issue of political justice is as hard for Eastern Europe as it was for a divided parliament in Paris 200 years ago. To post-communist societies, making the right sort of reckoning with those who ran them under communism matters vitally, both for the health of fledgling democracy and for the speed of economic reform.

Any new order has a fundamental decision to make about the old. Should it draw a line under the past, even at the cost of ignoring injustice and leaving old bureaucrats in place? Yes, think some of the bravest opponents of communism, including President Vaclav Havel in Czechoslovakia and President Lech Walesa in Poland. Hungary's President Arpad Goncz advocates tolerance. Germany's head of state, Richard von Weizsäcker, as a young lawyer defended his father, a former official head of Hitler's foreign ministry, at one of the later Nuremberg trials. He now speaks out against witch-hunts and character assassination.

But these sentiments are not universally shared. Others believe that a new society must punish and purge. Democracy, many right-wing members of parliament in Czechoslovakia, Hungary and Poland believe, requires "debolshevisation". They see widespread signs of public apathy or disillusion, and lay much of the blame on a failure to punish and root out communists.

Liberty and the blood of tyrants

Given a choice between blanket amnesty and a clear-out, a few, brutal examples might look like a good compromise. "The tree of liberty must be refreshed from time to time with the blood of patriots and tyrants," said Thomas Jefferson, America's third president and one of its first ambassadors in Paris. But exemplary justice has its pitfalls. The intended lesson may be misunderstood. Nicolae Ceausescu, the dictator of Romania, and his wife were shot after a kangaroo trial which convinced many Romanians that the communists were still in charge. A show trial of four henchmen, with shaved heads and wearing striped prison pyjamas, soon followed. It did little to change Romanians' minds. The defendants, accused of genocide, were swiftly convicted and jailed. Though hated, these men were widely seen as scapegoats.

The courts may be above reproach. The offences may have been recognised as crimes at the time they were committed. Yet trials of old leaders can, all the same, make the law look anything but smooth or just. The trial of Todor Zhivkov, the former boss of Bulgaria, for embezzlement and abuse of power has been interrupted because of his health so many times it may never finish. The Germans say they want to try Erich Honecker, the former ruler of East Germany, for the shoot-to-kill policy at the Ber-

lin Wall. But he is in Chile's Moscow embassy and, it is said, dying of kidney cancer.

Communist leadership was collective. If Mr Zhivkov and Mr Honecker deserve punishment, do not others? In theory, yes, and many of them. In practice, prosecutors are concentrating on the most detested and (now) visible symbols of the old order: former senior secret-policemen. Even this is not always straightforward. In Germany, judicial authorities last year decided not to proceed with a prosecution of Erich Mielke, former boss of East Germany's security and of the Stasi, its sinister secret police. Plenty of former high-ranking Stasi officers are walking about free. Meanwhile several border guards who merely acted on orders to kill have been convicted. Mr Mielke, who is 84, was later put on trial—for the murder of two policemen in 1931, on evidence that was originally secured by Nazi prosecutors using torture. Are these the lessons in justice that democrats should be teaching?

Czechoslovakia's parliament has, in effect, banned former senior communists from public jobs (though not parliament) for five years. Bulgaria's banking privatisation law bars them from holding any position in a private-sector bank for the same period. To make possible the prosecution of those who helped put down the 1956 uprising, Hungary's parliament last year lifted the statute of limitations for political murders and treason (though the constitutional court in Budapest has just struck down this law). Many of Hungary's former top communists have had to tell a parliamentary committee, on oath, how they came by their money.

These laws and procedures appear to break normal rules of criminal justice: a statute of limitations should not be lifted to make prosecutions possible after time has run out; all are equal before the law; guilt, being individual not collective, must be individually proved; punishment must fit the crime. But communism, the sponsors of such bills reply, was never normal. Revolutionary justice must sometimes bend the rules. Besides, the punishments are more political than criminal.

How—and how far down?

Breaking with communism and creating democracy in Eastern Europe is a many-layered business. It involves issues of justice (moral, political and criminal), of economic control and of social privilege. The answers may be conflicting. How are they to be resolved?

Many would agree with President Walesa that moral reckoning is a private affair. Some think it enough that once-ruling communists, who thought history was on their side, should be swept from power in a historic defeat. If they are to be further punished, how can conflicts of criminal law and natural justice be reconciled? Is it fair to restrict their political rights, even if no criminal guilt is proved?

And how far down is the process to be pursued? The advocates of tolerance ask how the untainted half of society (or was it a quarter, or an eighth?) can pass judgment on the rest. Dissidents were rare, communists many. In 1980, 20% of Romanians over the age of 18 belonged to the communist party. In East Germany the figure was 18%, in Czechoslovakia 14%, in Bulgaria 13%, in Poland 12½%, in Hungary 10%. Some cite these figures to underline the urgency of smoking out the old elite and removing their perks and hidden powers. To others, the figures show, on the contrary, that Eastern Europe's new societies can but be imperfect grafts upon the old.

Hardly anyone believes that the crimes of East European communists approached Stalin's, let alone Hitler's. A special tribunal for crimes against humanity—a category created by the victors of the second world war for heinous acts, such as genocide, that might escape the net of national law—is nowhere in question. There are still many cases of violence that call for trial under ordinary criminal law. The victims and their families demand justice. In a perfect world, they would get it. But the problems—who to indict, how to assemble evidence so long after—are formidable. No wonder many prosecutors and justice ministers would like to draw a sponge over the past.

The priority, others argue, is not the past at all, but the future: not justice but economics. In the break with communism, the most urgent task, on this view, is privatisation. That would cut the links between ministries and factories. Once free enterprise takes root and government no longer runs the economy, it will not matter whether ex-communist officials are secret Leninocrats, democrats or just bureaucrats.

That may sound like double-talk to those East Europeans who suspect capitalism as a way for ex-communists to re-emerge on top. They resent the members of an old elite who, as last-minute democrats, not only hung on to jobs, perks and villas, but now sit on the boards of private-sector companies. Restitutive justice, as it is called, has not been ignored. In Czechoslovakia, for example, communist-party property reckoned to be worth more than $400m has been confiscated and given to charity or to welfare bodies. Across Eastern Europe, people who lost land or firms to nationalisation have some chance of compensation or return of their property. But these measures do not seem to have allayed populist resentment against the old (new?) elite.

Beyond these issues lies the task of coming to terms with the past in a broader sense: finding ways to put Eastern Europe's recent experience into a historical context. The region's dark ages did not begin in 1945, nor were communists its only abusers of power. Nor is its experience unique. Many countries—America in 1865, France and Germany in 1945, Spain, Portugal, much of the third world—have lived through the bitter aftermath of civil war, foreign rule or home-grown dictatorship.

How patience wore thin

At first, most people's instinct in Eastern Europe was to put the past aside. Peaceful, rich post-Franco Spain was held out as a model. In Poland, a more or less explicit deal was struck in 1989 between the communists and Solidarity: no vendettas, in exchange for power-sharing.

Latin America offered a lesson. Brutal military regimes there had handed power to democrats during the 1980s, on condition there be general amnesties. Argentina, where more than 9,000 people died under military rule in 1976-83, was an exception; but even there the efforts of the new democratic government to put on trial more than a handful of senior officers came to nothing, in the face of barracks rebellions and mutinies.

By last summer the mood in Eastern Europe had hardened. Public resistance to the pain of economic transition was growing. Communist officials, it was said, were blocking reform. The attempted coup in Moscow last August shocked Eastern Europe. Right-wing parliamentarians in Czechoslovakia, Hungary and Poland hurried to push forward anti-communist legis-

lation. In Germany the opening this January of the files of the Stasi has produced a national drama of soul-searching and recrimination.

The law passed by Czechoslovakia's parliament last October bars senior communist officials, members of communist militias, secret policemen and their informants from jobs in government, state firms, armed forces, courts or universities (though not parliament) for five years. Communists who held high rank only during the "Prague spring" of 1968 are excluded. By putting down 1,000 crowns, about $35, anyone can have a senior official investigated, though the deposit is lost if the victim falls into none of the four forbidden categories. President Havel signed this bill with reluctance. Deputies of the centre-left—the broad family to which he belongs—wanted the bill to apply only to leading communists who had flouted human rights. Right-wing deputies threw that clause out. As passed, the law applies to the head of the former security services and to the Prague Castle bandmaster alike. The federal parliament has also decided that preaching communism is not just a folly but a crime.

In Hungary, the bill to amend the statute of limitations was sponsored by Zsolt Zetenyi, a member of the centre-right Democratic Forum. The number of trials, it was reckoned, could range from zero to 1,000. President Goncz objected to the bill. Nobody really knows what the ill-drafted treason statute to which it refers means, and it was with this that the constitutional court found most fault.

Hungary's liberals had a broader criticism. They questioned the bill's fairness. Who was it aimed at? The prosecutor of Imre Nagy, the Hungarian leader executed after the 1956 uprising, is alive. But most of those who sided with the Russians, including Janos Kadar, their leader, are dead. Kadar, who ruled Hungary for more than three decades, made a Faustian bargain with the Soviet Union: political obedience for economic liberty. No Hungarian is proud of this. But, given the alternatives, few think it a punishable offence. Were the sins of 1956 not mitigated or atoned for by Hungary's (relative) tranquillity and economic success in the decades since? By the late 1980s, many Hungarian communists were out-and-out reformers.

In Poland, the party by then was a spent force. On foreign money borrowed in the 1970s, the old order had sleepwalked on, watched over by the army and police. General Jaruzelski's martial law, imposed in 1981, was harsh at first and some strikers were killed (though not on the scale of Poznan in 1956 or Gdansk in 1970). But gradually the old order accepted the inevitable. The policemen who killed Father Jerzy Popieluszko, a Solidarity priest, were tried in 1985 and jailed (though not those higher up who may have sanctioned the murder). For Solidarity leaders such as Adam Michnik and Bronislaw Geremek, not prosecuting past crimes was a fair price for a peaceful revolution. General Jaruzelski—who can fairly claim to have saved his country from a Russian invasion—remains at liberty, peaceably writing his memoirs.

With democracy, the ministries of the interior and of justice were slowly purged. But in the rest of the government, including the defence ministry, old faces simply changed labels. Last year, rightist deputies in the Sejm, the lower house of parliament, introduced a bill to ban ex-communists who had jobs at provincial level or above (Poland has 49 provinces) from public office for 10 years. However, in the hopelessly split parliament elected last November, progress on any legislation is difficult. Opposed by liberals who think it unjust and unnecessary, the bill languishes in committee.

Those miles of files

East Germany, like Czechoslovakia, was, to the end, a police state. This may explain why anti-communism is fiercest in these countries. Meticulous Stasi officials left plenty of evidence behind them—125 miles of files, even after some were burned or left to rot in the rain as communism crumbled. And the files are being used (unlike those of Poland, whose first democratic interior minister, Krzysztof Kozlowski, reckoned its secret-police files such a stew of innuendo and report-padding that he locked them up). Some Germans—and not just the estimated ½m informers who risked exposure— wanted the Stasi files burned or buried. According to Joachim Gauck, however, the pastor in charge of the archive in Berlin, it is clear from them who was a victim of the Stasi and who a consenting spy. The victims, parliament decided, had a right to know. This January the files were opened, though initially only to those who had been policed or those who policed them.

Horrors spilled out. Vera Wollenberg, a well-known dissident, learned that her husband had turned informer. The Stasi had had a plan to break the will (and destroy the marriage) of two other dissidents, Gerd and Ulrike Poppe. An anti-communist priest, Heinz Eggert, discovered that his doctor, a Stasi agent, had prescribed him drugs that could lead to psychosis.

Even before the files were opened, many of eastern Germany's democratic leaders had been judged below the required standard of purity. Ibrahim Böhme, who helped to found the Social Democrats there, Lothar de Maizière, East Germany's first democratic prime minister, and Manfred Stolpe, premier of Brandenburg and once talked of as a possible future German president, all had had contacts with the Stasi. Whatever their justification, to many easterners they are now damned.

Unduly damned, some other east Germans argue. They say the climate of accusation and guilt mainly serves western Germany. First, it makes a depressed and defeated east easier to repossess. Second, it is a moral substitute for denazification, for which the west had no stomach. East Germany's communism may have been bad, the argument goes, but neither morally nor politically was it as bad as Nazism. Its means were less vile, its declared aims foolish but not ignoble. And it was imposed by Russian force and (in 1953) fought against, whereas Nazism was voted for by many Germans, and accepted by most. Maybe, comes the rejoinder, but for the past 50 years, democracy was in the west, the police-state in the east. So the debate about the past rolls on, in television discussions and the weekly press. An official historical commission is now to delve into these muddied waters.

The psychological damage in eastern Germany is real enough. There is a common feeling there that everything that came out of East Germany is worthless. Writers such as Christa Wolf, once seen as critics of the old regime, are now widely treated as stooges. Nothing, it seems, need be rescued from the rubble, because the west can provide it all: money, telephones, writers and politicians. Other post-communist countries have to rebuild by themselves with what they have. That may be one reason why, even in Czechoslovakia, the anti-communist fury there is less intense.

Article 18

DECEMBER 1991   MULTINATIONAL MONITOR

CONQUERING THE EAST

By Jim Ridgeway

BUDAPEST — For the businessmen in their Mercedes now hurtling down the *autobahns* of Central and Eastern Europe, the East is the last great market left in the world. And for the Germans, who already are the

Jim Ridgeway is a columnist for the Village Voice.

dominant force here, its conquest promises to give them the power they could not achieve in two world wars.

The true enormity of the economic difficulties facing Central and Eastern Europe are only now coming into focus. And while there can be little doubt that this region will soon become an economic province of Germany, its economic well-being will require what amounts to a reinvention of the cohesion that marked the old Austro-Hungarian empire. Corporations are looking first to the revival of the economy in the Czech and Slovak Federal Republic, with its highly skilled workforce and finishing industries that need far less retooling than those elsewhere. Their eyes will next turn to Hungary, with its robust, competitive agricultural economy and a stream of new bootstrap service-based industries. As for the Slovakia part of old Czechoslovakia, businessmen wish it and its Stalinist heavy industry would drop off the face of the earth. They have some hope for Poland, although that country seems forever trapped by determinist forces, whether it be Stalin or the Pope.

Inferior infrastructure

The infrastructure of much of Eastern Europe predates World War II, and imperils both human health and economic productivity. The sanitation systems are outmoded. Bratislava, for example, has a refinery virtually in the middle of the city, and the communists who built it there in order to make Slovakia the center of a plastics and chemical industry cheerfully paid the fines for violating the country's anti-pollution laws rather than cleaning up or halting the emissions. As a result, the children of Bratislava are literally all sick with bronchial infections, prompting the government to decree that each child may spend two to three weeks in the countryside. The phone systems are impossible. While there are some efforts to bypass existing antiquated machinery by skipping a technological generation and installing cellular phones, cities like Prague are not likely to have a decent functioning phone system for at least 10 to 15 years. Few people even have access to the poor system that is currently in place. In Budapest, 39 percent of the households have phones. Outside the capital, however, only 10 percent of the population is served by a phone system. The waiting period to get a phone is 12 years.

The most fundamental infrastructure problem is energy. While the countries of the Eastern bloc have no oil and little natural gas production, the Soviet Union is the largest producer of oil and gas in the world, and ought to have provided a modern energy base for the Eastern bloc. But instead of shipping natural gas to Central Europe, the Soviets sold the gas for hard currency to the West Germans, leaving East Germany, Czechoslovakia, Hungary, Poland and the rest of the East ever more dependent on burning dirty, energy-inefficient brown coal to produce electricity. This created a blanket of deadly chemical smog over the forests and cities of central Europe, which, when the wind blew, drifted back across the Ukraine, Byelorussia and Russia. Even worse, the Eastern bloc countries con-

structed rickety nuclear power plants which are just waiting to blow up like Chernobyl did.

Today, little has changed. Environmentalists and ecologically minded legislators in Eastern European countries are struggling to dismantle or make safe nuclear power plants, searching for ways of burning lignite more cleanly and efficiently, talking wildly of schemes for alternative energy and attempting to persuade their governments to adopt the kinds of energy conservation programs that U.S. environmentalists first urged on President Carter in the 1970s and now are demanding of President Bush.

Oil still comes from Russia, although at higher prices. High in sulphur content and vanadium, it poses serious toxic threats to the population, especially children.

The former East bloc countries are reluctant to maintain any energy dependence on the Soviet Union, though there does not appear to be any long-term alternative. There seems to be little doubt that they will be buying oil and gas, and conceivably importing electricity, from Russia and the Ukraine.

Eastern Europe can no longer rely on oil supplies piped from the Middle East up through the Adriatic, since they have been cut off by the civil war in Yugoslavia. Even if these pipelines were reliable, they would have to be expanded greatly to be sufficient to serve the region.

Water engineers hold on to the great illusion of generating inexpensive, clean power from dams on the Danube. But the Stalinist dam projects on the Danube would produce barely enough electricity to run the water treatment and other facilities required to protect the nearby populace from the side effects of the dam, such as poisoned underground aquifers. Misty-eyed Czech planners talk enthusiastically about coal liquifaction and gasification, although similar projects in other parts of the world have always been expensive and technologically dubious. (One need only remember the hype surrounding coal gasification during the Carter years, when U.S. experts confidently predicted coal could be turned into gas to supplement the supposed dwindling supplies of natural gas if only the price were permitted to rise.) It appears unlikely that the cash-starved countries of Eastern Europe will find the money to pay for coal gasification.

One near-term prospect is to convert a pipeline that runs through the former territories of East Germany so that it can carry oil from the North Sea ports into Czechoslovakia.

Waiting for privatization

But all efforts to create new economic relations in the region hinge on privatization. Here there is remarkably little progress.

In the former territories of East Germany, the efforts to sell off the Kombinats and other businesses have been slow and clouded with charges of corruption. Over the past year, the Truehand, the agency charged with overseeing East German privatization, has privatized 4,000 of 10,500 East German businesses, generating some $9 billion in revenues. More than 130 foreign companies — only 17 of which are based in the United States — have acquired 200 formerly East German companies.

Unemployment in East Germany is running at 20 percent and is expected to rise to 40 percent by next year. East German labor is paid at 60 percent of the West German scale. There is a great sense of abandonment, betrayal and bitterness on the part of the East Germans towards the communists who promised everything and produced little, and now towards the West German political parties that held out high hopes at the time of unification.

In Czechoslovakia, U.S. law firms are pushing the nation towards a system in which former state businesses are turned over to the people, who would be provided stock certificates. But this is a paper exercise, and the exact terms of the transfer are vague. The Czech republic has now delayed the implementation of the voucher plan until February, and the federal government fears the vouchers will not actually be sold until after the parliamentary elections next June.

Meanwhile, Swiss and Austrian businessmen sweep across the landscape, taking advantage of small busi-nesses wherever they can. To make it easier to rip off the East Europeans, the Swiss have rewritten their laws so that is possible to deduct bribes as business expenses.

In Hungary, capitalist accumulation seems to be moving more quickly since the government largely looks the other way when it comes to collecting taxes on new small business enterprises which operate in a fast and furious cash economy with no records. They, in turn, plow profits back into the new ventures.

"Thirty percent of the gross domestic product is in the private sector and most of that in newly formed enterprises, not the old socialist enterprises," according to Peter Rona, former president of the Schroder bank who now runs a closed-end investment company with investments in Hungary.

Concluding last year that the Soviet Union was going to collapse, Hungary stepped up exports and aggressively sought markets in the West. As a result, exports last year grew by 25 percent. This year, hard currency exports are expected to grow by 27 percent.

"For the Germans the East has to be the future," Rona says. "If there is instability and economic chaos in the East, Germany will bare the brunt of it. The French certainly won't feel it. ... Already 80 percent of the foreign investment capital in Poland, Czechoslovakia, Hungary and the European parts of the Soviet Union is German. These investments now total in excess of 90 billion *deutchmarks*." ■

Article 19

JUNE 1991   MULTINATIONAL MONITOR

CAPITAL GOES EAST

The Role of the IMF in Eastern Europe

By Paul Hockenos

BUDAPEST, HUNGARY — Every third month, an International Monetary Fund (IMF) delegation calls on Hungary's economic policymakers. It is a day of reckoning for the National Bank and Finance Ministry

---

Paul Hockenos is the Eastern Europe correspondent for the Chicago-based In These Times.

chiefs in Budapest. They know well that their progress on the IMF's economic stipulations holds the key to the country's financial solvency.

For Hungary, as for all of the former communist countries, IMF approval of its free market transition policies is critical to its short-term survival. Should the IMF deem the policymakers too lenient in the application of the austerity programs, loans would be halted, and the financially strapped countries would be forced to default on their looming debts.

Such a cutoff of loans, government economists claim, would extinguish any hopes of economic recovery. The IMF's word not only determines countries' access to its own reserves, but functions as a seal of approval, esteemed by all major private and government creditors, as well as investors. The fragile Eastern European economies could plunge into chaos if foreign loans were cut off.

Facing massive debts and politically committed to the free market principles of the IMF, Eastern Europe's new heads of state have not resisted the hard terms of the IMF's tight monetary packages. All of the postcommunist governments, whether IMF members or not, have dutifully implemented the general conditions of the IMF recipe: monetary restriction, price liberalization, deregulation and privatization. Top among the demands of the prescribed "shock therapy" are massive cuts in domestic expenditures — from investment to food subsidies — in order to meet balance-of-payment (the level of imports versus exports) targets.

While every government in the former East bloc ascribes to the ultimate goal of a free market transition, the issue is how radically to proceed. The unspoken question is how great a burden the people will bear without rebelling. The austerity policies combined with the demise of the East bloc market have sparked falls in living standards, sharp drops in output and rising inflation and unemployment. The net domestic product last year dropped in every East European country, from 3.1 percent in Czechoslovakia to 13 percent in Bulgaria and 19.2 percent in East Germany. The tight domestic budget targets allow no funds for programs to address soaring homelessness, crime and drug use.

The IMF's role has been to discipline governments which waver in their commitment to push forward with the transition. When, for example, Hungary's 1989 budget, under the reform communist government, showed an unexpectedly large negative balance of payments and budget deficit, the IMF halted stand-by loans. The government quickly drafted an emergency mid-year budget and loan access was restored.

While the exact terms of IMF contracts are secret, the influence of the Fund's money managers is plain to see. "When one reads between the lines," says economist Laszlo Andor of the Hungarian Trade Unions' Institute for Economic Research, "it's clear that the IMF is practically dictating Hungarian monetary policy." When politicians are challenged about the latest cuts in education or medical subsidies, for example, they openly admit that the IMF has tied their hands. "The IMF policies embody the full logic of Reaganomics, and one hears that in politicians' language," says Andor.

The power of debt

The IMF's influence in Eastern Europe stems largely, although not exclusively, from the region's massive indebtedness. Eastern European countries desire IMF contracts which guarantee annual loans they need to help service their debts. Even the less indebted countries, in part because of their desire to be in the IMF's good graces and receive loans from the Fund, generally adhere to the IMF's policy prescriptions. Romania, for example, with almost no debt, has eagerly applied a radical version of the IMF calculus to its ailing economy. Along with Poland, Hungary, Czechoslovakia and Bulgaria, Romania as of April 1991 can negotiate credit and reform packages with the IMF. The country's first reward: a $295 million loan from the Export Deficit and Crisis Fund to soften the fallout resulting from cutbacks in Soviet aid and oil shortages caused by the Persian Gulf War.

With the exception of Romania, where the government pushed the people to starvation in the 1980s to cover the country's debts, all of the former East bloc countries suffer heavy indebtedness. Poland boasts the largest Central European debt at $47 billion and Hungary the highest per capita debt at $21 billion total. Bulgaria, whose foreign debt has more than doubled from $4.7 in 1986 to $10.8 billion, defaulted in spring 1990. Czechoslovakia stands in somewhat better shape with $8 billion outstanding. Yugoslavia and the Soviet Union owe foreign creditors $17 and $52 billion respectively.

While each country's case varies, the pattern of Eastern bloc indebtedness has its roots in the early 1970s. The East Europeans, along with the Third World countries, borrowed heavily, taking advantage of the rock-bottom interest rates which lasted until the mid-seventies. The plan was to use the borrowed funds to switch to import-led growth strategies, fueling domestic growth through technology and capital imports from the West. In theory, the export of the derivative manufactured goods back to the West would cover the accrued debts.

The expected export payoff on the world market never materialized, however. Industrial goods were peddled instead to the Soviet Union for rubles, leaving balance-of-payment deficits in internationally traded currencies. When the oil-price shocks hit, followed by the 1979-1982 world recession, the Eastern Europeans, Africans and South Americans plunged together into an abyss of debt. As interest rates skyrocketed, debtors' foreign deficits, of which only a fraction had ever been invested, soared. Hungary, for one, had invested only $3.5 billion of the $12 billion that it owed by 1981.

Trapped in debt

When the debt crisis came to a head in the early 1980s, Hungary and others sought out the IMF for help. The structural adjustments and debt-financing schedules began a vicious circle of borrowing that would double and triple the East Europeans' debts during the decade. Hungary continued to borrow, paying off its early 1980s principle three times over, while the total amount of its debt doubled. Poland also paid back its initial debt at least once, as its total indebtedness increased dramatically.

Hungarian sociologist Andrea Szego sees the dilemmas of the East European countries as classic examples of the "international debt trap." Governments take out new credits simply to finance old ones, and countries' entire economies then become geared toward exports. "Once a country is stuck in the debt trap, it is forced to export at any cost for foreign currency. The forced growth of exports leads to domestic losses that are taken out at home," she says.

The credit provided directly or indirectly by the IMF failed to translate into any significant growth in the debt countries, Szego explains. "After the first period of borrowing, the vast majority of funds went directly to financing debt payment. The debt-servicing plans were simply implemented to protect the international monetary system from collapse." She notes as well that the Hungarian Communist Party's attempt to sell the conservative IMF adjustment policy as a Marxist-Leninist program of renewal precipitated its fall. "This caused not only their own defeat, but the crisis of Marxism as well."

Today, the nationalist-conservative Hungarian Democratic Forum (HDF) government grapples with the same tight conditions as the communists. Hungary's pact with the IMF stipulates that the country's export surplus and tourism revenue must cover $1.6 billion in interest payments if it is to receive $2.35 billion in loans to pay off part of the principle on its debt.

The president of the Hungarian National Bank optimistically points out that the country's debt service ratio (servicing costs as a percent of total export earnings) has fallen to "only" 40 percent from 70 percent three years ago. But the collapse of the COMECON trade bloc and conversion to dollar-based trade with the Soviet Union (particularly for oil) has the government predicting a 14 percent drop in the terms of trade for 1991. Hungary's trade with the Soviet Union accounted for 30 percent of its total trade in 1980 but only 20 percent last year. The 10 percent increase in the volume of 1990 hard-currency exports to the West helped offset a 26 percent decline in ruble trade. But with the East now competing with the West on an equal basis for Soviet markets, the boom in westward exports will not cover Hungary's losses this year.

According to IMF rationale, the only recourse is harsher austerity at home. Last year, the additional 5 percent of gross domestic product extracted from the Hungarian economy to bolster the balance of payments came in large part from workers' pockets. With over a third of the population living at or below the poverty line, the government cut real wages through a calculated inflationary policy. The closure of "inefficient, centralized" industries — the same targets of investment cuts in the 1980s — is another means to trim the domestic budget. The much-heralded privatization of the industrial sector, which government economists hoped would bring in foreign currency, has fallen catastrophically short of expectations. Western investment is only a trickle, leaving the countries in the lurch, falling more than $10 billion short of anticipated totals.

"The economy is expected to [shoulder the] burden [of] higher and higher financing costs from a stagnating GDP," says Andor. "In the long run, the chances of repayment could only be improved if the economy developed competitive, productive industries. But, with these restrictive monetary policies, there's no chance for development. Internal investment is almost nonexistent because everything is going to the debt."

The human costs of austerity are daily more visible on the streets of every East European city. Domestic consumption fell last year in Czechoslovakia, Hungary, Poland, the Soviet Union and Bulgaria. The drops have forced even mid-level wage earners to take second or third jobs. Inflation jumped high above estimates in every country, with the exception of Hungary and East Germany. In Budapest, the train and subway stations are filling with homeless people and families. Slowly, economists and citizens alike are recognizing that the "belt-tightening" that politicians in 1989 promised would last only three to five years will be a fact of life for much longer.

Alternatives to austerity

Despite these consequences, opposition to the IMF's policies is almost nowhere to be seen. In Hungary, the entire spectrum of parliamentary parties backs prompt debt servicing and adherence to the general terms of the IMF contract. Politicians feel that "there's no alternative." The ruling HDF-led coalition has resisted the all-out "shock therapy" that IMF bankers pushed through in Poland. Yet, their somewhat more "gradual" approach is only a revised version of the same economic program that all of the parties endorse.

The major opposition party, the former dissident-led Free Democrats, supports even more draconian policies. The party's top economist, Attila Soos, sees the IMF role in Hungary as positive. In contrast to Andor and Szego, he charges that mismanagement and waste, not the debt cycle, are at the heart of the country's economic woes. "The IMF has been essential in pushing the government toward a capitalist market economy," he says. "Much of the HDF program is accepted only under IMF pressure." A year ago, he notes, the HDF advocated a "third way between capitalism and socialism. It was the IMF that pressured them to abandon this idea."

But André Gunder Frank, of the University of Amsterdam, recently in Prague to discuss the debt crisis, and others dispute the contention that there is "no other alternative" than to suffer from austerity measures implemented under the yoke of debt. "Debts have come and gone for ages," says the expert on debt issues. He sees three ways in which Third World and East European debts could be reduced or eliminated. The first is to pay them back, the path taken by Romania's dictator, Nicolas Ceausescu, with its well-known consequences. The second avenue is to default, which many countries did in the 1920s and 1930s. Another alternative is for creditors to write debts down or forgive them entirely. This option is not without precedent. The Allies wrote off West Germany's remaining war debt at the 1948 London Conference. East Germany's domestic debt was simply taken over last year by West Germany.

The most dramatic breakthrough in this regard came in spring 1991, when the Paris Club, an informal grouping of the world's 17 leading industrial countries, announced that it would halve Poland's enormous debt and reduce accumulated interest by 80 percent. The creditor governments agreed that economic recovery for Poland was inconceivable without substantial debt reduction. Unlike Hungary and the other East European countries, an unusually high proportion of Poland's debt was owed directly to foreign governments rather than banks or multilateral agencies.

The decision, however, was no act of charity. The Western countries knew well that Poland had no prospect for full repayment. The wave of strikes and strike threats against the government's "shock therapy" dangerously jeopardized the reform process. The finance ministry finally convinced the IMF and member states that the population would not endure the crisis without greater support. As the London-based *Economist* warned, "Debt relief is a reward and an incentive, not a right. ... When a company nears bankruptcy, creditors will reduce its debts only if they think doing so stands a chance of making the firm able to survive in the longish term and this to repay or service those debts that remain. It is the same with countries. ... Debt relief could be — and was — made conditional on those reforms staying in place during the next four years."

The mechanism for that control is the gradual lifting of debt burdens. In the first phase of three years, 30 percent of the agreed sum of $33 billion will be dropped. A further 20 percent will go in 1994 if Poland's recently sealed pact with the IMF is deemed "successful," states the Paris Club communiqué.

Until then, Poland must haggle with the individual governments as well as private banks over the exact terms of reduction. Germany and Japan have put up the fiercest resistance. The "Polish precedent" piqued no one more than the German banks, which hold the lion's share of Poland's debt as well as that of many other East European countries. The United States' elimination of 70 percent of Poland's debt to U.S. banks upon President Lech Walesa's March visit raised a furor in Vienna and Frankfurt. "The whole $3.8 billion that Poland owes the USA is only a fifth of what the country owes little Austria," complained the Vienna daily *Die Presse*. "It will be difficult now to prevent a chain reaction [across Eastern Europe]."

Already, the "Polish precedent" has triggered the feared murmurs of dissent in Hungary. A leading politician's claim that the government was "split over asking for a debt reduction" unleashed a storm in the Budapest financial community. Politicians, bankers, and experts rushed to deny the charge. "The government," a spokesperson reassured the press, "is fully united on the question of debt repayment."

Closing the third way

In the immediate aftermath of the 1989 revolutions, proponents of neo-classical free market reform were just one voice among many. From Berlin to Sofia, somewhat vague but nevertheless different ideas of "third ways," "social market systems" and "social ecological economies" were bandied about by the parties now in office. But the IMF moved fast to see that these alternatives never saw the light of day. In a spring 1990 brief on Eastern Europe policy, the IMF managing director wrote that "any attempts to find a third way between central planning and a market economy" must be ruled out. The debt trap ensured the IMF the leverage that it needed to encourage countries to follow a free-market trajectory. The results may please Western governments, bankers and industrialists, but the consequences have been devastating for the people of Eastern Europe, who, having earned a measure of political freedom, are finding themselves under the thumb of a new tyrant. ∎

Article 20   *Europe, March 1992*

Going to Market

Bruce Barnard

The European Community is facing one of its toughest challenges ever as its east European neighbors brace for a make or break effort to pull off their unprecedented move from a Communist planned economy to a market economy.

The Community is already deeply involved in helping eastern and central Europe's transition to capitalism through a mixture of financial aid packages, technical assistance and trade agreements. But the sheer scale of the economic and political transformation means that the E.C. will have to deepen its commitment to the fledgling democracies during the rest of the decade.

Brussels will be distracted by other events, not least the economic rescue of the former Soviet Union. And after two years of intense contacts with its east European neighbors, the E.C. is turning to more domestic matters like completion of its single market program, reform of the Common Agricultural Policy, and agreeing on a new budget.

Meanwhile, the east Europeans themselves fear they will be overlooked as the West becomes preoccupied with bailing out the former Soviet republics. "The legitimate economic and trade interests of the fragile . . . east European states should be duly taken into account" in working out aid for the former Soviet republics, the foreign ministers of Czechoslovakia, Hungary, and Poland said in a joint statement to a recent 47-nation conference in Washington on emergency aid to Russia and the other republics.

The E.C. can boast a credible track record in responding to the quicksand collapse of European Communism. The former eastern Germany is now just another region in the Community like southern Italy or Northern Ireland. The E.C. recently signed trade agreements with Hungary, Poland and Czechoslovakia involving a 10-year transition to free trade. Now the Community is moving to establish a closer trading relationship with the less developed economies of Bulgaria and Romania as well as the three Baltic republics.

The E.C. has taken overall charge of the West's assistance to eastern and central Europe through its coordination of the so-called Group of 24.

The total commitments of the G-24 nations for aid and investment in Eastern Europe now totals some $45 billion, of which the E.C. accounts for the lion's share.

The Community also played a pioneering role in establishing the European Bank for Reconstruction and Development (EBRD) which opened its doors in London last April.

However, while the numbers look impressive they may only have a marginal impact on long-term prospects of the recipients. And the volume of the handouts, pledges, and commitments has already peaked. The day of massive transfers from West to East is over. Sir Leon Brittan, the E.C. Competition Commissioner, put it quite bluntly: "There is an erroneous belief in some quarters that when the going really gets tough, money will be miraculously forthcoming."

But east European leaders say they aren't looking for handouts but simply the chance to break into the huge E.C. market of 345 million consumers.

The "Europe Agreements" signed in Brussels last December have thrown a lifeline to Czechoslovakia, Hungary, and Poland as they struggle to break into the global trading system via the European Community. Just as important as the 10-year transition to free trade with the world's biggest single market was a reference to their eventual membership in the Community.

"The short-term benefit will be better access to E.C. markets, while the long-term benefits will include stable and predictable policy as we work to adapt our regulations to those of the E.C. over 10 years," said Jaroslav Mulewicz, Poland's chief trade negotiator.

The agreement will open up Hungary to foreign investment as well as trade, according to Endre Juhasa, director general of the Ministry of International Economic Relations. Czechoslovakia's Deputy Foreign Minister Zenon Pirek said the accord would help his country to rejoin Western democracy.

The agreements were forged after a year of tortuous negotiations that pitted the east European's desire for improved market access for their most competitive exports (steel, textiles, and farm produce) against several E.C. industries. Portugal tried to delay a decision on ending textile quotas until the GATT trade talks were concluded. Spain and Italy pushed for a safeguard clause to block steel shipments, and France rejected proposals for more market access for Polish beef.

These rows led to clashes within the E.C. and prompted a Polish threat to walk away from the talks. Negotiators were bogged down in the most unseemly haggling right up to the very last minute.

The agreements could yet renew tensions between E.C. and east European producers in sensitive sectors. Eurofer, the E.C. steel producers' organization, which lobbied against improved market access for East European imports, is poised to launch an anti-dumping complaint against Polish steel beams. It has also warned that east European producers may interpret the trade agreements as a carte blanche to flood the Community market with cheap steel.

The agreements will provide an export lifeline for the east European trio following the collapse of the Soviet Union, which had accounted for about half of their total trade. Their exporters are raring to go. The E.C.'s decision to abolish scores of quotas on manufactured goods in 1990 triggered a 40-50 percent leap in Hungarian and Polish exports to the Community last year.

E.C. leaders are sure to face a test of political courage later this year when protectionist lobbies demand curbs on competitively-priced east European imports. The less developed, southern E.C. states, like Spain and Portugal, fear that funds will be diverted to the eastern "outsiders" and that private investment also will be funneled eastward.

Yet apart from the sensitive sectors, east Europe represents a minor irritant to E.C. firms which face a massively greater threat from Asia. And apart from the auto industry and a few other isolated instances, inward investment in eastern Europe has been at very modest levels, though there are encouraging signs of an increase.

Eastern Europe is a minnow in world trade. Czechoslovakia, Hungary, and Poland had a combined share of world trade in 1988 that was below the 1970 levels of any of the Asian tigers, Hong Kong, South Korea, Singapore, and Taiwan.

Under Communism, east European exporters were sealed off from the giant market on their doorstep. In 1988, 74 percent of western Europe's manufactured imports came from other west European countries, while eastern Europe accounted for only 1.3 percent of their purchases.

Jacques Attali, president of the EBRD, says the Europe Agreements are "not enough and too slow" and should give way to an agreement incorporating the E.C., the seven-nation European Free Trade Association, eastern Europe, and the former Soviet republics. This would be complemented by a trade financing organization to help countries through hard currency shortages.

The EBRD intends to hold a conference in London in March to float its plans, though most observers say it is too far ahead of its time to succeed.

However events are proceeding at such a pace that nothing can be ruled out.

A year ago, President Mitterrand of France said it would take "tens and tens of years" before the east Europeans would be ready to join the Community. But by January, Douglas Hurd, the British Foreign Secretary, said he hoped Czechoslovakia, Hungary, and Poland would be E.C. members by the year 2000. "Enlargement of the European Community toward the East will be a priority of the British presidency of the E.C." in the second half of the year, Hurd said.

Meanwhile, west European companies are building up their investments in eastern Europe, though the pace of spending has been held back by political and legal uncertainties. Front-runners like the car manufacturers Volkswagen, Fiat, and Opel; Ikea, the furniture concern; Asea Brown Boveri, the Swiss-Swedish electrical engineering group, have captured the headlines. But a host of smaller deals are cut every day that never make the headlines. Austrian firms, for example, have pumped $300 million of direct investment into Hungary alone and the Vienna stock exchange trades in the shares of more than 20 Hungarian companies.

Dow Europe's recent announcement that it will invest around $150 million in a Czech chemical company to serve as its eastern European distribution and marketing unit underlines the growing attractiveness of the region.

The EBRD says it expects a rise in major equity investment in eastern Europe in the coming months. The bank has been involved in several key transactions, including Air France's purchase of a 40% stake in CSA, the Czech airline, and investment by BSN of France and Nestle in the Czech food industry.

The bank says it is reviewing 15 Czech investments in the petrochemicals, pulp, paper, and aerospace sectors and studying a further 150 projects elsewhere in eastern Europe.

Meanwhile the outlook for eastern Europe, though still menacing, seems to be getting brighter. The Organization for Economic Cooperation and Development reckons output will still fall this year but at a slower rate of 2.2 percent overall compared with nearly 10 percent in 1991.

Bruce Barnard is the Brussels correspondent for *The Journal of Commerce*.

Article 21

The Christian Science Monitor
Wednesday, January 22, 1992

Bulgaria Starts Down Hard Road of Reform

Election of dissident confirms demise of communist regime

By Klas Bergman

Special to The Christian Science Monitor

SOFIA, BULGARIA

BULGARIA is slowly but steadily sweeping away its communist past.

After Bulgaria's first two free elections since the communist takeover after World War II, the opposition Union of Democratic Forces (UDF) has formed the country's first noncommunist government. And the nation's former leading dissident during the communist era, philosophy professor Zhelyu Zhelev, has become Bulgaria's first democratically elected president in the runoff election on Jan. 19.

Professor Zhelev won 53.5 percent of the vote to 46.5 percent for challenger Velko Valkanov of the former Communist Party, renamed the Bulgarian Socialist Party (BSP). Although the victory was narrow, still showing wide support for the former communists, it ensures the continuation of reform efforts.

The old communist guard still tries to hang on. Recently, the orthodox wing of the BSP held a rally in downtown Sofia to protest

American University Brings Surprises for Students, Teachers

BLAGOEVGRAD, BULGARIA

THE American flag flies over a new, almost luxurious building in the town of Blagoevgrad, among the mountains of southern Bulgaria.

The building was meant to be the local Communist Party headquarters, but as the wave of democracy swept through Bulgaria in the winter of 1989-90, the Communists never moved into the building.

Instead, the flag marks the site of the American University in Bulgaria, the first American institution of higher learning in Eastern Europe.

After almost 50 years of total domination by Soviet culture and communist ideology, young Bulgarians can learn for the first time about democracy and capitalism in an atmosphere of freely flowing ideas.

"We think that the American University here is the best thing that has ever happened in Bulgaria," says Kossara Marchinkova, a member of the first freshman class.

"Before, you didn't have freedom," adds Deyan Vassilev, another freshman. "So you cried freedom. But now you have freedom here, and it turns out not to be so easy. It is the most difficult thing to have freedom."

The university was founded last September with the help of the United States and Bulgarian governments and the University of Maine. Half of those who applied were accepted – 225 students in all. University administrators were astounded by the high quality of the applicants, who scored on average 1,103 out of a possible 1,600 on the combined Scholastic Aptitude Tests. The average score among American high school students is 900.

The choice to attend the American University of Bulgaria was not accepted by all members of the students' families. Christo Grozev says that although his parents practically forced him to come here, his grandparents were hesitant.

"My grandparents are both communists," he says, "and for some time my grandfather was enthusiastic about the idea. Then he met with one of their party officials who said it was an ideological institution and it was going to indoctrinate us with American ideas. And he said, well, I shouldn't go there. So the older generation is still afraid and suspicious."

The students speak English remarkably well, and members of the American faculty say they underestimated their new students.

Robert Phillips is a young political science professor from Gaffnee, South Carolina. He says that his Bulgarian students are a lot like American freshman, but that some of them are more sophisticated in their analysis.

"They are able to challenge you because they have this educational background. They are able to challenge you in different ways which American students just are unable to do."

His colleague, economics professor Baldwin Ranson from Western State College in Colorado, is teaching the Bulgarians traditional economics and capitalism.

"We were afraid at first that we couldn't communicate easily, and secondly that they might not understand complex ideas. That's no problem at all," he says.

"We're finding in economics that we must speed up what we do to get to their level of understanding."

Says Mr. Vassilev: "What I see in this education for the first time is the diversity, the pluralism of ideas. I never studied a science before which would give me contradicting views of the matter which would make me think and doubt."

The students say they are no longer interested in ideologies and try to move away from them and set up their lives in the most broad-minded fashion possible.

"I'm firmly convinced there are many resources in Bulgaria, especially human," Professor Ranson says. "And if they can be put on the right path, I think they can make this country bloom."

– K. B.

proposed laws that would expropriate the party's property. Red flags filled the air and the crowd of about 8,000 mostly older people, led by party chairman Alexander Lilov, shouted "Solidarity, Solidarity" and "Fascists, Fascists" against the democratic opposition, UDF.

The BSP lost only narrowly in last October's elections. Capturing around one-third of the vote, it is still a major political force. And it still hopes to make a comeback, says George Pirinsky, a longtime party member. But he admits that its biggest problem is a serious credibility gap – many Bulgarians still doubt that the party has really changed.

Bulgaria's first noncommunist prime minister in 45 years, Filip Dimitrov, says the communists have not changed, and he refuses to call them "socialists." He sees his government as the political guarantor that things have really changed in Bulgaria.

"Of course," he tells the Monitor, "I know well that we cannot bring better standards in a couple of months. But at least the grounds for hope should be established."

The young, quiet, and unassuming lawyer who now leads Bulgaria clearly feels the responsibility for bringing that hope.

"We have to succeed but it's neither easy nor lacking risky elements," he says in clear English.

Though social upheaval is one primary risk, Mr. Pirinsky says: "In general, the population is ready to make the effort connected with the harshness of reform. People are willing to reorient their lives, to acquire new skills, to put in a more intensive working day."

Today, Sofia is a different place than in the somber days of communism. Everywhere, private commerce is taking place. And on Sundays, people fill the magnificent Nevski Cathedral behind the parliament to worship in the new spirit of religious tolerance after the overthrow of communism.

The architect of the Bulgarian communist state, Giorgy Dimitrov, is no longer buried in his Lenin-like mausoleum in the center of Sofia. He was quietly moved one night to a common cemetery on the outskirts of the city. The mausoleum now stands empty

GUY STUART – STAFF

and the colorful honor guard is gone.

The transition from communism to democracy took two years, but little has taken place in the way of economic reforms.

Bulgaria's economic problems are daunting. Inflation is more than 70 percent and unemployment now exceeds 10 percent. The vital Soviet market—which used to make up half of Bulgaria's exports—has collapsed, and new Western markets have not yet been developed.

The country's foreign debt is $12 billion. The Bulgarian leva is almost worthless on the international markets, and hard currency is seriously lacking. Small businessmen who have established joint ventures with Western firms and who have to pay their bills in dollars or deutsche marks are particularly hard-hit by the currency crisis. Because the national bank needs the hard currency to pay off foreign debt, it often will not sell it to businessmen.

"We believe that in two to three years we could increase the ability of the country to pay its foreign debts and start the new development of the country," says Emil Harsev, executive director of the Bulgarian National Bank. "But probably it will take about five to 10 years for the Bulgarian economy to recover from this collapse, which was actually the reason for the end of the old regime."

"We actually have taken the decisive step, which means that things cannot go back," says Prime Minister Dimitrov.

Still, he admits that turning this old communist state-run economy into a private enterprise system is not easy.

Despite encouraging signs of change, much remains the same, especially in the countryside. Life there is still harsh. The local market in Samokov, a little town outside Sofia, offers practically nothing for sale but a large pile of cabbage. Cars are still more scarce than horses and shepherds.

Article 22

U.S.NEWS & WORLD REPORT, OCTOBER 28, 1991

Fear of flying in Czechoslovakia

The velvet revolution is facing its toughest tests

In the current production of "The Odyssey" by Laterna Magika, Prague's famed theater of illusionary light and human movement, a ship carrying Ulysses and his crew floats across the stage against a backdrop of idyllic blue seas. Suddenly, the storms of reality and fate send it crashing to the boards.

Two years after playwright-President Vaclav Havel's "velvet revolution" freed Czechoslovakia from communism and sent its hopes soaring, Havel and his 15 million people are bickering about how to keep their ship from foundering. "We're caught in a neurotic, vicious cycle," says Miroslav Macek, the vice chairman of the new Civic Democratic Party, during a brief break in an angry debate in the Federal Assembly over everything from how to rid the nation of Communist bureaucrats to laws facilitating desperately needed foreign investment.

Economic worries have triggered old resentments that now threaten to unravel the fragile confederation of Czechs and Slovaks. The two were uneasily bound together in the wake of World War I, a move that caused British statesman David Lloyd George to say that "Czechoslovakia isn't a country; it's a sausage."

So far, neither the sausage nor the bubble of enthusiasm for change has burst. "Of course it's not easy," says Hana Reznickova, a 36-year-old mother of two. "Everything is more expensive,

more uncertain. But look around you—do you see anyone who isn't happy?"

In Prague, smiling people sport what Prague student Katerina Stejskalova calls "new, happy clothing." Private shops now sell everything from Japanese video cameras to German refrigerators. Although inflation has leveled off, the cost of living has risen nearly 160 percent in the last year, average wages remain just a little more than $100 a month and few Czechoslovaks can afford local consumer goods, let alone imported ones.

To the outrage of many, a new class of got-rich-quick Czechoslovaks—some former Communist apparatchiks, others fronting for foreign entrepreneurs and speculators—have been the first winners in federal auctions privatizing small businesses. Unhappy that many former Communists still wield power, as they do elsewhere in Eastern Europe, parliament wants to bar ex-Communists from state jobs for five years. But in response to this process of *lustrace* (purification), some old apparatchiks are converting their old political clout into economic power by starting private businesses.

Frustration and fear are worst in the country's grossly overindustrialized and oversubsidized rural areas. Farmers in Bohemia—still strapped by cumbersome Marxist marketing systems and angered that some imported produce is cheaper than the food they grow—have begun blocking highways with their aging trac-

tors. In the grim industrial towns, tens of thousands of factory workers look ahead to a winter of unemployment.

Collapsing. The Poldi steelworks at the bleak town of Kladno, once among the nation's most formidable industrial complexes, already is in dire straits. Orders from the Soviet Union and other East-bloc customers have shrunk by 75 percent and could vanish altogether. Four thousand of the plant's 18,000 workers have been laid off. But Poldi remains exorbitantly overstaffed, and potential French and American investors say they won't touch the company unless thousands more are fired. Recently, the Czechoslovak national gas company threatened to cut off the power unless Poldi paid its $5 million back bill. "Everything's collapsing," frets Lukas Jindrich, a 50-year-old Poldi engineer as he pulls his blue jacket tighter against the autumn winds.

"It's part of the unavoidable cost of converting to a free-market economy," says Miroslav Zamecnik, Havel's economic adviser, who says "we desperately need Western investment and technical assistance to learn to properly produce and market our products, develop new profitable ones and overcome the shocks of change." Havel will make the same pitch this week when he visits Washington.

The revolution has exacted social as well as economic costs. Tourists are

HUNGARY'S PRESIDENT SPEAKS

'The society is drifting apart'

Hungarian President Arpad Goncz spent five years in jail after his country's 1956 revolution was crushed by Soviet tanks and 30 years eking out a living translating such American authors as Hemingway, Doctorow and even George Bush. He discussed his country's passage from communism to democracy with Marianne Szegedy-Maszak.

Political changes. We thought it would be a very, very hard task to topple communism and that the transition period would be very easy and pleasant. But we were wrong. Communism toppled by itself and annihilated itself quite easily, and the transition period is terribly difficult. ... It is sometimes hard to distinguish between the communist and the post-communist periods. Sometimes the mentality of the communists surfaces in the anticommunists, too. [It is] authoritarian on one side and obedient on the other. After 40 years of being ordered around, it is inevitable that everyone has the tendency to give orders and to obey orders.

Building a market economy. We don't have any model for privatization, so the first step has been an absolutely spontaneous privatization. This basically changed only the superficial aspects of the enterprise.... We have no idea of what the real price or the real value of our factories and our companies is, so we have no way to determine the fair market price of anything.

... The problem is that social priorities and economic priorities are in conflict with each other. We have to somehow create a social network to defend the people, but if we want to be successful in giving complete priority to the economy then it is impossible to create such a network. We have no money for it. ... The political efforts are all focused on handling the economic questions, but the society is drifting, drifting, step by step, further and further apart.

The younger generation. Our young people are a time bomb that is ticking. Until recently, many of the young men went into the Army when they were 19. Today, the size of the Army has decreased by about 50 percent. There are no jobs. The housing problem they face is absolutely hopeless. Youngsters who thought that they could go into a factory after they acquired a skill at the age of 16 or 17 now discover that the workplace is closed to them. Many of the trade schools these youngsters attended depended on the factories that now are bankrupt. So today there is a large age group that has no hope and no vision of the future.

Outside assistance. We don't really have the right to complain. We are trying to stand on three legs: the European Community, the Pacific Rim and the U.S.... Politically we have received very much help from Germany. About 60 percent of all the private investment is coming from the United States, as well as lots of advice. We have received serious monetary help in the form of credits from Japan.

Agriculture. ... There is a very deep overproduction crisis because our most important market was the Soviet Union, and now it is closed to us because they can't pay. ... So we have to go back to the Stone Age and barter: I give you a jar and you give me three arrowheads.

---

flocking to Prague, but some of the city's historic corners have been trashed with fast-food shops and currency-exchange booths. Enterprising Czechs have filled their medieval town squares with stands selling everything from Bohemian crystal to American popcorn to Soviet Army garb left behind when Moscow withdrew its 73,500 troops in 1990.

The crime rate, though still lower than Germany's, has more than doubled in two years. Wenceslas Square, where Czechs shouted down their Communist bosses in November 1989, has become a nightly market for teenage prostitutes and a haven for nimble pickpockets. Czech TV, once a humdrum Communist propaganda mill, has become a lively forum of open debate and Western programming. One result: Attendance at Prague's theaters, once the guardians of free expression, has fallen off so dramatically that four have been forced to close.

Havel's vision of a nation renewed by democracy, tolerance and reform is facing its toughest test in Slovakia, the country's eastern republic. Dependent on subsidized agricultural cooperatives and unprofitable, polluting industries, Slovakia's 5.4 million people have been hardest hit by free-market reforms. The unemployment rate is 9.5 percent, compared with the Czechs' 6.2 percent.

Secession? Slovakia's nationalist fires are being stoked more by resentment of Czechs than by Slovak pride. "We see no reason why 5 million Slovaks cannot sit as a nation in international bodies and not be represented by Czechs," says Vladimir Meciar, the former Slovak premier. Meciar's chief rival, Jan Carnogursky, head of Slovakia's Christian Democratic Movement and current premier of the regional government, sees Slovakia becoming an "independent subject" in Europe with only loose ties to the Czechs.

But Slovakia's autonomists are short on concrete plans for how they'd manage on their own. Much of their vague sense of nationalism harks back to the World War II-era "independent" Slovakia — an ignoble Nazi puppet state that shipped tens of thousands of its Jewish citizens to German death camps.

Not all Slovaks have fallen for the neonationalist pitch. "We are about two generations less developed than the

DEMOCRACY IN BULGARIA

An uphill battle

In Bulgaria, elections this month ended 47 years of communist control, but the vote raised more questions than it answered.

The Union of Democratic Forces, an umbrella movement like Solidarity in Poland and Civic Forum in Czechoslovakia, won 34 percent of the vote and now controls nearly half the seats in parliament. But in order to govern, the UDF must hold its own 12 parties and four main factions together; compromise with a party representing Bulgaria's million-strong Turkish minority; outmaneuver a Socialist (formerly Communist) Party that won a third of the vote, and control the communist-dominated bureaucracy, Army and police force. At best it will have to water down its plans for sweeping reform. At worst it could split apart even before taking office.

Severe inflation, falling output, a $12 billion foreign debt and growing food and fuel shortages do not favor either stability or gradualism. Despite the elections, democracy is still fighting an uphill battle in Bulgaria.

Czechs," admits Jana Krejcikova, an English teacher in Bratislava. "But the solution is to work harder, not to slow down reform. We don't have time for all this nationalist nonsense!" Banking on what he believes is a silent majority in Slovakia, Havel—who believes more symbolic autonomy for the Slovaks will save the federation—now proposes a referendum on the republic's future.

Havel himself still forgoes the elegant presidential castle for his own simply fur-

nished apartment overlooking the Moldau. But the jeans and sweater he once wore when receiving state visitors have given way to tailored suits, and his Renault "limousine" has been replaced by a fleet of BMWs that ferry the president and his minions. Still, recent polls give him an 83 percent approval rating among Czechs and 58 percent in Slovakia.

But even Havel, who may be preparing to seek another presidential term in 1992, can run out of time. On a hill

overlooking Prague, in the same spot where a gargantuan statue of Joseph Stalin once stood, Czechoslovakia's new leaders have placed a whimsical kinetic sculpture—a giant, brightly painted metronome. Its beat is steady, but it may be a touch slow. ■

BY RICHARD Z. CHESNOFF IN PRAGUE
AND PETER S. GREEN IN BRATISLAVA

Article 23

The **UNESCO COURIER**
NOVEMBER 1991

Hungary: the pitfalls of growth

Since 1990 Hungary has been trying to redress an economy long tilted in favour of pollution-prone heavy industry

by István Láng

AT the end of World War II, Hungary found itself politically and economically attached to the Communist bloc. From the beginning of the 1950s, a system of central planning and management was gradually developed. Companies came into State ownership, co-operative farms were formed and most of the service sector was brought under the control of the State or of co-operatives.

Quantitative growth at all costs became the watchword of industrial production. The development of heavy industry was given priority, energy-intensive technologies spread and raw materials were used with scant regard for economy. Nevertheless, the quantitative growth that occurred between 1950 and 1975 made it possible to raise the standard of living and well-being of the population as compared to the levels of the pre-war period.

After the first oil crisis, however, the limitations of the centrally planned system, its inability to adapt and its lack of competitiveness, soon became apparent. Failure to modernize the infras-

ISTVÁN LÁNG
is Secretary-General of the Hungarian Academy of Sciences in Budapest and a member of the Executive Board of the International Council of Scientific Unions (ICSU). He is also a member of the editorial advisory board of the World Resources Institute in Washington D.C. From 1984 to 1987 he was a member of the United Nations World Commission on Environment and Development (the Brundtland Commission).

tructure and to introduce computer technology meant that Hungary, like the other countries of Eastern Europe, began increasingly to lag behind Western Europe. The position was made even worse by increasing external debts and the slowing down of economic development.

This falling behind in the economic field was matched by a delay on the part of political leaders in East European countries, including Hungary, in recognizing the importance of environmental protection. Although Hungarian scientists participated in UNESCO's Man and the Biosphere programme from its inception, government agencies took six to seven years to react to the environmental challenges raised.

During the 1980s, Hungary faced growing economic difficulties. During the decade 1977 to 1987 the country's external debt grew from $43 million to $18,957 million. Various economic reforms were carried out and central control of planning and management was gradually reduced, but this was not sufficient to lead to a smoothly functioning, market-oriented economy. So when the importance of environmental protection was finally recognized, Hungary was already in a period of economic decline and it was not possible to make the big investment needed to replace polluting technologies or the energy-intensive and raw-material-intensive structure of industry.

The period 1989-1990 saw the beginning of radical, but peaceful, political change. In spring 1990, free elections were held and with a new Parliament and a new government Hungary has set out on the road to parliamentary democracy, with a multi-party system, a market-oriented economy and independence from military blocs.

However, the new government inherited the old environmental problems and it takes a long time to change old production structures. Nevertheless, data on the state of the environment have been made public and municipalities and voluntary environmental groups are being encouraged to play a larger part in pollution control by means of public debates and hearings.

Preparations for the 1992 United Nations Conference on Environment and Development have begun. A National Commission has been set up, and an action programme for the solution of local and national environmental problems has been drawn up with the aim of arousing public awareness. A panel of high-ranking experts has been formed with the task of working out, on the basis of the recommendations of the Rio Conference, a Hungarian strategy for the attainment of sustainable development.

What, then, is the present position in key policy sectors and what changes can be expected?

ENERGY POLICY

Energy policy is a key issue in the Hungarian debate on environmental protection. For decades, energy has been wasted on a vast scale in Eastern Europe, including Hungary. Owing to the use of out-of-date technologies, energy consumption per unit of product (e.g. per ton of steel or per ton of wheat) is on average 40 to 50 per cent higher than in the Western European countries and the proportion of energy-intensive sectors within industry is high. Energy consumption per capita, for example, in Austria and Hungary is practically the same, but, in relation to Gross National Product, Hungary consumes five times as much energy as Austria.

Energy policy for the future has two main objectives: to increase the efficient use of energy and to reduce dependence on external sources of energy. At present there is intense public debate as to whether or not a second nuclear power plant

should be built, and if not, on what primary fuel additional electrical energy will be based. This is a matter of great public concern because, although technological reconstruction of some existing power plants has led to some improvement with regard to the emission of pollutants, 44 per cent of the population live in areas where, at certain times of the year, the quality of the air does not meet minimum health standards.

INDUSTRY

Transition to sustainable industrial development and to market mechanisms entails considerable economic and social change. One example of this is that the previously established principle that "the polluter pays" seems to be being replaced by the new principle that "the polluter pays and the consumer pays". Another is that because of rising prices of raw materials and energy, coupled with decreasing government support, heavy industry is in crisis, with the unfortunate social consequence that unemployment has increased to an unprecedented degree. Paradoxically this is also an environmentally favourable phenomenon, since it means a decline in a sector of industrial activity which pollutes the environment the most.

Privatization of Hungarian companies has begun, mainly with the help of foreign capital. This will have a positive effect on the modernization of technological processes and thus will benefit the environment. Some environmentalists, however, are worried about this, since they fear that polluting processes that are no longer permitted in the European Community countries will be transferred to Hungary. It is the generally accepted opinion in Hungary that industrial development must be judged on the basis of European norms.

AGRICULTURE

Hungary's climate and soil are suitable for intensive agricultural production. In the 1980s, two-thirds of the country's agricultural produce was sold on the internal market, ensuring an ample food supply (exceptional in Eastern Europe), while one third was exported. However, intensive soil cultivation and the use of large amounts of artificial fertilizers and pesticides, as well as concentrated animal husbandry, have led to some degradation of the environment. Damage caused by wind and water erosion affects some 40 per cent of the land, a significant part of the groundwater contains an excess of nitrates, acidification of the soil can be observed on one third of the arable land and, as a result of irrigation, salinization has developed in many areas.

Privatization of the land has begun and there will be considerable decentralization in both land use and animal husbandry in the coming years. On the whole this is expected to have favourable environmental effects, but problems may arise in ensuring the proper use of agro-chemicals.

When Hungary joins the European Community (this is thought likely to occur in the second half of the 1990s), Hungarian agricultural exports will probably decrease. This will make it possible to shape the model of a low-energy-input agriculture.

TRANSPORT

Transport is one of the biggest sources of pollution in Hungary. Some 45 to 50 per cent of the carbon monoxide, 40 to 45 per cent of the nitrogen oxides and 90 per cent of the lead emitted into the air come from transport. Road transport has the greatest share in this emission with more than 85 per cent, the railways being responsible for 12 to 13 per cent and air transport for one to two per cent. The development of the means of mass transport is being given priority in the plans of both national and municipal authorities.

NATURE CONSERVATION

Some 626 hectares of Hungary's total territory of 93,000 square kilometres are protected. Altogether there are four national parks, 44 protected regions and 137 nature conservation areas. All the 2,500 caves, 415 plant species and 619 animal species are protected. In addition there are 877 locally protected areas.

The national parks have been established partly in forest areas and partly in lands which are very valuable for nature conservation but not easily usable for agriculture. Some problems have arisen because the national parks are not all fully owned by the State authorities responsible for conservation. With the privatization of land, this problem is growing more acute. The general trend, however, is for protected nature conservation areas to remain under State ownership and for their exploitation (for logging, grazing, fishing, etc.) to be fully controlled by the nature conservation service.

As can be seen from this short review, Hungary has inherited an onerous legacy from earlier regimes. Under new circumstances the intention is to adopt new methods to achieve sustainable development. Environment and development will figure jointly in the government's programme and an environmentally aware public will be there to encourage action and to ensure that the proper decisions are made. ∎

Article 24　　　　　*A N A L Y S I S*　　　　THE WORLD & I
JANUARY 1992

Poland's Leap to Democracy

by Brian A. Brown

"The government is incompetent," the taxi driver gripes, between puffs on his Marlboro cigarette, as he roughly drives me away from the Okecie Airport in Warsaw.

"The factories are closing," he complains, apparently unappreciative of his recently acquired right of free speech. Like most Poles, he is concerned more with the economic benefits of democracy than the political rights it bestows.

The taximeter—not calibrated to reflect the recent inflation—clicks on. I had heard of the "taxi mafia," which charges as much as $50–100 for a ride from the airport to downtown Warsaw. Those insisting on paying the usual $6 are physically threatened or worse. My driver, like most, is honest.

THE SHOPS ARE FULL

The changes, since my last visit in the summer of 1988, are

immediately apparent even from the backseat of the exhaust-spewing Polski Fiat. The Poles opened their borders and got at least a piece of what they always wanted: America.

Rumbling and rocking down the tracks alongside the taxi was a beat-up, state-run trolley car covered with a massive painting of the

are good, but I can't afford anything" is the most common refrain heard in Poland.

The economy is weighed down by 40 percent annual inflation, increasing unemployment (already at 10 percent), unsalvageable state factories, debts to the West, a substantial reduction in Soviet trade, Western trade barri-

dle ground by restructuring state industries is an unlikely prospect. Most of the enterprises are unsalvageable and only a few have attracted outside investors.

The economic quandary has led to political indecision. A recent cartoon captures the mood. Two relatively well-dressed Poles are being followed down the street by a vagrant. One of them nervously looks back and exclaims, "The idea of social equality keeps following me."

Politicians are wincing at the idea of continuing with the same intensity of reforms.

American flag advertising tours to the center of capitalist decadence.

The cowboys have arrived, too, and they're larger than life. A billboard of a walrus-mustached cowboy squatting in his Lee jeans stares down at the chaos left by the communists. Another fingers his Marlboro cigarette as he looks past an expansive Western landscape onto smoggy Warsaw—two unconquered frontiers merge.

Western businessmen, the modern-day pioneers, scurry about in a frantic attempt to capture consumer loyalty. Their first concern is to lock up the market, their second worry is whether anyone can afford their products. The faded red signs touting the glories of communism are obscured by neon lit shop signs proclaiming the grandeur of ownership.

In the shops, the gray shelves that until recently offered only a few dingy items are now full of colorful new products. From cars to condoms, Western and Japanese goods have flooded the market. But the average monthly salary of $163 is so low that few Poles can afford the comforts of capitalism. "The political changes

ers, and an immense, stifling bureaucracy. These problems caused President Lech Walesa, one of the driving forces behind the reforms, to complain that "we listened to the West, and we made too big a leap." Whether this was a genuine admission or an attempt to garner votes from a reform-weary populace before the recent parliamentary elections is not clear. What is clear, however, is that the Poles, once the most forceful proponents of radical market reforms in Eastern Europe, are today not sure where to go.

AN ECONOMIC QUANDARY

The reform movement that was moving full speed ahead through the uncharted waters between communism and capitalism has begun to drift in the face of inconclusive debates about monetary policy and unproductive state industries. The Poles are confounded by the catch-22 that state enterprises present: The state cannot forever subsidize uncompetitive businesses, but it is apparently unwilling to accept the massive unemployment their failure would cause. Attaining the mid-

Even if the Poles do eventually decide that they want some form of social democracy, with unemployment benefits and other state services, they will have to be able to pay for it. Most of the state services face severe shortages. The state hospitals, for instance, are deficient in the most basic necessities, including disposable syringes, analgesics, surgical tools, disposable gloves, and many other items and machinery. The shortages have forced doctors to wash surgical gloves and salvage pacemakers from cadavers for reuse. Revenues must be generated to support even the most basic state services. These revenues will not be produced by failing state enterprises.

Confronting these realities, Leszek Balcerowicz, Poland's finance minister and reform architect, has been attempting to spur the economy. Balcerowicz, among other things, has been knocking at Europe's back door. The European Community (EC), fearful of cheap Polish products, is in no rush to let its neighbor in. The EC insisted that Poland open its market but then did not reciprocate—it has erected barriers in the very industries in which Poland can most effectively compete: food, textiles, and steel. The Poles, in turn, implemented their own restrictions.

In Warsaw, it is possible to find Dutch hams selling at half the price of Polish hams. A number of EC members have already called for loosening restrictions on Polish meats. There has been significant progress in the talks and a trade accord with the EC may soon be reached.

Despite difficulties, the reforms have brought a flurry of entrepreneurial activity, made the out of control inflation manageable, brought the prices roughly in line with the market, and compelled the West to forgive a large portion of the national debt. More than 500,000 new businesses, accounting for 20–35 percent of the gross national product, were started last year. In addition, Polish exports to the West increased dramatically last year despite trade barriers.

The real question concerning the reforms and their success is

slowed as the communist dominated parliament debated what was to be done.

Parliamentary elections on October 27 finally gave Poles their first opportunity to elect a government that does not have seats set aside for those in the previous communist government. But in recognition of their plight, the Poles have turned somewhat apathetic. Despite the newness of their democracy, the election brought out only 40 percent of the voters. This meager turnout was, in fact, a referendum on the Polish reforms.

The few who did vote elected a fragmented Parliament. With more than 80 parties, including the Polish Friends of Beer Party, it was predictable that no clear majority would surface. Nonetheless, the outcome surprised most. Finishing first, with a paltry 12.8 percent of the vote, was former

same number of seats in the Sejm, or lower house, as the Democratic Union. The Peasant Party, which was once allied with the communists, got about 10 percent; the antiabortion Catholic Electoral Committee, the rightist Center Alliance and the nationalist Confederation for an Independent Poland both received approximately 8 percent of the votes. Even the Polish Friends of Beer Party, headed by a nationally known comedian, managed a respectable 12 seats, or 3 percent, in the 460 seat Sejm.

The Polish constitution allows President Walesa to dissolve the parliament in three months if it is unable to form a government. If so, new elections would be held.

While the splintered vote made it clear that there was no mandate for the current reforms, there did not appear to be a mandate for anything. The voters did not know which way to turn. With the stalling reforms, perpetually low salaries, and growing unemployment, the Poles were not sure which party or policy could save them. The parties themselves, and their respective advisers, hold specific beliefs concerning which course to chart, but the bottom line is that no one is sure as to where exactly a given policy will lead as Poland treads the virgin ground between communism and capitalism.

The debate will probably focus on whether a tight, anti-inflationary, monetary policy should be favored over antirecessionary plans, which may cause renewed inflation. However, either course is likely to bring hardship and further test the country's patience. The danger is that due to political bickering or voter impatience, no unified coalition may last long enough for its economic policies to take effect.

■

The economy is weighed down by increasing unemployment, unsalvageable state factories, debts to the West, and a substantial reduction in Soviet trade.

■

whether Poland will be able to regain its initial direction and end the drifting. This is largely a political question.

POLITICAL APATHY

The initial economic successes are largely due to Poland's quick and much ballyhooed economic reforms. But the changes

Prime Minister Tadeusz Mazowiecki's party, Democratic Union. The shocker was that the left of center Solidarity-connected Democratic Union finished almost even with the Democratic Left Alliance—the party established by the former communists.

The rest of the parties split the vote, which allowed the former communists to attain the

The Poles are hoping for a savior to transform the country—this is why Stanislaw Tyminski, the mysterious millionaire, Polish-Canadian businessman with an air of economic wizardry, was able to appear out of thin air and threaten Lech Walesa in the 1990 presidential elections.

President Walesa has been struggling to pull Poland up by the boot straps. Even though his hero status remains greatly untarnished around the world, most Poles have tired of him.

"He can't even speak proper Polish," is often the first complaint voiced against him. A popular joke quotes Walesa declaring, in phonetically flawed Polish, "I will be president, then I will be king."

More substantive criticisms usually go to his inability to pull Poland from the quagmire, his "arrogance," his "Machiavellian politics," or the "disloyalty" he displayed toward those in Solidarity as he climbed the presidential podium. A recent BBC documentary, admittedly anti-Walesa, showed an unrepentant Walesa wresting power from a number of powerful Solidarity intellectuals, many who, like him, were imprisoned under communism.

Part of the problem may be his isolation and handling by the famous Kaczynski brothers, who recently resigned. His two round-faced advisers, some say schemers, were constantly at Walesa's side. They had no compunction about appearing as manipulators, angling to get on camera or whispering in Walesa's ear on national television as he talked with Boris Yeltsin during the recent putsch.

The few defending Walesa insist he is a decision maker, while the intellectuals of Solidarity's Democratic Union, and others, are indecisive theorists interested in establishing a social democracy.

Either way, those in Democratic Union and Walesa bitterly dislike each other and the conflict could be the proverbial wrench in the already sputtering engine. Whether battles develop between Walesa and his old friends in Solidarity, or between any others in the coalition government, the ingredients exist for Poland to revisit its pre-World War II history when a splintered parliament brought the country to a standstill and a charismatic, authoritarian leader, Commander Pilsudski, took control.

Today, the danger is that divisive political minutiae will distract the politicians from the task at hand—continued economic reforms, and most importantly, increased privatization. In the face of collapsing state enterprise and heretofore unknown levels of unemployment, the politicians are wincing at the idea of continuing with the same intensity of reforms. But the *Economist* warns that "the growing acceptance of such gradualism is the greatest peril now facing the countries of Eastern Europe."

The Poles need to rise to the occasion. The politicians need to remain focused on a single package of dynamic market reforms, learn to compromise and put aside differences. And the people must recognize that impatience may impede their own progress.

THE UNCHANGED COUNTRYSIDE

The initial political and economic successes fueled the cities' sprint to catch the West, but the countryside remains, for the most part, stuck in a time warp.

On the road to Katowice, a major southern city, one can still see horses pulling wooden carts filled with coal or produce and peasants methodically swinging scythes back and forth. Rarely might you see a huge, bright orange harvester rumbling across a field.

Along the way I had an experience that exemplifies that Poland has a long road to travel. My host and I had passed three broken-down cars and when we stopped, to buy what turned out to be small, deformed sour apples, our Soviet car, a Samurai Lada, wouldn't start.

Two hours of fiddling and bug bites resulted in a diagnosis: The distributor cap was broken. In the last four decades every Pole had learned to be a mechanic, a plumber, an electrician, or a carpenter. But without spare parts, you are stranded—there are no phones, no tow trucks, and no AAA. My host driver carried a duplicate of just about every engine part, but not the one we needed.

> ## The EC insisted that Poland open its market but then did not reciprocate.

Many an uninterested Pole whizzed by us, but we ourselves had done the whizzing a few moments earlier. Suddenly another Lada screeched to a halt in front of us and out jumped a large, smiling Russian. He, like many others, was fleeing what was left of the Soviet Union in search of higher pay.

He towed us to a hotel. My host entered the smelly structure to discover that there was no phone. Sitting in the car to ensure no vital parts were stolen, I saw some capitalism sprouting—boys, as they do in London and Manhattan, were washing windshields for a few thousand zlotys (a few cents).

But a vestige of communism stared out at me. A large Ursus tractor, sitting on wood blocks, looked at me and the hustling boys with its broken headlights. This mechanical carcass came from what was the 13th largest company in Poland. Cannibalized for spare parts, it was destined to remain motionless, a monument to communist inefficiency.

The Ursus factory, once the great hope of the reformers, had just been shut down indefinitely—twelve thousand workers were laid off—another blow to an industrial output that dropped by a third last year.

After an exorbitant $30-a-night stay in a sub-standard Motel 6, my host, knowing there were no auto-parts stores around, found a used distributor cap in a local flea market. In the country, supply certainly has not yet caught up with demand.

After nearly 50 years of bare shelves, many Poles have become habitual complainers, but the question of economic prosperity is when, not if. So far, they have experienced fantastic economic changes, but at the same time the Poles face immense economic obstacles.

"All we do is import. We don't produce anymore; the government is not responding," complained a 50 year old who has known nothing but communism and is now making a healthy profit from her newly acquired pharmacy. When will she be happy? "When everything is private!"

The pace of privatization has already slowed. There is a good possibility that the newly formed government will continue to slide into the quagmire of economic indecisiveness and be unable to extricate itself. This means, among other things, that the dismantling of the stifling bureaucracy will slow, the foreign banks and investors will become more wary, and the state-owned industries will continue sucking out precious capital.

But below this gloomy macropicture is a small, though developing force of the new entrepreneurs, battling taxes and bureaucracies to create new enterprises and build a middle class. This activity will feed on itself and provide the growth, albeit slow, that Poland requires to move toward a market economy. Poles will prevail more because capitalism is in their blood and less because of grand, panacean, macroeconomic theories.■

Brian A. Brown, recently returned from Poland, is special adviser to the executive director of Freedom House, the New York-based human rights organization.

Article 25

THE WORLD & I
FEBRUARY 1992

Post-Communist Nationalism: The Case of Romania

by Juliana Geran Pilon

The collapse of the Soviet empire, exhilarating as it may be for the people who may now realistically hope for a freer life, brings with it serious aftershocks. The legacy of nearly five decades of communist rule is no small problem: A populace economically impoverished, subjected to lies and complete political control, has emerged traumatized and tired.

Perhaps the most urgent need before the people who have recently undergone a change of regime, no matter how incomplete (as in Romania), is to carve out an identity; hence post-communist nationalism. The attainment of self-definition may provide a healthy sense of self-worth and renewed confidence. Through continuity to their past and their rich—if sometimes checkered—traditions, the nations of East-Central Europe may yet be able to breathe, create, and survive once more.

The danger, however, is that instead of a healthy reappraisal of those traditions, there will be cheap jingoism and an inability to either forgive or move on to another historical level. Specifically, there is a chance that the pathology of the past half-century will be deliberately exploited by the defeated elite—the *nomenklatura*—in cooperation with delinquent, chauvinistic fringe elements, to create a lethal implosion. Hate-filled, racist, and xenophobic nationalism destroys any hope for democracy.

Yet it is possible for a nation to be both liberal—in the classical sense, respecting the individual and his voluntary associations—and national, or even multinational. The case of the United States stands as a promising example that such an ideal is not unrealistic.

It would be easy to dismiss nationalism as nineteenth-century romanticism, or as chauvinism with a thin veneer of ideological respectability. There are even those who deplore the demise of communism, which they argue "kept the lid on" nationalist feelings. While there is certainly some truth to this—communism kept the lid on most of the captive people's feelings—there is no point in denying the real issues, which involve man's place in history and society.

I do not consider "nationalism" to be just a vague mixture of ethnicity, self-interest, and xenophobia. The concept deserves closer analysis—particularly in the context of the traumatized East-Central European nations. While a detailed philosophical inquiry must be left for another time, a case study will help illustrate some of the components of the concept in a current setting: the case of Romania.

ROMANIA: A BRIEF CASE STUDY

Romania's democratic heritage was fragile at best at the time of Soviet takeover in August 1944. But then came the deluge: Romania was subjected first to a ruthless and then to a demonic form of communism, under Gheorghe Gheorghiu-Dej and Nicolae Ceauşescu respectively. The revolution of 1989, moreover, did not put an end to the communist regime, the revolt having coincided with a "palace coup" that quickly proceeded to "hijack" the revolution and put an end to its high hopes for systemic overhaul.

Thus, while currently undergoing privatization—or at least some version of it—the country continues to be ruled by members of the old regime whose commitment to democracy is questionable at best. Meanwhile the dissident opposition—surprisingly well organized in light of its recent birth—is still embryonic.

The country's ethnic minorities make up at least 12 percent of Romania's population. They are Hungarians (the largest group, over 2 million people), Germans, Serbs, Ukrainians, Gypsies, and others. The large Hungarian contingent is also relatively mature politically and is determined to preserve its cultural identity. The Jewish population dwindled to about 18,000 from over 800,000 as a result of World War II deportations and murders (accounting for some 400,000 deaths) and massive postwar emigration. Numbers aside, their cultural presence has outlived them, and the East-Central European phenomenon of "anti-Semitism without Jews" is alive and well.

The curse of anti-Semitism is, in fact, a microcosm of the problem at hand. Writes Henry Kamm in the *New York Times* of June 17, 1991:

Jews and other Romanians, as well as foreign diplomats, venture various guesses at the motivation of the growing anti-Semitism. Most cite the general rise of nationalism, of which slander against Jews is a classical component. ... Others note that Jews, as well as ethnic Hungarians, were prominent among the early communists, whom Moscow installed in power in 1944.

Hence a mixture of ethnic, ideological, and geopolitical considerations all play a part.

A legacy of communist anti-intellectualism is partly responsible for the deliberately populist theme embraced by the amorphous National Salvation Front (NSF)—the current political group in power—in the May 1990 elections, which gave it an overwhelming victory. Those elections, if not "free" in any reasonable Western sense of the word, certainly were not rigged, and they are widely accepted as having reflected popular sentiment at the time.

Without question, the most alarming and aggressive anti-intellectual outburst in East-Central Europe was the miners' brutal suppression of students and intellectuals in Bucharest in mid-June 1990, which had all the marks of a pogrom. An astonishing 67 percent of those polled by the Romanian Institute for Public Opinion Research supported the appeal to the miners, and 55 percent approved of their arrival. Classical scholar Andrei Cornea, writing in the *Journal of the Group for Social Dialogue*, finds that the image of the Jew as the rootless cosmopolitan individualist, supported by and supporting foreign capital, has been "supplanted" (one might add, supplemented) by that of the intellectual.

It was not surprising, therefore, that the NSF would make common cause with the extreme nationalist, anti-Hungarian organization Vatra Romaneasca (Romanian Hearth), which was established in January 1990 to oppose Hungarian demands for equal rights and ethnic recognition. Several prominent sympathizers of Vatra Romaneasca were co-opted by the NSF and elected on its lists in May 1990. The first issue of the NSF daily *Azi* (Today) included an article by a member of the Vatra Romaneasca—playwright Ion Coja—whose references to Hungarians were plainly racist. With time, the publication only worsened. *Azi* attacks not only Hungarians (and, of course, Jews); it has recently started a venomous campaign against Romania's Uniate (Eastern Catholic) community as well.

In addition, another neo-fascist weekly journal *Romania Mare* (Great Romania) is edited by Corneliu Vadim Tudor and Eugen Barbu, both former Ceauşescu sycophants with notorious ties to the Securitate (the secret police, which has since been renamed but not eliminated). This journal is suspected of receiving funds from Iosif Constantin Dragan, an émigré who amassed a fortune in Italy and is alleged to

be a former member of the Iron Guard.

The fact that former Ceauşescu sympathizers are involved in what is clearly an antidemocratic, hate-mongering group should come as no surprise. What cannot be underestimated is their extraordinary skill in manipulating Romanian sentiments.

Thus the rampant anti-Semitism that spread like an epidemic throughout the country in the summer of 1991 led Rabbi Moses Rosen to urge the emigration of all Jews left in the country. And who can blame him? The minister of the interior, for example, as recently as June 14, 1991, awarded a prize to *Great Romania* for "high-level professionalism" and "patriotism."

Petre Mihai Bacanu, the editor in chief of *Romania Libera*, the nation's main newspaper, told the Human Rights Caucus on August 8 that the journal *Romania Mare* and the Vatra Romaneasca enjoy the support of former Securitate members. And indeed, Vatra Romaneasca's statement of principles contains the strongest endorsement of the Securitate. Ceauşescu himself is lauded by *Romania Mare* as a Romanian patriot.

What, then, are the minorities or Romania to do? They must live with the fact that an organization such as Vatra Romaneasca states in its "Secret Program Statement" of February 20, 1990, the following strategy:

The popularity of Vatra Romaneasca will be secured throughout the world by way of propaganda activities, appealing to the anti-Hungarian, anti-Gypsy, and anti-German sentiments which have deep roots in the souls of Romanians.

From the very outset, we want every Romanian to be clear about our final goal: a Greater Romania in which alien elements have no place and will not be tolerated.

This attitude leaves little room for subtlety.

Hungarians continue to hope that Hungarian-language TV broadcasts will be reestablished, that Hungarian students will be allowed to study in their native language, the four-centuries-old Hungarian Bolyai University in Cluj (Kolozsvar) will be reopened, and proper legal measures will be taken against those responsible for the anti-Hungarian massacres in Targu-Mures (Maros-Vásárhely) in March 1990. In ideological terms, as the Hungarian Human Rights Foundation put it in a memo to the CSCE in June 1990, this means "the restoration of cultural, linguistic, and educational rights within Romania. These are rights that Romania has already guaranteed, on paper, to its national minorities as signatory to the UN human rights covenants and the Helsinki Final Act." However flawed these documents are, especially the decidedly socialist International Covenant on Economic, Social, and Cultural Rights, they offer a useful device to press for the rights of minorities.

The dilemma facing minorities in Romania was succinctly and cogently summarized by sociologist Nicolae Gheorghe, a distinguished leader of the Romani (Gypsy) community, on June 13, 1991, at a conference on the nationality question sponsored by the Washington-based Institute of Peace: "The problem is that the Romanian government opposes the idea of 'collective rights.' While I and others realize that our ideal is the promotion of individual rights, respect for each individual equally before the law and a democratic system, we have questions about how to pursue this goal strategically."

Since authoritarianism (in fact, neo-communism) is still entrenched in Romania, with privatization having just barely started and civil society still merely embryonic, the Hungarian community has understandably opted for embracing the concept of "collective rights." For the moment at least, the state must provide the money for education and control the media. Inevitably, therefore, the ethnic conflicts will have to play themselves out in the public arena. But there is little doubt that the sooner the public arena shrinks and the private sector develops, the better for minorities—as for majorities as well.

In fact, the newly formed Civic Alliance, created on November 7, 1990, and branched into a party in mid-July 1991, is dedicated to equal rights and a Western-style democratic system, which necessarily implies respect for all individuals and minorities in particular, for it is clear that without such respect there will not be a future for Romania.

The Civic Alliance follows in the spirit of Timisoara, the cradle of the December revolution, a multiethnic town where the spirit of pluralist cooperation is alive and well. According to George Serban, the president of the Timisoara Society and an author of the Timisoara Proclamation:

What the people of Timisoara have in common is one week of fighting during which we were all together: workers, intellectu-

als, men, women, Romanians, Hungarians, Germans. We all saw the tanks, the bullets, the dead and mutilated bodies. It was the only place psychologically ready for a revolution. Because here we all had a sense of history. We always knew we belonged to Europe—that we were once at its center—and we resented being cut off from it.

So there is clearly some hope. Unless the forces of hatred win out and cut off Romania once more from civilization, there is a good chance that this nation will once more return to Europe, perhaps even to its center. But whether the newly created Alliance will be able to achieve this is still very much an open question. It will not be easy.

For the moment, the Romanian situation is volatile, and critical: Without a system of individual freedom, Romania will never achieve prosperity or political respectability, and its citizens will continue to emigrate in droves.

But is individual freedom possible in a setting steeped in nationalist sentiments? Isn't individualism necessarily cosmopolitan and antinationalist? Not necessarily. The fact that individual freedom is reconcilable with nationalism—although not virulent chauvinism—was eloquently explained by Austrian philosopher Ludwig von Mises in his 1919 essay "Nation, State and Utopia."

THE CLASSICAL LIBERAL MODEL

The experience of the United States cannot but encourage the people of East-Central Europe with a promise of pluralism and democracy. Throughout U.S. history, orators have emerged to

articulate *the principle of tolerance* that is responsible for the success of the American experiment.

Take one example from the last century regarding discrimination on the basis of religion. In 1819, Judge Henry M. Brackenridge delivered a moving speech supporting repeal of an old law that forbade Jews to practice law or hold elective office: "Our political compacts are not entered into as brethren of the Christian faith," said Brackenridge, "but as men, as members of a civilized society. In looking back to our struggle for independence, I find that we engaged in that bloody conflict for the rights of man, and not for the purpose of enforcing or defending any particular religious creed." This did not seem obvious to everyone; efforts to repeal that law failed until 1825, when the arguments of reason and Constitution prevailed.

But what about the reality of political setting? Applying such principles will require forgetting past wrongs and tolerating differences. Perhaps it is emotionally too much to ask, after all the pain suffered in the recent past. The alternative, however, is to perpetuate hatred and continue sitting in a political minefield. No one really benefits from that in the long run, and usually not in the short run either.

The concept that associations ought to be voluntary, whether they be religious, economic, or political, is essential to a free society. And only a free society can be prosperous. All other roads, whatever their apparent value, lead to serfdom and penury. This idea was lucidly explained by Friedrich Hayek in *The Road to Serfdom*, first published in 1944, disseminated underground throughout East-Central Europe, and now being printed and published officially even in Romania. The Humanitas Press in Bucharest is preparing an edition complete with commentaries explaining the main ideas.

Hayek defended freedom primarily from the point of view of economic efficiency. He distrusted all forms of collectivism that were necessarily exclusionary, violating the rights of minorities. He writes: "It may, indeed, be questioned whether anyone can realistically conceive of a collectivist program other than in the service of a limited group, whether collectivism can exist in any form other than that of some kind of particularism, be it nationalism, racialism, or classism." To distrust particularism as a political form, however, is not to oppose voluntary associations—on the contrary. It is in the interest of freedom that he attacks state-sanctioned intolerance and oppression no matter what its rationale—be it religious, ethnic, or otherwise.

A century earlier John Stuart Mill also captured, in elegant language, the desirability of cultural, aesthetic, and other organic human groupings, directly contradicting the Marxist anti-utopia of forcefully fabricated "socialist man." "It is not by wearing down into uniformity all that is individual in themselves," writes Mill in the essay "On Liberty,"

> but by cultivating it and calling it forth, within the limits imposed by the rights and interests of others, that human beings become a noble and beautiful object of contemplation, [for] by the same process human life also becomes rich, diversified, and animating.

Pluralism adds nobility and diversity to the tapestry of human endeavor. Far from wishing to suppress such diversity, classical liberalism only wishes to limit its expression within the confines of civil society.

CONCLUSION

From a practical point of view, it is impossible to expect the nations of East-Central Europe to immediately forget ethnicity and embrace classical liberal toleration of individuality and universal rights. It will not do simply to say, for example, that Romania ought to allow Hungarians to run their own schools: Where will the money come from, when all education has been state run for nearly five decades, and people have no personal property to speak of? At the outset, therefore, the problems of allocation of public funds to different national groups will be insuperable. Minorities throughout East-Central Europe will be in need of special assistance and special considerations.

These problems of transition will require great sensitivity on the part of legislators and special understanding on the part of majorities. It is important to remember, however, where this should all lead, and that ultimately, the problems will be solved only when government gets out of the way, when individuals are allowed to pursue their own goals with their own resources, unhindered by bureaucrats.

If this is utopia, so be it. It takes men as they are, individual people with national and ethnic attachments. It is not unattainable. Given a modicum of reason, it is possible that ours may yet become—in words coined during the eighteenth century—the best of all possible worlds.■

Juliana Geran Pilon teaches history of ideas at Johns Hopkins University. She has recently completed a book on nationalism in Eastern Europe.

Article 26   *The New York Review*
January 30, 1992

The Massacre of Yugoslavia

Misha Glenny

1.

An unexpected drizzle one gloomy morning late last August served to heighten the tension as I left the northern Croatian town of Karlovac and was waved through the front line by a Croat National Guardsman. Violence had become so common in Croatia by then that nobody bothered to mention the dangers of crossing from one side to another. The checkpoint on the other side was jointly patrolled by the federal army (JNA) and Serb irregulars called Marticevci, from the town of Knin, one hundred miles to the south. The federal soldiers were polite, although they appeared unconcerned when the Marticevci shoved their automatic weapons into my stomach and subjected my car to a meticulous search. They ripped the film out of my cameras, took away my tapes to examine them, and inquired about my presumed relationship to the Croatian National Guard. Eventually I persuaded them that I was only trying to get an interview with Milan Babic, the Luger-toting prime minister of the self-proclaimed Serbian Autonomous Region (SAO) Krajina, the center of radical Serb nationalism in Croatia, and I was allowed to continue on my way.

To travel through Marticevci country is one of the more unnerving experiences of covering the war in Yugoslavia. The Marticevci, now the largest Serb paramilitary force, emerged when the first serious fighting between Serbs and Croats broke out in Knin in August 1990. Many of them had been Serb policemen who were thrown out of their jobs by the new Croatian government. They got their money, their weapons, and their name from Milan Martic, the first interior minister of the SAO Krajina, who like Babic is supported by both the Serbian president, Slobodan Milosevic, and the JNA leadership.

During World War II, Knin was the major center of the Serb nationalist Chetnik movement inside Croatia. In other parts of Croatia Serbs mostly joined or supported Tito's Partisans, whose internationalist ideology dominated the Croatian resistance movement. In their tactics and political attitudes the Marticevci have been heavily influenced by the traditions of the Chetnik movement of World War II. They are, however, an integral part of the self-proclaimed SAO Krajina and as such command greater respect among most Serbs than the wilder new Chetnik units from the Serb heartlands, who are largely beyond any systematic control. After reporting for more than a year on the reborn Chetnik movement in Serbia I have found its most striking characteristic to be its

obsession with violence. Its members apparently take pleasure in torturing and mutilating civilian and military opponents alike.

In the fall of 1990, President Tudjman of Croatia and President Milosevic of Serbia, the latter working through Milan Babic, his man in Knin, began their struggle for control of three districts with mixed Serb and Croat populations that lie south of Zagreb—Lika, Kordun, and Banija. Initially, most of the conflicts in these districts were provoked by the Croat authorities. President Tudjman and the government of his Croatian Democratic Union were determined to create a new state identified exclusively with the Croat nation, and the new regime in Croatia took steps to

"Literary Croatian," which uses the Roman alphabet, became, according to the new Croat constitution, the only official language in the republic.

Tudjman also refused to offer the Serb population of at least 600,000 cultural autonomy, including, for example, control over schools in districts where Serbs were a majority, or the right to use Cyrillic script in official documents. He ordered the Serb police in such districts to be replaced by Croats, and Serbs in key positions in the local administration were dismissed. At the same time, the principal Yugoslav symbol, the red star, was replaced everywhere by the most important insignia of Croatian statehood, the red-and-white checkered shield, the coat of arms of the historic

discriminate against the Serbs, who make up between 12 and 20 percent of Croatia's population, depending on whose statistics you believe—there are no reliable figures. After the elections of April 1990, which brought Tudjman to power, the Serbs were stripped of their status as a constituent (drzavotvoran) nation within Croatia.

Croat kingdom, which had also been widely used by the Ustasi, the murderous Croat fascist organization installed by the Nazis as rulers of Croatia in 1941. One now sees the shield, without the Ustasi "U," everywhere in Croatia, whether on official buildings or on police helmets. Serbs view the red star not just as a Communist symbol but as a sign legitimizing their equal status with Croatians, and they believe the ubiquitous presence of the checkered shield underlines the loss of that equality.

When the Interior Ministry in Zagreb tried to impose Croat police forces on Serbian villages, Milan Babic would send his political and military representatives to demand that the local Serb mayor order the storming of the district police station by armed villagers, who were expected to drive out the Croat police. If the local mayor refused, the Marticevci would often get rid of him either by packing the local council, of which the mayor is president, or by intimidating him with threats or physical attack. Beginning in April 1991 Babic was able to take over another local administration every two weeks or so, and, in many parts of Lika and Krajina, force the Croat police out without a struggle.

The insensitivity with which the Croats carried out their nationalist policies is well illustrated in the case of Glina, a small town forty miles southeast of Zagreb in Banija with some ten thousand inhabitants, 60 percent of them Serbian. In peacetime, Glina is a picturesque town resting in a gentle, shaded valley between two ranges of hills, which were Partisan strongholds during World War II. The town was the scene of two notorious massacres by the Ustasi. In 1941 some eight hundred Serbs were slaughtered in Glina's Orthodox church, while later over a thousand more lost their lives on the outskirts of town. The memory of Croat atrocities in Glina remains vivid.

Beginning in the early autumn of 1990 Croat police came into Glina in what the local citizens described as "raids." The Croat police took away the weapons of the Serbian policemen, first the reserve police and later on the regular police, and reinforced the Glina station with members of the Croat militia, thereby insuring that most of the armed police in Glina would be Croats. They made it clear that they were now in control, and Serbs from Glina told me that they felt intimidated by them. Tudjman's officials also insisted on displaying the Croat flag throughout the town.

Despite the sense of alarm that first spread through the Banija district in September 1990, the local Serb leaders in Glina maintained regular contact with the Croatian government in Zagreb. They appealed to the government and the local police chief in the nearby town of Petrinja not to continue intimidating local Serbs by a show of force. The authorities in Zagreb refused to change their tactics. The local Serb leaders tried to keep out of the growing political struggle between Milan Babic's organization in Knin and the government in Zagreb. But when Croatian independence was declared on June 25 of this year, Glina's Serbs, fearing the worst, sided with the thuggish forces of the Marticevci.

On an extremely hot day early last July, while all attention was concentrated on the fighting in Slovenia, the Marticevci began their first sustained attack in Central Croatia. Several hundred of them swarmed into the town from their stronghold in the surrounding forest. Despite dozens of reinforcements sent by the Croats into Glina, the Marticevci sealed off the town in a matter of hours. Several Croat policemen were killed before the police station surrendered. At the time it was still possible to surrender—six months later such incidents almost invariably become fights to the death. On the same day, tanks of the federal army, which has a majority of Serbian officers, started to separate the Serb fighters from the Croat reinforcements sent into the district. While the army announced that it would stop the bloodshed between the two nationalities and did so, it also protected the territorial gains of the Serb militia.

With the fighting in Glina, a real war started in Croatia. This war is largely the consequence of aggression sponsored by the Serbian regime in Belgrade and the JNA, but it also partly originated in the contemptuous treatment of the Serb minority by the Tudjman government. It is also, too, partly a revival of civil war, although in a purer, more nationalist form than was the case between 1941 and 1945, when almost two thirds of the Partisan fighters in Croatia were Croats opposed to the Ustasa state. In the current war the two sides are divided almost entirely along national lines. Croatian officials say that this is not a nationalist war but a struggle between a Bolshevik administration in Belgrade and their own free-market democracy—a claim as misleading and contemptible as the Serbian view of the conflict as a war of liberation against a revived fascist state. Tudjman and his elected government, like Milosevic's government, still have many connections with the old Communist bureaucracy, and they have acted harshly and provocatively toward Serbs; but they have not revived a fascist state.

2.

By the end of September 1991, the Marticevci and the JNA had occupied all but a long narrow strip of land in the Kordun district below the Kupa River in central Croatia. About 25,000 peasants live in this fertile land between the towns of Karlovoc and Sisak. Most of the villages are Croat, but they traditionally had good relations with the nearby Serb and mixed villages. On October 1 a joint force made up of the JNA, Chetnik units from Serbia, the Marticevci from Knin (100 miles to the south), and conscripts and volunteers from the local Serb villages began one of the most ruthless offensives of the entire war. Its victims were the defenseless Croat villagers living near the Kupa River, most of them older people, the younger inhabitants having left to work in northern Europe, mainly Germany, since Kordun, in spite of its fertile land, is one of Croatia's poorer regions.

According to several Serb spokesmen, the Serb forces attacked in revenge for the murder, on September 21, of thirteen JNA prisoners of war on the Korana bridge on the outskirts of Karlovac—killings that even the Croat Interior Ministry admitted had taken place. This willingness to justify one atrocity by pointing to another committed by the opposing side has helped to create the current pattern of reciprocal massacre in Yugoslavia.

The tactics of the JNA forces and the Chetniks in northern Kordun were repeated from village to village. First the artillery would "soften up" the villagers, with bombardments lasting between twenty minutes and four hours. If there was no resistance (as was the case in all but a few of the villages), JNA officers would enter the town and demand the surrender of any National Guardsmen or Croat police, and they would then allow the Serb irregulars to come into the town. In the eastern part of Kordun, it was mainly the Serb irregulars from neighboring villages in their improvised uniforms who arrived first. In the western part of Kordun, the Chetnik detachments were made up primarily of men from Loznica and Valjevo, two towns from Serbia's Chetnik heartland about 250 miles away. Both groups set about burning and looting the villages, and each village was bombarded continually with gunfire and grenades for between twelve and twenty hours. Houses were searched for weapons and for any young Croat men in hiding. The buildings were then thoroughly plundered.

Croats in the villages to the east were fortunate, since their neighbors from Serb villages warned them to travel north across the Kupa River as fast as they could. While hundreds of people in boats desperately paddled to reach the northern river bank, the JNA pounded them with mortar and tank fire. In Karlovac's hospital, I talked to survivors with appalling shrapnel wounds who described how their friends and neighbors drowned or were blown apart before they were able to cast off.

The people in the nearby villages of Vukmanic, Skakavac, and Kablar suffered even worse treatment. Witnesses from Skakavac told me of an extensive massacre of Croat civilians there. The numbers of dead are unknown since the JNA has refused to allow the Croat Red Cross into Skakavac to claim the bodies. In Vukmanic, all seven members of the Mujic family were killed after being denounced by a local Serb who had a grudge against them; the Chetnik brigade that took over the village of Kablar slaughtered the remaining men in cold blood, including an eighty-two-year-old Croat. Here, too, the bodies have not been turned over to the Red Cross.

In Kamensko and other villages, the bodies of Croats killed during the fighting were allowed to lie decaying in the streets. Between eight and twelve days after their deaths, the JNA finally permitted the Karlovac Red Cross workers to come to collect them. The eighteen bodies I saw were so badly putrified that the chief pathologist at Karlovac hospital could no longer say with any certainty which injuries had been the cause of death. Whether they were caught in crossfire or deliberately slaughtered, the JNA and the Chetniks had afforded them no dignity in death. The desecration of the Croat villages was complete—churches and schools were destroyed while JNA tanks ran over the local cemeteries.

The attack on northern Kordun was among the most barbaric suffered by Croats during the current war. Nonetheless it remains one of the least known abroad, mainly because major towns such as Vukovar, Osijek, and Dubrovnik were not involved. But at least it can be said that their visible destruction alerted the world to the crimes being committed by the JNA and the Chetniks at the expense of Croats. Unfortunately the suffering of the innocent Serbs in Croatia has had no such attention.

3.

During July and August of 1991, eastern Croatia became one of the most violent fronts in the war. As fighting spread through the villages in northeastern Croatia, small shops and kiosks, owned and run almost entirely by local Serbs in Osijek, the regional capital, were destroyed systematically in a series of bomb attacks. A pattern of intimidation and arbitrary violence against Serbs in Croat-held areas then spread through most of the regions in Croatia where fighting had broken out.

In August respected Serbs began disappearing in one town after another, even in the larger cities—including Zagreb—which had been spared the worst violence. Among those who disappeared, to name only two of many, were Dusan Trivuncic, a member of the Croat Parliament for the SDP, the reformed Communist Party, and Dragan Rajsic, the retired head of the safety department at the Sisak oil refinery, thirty-five miles southeast of Zagreb. Both were kidnapped by armed Croats in uniform; the Croat minister of interior, Ivan Vekic, says he has been unable to find out what happened to them.

Attacks on Serbs have since sharply increased. The bodies of thirteen murdered Serbs were discovered in the Sisak region, which has been under extremely heavy bombardment from JNA units in Petrinja—bombardments that virtually everyone I talked to agreed made the Croat forces there treat local Serbs all the more brutally. In September thousands of Serbs began leaving their homes in the port town of Zadar after many people were beaten in the streets by Croats and forced out of their apartments; several were lynched. Many Serbs leaving Croat towns who have relations in other European countries have tried to find temporary refuge abroad. But most are forced to go to Serbia or Montenegro, although few have any desire to go to either place. A large minority has also left Croatia for the multi-ethnic republic of Bosnia-Hercegovina. Again the wave of uncontrolled Croat anger apparently was provoked by the violent attacks by JNA units in the region.

Before long I heard reliable reports of a massacre carried out by right-wing Croats. This happened in Gospic, a mixed town in the western part of Lika, which was first attacked by Chetnik and JNA units in late August. As with many towns in Croatia, the division between nationalities in Gospic is reflected in the town's geography. All but a few of the residents of the eastern part of the town were Serbs, who fled behind JNA lines as soon as the first attacks began. But a considerable number of Serbs also lived in the western, largely Croat, part of town and, in response to the appeals of the Croat government, they remained there. These are colloquially known as "loyal Serbs," or slightly more frivolously, "Hrbi" (a conflation of the words for Croats and Serbs in Serbo-Croatian).

On October 16, an alarm signaling a Serb artillery attack sounded in the town, and once again the miserable inhabitants of Gospic took refuge in cellars. Life in the bomb shelters in Croatia is a humiliating experience. After the first rush of intense anger and frustration toward an enemy who only reveals himself in a shower of deadly projectiles, people become apathetic and gullible, ready to accept any orders or demands made of them. When groups of uniformed Croats entered several of Gospic's cellars on the night of October 16 and took away over one hundred Serbs who had taken shelter in them, witnesses told me, they complied without protest.

Most of the Serbs were professionals working in Gospic's local administration. They included the town's deputy district attorney and the deputy head of Gospic's prison, to which, with terrible irony, they were at first taken. After this at least twenty-six were murdered, according to a list later obtained by the Croatian government. The final figure of the massacre victims is still to be confirmed, although over seventy-five Serbs, including many women, are unaccounted for. The only Serb minister in the Croat government, Zivko Juzbasic, says he fears that over one hundred were killed in the Gospic massacre. Ten weeks after it took place, Interior Minister Vekic has not given any explanation of what happened, although he has said his ministry is preparing a statement on the case.

If a UN peacekeeping force is not deployed, the civil war will very probably intensify in Croatia and in all likelihood spread to Bosnia-Hercegovina, as Serbian forces continue their merciless attacks. Meanwhile Serbian civilians in Croatia face serious threats to their lives every day. The Serbian Democratic Forum, a movement which has attracted most of the prominent Serb intellectuals and professionals in Croatia, has appealed to the government in Zagreb to arrange the orderly evacuation of Serbs from Croatia under international supervision. The appeals have so far been ignored. Those who rightly denounce the Belgrade regime for its aggression should be concerned about aggression against the Serbs in Croatia as well.

The Zagreb government has in effect done nothing to stop the violence against Serbs for two reasons. The war has intensified radical chauvinist sentiment among the Croat population and in particular among its fighting forces, which now include thousands of fascist Black Legionaires, and members of the Ustasi and of the extremist paramilitary organization called HOS. Many Croats would regard strong statements of public concern for Serbs as a demonstration of weakness by President Tudjman and his government. Croatia also presents itself as a democratic state which abides by Western European standards on human rights. Instead of confronting violations of human rights, the Croat government attempts to hide them in the hope that they will disappear, and escape the attention of the West. This policy cannot work for long and can only bring dishonor to the Croat cause.

4.

Notwithstanding the marked nationalist character of the conflict, the federal army has claimed from the very beginning that it represents Yugoslavia. In fact, the assumption that behind the war lies a well-coordinated Greater Serbian plan is a serious misconception, and one that makes a diplomatic solution to the crisis all the more difficult. "Serbian" policy is determined by three political forces—Milosevic, the JNA officer corps, and the leaderships of the self-proclaimed Serb republics in Croatia and Bosnia. Each has its own program which sometimes coincides with the others, but frequently differs. In addition, there are often bitter divisions within the officer corps and among the leaders of Serbian enclaves, and these disagreements can have unpredictable and dangerous consequences.

One often hears how the army is "Serbian-led" or "Serbian-dominated," which it is, but this does not mean that the first concern of many of the top officers is to serve the cause of greater Serbian unity. The Hague Peace Conference, which first convened last September under Lord Carrington's chairmanship, tried to find solutions acceptable to all the republics and ethnic groups in Yugoslavia; but it failed to take into account the political motives of the men who are doing most of the fighting. The JNA officers have tried to justify their military attacks by claiming that the rights of Serbs (i.e., Yugoslav citizens) were threatened by Croatia's secessionist government. They were, however, primarily concerned with the need to protect their own status and privileges. No federal Yugoslavia would mean no JNA. The diplomats and politicians trying to stop the war realized too late that this powerful army could not just be wished away.

Although the primary allegiance of the army officer corps has been to Yugoslavia and not Serbia, the decay of federal institutions has aroused the latent Serb nationalism within the army. Seventy percent of the officers are Serb, and no doubt they are as much affected by the spread of irrational nationalism as everyone else. Early in the Yugoslav conflict, two main factions formed within the army leadership. The first was associated with the federal defense minister, General Veljko Kadijevic, and his deputy, the Slovene Stane Brovet, two of the three-man joint chiefs of staff. With a Serb father and a Croat mother, General Kadijevic has always associated himself with Yugoslavia and not with Serbia. The Serbian nationalist press has heaped abuse on him during the past three months, accusing him of undermining the war effort because he refuses to support Serbia's chief war aim—the expansion of Serb territory by military means. Kadijevic, it seems, genuinely believes in a political solution that has by now become a fantasy: the restoration of the Yugoslav state, including parts, or even all, of Croatia.

At the same time, a powerful network of Serb nationalists emerged among the officer corps to compete with Kadijevic's Yugoslav ideology. Its best-known representative is Blagoje Adzic, a Serb from Croatia whose entire family was slaughtered by the Ustasi during the war. As the member of the three-man joint chiefs of staff who is responsible for operations in the field, Adzic is in a position to decide military strategy. From the beginning of the conflict, he has advocated that Yugoslav federal ideology be cast aside and the JNA be converted into a Serbian army which would integrate the Chetnik fighters into its command.

Adzic is also linked politically to one of the most powerful men in the army high command, General Marko Negovanovic, the former head of the military intelligence organization KOS, which has an immensely effective network of agents and informants throughout the army and indeed in all the Yugoslav republics. General Negovanovic and the KOS have put their weight behind the army's nationalist wing. Negovanovic's influence recently increased further when he was appointed the Serbian minister of defense. As the federal government fades steadily in importance, the new republican cabinet in Serbia, which in addition to Negovanovic includes some other ambitious nationalists, has further undermined the position of the federal defense minister, General Kadijevic.

Such overt Serbian nationalism presented Milosevic with a diplomatic problem since his strategy depended on maintaining the increasingly dubious concept of a federal Yugoslav state. At international negotiations, and particularly at the Hague Peace Conference, he tried to disguise Serb aggression against Croatia by defending the right of Yugoslavs (notably the

Serb minority in Croatia and the Serbs in Bosnia) to remain where they are in Yugoslavia. If he were to agree to General Adzic's demands that the national army should be transformed into a Serbian army, the war of the Yugoslav state against irredentists would become simply an expansionist war guided by a Greater Serbian ideology at the expense of Croatia, which has an elected government.

Their mutual need to cling to the Yugoslav idea led to the close relationship between Milosevic and General Kadijevic. Recently they have made it clear that they want a political solution to the crisis. They have done so largely because Milosevic needs international support for his republic if he is to remain in power after the war. His flexibility was demonstrated during the crucial session of the Hague Peace Conference in the middle of November, when he agreed in private to drop the demand that the Serbian-dominated areas in Croatia be allowed to detach themselves from Zagreb's rule. He did so against the wishes of both radical Serb leaders like Babic, who publicly denounced his decision, and the army's nationalist wing. Just as the document with this concession was about to be signed, however, the nationalist officers ordered the heavy bombardment of Dubrovnik, completely undermining Milosevic's position.

In early December, General Kadijevic was close to an agreement with Cyrus Vance on a cease-fire that would allow a UN peacekeeping force to be deployed. Once again Dubrovnik was bombarded and the agreement undermined. Kadijevic was forced to apologize and he called for an investigation to find out who had ordered the attack—an implicit and humiliating admission that he did not control all his forces. Vance returned to the UN aware that while he could talk for hours with Kadijevic, any agreement would depend on the will of others.

Although it is Croatia that has had to suffer the violence of the war, the divisions in the Yugoslav or Serbian camp now threaten the stability of the current regime in Serbia, the very exis-

tence of the federal army, and the security of the Serb mini-states in Croatia. The possibility that Milosevic, the JNA leadership, and the Serb leaders in Croatia and Bosnia could fulfill their disparate aims is receding steadily. According to senior army officers with whom I recently spoke, the JNA is beginning to break up for three reasons. First, the military is buckling under pressure of ideological divisions within its own ranks; second, in the wake of the economic collapse throughout eastern Yugoslavia, the army is no longer guaranteed a sponsor; and, finally, the army is unable to attract anything approaching the number of recruits it requires to wage a long war.

In early January, Milosevic and Kadijevic were working hard to bring about a cease-fire and thus create the conditions for the arrival of a UN peacekeeping force in Yugoslavia. This is not because these thoroughly unattractive men believe in the inherent justice of a UN-led solution but because without a UN buffer zone in Croatia, they see a political and even a military defeat staring them in the face. Their moderate alliance has in turn produced a new flock of hawks including the Serb nationalists in the army and Milan Babic in Knin, who has warned that any UN troops deployed inside the Krajina are likely to be fired on. The hawks continue to believe, wrongly I suspect, in the efficacy of a nationalist war. Yet the JNA cannot sustain its operations indefinitely. It will, however, cause further havoc in Croatian towns, and may ignite a new conflict in Bosnia if a political solution is not found. Ironically, without a UN peacekeeping force in Krajina, Bosnia, and Eastern Slavonia, the Croatian National Guard, bolstered by the support which international recognition promises, stands an excellent chance of regaining most of the territory containing a considerable Serb population that it has lost to the Serb irregulars and the JNA. Such a defeat for Serbia would create a new nationalist grievance in the Balkans comparable in its emotional force to the hatred of the Versailles treaty in Weimar Germany.

5.

Meanwhile the decision of the European Community Foreign Ministers on December 16 to accept the independence of the Yugoslav states that ask to be recognized as such has far-reaching implications. First, it reinforces the growing confidence of Germany in foreign policy matters, since throughout the autumn the United Kingdom, the United States, and the United Nations publicly asked that recognition of Croatia and Slovenia be postponed until a comprehensive settlement had been agreed on by all parties. Germany ignored this request and in mid-December announced that it would recognize Croatia and Slovenia on January 15.

The French, who are traditionally suspicious of the US and Britain and fear playing second fiddle to Bonn, proposed a compromise: that only the republics that met democratic standards should be recognized. Unfortunately, the French plan, commendable in principle, was thrown together in haste simply to prevent an open split in the European Community. Germany showed that the issue of democratic standards was not decisive when it announced that it would recognize Croatia and Slovenia "unconditionally."

Until now Germany's recent policies in Eastern Europe have been much more beneficial to the countries there than those of the United Kingdom or the United States. Despite its preoccupation with the former GDR, German business has been investing steadily in Eastern Europe, notably western Poland, Bohemia, Moravia, and Hungary; in doing so Germany is contributing more toward regional stability than any other Western nation. Mrs. Thatcher's nightmare of German expansion would carry some political weight if her government or that of John Major had shown the slightest inclination to encourage investment in Eastern Europe.

In its new policy toward Yugoslavia, Germany demonstrated for the first time that it could, on a major issue, openly oppose the stated aims of American policy, which are often transmitted to the Europeans through the United Nations or through British diplomats within the European Community and at the Hague Peace Conference. From the point of view of the diplomatic power game, the unilateral German move is understandable, especially since American and British policy in Yugoslavia has been concerned to restrict the growth of German influence in the region. But it is most disturbing that the place selected for this test of strength should be Yugoslavia. Serbia, for its part, interprets the determination of Germany (together with Italy and Austria) to recognize Croatia as a revival of the wartime Axis alliance. This could be said to be true only in the sense that Germany now has strong economic interests in some of the same regions that it did in the 1930s—western Poland, Bohemia, Moravia, Hungary, Austria, Slovenia, Croatia, and northern Italy. The Belgrade government also believes that the Catholic Church has had an important part in bringing about this alliance, a claim that is not entirely without foundation. The recognition of Croatia now is likely to open still further the breach between the Orthodox and Catholic churches.

The decision of the Kohl government to recognize Croatia "unconditionally" is unfortunate in several ways. It implies that Germany has such a single-minded concern for its own interests that it is willing even to recognize East European republics that are unable to guarantee the safety of citizens under their control. The massacre in Gospic, for example, was not carried out by irregulars but by forces of the Croat state. Britain, which is under pressure not to undermine the unity of the EC, may follow Germany's lead and also recognize Croatia. And now that the federal prime minister Ante Markovic, Washington's main ally in Yugoslavia, has resigned, the United States, too, may recognize the Tudjman regime.

But recognition will not stop the fighting. The army and the Serbs have said they will not withdraw if Croatia is recognized but will fight all the harder. If Germany uses recognition to supply Croatia with weapons—which it has not been able to do so far because of the UN arms embargo against Yugoslavia—then the conflict will be fairer but it will be much bloodier as well. Recognition probably also means an end to the Hague Peace Conference, which presumed that a comprehensive settlement would be arranged before recognition was granted to anybody. It also makes the work of the United Nations more difficult. But, above all, it raises the possibility of the war spreading to Bosnia-Hercegovina. The German recognition of Croatia and Slovenia has forced the president of Bosnia, in which Croats and Muslims make up the majority, to apply for recognition. The Serb leaders in Bosnia immediately said that if the republic were recognized they would form their own state within Bosnia. The Muslims warned in return that such a step would lead to "tragedy." Such a possible chain of events underlines the urgent need for the deployment of UN troops inside Croatia. If they are deployed in the three regions with large Serb populations, as proposed by Cyrus Vance, then these would assume the status of demilitarized zones under UN control. The three regions would belong neither to Croatia nor to any Yugoslav or Serbian state. This is clearly not a satisfactory long-term solution—and it depends as I write on the ceasefire of January 3 holding up—but if UN troops are deployed, the military conflict should come to an end, without doubt the most important task at the moment.

No doubt the Serbian politicians, by their aggressive and irrational behavior, have contributed greatly to the current tragedy, but Croatia bears a share of responsibility as well, and therefore Germany's unilateral move to recognize Tudjman's regime is of dubious moral value. In its practical consequences, recognition risks causing more death and destruction. As a model for a future approach to disputes in Eastern Europe and the former Soviet Union, moreover, it is nothing short of catastrophic ☐

—January 3, 1992

Credits

Glossary of Terms and Abbreviations

Anti-Party Group Nikita Khrushchev's opponents in the Soviet Communist Party's Politburo/Presidium who tried but failed to force his resignation as first secretary in June 1957.

Apparat The bureaucracy of the Soviet Communist Party. Bureaucrats who work in the bureaucracy are called *apparatchiki*.

Bolshevik The left wing of the Russian Social Democratic Party (RSDP); Bolshevik members of the RSDP believed in the necessity of the violent overthrow of the Czarist order to achieve change.

Brezhnev Doctrine A set of ideas attributed to Leonid Brezhnev, calling for collective intervention of Socialist countries to prevent counterrevolution and justifying the Soviet-led Warsaw Pact intervention in Czechoslovakia in August 1968.

Charter 77 Movement A group of Czechoslovak dissidents who criticized the human-rights violations by the government in Prague in a document (charter) in January 1977 and who continued their criticism despite regime harassment and punishment of its members.

C.I.S. Commonwealth of Independent States, the name now used to define the 11 republics that constitute what is left of the old U.S.S.R. Four of the original 15 republics elected not to join the new C.I.S.: Estonia, Latvia, Lithuania, and Georgia.

CMEA (Council for Mutual Economic Assistance) Established in January 1949 and consisted of Bulgaria, Czechoslovakia, East Germany, Hungary, Poland, Romania, and the Soviet Union. Its long-term objective was the economic integration of Soviet Bloc countries.

Cold War A sharp deterioration of Soviet-American relations immediately following the end of World War II because of a worldwide ideological and political rivalry that occasionally threatened armed conflict.

Collectivization The forced amalgamation under collective communal management of farms formerly owned privately.

Collegialism Collective decision-making in which no single person dominates the process by which agreement is reached.

Cominform The Communist Information Bureau established in September 1947 to disseminate Soviet ideological principles among the European Communist parties.

Comintern The Third (Communist) International established in March 1919 to unify the world's Communist parties in their combat of capitalism. Unlike the Cominform, the Comintern required abject loyalty of its members to directives issued from its headquarters in Moscow. The Comintern was dissolved in World War II.

Committee for Social Self Defense The new (1977) name of the Committee for the Defense of the Workers set up in 1976 by Polish intellectuals to help Polish workers arrested by the Warsaw regime for involvement in the 1976 strikes against increases in food prices.

Communism The ideal classless and stateless communal societies that workers in Socialist countries are striving to create in accordance with the teachings of Karl Marx and Vladimir Lenin.

CPSU (Communist Party of the Soviet Union) The successor of the Bolshevik Party that seized power in Russia in November 1917.

Cultural Autonomy The right of an ethnic group in a multinational society to speak its own language, preserve other aspects of its cultural identity, and enjoy a measure of self-administration.

Czarism The theory and practice of government under the Russian czars, notably those of the Romanov dynasty from 1614 to 1917.

Democratic Centralism The principles authored by Vladimir Lenin on which the organizational structure and behavior of Communist parties are supposed to be based.

Democratization A broadening of popular participation in electoral processes within the party, government, and the workplace.

Detente Relaxation of tensions between the Soviet Union and its allies and the Western countries.

Duma The national legislature of imperial Russia established for the first time in 1906; after the Bolshevik Revolution of 1917 it was succeeded by a new national legislature called the Supreme Soviet, established in the 1922 Soviet Constitution.

Eastern Bloc Another name for the Soviet Bloc, which consisted of the Soviet Union and its Warsaw Pact allies in Eastern Europe.

Eurocommunism A set of ideas and practices embraced in different ways at different times and with different consequences by the Italian, French, and Spanish Communist parties beginning in the late 1960s that brought them into ideological and policy conflict with the Soviet Communist Party.

Fascism A set of ideas and practices calling for the establishment of an authoritarian political system to preserve the societal status quo against challenges from the "left"; for example, in Italy and Spain in the 1920s and the 1930s.

Fatherland Front A loose coalition of anti-Fascist groups dominated by the Bulgarian Communists that facilitated the expansion of their political influence in Bulgaria during and immediately following the end of World War II.

Glasnost Refers to a new openness or candor of political and ordinary citizens on national issues and problems.

Gosizdat Literally "published by the government" and meaning publications officially approved for public circulation, and thus the opposite of Samizdat.

Gosplan A national state planning agency in the Soviet Union that was responsible for drafting the so-called 5-year national plans of the Soviet state.

Great Purge The arrest, conviction, and punishment by death or imprisonment of high-ranking Soviet Communist Party and government officials by Joseph Stalin's regime in the mid-1930s.

Institutional Pluralism A term used to describe the appearance of interest groups and a broadening of the channels of political communication in a monolithic and authoritarian political system.

Interlocking Directorate A term used to characterize a situation in Socialist countries in which officials occupy simultaneously at least two administrative posts, one in the Communist party and the other in the government.

KGB (Committee of State Security) In the Soviet Council of Ministers, a secret investigatory agency of the former Soviet government responsible for, among other things, internal and external security and both strategic and counterintelligence work.

Komsomol The national youth organization or "Communist Youth League" of the former Soviet state. Its members ranged in age from 15 to 27 years.

Kulak Tough and resourceful Russian peasants who became wealthy and offered violent resistance to the collectivization policies of the Stalinist regime in the early 1930s.

Narodniki The "Populists," a movement of teachers, students, lawyers, physicians, and some aristocrats who tried to arouse the Russian peasantry against the Czarist regime in the early 1870s.

NATO (North Atlantic Treaty Organization) Established at the height of the Cold War in 1949 to defend Western countries against a threat to their security.

NEM (New Economic Mechanism) Established in Hungary in 1968, NEM introduced elements of a market economy with pricing and other techniques reminiscent of a capitalist economy involving a decentralization of planning and emphasis on managerial expertise and competitiveness in production. Bulgaria and Romania subsequently introduced versions of the Hungarian NEM, calling their changes by the same name even though they were not identical to those made in Hungary.

NEP (New Economic Policy) Under Vladimir Lenin, the development of the mixed Soviet economy in which some private ownership of the means of production continued, especially in agriculture, but other sectors of the economy, notably industry, were nationalized.

Nomenklatura The lists of positions in the party and state heirarchies to be filled only with the approval of the appropriate party officials.

Ostpolitik The policy of reconciliation and the maintenance of good relations with Socialist countries in the Soviet Bloc pursued by West Germany starting in the late 1960s.

Parallelism The existence of party organization that parallels and at the same time monitors the organization of government on all levels of administration from the top at the center of the country to the bottom or grass-roots level.

People's Democracy A term used to designate the establishment of a Communist party dictatorship in Eastern Europe in the late 1940s and to distinguish the new and therefore less developed socialism of the Eastern European countries from the older and more developed socialism of the Soviet Union.

Perestroika A restructuring of the Soviet economy involving decentralization of business and production, producing a limited expansion of entrepreneurism in the retail sector of the economy and the introduction of profit and loss in the management of economic enterprises.

Personality Cult Popular worship of the individual, encouraged by a political leader to increase his power.

RSDP (Russian Social Democratic Party) A Marxist party established in 1898 to work for the improvement of the conditions of the Russian proletariat and divided initially between evolutionists and revolutionaries, from which developed the Bolshevik party that seized power in 1917.

Russia The largest, most populous, most ethnically diverse, and most influential of the 11 constituent union-republics of the C.I.S.

Samizdat Literally "self-published" and meaning publications produced clandestinely because their content is forbidden by the state.

Serfdom The system of economic and political servitude prevalent in Czarist Russia until its abolition in 1861 by Czar Alexander II.

Socialism A set of ideas and practices that call for community management and control of the scarce factors of production to achieve equality of well-being. Different kinds of socialism (Marxian socialism, Arab socialism, Indian socialism, etc.) in different national settings at different periods of national development determine the precise degree of political power assigned to the community to achieve social justice.

Soviet Bloc A term used to describe the Soviet Union and its Warsaw Pact allies in Eastern Europe.

Soviet (local governing body) A legislative organ of government consisting of representatives of an administratively defined community and endowed with limited authority that is at all times subject to the review of higher government bodies.

Soviet (person) A citizen of the former Soviet Union.

Soviet Federalism The federal type of intergovernmental relations established in the Soviet Union in 1922 wherein the bulk of administrative decision making is concentrated in the central government in Moscow, and constituent units, in particular the largest and most populous, are based on the ethnic principle but enjoy little autonomy in contrast with the constituent units of federal systems in the West, where there is more equitable balance of power between central and local government.

U.S.S.R. (Union of Soviet Socialist Republics) The Soviet Union, successor in 1922 of the Russian Soviet Federated Socialist Republic founded originally in 1917. On December 26, 1992, the Supreme Soviet passed a resolution acknowledging the demise of the U.S.S.R.

War Communism Sometimes called "militant communism," this term refers to efforts of the Bolsheviks between 1917 and 1921 to respond to emergency conditions resulting from World War I and the Revolution of 1917, such as acute shortages of food, and simultaneously to inaugurate the Socialist transition to communism, for example, by nationalizing industries, redistributing land, and replacing money as a medium of exchange with a barter system. War communism, along with the Civil War and the allied blockade of Russia, caused the near total collapse of the Russian economy and was superseded by the New Economic Policy starting in 1921.

Warsaw Pact An alliance of six Eastern European countries and the Soviet Union, linking them closely together in matters of defense. Established in 1955, ostensibly in response to West Germany's entry into NATO, the alliance, which was dominated by the Soviet Union, by far its most militarily powerful member, became another instrument of Soviet influence and control in Eastern Europe. With the dissolution of the U.S.S.R., the Warsaw Pact ceased to be a viable alliance.

Young Pioneers A Soviet state organization for children between the ages of 10 and 15 years which provided extensive recreational activities with strong political overtones. Membership in the Young Pioneers was a prerequisite for joining the more advanced youth group known as the Komsomol.

Zemstvos The local legislative bodies established by Czar Alexander II in a law of 1864 in which nobility, townspeople, and peasantry were to be represented and which were endowed with power to levy taxes for local economic and social needs such as roads, bridges, schools, and hospitals.

Bibliography

THE SOVIET UNION

Domestic Developments

Abel Aganbegyan, *The Economic Challenge of Perestroika* (Bloomington: Indiana University Press, 1988).

The director of the economics section of the Soviet Academy of Sciences and Gorbachev's chief economic adviser analyzes the goals, methods, and limits of perestroika.

Leon P. Baradat, *Soviet Political Society*, 2nd ed. (Englewood Cliffs: Prentice Hall, 1989).

Written with the student in mind, this edition investigates the broad scope of Soviet political life, examining not only the government and the party but also the economy and society.

Donald D. Barry and Carol Barner-Barry, *Contemporary Soviet Politics*, 4th ed. (Englewood Cliffs: Prentice Hall, 1991).

This book is problem-oriented and devotes a great deal of attention to policy matters with an emphasis on the Gorbachev era.

Seweryn Bialer, ed., *Politics, Society, and Nationality Inside Gorbachev's Russia* (Boulder: Westview Press, 1988).

The best brief analysis of the character and consequences of Gorbachev's reforms.

_____, *The Soviet Paradox: External Expansion, Internal Decline* (New York: Vintage, 1986).

An invaluable study of Soviet politics during the Andropov-Chernenko interregnum that analyzes the conditions that led to Gorbachev's ascendancy and to the formulation of his ambitious program of reform.

Zbigniew K. Brzezinski, *The Grand Failure: The Birth and Death of Communism in the Twentieth Century* (New York: Scribners, 1988).

A thought-provoking analysis of the problems confronting the Soviet Union and Central/Eastern Europe under socialism that explain the urgency of reform.

Stephen F. Cohen, *Rethinking the Soviet Experience: Politics and History Since 1917* (New York: Oxford University Press, 1985).

A thoughtful reassessment of the historical evolution of the Soviet political system.

Stephen F. Cohen and Katrina vanden Heuvel, eds. *Voices of Glasnost: Interviews with Gorbachev's Reformers* (New York: Norton, 1989).

An account of the personal and political difficulties of carrying out perestroika by 14 Soviet public figures.

Joan Francis Crowley and Dan Vaillancourt, *Lenin to Gorbachev: Three Generations of Soviet Communists* (Arlington Heights: Forum Press, 1989).

A look at Soviet political evolution in terms of generation theory. Communist rule of the Soviet Union is studied in terms of the personalities and ideas of Lenin, Stalin, Khrushchev, Brezhnev, and Gorbachev.

Viktor Danilov, *Rural Russia Under the New Regime* (Bloomington: Indiana University Press, 1988).

A study of agricultural problems in the Soviet Union and Gorbachev's efforts to address them.

Anthony Jones, Walter Connor, and David E. Powell, eds. *Soviet Social Problems* (Boulder: Westview Press, 1991).

An account of the social problems that Soviet society accumulated over its history.

Basile Kerblay, *Modern Soviet Society* (New York: Pantheon Books, 1983).

The definitive study of Soviet society that places the Soviet Union in an international context through comparisons with other industrialized countries, notably France, the United States, and Japan. Still a classic.

Amy W. Knight, *The KGB: Police and Politics in the Soviet Union* (Winchester, Allen and Unwin Hyman, 1988).

Based on a wide range of published materials from Russian and Soviet sources, this book provides an informative and objective study of the Soviet secret-police apparatus.

Gail Warshofsky Lapidus, ed., *Women, Workers, and Family in the Soviet Union* (Armonk: M. E. Sharpe, 1982).

A collection of articles on what the Soviets themselves say about the dilemma of female employment in the Soviet Union.

Walter Z. Laquer, *The Long Road to Freedom: Russia and Glasnost* (New York: Scribners, 1988).

A thorough investigation of the roots, causes, and impact of glasnost.

D. Richard Little, *Governing the Soviet Union* (New York: Longman, 1989).

A general introduction to the Soviet political system. Distinctive features include an emphasis on how policies were made and an explanation of the Soviet citizen's public and private behavior.

David R. Marples, *The Social Impact of the Chernobyl Disaster* (New York: St. Martin's Press, 1988).

A thorough, readable analysis of the economic, social, and political consequences of the Chernobyl accident.

Roy Medvedev, *Let History Judge: The Origins and Consequences of Stalinism* (New York: Columbia University Press, 1989).

A revised and expanded version of the first edition of this classic work. It provides new light on the Stalinist past using Western scholarship as well as Russian sources.

Cameron Ross, *Local Government in the Soviet Union* (New York: St. Martin's Press, 1987).

A study of the role and functions of local Soviets helpful in understanding Gorbachev's administrative reforms.

Michael Ryan, *Doctors in the Soviet Union* (New York: St. Martin's Press, 1990).

An important contribution to the growing literature on the Soviet health-care system.

Richard Sakwa, *Gorbachev and His Reforms 1985–1990* (Englewood Cliffs, Prentice-Hall, 1990).

A comprehensive review of the scope and significance of the key aspects of Gorbachev's reform program based on a wide reading of Soviet and Western sources.

Fred Schulze and Gordon Livermore, eds., *The U.S.S.R. Today: Perspectives From the Soviet Press* (Columbus: Current Digest of the Soviet Press, 1988), 7th ed.

An invaluable source of information on problems in Soviet domestic politics and foreign relations that includes commentary on the economy, health and welfare, education, religion, and the arts.

Dora Shturtman, *The Soviet Secondary School* (New York: Routledge, Chapman and Hall, 1988).

A study of the structure and behavior of Soviet secondary education that points out problems that Gorbachev was trying to address.

Gordon B. Smith, *Soviet Politics: Struggling With Change* (New York: St. Martin's Press, 1992).

One of the most up-to-date studies of the Soviet system on the eve of its collapse with attention to steps toward democratization, the process of economic collapse, and the worsening of the nationalities problem.

Graham Smith, ed., *The Nationalities Question in the Soviet Union* (New York: Longman, 1990).

Written by a team of international experts, this book provides systematic and authoritative coverage of the 20 most important nationalities, with emphasis on the response of each to the Gorbachev reform program.

Hedrick Smith, *The New Russians* (New York: Random House, 1990).

Based on hundreds of interviews with Soviet citizens from all walks of life, Smith explores the roots of Gorbachev's reforms, the problems of implementing them, and reasons why they failed to save the Soviet system.

Isaac J. Tarasulo, ed., *Perils of Perestroika: Viewpoints From the Soviet Press 1989–1991* (Wilmington: Scholarly Resources, 1992).

A collection of articles by Soviet analysts on change in the Soviet Union under Gorbachev, covering popular political attitudes, the changing role of the party, economic problems and policies, the military, and foreign affairs.

Boris Yeltsin, *Against the Grain: An Autobiography* (New York: Summit Books, 1990).

The political life of Russian President Yeltsin focuses on not only his rise to political prominence and national leadership but also the workings of the Soviet Communist Party Politburo.

Tatayana Zaslavskaya, *The Second Socialist Revolution: An Alternative Soviet Strategy* (Bloomington: Indiana University Press, 1990).

An incisive analysis by a Soviet sociologist and contributor to the ideas underpinning perestroika of the difficulties that the Gorbachev leadership had in overhauling the Soviet system, especially having to do with popular attitudes and prejudices toward change.

Foreign Policy

Jonathan R. Adelman, *The Dynamics of Soviet Foreign Policy* (New York: Harper & Row, 1989).

A brief introductory overview of Soviet foreign policy. Distinctive features of the book are its chapters on how to examine and interpret Soviet foreign-policy problems.

Raymond L. Garthoff, *Détente and Confrontation: American-Soviet Relations From Nixon to Reagan* (Washington, D.C.: Brookings Institution, 1985).

An encyclopedic analysis of American-Soviet relations during the 1970s with emphasis on the Nixon, Ford, and Carter years and with substantial coverage of the Afghan crisis.

Mikhail Gorbachev, *Perestroika: New Thinking for Our Country and the World* (New York: Harper & Row, 1987).

After a definition of the purposes and methods of his reform program, the Soviet leader presents his views on the significance of perestroika for Soviet foreign policy.

Steve Hirsch, ed., *MEMO: New Soviet Voices on Foreign and Economic Policy* (Washington, D.C.: The Bureau of National Affairs, 1990).

A collection of scholarly articles dealing with Soviet-American relations, the Third World, Gorbachev's New Thinking, and perestroika's impact on Soviet foreign policy.

Allen Lynch, *Gorbachev's International Outlook: Intellectual Origins and Political Consequences* (New York: Institute for East-West Security Studies, 1989).

Analysis of the principles of Gorbachev's New Thinking on foreign policy.

Michael McGwire, *Perestroika and Soviet National Security* (Washington, D.C.: The Brookings Institution, 1991).

The most thorough study of the impact on Soviet international policies of perestroika.

Karl W. Ryavec, *United States-Soviet Relations* (New York: Longman, 1988).

A comprehensive analysis of the major issues in recent Soviet-American relations, such as arms control, regional rivalries, and trade. This book is an invaluable aid in understanding Gorbachev's policies toward the United States.

Sylvia Woodby, *Gorbachev and the Decline of Ideology in Soviet Foreign Policy* (Boulder: Westview Press, 1989).

This book explains Gorbachev's approach to ideology and the

ways in which he diminished its importance as a determinant of Soviet international behavior.

Peter Zwick, *Soviet Foreign Relations: Process and Policy* (Englewood Cliffs: Prentice Hall, 1989).

An analysis of Soviet foreign policy that emphasizes goals and methods of policy formation as well as policy actions.

CENTRAL/EASTERN EUROPE

Regional Studies

Aurel Braun, ed., *The Soviet-East European Relationship in the Gorbachev Era: The Prospects of Adaptation* (Boulder: Westview Press, 1990).

A collection of essays assessing the policies of the Central/Eastern European countries toward the former Soviet state and their perceptions of their relationship with the Kremlin.

J. F. Brown, *Eastern Europe and Communist Rule* (Durham: Duke University Press, 1988).

Analyzes the major political and economic developments in Central/Eastern Europe over the last quarter-century, discussing both the region as a whole and its components, with individual coverage of the countries of the former Warsaw Pact plus Yugoslavia and Albania. It focuses on common themes.

Karen Dwisha and Philip Hanson, eds., *Soviet-East European Dilemmas: Coercion, Competition, and Consent* (New York: Holmes and Meier, 1981).

Essays on Central/Eastern European political, economic, and military relations with the Soviet Union and the West.

Charles Gati, *The Bloc That Failed: Soviet-East European Relations in Transition* (Bloomington: Indiana University Press, 1990).

A synthesis of the postwar evolution of Soviet-Central/Eastern European relations and analysis of the revolutionary events in the region.

William E. Griffith, ed., *Central and Eastern Europe: The Opening Curtain* (Boulder: Westview, 1989).

Essays by outstanding scholars who discuss economic, social, political, and trade problems within and among the Central/Eastern European countries and between them and the Soviet Union, Western Europe, and the United States.

Bernard Gwertzman and Michael T. Kaufman, eds., *The Collapse of Communism* (New York: Times Books, 1990).

A collection of articles on the collapse of Communist party regimes in Central/Eastern Europe in 1989.

Peter Havlik, ed., *Dismantling the Command Economy in Eastern Europe: The Vienna Institute for Comparative Economic Studies Yearbook III* (Boulder: Westview Press, 1991).

Analyzes the general problems of economic transition in the countries of the former Soviet Bloc.

Lyman H. Legters, ed., *Eastern Europe: Transformation and Revolution 1945–1991, Documents and Analyses* (Lexington: D. C. Heath, 1991).

A collection of essays by Western scholars and Central/Eastern European analysts and politicians on various aspects of political development in particular countries in the era of communist rule. This book includes essays on the revolutionary events of 1989 and the post-Communist era of the early 1990s.

Joni Lovenduski and Jean Woodall, *Politics and Society in Eastern Europe* (Bloomington: Indiana University Press, 1988).

A general introduction that provides a good background for understanding the changes and reforms in 1989.

Hugh Seton-Watson, *The East European Revolution* (New York: Praeger, 1956).

A historian's explanation of how Communists came to power in Central/Eastern Europe.

Peter F. Sugar and Ivo J. Lederer, eds., *Nationalism in Eastern*

Europe (Seattle: University of Washington, 1969).
Explores the historic development of political nationalism among the peoples of Central/Eastern Europe, from the beginning of their development to the Communist ascendancy.

Vladimir Tismaneanu, *The Crisis of Marxist Ideology in Eastern Europe* (New York: Routledge, Chapman, and Hall, 1988).
A useful study of the failure of the Marxist-based regimes in Central/Eastern Europe to achieve ideological legitimacy.

Country Studies
The following studies provide insight into the particular characteristics of individual Central/Eastern European nations.

Albania
Elez Biberaz, *Albania: A Socialist Maverick* (Boulder, Westview Press, 1990).

Anton Logoreci, *The Albanians: Europe's Forgotten Survivors* (London: Gollancz, 1977).

Ramadan Marmullaku, *Albania and the Albanians*, Margo and Bosco Milosavljevic, trans. (Hamden: Archon Books, 1975).

Orjan Sjoberg, *Rural Change and Development in Albania* (Boulder: Westview Press, 1991).

Bulgaria
James F. Brown, *Bulgaria Under Communist Rule* (New York: Praeger, 1970).

Bogoslav Dobrin, *Bulgarian Economic Development Since World War II* (New York: Praeger, 1983).

Nissan Oren, *Revolution Administered: Agrarianism and Communism in Bulgaria* (Baltimore: Johns Hopkins, 1973).

Czechoslovakia
Vladimir Kusin, *From Dubcek to Charter 77: A Study of Normalization in Czechoslovakia 1968-1978* (New York: St. Martin's Press, 1978).

Zdenek L. Suda, *Zealots and Rebels: A History of the Czechoslovak Communist Party* (Stanford: Hoover Institution Press, 1980).

Bernard Wheaton and Zdenek Wheaton, *The Velvet Revolution: Czechoslovakia 1988-1991* (Boulder: Westview, 1992).

East Germany
David Childs, *The G.D.R.: Moscow's German Ally* (London: George Allen and Unwin, 1983).

Henry Krisch, *The German Democratic Republic: The Search for Identity* (Boulder: Westview, 1985).

Gregory Sandford, *From Hitler to Ulbricht* (Princeton: Princeton University Press, 1983).

Hungary
Charles Gati, *Hungary and the Soviet Bloc* (Durham: Duke University Press, 1986).

Joseph Held, ed., *The Modernization of Agriculture: Rural Transformation in Hungary* (New York: Columbia University Press, 1980).

Tibor Palankai, *The European Community and Central European Integration: The Hungarian Case* (Boulder: Westview, 1991).

Poland
Timothy Garton Ash, *The Polish Revolution: Solidarity* (New York: Vintage Books of Random House, 1985).

Jan B. deWeydenthal, *The Communists of Poland: An Historical Outline* (Stanford: Hoover Institution Press, 1979).

John Moody and Roger Boyes, *The Priest and the Policeman: The Courageous Life of Father Jerzy Popieluszko* (New York: Summit Books, 1987).

Carole Nagengast, *Reluctant Socialists, Rural Entrepreneurs: Class Culture and the Polish State* (Boulder: Westview Press, 1991).

George Sanford, *Polish Communism in Crisis* (New York: St. Martin's Press, 1983).

Thomas Swick, *Unquiet Days: At Home in Poland* (New York: Ticknor and Fields, 1991).

Lawrence Wechsler, *The Passion of Poland* (New York: Pantheon, 1984).

Romania
Mary Fischer, *Nicolae Ceausescu: A Political Biography* (Boulder: Lynne Rienner Publishers, 1989).

Stephen Fischer-Galati, *The New Rumania: From People's Democracy to Socialist Republic* (Cambridge: MIT Press, 1967).

Trond Gilberg, *Nationalism and Communism in Romania: The Rise and Fall of Ceausescu's Personal Dictatorship* (Boulder: Westview Press, 1990).

Robert R. King, *History of the Rumanian Communist Party* (Stanford: Hoover Institution Press, 1980).

Daniel N. Nelson, ed., *Romania After Tyranny* (Boulder: Westview Press, 1991).

Yugoslavia
April Carter, *Democratic Reform in Yugoslavia: The Changing Role of the Party* (Princeton: Princeton University Press, 1982).

Dushko Doder, *The Yugoslavs* (New York: Random House, 1978).

Harold F. Lydall, *Yugoslavia in Crisis* (New York: Oxford University Press, 1989).

Pierre Maurer and Marko Milivojevic, eds., *Yugoslavia's Security Dilemmas* (New York: St. Martin's Press, 1988).

Pedro Ramet, *Nationalism and Federalism in Yugoslavia* (Bloomington: Indiana University Press, 1984).

Dennison Rusinow, *The Yugoslav Experiment 1948-1974* (Berkeley: University of California Press, 1977).

Dennison Rusinow, ed., *Yugoslavia: A Fractured Federalism* (Lanham: The Wilson Center Press, 1988).

CURRENT EVENTS

To keep up to date on the Soviet Union and Central/Eastern Europe, the following are especially useful.

New Times (Moscow)
A weekly journal containing articles on world affairs.

Yearbook on International Communist Affairs
Summarizes in brief but succinct country essays the current development of the world's Communist parties.

Facts on File and *Keesings Contemporary Archives*
Standard brief summaries of current events, issued annually.

The New York Times, The Christian Science Monitor, The Washington Post, The London Times, and *Le Monde*
Among the best of the daily newspapers in the West on international and communist affairs.

Radio Free Europe and *Radio Liberty* (Munich)
Research agencies that report on current developments in the former Soviet Bloc by monitoring the media of individual countries. Reports are written by area experts and are distributed to various libraries in mimeograph form.

SCHOLARLY JOURNALS

Problems of Communism
International Communication Agency
1776 Pennsylvania Ave., NW, Rm. 964
Washington, DC 20547
Devoted exclusively to domestic and international developments relevant to socialist countries and Communist parties.

East European Quarterly
University of Colorado
Box 29 Regent Hall
Boulder, CO 80309
Concentrates on articles about recent and current developments.

Soviet Studies
M. E. Sharpe, Inc.
901 N. Broadway
White Plains, NY 10603
Deals with a variety of topics.

World Today
10 St. James's Square

London SW1Y 4LE, England
Brief but informative articles on current international problems and crises.

International Affairs
Moscow
Articles on different problems in Soviet foreign policy.

Orbis: A Journal of World Affairs
Foreign Policy Research Institute
3508 Market St., Suite 350
Philadelphia, PA 19104
Articles on current international issues.

Foreign Affairs
Council on Foreign Affairs, Inc.
58 E. 68 St.
New York, NY 10021
One of the most prestigious American journals covering international affairs. Articles consist of essays by well-known writers and government officials both in the United States and abroad.

Sources for Statistical Reports

U.S. State Department, *Background Notes* (1988–1991).

The World Factbook (1992).

World Statistics in Brief (1991).

The Statesman's Yearbook (1990–1991).

Demographic Yearbook (1991).

Statistical Yearbook (1992).

World Bank, *World Development Report* (1991).

Ayers Directory of Publications (1991).

World Almanac (1992).

Macedonia, 115, 195, 196, 232; *see also,* Yugoslavia

Made, Tiit, 78

Major, John, 105, 265

Manolescu, Nicolae, 167

market economy: in Central/Eastern Europe, 104–105, 112, 125–126, 240, 248, 250; Soviet, 72–73, 77, 188, 190, 216–217

Markovic, Anton, 174, 176, 177, 179

Marticevci, Serbia's, 260, 261

Marx, Karl, 4, 5, 6–7, 8–9, 14, 24, 29, 31, 34, 36, 37, 43, 59, 67, 88, 92, 109, 111, 115, 134, 166, 176, 185, 188, 241, 259

Mazowiecki, Tadeusz, 154, 155, 158, 159, 160, 253

Meciar, Vladimir, 248

media, Soviet, 14, 22, 45, 46

Mesic, Stipe, 176

Meskhetian people, in Georgia, 65–66, 194, 214

Michael, Romania's King, 162, 166

Michnik, Adam, 149, 154, 237

Mielke, Erich, 235

Mikulic, Branko, 172

military, influence of Soviet, 15, 18–19, 41, 53, 55–56, 68, 71, 73–76

Mill, John Stuart, 259

Milosevic, Slobodan, 112, 171, 174, 176, 177, 178, 179, 260, 264

Mitchell, Jay, 209

Mitterrand, François, 59, 100, 105, 244

Mladenov, Petar, 116, 117

Modrow, Hans, 132, 133–134

Moldova, 2, 50, 65, 70, 75, 84, 88, 168, 192, 195, 210

Molotov-Ribbentrop Pact, 160

monarchical socialism, in Romania, 162

Mongolia, Soviet Union and, 60

Moravia, 234, 265

Moruhov, Mikhail, 217

Mozambique, Soviet Union and, 59

Muslim religious groups, in the Soviet Union and Central/Eastern Europe, 32, 33, 35, 50, 65, 80, 191, 208, 210–215, 219, 220, 221–222, 227–230

Nagorno-Karabakh, 50–51, 75, 76, 194, 195, 204

Nagy, Imre, 140, 146, 236

Nano, Fato, 111, 112

narodniki, 6

"Nation, State, and Utopia" (von Mises), 258

National Wealth Management Funds, 155

NATO (North Atlantic Treaty Organization), 27, 28, 57, 59, 78, 91, 98, 100, 105, 130, 136, 145, 157, 163, 179

Nazarbayev, Nursultan, 73, 77, 191, 199

Nazis, 86, 87, 88, 90, 121, 128, 130, 137, 140, 158, 162, 185, 188, 189, 221, 235, 237, 248, 261

Negovanovic, Marko, 264

neo-Nazis, 137

New Class (Djilas), 172

New Economic Mechanism, Hungary's, 141

New Economic Policy (NEP), Lenin's, 10, 11, 82, 186

New Economic System, East(ern) Germany's, 131

New Thinking, Gorbachev's, 56, 77, 203

Nezhay, Aleksandr, 223

Nicaragua, Soviet Union and, 59

Nicholas II, Czar, 5, 6, 7, 33, 82

Nine Plus One Agreement, 64, 68, 69, 70

Nixon, Richard, 163, 169

NKVD, 157

nomenklatura, 18, 19, 25, 70, 211, 223, 256

North Korea, Soviet Union and, 3, 57, 188

North Vietnam, Soviet Union and, 3, 57, 60, 188

Novotny, Antonin, 121, 128

nuclear weapons, Soviet, 15, 19, 56, 57, 75–76, 77, 79, 100, 214

Oder-Neisse line, 159, 195

Olszewski, Jan, 155, 156

Organization for Economic Cooperation and Development (OECD), 244

Orlov, Yuri, 36

Ossetian people, Georgia's, 65–66, 195, 197

Ostpolitik, West Germany's, 97, 163

Ottoman Empire, 188, 189

Overseas Investment Corporation, 119, 127

Pakistan: 80; Soviet Union and, 29, 32

Palestine Liberation Organization (PLO), 59, 174, 188

Pamyat, 45, 221

Papandreou, Andreas, 109

paradnost, 24

parasitism, in the Soviet Union, 34

Paris Charter, 196

Paris Club, 242

Pashko, Gramoz, 110

Pavlov, Valentin, 67, 68–69, 204, 215

people's assessors, Soviet, 22

perestroika, 4, 5, 14, 15, 16, 41–45, 48, 52, 57, 66, 71, 83, 99, 131, 172, 197, 203, 204, 205, 206, 211, 212, 214, 220; in Bulgaria, 115–116, 117; in Central/Eastern Europe, 101, 102, 109; in Czechoslovakia, 122, 123; in Hungary, 141, 145; in Poland, 152–153, 156; in Romania, 164, 165

personality cults: Romanian, 162; Soviet, 12, 13, 187

Petrakov, Nikolai, 62, 63

Petrov, Vladislav, 226

Pilsudski, Josef, 154–155

Pirek, Zenon, 243

Pirinsky, George, 246

Pirvulescu, Constantin, 165

pluralization, of Soviet politics after 1989, 66–71

Poland, 84, 85, 86, 87, 88, 90, 93, 94, 95, 96, 97, 98, 99, 100, 101, 102, 104, 105, 106, 136, 145, 169, 190, 191, 195, 198, 200, 216, 218, 230, 231, 232, 233, 234, 235, 236–237, 238, 240, 241, 242, 243, 244, 248, 265; Bulgaria and, 118, 119; Czechoslovakia and, 121, 122, 124, 126; democracy in, 251–255; overview of, 148–160; Soviet Union and, 36, 41, 46, 58, 59, 78, 189; Yugoslavia and, 173, 174

Politburo, Soviet, 16, 17, 18, 20, 21, 30, 35, 47, 52, 61, 71, 204

political dissent: in Poland, 149–150; in the Soviet Union, 13, 23, 36–38, 45–46, 55, 57, 214

political education, Soviet, 14–15

Pomerania, 158, 159

Popieluszko, Jerzy, 237

Popov, Dmitri, 118

Popov, Gavril, 66, 69, 198, 199

popular fronts, Soviet, 52

Portugal, 244

Pozsgay, Imre, 142, 143, 145

Prague Spring, 121–122, 123, 124, 125, 236

prices, decontrol of, in the Soviet Union, 72–73

Primakov, Yevgeni, 63

privatization: in Albania, 112; in Czechoslovakia, 125–126, 247, 248; in East(ern) Germany, 135, 238–239; in Hungary, 142, 144, 240, 250–251; in Poland, 154, 155, 255; in Romania, 167, 256; in the Soviet Union, 61, 62, 63, 72, 73; in Yugoslavia, 172–174

profitability, *perestroika* and, 42

Protocols of the Elders of Zion, 221

Prunskiene, Kasmieria, 159

Pugo, Boris, 67, 68, 69, 70, 203

Puklatov, Abdul Rakhman, 81

purges: in Albania, 108; in East(ern) Germany, 130; Stalin's, 10–11, 12, 19

Rajsic, Dragan, 262

Rakosi, Metyas, 140

Rakowski, Miecyslav, 152, 153

Reagan, Ronald, 100, 109, 145

Red Army faction, 138

reform communism, 66, 67

religion, 104; in the Soviet Union, 5, 6, 32–34, 36, 45, 50, 191, 219–223; *see also,* Jews; Muslims; Roman Catholic Church; Russian Orthodox religion

restitutive justice, 236

reunification, German, 134–136, 158, 190–191, 195

Revolution of October 1905, Russia's, 7, 82

Road to Serfdom, The (Hayek), 258–259

Roman Catholic Church: in Central/Eastern Europe, 96, 97, 122, 171, 191, 265; in Poland, 149, 150–151, 152, 156

Romania, 50, 58, 84, 85, 86, 87, 88, 95, 97, 98, 99, 100, 101, 103, 110, 114, 119, 132, 195, 230, 232, 233, 234, 235, 236, 240, 242; Hungary and, 144, 145, 146; nationalism in, 255–259; overview of, 161–170; Poland and, 151, 157; Soviet Union and, 188, 189, 190

Romanov, Grigori, 203

Romanov family, Russia's, 5–8

Rona, Peter, 239

Rosen, Moses, 257

Rukh, 49

Russia, 2, 4, 62, 63, 64, 65, 66, 70, 71, 72, 74, 75, 76–77, 80, 83, 84, 85, 190, 191, 192, 193, 194, 195, 196, 209, 215, 238; dominance of, 30–32, 81, 83, 87–88, 191, 208; entrepreneurs in, 217–219; women in, 227–230; *see also,* Commonwealth of Independent States; Soviet Union

Russian Orthodox religion, 5, 6, 32, 33, 36, 45, 50, 115, 185, 210, 219, 220, 222, 223

Russian Social Democratic Party (RSDP), 6–7

Ruthenian people, 190

Rutskoy, Aleksandr, 67, 76, 199

Ryzhkov, Nikolai, 54, 63, 64, 67, 145, 185, 203, 204

Sachs, Jeffrey, 200

Sagers, Matthew, 208

Sakharov, Andrei, 36, 37, 54, 66, 67, 198, 203

Salik, Muhammed, 80

SALT (Strategic Arms Limitation Talks), 27, 83

Samizdat, 37

satellization, of Central/Eastern European countries, by the Soviet Union, 85, 89–91, 125, 145

Saudi Arabia, 80; Soviet Union and, 32, 33, 220